An Anthology

INTRODUCING THE DRAMA

by John Gassner, Sterling Professor of Playwriting and Dramatic Literature

Yale University

and Morris Sweetkind, Chairman, Department of English

The Cheshire Academy, Cheshire, Connecticut

HOLT, RINEHART AND WINSTON, INC.

New York

COPYRIGHT © 1963 BY
HOLT, RINEHART AND WINSTON, INC.
ALL RIGHTS RESERVED
03-003650-X
PRINTED IN THE UNITED STATES OF AMERICA
90123   22   109876

The editors wish to thank the following authors, publishers, and other holders of copyright for permission to use copyrighted materials:

Mrs. Christy MacKaye Barnes for "The Scarecrow" by Percy MacKaye. Copyright 1914 by Percy MacKaye; Copyright 1942 by Mrs. Christy MacKaye Barnes.

Samuel French, Inc. for "The Late Christopher Bean" founded upon "Prenez garde à la peinture" by René Fauchois, Copyright 1932 (under title of "Muse of All Work") by Sidney Howard; Copyright 1933 by Sidney Howard; Copyright © 1959, 1960 (in renewal) by Polly Damrosch Howard. All rights reserved.

John Gassner for his version of "Everyman." Copyright 1935, 1951 by John Gassner.

Ninon Tallon Karlweis (exclusive agent for the Giraudoux Estate) for "The Apollo of Bellac" by Jean Giraudoux, adapted by Maurice Valency. Copyright (under title of "L'Apollon de Marsac") 1942 by Jean Giraudoux; Copyright (under title of "L'Apollon de Bellac") 1947 by Jean Giraudoux.

Little, Brown and Company for "The Barretts of Wimpole Street" by Rudolf Besier. Copyright 1930,-1958 by Rudolf Besier.

Putnam & Co. Ltd. for "A Night at an Inn" by Lord Dunsany. Copyright 1915 by *The Smart Set*; Copyright 1916 by Sunwise Turn, Inc.; Copyright 1917 by John W. Luce & Co.; and published simultaneously in New York and London by G. P. Putnam's Sons in *Plays of God and Men*.

Random House for "The Glass Menagerie" by Tennessee Williams. Copyright 1945 by Tennessee Williams and Edwina D. Williams. Reprinted from *Six Modern American Plays*.

The Society of Authors, The Public Trustee, and Dodd, Mead and Company, Inc., for "Arms and the Man" by George Bernard Shaw. Copyright 1898, 1926 by Bernard Shaw; Copyright 1913, 1941 by George Bernard Shaw.

Maurice Valency, and his representative, Audrey Wood, Ashley-Steiner-Famous Artists, Inc., for "The Apollo of Bellac" by Jean Giraudoux, adapted by Maurice Valency. Copyright 1954 by Maurice Valency.

The editors also wish to thank the following for their help in supplying photographic and other illustrative material pertaining to drama and literature:

George Freedley, chief of the New York Public Library Theatre Collection; Professor Henry W. Wells, curator of the Columbia University Brander Matthews Dramatic Museum, and also his assistant, Miss Elsa Pinthus; and chiefs of photo archives at The American National Theatre and Academy; The British Travel Association; The French Government Tourist Office; The Greek Government Information Center; The High School of Performing Arts, New York City; The Hofstra College Shakespeare Festival, Hempstead, N.Y.; The Horace Mann School for Boys, Riverdale, N.Y.; and the Colorado State College "Little Theatre of the Rockies," Greeley, Colorado.

Photo credits: Cover photograph showing Theatre of Dionysus, by Philip Gendreau. "Antigone" scene, Copyright by Roy Stevens, N.Y.C.; London production scene of "School for Scandal," Copyright by Angus McBean, London, England.

Also scenes from "Romeo and Juliet," by Friedman-Abeles, N.Y.C.; "The Barretts of Wimpole Street," by Menasco Studio, Shrevesport, La.; "A Night at an Inn," by White Studio, N.Y.C.; "The Glass Menagerie," by Photographic Laboratory, Univ. of Minnesota; "The Barretts of Wimpole Street," by Avery Willard, N.Y.C.; "An Enemy of the People," by Lucas-Pritchard, N.Y.C.; "Arms and the Man," by Skeets Calvin, Greeley, Colo.; scene showing view of Theatre of Dionysus, by David Sweetkind, New Haven, Conn.; and "The Passion Play" scene by Bernand, Paris, France.

Caution

All the plays listed above are fully protected under copyright laws of the United States of America, the British Empire, including the Dominion of Canada and all other countries members of the Copyright Union. All rights including professional, amateur, motion pictures, recitation, public reading, radio broadcasting, televised performance, and the rights of translation into foreign languages are strictly reserved in their present form. These plays are for the reading public only. All inquiries for such rights must be addressed to the copyright owners.

PREFACE

This anthology represents an effort to introduce students to the subject of dramatic literature. For this purpose the plays are grouped under headings that show various types of drama proven to be popular and successful over the years. These types are not presented, however, as absolute categories. They are approximate classifications allowing for much leeway in defining plays in order to take into consideration the existence of borderline cases and the tendency of one category to blend into another. Thus "comedy" in a particular instance may border on "farce" or contain farcical elements; and "farce" may verge on "comedy." Our prime objective is to enable students to experience and judge drama in its amplitude and variety.

Although a brief survey is presented in the *Introduction,* no attempt has been made to represent the history of the drama through the selections. For this reason, no elaborate explanations need be offered for the omissions the teacher will observe and may wish to repair with assignments outside the scope of the present volume. Nevertheless, we have inevitably included the work of the major periods and dramatists from classical antiquity to the twentieth century, and from Sophocles to Tennessee Williams. Many authors have been represented by some major work; those who have not been so represented for pedagogical or related reasons, reveal the essential attributes of their work in the minor play chosen here.

An explanation concerning the editorial matter in the book may also be in order. We have left it to the individual teacher to decide how to proceed in arousing and sustaining class interest. An introduction to each of the sections is offered along with brief discussions at the beginning of each individual selection.

Suggested topics for further discussion and study are included at the end of each selection. Much, however, is left to the individual teacher who may want to supplement the introductory material, and pursue close study of some or all the plays.

It should further be noted that the arrangement of selections in this anthology is not in chronological order except under the various subdivisions of the book. Primarily, it has been our intention to introduce students to some major varieties of dramatic composition . . . not to *all* of them of course, and not without allowing for the possibility that a particular play might also fit more or less into a different subdivision than the one in which it has been placed. Our object has been to bring some order into a student's impressions of the drama and the theatre as a greatly diversified enterprise. It was not our aim to reduce the drama to cut-and-dried definitions even though our selections illustrate well established types of drama. By offering the best known types— tragedy, social drama, melodrama, allegory, comedy, and farce—we have presented types of drama with which students should be familiar. These classifications represent different ways of looking at life, and may introduce students to an understanding of life, in addition to enabling them to acquire some knowledge of the stage and its literature.

We cannot close without expressing our deep gratitude to the many people who have helped us carry this project through to fruition including Arthur N. Sheriff, headmaster of Cheshire Academy; and also the kind and generous assistance of our wives, Mollie Gassner and Betty Sweetkind.

THE EDITORS

John Gassner, Yale University, New Haven, Conn.
Morris Sweetkind, Cheshire Academy, Cheshire, Conn.

CONTENTS

Preface	iv
General Introduction: Drama and Theatre	1
Selected Illustrations: Drama and Theatre (*following page 12*)	

PART ONE: TRAGEDY, SOCIAL DRAMA, AND MELODRAMA

Introduction to Part One (*Tragedy, Social Drama and Melodrama*)	13
Sophocles (*short biography*)	20
Introduction to "Antigone"	21
Sophocles: "Antigone" (*English version by John Gassner*)	23
Questions and study aids for "Antigone"	42
William Shakespeare (*short biography*)	43
Introduction to "Romeo and Juliet"	45
Shakespeare: "Romeo and Juliet"	47
Questions and study aids for "Romeo and Juliet"	131
Henrik Ibsen (*short biography*)	133
Introduction to "An Enemy of the People"	135
Ibsen: "An Enemy of the People"	137
Questions and study aids for "An Enemy of the People"	193
Lord Dunsany (*short biography*)	195
Introduction to "A Night at an Inn"	195
Dunsany: "A Night at an Inn"	196
Questions and study aids for "A Night at an Inn"	203

PART TWO: BIOGRAPHY AND AUTOBIOGRAPHY

Introduction to Part Two (*Biography and Autobiography*)	205
Rudolf Besier (*short biography*)	208
A note on the Brownings	208
Introduction to "The Barretts of Wimpole Street"	210
Besier: "The Barretts of Wimpole Street"	211
Questions and study aids for "The Barretts of Wimpole Street"	264
Tennessee Williams (*short biography*)	265
Introduction to "The Glass Menagerie"	267
Williams: "The Glass Menagerie"	268
Questions and study aids for "The Glass Menagerie"	305

PART THREE: ALLEGORY AND FANTASY

Introduction to Part Three (*Allegory and Fantasy*)	307
Introduction to "Everyman"	308
(Anonymous): "Everyman" (*Modernized version by John Gassner*)	309
Questions and study aids for "Everyman"	331

Percy MacKaye (*short biography*)	333
Introduction to "The Scarecrow"	333
MacKaye: "The Scarecrow"	334
Questions and study aids for "The Scarecrow"	377

PART FOUR: COMEDY AND FARCE

Introduction to Part Four (*Comedy and Farce*)	379
Molière (*short biography*)	383
Introduction to "The Pretentious Ladies"	383
Molière: "The Pretentious Ladies" ("*Les Précieuses ridicules*": English version by John Gassner)	384
Questions and study aids for "The Pretentious Ladies"	396
Richard Brinsley Sheridan (*short biography*)	398
Introduction to "The School for Scandal"	398
Sheridan: "The School for Scandal"	399
Questions and study aids for "The School for Scandal"	448
George Bernard Shaw (*short biography*)	450
Introduction to "Arms and the Man"	452
Shaw: "Arms and the Man"	454
Questions and study aids for "Arms and the Man"	493
Anton Chekhov (*short biography*)	495
Introduction to "Then and Now"	495
Chekhov: "Then and Now" (*An adaptation and arrangement of "The Marriage Proposal" and "The Harmful Effects of Smoking" by John Gassner*)	496
Questions and study aids for "Then and Now"	507
Sidney Howard (*short biography*)	508
Introduction to "The Late Christopher Bean"	508
Howard: "The Late Christopher Bean"	509
Questions and study aids for "The Late Christopher Bean"	563
Jean Giraudoux (*short biography*)	565
Introduction to "The Apollo of Bellac"	566
Giraudoux: "The Apollo of Bellac" (*Adaptation by Maurice Valency*)	567
Questions and study aids for "The Apollo of Bellac"	583

GENERAL INTRODUCTION: DRAMA AND THEATRE

When, seated in a modern theatre, expectantly we watch the rise of the curtain, we are the heirs of a tradition that is as old as mankind. From savage to civilized man, for countless centuries in all parts of the world, people have participated in the unique experience that we characterize as dramatic. Religious exaltation, profound tragedy, joyful laughter, and clownish buffoonery—all the emotions of humanity have been enacted by performers on a stage before an assembled audience. Let us view some of these performances to catch a glimpse of the changing conditions under which this universal art has been practiced.

The Drama of Primitive Peoples

First, let us go back several thousand years to southeastern Australia among a tribe of primitive people. On a dark night by the light of fires and burning torches, we see enacted a strange drama. Seated around a semiclearing are several hundred women, children, and warriors. An old man leaning on a staff totters into the center and peers into a hollow log. Pretending to spy an animal in the trunk of the fallen tree, he tries to poke it out with his stick, meanwhile uttering appropriate words. From the nearby brush a warrior masked as an animal creeps out stealthily and claws the leg of the old man. The latter, pretending to be greatly frightened, utters some cries and hits the supposed beast with his stick. This actor then dodges around on all fours trying to evade the blows but finally lies down feigning death. The old man goes back to the log and another warrior dressed as a beast crawls out. The same pantomimic actions are performed and the same words uttered until several supposed animals are "killed." The old man then utters a shout of triumph; then all join around the fire in a joyous chant and dance accompanied by the music of drums, rattles, and clashing boomerangs.

Now this little drama which is of absorbing interest to all the spectators, we soon discover, has not been enacted primarily for the entertainment of the tribe. Its purpose is to communicate to the all-powerful spirits or gods the desires of these primitive people, in this case, a successful hunt. This ceremony performed carefully by trained actors according to a traditional ritual is religious in nature. It is a kind of dramatic prayer in which the suppliants plead with the invisible powers to give the tribe a plentiful food supply. Were we to return during the dry season, we might see three members of the same tribe (if it was also dependent on agriculture) perform a different playlet. One actor, the weathermaker, would climb a tree and sprinkle some water on the ground to represent rain. A second would hit two stones together to represent thunder; and a third would strike a fire brand until the sparks flew to represent lightning. The tribe might then join in a joyous chant and dance. A more elaborate rain-making drama still survives in the annual snake ceremony of the Hopi Indians of America. Thus primitive man by the use of sympathetic or imitative magic expresses his needs and his hopes for their fulfillment.

From such ceremonials—lasting hours or days—performed by peoples all over the world arose the earliest drama, unwritten but preserved from generation to generation by tribal and religious sanctions. Thus all the important elements of dramatic representation may be found among even the most primitive peoples of the past or present: the acting out of a story by means of imitative movements, gestures and words; the use of masks or disguises to represent different characters—departed ancestors, spirits, animals, or gods; the effective combination of the dance, chant, and instrumental music to stir the emotions of the participants and observers; and lastly, an absorbed audience in an improvised outdoor "theatre" watching the religious performance.

The Greek Theatre

Let us now go from Australia to Athens in 429 B.C. to see the first production of Sophocles' *Oedipus the King*, one of a group of plays presented at a public dramatic festival. During the annual festival held in honor of Dionysus, the god of vegetation and wine in Greece, three days were set aside for dramatic contests. Each competitor wrote three plays (hence the name *trilogy*), usually, in the days of Sophocles' great predecessor Aeschylus about a quarter of a century earlier, dealing with the tragic events befalling one family. The dramatist was also expected to write a fourth play, a boisterous satyr-drama, dealing with the same or loosely related material humorously. The four plays—three tragic and one comic—would make up a *tetralogy*. How different in presentation and yet how similar in spirit this cultured drama seems when compared to the ceremonial plays of early man.

The theatre is still in the open, but instead of being in a jungle clearing it is on the southeastern slope of the Acropolis just below the clean-cut Parthenon, which gleams like a jewel in the bright Aegean sunshine. At the bottom of the hill is a large circle (the orchestra) for the Chorus with an altar in the center. From this circular space branch out rows of stone seats arranged symmetrically up the hillside in the form of a semicircle. A few feet in back of the circular orchestra is a long wooden building which serves as a dressing room, as a scenic background for the action, and as a means of exit and entrance for the actors. As we gaze around us we see this symmetrically designed theatre rapidly filling up with people drawn from all classes of society (slaves excepted) until about fifteen or twenty thousand have jammed their way in. Though the spectators seem as lively and excited as a modern football crowd, they are here not simply for entertainment. True, the crowd is as expectant as only an audience of "first-nighters" or athletic "rooters" can be, for competition among the dramatists is keen and each playwright has his loyal supporters who hope their favorite will win the prize this year. But we quickly observe that the dramatic contest is simply part of a great religious festival, because the statue of Dionysus (the patron of the theatre) stands in the center of the orchestra, and perhaps the most honored spectator is the priest of the vine-god who sits in a special seat of the front row.

Oedipus the King opens with Oedipus addressing a group of despairing suppliants whose spokesman, an old priest, begs the ruler to remove the strange plague that has fallen on Thebes. Creon, the brother of Queen Jocasta, arrives and informs Oedipus that the oracle at Delphi has pronounced that only by the discovery and punishment of the murderer of Laius, the previous king, can Thebes rid itself of the defilement. Wise and confident Oedipus, who had solved the riddle of the sphinx, promises to carry out the divine edict. The Chorus, consisting of fifteen men who are supposed to be the elders of Thebes, then enters and chants an eloquent prayer of supplication to the god Apollo and the goddesses Athene and Artemis.

Oedipus after denouncing the unknown murderer then begins his ironical quest. In his passionate search for the truth the suspicious and angry Oedipus quarrels with the blind prophet Teiresias and with Creon. As the past is gradually revealed, the hopes of the king rise and fall. Both Jocasta and the shepherd try to stop him in his impetuous search for the truth. The Chorus sways from belief in the king's innocence, to doubt, to pity for his suffering. When the final revelation confirms Oedipus' guilt, the doomed king rushes into the palace after the queen.

A messenger informs the audience of the suicide of the queen and the self-punishment of the king. (One of the strongest conventions of Greek drama was that violent deeds should be committed off-stage.) Oedipus now enters (with a bloody mask indicating his blindness). Tragic self-knowledge has humbled the king, and in a touching tableau he embraces his two daughters and weeps for their unhappy future.

The performance of the tragedies of Aeschylus, Sophocles, and Euripides and the comedies of Aristophanes differed from a modern production not only in the use of a chorus, but in other details. Greek actors wore masks made of linen, cork, or wood with large mouth openings so that they could project their voices to the distant spectators, although the Greek amphitheatre possessed excellent acoustics. The actors' stature was abnormally raised by colorful high-heeled boots and lofty headdresses. Facial expression, of course was missing, but voice quality and gesture were important in conveying emotion. Acting was stylized rather than realistic.

Greek plays both in content and presentation attained a very high level of artistic excellence. They are, first of all, "good theatre" holding the interest of a large audience by the tragic sufferings of legendary figures presented in the form of a clearly articulated flow of events carefully built up to tremendous climaxes. Though much of the material when boldly summarized in prose seems lurid—hereditary sins, murders, and even incest often form the plot basis—yet the Attic dramatists fashioned their material into such beautiful forms, and expressed it in such lofty poetry that their tragedies rose to an epic dignity and a solemn grandeur that have perhaps never been surpassed in dramatic literature. Furthermore, the rhythmic movement and postures of the chorus figures dressed in colorful, draped costumes, together with the lyrical chants of trained voices accompanied by instruments playing specially composed music, combined to form an artistic spectacle that must have been as satisfying to the eye and the ear as it was in evoking emotional and intellectual responses.

The Medieval Theatre

The glory that was Greece passed away; her splendid temples and amphitheatres fell into ruins; her plays were either lost forever or the few surviving ones forgotten for many centuries. However, the dramatic instinct in man is too powerful a force not to assert itself. Dead for several centuries, European drama started all over again. About the ninth century A.D. there began to appear in the churches of Europe simple playlets (developed from liturgical chants) enacted as part of the Easter or Christmas service. These became more elaborate; as they grew in popularity they became separated from the liturgy, and were performed outside the church. Later the trade associations or guilds of the medieval cities took them up, and local poets composed whole cycles of plays dealing with all the events of Biblical history from the Creation to the Judgment Day. This religious drama was split up in thirty, forty, or fifty episodes, and each one was put into the hands of an appropriate guild. Let us watch one of these English pageant plays performed at Wakefield in the summer of 1442, about nineteen centuries after Sophocles won his first prize for a group of plays at Athens.

Very early in the morning we are part of a large crowd of spectators standing at one of several gathering places in town awaiting the arrival of the first pageant-wagon. Several days before, banner-bearers announced that this particular performance would consist of thirty-two scenes. All guild members have been taxed to support this local dramatic project; and since there is much rivalry between the different guilds as to which one will put on the best show, the audience is eager to view the dramatic presentation of the Bible story and to cheer on the local actors.

At last appears the first pageant-wagon, a gaily decorated vehicle similar to a "float" in a modern parade, except that it has two stories: the upper one an open platform which is used as the stage; and the lower one enclosed by curtains serving as a dressing room. On this movable stage is then enacted in a naive but sincere fashion the first scene of this long mystery play, the creation of heaven and the revolt of Lucifer. (A dramatization of Biblical events is known as a *Mystery* play; a presentation of an episode in the life of some saint or some prodigy performed in behalf of religion based on church history or tradition is a *Miracle* play.) The cart then moves on to the next station while the second cart draws up before us to present the creation of earth and all its creatures, the making of Adam and Eve, the temptation scene in Paradise, and the expulsion. The third scene represents the story of Cain and Abel; but perhaps the most interesting is the next one, the episode of Noah and the flood. This pageant-wagon made by the fisherman's guild is roughly built in the shape of an ark, and the incidents enacted on it meet with the hearty approval of the spectators because of the comic quarrels between Noah and his stubborn wife, with fists flying freely. The plea of the three sons and the rising flood quickly end this family dispute. And so for many hours (and sometimes for several days) the medieval theatre in the form of a moving pageant is brought to the people for their amusement and religious instruction.

About a century and a half after the miracle plays became popular, plays dealing with the struggle for man's soul and using abstract, or allegorical, characters (personifications of the virtues and the vices, etc.) came into vogue. Together these so-called morality plays or "moralities" and the mystery play cycles formed an essential part of the life and entertainment of the middle ages. The moralities, didactic in tone, are more unified as separate plays than the rather chaotic mystery plays. Portraying a conflict in man's soul between good and evil forces, usually represented as abstractions, these plays appealed to medieval spectators, for they enjoyed allegory, were accustomed to sermons or homilies, and were greatly occupied with the coming of death and the terrors and promises of an after-life.

The serious tone, the dramatic conflict, and the vitality of the allegorical characters in moralities like *Everyman* showed possibilities of later developing into secular tragedies. The "Vice," a mischievous character in these plays, later became a stock comic figure. (In Shakespeare's *Henry IV, Part One*, Prince Hal characterizes Falstaff as "that reverend *vice*, that grey iniquity, that father ruffian.") The moralities became an important link between the medieval religious play and Elizabethan drama.

Shakespeare's Theatre

In 1576 James Burbage, the father of Richard Burbage, the actor, built the first public London playhouse. This venture proving profitable, several other theatres were soon erected; one of these, the Globe, housed Shakespeare's acting company. Let us attend the opening night performance of Shakespeare's *Romeo and Juliet*.

On a pleasant day in the spring of 1596 we wend our way outside the city limits to the other side of the Thames River in Southwark where the octagonal open-air Globe theatre is about to give a performance. The flag flying from the turreted hut informs us that a performance will be given that afternoon. (Plays are performed every pleasant afternoon, except Sundays.) Shortly after we enter (about 3:00 P.M.) a trumpeter announces that the play is about to begin. From our crowded vantage point in the pit (which corresponds to our modern orchestra) where we stand throughout the play with the so-called groundlings, we notice that the stage is a raised platform open on three sides extending right into the audience. Behind this uncovered, uncurtained stage is a decorated wall with a couple of doors, and between them a hanging arras which can be drawn aside, if needed, to reveal or suggest some interior scene such as a bedroom, tomb, or cave. Directly above is a windowed balcony, supported by pillars, which can serve as an upper stage. All around the theatre are thatch-covered galleries with seats for the upper class patrons who pay a higher admission fee than the "groundlings." On the edge of the front stage are seated some young Elizabethan fops showing off their richly-colored clothes and exchanging bantering remarks with the spectators. The closeness of the audience to the actors immediately creates an atmosphere of intimacy in which soliloquies and whispered asides seem not at all unnatural. Though the garments of the actors are splendid, the stage properties are quite simple. A tree represents a forest, and a chair a throne. But the sparseness of realistic scenery and the absence of lighting effects are more than compensated for by the rich descriptions, stimulating to the imagination of the listeners, that the poet-dramatist puts into the mouths of his actors.

> "The grey-ey'd morn smiles on the frowning night,
> Chequering the eastern clouds with streaks of light"

In these words Friar Laurence describes the dawn as he sees it from his cell. It is on this almost medieval stage, before a cross-section of London citizens ranging from educated aristocrats to the boisterous groundlings, that Shakespeare's early tragedy is enacted.

An actor steps to the front of the stage and recites the sonnet prologue that informs us that we are to witness the tragic spectacle of a "pair of star-crossed lovers" who will be destroyed by an old family feud. He bows and makes his exit. Servants of the two rival houses of the Capulets and Montagues enter and egg each other on. Then members of both houses become embroiled, and the Prince of Verona issues a stern warning to them to keep the peace. With no pause between the swiftly moving scenes and with rising tension, the play advances to the meeting of the lovers, their romantic first balcony scene, and their hasty, secret marriage. But the deaths of Romeo's friend Mercutio and of Juliet's kinsman Tybalt, who slew Mercutio and was then slain by Romeo, separate the young lovers. Juliet (played, as were all female characters, by a boy-actor) resorts to the desperate stratagem of feigned death, probably thrilling the audience with her blood-curdling soliloquy before she drinks the potion. The final misadventures overtake the lovers, and the play ends with the tragic reconciliation of the surviving Capulets and Montagues.

Our "two hours' traffic" of the stage is over, but what a moving experience it has been! The thunderous applause and cheers indicate that a new hit play is born. When Queen Elizabeth hears of the success of this or some other play, she may command the Lord Chamberlain's Men (Shakespeare's acting company) to present it at court. It is known that she took immense delight in such private performances of Shakespeare's plays; her favorite character was the great comic figure of Falstaff in the *Henry IV* plays.

The Comic Theatre of Molière and Sheridan

When at the end of the sixteenth century, Londoners were enjoying Shakespeare's *Romeo and Juliet* and his *Bolingbroke Tetralogy*, Frenchmen in the provinces were being entertained by itinerant companies of male and female players who performed in the houses of nobility, in town halls, and in open squares. In 1629 one of these companies obtained a permanent lease of the Hôtel de Bourgogne; and twelve years later Louis XIII, encouraged by his Prime Minister, Cardinal Richelieu, who loved the theatre, bestowed upon these actors the title of Troupe Royale and awarded them an annual subsidy. Two other companies, one consisting of Italian comedians, also established themselves in Paris. Poets and dramatists were encouraged and pensioned to write plays. Thus under royal patronage the French theatre was launched on its spectacular career.

When Cardinal Richelieu built his splendid new palace, he included as part of the elaborate building project the most commodious and ornate playhouse in France, the Théâtre du Palais Royale. The auditorium was a lofty hall measuring seventy feet by sixty. Lit by four crystal chandeliers, this hall had a stage behind an ornamented proscenium frame. Along each side were three galleries divided into compartments; the lower two, decorated in gold, were occupied by high society; the third, undecorated, by commoners. In the front part of the hall, as in the Elizabethan theatre, stood the groundlings. Behind them were seats for the middle-class public. On two sides of the stage sat the dandies. This theatre could accommodate about one thousand spectators. Not to be outdone, Louis XIV also built an elaborate theatre, the Petit-Bourbon Palace, which was taken over by the Italian comedians.

At this theatre in 1659 Molière's acting company, in the presence of the king and other notables, put on a performance of *The Pretentious Ladies* (see page 384). This gay satire on the affectations of people aping the latest fashions in behavior, speech, and dress was an immediate success. Molière received a cash gift from the king, and from that time on his company, under royal patronage, was the envy of his rivals. When the Petit-Bourbon theatre was demolished, Molière's troupe performed, usually three days a week—Sundays, Tuesdays, and Fridays—at Richelieu's theatre.

Molière's "high comedy," satirizing the ridiculous fashions of contemporary society and the universal frailties of human nature, had little use for the elaborate scenery and stage machinery imported from Italy. Molière even dispensed with the unique proscenium curtain which Richelieu had taken pains to install. A simple set with a table, a few chairs, and a writing desk was sufficient for Molière's purposes. He eschewed the spectacular in the pursuit of wit and satire, reserving spectacle for special occasions. After the success of *The Pretentious Ladies*, the prolific dramatist produced in this theatre until his death in 1673 twenty plays that have been ever since the delight of the civilized world.

While the sparkling comedies of Molière, and the tragedies of Corneille and Racine were raising seventeenth-century French drama to new heights, English drama after the Elizabethan period was steadily declining, both aesthetically and ethically. Noble tragedy degenerated into crude melodrama; thrilling poetry, into bombastic rhetoric. The normal was debased into the abnormal; sensitivity was replaced by inhuman cruelties and gross passions. When the Puritans (always enemies of the theatre) rose to power and civil war broke out in 1642, they promptly issued an official ordinance, "Publik Stage-Plays shall cease." The theatre was abolished in England until 1660 when the English monarchy was restored, and Charles II and his courtiers returned from their exile in France.

The king promptly established two acting companies and opened two theatres. However, the theatre of the period known as the Restoration (1660-1700) was primarily for the entertainment of the aristocracy. The plays that appealed to the taste of fashionable society were either artificial tragedies stressing the conflict of love and honor, or witty, often immoral, comedies that owe their reputation to their polished dialogue. Sophisticated wit replaced hearty humor; the city was glorified; the countryside ridiculed. The betrayed husband became the butt of jests; the seducer, the hero. The only two important theatrical innovations of the period were the employment of women as performers and the introduction of movable scenery.

In the eighteenth century when the middle classes became dominant, a strong reaction against immorality in the theatre set in. Audiences now enjoyed operas, spectacles, and sentimental plays. The age reacted violently against not only the sophisticated coarseness of Restoration comedy, but against robust, Falstaffian humor. Richard Steele considered laughter "a distorted passion"; and Lord Chesterfield, the arbiter of eighteenth century good taste, told his son, "It is the characteristic of folly and ill manners . . . it is a disagreeable noise that distorts the face." Not until the last quarter of the century did Oliver Goldsmith and Richard Brinsley Sheridan restore laughter and wit to the stage in England, while Beaumarchais, who smuggled arms to the American colonies while they were waging their war for independence, invigorated the French stage with his famous comedies, even better known as operas, *The Barber of Seville* and *The Marriage of Figaro*.

When David Garrick, the famous actor and director, retired in 1776 from the management of the Drury Lane Theatre, Sheridan, with the help of his father-in-law and other investors, took over the theatre. On May 8, 1777, at the age of twenty-six, he presented *The School for Scandal*, his brilliant social comedy, that was an immediate success. A century after the death of Molière, his spirit came to life again. The next morning the reviewer in *The Public Advertiser* wrote that the screen scene "produced a burst of applause beyond anything ever heard perhaps in a theatre." After seeing the play, Horace Walpole wrote, "It seemed a marvelous resurrection of the stage." The only member of the audience who sat unmoved through the performance was Richard Cumberland, the author of contemporary sentimental plays. When informed of this, Sheridan's comment was, "Lud! How ungrateful the man for not smiling over my comedy! Not a fortnight ago, I went to a tragedy of his at Covent Garden, and laughed from the beginning to the end."

The Modern Theatre

In their attack upon sentimentalism, Goldsmith and Sheridan, it soon turned out, had won only a battle, not a war. They had no real successors until a century later when Shaw wrote *Arms and the Man*. In the English as well as the European theatre the drama as an escape from reality rather than a criticism or interpretation of life re-established itself in the form of pathetic plays popularly known, later on, as "tear-jerkers," extravagant spectacles and pantomimes, comic operas, vaudevilles, farces, and melodramas.

To handle the new audiences, larger playhouses were built, more elaborate stage sets and lighting were used, and the role of the actor became more important than that of the playwright. Famous actors exploited their personalities instead of honestly interpreting the characters of classic revivals. Nahum Tate's atrocious version of Shakespeare's *King Lear* (giving the play a happy ending) made in 1681 survived in the British theatre until 1823.

In France Victor Hugo raised the standard of romanticism with the presentation of his *Hernani* at the Théâtre Français in 1830. Fists flew and duels were fought between the embattled classicists and the romanticists. When the struggle was over, the triumph of Victor Hugo and his followers—De Musset, de Vigny and Dumas père—was complete. This wave of "poetic," sentimental romanticism, however, was short-lived, for the pendulum of popular taste swings easily from one extreme to the other. The fickle public now turned to the facile prose concoctions of the prolific playwright Scribe, who wrote from 1830 to 1860 more than four hundred vaudeville sketches, plays, and operas.

With his mastery of all the theatrical devices of clever plots, surprises, pathetic incidents, and happy endings, Scribe perfected the formula of the so-called well-made play. Catering to the taste of his middle-class audiences, he won immense popularity. When elected to the French Academy in 1836, he expressed the sentiment of the age and justified his dramatic philosophy in these words: "You go to the theatre, not for instruction or correction, but for relaxation and amusement. Now what amuses you most is not truth, but fiction. To represent what is before your eyes every day is not the way to please you; but what does not come to you in your usual life, the extraordinary, the romantic, that is what charms you, that is what one is eager to offer you." After the death of Scribe in 1861, Sardou continued this tradition for the next generation. In Europe and in England, practitioners of the well-made play soon mastered the theatrical tricks of the trade; the success formula for winning audiences was given classic utterance by Wilkie Collins, "Make 'em laugh; make 'em weep; make 'em wait."

A reaction against this "escape philosophy" of the theatre as popular entertainment was inevitable. The innovators who tried to bring realism into the theatre in the form of the thesis or problem play were Eugène Brieux in France, and T. W. Robertson, Sir A. W. Pinero and Henry Arthur Jones in England. But the most influential rebel, who proved to be the father of modern drama, was Henrik Ibsen, the Norwegian (page 133). When in 1879 he presented *A Doll's House,* a dramatic bomb exploded whose repercussions are still felt in the theatres of the western world. His next play, *Ghosts,* in 1881 proved even more shocking and he was denounced by many while praised by a few adherents; and in 1882, Ibsen replied to his critics with the defiant comedy, *An Enemy of the People* (see page 137). Even more violent and lasting than the 1830 battle between the French romanticists and classicists was the conflict now waged between the realists and romanticists.

In truthful observation and technical experimentation the drama had fallen far behind the realistic novel. France had produced Flaubert; Russia, Tolstoy, Turgenev, and Dostoyevsky; England, George Eliot and Hardy; and America, Henry James. With the rapid development of industrialism, the growth of democracy, and the rising influence of science in the modern world, a host of new problems emerged that called for dramatic treatment. Ibsen, Strindberg and their followers with passion and close observation of real life tackled these new complex problems—both in their sociological and psychological aspects—and in a series of powerful prose plays quickly destroyed the flimsy foundations on which the sentimental and romantic theatre had rested for a century. The conventional ideas of Victorian society now came under the close scrutiny of alert dramatists who re-examined society's ideas of marriage, sex, democracy (see *An Enemy of the People*, page 137) and made the playhouse an arena for the discussion of contemporary problems. As the concepts of Darwin, Marx, and Freud flowed into the popular current of ideas, modern dramatists represented life on the stage not only in realistic but in naturalistic terms, stressing the sordid, ugly aspects "scientifically" and presenting human beings as helpless victims of biological, social, and economic forces.

The theatre in which these realistic and naturalistic plays were performed underwent a parallel revolution. The apron stage projecting into the audience now disappeared, and the actors now stepped back and performed inside the picture-frame stage of the modern theatre. The sets became more realistic and solid. The audience now watched the "real-life" events enacted in a room from which the fourth wall had been removed.

Pioneers in Germany, France, England, and Russia welcomed the new plays and developed acting techniques and production methods suitable to their presentation. In 1874 the Duke of Saxe-Meiningen created a new acting company which gave realistic productions; in 1887 the gas clerk André Antoine founded the progressive *Théâtre Libre* (The Free Theatre) in Paris and developed ultrarealistic stage techniques; and in 1899 the critic Otto Brahm founded *Die Freie Bühne* (The Free Theatre) in Berlin for the promotion of realism in plays and play productions. In 1891, Jacob T. Grein established his Independent Theatre in London for the same purpose, and gave Bernard Shaw his first stage production. The best known and most influential leader of realism, the famous Moscow Art Theatre, was established half a dozen years later by Stanislavsky and Nemirovitch-Dantchenko. It became especially known for developing a superb acting company and a system of intensifying the reality of the actor's performance that came to be known as the Stanislavsky system and the "Method." This theatre was particularly successful in producing Chekhov's plays. (See Introduction to Chekhov, page 495.)

A short-lived reaction against didactic realism and naturalism was initiated by the romantic plays of Rostand and by the symbolic dramas of Maeterlinck. *Cyrano de Bergerac* for example, written especially for the talented French actor Constant Coquelin, was a tremendous success in 1897, and has held the stage ever since, satisfying the perennial longings of the human heart for poetic romanticism, heroic actions, and nobility of soul. Sarah Bernhardt, Richard Mansfield, and Walter Hampden found the play to be a splendid popular vehicle for their formidable acting talents. The symbolism and fantasy of Maeterlinck, a leader of the revived romanticism of the last decade of the nineteenth century, were appropriated by twentieth-century dramatists who produced an interesting amalgam of romantic, fantastic, and realistic elements in many of their plays. (See *The Scarecrow*, page 334, *The Glass Menagerie*, page 268, and *The Apollo of Bellac*, page 567.)

So we see that the modern theatre has been a fertile field for dramatic experimentation on an international scale. Every intellectual current of our day has found expression in the theatre: the naturalism of Zola, the existentialism of Sartre, and the Theatre of the Absurd in our troubled days.

In the twentieth century, too, the American theatre, beginning with O'Neill, came of age. His plays and those of Tennessee Williams and others received productions all over the world. "The fabulous invalid," as the theatre has been called because of its instability and its high percentage of failure, refuses to die. Drama, for twenty-four hundred years the most popular of the arts, will continue to express the struggles and aspirations, the tragedies and triumphs of the human spirit.

Some Illustrations of Drama and Theatre

Soldiers guard Antigone while elders watch as she is about to be entombed alive. Scene is from a television production of the famous Greek tragedy.

Theatre of Dionysus in Athens, Greece (340-330 B.C.), had room for more than 17,000 spectators. A portion of the skene and the stage at left center is shown on the cover photograph of this book.

Harlequin. Zany Corneto. Il Segnor Pantalon.

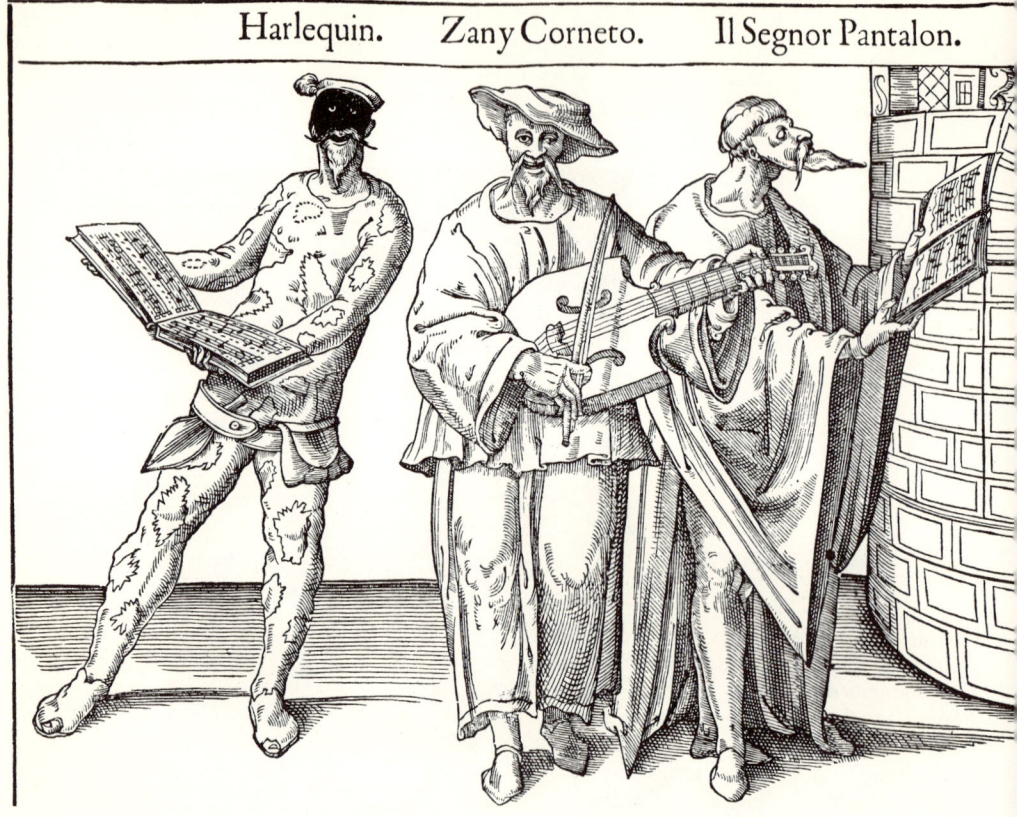

Stock commedia dell' arte characters of the 15-16th century. Players such as these were skilled at improvising lines around various comic situations.

A modern performance of a "mystery" play in York, England, shows *The Adoration of the Magi.*

Model of a familiar sight in medieval England: a pageant-wagon presentation of a biblical story. Scene here is performance of *Noah and the Flood.*

Scenes from modern productions of *Everyman* show Death summoning Everyman, and then Everyman descending into a grave.

A modern performance of *The Passion Play*, on the steps of Notre Dame cathedral, Paris, France, shows crucifixion scene.

Flautin, another commedia dell' arte type, shown playing a guitar. Pantomime tradition dates back many centuries, and many performers keep it alive today. Above, pantomimist Jean Louis Barrault in clown-like costume chases elusive imaginary butterfly.

16. S. Anthoines.	19. the Duth Chucche.	22. Leadne Hall.	25. S. Andrew.
17. S. Laurens Poultney.	20. S. Michaelis.	23. Fichmongeeshal.	26. S. Dunston in
18. The Exhange.	21. S. Peter.	24. S. H...	de cast.

A view of London during Shakespeare's time. Buildings with flags at lower left are playhouses. The famous Globe theatre where Shakespeare's plays were performed is at number 37 in this scene from an old print.

A portrait of William Shakespeare.

A private performance of a play for Queen Elizabeth and members of her court.

A diagrammatic reconstruction of the Globe stage. Note flexible play area.

A scene from a 16th century English comedy, *Gammer Gurton's Needle*, as performed by high school students. Here a lost needle is discovered.

Model of an English courtyard where plays were performed. The Globe's design was an outgrowth of the earlier courtyard stages.

Romeo and Juliet meet for the first time in Shakespeare's ageless love story. Lovers are shown at left.

A model of a portion of the Globe theatre showing balconies at left, and also part of the stage with black drapes indicating that a tragedy is being performed.

The Nurse watches carefully as Romeo speaks to Juliet.

Scene from a performance of Sheridan's *School for Scandal* by an English company in London's Theatre Royal. In library are, left to right, Moses, Careless, and Sir Oliver Surface.

Two old prints show comic highlights of *School for Scandal:* (top) Charles Surface auctions the family portraits; and (bottom) the screen scene showing Lady Teazle being discovered in the apartment of Joseph Surface.

The comic tradition of Molière is continued at the Comédie Française in Paris, France. Scene here is from Molière's *School for Wives*. Note style and costumes.

Line drawing shows detail of Hindu God in Lord Dunsany's *A Night at an Inn*.

Scene above shows entrance of the Hindu God in a notable performance of the play off-Broadway in New York City.

In another scene from Ibsen's play (above), Dr. Stockmann is restrained by his wife Katherine, and daughter Petra, from hitting the wily printer Aslaksen with an umbrella.

At left, an angry mob threatens Dr. Stockmann and members of his family in a scene from a Broadway production of Ibsen's *An Enemy of the People*. Here the Doctor is named a traitor.

Scenes from a high school production of Lord Dunsany's *A Night at an Inn* show (above) one of the Hindu God Klesh's priests stealthily entering the inn room; and (below) another version of Klesh as he arrives to mete out justice to the cowering Toff, at right, and his henchmen.

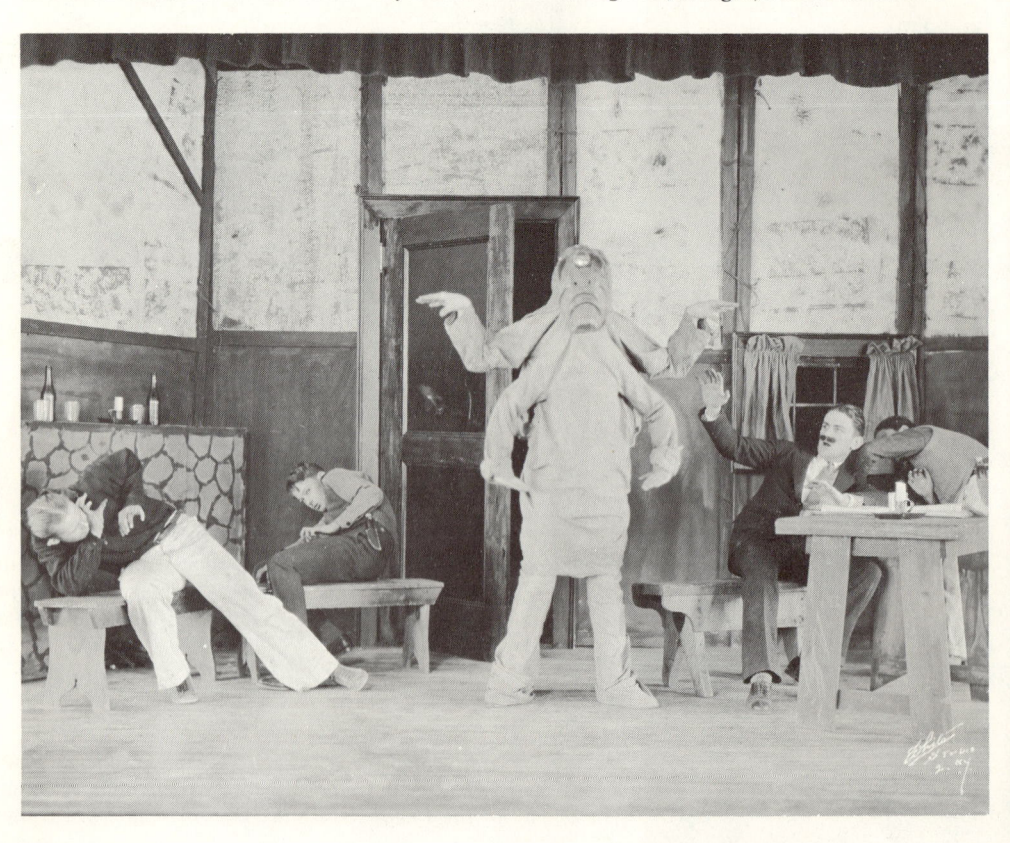

Elizabeth Barrett's father, left, confronts his daughters concerning a clandestine visit by a suitor, Captain Surtees Cook, in a scene from a high school production of Rudolf Besier's *The Barretts of Wimpole Street*. A favorite of theatre groups, the play has many exciting moments.

In a community theatre production of Besier's play, Barrett, the father, is shown forcing a confession from his daughter Henrietta as other members of the family react to the tense action.

Tom Wingfield recalls a portion of his life as his sister and mother re-enact the action in Tennessee Williams' memory play, *The Glass Menagerie*. Scene is from a university production. Stage setting is simple, but effective for play's delicate mood.

In a state college production of Shaw's *Arms and the Man*, Captain Bluntschli reads a list of his possessions in the final scene of the comedy. Listening are: Raina, Louka, Major Saranoff and Madame Petkoff.

In one of the first performances of Percy MacKaye's tragedy of the ludicrous, *The Scarecrow*, university players impersonating Goody Rickby, left, and Dickon, right, are seen as they watch the result of magical spells bring their creation, Lord Ravensbane, staggeringly to life.

Dr. Haggett, his wife and his daughter, at left, receive startling news about some paintings, and Abby, their maid, offers an explanation in Sidney Howard's comedy, *The Late Christopher Bean*. Scene is from Broadway production starring Pauline Lord, right.

Dr. and Mrs. Haggett admire a portrait of Abby. She removes frame, but won't give up picture.

TRAGEDY, SOCIAL DRAMA AND MELODRAMA

Three more or less distinct types of serious drama have appeared frequently in the theatre of the Western world. *Tragedy* takes life seriously by dealing with meaningful suffering and showing men and women struggling with their fate. *Social drama* examines life in society and focuses attention on its problems and conflicts. *Melodrama*, in concentrating on crimes and catastrophes that keep the playgoer in suspense or fill him with excitement, highlights—often quite sensationally—the world of good and evil with which men are concerned in reality and in fantasy. In reality, because there is always violence or the possibility of violence in the world; and in fantasy because our anxieties fill our imagination and our dreams with weird discoveries and strange terrors.

In all the above-mentioned types of drama the dominant tone is serious and at times even somber, even though the play may also include comic elements. Only one other major form of drama is not quite covered by the terms *tragedy*, *social drama*, and *melodrama*. Simply called "drama" or designated by the French word *drame*, this type of play is a blend of tragedy and comedy. It produces concern for some character or group of characters without developing the exalted passions associated with tragedy, without focusing directly (or exclusively) on the subject matter of social drama, and without seeking exciting action solely for the sake of the excitement or "thrill," as in melodrama. An outstanding example of this type of play is Tennessee Williams' most attractive drama *The Glass Menagerie*, presented in another section (page 268). The subject is serious, for the author recalls his unhappy boyhood when he lived in genteel poverty with his well-intentioned but scatterbrained mother and his lovable but helpless sister. The author's treatment is no less serious, for he takes a sympathetic yet critical view of his tense home life, and reflects on the necessity of facing reality, as neither his mother, a former Southern belle, nor his painfully shy sister was capable of doing. But *The Glass Menagerie* presents little people in wholly private circumstances who are important only to themselves. They move us with their simple humanity, and that is just about all that Tennessee Williams intended. He did not try to inflate his little people into heroic characters or their private situations into public ones. Since most people do not stir up the world with their problems, and since many situations in life are inconspicuous yet capable of arousing our interest, there is a place in the theatre for modest plays like *The Glass Menagerie*.

"Drama" or *drame* has had a large hold on the twentieth-century stage. But it does not monopolize the theatre because we still need the uplifting experience of *tragedy*, the challenge to public action contained in *social drama*, and the sheer excitement of *melodrama*. Tragedies continue to be written and the best tragic plays of earlier periods continue to be presented on the stage. If we say that *drame* is the drama of "little" people, we must bear in mind that we also like to consort with people who rise above the common levels of life. We can be stirred and instructed by being kept in touch with great hopes, struggles, and disasters that test the resources of the human spirit.

Many nontragic plays like *The Glass Menagerie*, besides *are* "social dramas" or contain elements of social drama. In *The Glass Menagerie* Tennessee Williams presents little people of his play against the background of the economic depression of the 1930's and World War II. The best known nontragic plays of Chekhov, among which is the modern dramatic masterpiece *The Three Sisters*, also give importance to the social background. He is concerned especially with the pettiness and boredom of provincial life in Russia, the lack of incentives, and the frustration felt by sensitive and intelligent people.

To some degree "social drama" is likely to be encountered almost everywhere in the modern theatre because of our great interest in political conflict, social ideas, and the influence of environment. Man is a social animal, and naturally interested in the stability and welfare of his society. He is also apt to be concerned with problems of social behavior and government that require active participation on his part and that make him choose one side or another in a controversy or a political conflict. In the modern theatre, which reflects the modern world, playwrights have often dealt directly with social and economic problems. They have done so "topically," presenting a specific "topic" of immediate interest and urgency as in plays about presidential elections such as *State of the Union* by Howard Lindsay and Russel Crouse, and in *The Best Man* by Gore Vidal; or they have written about society in terms that are neither topical nor local in essence but "universal." Such a play is *An Enemy of the People*, written in 1882 by Henrik Ibsen. Its subject is the conflict between the individual and his community when his conscience clashes with the materialistic interests of his fellow citizens. The term *social drama* is used most appropriately when a play gives unmistakable priority to the social or political conflict, and our attention is not diverted from it by other considerations.

The existence of this type of drama is taken for granted today, and it often arouses a great deal of public interest. Yet it has had only qualified acceptance from critics who have high standards and expect poetry, imagination, and even profundity from dramatic literature. For such critics, social drama stands only on the foothills of great art. The heights can be occupied only by tragedy, and it must be admitted that these heights have been infrequently attained even by modern playwrights. It would appear, in fact, that the modern mind and spirit have been unfavorable to the development of distinctively *modern* tragedy.

Most tragedies written in modern times have dealt with the past, more or less in the idiom of the past, or have been set in places remote from the modern industrial world. Only few periods of human history have given rise to plays that have been accepted without reservation as genuine tragedies. These have been chiefly the fifth century B.C. classic Greek, the sixteenth and early seventeenth century Renaissance (which includes the Elizabethan "Age of Shakespeare"), and the "Neo-Classic" late seventeenth century in France in which Jean Racine wrote half a dozen distinguished tragedies, among which his *Phaedra* is the most famous. In the present book tragedy is represented by Sophocles' *Antigone*, one of the great examples of classical Greek drama; and also an example from the Elizabethan age: Shakespeare's *Romeo and Juliet*. Other Shakespearean tragedies such as *Hamlet*, and *Macbeth*, and also Sophoclean tragedies such as *Oedipus Rex*, and *Oedipus at Colonus*, are readily available in library theatre collections for further student study.

It may be useful to start with a broad distinction between *pathos* and *tragedy*. The word *pathos* is of Greek origin and means "feeling" or "suffering." A play may enable us to feel a great deal of sympathy with a character and make us pity him. Such a play, which we may like or even esteem highly if it isn't crudely emotional and extravagantly sympathetic, is *not* a tragedy: it is simply a drama or *drame*. (See above, page 13.)

Another distinction should be made between ordinary people and extraordinary, tragic figures since the suffering character in tragedy should be impressive. He must have more than ordinary human qualities, especially a more than ordinary capacity for doing good and evil, if we are to feel more than pity for him. His personality and situation must fill us with fear or terror, as well as with pity, if his fate is to make an extraordinary impression on us. Our being able to pity him is not enough. A play is not a tragedy simply because it is "serious" and gives the impression of dealing with "real" people and "real" emotions. The application of the word "tragic" to any kind of misfortune or misery is undiscriminating, and should be avoided, especially in defining a play or, for that matter, a novel.

Still another distinction needs to be made between a "true" report on some character's fate and a tragic presentation of his fate. The latter is true not to the literal facts, but to the *essence* of the experience—that is, to its universal and meaningful aspects. *Tragedy* is, therefore, imaginative rather than reportorial, and poetic rather than prosaic. Tragedies are normally written in verse or in poetic prose—that is, prose highly expressive, intense, and more or less imaginative or metaphorical. Even when written in prose, a tragedy *transcends* commonplaceness, *recreates* experience, and gives intense (frequently, indeed eloquent) expression to its subject matter. In these respects a tragedy may even be described as a distinctly poetic type of drama or, perhaps, a dramatic form of poetry.

Tragedies usually conclude with the defeat or the actual death of the chief character. But the author of a true tragedy has not provided the catastrophe for the purpose of merely frightening or shocking the audience, as in the case of melodrama. In other words, the catastrophe must have some point and carry some meaning. It must ultimately be based on our sense of reality, and must not be purely accidental. If I walk down the street and a flowerpot drops on my head, the event cannot be properly called a tragedy. Even when accidents do occur, the sufferer must collaborate with his fate, so to speak; his character or will and his actions or decisions must help to bring about his misfortune before his suffering can attain any significance.

A play devoid of emotional power is not a tragedy; neither is it a tragedy if it is merely fanciful and arbitrary. A tragedy, no matter how poetic, discovers significance of a spiritual and moral nature in life, even if the tragic character himself should conclude, as Macbeth does, that

"Life's but a walking shadow, a poor player
That struts and frets his hour upon the stage
And then is heard no more";

or a tale

"Told by an idiot, full of sound and fury,
Signifying nothing."

It is no wonder, then, that tragic art has been regarded as the most distinguished form of drama. It is no wonder, either, that in a good tragedy we are expected to emerge from the experience of suffering purged by the "pity and terror" we have felt, having had a so-called *catharsis* (*katharsis*). The spectacle of tragedy awakens and refreshes us, and we leave it enriched with insight and strengthened in spirit. It is the "paradox of tragedy" that we derive pleasure from the pain it gives us. Its rhythm or pattern is one of defeat culminating in spiritual victory, of a sort of death-and-resurrection ritual out of which tragic art emerged some twenty-five centuries ago.

We may say, then, that tragedy is an art that enables us to retain some mastery over life, to heal its wound, and to overcome its apparent accidental character. We observe men, trying to realize their wishes (developing a *purpose*), become embroiled as a result in inner and outer conflicts (*passion*), and arriving after much suffering at last, at some understanding (or *perception*), of themselves and their fate. This is the "tragic rhythm" that has been defined as a dramatic movement from PURPOSE, to PASSION, to PERCEPTION.

Tragedy has been one way in which man has attempted to make sense out of the trials of life. It is one way in which he has tried to make order out of disorder, confusion, and failure in the world. It is not surprising that many great tragedies are thoroughly grounded in the great religious and moral questions that have concerned mankind throughout history. These, moreover, have ramifications in other areas of human interest, the psychological, as in *Hamlet*, and the social or environmental, as in *Antigone*, and even in that tragedy of young love *Romeo and Juliet*, since civic disorder is a major cause of the catastrophe. Men's fate, whether they are kings like Oedipus, or young girls like Antigone and Juliet, is involved in the dramatic complications, and the destiny of states like the Thebes of Oedipus, Creon, and Antigone, and may hinge on the decisions of the main characters.

Tragedy is not only the most exalted, but also the most comprehensive of the arts. Its great range is exemplified by the first two plays in the following section: *Antigone*, with conflict between religion and the state, or between an individual's conscience and the law; and *Romeo and Juliet*, with the experience of love and hate in a world of passion and unreason.

Tragedy, social drama, melodrama, and every other recognizable type of play may appear in verse or prose, or partly in verse, and partly in prose. Structure or form may also differ radically: Greek tragedy follows a formal pattern consisting, in the main, of an alternation of dramatic scenes (*episodes*) and choral songs and recitations. Shakespeare's tragedies, on the other hand, consist of a continuous flow of varied events which may move rapidly from place to place over considerable periods of time. Classic Greek tragedies, by contrast, tend to adhere to the so-called "unities of time, place, and action," with the action rarely occurring in more than one place or consuming more than a single day or "a single revolution of the sun." Neo-classic drama, as represented by the plays of Pierre Corneille and Jean Racine in seventeenth century France, follow these "unities" even more strictly. Classic and neo-classic tragedies have single plots, and mingle serious and comic scenes only very rarely, as in the Sentry's first scene with Creon in Sophocles' *Antigone* (see page 27). Whereas Elizabethan tragedies may include comic scenes, and combine a main plot with a subplot. Modern tragedies may have loose structure or may be very tightly constructed as shown in plays of Ibsen and Strindberg; or modern playwrights may follow a formal pattern and even include choral passages—as T. S. Eliot did in *Murder in the Cathedral*.

Aristotle, the fourth century B.C. Greek philosopher, wrote the first known study of tragedy in his *Poetics*, a work that has been closely studied, interpreted, and sometimes misinterpreted. His definition of tragedy has had wide currency.

Tragedy, according to Aristotle, is a serious drama which arouses "pity" and "fear"—"pity" for unmerited misfortune, and "fear" that we may be overcome by the same evils as the characters in the tragedy. The pity and the fear experienced by us in witnessing the tragedy are supposed to bring about a purgation or *catharsis* of the fear and pity, and similarly disturbing emotions we harbor in ourselves. Exactly how this purgation is produced in us is not clearly explained by Aristotle, and has been the subject of considerable dispute.

But there is much agreement on the opinion that we *are* somehow purged and fortified by the tragic experience, and that this is possible because we are able to identify ourselves with the tragic character. We can sympathize with him, and feel that what happens to him may happen to us, too. For this reason, according to Aristotle, the tragic hero should not be an entirely evil man or downright villain, a type of character often found in melodrama. We cannot believe ourselves to be wholly bad and cannot therefore identify ourselves with such a character. Moreover, we cannot truly sympathize with him when he gets into trouble or is destroyed; we can only conclude that he is getting what he deserves and reaping as he has sown. Nor can the tragic hero be a wholly good man, according to Aristotle and his followers, because the destruction of such a character may outrage our feelings, so that our anger and revulsion may take precedence over our "pity and fear."

There can be some dispute over this last-mentioned point, and the need to modify it is made evident by a closer examination of the Sophoclean tragedy, *Antigone*. There can be little doubt that Sophocles saw no moral fault in the heroine after whom the play is named. She violated an edict forbidding the burial of one of her brothers, and this law, pronounced arbitrarily by the new ruler of the state, Creon, violated decency and religion in addition to outraging the heroine's private sentiments. But it can be argued that although she is morally in the right, she makes errors of judgment that prove costly even if they leave her heroism unstained. She is intemperate in dealing with the king, who is her uncle, and it may also be maintained that she would not have killed herself so soon after being walled up alive in a cave if she had been less impetuous. Her strong character and all her other virtues, added to her error of judgment (her impractical idealism), brought about her suffering and death. With this in mind, we can understand what Aristotle meant when he said that the tragic character should be a good person who suffers as a result of some tragic flaw (*hamartia*); the misfortune results from either some flaw in character (Macbeth becomes a murderer because he is impelled by extreme ambition to become king of Scotland) or some error in judgment or in policy. Thus Antigone encompasses her own destruction through her incautious nobility, and Oedipus (who murdered his father and committed incest unwittingly) destroys himself with his persistent pursuit of the truth and violent reaction to his terrifying discovery. The headlong passion of the pure love of Romeo and Juliet contributes to their undoing.

No matter how we interpret the details of the dramatic action in these and other famous tragedies, we must concede that the tragic action arises from the characters and reflects human nature as well as the outside world of circumstance and accident. At least this much truth is present in the Aristotelian idea that a tragic character is destroyed by a "tragic flaw" in an otherwise good or admirable person.

This more or less close relationship between character and fate is an important factor in distinguishing between true tragedy and simple *melodrama*, a play that may interest and excite the playgoer, but that cannot be taken very seriously after the play is over, because in a melodrama the author merely *pretends* to be serious but is really interested only in providing excitement. The action in a melodrama (even in the case of so excellent an example as Lord Dunsany's *A Night at An Inn*, page 196) does not arise from the characters but from their situation and from supernatural intervention: the characters are simply thrust into such a play in order to perform actions required by the playwright for his plot. The characters therefore tend to be types—heroes or villains—rather than fully created individuals. And at the conclusion we may be left excited or thrilled, but neither enlightened nor calmed. We do not attain the peace of tragedy that the poet John Milton described as "calm of mind, all passion spent"—which is also an apt definition of tragic catharsis.

SOPHOCLES (495-406 B.C.)

Of the three famous tragic dramatists of ancient Greece, Sophocles is probably the greatest. Aeschylus was more preoccupied with profound religious and ethical problems, such as the meaning of divine justice; Euripides, the psychologist and skeptic, with the tangled emotional conflicts that war, religion, and politics engender in the souls of men, and especially women. But Sophocles, with his "even-balanced soul," was interested primarily in man as a complex human being heroically and painfully striving to attain knowledge and happiness in a world governed by inexorable laws. Less the religious idealist than Aeschylus, less the social critic than Euripides, Sophocles was the realistic, sympathetic humanist "who saw life steadily, and saw it whole."

His life spanned almost the whole of that remarkable fifth century when Athens reached the height of her glory in drama, philosophy, art, and architecture. Sophocles' ironic and tragic vision of life was not the result of any personal misfortunes. Sophocles lived a long, happy, fruitful life writing more than 120 plays. At the age of ninety he wrote his valedictory to the Attic stage, his beautiful mystical play *Oedipus at Colonus*. Upon him the gods showered their abundant gifts: riches, beauty, health, genius, fame, a long life, and a peaceful death.

He was born about 495 B.C. in Colonus, a suburb on a lovely hill about a mile from Athens. His well-to-do family gave him the best education obtainable, and he grew up to be a handsome, intelligent youth, an accomplished musician, and an excellent athlete. At the age of fifteen he was chosen to lead a boys' chorus celebrating the victory at Salamis. When he was only twenty-seven, he defeated Aeschylus in the annual dramatic competition. Because of his long dramatic career and his consummate art, Sophocles won the first prize more than any other competitor. Unfortunately, only seven of his plays have survived: *Ajax, Antigone, Maidens of Trachis, Oedipus the King, Electra, Philoctetes,* and *Oedipus at Colonus*.

He distinguished himself equally in civic affairs. With Pericles he was chosen one of the ten generals, the highest elective office in Athens, and served with him in the war against the Samian revolt. Later he was put in charge of the Greek confederacy funds. His contributions to the drama, and his zeal in public affairs won for him the respect of the whole community. Besides his fellow dramatists, his friends included Herodotus and Thucydides, the historians; Socrates, the philosopher, and young Aristophanes, the comic dramatist. Sophocles died in 406 B.C. honored by all the citizens whom he had served so well.

Sophocles, the dramatist, made several important contributions to the development of Greek tragedy. By introducing a third actor, he made both the plot and characterization more complex. Though for choreographic reasons he increased the size of the chorus from the customary twelve to fifteen, he subordinated its function and laid increased emphasis on the plot and dialogue. He made each play of the conventional trilogy a separate organic unit. He delineated characters more subtly, and created better parts for the actors. By stressing action on the stage rather than lengthy narration by messengers, he increased the dramatic interest in his plays. By his improved dramatic technique he motivated the entrances and exits of his characters. He made costume innovations, and finally, he is credited by

INTRODUCTION TO *Antigone* 21

the philosopher Aristotle with inventing painted scenery. It is no wonder that Sophocles was honored both as a man and dramatist many years after his death.

INTRODUCTION TO *ANTIGONE*

For almost three thousand years the poignant story of Oedipus and his family has held a strange fascination for mankind. Though mentioned but briefly by Homer in the *Odyssey*, the legend became a popular subject for Attic dramatists. Sophocles wrote three tragedies dealing with the family; the earliest was *Antigone* (about 441 B.C.), the next was *Oedipus the King* (about 430 B.C.), and the last was *Oedipus at Colonus* (401 B.C.). The modern reader or spectator will understand and enjoy a play like *Antigone* better if he familiarizes himself with the background of the story. What follows is a very brief account of the main events.

Warned by an oracle that their newborn son would murder his father and marry his mother, Laius, the king of Thebes, and his wife, Jocasta, exposed the infant to die. The child, called Oedipus, or Swellfoot, survived. Years later, however, while running away in an attempt to escape the prophecy, Oedipus unknowingly killed his father in a highway brawl. His travels soon took him to Thebes where he rescued the Thebans from the terror of the Sphinx by answering the riddle she posed. The grateful Thebans thereupon made Oedipus their king, and he married the queen, Jocasta. Thus, both prophecies were fulfilled.

For years he reigned as a popular and beloved ruler, with Jocasta and their two sons, Polynices and Eteocles, and their two daughters, Antigone and Ismene. Then, a devastating plague struck the kingdom, and the oracle warned that the country would be spared only if the murderer of Laius were exposed and punished. After an agonizing search, Oedipus discovered the truth and blinded himself; and Jocasta committed suicide. The plague was at last lifted.

For twenty years Oedipus lived on in Thebes, until Creon, now the regent of Thebes, expelled him. Accompanied only by Antigone, blind Oedipus wandered from place to place. His son Polynices sought him out to ask help in the civil war, but Oedipus denounced both his sons for their faithlessness, and predicted their deaths. Oedipus died in Colonus, where he had been given haven by Theseus, king of Athens.

Civil war continued in Thebes until it was agreed to settle the issue through single combat of Eteocles and Polynices. Oedipus' prophecy was fulfilled as the two died by each other's hand.

Creon decreed that Eteocles should be buried a hero, but that Polynices, an enemy of the state, should remain unburied. However, in response to her brother's last request to her (that she bury him in the event of his death while fighting against Thebes), Antigone defied Creon's decree. It is at this point that the play *Antigone* opens.

One of the most persistent conflicts in human history has been the opposition of the individual soul or conscience to delegated authority, or the clash of human and divine law. Socrates heroically faced his Athenian judges; Joan of Arc, her inquisitors; Thomas à Becket and Sir Thomas More, their English sovereigns; Anne Hutchinson, her Puritan accusers; and Thoreau refused to pay a tax to support slavery and a war he considered morally indefensible. Twenty-four hundred years ago Sophocles dramatized this age-old ethical problem in his play *Antigone*.

The tragic, blind Oedipus wept prophetic tears when he lamented the bitter fate that he foresaw for his two daughters. In the opening scene of the *Antigone* Sophocles quickly informs us of Antigone's firm resolution to defy King Creon's decree. The eternal battle, between the individual conscience upholding what she calls the eternal unwritten laws of God and the secular law of the state, is once more joined.

Sophocles does not sentimentalize this conflict by portraying Antigone as a perfect, starry-eyed heroine, and Creon as a conscienceless villain. In the end heroic goodness does not triumph over evil. The Attic dramatist was too much the realist, and was too familiar with human frailties to falsify life in this way. Admirable as Antigone is in her love for her brother, her respect for the dead, her reverence for the higher unseen law; and heroic as she is in her defiance of Creon, the king of Thebes, she is presented as contemptuous of her gentle sister Ismene, fierce in her denunciation of those who disagree with her, and boastful in justifying her martyrdom. Despite her weaknesses, what makes her a universal tragic figure like Oedipus is her fanatical zeal in clinging to a noble ideal even though it leads to her destruction. Creon is as stubborn and sincere as she is in upholding what he considers to be the security of the state and his duty as king. He is a new, inexperienced ruler who finds it difficult to withdraw his first edict, so openly defied by a young girl. How evenly balanced the two antagonists are in their dramatic debate is evident from the fact that the chorus, which has been described as "the ideal spectator," is easily swayed from one to the other.

Yet that Sophocles wants us finally to sympathize with Antigone is clearly evident. Sophocles, the traditionalist, believed that human authority and divine law should be compatible. However, if a conflict should ever arise between the two concepts, the eternal law of the gods should prevail. After all, the virtuous Haemon, Teiresias the prophet, and finally Creon himself accept this truth. At the conclusion of the play, the broken Creon, like the blind Oedipus, learns the bitter lesson of the fallibility of man and the limitations of his power in a complex but morally-ordered universe.

ANTIGONE

SOPHOCLES

ENGLISH STAGE AND TELEVISION VERSION BY JOHN GASSNER

CHARACTERS

ANTIGONE, *Creon's niece and the younger daughter of Oedipus*
ISMENE, *her sister*
CREON, *new king of Thebes (pronounce Thēbz)*
SENTRY
HAEMON, *Creon's sole surviving son*
TEIRESIAS, *the blind old prophet of Thebes*
EURYDICE, *the queen, Creon's wife and Haemon's mother*
Chief elder, *the chorus leader of Choragus (Choragos)*; chorus of the elders of Thebes, *(consisting of 15 men together with the "chief elder")*; guards and attendants; messenger; boy *who leads Teiresias*; and attendants of the queen.

NOTE ON THIS VERSION: *The matter enclosed in parentheses was intended for television production by the Omnibus television program sponsored by The Ford Foundation in the 1950's. It may assist the student in visualizing a possible stage production, but it cannot stand for a stage production in Sophocles' own times except for the presence of a permanent building which represents Creon's palace, a flight of front steps, and a circular area (the orchestra) facing the palace and serving the chorus of the elders of Thebes as a place for dancing and recitation. Entrances and exits are at the right and the left between the palace and the orchestra. In the television directions, the word "percussion" refers to drums, tympani, etc.; "theme up" means rising volume and "under" signifies decreasing volume when the music or the percussion fades under the words of the characters or the chorus.*

A key to pronunciation of characters' names is as follows:

OEDIPUS	Oed-i-pus
ANTIGONE	An-tig-o-ne
ISMENE	Is-me-ne
POLYNICES	Pol-y-ni-ces
TEIRESIAS	Ti-re-si-as
CREON	Cre-on
HAEMON	He-mon
EURYDICE	U-rid-i-ke
ETEOCLES	E-te-o-cles

Music (Theme)
Theme Up
Theme Under

NARRATOR: The greatest of all legends about human fate is the ancient story of King Oedipus and his family. Oedipus, upon discovering that he had killed his father and married his mother unknowingly, was so overcome with horror that he blinded himself and exiled himself from his kingdom. His two sons Eteocles and Polynices, succeeded him, with the understanding that they would alternate as kings of Thebes. When Eteocles refused to yield the crown to his brother, Polynices laid siege to Thebes with the help of an army from the neighboring kingdom of Argos. In the ensuing battle the two brothers slew each other in hand to hand combat. The army from Argos, however, was driven off by the Thebans and the crown passed on to Creon, uncle of the slain brothers and their sisters Antigone and Ismene. Peace, one might have thought, had come at last to the long-suffering kingdom of Thebes. But, no! Fate, operating through the blind heart and will of man, was not yet satisfied. It continued to exact its toll of human suffering, as you shall see.

(*Dissolve to a view of the city of Thebes in moonlight. Then move to a medium shot of the palace of Thebes, a columned edifice with three doors. Center door is the largest. A ramp of steps leads up to the palace, facing which is a semicircular —actually circular—area, with an altar in the center. Entrances to the right and left between this area and the palace steps lead presumably to gates of the city. Music up, then out.*)

(ANTIGONE *and* ISMENE *come out of the palace, door left:* ANTIGONE, *holding a small bronze vase, is in a state of great agitation.*)

ANTIGONE: Ismene, dearest sister, my only one, is there any grief, or any misery, inherited from our father that we have been spared? Sorrow and shame, distress and anguish—all the evil that life can bring has befallen us: You have heard the news perhaps, the outrage Creon has committed against us. Have you heard?

ISMENE: I have heard nothing, Antigone, but that the enemy fled in the darkness; and nothing more I know than that two miserable sisters have lost two unfortunate brothers who died by each other's hand.

ANTIGONE: I knew you hadn't heard, and that is the reason I called you out here. Something must be done at once.

ISMENE: Some strange thing distresses you: What is it, Antigone?

ANTIGONE: What else but that a great disgrace befalls our family? Our brother Eteocles has been buried with due honor and with all customary rites. But Polynices, no less our brother, who died so miserably, lies, I hear, unburied in the field—for the birds of prey to swoop down and feast upon him, a welcome carrion for them, unwept and unhonored: and this is what Creon, our kinsman, our *virtuous* Creon, decreed! And soon the entire city will hear of it; he is coming here to proclaim the edict to all who do not yet know it. No one shall bury Polynices or mourn for him upon pain of death by stoning before all the people; Creon dares give such orders! Now you know all—and now is the time to show yourself the daughter of a noble line or a base common-born woman.

ISMENE: Poor sister, how can I help you?

ANTIGONE: You must decide at once. Will you help me or not?

ISMENE: In what rash, what dangerous thing? What would you have me do?

ANTIGONE: Will you help me remove the dear dead one?

ISMENE: You would dare to do this when it is plainly forbidden?

ANTIGONE: I will not disgrace my birth! I shall do my part—and yours, too, if necessary, by a brother, who is your brother, too.

ISMENE: Oh, overbold one—when Creon forbids it?

ANTIGONE: Creon has no right to keep me from my own.

ISMENE: Oh, remember, sister, how our father perished? How he was loathed and scorned for what he himself so bravely brought to light? And how he ripped out his eyes with his own hands in his anguish! Remember, too, how our own mother died—*his* mother and yet *his* wife! How she, poor woman, twisted out her life in a noose. And now, our two brothers having fallen in a single day, each shedding, each hapless one, the other's blood. We alone are left. So think, Antigone, how we, weak women, shall perish if we disobey the law. I shall pray to the dead to forgive me but, helpless as I am, I shall submit to him who has the power. It is senseless to meddle!

ANTIGONE: I will not urge you then. Remain what you choose to be: I would not let you help me now even if you changed your mind. But *I* will bury him, though I die for it: I shall have peace then, at last, lying by the side of him I loved, sinless in sinning. It is to the dead that my allegiance belongs, in their world I shall abide forever.

(*She starts to move toward the City's Walls*)

And now I leave you since the gods' eternal laws are nothing to you.

ISMENE: I too honor the gods, but I am a frail woman and I cannot defy the laws of the state.

ANTIGONE: Let that be your pretext, if you will. As for me, I am going to raise a mound, heaping the earth on a brother I love.

ISMENE: How I fear for you, Antigone!

ANTIGONE: Have no fear for me. Fend for yourself!

ISMENE: Oh, sister, sister: if you must, be sure to tell nobody; keep it hidden, and I shall keep it hidden too.

ANTIGONE: No, no, I shall hate you if you remain silent: Let everyone know, for from now on I intend to please no one alive! Think, too, what the king will do if you fail to tell him.

ISMENE: How that hot heart of yours makes my blood run cold!

ANTIGONE: I am doing what I must do, pleasing whom I most wish to please.

ISMENE: If only you could! But I know that you cannot. And you must know you propose more than you can do.

ANTIGONE: (*resolutely*) When I have done *all* I can, I shall do no more!

ISMENE: Impossible things should not be attempted at all.

ANTIGONE: No more! I shall come to hate you for your hateful words, and the dead shall hate you, too. Now, leave me to what you think is my madness. I am not afraid, for if I die I shall not die dishonorably.

ISMENE: Go, then, on your way, but remember this: Wild as you are, all who love you must love you still.

(ANTIGONE *goes out right, and* ISMENE, *wringing her hands, runs anxiously, fearfully, into the palace through door left, where the sisters' quarters are presumably located.*)

(*Percussion music as one by one, or in small groups, the* ELDERS *of Thebes approach the palace and take their stand in front of it, a short distance from the lowest step, gradually forming a chorus. Day is breaking as they start to recite:*)

CHORUS OF ELDERS:

O Light of the rising sun,
Brightest beam that ever shone on Thebes
   of the seven gates:
How you have sped in the night the warrior king who with white shield
Came from Argos to destroy our land
As an eagle shrieking shrill with snow-white wing,
Stirred up by the prince Polynices to support his claim.

He raged above the roofs of the city,
Encircling our wide portals with thirsty spears;
But he sped before he could fill his jaw with the blood of our men,
Before the fire-god seized our crown of towers:
So loud the din of battle

We raised against the foe as we smote him
   down!

Crashing to earth he fell
The man who, torch in hand, with mad-
   man's haste
Swept over us with the blast of hate;
And Mars, the god of war, brought each
   foe his fate:
Each captain, matched by captain at one
   gate,
Yielded his armor to the god and fled—
All but the fated ones,
Who, from one father and one mother
   sprung, brother against brother,
Driving their spears to the desperate end
   gave to each other a common death.

But now that victory
Has come to Thebes the glorious land,
Let joy be great;
Learn we forgetfulness,
Taking leave of war;
And all night long, with dance and hymn
Let us go round in state
To the temples of our gods;
And may Bacchus lead us, whose dancing
   shakes the earth.

(*Percussion out. A trumpet sounds. The center door opens.* CREON, *now King of Thebes and wearing the crown, comes out with attendants.*)

AN ELDER OF THE CHORUS: But here at last comes our new king, Creon, crowned by chance, the providence of god. We shall hear now why he has summoned us, the elders of our city at this hour.

(*They range themselves in front of the lowest step, bowing lightly, as* CREON *descends one step to address them, flanked by attendants. He holds a scroll in his hand. An elderly reverent man, the chief of the elders, steps forth to greet him, then goes back to join the chorus and to act as its leader.*)

(*Trumpet. Then drum-beat under.*)

CREON: Elders of Thebes, the ship of state vexed by the gods' wild waves has been safely righted again and stands steady. I have summoned you here separately to establish at once with you, before the rest of Thebes, my right to the throne as next in the royal line now that the sons of Oedipus are dead. You were loyal to Oedipus when he ruled the land, and then loyal to them when they became the rulers of Thebes, and I expect you now to be loyal to *me* now that I possess the throne and its power. I realize of course that no ruler can be known in mind and spirit until his judgment has been tested. But you will know *my* mind, since I have summoned you for this purpose. You will see me at once as a man who puts his country's welfare above all the claims of friendship and kinship, for I set nothing above the state. I hold him most base who keeps his lips locked tight when the nation's welfare is at stake; and I have only contempt for a man who puts his friend ahead of his country. Let Zeus be my witness, Zeus who sees everything, that I would never hesitate to speak out full and clear if I saw my people heading for disaster. Nor will I ever treat as friend my country's foe, never forgetting that only while the ship of state prospers and keeps us safely afloat can we have true friends. It is in conformity with these principles, which secure the city's welfare, that I have had Eteocles, who fell fighting for our city, buried with full honors as becomes a hero. But I have left the body of his miserable brother, traitorous Polynices, unburied where he fell outside the city's gate. He sought to destroy his city and consume the altars of his fathers and their gods with fire. He sought to spill his kinsmen's blood or else enslave his countrymen. I shall never reward evil with virtue's due! And now, having drawn up my decree, I have summoned you to hear it.

(*Unrolling the scroll, he reads from it.*)

"Whereas Polynices came to Thebes with fire and sword to claim the throne from his brother, who died fighting for our land; whereas Polynices waged war against Thebes, it is my will and command that no man shall touch his body or pray for him on pain of death. Unburied he shall lie, a shameful sight, for the birds and the dogs to have their fill of him." So you know the bent of my mind. As long as I rule, only the friend of the state, living or dead, shall receive any consideration.

CHIEF ELDER: That is your will, Creon, son of Menœceus, touching the city's foe, and yours is the power to order things for the living as well as for the dead.

CREON: You are to heed this order, and see to it that there is no disobedience.

CHIEF ELDER: But would that the burden were placed on younger shoulders than ours! We are too old to carry out this task.

CREON: I do not require this of you that you should keep watch. I have posted sentries to watch the corpse.

CHIEF ELDER: Then what task do you require us to perform?

CREON: I require nothing more from you than this: That you refrain from giving support to those who violate my decree.

CHIEF ELDER: Who would dare? Only fools are in love with death.

CREON: And death *is* the penalty I have established for this crime. Yet bribery flourishes and the love of profit has lured many a man to his ruin.

(*The* CHORUS *is about to speak when a soldier, the* SENTRY, *enters the scene from the right, troubled and hesitant, but trying to put on a bold face as far as possible.*)

SENTRY: I would not say, my lord, that I have come breathless with speed; I will not say I came plying nimble feet, for I had many halting points of thought and I felt like turning back. My mind kept on saying to me, "You ox! why must you go to your doom?" But then I reflected that if Creon gets the news from someone else, it will be worse for me. So, revolving all this in my mind, I came in haste—but *slow*, and made a short road long. So here I am ready to speak out, though what I have to say doesn't make any sense. After all, whatever happens, I said to myself, I can suffer only my fate.

CREON: Come, come! What is your trouble, man?

SENTRY: First, I want to say a word about myself: Let it be understood, my lord, *I didn't do it, and I didn't see who did*. It wouldn't be right if I were punished for it.

CREON: You are very good at fencing —or putting a fence around yourself. You must have something very curious to report. What is it?

SENTRY: A man bringing dreadful news, you know, has reason to hesitate.

CREON: You have hesitated enough— out with it, man!

SENTRY: Well, I suppose I must. The corpse, my lord—someone gave it burial. Someone sprinkled it with dust, performing the proper rites for the dead, and— disappeared.

CREON: What are you saying, soldier? *What man dared?*

SENTRY: I don't know. There was no stroke of axe in the dry ground, and the earth was not dug up. We found no chariot-wheel tracks in the dust, and he who did it went and left no sign. There was no sign whatever that human hands had done the deed. When the first day-watchman came to relieve us, it was he who showed us what had been done—the dead entirely hidden under dust, as if someone had tried to avert the curse that lies on those who are left unburied. And the wonder of it is that no dog nor wild beast had been there to disturb the body. Words then flew fast, each man accusing the other, until we nearly came to blows. Every man was accused, though no one could be proved guilty; each man was willing to take a red-hot iron in his hand or walk through fire to prove his innocence. Then when we saw that nothing was to be gained by wrangling, someone spoke up sensibly, and his advice was to bring the news to you. So we threw the dice—and I, *I* it was who won the *precious* prize. So here I am.

(CREON *has been silent throughout this report—cold and erect.*)

CHIEF ELDER: My mind, our king, has long been whispering: Can the gods have done this thing by themselves?

CREON: Stop this nonsense, before I call you a ripened fool! This cannot be! Would the gods favor the corpse of man who vowed to lay their temples low? You anger me! Would the gods favor a wretch who came, with a foreign army, to burn the land over which they watch and to flout their laws? But I have long had reason to suspect men of murmuring in secret, of wanting to lift their head against me, resenting my orders and my rule: I say there are foul conspirators afoot—men who never yet learned to put their haughty neck beneath the yoke of law: I do not doubt that they have bribed the soldiers with the clink and color of gold. This base metal lays cities low. *This* drives men from their peaceful dwelling-places; money it is that warps the minds of even honorable men, and teaches them corruption. But they who yielded to their greed and allowed themselves to be bribed shall rue their villainy in time; they shall be found out!

(*To the* SENTRY, *coldly*)

Sentry, hear my solemn oath by Zeus before you go! Unless you find the man whose hand was in this plot and produce him before me here, you will come to consider death itself a mercy, for death shall not be enough for you. I shall keep you hanging half-alive until you confess who bribed you.

SENTRY: (*quaking*) May I speak? Or shall I turn at once and go without a word?

CREON: Even your voice offends me. Stop your babbling, fool, and *go*!

SENTRY: I may be a babbler, my lord, but I am no traitor. I didn't bury the corpse; I am not guilty.

CREON: Not guilty? You sold your soul for silver, miserable fellow, didn't you? You pain me.

SENTRY: Not I, my lord; the doer of the deed does, but not I. It is a terrible thing, surely, when judges make errors in judgment and misjudge one.

CREON: (*vehemently*) Judgment or no judgment, play with your words as you will, you will get judgment aplenty unless you bring me the man who did it.

(CREON *turns abruptly from the* ELDERS *and starts up the steps. The* CHIEF ELDER *starts to follow him hesitantly, but returns to the* CHORUS *as* CREON *enters the palace through center door.*)

SENTRY: (*half to the* ELDERS, *half to himself*) Bring the man? I'd like to know how I am to find him! Still, I didn't think to come away alive; so having escaped beyond my hopes, I'll just thank the gods for my safety—and make myself scarce....

(*The* SENTRY *goes off right. The* ELDERS, *greatly troubled, however, merely move away a little from the palace steps and arrange themselves as a* CHORUS *facing the palace. Percussion up.*)

CHORUS of ELDERS:

Many are the wonders of the world,
But nothing more wonderful than man!
He makes a path in the whitening storm-tossed waters,
He makes the crests of the waves do his work.
Earth, eldest of the gods, immortal and tireless,
He also masters, turning up the soil year after year
With his plows and the labor of yoked stallions.

The light-winged race of the birds
The beasts that roam savage in the fields,
The sea-brood in the deep—he cunningly
  snares them all in his woven nets,
And by his subtle arts he brings the binding yoke
Upon the neck of the rough-maned horse
  and the shoulders
Of the mountain bull.

And speech, and thought swift as the wind,
And a tempered mood for the civic work
  of states
Has he taught himself;
And how to escape the nip of the frost
  under the winter skies,
And the arrows of the rain.
Man is all-provided!
Against death alone is he unprovided,
  but he has mastered even disease by
  his art.

Cunning is he beyond all measure of
  thought
With his intelligence and skill to plan
Now for evil, now for good.
And holding fast to the laws that rest
  upon the justice of God,
A city can proudly stand.
But there is no city for the man
Who lets his mind dwell with evil.
Never shall he, an outcast for his presumption,
Share my heart and my thoughts who becomes reckless.

(*The* SENTRY *appears from the right, leading* ANTIGONE *who holds herself erect with pride and defiance.*

CREON *who had come out of the palace during the last part of the chorus, begins to descend the steps.*)

CHIEF ELDER: But what is this, what strange vision fills me with wonder? I know the maiden. Oh, doom from God, this is Antigone, unhappy daughter of an unhappy father. (*to* ANTIGONE) Surely it isn't you who braved the king's decree, and are brought here for judgment!

SENTRY: We caught her burying the dead man again after we had uncovered the corpse. Where is the king?

CHIEF ELDER: There he comes from the palace door, arriving in time.

(CREON *enters*)

CREON: Why "in time"?

SENTRY: Men, my king, should bind themselves to nothing by oaths, for after the lashing you gave me I swore that you wouldn't see me here again for a long time. But a welcome surprise makes me break my vow—and no casting of lots brings me to you this time for the prize is mine; I bring the maid. (*pushing* ANTIGONE *forward*) Take her, my lord, and question her—she is yours now, and I can depart well rid of it all.

(*The* SENTRY *starts to walk out, when* CREON *stops him imperiously as he regards* ANTIGONE *with great anger.*)

CREON: But your prisoner is—Come back here! Tell me how and where you found her.

SENTRY: In the act of burying the dead.

CREON: Are you telling the truth?

SENTRY: I saw her burying the corpse myself.

CREON: But how could this be?

SENTRY: After sweeping away the dust that had been heaped on the body, and laying bare the tainted corpse, we sat on a hill to windward, shunning the infected air, and watched the cadaver from there. Every man was awake, and was keeping the next one awake, remembering your threats. So it was until the white sun stood straight above us, when suddenly a high wind leaped from earth, and a storm of dust, stripping the woods of their leaves, made us close our eyes. The storm lasted a long while. But when it passed at last, and we looked up she was there looking at the corpse at her feet. With a cry shrill as a bird's when it beholds the nest robbed of its young brood, there she stood calling down curses on those who had uncovered the body. Dust she had brought, and from a vase of bronze she sprinkled the sacred water over the dead. When we ran down and charged her with the deed she denied nothing, and this was a relief to me, though it made me uneasy, too. (*apologetically, to the* ELDERS, *but as if to* ANTIGONE) To make trouble for anybody—it's not my way, but I like to protect my skin, I do.

CREON: (*dismissing him, and turning to* ANTIGONE *who has kept her head lowered during the* SENTRY'S *report*) You, then, who bend your face to the ground, do you deny his words?

ANTIGONE: He speaks the truth; I deny nothing.

CREON: (*to the* SENTRY) Dismissed! Be thankful you are clear of a heavy charge.

(*The* SENTRY *leaves quietly, with a troubled look sweeping* ANTIGONE *and the* ELDERS)

CREON: Tell me now, Antigone, did you know I had forbidden it?

ANTIGONE: I knew. (*reproachfully*) How could I not know when your edict was proclaimed everywhere?

CREON: You disobeyed the edict then. You dared?

ANTIGONE: I dared: The edict was not from the God who rules above: Nor was it Justice, she who dwells with the gods who reign below, that ordained this: No law of yours, you being a mortal man, can supersede the never-changing unwritten laws of heaven! These are not of today or yesterday—no man knows when first they came into being, but they are for all time. I would be a weakling to set them aside for fear of earthly judgment; and if I must die before my time for what I have done—well, then, I die, and for one who has suffered as *I* have suffered, there is only gain in this, and no loss.

(CREON *smiles grimly at her*)

Yes, I would have had reason to grieve only if I had left my mother's sow unburied, and if in doing what I did I seem foolish to you, perhaps—perhaps the reason is no other than that the judge who condemns me is himself a *fool*!

CHIEF ELDER: Perverse and obstinate, headstrong child of a headstrong father, when will she learn to yield?

CREON: Know then, passionate fool, that hardest steel can be broken, and horses have been made tame with a bit in their wild teeth!

(*To the* ELDERS)

Guilty in transgressing my law, she is twice guilty now with her insolence; sister's child though she be and so near in blood, I say she is the guilty man— and I am no man at all, if I let her escape the full penalty of the law.

(*As the* ELDERS *react with horror*)

Yes, she—*and her sister*—shall not escape their doom.

(*As the* ELDERS *and* ANTIGONE *are about to protest*)

I found the other one sniveling indoors and distraught; I have no doubt that she is guilty, too; though most I hate those who when trapped at last

(*Looking at* ANTIGONE)

try to brazen out their crime with reasons and call it a *glorious* deed.

(*At a gesture from him, attendants go into the palace for* ISMENE)

ANTIGONE: No man standing before you thinks otherwise, but their tongues are tied; there is nothing base in honoring our own blood.

CREON: Yes, if you honor the good.

ANTIGONE: The dead man was a brother! No less than the other man.

CREON: Brother, indeed, a man bent on laying waste his land while the other brother defended it! And died its champion. An evil man shall not be accorded the same honors as a blameless man.

ANTIGONE: Which of us can say who is blameless and who is not? Polynices had an equal right to the throne he claimed. But if no other reasons move you, remember, Creon, that Hades, the lord of the dead, claims equal rights for all.

CREON: Not when the man dies an enemy of the state; then he becomes unholy.

ANTIGONE: Who knows what is holy or unholy below!

CREON: I know one thing, which you appear not to know: an enemy should be hated even in death.

ANTIGONE: But I was made for love, and not for hate.

CREON: Go then, and love below, in the world of the dead: While I live, I shall not take my law from any woman.

(ISMENE *comes out of the palace door at the right, guarded by* CREON'S *attendants. She rushes down the steps, tearfully.*)

COUNCILOR: (*to the other* ELDERS, *but intending his words for* CREON) Those are a sister's tears; and that is guiltless, gentle sorrow dropping down like rain.

CREON: (*turning fiercely on* ISMENE) You, too, there, creeping like a viper in my house, secretly draining me of my blood, scheming with the other one to thrust me from my throne! Come now, answer me: Will you wail out your innocence, or will you confess your guilty part in this?

ISMENE: (*impulsively, looking desperately at* ANTIGONE) Yes, I have done the deed—that is, if she will let me have my share of suffering.

ANTIGONE: No! Justice will not suffer this. I would not give you a share in my glory now. The deed was *mine* alone!

ISMENE: Don't reject me, sister. Let me die with you.

ANTIGONE: I want no friends in words. You had no hand in it; so let my death alone be enough.

ISMENE: And what life will I have here *alone;* what will life be worth without you, Antigone?

ANTIGONE: Ask Creon! You have no ears for anyone else!

ISMENE: You are laughing at me, sister. Does my grief give you such pleasure?

ANTIGONE: There is no pleasure in my laughter.

ISMENE: Let me help you.

ANTIGONE: No. Save yourself. I don't begrudge you your life.

ISMENE: But I want to share your fate.

ANTIGONE: A little while ago you chose to live: Live, then, Ismene.

ISMENE: Antigone! Oh, sister, remember I warned you.

ANTIGONE: Yes, I know, and your wisdom is approved in this world; mine will be approved in the other: *My* life I gave up long ago.

(CREON *has been listening to them mockingly. It is evident that he has never had a high opinion of* ISMENE, *the weaker sister.*)

CREON: (*to the* ELDERS) Of these two girls, the one (*pointing to* ANTIGONE) is only recently gone mad; the other (*he looks at* ISMENE) has been foolish ever since her life began.

ISMENE: O Creon, the miserable are always foolish—

CREON: *You* certainly are to want to join the guilty.

ISMENE: But how shall I go on living when she is not here?

CREON: That is simple: *She* is no longer here.

ISMENE: But how can you kill Antigone when she is betrothed to your son?

CREON: Death will annul the betrothal. (*brutally*) There will be other fields for him to plow.

ISMENE: He will never espouse anyone so dear to him.

CREON: I don't want a wild slut like your sister for Haemon!

ISMENE: O dear Haemon, how your father wrongs you!

CREON: Enough of your love and marriage prattle. You bore me.

CHIEF ELDER: You are determined, then, to deprive your son of his bride?

CREON: (*grimly*) I won't! But death will!

CHIEF ELDER: (*troubled*) So she must die?

CREON: I am determined that she shall.

(*To his* ATTENDANTS)

Take them inside: they are women and are not to roam about, either of them, like men.

(*Looking at* ANTIGONE)

And guard that one well. Even bold natures take to their heels when they see death closing in on them.

(ANTIGONE *and* ISMENE *are taken to their quarters in the palace, while* CREON *starts pacing about angrily on the lowest step. Meanwhile, the* ELDERS *have moved away a little from their previous positions: and, much troubled, they talk among themselves. Their lines merge into another choral recitation. Percussion up, then under.*)

CHORUS of ELDERS.

Blessed are they who have never known the taste of suffering,
But once a house has been shaken by the wrath of heaven,
The curse never fails, passing from life to life.
Doom swirls from generation to generation
Like thunderous wave upon wave in the black main.
The whirlwind roars, whirling up the damp sand from the depths,
As every mountain peak sends from the north
Blast upon blast to beat upon the shore.

We have seen the gathering evils of this royal house
Whirl on and bring grief upon grief
From age to age, father to son without end;
Surely some god smites them down.
And now the last green sprig of the race of Oedipus is brought low.
A sprinkle of blood-stained dust due to the gods of the underworld
An angry speech spoken in folly
And a seizure of frenzy at the heart have cut it down.

Can the arrogance of man
Check the power of the god whom neither sleep nor age subdues?
Zeus dwells in dazzling splendor forever young
And his law is ever the same:
Nothing that is extreme
Enters the life of men without bringing unhappiness.

As for hope, it comes to many
In wide wanderings so often as a lure of giddy desire
That man knows nothing of what will befall him until he has scorched his feet against the treacherous flames.
A knowing man was he who spoke in years gone by
That evil things seem ever good to those whom fate draws to their destruction:
Short is the hour free from grief.

(*Percussion out. Then* HAEMON, *who has quietly entered from the right side of the stage, starts moving slowly toward his father.*)

CHIEF ELDER: Here comes Haemon, the last of your sons, Creon, brought here by grief for his bride, or is it anger that brings him?

CREON: We shall know soon enough without having to consult any diviners.

(*Moving somewhat less than confidently to* HAEMON)

Son, I know why you have come out: you have been told about the judgment on Antigone. You have not come here in a rage against your father, surely! We are still the good friends we have always been, whatever I did?

HAEMON: I am your son, father, as ever. Your wisdom at the helm of state means more to me than any marriage.

CREON: Spoken like a true son! Fix your heart on nothing but this—obey your father and all will be well. This is what all men pray for: to see dutiful sons growing to manhood in their houses. Whoever breeds undutiful sons breeds trouble and delights his enemies.

(*To* HAEMON)

Do not lose your reason, my son, over an unprofitable woman for the sake of a little pleasure; know that the pleasures of marriage soon grow stale, and cold are the embraces of a wife when she proves worthless. Since I caught the girl disobeying me, the only one in the entire city, and she defied me in front of all the people, I had no choice: I would have made myself out a liar if I had let her go. She must die! Let her appeal as much as she wants to the ties of kinship, she must pay the penalty.

(*As* HAEMON *remains silent*, CREON *becomes agitated*)

Haemon, a city needs the rule of a man, and no man rules the state if he doesn't rule his household. No one may dictate to the ruler or overrule him. Disobedience ruins cities; disobedience makes desolate the homes of men; disobedience in little things and great breaks the ranks of armies. It is better, in truth, to have death than disorder.

(*As* HAEMON *starts to speak*)

Remember, my son, the will of a mere woman must never sway us; I would rather resign from the throne than let a woman defeat me.

HAEMON: The gods, my father, have bestowed reason upon man; and no greater gift has been given to us. Far be it from me to say to you that you are not always in the right; I could never bring myself to reprove you. Yet, father, the reason that has been implanted in all men requires us to heed other men's thoughts as well as our own; and I, who have made it my business to hear words men withhold from you out of fear, I have heard whisperings in the city that in this you are not right. "No woman," men say, "ever deserved this judgment less, none was treated more shamefully for a nobler deed." It is your welfare and your good name that concern me most. No, father, these are not trivial murmurings, but words to be weighed.

CREON: (*his anger rising*) The words of common people, little better than slaves?

HAEMON: (*eagerly*) Father, we must never think that only *our* words are wise. Look how the trees must yield their leaves to the winter leaf by leaf; look how the sailor must slacken his sheets of sail to keep his ship afloat. Father, relent to the reason of others; forget your anger and forgive.

CHIEF ELDER: The lad has spoken well and, you, my king, have also spoken well. So each of you can learn from the other.

CREON: (*exploding*) Shall a man of our years learn wisdom from a boy?

HAEMON: (*pleading*) Consider only my words, father, not my years.

CREON: Tell me this: Is it intelligent to sanction lawlessness?

HAEMON: I do not plead for the lawless.

CREON: Who dares say it is not lawless to do what she did?

HAEMON: *All* the people, father!

CREON: (*raging*) Shall the Thebans prescribe to me?

HAEMON: Father, there is no state where one man's will is supreme.

CREON: Is not the state his who governs it?

HAEMON: A state for one man is no state. What you want is to govern alone, and that is to rule only in a desert.

CREON: (*to the* ELDERS) So I am not to be allowed to punish traitors! I see I have given life to a weakling, who is a slave to a woman; that boy of mine has become a woman's champion.

HAEMON: Only, father, if you are a woman; because I am concerned for you alone.

CREON: An excellent concern!—to wrangle with one's father!

HAEMON: Only when I find him offending against justice and doing wrong.

CREON: So *I* do wrong when I respect my rights? I would not make a liar of myself, I had no choice but to carry out my decree! Whatever you say, you will never marry her in *this* world.

HAEMON: Then she shall die—and in dying cause another to die.

CREON: (*misunderstanding*) So, you've come at last to this and dare threaten your father!

HAEMON: (*puzzled*) How have I threatened you in calling your decision unwise?

CREON: You woman's bondsman, you dare answer me again?

HAEMON: Would you speak and expect no answer?

CREON: (*furiously*) So you taunt me, too. This passes all bounds, and you shall smart for it at once. (*shouting to the* ATTENDANTS) Bring out the loathsome girl and let her be slain immediately—*in his presence.*

HAEMON: Never think of it! And never shall you see my face again.

(HAEMON *runs out*)

CHIEF ELDER: (*worried, while the other* ELDERS *murmur among themselves, distressed*) The boy has run out in a rage. A young mind, Creon, is dangerous when it is goaded.

CREON: (*beside himself, yet a little uncertain*) Let him run! Where he will, do or dream to do what no man can do: He shall not save these two girls from their doom.

CHIEF ELDER: Will you have *both* slain?

CREON: (*reconsidering*) No, of course; you do well to remind me. Only the one who performed the burial shall die.

(*As* ANTIGONE, *her hands tied, is led out of the palace through the side door, he starts to go up to the center palace door.*)

CHIEF ELDER: And what death have you decreed for her?

CREON: (*He hasn't thought of this and is taken aback by the directness of the question. Perhaps he has gone too far! He hesitates and begins to back down a little, but not without trying to bluster his way out*) There is the open rock by the old abandoned road, where it is loneliest. Let her be taken there, and let the cave be walled up there in the rocky vault. I have no wish to make the mistake of tainting the city with her blood, *but still living* shall be buried there. Then let the unseen powers of the underworld, whom she has loved so well, take her in charge. Let her pray to *them* to release her; let her learn, though she learns too late, how vain it is; that it is lost labor to revere the dead.

(CREON *goes up the steps into the palace without looking at the* ELDERS, *as* ANTIGONE, *her hands bound, comes out of the door right. Seeing her, he makes a sign to the* ATTENDANTS *to unbind her hands—and enters the palace. As the* ELDERS *gather together to form the chorus, we see* ANTIGONE'S *hands being unbound, and:* ISMENE *runs out distractedly to her, but she is dragged back by* ATTENDANTS. *Percussion up, then under.*)

CHORUS of ELDERS.

O love, invincible,
That preys upon a rich man's substance
   and wins everything
While lying in wait in the smooth cheek
   of a girl!
You roam about at will over the widest
   sea

And invade the homes of the dwellers in the wilderness.
Not even the undying gods can escape you,
Nor can any mortal man whose life is but for a day!
Your beauty drives him to distraction.

You turn astray the souls of just men to their eternal ruin;
And here in our city you have brought strife between father and son,
And victory belongs only to the love-light in the eyes of a bride. You sit enskied
Equal with the eternal powers!
Immortal Aphrodite, once more
You have worked your invincible will.

(*Percussion out. By now* ANTIGONE *has been brought down and is passing the* ELDERS, *who range themselves in two files for her to pass through.*)

CHIEF ELDER: And now I, myself, am brought beyond the bounds of strict loyalty; for I cannot hold back my tears as I see before me Antigone, the young bride, hurried to the bridechamber where all must lie.

ANTIGONE: Yes, look upon me, men of my fatherland, as I leave the sunlight, never to look upon it again. Hades leads me, death who welcomes all to his black shore, an unwed wife for whom no bridal song shall ever be sung; no dawn for me will shine again as I go my way.

CHORUS: But honor is yours, girl of the noble heart! You depart with glory to the place of the dead, not smitten by the sickness that decays, untouched by the edge of the sword, of your own free will, alone among mortals, you go down to the world below forever young.

ANTIGONE: In days gone by I used to hear of one, the daughter of Tantalus, from whom I trace my descent, how the stones clung about her, like ivy, on the high rock; and how she wastes there still while the rains pelt her body and the snows fall and her tears forever flow. I can feel her sufferings in mine, soon to be imprisoned like her in my tomb.

CHORUS: But she was sprung from the gods, and you and we are mortal. To win renown with the gods in sharing their fate should assuage your pain.

ANTIGONE: You only mock me when you praise. In the name of our fathers, do not taunt me to my face. O holy ground of the Thebans who drive many chariots, O fountains of Dirce in this land, bear witness how unwept of friends and by what cruel laws condemned I pass on to my rock-closed prison with no home on earth or in the shades below, no home either among the living or the dead.

CHORUS: If only you had been less bold, unfortunate daughter of a fated race. Not for yourself alone you suffer—like your father, you dared too much, and your father's guilt has undone you.

ANTIGONE: My father's guilt! You have come to that at last, my bitterest thought, rewakening my grief for my father and the doom of our great house, for the bridal horror of mother and son, the infection of the marriage: From what parents did I draw my miserable life? O Oedipus, my father, from the grave have you smitten me down? And, brother, my unfortunate brother, it is certain your dying has brought me to death.

(CREON *has come out of the center door of the palace glowering. Some of the* ELDERS *see him and move guiltily away from* ANTIGONE.)

CHIEF ELDER: Your headstrong will has brought you to this pass. Reverence for the dead is due reverence, but laws enforced with power cannot be safely defied. You have chosen your doom with your rashness.

ANTIGONE: Unwept, then, and friendless I must journey on this road that lies open for my fate! No longer shall I behold the daystar's sacred light, no tear shed, no moan of a friend for me!

CREON: (*coming down the steps*) Enough! Take her away: If all who are condemned to death were given time to wail at their will, their lamentations would keep them alive forever. Block up the vault and leave her there alone—let her live there as long as she wants or let her die there. *Our* hands shall be clean, not having shed her blood: I want only this, that she shall not share the light of day with us.

(*He makes a gesture, as if saying "Is this an unreasonable thing to wish?" and with a sign from him* ANTIGONE *is led away.*)

ANTIGONE: I go to find my own in death! My unhappy father will bid me welcome; my miserable mother, too; and you, my wounded brother Polynices, whom I tended in his death. None of you will blame me, I know; for I transgressed no law of God; if I *have* done wrong, I shall come to know my sin there from the gods themselves; (*looking hard at* CREON, *who averts his face from her*) but if the guilt is *his* who judges me here, I say, may *he* suffer for it *there* in equal measure!

CHIEF ELDER: (*shaking his head*) Still the same tempestuous heart, driven by the same contentious winds!

CREON: The guards who let her tarry here so long shall be punished for the delay.

ANTIGONE: Ah! that man's voice sends me to my death.

CREON: (*sarcastically*) I would not deceive you by letting you think otherwise!

ANTIGONE: I go, the last of the noble line that gave you *kings*, men of Thebes! Remember what I suffer—*and at whose hands!*—because I would not disregard the laws of god!

CHORUS: (*Percussion up, then under*)
So did another princess, Danaë of old,
Upon whom Zeus descended in a golden shower,
Lose the light of heaven
In a tomb-like chamber enclosed—
Strange and dreadful is destiny. . . .

So was another shut in a cave,
A king who defied the wine-god
And made light of his worshipers
With his words of scorn.

So did another fated man
See his violent wife
Deal wounds of death with a sharp spindle
To his two sons.

So did a mother suffer
A woman wedded with a curse.
Reared though she was by gods,
The fates fell upon her hard. . . .

(*Suddenly, as they turn around, they are thunderstruck, and* CREON *himself is visibly startled. For suddenly a majestic figure appears, wearing a prophet's robes and an ancient priestly mask. There stands* TEIRESIAS *among them, his left hand holding a boy, a novice of the priesthood, by the hand—that is, the boy who leads him, for* TEIRESIAS *is not only very old, but blind. Nobody was apparently prepared for his coming. It is as if he had come out of the earth mysteriously. He must have approached them soundlessly, walking on light feet. And, indeed, there is something unreal and eerie about him. He raises his right hand.*)

TEIRESIAS: (*to the* ELDERS) Princes of Thebes, we have come with linked steps, this boy and I, having only one pair of eyes between us; a blind man can move only with a guide's help.

CREON: What is the meaning of all this?

TEIRESIAS: I will tell you, Creon, and see to it that you heed my words.

CREON: It was never my custom to slight your counsel before, Teiresias.

TEIRESIAS: You steered the city's course well then, and you prospered when you did!

CREON: I can attest to the benefits, and gladly acknowledge my debt.

TEIRESIAS: In that case listen to me now. You stand once more on the fine razor edge of fate.

CREON: What is it? Your words fill me with dread.

TEIRESIAS: Hear my warning then! Sitting as of old on the throne of prophecy by the ancient shrine where birds are wont to gather about me, a noise of doom came to me. Creon, birds were screaming at the altar, and fearful was their shrieking passion; then my ears, that serve me for eyes in my blindness, then my ears accustomed to know the whir of wings, told me they were tearing each other's flesh with murderous talons. I then made a trial of sacrifice at the altar, but the fire of God would not light; a sorry trickle oozed down from the sacrificial flesh, and the embers smoked and sputtered—then I knew everything!

CREON: What riddle are you spinning out for me, Teiresias?

TEIRESIAS: (*sternly*) No riddle at all, Creon: the city's altars are polluted, dogs and unclean birds have tainted them with carrion from the miserable corpse of the son of Oedipus. The gods reject our prayer now that bird and beast have tasted human flesh at the walls!

CREON: What is your drift?

(*He regards* TEIRESIAS *narrowly*)

TEIRESIAS: It is you who have done this and brought evil upon Thebes with your folly, for what glory, rather than folly, is there in slaying the slain?

(CREON *makes an angry gesture*)

Think on this, my son! To err is the common lot of men, but having once erred, he is not blest who stands obstinate. Yield to the dead, Creon! Commit no outrage against a corpse: I speak only for your own good, and such counsel should be welcomed, not scorned or resented.

CREON: It seems I have been the target of every man's arrow: soothsayers have been bribed to deter me from my purpose—prophets have made merchandise of me all my life. I tell you, old man, you may aim all your shafts at me, you may get all the gold of India and fill your house with every sort of gifts, yet that corpse shall have no grave, though eagles themselves take up that traitorous flesh morsel by morsel to the throne of heaven. Teiresias, it is a shameful thing when so old a man as you barters his wisdom in the market place!

TEIRESIAS: (*desperately*) Does no man know—no man understand?

CREON: (*sarcastically*) What, Teiresias? Quick; read me your little lecture.

TEIRESIAS: I have nothing to say that you did not learn from me before, that a word in season is worth all of a man's wealth—

CREON: (*jeering*) Tell me how high you set your fee! The tribe of prophets has always loved gold.

TEIRESIAS: And kings have always loved power.

CREON: Do not forget yourself, Teiresias; you are speaking of your king!

TEIRESIAS: I have good reason to know it, since it was I who made you king.

CREON: I admit you have some skill as a seer, but you are inclined to be dishonest.

TEIRESIAS: Stirred as I am, I shall speak words I have left unspoken—

CREON: By all means! But don't expect to be *paid* for them.

TEIRESIAS: In this alone you are right: Creon, you will not want to pay me for *these* words, but listen well: The sun will not have driven his chariot far before— *corpse* for *corpse*—you have given something of your own flesh to death. The furies of hades are awakened, the dread avengers, because you have thrust children of the sun into darkness, lodging the living in the grave, while, in denying burial to a corpse, you have kept a soul in the world that belongs to the dark gods below! Hear then a prophecy *unpaid* by any man.

(*Swaying as he speaks, almost in sing-song fashion, but strong and clear*)

Yet a little while, a very little while, and a wail of men and women shall fill the house of Creon. Yet a little while, and the angry cities of men shall look with loathing on the one who gives human limbs to dogs and beasts. *These* are arrows for your heart, proud man, and they will reach their mark without fail. (*to the* BOY) Now lead me away, my boy, that he may vent his scorn on *younger* men or learn to keep a *better* tongue in a *clearer* head.

(*He leaves the scene with the* BOY *leading him by the hand*)

(*The* ELDERS *and the* COUNCILOR *have covered their faces with their hands at the dreadful prophecy, and* CREON *himself has been visibly affected. He stands like a dazed man, saying nothing. He seems unaware of the departure of* TEIRESIAS, *who has slowly gone toward the exit at the left, watched by the* ELDERS *until he is enveloped in a mist and disappears. There is a pause. Then the* COUNCILOR *moves forward from the* CHORUS.)

CHIEF ELDER: The man has gone, my king, leaving behind dire prophecies. I have never known him to be mistaken.

CREON: (*reluctantly*) Nor I; it is this that troubles me. The choice is hard: To submit is bitter, but not to give in may be dangerous.

CHIEF ELDER: Creon—

CREON: What would you like me to do?

CHIEF ELDER: Free the girl from her tomb—and give the unburied man a grave.

CREON: So you want me to yield—renounce my intention—

CHIEF ELDER: (*impulsively*) Yes, Creon—yes! And with all speed, for the vengeance of god is swift-footed . . .

CREON: It is hard to give in; but I cannot fight with destiny.

CHIEF ELDER: And do not leave this to others: You must go yourself.

CREON: You are right: I must undo the evil myself. My heart misgives me, and I realize now that the gods' laws must be heeded by man to the very end of his days. (*to* ATTENDANTS) Quickly now, take axes to open the tomb; but since mine was the judgment, I will release her myself.

(*He places himself at the head of his followers*)

(*Percussion up—a wild, uneven drumbeat as* CREON, ATTENDANTS, SERVANTS, *rush out in disorder. And as they leave,* EURYDICE, *the queen, a subdued but intense and evidently long-suffering woman, comes out of the center door with great anxiety. Unaccompanied. She watches the departure, glances hesitantly at the* ELDERS *who have moved away from the steps of the palace and have been forming two groups as a chorus.*)

(*The* CHORUS *is muffled here. Its speech is rapid, full of tension. Some of the* ELDERS *are in an attitude of prayer: some, in attitudes of ecstasy, arms outspread to Heaven, with hopefulness and relief. The two groups are in sharp contrast: the* ELDERS *at prayer are fervidly murmuring words that cannot be heard. Only the* ELDERS *who are in a hopeful ecstasy can be heard—when their voices rise in pitch.*)

(*Drums in "counterpoint": two drums— perhaps a low bass drum and a snare drum. The total effect is one of counterpoint between the two groups.*)

(*The praying group sways toward the ground, as if praying to the awe-inspiring gods of the underworld. The ecstatic group has begun to swing branches, and, now and then, the words come over. But the effect should be weird rather than joyful.*)

(EURYDICE, *showing concern, during this scene goes into the palace—into the door at the left, which we presume led to* AN-

TIGONE's and ISMENE's *apartment—as if she were concerned.*)

CHORUS:
>God of the vine . . .
>>immortal Dionysus . . .
>Your torches of pine
>>flare forth in dance . . .
>On the ivied slopes of hills
>>and vine-clad promontories,
>Your name rings out with hope.

>God who dwells in Thebes . . .
>>god of mystery . . .
>Visit the streets of the city . . .
>Protect . . .
>>Save . . .
>Come with cleansing tread
>>from the mountain slopes . . .
>And over the moaning waters
>>of the inlets of the sea . . .
>God of the many names.
>>Appear . . . appear!

(*As their cries of jubilation, growing louder each instant, drown out the hushed voices of prayer by the second group,* EURYDICE *comes out with* ISMENE. *And the* CHIEF ELDER, *who had led the praying first group, noticing them, detaches himself from the* ELDERS *and moves toward them, mounting the steps.*)

(*A loud discord of tympani*)

(*Suddenly, however, a nearly breathless messenger, one of the* ATTENDANTS *who followed* CREON, *runs in from the right, and seeing only the* CHIEF ELDER *runs up to him, falling down on his knees. The second chorus sees him, becomes silent, and moves closer—hopefully. The first chorus continues, very low, noticing nothing at first.*)

MESSENGER: (*breathlessly*) House of the king, what news I bring! How inexorable is fate to mortal man! Creon was blest once, a savior of this land who was given dominion, but fortune raises up and fortune casts down: Now he has lost everything, and man bereft of all joy is no more than a breathing corpse—let him heap up riches in his house, and let him live royally, if he has no happiness I would not give the shadow of a vapor for everything he possesses.

(EURYDICE *mounts down a step, with* ISMENE *and other women following her*)

CHIEF ELDER: What is this fresh affliction that has come upon us?

MESSENGER: Death! Both are dead, and a man still living bears the guilt.

(*By now the first* CHORUS *has risen from its prayers and moved closer to the* MESSENGER)

Haemon the prince is dead, and his blood shed by no stranger.

CHIEF ELDER: Who, then, is the slayer? Surely not his father!

MESSENGER: By his own hand, in anger with his father is Haemon slain.

CHIEF ELDER: O prophet Teiresias, how are your words proved true!—But here comes the queen—by chance or has she heard everything?

(EURYDICE *approaches the* MESSENGER)

EURYDICE: (*to the* MESSENGER) I heard mention of fearful news, whereupon I fell into my handmaids' arms as one bereft of sense. Give your news again; I shall listen calmly—grief and I have not been strangers.

MESSENGER: I shall report what I saw, and not conceal what will be revealed soon enough. First we stopped outside the wall to give Polynices' corpse a proper burial. But we found the body so cruelly mangled by dogs that we washed the little that remained, pouring sanctified water and praying for forgiveness to Pluto and to the dread goddess of the crossroads, and we burned the remains on freshly-cut branches. Then above his ashes we raised a high mound in his memory, heaping the earth of his mother-land over him. Then, delaying no longer, we hastened to the doomed maiden's nuptial chamber in the rock. But soon from far off one could hear a man's loud voice lamenting and we ran to tell the king, and Creon coming nearer raised his voice in anguish, calling out "I have a foreboding that this is the hardest road I have yet to traverse, for I hear my son's voice. Run quickly to the tomb, my men, where the stones have been wrenched away, leaving a gap, then look through the crevice and tell me if it is Haemon you see there—or are the gods deceiving me?" His despair speeding us on, we soon arrived at the cave, and looking in through the crevice, we caught a glimpse of the girl lying strangled in a noose she had made of her fine linen.

(*At this* ISMENE *crumples in a heap on the stones of the steps*)

There also, beside her, we saw Haemon, his arms around her waist, lamenting the loss of his bride and cursing his father's crime. Creon went in to him, then, calling to him, "What is it, my son, that is unhinging your mind? Come forth, my child—I implore you to come out." But the youth, fiercely glaring at his father, saying not a word, spat at the father beside him; and drawing his sword, he thrust it at Creon. But missing his aim, and in anger at himself, Haemon leans with all his weight against the blade and drives the sword into his own breast: He falls and gathering the maid in his arms feebly, his blood staining her white cheek, he gasps out his life. Dead is the bridegroom with his bride, corpse grasping corpse, keeping his nuptials in the house of death, a witness that of all the misfortunes afflicting men nothing is so dire, nothing so evil, as unwisdom.

(*Saying nothing*, EURYDICE *goes up the steps blindly, watched by the stunned* ELDERS *as she enters the palace.*)

CHIEF ELDER: What are we to make of this? The queen has left us without a word.

MESSENGER: I, too, am troubled by her silence—but she may have deemed it more seemly to grieve in private.

CHIEF ELDER: Yet a grief so quiet portends no less a danger than excessive grief.

MESSENGER: We must see whether she has not hidden some purpose in her troubled heart. Silence so unnatural is too desperate!

(*He goes into the palace*)

CHIEF ELDER: See the king himself approaching—bringing with him, if I dare say it, no stranger's evil, but his own.

(*And now* CREON *enters with heavy steps, followed by his* ATTENDANTS, *bearing the body of* HAEMON. *At this the* ELDERS *move toward him, and the* CHIEF ELDER *comes down the steps from the palace, making a gesture of compassion toward* CREON. CREON *steps away from the outstreched arm.*)

CREON: There is nothing so blind as the unseeing heart, and my wretched blindness has undone me: You behold a father who killed his son, and a son who perished young not by his own but by his father's folly.

CHIEF ELDER: Would that wisdom had not come so late, alas!

CREON: O I have learned a bitter lesson! Yet I think some god not to be resisted by man hurled me down the paths of cruelty on which I trampled out the life I held most dear.

(*A sound of lamentation comes from the palace. Then the great central door opens, flung open by the* MESSENGER.)

MESSENGER: (*speaking hesitantly, before the body of* EURYDICE *is revealed*) You have brought a heavy burden with you, my king, but another awaits you within.

CREON: What worse misfortune follows my misfortune?

MESSENGER: Your wife, the mother of the corpse you bring, freshly stricken, is dead.

CREON: O god of the underworld,

whom nothing appeases, have you no mercy for me!

(*To* MESSENGER)

And bearer of such bitter news, what words are you speaking? I was already a dead man before you smote me anew. My wife dead?—death heaped on death?

(ATTENDANTS *have brought out* EURYDICE *and placed her body on the top step of the stairs fronting the palace.*)

MESSENGER: You may see for yourself; it is no longer hidden.

CREON: But lately I held my son in my arms, and now another corpse—his unhappy mother—O wife! O son!

MESSENGER: I found her at her altar, crying out that her son, the last of her womb, was gone; then calling you a slayer of sons, she took the knife from the altar and struck at her heart.

CREON: (*bowing his head*) Would that someone had struck at mine! Is there no one to thrust a sword into my bosom? My guilt is great and it weighs on no one but myself; wretched that I am, I was the slayer, not she who slew herself—it was I alone!

(*To his* ATTENDANTS)

Away—lead me away with all speed; my life is nothing but a death!

CHIEF ELDER: You do well to depart, my master—if anything can be well in so much misfortune. To be brief when trouble comes our way is the best course.

CREON: Let it come, let it: the best fate for me would be death. May I never look upon the light of another day.

CHIEF ELDER: Death will come when it will, and the future rest where it must. Meanwhile there is much to be done.

CREON: This is true, but all my desire was in that prayer; I do not wish to live.

CHIEF ELDER: In vain your prayer!—mortals are not spared their destined pain.

CREON: Then lead me away at least, a rash and foolish man

(*Looking down at his son's body and then toward his wife's above*)

who slew you, my son, and you, too, my wife. Where to turn, where to find support, I wish I knew: Everything has gone amiss with me, everything I had in hand has come to nothing—a heavy fate has crushed me to earth!

(CREON *is led up the stairs, followed by* ATTENDANTS *who bear the body of* HAEMON *inside. Then another bier is brought in by other* ATTENDANTS *who have been in the background throughout this scene. It is the body of* ANTIGONE. *And* ISMENE, *who has recovered during the previous action and has remained behind realizes it is her sister. She throws herself at the bier, calling out*

"*Antigone!*"

and follows the body as it, too, is brought into the palace—through the center door, the ATTENDANTS *taking their cue from the* CHIEF ELDER, *who bows and points to the center door; as if to indicate she should be placed near* HAEMON *her lover. Whereupon—as the door closes on* ANTIGONE—*the* ELDERS, *forming the* CHORUS, *speak with one voice—simply and without accompaniment*)*

CHORUS:

Nothing secures happiness so much as wisdom,
And in matters touching God it is best to be reverent!
Great pride in man is punished with great blows,
And after many years, in old age,
Chastening sorrows teach us at last to be wise.

THE END

---

* The reader should note that the stage direction in parentheses is solely for a television production. In the original there is no reference to Antigone in this scene.

QUESTIONS

A. Understanding the action:

Various theatre critics have commented on the fact that although *Antigone* is the title of Sophocles' play, the title is a misnomer because the play is really built around Creon.

1. Do you agree with this statement? Are Antigone and Creon of equal importance? Give reasons for your answers.

2. Why is the opening of the play considered a masterly scene of exposition? But what information does Sophocles withhold in the opening scene? How might he be justified in withholding this information for dramatic purposes?

3. In ancient Greece the decree of a king or tyrant not sanctioned by the people was often denied the status of law. Was Creon's decree considered invalid by any of the characters besides Antigone?

4. Describe and criticize Creon's philosophy of government as proclaimed in his edict.

5. When writing tragedy Greek dramatists did not usually introduce comic scenes or characters. Are there any comic scenes in *Antigone*, and is there dramatic justification for including such scenes? How is unity of mood and action achieved?

6. The third ode is a hymn to the power of love in human affairs. Why doesn't Sophocles show the two lovers, Haemon and Antigone, together?

7. What defense does Antigone make of her action? What are Creon's arguments?

8. Sophocles apparently added Haemon to the original Antigone story. What does the play gain by this addition?

9. In the quarrel between Haemon and Creon, the Chorus first siding with the son, then with the father, comments, "Both speak well." What is the final decision of the Chorus?

10. Is Haemon upholding democratic ideals and Creon totalitarian ones? Discuss.

11. Does Creon suspect that his son is going to commit suicide? Discuss your answer.

12. What is the function of Teiresias in the action?

13. Why does Eurydice commit suicide? How is this incident essential to the play?

B. Understanding the characters:

1. How do the two sisters differ in character? Do they change in the course of the play—that is, are they static or dynamic characters?

2. Are Antigone and Creon entirely responsible for their actions or is there some divine intervention in their lives? Is the suffering of the two the same or different? Is it justified?

3. Are Creon's reasons for refusing to bury Polynices sound or fallacious? In what way?

4. Where does Ismene show herself weak? Strong?

5. What traits has Antigone inherited from her father?

6. What is revealed about the character of Creon by his accusation of bribe-taking directed against the sentry and Teiresias?

C. Comparisons:

1. What democratic ideals are expressed in the plays *Antigone* and *An Enemy of the People*?

2. Compare the sister relationship in *Antigone* and *The Barretts of Wimpole Street*.

3. What is the difference in the nature of the conflict of Dr. Stockmann, the individualist (in *An Enemy of the People*), against "the compact majority" and that of Antigone against Creon? Are both triumphant in defeat? Are they both tragic figures?

WILLIAM SHAKESPEARE (1564-1616)

The Elizabethan Age

When Shakespeare, the world's greatest dramatist, was born in 1564, Queen Elizabeth had already been ruling for six years. Her reign, from 1558 to her death in 1603, was the high noon of the English renaissance, which had begun in the late fifteenth century after a succession of national disasters—defeat in the Hundred Years' War, the loss of England's possessions in France, and the civil conflict of the Wars of the Roses.

Shakespeare was born into a world of rapid change in religion, politics, and trade, into a world of great intellectual ferment. The Protestant Reformation was now complete. A strong, patriotic fervor imbued the English people now united under Elizabeth, their nationalism intensified by the defeat in 1588 of the Spanish Armada. The restrictions of medieval feudalism crumbled under the impact of increased trade and manufacturing. As the canny and frugal queen kept her country from being embroiled in costly European wars, England's new merchant class prospered and the common people gained more comforts; and soon after Elizabeth's death the founding of new colonies in America was the beginning of a worldwide empire. Francis Bacon, philosopher and scientist, declared, "I have taken all knowledge for my province." Poetry and music flourished. The theatre became the most popular form of entertainment encouraging a host of interesting dramatists to write for it. John Milton looking back on the England of Elizabeth characterized it as "a noble and puissant nation, arousing herself, like a strong man after sleep and shaking her invincible locks."

Shakespeare's Life and Work

William Shakespeare of Stratford-on-Avon, the eldest son and third child of John and Mary Arden Shakespeare, was baptized on April 26, 1564. He attended the free grammar school of Stratford, where he evidently received a sound elementary education that stressed a knowledge of the *Bible* and Latin. The rest of his formidable intellectual background was the result of a lifetime of self-education. At the age of eighteen he married Anne Hathaway, eight years his senior. The following year their first child, Susanna, was born and two years later twins, Hamnet and Judith. Shakespeare's only son, Hamnet, lived only eleven and a half years. His two daughters later married Stratford gentlemen.

After teaching school for a while, Shakespeare in 1585 left Stratford to seek his fortune in London. Here he probably became connected with the theatre, first as an actor and then as an adapter of older plays like the three parts of *Henry VI*. He also tried his hand at writing poetry. His two narrative poems on classical subjects, *Venus and Adonis* (1593) and *Lucrece* (1594), he dedicated to the Earl of Southampton. About this time he was also writing his famous sonnets, which, however, were not published until 1609. Had Shakespeare written nothing but these 154 sonnets, he would still be considered one of the world's great poets.

Shakespeare's intimate connection with the theatre as actor, playwright, director, and owner lasted for eighteen years. He was a very prolific dramatist averaging two plays a year. His early comedies such as *Love's Labor Lost* and *Two Gentlemen of Verona* show great verbal felicity. He then wrote a series of historical plays, the greatest of which is his Bolingbroke Tetralogy consisting of *Richard II, Henry IV Parts One and Two* and *Henry V*. Then came his more mature comedies: *Much Ado about Nothing, As You Like It,* and *Twelfth Night*. From 1601 to 1609 for reasons that we can only conjecture, a tragic gloom darkened his mind; and he wrote bitter problem "comedies" like *Measure for Measure* and the four great tragedies: *Hamlet, Othello, King Lear,* and *Macbeth*. In his final period after the dark cloud of obsession with evil had lifted, he wrote his last three comedies of reconciliation: *Cymbeline, The Winter's Tale,* and *The Tempest.*

In his age Shakespeare was a popular and successful dramatist. His plays were often performed at court for Queen Elizabeth and, after her death in 1603, for King James I. As early as 1597 Shakespeare was wealthy enough to purchase New Place, the second largest house in Stratford. Here with his family he spent the last five years of his life in quiet retirement as a country gentleman. He died on April 23, 1616.

The First Folio

To two actor friends of Shakespeare, John Heminge and Henry Condell, we must be eternally grateful, for in 1623 they collected in one volume the first complete edition of Shakespeare's plays. This book (with the possible exception of the King James' Version of the *Bible* published in 1611) is the most important in English literature. *The First Folio,* as it is called, contained thirty-six of Shakespeare's plays; only *Pericles* was missing. Here for posterity were twenty plays that had never before been printed, including such important ones as the three Roman or "Plutarch" plays: *Julius Caesar, Coriolanus,* and *Antony and Cleopatra;* the charming comedies *Twelfth Night* and *The Tempest;* and the tragedy *Macbeth*. What an incalculable loss world drama would have suffered had these two actors not had the thoughtfulness to issue this memorial volume of 454 pages as a tribute to their old friend!

The First Folio contained an engraved portrait of the dramatist, dedicatory epistles, poetic tributes, a list of the principal actors who had performed his plays, and Ben Johnson's eulogy:

> "Soul of the age!
> The applause, delight, the wonder of our stage!
> . . . .
> Triumph, my Britain! Thou hast one to show,
> To whom all the scenes of Europe homage owe.
> He was not of an age, but for all time."

Perhaps to publicize the forthcoming volume as well as to pay a further tribute to their beloved friend, Heminge and Condell with a group of London actors came to Stratford to perform a Shakespearean play. They were, however, not given a warm reception. Susanna, Shakespeare's daughter, had married a devout Puritan, Dr. John Hall. The Puritans (whom Shakespeare and other Elizabethan dramatists had persistently ridiculed for their opposition to the theatre) objected, for in the Stratford Register we find this curious entry: "Item to King's Players for not playing in the Hall on Jan. 10, 1623, ten shillings." Prevented from putting on a performance, the Globe actors did, however, erect a bust of Shakespeare as a tribute to his genius.

On November 8, 1623, *The First Folio* was registered in Stationers' Hall and put on sale for what was at that time the considerable sum of £1. Today a copy in good condition is valued at about $50,000.

INTRODUCTION TO *ROMEO AND JULIET*

Shakespeare was about thirty years of age when he wrote his first tragedy, *Romeo and Juliet*. Although the play has always been very popular, it differs in many respects from his later tragedies: *Hamlet, Lear, Othello* and *Macbeth*.

These latter tragedies are similar in dramatic conception. They all present a dominating figure of royal rank who, with all his virtues, possesses some fatal flaw which eventually brings about his downfall and death. The actions of such a tragic hero influence the destinies of the state. Shakespeare's *Romeo and Juliet*, however, is not essentially a tragedy of character but of fate. Romeo and Juliet are "a pair of star-crossed lovers" destroyed by chance events and a family feud, both circumstances over which they have no control. The young lovers may act rashly, but they possess no tragic flaws comparable to Lear's vanity and folly or Macbeth's evil ambition. The death of the lovers does not affect the welfare of a whole country; it is the tragedy of two families of Verona. Romeo and Juliet are more the victims of adverse fate than of inherent character flaws.

This play also differs from Shakespeare's great tragic quartet in that almost half of it is humorous. The exuberant, young Shakespeare introduced several comic scenes centering around the garrulity and ineptitude of the bumbling nurse, the stupidity of Peter, and the cynical, punning wit of Mercutio. The older Shakespeare would certainly have curtailed the drawn-out battle of puns between Romeo and Mercutio in Act II Scene 4 and the lyrical but undramatic Queen Mab speech. Another indication of Shakespeare's youthfulness in this play is the large number of artificial verse forms. The introductory chorus and the prologue to the second act as well as the first conversation of the lovers at the Capulet party are Shakespearean sonnets. Juliet's soliloquy in Act III Scene 2 is an Elizabethan marriage hymn or epithalamium. Many of the moralistic speeches of Friar Lawrence are rhymed couplets.

Yet in spite of these shortcomings, *Romeo and Juliet* has held the interest of audiences for over three centuries. It is perhaps the most passionate and beautiful portrayal of youthful love in dramatic literature. Dealing with a universal theme, the sweetness and bitterness of love, it tells a story whose essential details go as far back as a fifth century Greek romance. Italian writers of the sixteenth century also dealt with the story. Shakespeare's chief sources were an English poem by Arthur Brooke called *The Tragicall Historye of Romeus and Juliet* published in 1562 and a prose version found in an anthology, Painter's *Palace of Pleasure*, published in 1567.

Though Shakespeare's plot may contain some improbable and melodramatic incidents, it moves with mounting interest and headlong haste to its predestined end. From the opening scene of the renewal of the ancient feud by stupid servants to the solemn reconciliation of the two families over the dead bodies of the young victims, the play captures our undivided attention. Individual scenes reveal a masterly sense of the theatrical. What audience can fail to be stirred by the dramatic impact of the bustling party scene; of the two contrasting balcony scenes—one drenched in the romantic moonlight of youthful passion, the other bathed in the cold dawn of despairing lovers parting for the last time; of the tragic duel of Mercutio and Tybalt; of the blood-curdling visions of young Juliet in the potion scene; of the exciting tomb scene?

Another important reason for the popularity of the play is its rich poetry. In *Romeo and Juliet* Shakespeare reveals a complete mastery of imagery, rhythm, and poetic diction to express a wide and deep range of emotion and thought. How forcefully the dramatist communicates to us the superficial nature of Romeo's calf-love for Rosaline by forced antitheses:

"O heavy lightness! serious vanity!
 Mis-shapen chaos of well-seeming forms!
 Feather of lead, bright smoke, cold fire, sick health"

and by Romeo's sentimental definition,

"Love is a smoke made with the fume of sighs."

How different are the sharp images that well up in Romeo's poetic soul so expressive of his genuine love for Juliet when he first sees her!

"O! she doth teach the torches to burn more bright!
 It seems she hangs upon the cheek of night
 Like a rich jewel in an Ethiop's ear;
 Beauty too rich for use, for earth too dear!
 So shows a snowy dove trooping with crows,
 As yonder lady o'er her fellows shows."

How perfectly Shakespeare's poetry expresses the joyful passion of the lovers in the first balcony scene and their fears in the second, the terror of young Juliet before she drinks the potion, the cold moralizing of the Friar, and the heartbreaking grief of Romeo in the tomb scene! In this play perhaps for the first time Shakespeare's poetic powers meet the challenge of effective dramatic communication magnificently.

In his first tragedy Shakespeare already reveals his remarkable gifts of three-dimensional characterization. Aside from the protagonists perhaps his two most lifelike portraits are the contrasting ones of the sensual, loquacious Nurse, who gets vicarious thrills in participating in the secret love affair, and of the capricious, loyal, witty Mercutio, who dies with a pun on his lips, "Ask for me to-morrow, and you shall find me a grave man." Fiery Tybalt, stubborn old Capulet, sensible Benvolio, philosophic old Friar Laurence —all come to life under Shakespeare's magic pen.

Finally, in *Romeo and Juliet* Shakespeare has something significant to say about the nature of love and the relation of parents and children. In a short space of time, we see two young innocents mature from children to adulthood. Suddenly involved in a series of uncontrollable events, the dreamy, sentimental Romeo, learning the complex nature of human love, becomes a brave man of action, a sincere lover who cannot imagine himself living in a world without Juliet. In the same manner, the subservient young Juliet matures quickly into an intelligent, passionate woman who faces the realities of a cruel world with courage. In this play Shakespeare shows us various concepts of love and marriage. To the vulgar Nurse physical love is the only foundation for happy marriage; to the parents of Juliet money and social position are all-important; to the gay bachelor Mercutio women are but playthings. Against the materialistic background of these views, the ideal love of Romeo and Juliet sparkles and glows like the evening star. The play is a poetic tribute to the glory of true love. By his consummate skill as poet and dramatist Shakespeare has immortalized for all mankind the ecstasies and agonies of youthful love.

THE TRAGEDY OF ROMEO AND JULIET

WILLIAM SHAKESPEARE

CHORUS, *an Actor who addresses Audience*
ESCALUS, *Prince of Verona*
COUNT PARIS, *a young kinsman to the Prince*
MONTAGUE*
CAPULET
AN OLD MAN, *a member of the Capulet family*
ROMEO, *son to Montague*
MERCUTIO, *kinsman to the Prince, and friend to Romeo*
BENVOLIO, *nephew to Montague, and friend to Romeo*
TYBALT, *nephew to Lady Capulet*
FRIAR LAURENCE
FRIAR JOHN
BALTHASAR, *servant to Romeo*
ABRAM, *servant to Montague*
SAMPSON ⎫ *servants to Capulet*
GREGORY ⎭
PETER, *servant to Juliet's nurse*
AN APOTHECARY *in Mantua*
THREE MUSICIANS
AN OFFICER
LADY MONTAGUE, *wife to Montague*
LADY CAPULET, *wife to Capulet*
JULIET, *daughter to Capulet*

Nurse to Juliet, Citizens of Verona, Gentlemen and Gentlewomen of the houses of Capulet and Montague, Masked Guests, Torchbearers, Pages, Guards, Watchmen, Servants, and Attendants

The main action occurs in Verona, a city in Northern Italy. SCENE I *of* ACT V *occurs in Mantua, Italy.*

PROLOGUE

Enter Chorus.

CHORUS: Two households, both alike in dignity,
   In fair Verona, where we lay our scene,
From ancient grudge break to new mutiny,
   Where civil[1] blood makes civil hands unclean.
From forth the fatal loins of these two foes
   A pair of star-crossed[2] lovers take their life;
Whose misadventured piteous overthrows
   Doth with their death bury their parents' strife.[3]

[1] citizens'
[2] frustrated by unfavorable stars (as in the teachings of astrology).
[3] their parents' strife is ended by the deaths of the young lovers.

---

* Both Montague and Capulet are referred to as "old" in the original text, but they would not be considered really aged in our century. They are the heads of the noble houses of Montague and Capulet, in Verona.

The fearful passage of their death-marked love,
And the continuance of their parents' rage,
Which, but their children's end, naught could remove,[4]
Is now the two hours' traffic[5] of our stage;
The which if you with patient ears attend,
What here shall miss, our toil shall strive to mend.

[4] the continuance of the parents' anger could not be ended except by their children's death.
[5] business.

ACT I SCENE I

Enter Sampson *and* Gregory, *of the house of* Capulet, *carrying swords and bucklers.*

SAMPSON: Gregory, on my word, we'll not carry coals.[6]
GREGORY: No, for then we should be colliers.[7]
SAMPSON: I mean, an we be in choler, we'll draw.[8]
GREGORY: Ay, while you live, draw your neck out of collar.
SAMPSON: I strike quickly, being moved.
GREGORY: But thou art not quickly moved to strike.
SAMPSON: A dog of the house of Montague moves me.
GREGORY: To move is to stir, and to be valiant is to stand.
Therefore, if thou art moved, thou runn'st away.
SAMPSON: A dog of that house shall move me to stand. I will take the wall[9] of any man or maid of Montague's.
GREGORY: That shows thee a weak slave, for the weakest goes to the wall.
SAMPSON: 'Tis true; and therefore women, being the weaker vessels, are ever thrust to the wall. Therefore I will push Montague's men from the wall and thrust his maids to the wall.
GREGORY: The quarrel is between our masters, and [between] us their men.
SAMPSON: 'Tis all one. I will show myself a tyrant. When I have fought with the men, I will be cruel with the maids—I will cut off their heads.

[6] We shall not endure insults.
[7] coal-dealers—a pun on "carrying coals"—that is, on suffering insults.
[8] if we be in anger, we'll draw our swords.
[9] take the inner, (cleaner, therefore preferred) part of the sidewalk. The rest is punning and low jesting by the servants.

GREGORY: The heads of the maids?
SAMPSON: Ay, the heads of the maids, or their maiden heads. Take it in what sense thou wilt.
GREGORY: They must take it in sense that feel it.
SAMPSON: Me they shall feel while I am able to stand; and 'tis known I am a pretty piece of flesh.
GREGORY: 'Tis well thou art not fish; if thou hadst, thou hadst been poor-John.[10] Draw thy tool! Here comes two of the house of Montagues.

Enter two other Servingmen, Abram *and* Balthasar.

SAMPSON: My naked weapon is out. Quarrel! I will back thee.
GREGORY: How? turn thy back and run?
SAMPSON: Fear me not.
GREGORY: No, marry.[11] I fear thee!
SAMPSON: Let us take the law of our sides; let them begin.
GREGORY: I will frown as I pass by, and let them take it as they list.
SAMPSON: Nay, as they dare. I will bite my thumb[12] at them, which is disgrace to them if they bear it.
ABRAM: Do you bite your thumb at us, sir?
SAMPSON: I do bite my thumb, sir.
ABRAM: Do you bite your thumb at us, sir?
SAMPSON: (*to* GREGORY) Is the law of our side if I say ay?
GREGORY: No.
SAMPSON: No, sir, I do not bite my thumb at you, sir; but I bite my thumb, sir.
GREGORY: Do you quarrel, sir?
ABRAM: Quarrel, sir? No, sir.
SAMPSON: But if you do, sir, I am for you. I serve as good a man as you.
ABRAM: No better.
SAMPSON: Well, sir.

Enter Benvolio.

GREGORY: (*to* Sampson) Say 'better.' Here comes one of my master's kinsmen.
SAMPSON: Yes, better, sir.

[10] a cheap fish, dried hake.

[11] indeed (from the oath, "by Mary"—that is, by the Virgin Mary)

[12] biting one thumb at someone was an insult.

ABRAM: You lie.
SAMPSON: Draw, if you be men. Gregory, remember thy swashing blow.
BENVOLIO: Part, fools!
Put up your swords. You know not what you do.

Enter Tybalt.

TYBALT: What, art thou drawn among these heartless hinds?[13]
Turn thee, Benvolio! look upon thy death.
BENVOLIO: I do but keep the peace. Put up thy sword,
Or manage it to part these men with me.
TYBALT: What, drawn, and talk of peace? I hate the word
As I hate hell, all Montagues, and thee.
Have at thee, coward!
They fight.

[13] cowardly servants.

Enter an Officer, *and three or four* Citizens *with clubs or partisans.*

OFFICER: Clubs, bills, and partisans![14] Strike! beat them down!
CITIZENS: Down with the Capulets! Down with the Montagues!

[14] the officer calls for arms with which to put down the riot; he calls for weapons consisting of a long shaft with a sharp spear-head and a cutting-blade.

Enter old Capulet, *in his gown, and* Capulet's Wife.

CAPULET: What noise is this? Give me my long sword, ho!
WIFE: A crutch, a crutch! Why call you for a sword?
CAPULET: My sword, I say! Old Montague is come
And flourishes his blade in spite of me.[15]

[15] to spite me, in defiance of me.

Montague [*"old Montague"*] *and his* Wife *enter.*

MONTAGUE: Thou villain Capulet!—Hold me not, let me go.
MONTAGUE'S WIFE: Thou shalt not stir one foot to seek a foe.

Enter Prince Escalus, *with his* Attendants [*"Train"*].

PRINCE: Rebellious subjects, enemies to peace,
  Profaners of this neighbor-stainèd steel—
  Will they not hear? What, ho! you men, you beasts,
  That quench the fire of your pernicious rage
  With purple fountains[16] issuing from your veins!
  On pain of torture, from those bloody hands
  Throw your mistemperèd[17] weapons to the ground
  And hear the sentence of your movèd[18] prince.
  Three civil brawls, bred of an airy word
  By thee, old Capulet, and Montague,
  Have thrice disturbed the quiet of our streets
  And made Verona's ancient citizens
  Cast by[19] their grave beseeming ornaments
  To wield old partisans,[20] in hands as old,
  Cank'red[21] with peace, to part your cank'red[22] hate.
  If ever you disturb our streets again,
  Your lives shall pay the forfeit of the peace.
  For this time all the rest depart away.
  You, Capulet, shall go along with me;
  And, Montague, come you this afternoon,
  To know our farther pleasure in this case,
  To Villafranca, our common judgment place.*
  Once more, on pain of death, all men depart.

[16] blood spurting from your veins.
[17] misused, abused.
[18] angry.
[19] cast away, throw away.
[20] weapons,—see above.
[21] cankered—rusted or rotted by peace.
[22] malignant, diseased hate.
* A standard reading of this line is, "To old Freetown (the meaning of Villafranca), our common judgment place."

All but Montague, *his* Wife, *and* Benvolio *leave the stage.*

MONTAGUE: Who set this ancient quarrel new abroach?[23]
  Speak, nephew, were you by when it began?
BENVOLIO: Here were the servants of your adversary
  And yours, close fighting ere I did approach.
  I drew to part them. In the instant came
  The fiery Tybalt, with his sword prepared;
  Which, as he breathed defiance to my ears,
  He swung about his head and cut the winds,
  Who, nothing hurt withal, hissed him in scorn.
  While we were interchanging thrusts and blows,
  Came more and more, and fought on part and part,
  Till the Prince came, who parted either part.
[MONTAGUE'S] WIFE: O, where is Romeo? Saw you him to-day?
  Right glad I am he was not at this fray.
BENVOLIO: Madam, an hour before the worshipped sun
  Peered forth the golden window of the East,
  A troubled mind drave me to walk abroad;

[23] Who reopened this old quarrel?

Where, underneath the grove of sycamore
That westward rooteth from this city side,
So early walking did I see your son.
Towards him I made, but he was ware[24] of me
And stole into the covert of the wood.
I, measuring his affections by my own,
Which then most sought where most might not be found,[25]
Being one too many by my weary self,
Pursued my humor, not pursuing his,
And gladly shunned who gladly fled from me.

MONTAGUE: Many a morning hath he there been seen,
With tears augmenting the fresh morning's dew,
Adding to clouds more clouds with his deep sighs;
But all so soon as the all-cheering sun
Should in the farthest East begin to draw
The shady curtains from Aurora's bed,[26]
Away from light steals home my heavy[27] son
And private in his chamber pens himself,
Shuts up his windows, locks fair daylight out,
And makes himself an artificial night.
Black and portentous must this humor prove
Unless good counsel may the cause remove.

BENVOLIO: My noble uncle, do you know the cause?

MONTAGUE: I neither know it nor can learn of him.

BENVOLIO: Have you importuned him by any means?

MONTAGUE: Both by myself and many other friends;
But he, his own affections' counsellor,
Is to himself—I will not say how true—
But to himself so secret and so close,
So far from sounding and discovery,
As is the bud bit with an envious worm
Ere[28] he can spread his sweet leaves to the air
Or dedicate his beauty to the sun.
Could we but learn from whence his sorrows grow,
We would as willingly give cure as know.

[24] aware or wary of me.
[25] desired solitude.
[26] dawn. Aurora is goddess of the dawn.
[27] depressed, melancholy.
[28] before.

Enter Romeo.

BENVOLIO: See, where he comes. So please you step aside,
I'll know his grievance, or be much denied.

MONTAGUE: I would thou wert so happy by thy stay
To hear true shrift.[29] Come, madam, let's away.

[29] confession.

Montague *and* Wife *leave the stage.*

BENVOLIO: Good morrow, cousin.
ROMEO: Is the day so young?
BENVOLIO: But new struck nine.
ROMEO: Ay me! sad hours seem long.
Was that my father that went hence so fast?
BENVOLIO: It was. What sadness lengthens Romeo's hours?
ROMEO: Not having that which having makes them short.
BENVOLIO: In love?
ROMEO: Out—
BENVOLIO: Of love?
ROMEO: Out of her favor where I am in love.
BENVOLIO: Alas that love, so gentle in his view,[30]
Should be so tyrannous and rough in proof!
ROMEO: Alas that love, whose view is muffled still,[31]
Should without eyes see pathways to his will!
Where shall we dine? O me! What fray was here?
Yet tell me not, for I have heard it all.
Here's much to do with hate, but more with love.
Why then, O brawling love, O loving hate,
O anything, of nothing first create!
O heavy lightness, serious vanity,
Misshapen chaos of well-seeming forms,
Feather of lead, bright smoke, cold fire, sick health,
Still-waking sleep, that is not what it is!
This love feel I, that feel no love in this.
Dost thou not laugh?
BENVOLIO: No, coz,[32] I rather weep.
ROMEO: Good heart, at what?
BENVOLIO: At thy good heart's oppression.
ROMEO: Why, such is love's transgression.
Griefs of mine own lie heavy in my breast,
Which thou wilt propagate, to have it prest
With more of thine. This love that thou hast shown
Doth add more grief to too much of mine own.
Love is a smoke raised with the fume of sighs;
Being purged, a fire sparkling in lovers' eyes;
Being vexed, a sea nourished with lovers' tears.
What is it else? A madness most discreet,
A choking gall, and a preserving sweet.
Farewell, my coz.
BENVOLIO: Soft! I will go along.
An if you leave me so, you do me wrong.

[30] in appearance.
[31] whose sight is still blindfolded.
[32] cousin.

ROMEO: Tut! I have left [lost] myself; I am not here;
This is not Romeo, he's some other where.
BENVOLIO: Tell me in sadness,[33] who is that you love?
ROMEO: What, shall I groan and tell thee?
BENVOLIO: Groan? Why, no!
But sadly tell me who.
ROMEO: Bid a sick man in sadness make his will.
Ah, word ill urged to one that is so ill!
In sadness, cousin, I do love a woman.
BENVOLIO: I aimed so near when I supposed you loved.
ROMEO: A right good markman. And she's fair I love.
BENVOLIO: A right fair mark, fair coz, is soonest hit.
ROMEO: Well, in that hit you miss. She'll not be hit
With Cupid's arrow. She hath Dian's[34] wit,
And, in strong proof[35] of chastity well armed,
From Love's weak childish bow she lives uncharmed.*
She will not stay the siege of loving terms,
Nor bide th' encounter of assailing eyes,
Nor ope her lap to saint-seducing gold.
O, she is rich in beauty; only poor
That, when she dies, with beauty dies her store.
BENVOLIO: Then she hath sworn that she will still live chaste?
ROMEO: She hath, and in that sparing makes huge waste;
For beauty, starved with her severity,
Cuts beauty off from all posterity.
She is too fair, too wise, wisely too fair,
To merit bliss by making me despair.
She hath forsworn to love, and in that vow
Do I live dead that live to tell it now.
BENVOLIO: Be ruled by me; forget to think of her.
ROMEO: O, teach me how I should forget to think!
BENVOLIO: By giving liberty unto thine eyes.
Examine other beauties.
ROMEO: 'Tis the way
To call hers exquisite in question more.
These happy masks that kiss fair ladies' brows,
Being black puts us in mind they hide the fair.
He that is strucken blind cannot forget
The precious treasure of his eyesight lost.
Show me a mistress that is passing[36] fair,
What doth her beauty serve but as a note
Where I may read who passed that passing fair?

---

[33] in earnest, seriously. In the next few lines, Romeo puns on the word "sadness."

[34] Diana's, the moon goddess and the virgin goddess of the heart.

[35] armor.

* Another reading is "unharmed"; "uncharmed" has a similar meaning here—that is, "unbewitched" or "unbeguiled."

[36] surpassing.

Farewell. Thou canst not teach me to forget.
BENVOLIO: I'll pay that doctrine,[37] or else die in debt.
Exeunt.

[37] I'll make you change your opinion.

SCENE II [*A street*]

Enter Capulet, Count (County) Paris, *and the* Clown.

CAPULET: But Montague is bound as well as I,
In penalty alike; and 'tis not hard, I think,
For men so old as we to keep the peace.
PARIS: Of honorable reckoning are you both,
And pity 'tis you lived at odds so long.
But now, my lord, what say you to my suit?
CAPULET: But saying o'er what I have said before:
My child is yet a stranger in the world,
She hath not seen the change of fourteen years;
Let two more summers wither in their pride
Ere we may think her ripe to be a bride.
PARIS: Younger than she are happy mothers made.
CAPULET: And too soon marred are those so early made.
The earth hath swallowèd all my hopes but she;[38]
She is the hopeful lady of my earth.
But woo her, gentle Paris, get her heart;
My will to her consent is but a part.
An she agree, within her scope of choice
Lies my consent and fair according voice.
This night I hold an old accustomed feast,
Whereto I have invited many a guest,
Such as I love; and you among the store,
One more, most welcome, makes my number more.
At my poor house look to behold this night
Earth-treading stars[39] that make dark heaven light.
Such comfort as do lusty young men feel
When well-apparelled April on the heel
Of limping Winter treads, even such delight
Among fresh fennel buds shall you this night
Inherit at my house. Hear all, all see,
And like her most whose merit most shall be;
Which, on more view of many, mine,[40] being one,
May stand in number, though in reck'ning none.[41]
Come, go with me. (*To the Servant, giving him a paper*) Go, sirrah, trudge about

[38] Capulet means that all his other children are dead.
[39] He is referring to his guests, the young ladies.
[40] He means his daughter Juliet.
[41] He means she is not to be "reckoned" among those maidens who will be desired in marriage.

Through fair Verona; find those persons out
Whose names are written there, and to them say,
My house and welcome on their pleasure stay.

He leaves the stage with Paris.

SERVANT: Find them out whose names are written here? It is written that the shoemaker should meddle with his yard and the tailor with his last, the fisher with his pencil and the painter with his nets; but I am sent to find those persons whose names are here writ, and can never find[42] what names the writing person hath here writ. I must to the learned. (*Seeing* Benvolio *and* Romeo *approaching*) In good time!

Enter Benvolio *and* Romeo.

BENVOLIO: Tut, man, one fire burns out another's burning;
One pain is less'ned by another's anguish;
Turn giddy, and be holp[43] by backward turning;
One desperate grief cures with another's languish.
Take thou some new infection to thy eye,
And the rank poison of the old will die.

ROMEO: Your plantain leaf is excellent for that.

BENVOLIO: For what, I pray thee?

ROMEO: For your broken shin.

BENVOLIO: Why, Romeo, art thou mad?

ROMEO: Not mad, but bound more than a madman is;
Shut up in prison, kept without my food,
Whipped and tormented and (*noticing the Servant*) —God-den,[44] good fellow.

SERVANT: God gi' go-den. I pray, sir, can you read?

ROMEO: Ay, mine own fortune in my misery.

SERVANT: Perhaps you have learned it without book. But I pray, can you read anything you see?

ROMEO: Ay, if I know the letters and the language.

SERVANT: (*misunderstanding him and turning away from him*) Ye say honestly. Rest you merry.

ROMEO: Stay, fellow; I can read. *He reads the letter.*
Signior Martino and his wife and daughters;
County Anselmo and his beauteous sisters;
The lady widow of Vitruvio;
Signior Placentio and his lovely nieces;
Mercutio and his brother Valentine;
Mine uncle Capulet, his wife, and daughters;
My fair niece Rosaline and Livia;

---

[42] can never "find out"; because he can not read.

[43] helped.
[44] Good evening; or, Good afternoon.

Signior Valentio and his cousin Tybalt;
Lucio and the lively Helena.

A fair assembly. Whither should they come?
SERVANT: Up.
ROMEO: Whither? To supper?
SERVANT: To our house.
ROMEO: Whose house?
SERVANT: My master's.
ROMEO: Indeed I should have asked you that before.
SERVANT: Now I'll tell you without asking. My master is the great rich Capulet; and if you be not of the house of Montagues, I pray come and crush[45] a cup of wine. Rest you merry. (*He goes off.*)
BENVOLIO: At this same ancient feast of Capulet's
   Sups the fair Rosaline whom thou so lov'st,
   With all the admirèd beauties of Verona.
   Go thither, and with unattainted[46] eye
   Compare her face with some that I shall show,
   And I will make thee think thy swan a crow.
ROMEO: When the devout religion of mine eye
   Maintains such falsehood, then turn tears to fires;
   And these,[47] who, often drowned, could never die,
   Transparent heretics, be burnt for liars!
   One fairer than my love? The all-seeing sun
   Ne'er saw her match since first the world begun.
BENVOLIO: Tut! you saw her fair, none else being by,
   Herself poised with herself in either eye;
   But in that crystal scales let there be weighed
   Your lady's love against some other maid
   That I will show you shining at this feast,
   And she shall scant[48] show well that now seems best.
ROMEO: I'll go along, no such sight to be shown,
   But to rejoice in splendor of my own.

[45] drink.
[46] unprejudiced.
[47] these eyes (who often drowned with tear).
[48] hardly.

SCENE III   [*A Room in the Capulet House*]

They leave the stage.
Enter Capulet's Wife *and* Juliet's old Nurse

WIFE: Nurse, where's my daughter? Call her forth to me.
NURSE: Now, by my maidenhead at twelve year old,

I bade her come. What, lamb! what, ladybird!
God forbid, where's this girl? What, Juliet!

Enter Juliet.

JULIET: How now? Who calls?
NURSE: Your mother.
JULIET: Madam, I am here.
What is your will?
WIFE: This is the matter—Nurse, give leave awhile,
We must talk in secret. Nurse, come back again;
I have rememb'red me, thou 's hear our counsel.
Thou knowest my daughter's of a pretty age.
NURSE: Faith, I can tell her age unto an hour.
WIFE: She's not fourteen.
NURSE: I'll lay fourteen of my teeth—
And yet, to my teen be it spoken, I have but four—
She's not fourteen. How long is it now
To Lammastide?[49]
WIFE: A fortnight and odd days.
NURSE: Even or odd, of all days in the year,
Come Lammas Eve at night shall she be fourteen.
Susan and she (God rest all Christian souls!)
Were of an age. Well, Susan is with God;
She was too good for me. But, as I said,
On Lammas Eve at night shall she be fourteen;
That shall she, marry; I remember it well.
'Tis since the earthquake now eleven years;
And she was weaned (I never shall forget it),
Of all the days of the year, upon that day;
For I had then laid wormwood to my dug,[50]
Sitting in the sun under the dovehouse wall.
My lord and you were then at Mantua.
Nay, I do bear a brain. But, as I said,
When it did taste the wormwood on the nipple
Of my dug and felt it bitter, pretty fool,
To see it tetchy and fall out[51] with the dug!
Shake, quoth the dovehouse! 'Twas no need, I
  trow,[52]
To bid me trudge.[53]
And since that time it is eleven years,
For then she could stand high-lone; nay, by th'
  rood,[54]
She could have run and waddled all about;
For even the day before, she broke her brow;

---

[49] Lammastide, which falls on the first of August, is a holiday that commemorates St. Peter's imprisonment and miraculous deliverance from prison.

[50] laid wormwood, a bitter herb, to her breast in order to wean the child.

[51] be angry with.

[52] believe.

[53] run away.

[54] cross.

And then my husband (God be with his soul!
'A was a merry man) took up the child.
'Yea,' quoth he, 'dost thou fall upon thy face?
Thou wilt fall backward when thou hast more wit;
Wilt thou not, Jule?' and, by my halidom,
The pretty wretch left crying and said 'Ay.'
To see now how a jest shall come about!
I warrant, an I should live a thousand years,
I never should forget it. 'Wilt thou not, Jule?' quoth he,
And, pretty fool, it stinted[55] and said 'Ay.'
WIFE: Enough of this. I pray thee hold thy peace.
NURSE: Yes, madam. Yet I cannot choose but laugh
To think it should leave crying and say 'Ay.'
And yet, I warrant, it had upon its brow
A bump as big as a young cock'rel's stone;
A perilous knock; and it cried bitterly.
'Yea,' quoth my husband, 'fall'st upon thy face?
Thou wilt fall backward when thou comest to age;
Wilt thou not, Jule?' It stinted and said 'Ay.'
JULIET: And stint thou too, I pray thee, nurse, say I.
NURSE: Peace, I have done. God mark thee to his grace!
Thou wast the prettiest babe that e'er I nursed.
An I might live to see thee married once,
I have my wish.
WIFE: Marry, that 'marry' is the very theme
I came to talk of. Tell me, daughter Juliet,
How stands your disposition to be married?
JULIET: It is an honor that I dream not of.
NURSE: An honor? Were not I thine only nurse,
I would say thou hadst sucked wisdom from thy teat.
WIFE: Well, think of marriage now. Younger than you,
Here in Verona, ladies of esteem,
Are made already mothers. By my count,
I was your mother much upon these years[56]
That you are now a maid. Thus then in brief:
The valiant Paris seeks you for his love.
NURSE: A man, young lady! lady, such a man
As all the world—why he's a man of wax.[57]
WIFE: Verona's summer hath not such a flower.
NURSE: Nay, he's a flower, in faith—a very flower.
WIFE: What say you? Can you love the gentleman?
This night you shall behold him at our feast.

[55] stopped crying.
[56] I was about the same age as you are now, Juliet. I was still a maiden when I gave birth to you.
[57] a model of a man.

Read o'er the volume of young Paris' face,
And find delight writ there with beauty's pen;
Examine every married lineament,[58]
And see how one another lends content;
And what obscured in this fair volume lies
Find written in the margent[59] of his eyes.
This precious book of love, this unbound lover,
To beautify him only lacks a cover.[60]
The fish lives in the sea, and 'tis much pride
For fair without the fair within to hide.
That book in many's eyes doth share the glory,
That in gold clasps locks in the golden story;
So shall you share all that he doth possess,
By having him making yourself no less.
NURSE: No less? Nay, bigger! Women grow by men.
WIFE: Speak briefly, can you like of Paris' love?
JULIET: I'll look to like, if looking liking move;
But no more deep will I endart[61] mine eye
Than your consent gives strength to make it fly.

[58] related feature.
[59] margin.
[60] that is, a wife.
[61] shoot or dart.

Enter a Servingman.

SERVINGMAN: Madam, the guests are come, supper served up, you called, my young lady asked for, the nurse cursed in the pantry, and everything in extremity. I must hence to wait. I beseech you follow straight.
WIFE: We follow thee. [*Exit the* Servingman.] Juliet, the County stays.
NURSE: Go, girl, seek happy nights to happy days.
[*Exeunt.*]

SCENE IV   [*A street*]

Enter Romeo, Mercutio, Benvolio, *with five or six other* Maskers, *accompanied by* Torchbearers.

ROMEO: What, shall this speech be spoke for our excuse?
Or shall we on without apology?

BENVOLIO: The date is out of such prolixity.[62]
    We'll have no Cupid hoodwinked with a scarf,
    Bearing a Tartar's painted bow of lath,
    Scaring the ladies like a crowkeeper;[63]
    But, let them measure us by what they will,
    We'll measure them a measure[64] and be gone.

ROMEO: Give me a torch. I am not for this ambling.
    Being but heavy, I will bear the light.

MERCUTIO: Nay, gentle Romeo, we must have you dance.

ROMEO: Not I, believe me. You have dancing shoes
    With nimble soles; I have a soul of lead
    So stakes me to the ground I cannot move.

MERCUTIO: You are a lover. Borrow Cupid's wings
    And soar with them above a common bound.

ROMEO: I am too sore enpiercèd with his shaft
    To soar with his light feathers; and so bound
    I cannot bound a pitch above dull woe.
    Under love's heavy burden do I sink.

MERCUTIO: And, to sink in it, should you burden love—
    Too great oppression for a tender thing.

ROMEO: Is love a tender thing? It is too rough,
    Too rude, too boist'rous, and it pricks like thorn.

MERCUTIO: If love be rough with you, be rough with love.
    Prick love for pricking, and you beat love down.
    Give me a case to put my visage in.
    A visor for a visor![65] What care I
    What curious eye doth quote deformities?
    Here are the beetle brows[66] shall blush for me.

BENVOLIO: Come, knock and enter; and no sooner in
    But every man betake him to his legs.[67]

ROMEO: A torch for me! Let wantons light of heart
    Tickle the senseless rushes[68] with their heels;
    For I am proverbed with a grandsire phrase,
    I'll be a candle-holder and look on;
    The game was ne'er so fair, and I am done.

MERCUTIO: Tut! dun's the mouse,[69] the constable's own word!
    If thou art Dun,[70] we'll draw thee from the mire
    Of this sir-reverence love, wherein thou stickest
    Up to the ears. Come, we burn daylight,[71] ho!

ROMEO: Nay, that's not so.

MERCUTIO: I mean, sir, in delay
    We waste our lights in vain, like lamps by day.

---

[62] such superfluous speeches (prolixity) by masked visitors are out of fashion now ("the date is out").

[63] scarecrow.

[64] dance a dance for them.

[65] a mask for a face that is a mask ("visor"), a pun on Mercutio's referring to his "visage" in the previous line.

[66] the beetling (overhanging) eyebrows of the mask he is wearing.

[67] let every man start dancing.

[68] the rushes strewn on the floor as a covering.

[69] be quiet as a mouse!

[70] "Dun" was the stock name for a horse.

[71] We waste time.

Take our good meaning, for our judgment sits
Five times in that ere once in our five wits.
ROMEO: And we mean well in going to this masque,
But 'tis no wit[72] to go.
MERCUTIO: Why, may one ask?
ROMEO: I dreamt a dream to-night.
MERCUTIO: And so did I.
ROMEO: Well, what was yours?
MERCUTIO: That dreamers often lie.
ROMEO: In bed asleep, while they do dream things true.
MERCUTIO: O, then I see Queen Mab[73] hath been with you.
She is the Fairies' Midwife, and she comes
In shape no bigger than an agate-stone
On the forefinger of an alderman,
Drawn with a team of little atomies[74]
Over men's noses as they lie asleep
Her wagon spokes made of long spinners' legs,[75]
The cover, of the wings of grasshoppers;
Her traces, of the smallest spider's web;
Her collars, of the moonshine's wat'ry beams;
Her whip, of cricket's bone; the lash, of film;
Her wagoner, a small grey-coated gnat,
Not half so big as a round little worm
Pricked from the lazy finger of a maid;
Her chariot is an empty hazelnut,
Made by the joiner squirrel or old grub,
Time out o' mind the fairies' coachmakers.
And in this state she gallops night by night
Through lovers' brains, and then they dream of love;
O'er courtiers' knees, that dream on curtsies straight;
O'er lawyers' fingers, who straight dream on fees;
O'er ladies' lips, who straight on kisses dream,
Which oft the angry Mab with blisters plagues,
Because their breaths with sweetmeats tainted are.
Sometimes she gallops o'er a courtier's nose,
And then dreams he of smelling out a suit;[76]
And sometime comes she with a tithe-pig's tail[77]
Tickling a parson's nose as 'a lies asleep,
Then dreams he of another benefice.[78]
Sometimes she driveth o'er a soldier's neck,
And then dreams he of cutting foreign throats,
Of breaches, ambuscadoes, Spanish blades,

---

[72] not wise.
[73] a Celtic name for the queen of the fairies.
[74] minute creatures.
[75] spiders' legs.
[76] a petition.
[77] tithe-pig is the pig reserved for the parson—the tenth pig.
[78] another source of revenue in the church.

Of healths five fathom deep; and then anon
Drums in his ear, at which he starts and wakes,
And being thus frighted, swears a prayer or two
And sleeps again. This is that very Mab
That plats the manes of horses in the night
And bakes the elflocks[79] in foul sluttish hairs,
Which once untangled much misfortune bodes.
This is the hag,[80] when maids lie on their backs,
That presses them and learns them first to bear,
Making them women of good carriage.
This is she—
ROMEO: Peace, peace, Mercutio, peace!
Thou talk'st of nothing.
MERCUTIO: True, I talk of dreams;
Which are the children of an idle brain,
Begot of nothing but vain fantasy;
Which is as thin of substance as the air,
And more inconstant than the wind, who woos
Even now the frozen bosom of the North
And, being angered, puffs away from thence,
Turning his side to the dew-dropping South.
BENVOLIO: This wind you talk of blows us from ourselves.
Supper is done, and we shall come too late.
ROMEO: I fear, too early; for my mind misgives
Some consequence, yet hanging in the stars,
Shall bitterly begin his fearful date
With this night's revels and expire the term
Of a despisèd life, closed in my breast,
By some vile forfeit of untimely death.
But he that hath the steerage of my course[81]
Direct my sail! On, lusty gentlemen!
BENVOLIO: Strike, drum.

[79] knots of hair.
[80] nightmare, a night hag or witch.
[81] He means God.

SCENE V [*The Hall in the Capulet House*]

They march about the stage, and Servingmen *come forth with their napkins.*

FIRST SERVINGMAN: Where's Potpan, that he helps not to take away? He shift a trencher![82] he scrape a trencher!

[82] a wooden platter.

SECOND SERVINGMAN: When good manners shall lie all in one or two men's hands, and they unwashed too, 'tis a foul thing.

FIRST SERVINGMAN: Away with the joint-stools, remove the court-cupboard, look to the plate. Good thou, save me a piece of marchpane and, as thou loves me, let the porter let in Susan Grindstone and Nell. (*He calls out.*) Anthony and Potpan!

These Servants *enter.*

THIRD SERVINGMAN: Ay, boy, ready.

FIRST SERVINGMAN: You are looked for and called for, asked for and sought for, in the great chamber.

FOURTH SERVINGMAN: We cannot be here and there too. Cheerly, boys! Be brisk awhile, and the longer liver take all.

Capulet, *Capulet's* Wife, Juliet, *other members of the house and* Guests, *greeting the* Maskers.

CAPULET: Welcome, gentlemen! Ladies that have their toes
Unplagued with corns will walk a bout with you.
Ah ha, my mistresses! which of you all
Will now deny to dance? She that makes dainty,[83]
She I'll swear hath corns. Am I come near ye now?
Welcome, gentlemen! I have seen the day
That I have worn a visor and could tell
A whispering tale in a fair lady's ear,
Such as would please. 'Tis gone, 'tis gone, 'tis gone!
You are welcome, gentlemen! Come, musicians, play.

Music plays, and the dance begins.

A hall, a hall![84] give room! and foot it, girls.
More light, you knaves! and turn the tables up,
And quench the fire, the room is grown too hot.
Ah, sirrah, this unlooked-for sport comes well.
Nay, sit, nay, sit, good cousin Capulet,
For you and I are past our dancing days.
How long it's now since last yourself and I
Were in a mask?

A SECOND CAPULET: By'r Lady, thirty years.

CAPULET: What, man? 'Tis not so much, 'tis not so much;

[83] She that hesitates.
[84] "clear the hall for dancing!"

'Tis since the nuptial of Lucentio,
Come Pentecost as quickly as it will,
Some five-and-twenty years, and then we masked.
SECOND CAPULET: 'Tis more, 'tis more. His son is elder, sir;
His son is thirty.
CAPULET: Will you tell me that?
His son was but a ward[85] two years ago.
ROMEO: (*addressing a* Servingman) What lady's that, which doth enrich the hand
Of yonder knight?
SERVINGMAN: I know not, sir.
ROMEO: O, she doth teach the torches to burn bright!
It seems she hangs upon the cheek of night
As a rich jewel in an Ethiop's ear—
Beauty too rich for use, for earth too dear!
So shows a snowy dove trooping with crows
As yonder lady o'er her fellows shows.
The measure done, I'll watch her place of stand
And, touching hers, make blessèd my rude hand.
Did my heart love till now? Forswear it, sight!
For I ne'er saw true beauty till this night.
TYBALT: This, by his voice, should be a Montague.
Fetch me my rapier, boy. What, dares the slave
Come hither, covered with an antic face,[86]
To fleer[87] and scorn at our solemnity?
Now, by the stock and honor of my kin,
To strike him dead I hold it not a sin.
CAPULET: Why, how now, kinsman? Wherefore storm you so?
TYBALT: Uncle, this is a Montague, our foe;
A villain, that is hither come in spite
To scorn at our solemnity this night.
CAPULET: Young Romeo is it?
TYBALT: 'Tis he, that villain Romeo.
CAPULET: Content thee, gentle coz, let him alone.
'A bears him like a portly gentleman,
And, to say truth, Verona brags of him
To be a virtuous and well-governed youth.
I would not for the wealth of all this town
Here in my house do him disparagement.
Therefore be patient, take no note of him.
It is my will, the which if thou respect,
Show a fair presence and put off these frowns.
An ill-beseeming semblance for a feast.

[85] a minor.
[86] a comic mask.
[87] scorn.

TYBALT: It fits when such a villain is a guest.
　　　　I'll not endure him.
CAPULET: 　　　　　　He shall be endured.
　　　　What, goodman boy! I say he shall. Go to!
　　　　Am I the master here, or you? Go to!
　　　　You'll not endure him, God shall mend my soul!
　　　　You'll make a mutiny among my guests!
　　　　You will set cock-a-hoop, you'll be the man![88]
TYBALT: Why, uncle, 'tis a shame.
CAPULET: 　　　　　　　　　　Go to, go to!
　　　　You are a saucy boy. It's so, indeed?
　　　　This trick may chance to scathe you. I know what.
　　　　You must contrary[89] me! Marry, 'tis time—
　　　　(*To the dancers*) Well said, my hearts!—(*To
　　　　Tybalt*) You are a princox[90]—go!
　　　　Be quiet, or—More light, more light!—For shame!
　　　　I'll make you quiet; what!—Cheerly, my hearts!
TYBALT: Patience perforce[91] with willful choler meeting
　　　　Makes my flesh tremble in their different greeting.
　　　　I will withdraw; but this intrusion shall,
　　　　Now seeming sweet, convert to bitt'rest gall.　*Exit.*
ROMEO: If I profane with my unworthiest hand[92]
　　　　This holy shrine,[93] the gentle sin is this;
　　　　My lips, two blushing pilgrims,[94] ready stand
　　　　To smooth that rough touch with a tender kiss.
JULIET: Good pilgrim, you do wrong your hand too
　　　　　much,
　　　　Which mannerly devotion shows in this;
　　　　For saints have hands that pilgrims' hands do touch,
　　　　And palm to palm is holy palmers' kiss.
ROMEO: Have not saints lips, and holy palmers[95] too?
JULIET: Ay, pilgrim, lips that they must use in
　　　　　prayer.
ROMEO: O, then, dear saint, let lips do what hands
　　　　　do![96] They pray; grant thou, lest faith turn to
　　　　　despair.
JULIET: Saints do not move, though grant for prayers'
　　　　　sake.
ROMEO: Then move not while my prayer's effect I
　　　　　take.
　　　　　　　　　　　　　　　　(*He kisses her.*)
　　　　Thus from my lips, by thine my sin is purged.
JULIET: Then have my lips the sin that they have
　　　　　took.
ROMEO: Sin from my lips? O trespass sweetly urged!

---

[88] You will be the leader and play the hero.

[89] You must go contrary to me.

[90] saucy youngster.

[91] enforced patience, forced self-control.

[92] Let the student understand that here Romeo addresses Juliet with a sonnet—a lyric poem of 14 lines, consisting (in the case of the English sonnet) of three quatrains (four-line stanzas), followed by a couplet (two rhyming lines—"sake," "take." —After this, a new quatrain is started, as if a second sonnet were in the making (the rhymes are "purged"—"urged," "took-book"); then the Nurse interrupts with "Madam, your mother craves a word with you."

[93] Juliet's hand.

[94] pilgrims visit shrines; Romeo's blushing (red) lips visit her hand, which he has just called a "holy shrine."

[95] pilgrims.

[96] That is, let our lips press each other in a kiss, just as hands press each other in a handclasp.

Give me my sin again.   (*He kisses her again.*)
JULIET: You kiss by th' book.[97]
NURSE: (*going to her*) Madam, your mother craves a word with you.
ROMEO: What is her mother?
NURSE: Marry, bachelor,
   Her mother is the lady of the house,
   And a good lady, and a wise and virtuous.
   I nursed her daughter that you talked withal.
   I tell you, he that can lay hold of her
   Shall have the chinks.[98]
ROMEO: Is she a Capulet?
   O dear account! my life is my foe's debt.[99]
BENVOLIO: Away, be gone; the sport is at the best.
ROMEO: Ay, so I fear; the more is my unrest.
CAPULET: Nay, gentlemen, prepare not to be gone;
   We have a trifling foolish banquet towards.
   Is it e'en so? Why then, I thank you all.
   I thank you, honest gentlemen. Good night.
   More torches here! Come on then, let's to bed.
   Ah, sirrah, by my fay,[100] it waxes late;
   I'll to my rest.
      All but Juliet *and* Nurse *leave the stage.*
JULIET: Come hither, nurse. What is yond gentleman?
NURSE: The son and heir of old Tiberio.
JULIET: What's he that now is going out of door?
NURSE: Marry, that, I think, be young Petruchio.
JULIET: What's he that follows there, that would not dance?
NURSE: I know not.
JULIET: Go ask his name.—If he be marrièd,
   My grave is like to be my wedding bed.
NURSE: His name is Romeo, and a Montague,
   The only son of your great enemy.
JULIET: My only love, sprung from my only hate!
   Too early seen unknown, and known too late!
   Prodigious birth of love it is to me
   That I must love a loathèd enemy.
NURSE: What's this? what's this?
JULIET: A rhyme I learnt even now
   Of one I danced withal.
      Someone calls within, 'Juliet.'
NURSE: Anon, anon![101]
   Come, let's away; the strangers all are gone.
      Exeunt.

[97] according to etiquette.
[98] wealth, money.
[99] "My life belongs to my foe."
[100] faith.
[101] Coming right away!

ACT II

Enter the Chorus.

CHORUS: Now old desire[102] doth in his deathbed lie,
    And young affection[103] gapes to be his heir;
That fair for which love groaned for and would die,
    With tender Juliet matched, is now not fair.
Now Romeo is beloved and loves again,
    Alike bewitchèd by the charm of looks;
But to his foe supposed he must complain,
    And she steal love's sweet bait from fearful
        hooks.[104]
Being held a foe, he may not have access
    To breathe such vows as lovers use to swear,
And she as much in love, her means much less
    To meet her new belovèd anywhere;
But passion lends them power, time means, to meet,
Temp'ring extremities with extreme sweet.

[102] Romeo's "old desire" for Rosaline.
[103] Romeo's "new affection" for Juliet "gapes"—is eager to open his mouth hungrily—to succeed the "old desire."
[104] Juliet must steal her love as a result of the family feud, and avoid being caught (as a fish is with "fearful hooks").

SCENE I   [*A path along the wall of Capulet's Orchard or Garden*]

Enter Romeo *alone.*

ROMEO: Can I go forward when my heart is here?
    Turn back, dull earth,[105] and find thy centre out.

[105] Romeo calls his body (as contrast with his soul or "heart") "dull earth."

Enter Benvolio *with* Mercutio, Romeo *hiding from them when he sees them approaching.*

BENVOLIO: Romeo! my cousin Romeo! Romeo!
MERCUTIO: He is wise,
    And, on my life, hath stol'n him home to bed.
BENVOLIO: He ran this way and leapt this orchard
    wall.
    Call, good Mercutio.
MERCUTIO: Nay, I'll conjure too.
    Romeo! humors![106] madman! passion! lover!
    Appear thou in the likeness of a sigh;
    Speak but one rhyme, and I am satisfied!
    Cry but 'Ay me!' pronounce but 'love' and 'dove';

[106] moods, whims.

Speak to my gossip Venus one fair word,
One nickname for her purblind son and heir
Young Abraham Cupid, he that shot so true
When King Cophetua loved the beggar maid![107]
He heareth not, he stirreth not, he moveth not;
The ape is dead, and I must conjure him.
I conjure thee by Rosaline's bright eyes,
By her high forehead and her scarlet lip,
By her fine foot, straight leg, and quivering thigh,
And the demesnes[108] that there adjacent lie,
That in thy likeness thou appear to us!

BENVOLIO: An if he hear thee, thou wilt anger him.
MERCUTIO: This cannot anger him. 'Twould anger him
To raise a spirit in his mistress' circle
Of some strange nature, letting it there stand
Till she had laid it and conjured it down.
That were some spite; my invocation
Is fair and honest: in his mistress' name,
I conjure only but to raise up him.
BENVOLIO: Come, he hath hid himself among these trees
To be consorted with the humorous[109] night.
Blind is his love and best befits the dark.
MERCUTIO: If love be blind, love cannot hit the mark.
Now will he sit under a medlar tree
And wish his mistress were that kind of fruit
As maids call medlars when they laugh alone.
O, Romeo, that she were, O that she were
An open et cetera, thou a pop'rin pear!
Romeo, good night. I'll to my truckle-bed;[110]
This field-bed is too cold for me to sleep.
Come, shall we go?
BENVOLIO: Go then, for 'tis in vain
To seek him here that means not to be found.
[*Exeunt.*]

[107] That is, Cupid hit the mark perfect ("so true") and made King Cophetua, the king in a folk ballad, fall in love with a beggar maid.
[108] domains.
[109] damp.
[110] trundle-bed.

SCENE II [*The Capulet's Orchard*]

ROMEO: He jests at scars that never felt a wound.

Juliet *appears above at a window.*

But soft! What light through yonder window breaks?
It is the East, and Juliet is the sun!

Arise, fair sun, and kill the envious moon,
Who is already sick and pale with grief
That thou her maid art far more fair than she.[111]
Be not her maid, since she is envious.
Her vestal livery is but sick and green,
And none but fools do wear it. Cast it off.
It is my lady; O, it is my love!
O that she knew she were!
She speaks, yet she says nothing. What of that?
Her eye discourses; I will answer it.
I am too bold; 'tis not to me she speaks.
Two of the fairest stars in all the heaven,
Having some business, do entreat her eyes
To twinkle in their spheres till they return.
What if her eyes were there, they in her head?
The brightness of her cheek would shame those stars
As daylight doth a lamp; her eyes in heaven
Would through the airy region stream so bright
That birds would sing and think it were not night.
See how she leans her cheek upon her hand!
O that I were a glove upon that hand,
That I might touch that cheek!

JULIET: Ay me!
ROMEO: She speaks.
O, speak again, bright angel! for thou art
As glorious to this night, being o'er my head,
As is a wingèd messenger of heaven
Unto the white-upturnèd wond'ring eyes
Of mortals that fall back to gaze on him
When he bestrides the lazy-pacing clouds
And sails upon the bosom of the air.

JULIET: O Romeo, Romeo! wherefore art thou Romeo?
Deny thy father and refuse thy name;
Or, if thou wilt not, be but sworn my love,
And I'll no longer be a Capulet.

ROMEO: (*aside—to himself*) Shall I hear more, or shall I speak at this?

JULIET: 'Tis but thy name that is my enemy.
Thou art thyself, though not a Montague.
What's Montague? It is nor hand, nor foot,
Nor arm, nor face, nor any other part
Belonging to a man. O, be some other name!
What's in a name? That which we call a rose
By any other name would smell as sweet.
So Romeo would, were he not Romeo called,

---

[111] The moon, the goddess Diana, is envious that Juliet is more fair than she.

Retain that dear perfection which he owes
Without that title. Romeo, doff thy name;
And for thy name, which is no part of thee,
Take all myself.

ROMEO: (*aloud, stepping out of the darkness a little*)
   I take thee at thy word.
Call me but love, and I'll be new baptized;
Henceforth I never will be Romeo.

JULIET: What man art thou that, thus bescreened in night,
So stumblest on my counsel?

ROMEO: By a name
I know not how to tell thee who I am.
My name, dear saint, is hateful to myself,
Because it is an enemy to thee.
Had I it written, I would tear the word.

JULIET: My ears have yet not drunk a hundred words
Of thy tongue's uttering, yet I know the sound.
Art thou not Romeo, and a Montague?

ROMEO: Neither, fair maid, if either thee dislike.

JULIET: How camest thou hither, tell me, and wherefore?
The orchard walls are high and hard to climb,
And the place death, considering who thou art,
If any of my kinsmen find thee here.

ROMEO: With love's light wings did I o'erperch[112] these walls;
For stony limits cannot hold love out,
And what love can do, that dares love attempt.
Therefore thy kinsmen are no stop to me.

JULIET: If they do see thee, they will murder thee.

ROMEO: Alack, there lies more peril in thine eye
Than twenty of their swords! Look thou but sweet,
And I am proof against their enmity.

JULIET: I would not for the world they saw thee here.

ROMEO: I have night's cloak to hide me from their eyes;
And but thou love me, let them find me here.
My life were better ended by their hate
Than death prorogued,[113] wanting of thy love.

JULIET: By whose direction found'st thou out this place?

ROMEO: By love, that first did prompt me to inquire.
He lent me counsel, and I lent him eyes.
I am no pilot; yet, wert thou as far

[112] overperch—fly over.
[113] postponed.

As that vast shore washed with the farthest sea,
I should adventure for such merchandise.

JULIET: Thou knowest the mask of night is on my face;
Else would a maiden blush bepaint my cheek
For that which thou hast heard me speak to-night.
Fain would I dwell on form—fain, fain deny
What I have spoke; but farewell compliment![114]
Dost thou love me? I know thou wilt say 'Ay';
And I will take thy word. Yet, if thou swear'st,
Thou mayst prove false. At lovers' perjuries,
They say, Jove laughs. O gentle Romeo,
If thou dost love, pronounce it faithfully.
Or if thou thinkest I am too quickly won,
I'll frown, and be perverse, and say thee nay,
So thou wilt woo; but else, not for the world.
In truth, fair Montague, I am too fond,
And therefore thou mayst think my 'havior light;
But trust me, gentleman, I'll prove more true
Than those that have more cunning to be strange.[115]
I should have been more strange, I must confess,
But that thou overheard'st, ere I was ware,
My true-love passion. Therefore pardon me,
And not impute this yielding to light love,
Which the dark night hath so discoverèd.

ROMEO: Lady, by yonder blessèd moon I vow,
That tips with silver all these fruit-tree tops—

JULIET: O, swear not by the moon, th' inconstant moon,
That monthly changes in her circled orb,
Lest that thy love prove likewise variable.

ROMEO: What shall I swear by?

JULIET: Do not swear at all;
Or if thou wilt, swear by thy gracious self,
Which is the god of my idolatry,
And I'll believe thee.

ROMEO: If my heart's dear love—

JULIET: Well, do not swear. Although I joy in thee,
I have no joy of this contract to-night.
It is too rash, too unadvised, too sudden;
Too like the lightning, which doth cease to be
Ere one can say 'It lightens.' Sweet, good night!
This bud of love, by summer's ripening breath,
May prove a beauteous flow'r when next we meet.

[114] etiquette.
[115] to be, or to pretend to be, aloof.

Good night, good night! As sweet repose and rest
Come to thy heart as that within my breast!
ROMEO: O, wilt thou leave me so unsatisfied?
JULIET: What satisfaction canst thou have to-night?
ROMEO: Th' exchange of thy love's faithful vow for mine.
JULIET: I gave thee mine before thou didst request it;
And yet I would it were to give again.
ROMEO: Wouldst thou withdraw it? For what purpose, love?
JULIET: But to be frank[116] and give it thee again.
And yet I wish but for the thing I have.
My bounty[117] is as boundless as the sea,
My love as deep; the more I give to thee
The more I have, for both are infinite.
I hear some noise within. Dear love, adieu!
            (*Someone—the* Nurse—*calls within.*)
Anon, good nurse! Sweet Montague, be true.
Stay but a little, I will come again. *She goes inside.*
ROMEO: O blessèd, blessèd night! I am afeard,
Being in night, all this is but a dream,
Too flattering-sweet to be substantial.

Juliet *returns.*

JULIET: Three words, dear Romeo, and good night indeed.
If that thy bent of love be honorable,
Thy purpose marriage, send me word to-morrow,
By one that I'll procure to come to thee,
Where and what time thou wilt perform the rite;
And all my fortunes at thy foot I'll lay
And follow thee my lord throughout the world.
NURSE: (*within*) Madam!
JULIET: I come, anon.—But if thou meanest not well,
I do beseech thee—
NURSE: (*within*) Madam!
JULIET: By and by[118] I come.—
To cease thy suit and leave me to my grief.
To-morrow will I send.
ROMEO: So thrive my soul—
JULIET: A thousand times good night!
            She disappears.

[116] free, liberal, generous.
[117] "My desire to give"—to give you my love.
[118] immediately.

ROMEO: A thousand times the worse, to want thy light!
Love goes toward love as schoolboys from their books;
But love from love, toward school with heavy looks.

Enter Juliet *again.*

JULIET: Hist! Romeo, hist! O for a falc'ner's voice
To lure this tassel-gentle[119] back again!
Bondage[120] is hoarse and may not speak aloud,
Else would I tear the cave where Echo lies
And make her airy tongue more hoarse than mine
With repetition of 'My Romeo!'
ROMEO: It is my soul[121] that calls upon my name.
How silver-sweet sound lovers' tongues by night,
Like softest music to attending ears!
JULIET: Romeo!
ROMEO: My sweet?
JULIET: At what o'clock to-morrow
Shall I send to thee?
ROMEO: By the hour of nine.
JULIET: I will not fail. 'Tis twenty years till then.
I have forgot why I did call thee back.
ROMEO: Let me stand here till thou remember it.
JULIET: I shall forget, to have thee still stand there,
Rememb'ring how I love thy company.
ROMEO: And I'll still stay, to have thee still forget,
Forgetting any other home but this.
JULIET: 'Tis almost morning. I would have thee gone—
And yet no farther than a wanton's[122] bird
That lets it hop a little from her hand,
Like a poor prisoner in his twisted gyves,[123]
And with a silken thread plucks it back again,
So loving-jealous of his liberty.
ROMEO: I would I were thy bird.
JULIET: Sweet, so would I.
Yet I should kill thee with much cherishing.
Good night, good night! Parting is such sweet sorrow
That I shall say good night till it be morrow.
She disappears.
ROMEO: Sleep dwell upon thine eyes, peace in thy breast!

---

[119] falcon—a male falcon.
[120] her state of "bondage," her fear of being watched, is such that she must speak softly.
[121] for Romeo, Juliet is his "soul."
[122] a playful child's bird.
[123] chains.

Would I were sleep and peace, so sweet to rest!
Hence will I to my ghostly[124] father's cell,
His help to crave and my dear hap[125] to tell.   *Exit.*

[124] spiritual.
[125] good fortune.

SCENE III   [*Friar Laurence's cell*]
Enter Friar Laurence *alone, with a basket.*

FRIAR: The grey-eyed morn smiles on the frowning night,
Check'ring the Eastern clouds with streaks of light;
And fleckèd darkness like a drunkard reels
From forth day's path and Titan's[126] fiery wheels.
Now, ere the sun advance his burning eye
The day to cheer and night's dank dew to dry,
I must up-fill this osier cage[127] of ours
With baleful weeds and precious-juicèd flowers.
The earth that's nature's mother is her tomb.
What is her burying grave, that is her womb;
And from her womb children of divers kind
We sucking on her natural bosom find,
Many for many virtues excellent,
None but for some, and yet all different.
O, mickle[128] is the powerful grace that lies
In plants, herbs, stones, and their true qualities;
For naught so vile that on the earth doth live
But to the earth some special good doth give;
Nor aught so good but, strained from that fair use,
Revolts from true birth,[129] stumbling on abuse.
Virtue itself turns vice, being misapplied,
And vice sometime 's by action dignified.
Within the infant rind of this weak flower
Poison hath residence, and medicine power;
For this, being smelt, with that part cheers each part;
Being tasted, slays all senses with the heart.
Two such opposèd kings encamp them still
In man as well as herbs—grace[130] and rude will;
And where the worser is predominant,
Full soon the canker death eats up that plant.

Enter Romeo.

ROMEO: Good morrow, father.
FRIAR: Benedicite![131]
What early tongue so sweet saluteth me?
Young son, it argues a distemperèd head

[126] the Sun's; in Greek mythology, the Titan Hyperion is the Sun.
[127] Willow basket.
[128] much.
[129] deviated from or revolts against its true nature and becomes corrupted ("stumbles on abuses").
[130] goodness, or the capacity to be good.

[131] "God blesses you."

So soon to bid good morrow to thy bed.
Care keeps his watch in every old man's eye,
And where care lodges, sleep will never lie;
But where unbruisèd youth with unstuffed[132] brain
Doth couch his limbs, there golden sleep doth reign.
Therefore thy earliness doth me assure
Thou art uprousèd with some distemp'rature;
Or if not so, then here I hit it right—
Our Romeo hath not been in bed to-night.

ROMEO: That last is true—the sweeter rest was mine.
FRIAR: God pardon sin! Wast thou with Rosaline?
ROMEO: With Rosaline, my ghostly father? No.
I have forgot that name and that name's woe.
FRIAR: That's my good son! But where hast thou been then?
ROMEO: I'll tell thee ere thou ask it me again.
I have been feasting with mine enemy,
Where on a sudden one hath wounded me
That's by me wounded. Both our remedies
Within thy help and holy physic lies.
I bear no hatred, blessèd man, for, lo,
My intercession[133] likewise steads my foe.
FRIAR: Be plain, good son, and homely in thy drift.
Riddling confession finds but riddling shrift.
ROMEO: Then plainly know my heart's dear love is set
On the fair daughter of rich Capulet;
As mine on hers, so hers is set on mine,
And all combined, save what thou must combine
By holy marriage. When, and where, and how
We met, we wooed, and made exchange of vow,
I'll tell thee as we pass; but this I pray,
That thou consent to marry us to-day.
FRIAR: Holy Saint Francis! What a change is here!
Is Rosaline, that thou didst love so dear,
So soon forsaken? Young men's love then lies
Not truly in their hearts, but in their eyes.
Jesu Maria! What a deal of brine
Hath washed thy sallow cheeks for Rosaline!
How much salt water thrown away in waste
To season love, that of it doth not taste![134]
The sun not yet thy sighs from heaven clears,
Thy old groans ring yet in mine ancient ears.
Lo, here upon thy cheek the stain doth sit
Of an old tear that is not washed off yet.
If e'er thou wast thyself, and these woes thine,
Thou and these woes were all for Rosaline.

---

[132] untroubled, unburdened.
[133] "My request benefits ("steads") my foe."
[134] that has no savor as yet.

And art thou changed? Pronounce this sentence then:
Women may fall when there's no strength[135] in men.
ROMEO: Thou chid'st me oft for loving Rosaline.
FRIAR: For doting, not for loving, pupil mine.
ROMEO: And bad'st me bury love.
FRIAR: Not in a grave
To lay one in, another out to have.
ROMEO: I pray thee chide not. She whom I love now
Doth grace for grace and love for love allow.
The other did not so.
FRIAR: O, she knew well
Thy love did read by rote, that could not spell.
But come, young waverer, come go with me.
In one respect I'll thy assistant be;
For this alliance may so happy prove
To turn your households' rancor to pure love.
ROMEO: O, let us hence! I stand on sudden haste.
FRIAR: Wisely and slow. They stumble that run fast.
Exeunt.

[135] steadiness, constancy.

SCENE IV [*A street*]

Enter Benvolio *and* Mercutio.

MERCUTIO: Where the devil should this Romeo be? Came he not home to-night?
BENVOLIO: Not to his father's. I spoke with his man.
MERCUTIO: Why, that same pale hard-hearted wench, that Rosaline,
Torments him so that he will sure run mad.
BENVOLIO: Tybalt, the kinsman to old Capulet,
Hath sent a letter to his father's house.
MERCUTIO: A challenge, on my life.
BENVOLIO: Romeo will answer it.
MERCUTIO: Any man that can write may answer a letter.
BENVOLIO: Nay, he will answer the letter's master, how he dares, being dared.
MERCUTIO: Alas, poor Romeo, he is already dead! Stabbed with a white wench's black eye; run through the ear with a love song; the very pin of his heart cleft with the blind bow-boy's butt-shaft;[136] and is he a man to encounter Tybalt?

[136] Cupid's arrow.

ACT II, SC. IV   THE TRAGEDY OF ROMEO AND JULIET

BENVOLIO: Why, what is Tybalt?
MERCUTIO: More than Prince of Cats,[137] I can tell you. O, he's the courageous captain of compliments. He fights as you sing pricksong[138]—keeps time, distance, and proportions; he rests his minim rests,[139] one, two, and the third in your bosom! the very butcher of a silk button, a duellist, a duellist! a gentleman of the very first house, of the first and second cause. Ah, the immortal passado![140] the punto reverso![141] the hay![142]
BENVOLIO: The what?
MERCUTIO: The pox[143] of such antic, lisping, affecting fantasticoes—these new tuners of accent! 'By Jesu, a very good blade! a very tall[144] man!' Why, is not this a lamentable thing, grandsir, that we should be thus afflicted with these strange flies, these fashion-mongers, these pardon-me's, who stand so much on the new form that they cannot sit at ease on the old bench? O, their bones, their bones![145]

[137] "Tybalt" is the name of the cat in the famous old beast-fable of Reynard the Fox.
[138] music that was fully written out for performance.
[139] rests in music—the shortest rests.
[140] a lunge with the duelling sword.
[141] a backhanded stroke.
[142] the thrust home.
[143] An expression of contempt.
[144] brave.
[145] bones—"bons" (in French)—their exclamations of "Good! Good," "Bons! Bons!"

Enter Romeo.

BENVOLIO: Here comes Romeo! here comes Romeo!
MERCUTIO: Without his roe, like a dried herring. O flesh, flesh, how art thou fishified! Now is he for the numbers[146] that Petrarch[147] flowed in. Laura, to his lady, was a kitchen wench (marry, she had a better love to berhyme her), Dido[148] a dowdy, Cleopatra a gypsy, Helen and Hero[149] hildings and harlots, Thisbe[150] a grey eye or so, but not to the purpose. Signior Romeo, bon jour! There's a French salutation to your French slop.[151] You gave us the counterfeit fairly last night.
ROMEO: Good morrow to you both. What counterfeit did I give you?
MERCUTIO: The slip, sir, the slip.[152] Can you not conceive?
ROMEO: Pardon, good Mercutio. My business was great, and in such a case as mine a man may strain courtesy.
MERCUTIO: That's as much as to say, such a case as yours constrains a man to bow in the hams.[153]
ROMEO: Meaning, to curtsy.

[146] verse.
[147] the famous Italian poet who celebrated his lady-love Laura in his poetry.
[148] Dido, the queen of Carthage, in Virgil's Latin epic poem the *Aeneid*.
[149] Helen of Troy and Hero, the heroine of the story of Hero and Leander, the subject of a long poem by Christopher Marlowe.
[150] Another romantic heroine beloved of Pyramus; whose story is crudely acted out in Shakespeare's *A Midsummer Night's Dream*.
[151] trousers.
[152] a pun, because "slip" also means a counterfeit coin.
[153] hips.

MERCUTIO: Thou hast most kindly hit it.
ROMEO: A most courteous exposition.
MERCUTIO: Nay, I am the very pink of courtesy.
ROMEO: Pink for flower.
MERCUTIO: Right.
ROMEO: Why, then is my pump[154] well-flowered.
MERCUTIO: Sure wit, follow me this jest now till thou hast worn out thy pump, that, when the single sole of it is worn, the jest may remain, after the wearing, solely singular.[155]
ROMEO: O single-soled jest, solely singular for the singleness!
MERCUTIO: Come between us, good Benvolio! My wits faint.
ROMEO: Swits[156] and spurs, swits and spurs! or I'll cry a match.[157]
MERCUTIO: Nay, if our wits run the wild-goose chase, I am done; for thou hast more of the wild goose in one of thy wits than, I am sure, I have in my whole five. Was I with you there for the goose?[158]
ROMEO: Thou wast never with me for anything when thou wast not there for the goose.[159]
MERCUTIO: I will bite thee by the ear for that jest.
ROMEO: Nay, good goose, bite not!
MERCUTIO: Thy wit is a very bitter sweeting;[160] it is a most sharp sauce.
ROMEO: And is it not, then, well served in to a sweet goose?
MERCUTIO: O, here's a wit of cheveril,[161] that stretches from an inch narrow to an ell[162] broad!
ROMEO: I stretch it out for that word 'broad,' which, added to the goose, proves thee far and wide a broad goose.
MERCUTIO: Why, is not this better now than groaning for love? Now art thou sociable, now art thou Romeo; now art thou what thou art, by art as well as by nature. For this drivelling love is like a great natural that runs lolling up and down to hide his bauble[163] in a hole.
BENVOLIO: Stop there, stop there!
MERCUTIO: Thou desirest me to stop in my tale against the hair.
BENVOLIO: Thou wouldst else have made thy tale large.
MERCUTIO: O, thou art deceived! I would have made it short; for I was come to the whole depth of my

[154] shoe.
[155] there is much punning here on "sole."
[156] switches.
[157] "I'll claim a victory."
[158] "Was I right on calling you a goose?"
[159] "When you were not there for chasing women"— another pun.
[160] a tart kind of apple.
[161] a kid-skin that stretches easily.
[162] an ell measured 45 English inches.
[163] the wand traditionally carried by a professional jester.

[164] pursue.
[165] stuff.

tale, and meant indeed to occupy[164] the argument no longer.

ROMEO: Here's goodly gear![165]

Enter Nurse *and her servant* Peter.

MERCUTIO: A sail, a sail!
BENVOLIO: Two, two! a shirt and a smock.[166]
NURSE: Peter!
PETER: Anon.
NURSE: My fan, Peter.
MERCUTIO: Good Peter, to hide her face; for her fan's the fairer face.
NURSE: God ye good morrow, gentlemen.
MERCUTIO: God ye good-den, fair gentlewoman.
NURSE: Is it good-den?[167]

[166] A man ("shirt") and a woman ("smock").
[167] afternoon.
[168] the indented mark on a sundial or on the face of a clock.
[169] said ("quoth") he. The nurse is pleased with Romeo's jest. "Mar" means to spoil.
[170] for want (or lack) of a worse.
[171] very well understood in faith.
[172] invite. The young men proceed to tease her by pretending to misunderstand her business in looking for Romeo, imputing dishonorable motives to her, and playing on words which cause her to feel abused, so that she scolds her servant Peter for not coming to her defense.

MERCUTIO: 'Tis no less, I tell ye; for the bawdy hand of the dial is now upon the prick of noon.[168]
NURSE: Out upon you! What a man are you!
ROMEO: One, gentlewoman, that God hath made for himself to mar.
NURSE: By my troth, it is well said. 'For himself to mar,' quoth 'a?[169] Gentlemen, can any of you tell me where I may find the young Romeo?
ROMEO: I can tell you; but young Romeo will be older when you have found him than he was when you sought him. I am the youngest of that name, for fault of a worse.[170]
NURSE: You say well.
MERCUTIO: Yea, is the worst well? Very well took,[171] i' faith! wisely, wisely.
NURSE: If you be he, sir, I desire some confidence with you.
BENVOLIO: She will endite[172] him to some supper.
MERCUTIO: A bawd, a bawd, a bawd! So ho!
ROMEO: What hast thou found?
MERCUTIO: No hare, sir; unless a hare, sir, in a lenten pie, that is something stale and hoar ere it be spent.   (*He sings*)

> An old hare hoar,
> And an old hare hoar,
> Is very good meat in Lent;
> But a hare that is hoar
> Is too much for a score
> When it hoars ere it be spent.

Romeo, will you come to your father's? We'll to dinner thither.
ROMEO: I will follow you.
MERCUTIO: Farewell, ancient lady. Farewell, lady, lady, lady.[173]   *Exeunt* Mercutio *and* Benvolio.
NURSE: I pray you, sir, what saucy merchant was this that was so full of his ropery?[174]
ROMEO: A gentleman, nurse, that loves to hear himself talk and will speak more in a minute than he will stand to in a month.
NURSE: An 'a speak anything against me, I'll take him down, an 'a were lustier than he is, and twenty such Jacks; and if I cannot, I'll find those that shall. Scurvy knave! I am none of his flirt-gills;[175] I am none of his skains-mates. And thou must stand by too, and suffer every knave to use me at his pleasure!
PETER: I saw no man use you at his pleasure. If I had, my weapon should quickly have been out, I warrant you. I dare draw as soon as another man, if I see occasion in a good quarrel, and the law on my side.
NURSE: Now, afore God, I am so vexed that every part about me quivers. Scurvy knave! Pray you, sir, a word; and, as I told you, my young lady bid me inquire you out. What she bid me say, I will keep to myself; but first let me tell ye, if ye should lead her into a fool's paradise,[176] as they say, it were a very gross kind of behavior, as they say; for the gentlewoman is young; and therefore, if you should deal double with her, truly it were an ill thing to be offered to any gentlewoman, and very weak[177] dealing.
ROMEO: Nurse, commend me to thy lady and mistress. I protest unto thee—
NURSE: Good heart, and i' faith I will tell her as much. Lord, Lord! she will be a joyful woman.
ROMEO: What wilt thou tell her, nurse? Thou dost not mark me.
NURSE: I will tell her, sir, that you do protest, which, as I take it, is a gentlemanlike offer.
ROMEO: Bid her devise
Some means to come to shrift this afternoon;
And there she shall at Friar Laurence' cell
Be shrived and married. Here is for thy pains.
NURSE: No, truly, sir; not a penny.

[173] Mercutio apparently sings the words "lady, lady, lady," which appear in an old ballad, *Chaste Susanna*.
[174] coarse joking.
[175] flirts.
[176] seduce her.
[177] improper, dishonorable.

ROMEO: Go to! I say you shall.
NURSE: This afternoon, sir? Well, she shall be there.
ROMEO: And say, good nurse, behind the abbey wall.
Within this hour my man shall be with thee
And bring thee cords made like a tackled stair,[178]
Which to the high topgallant[179] of my joy
Must be my convoy in the secret night.
Farewell. Be trusty, and I'll quit[180] thy pains.
Farewell. Commend me to thy mistress.
NURSE: Now God in heaven bless thee! Hark you, sir.
ROMEO: What say'st thou, my dear nurse?
NURSE: Is your man secret? Did you ne'er hear say, Two may keep counsel, putting one away?
ROMEO: I warrant thee my man's as true as steel.
NURSE: Well, sir, my mistress is the sweetest lady. Lord, Lord! when 'twas a little prating thing—O, there is a nobleman in town, one Paris, that would fain lay knife aboard;[181] but she, good soul, had as lieve[182] see a toad, a very toad, as see him. I anger her sometimes, and tell her that Paris is the properer man; but I'll warrant you, when I say so, she looks as pale as any clout in the versal world.[183] Doth not rosemary and Romeo begin both with a letter?
ROMEO: Ay, nurse; what of that? Both with an R.
NURSE: Ah, mocker! that's the dog's name. R is for the— No; I know it begins with some other letter; and she hath the prettiest sententious[184] of it, of you and rosemary, that it would do you good to hear it.
ROMEO: Commend me to thy lady.
NURSE: Ay, a thousand times (*Romeo departs*) Peter!
PETER: Anon.
NURSE: Peter, take my fan, and go before, and apace.
Exit, following Peter.

[178] a rope ladder.
[179] the highest on a sailing vessel.
[180] reward, requite.
[181] marry Juliet — literally, partake of the food.
[182] as gladly, as willingly.
[183] as any rag in the whole (universal) world.
[184] She has made the prettiest sentences, using words beginning with the letter "r," such as Romeo and Rosemary.

SCENE V   [*The Capulet Orchard*]

Enter Juliet.

JULIET: The clock struck nine when I did send the nurse;
In half an hour she promised to return.

Perchance she cannot meet him. That's not so.
O, she is lame! Love's heralds should be thoughts,
Which ten times faster glide than the sun's beams
Driving back shadows over low'ring hills.
Therefore do nimble-pinioned[185] doves draw Love,[186]
And therefore hath the wind-swift Cupid wings.
Now is the sun upon the highmost hill[187]
Of this day's journey, and from nine till twelve
Is three long hours; yet she is not come.
Had she affections and warm youthful blood,
She would be as swift in motion as a ball;
My words would bandy[188] her to my sweet love,
And his to me.
But old folks, many feign as they were dead—
Unwieldy, slow, heavy and pale as lead.

[185] swift-winged.
[186] the chariot of the goddess of Love, Venus is drawn by doves.
[187] the sun is at its zenith.
[188] speed.

Enter Nurse *and* Peter.

O God, she comes! O honey nurse, what news?
Hast thou met with him? Send thy man away.
NURSE: Peter, stay at the gate.
　　　　　　　(*Peter leaves the scene.*)
JULIET: Now, good sweet nurse—O Lord, why lookest thou sad?
Though news be sad, yet tell them merrily;
If good, thou shamest the music of sweet news
By playing it to me with so sour a face.
NURSE: I am aweary, give me leave awhile.
Fie, how my bones ache! What a jaunce[189] have I had!
JULIET: I would thou hadst my bones, and I thy news.
Nay, come, I pray thee speak. Good, good nurse, speak.
NURSE: Jesu, what haste! Can you not stay awhile?
Do you not see that I am out of breath?
JULIET: How art thou out of breath when thou hast breath
To say to me that thou art out of breath?
The excuse that thou dost make in this delay
Is longer than the tale thou dost excuse.
Is thy news good or bad? Answer to that.
Say either, and I'll stay the circumstance.[190]
Let me be satisfied, is't good or bad?
NURSE: Well, you have made a simple choice; you

[189] jolt.
[190] wait for the details of your report.

know not how to choose a man. Romeo? No, not he. Though his face be better than any man's, yet his leg excels all men's; and for a hand and a foot, and a body, though they be not to be talked on, yet they are past compare. He is not the flower of courtesy, but, I'll warrant him, as gentle as a lamb. Go thy ways, wench; serve God. What, have you dined at home?

JULIET: No, no. But all this did I know before.
What says he of our marriage? What of that?

NURSE: Lord, how my head aches! What a head have I!
It beats as it would fall in twenty pieces.
My back a t' other side—ah, my back, my back!
Beshrew your heart[191] for sending me about
To catch my death with jauncing up and down!

JULIET: I' faith, I am sorry that thou art not well.
Sweet, sweet, sweet nurse, tell me, what says my love?

NURSE: Your love says, like an honest gentleman, and a courteous, and a kind, and a handsome, and, I warrant, a virtuous—Where is your mother?

JULIET: Where is my mother? Why, she is within.
Where should she be? How oddly thou repliest!
'Your love says, like an honest gentleman,
"Where is your mother?"'

NURSE: O God's Lady dear!
Are you so hot? Marry, come up, I trow.[192]
Is this the poultice for my aching bones?
Henceforward do your messages yourself.

JULIET: Here's such a coil![193] Come, what says Romeo?

NURSE: Have you got leave to go to shrift to-day?

JULIET: I have.

NURSE: Then hie you hence to Friar Laurence' cell;
There stays a husband to make you a wife.
Now comes the wanton blood up in your cheeks:
They'll be in scarlet straight at any news.
Hie you to church; I must another way,
To fetch a ladder, by the which your love
Must climb a bird's nest[194] soon when it is dark.
I am the drudge, and toil in your delight;
But you shall bear the burden soon at night.
Go; I'll to dinner; hie you to the cell.

JULIET: Hie to high fortune! Honest nurse, farewell.
                                          Exeunt.

---

[191] Shame on you.

[192] By the Virgin; here's your punishment, I trust ("trow").

[193] such a fuss.

[194] that is, climb into Juliet's bedchamber.

SCENE VI [*Friar Laurence's cell*]

Enter Friar Laurence *and* Romeo.

FRIAR: So smile the heavens upon this holy act
That after-hours with sorrow chide us not!
ROMEO: Amen, amen! But come what sorrow can,
It cannot countervail[195] the exchange of joy
That one short minute gives me in her sight.
Do thou but close our hands with holy words,
Then love-devouring death do what he dare—
It is enough I may but call her mine.
FRIAR: These violent delights have violent ends
And in their triumph die, like fire and powder,
Which, as they kiss, consume. The sweetest honey
Is loathsome in his own deliciousness
And in the taste confounds the appetite.
Therefore love moderately: long love doth so;
Too swift arrives as tardy as too slow.

[195] equal.

Enter Juliet.

Here comes the lady. O, so light a foot
Will ne'er wear out the everlasting flint.
A lover may bestride the gossamer[196]
That idles in the wanton summer air,
And yet not fall; so light is vanity.
JULIET: Good even to my ghostly[197] confessor.
FRIAR: Romeo shall thank thee, daughter, for us both.
JULIET: As much to him, else is his thanks too much.
ROMEO: Ah, Juliet, if the measure of thy joy
Be heaped like mine, and that thy skill be more
To blazon[198] it, then sweeten with thy breath
This neighbor air, and let rich music's tongue
Unfold the imagined happiness that both
Receive in either by this dear encounter.
JULIET: Conceit,[199] more rich in matter than in words,
Brags of his substance, not of ornament.
They are but beggars that can count their worth;
But my true love is grown to such excess
I cannot sum up sum of half my wealth.

[196] spider's web.
[197] spiritual, religious.
[198] proclaim, set it forth.
[199] true understanding.

FRIAR: Come, come with me, and we will make short work;
For, by your leaves, you shall not stay alone
Till Holy Church incorporate two in one.

He leads them out.

ACT III   SCENE I   [*A street*]

Enter Mercutio, Benvolio, *and Men.*

BENVOLIO: I pray thee, good Mercutio, let's retire.
The day is hot, the Capulets abroad,
And, if we meet, we shall not 'scape a brawl,
For now, these hot days, is the mad blood stirring.

MERCUTIO: Thou art like one of these fellows that, when he enters the confines of a tavern, claps me his sword upon the table and says 'God send me no need of thee!' and by the operation of the second cup draws him on the drawer,[200] when indeed there is no need.

BENVOLIO: Am I like such a fellow?

MERCUTIO: Come, come, thou art as hot a Jack in thy mood as any in Italy; and as soon moved to be moody, and as soon moody to be moved.

BENVOLIO: And what to?

MERCUTIO: Nay, an there were two such, we should have none shortly, for one would kill the other. Thou! why, thou wilt quarrel with a man that hath a hair more or a hair less in his beard than thou hast. Thou wilt quarrel with a man for cracking nuts, having no other reason but because thou hast hazel eyes. What eye but such an eye would spy out such a quarrel? Thy head is as full of quarrels as an egg is full of meat; and yet thy head hath been beaten as addle as an egg for quarrelling. Thou hast quarrelled with a man for coughing in the street, because he hath wakened thy dog that hath lain asleep in the sun. Didst thou not fall out with a tailor for wearing his new doublet before Easter? with another for tying his

[200] by the time he has had his second cup draws his sword against the waiter who draws the wine.

new shoes with old riband? And yet thou wilt tutor me from quarrelling!

BENVOLIO: An I were so apt to quarrel as thou art, any man should buy the fee simple[201] of my life for an hour and a quarter.[202]

MERCUTIO: The fee simple? O simple!

Enter Tybalt *and other* Capulets.

BENVOLIO: By my head, here come the Capulets.
MERCUTIO: By my heel, I care not.
TYBALT: Follow me close, for I will speak to them.
Gentlemen, good-den. A word with one of you.
MERCUTIO: And but one word with one of us?
Couple it with something; make it a word and a blow.
TYBALT: You shall find me apt enough to that, sir, an you will give me occasion.
MERCUTIO: Could you not take some occasion without giving?
TYBALT: Mercutio, thou consortest with Romeo.
MERCUTIO: Consort?[203] What, dost thou make us minstrels? An thou make minstrels of us, look to hear nothing but discords. Here's my fiddlestick;[204] here's that shall make you dance. Zounds,[205] consort!
BENVOLIO: We talk here in the public haunt of men.
Either withdraw unto some private place,
Or reason coldly of your grievances,
Or else depart. Here all eyes gaze on us.
MERCUTIO: Men's eyes were made to look, and let them gaze.
I will not budge for no man's pleasure, I.

Enter Romeo.

TYBALT: Well, peace be with you, sir. Here comes my man.
MERCUTIO: But I'll be hanged, sir, if he wear your livery.[206]
Marry, go before to field, he'll be your follower!
Your worship in that sense may call him man.
TYBALT: Romeo, the love I bear thee can afford
No better term than this: thou art a villain.

[201] permanent lease.
[202] If I were as quarrelsome as you, my life would last about an hour and a quarter.
[203] Mercutio puns on the word "consort," which also meant a group of instruments or players' on a group of musical instruments.
[204] He means his dagger.
[205] an exclamation, meaning "by God's wounds!"
[206] servant's uniform from which it was possible to tell whom he served.

ROMEO: Tybalt, the reason that I have to love thee
Doth much excuse the appertaining rage
To such a greeting. Villain am I none.
Therefore farewell. I see thou knowest me not.
TYBALT: Boy, this shall not excuse the injuries
That thou hast done me; therefore turn and draw.
ROMEO: I do protest I never injured thee,
But love thee better than thou canst devise[207]
Till thou shalt know the reason of my love;
And so, good Capulet, which name I tender
As dearly as mine own, be satisfied.
MERCUTIO: O calm, dishonorable, vile submission!
Alla stoccata[208] carries it away. *He draws his sword.*
Tybalt, you ratcatcher, will you walk?
TYBALT: What wouldst thou have with me?
MERCUTIO: Good King of Cats, nothing but one of your nine lives. That I mean to make bold withal, and, as you shall use me hereafter, dry-beat the rest of the eight. Will you pluck your sword out of his pilcher[209] by the ears? Make haste, lest mine be about your ears ere it be out.
TYBALT: I am for you. *He draws.*
ROMEO: Gentle Mercutio, put thy rapier up.
MERCUTIO: Come, sir, your passado![210] *They duel.*
ROMEO: Draw, Benvolio; beat down their weapons.
Gentlemen, for shame! forbear this outrage!
Tybalt, Mercutio, the Prince expressly hath
Forbid this bandying in Verona streets.
Hold, Tybalt! Good Mercutio!
(Tybalt, *under* Romeo's *arm, stabs* Mercutio, *and then flees followed by his men.*)
MERCUTIO: I am hurt.
A plague on both your houses! I am sped.
Is he gone and hath nothing?
BENVOLIO: What, art thou hurt?
MERCUTIO: Ay, ay, a scratch, a scratch. Marry, 'tis enough.
Where is my page? Go, villain, fetch a surgeon.
(*A* Page *runs off-stage to call a physician.*)
ROMEO: Courage, man. The hurt cannot be much.
MERCUTIO: No, 'tis not so deep as a well, nor so wide as a church door; but 'tis enough, 'twill serve. Ask for me to-morrow, and you shall find me a grave[211] man. I am peppered, I warrant, for this world. A plague a both your houses! Zounds, a dog, a rat, a mouse, a cat, to scratch a man to

---

[207] realize, know.
[208] at the thrust.
[209] scabbard.
[210] lunge.
[211] a pun—"grave" in the double sense of being serious and occupying a grave.

death! a braggart, a rogue, a villain, that fights
by the book of arithmetic! Why the devil came
you between us? I was hurt under your arm.
ROMEO: I thought all for the best.
MERCUTIO: Help me into some house, Benvolio,
Or I shall faint. A plague a both your houses!
They have made worms' meat of me. I have it,
And soundly too.—Your houses!

He drags himself away, supported by Benvolio.

ROMEO: This gentleman, the Prince's near ally,
My very friend, hath got this mortal hurt
In my behalf—my reputation stained
With Tybalt's slander—Tybalt, that an hour
Hath been my cousin. O sweet Juliet,
Thy beauty hath made me effeminate
And in my temper soft'ned valor's steel!

Enter Benvolio.

BENVOLIO: O Romeo, Romeo, brave Mercutio is dead!
That gallant spirit hath aspired[212] the clouds,
Which too untimely here did scorn the earth.
ROMEO: This day's black fate on more days doth depend;[213]
This but begins the woe others must end.

Tybalt *returns.*

BENVOLIO: Here comes the furious Tybalt back again.
ROMEO: Alive in triumph, and Mercutio slain?
Away to heaven respective lenity,[214]
And fire-eyed fury be my conduct now!
Now, Tybalt, take the 'villain' back again
That late thou gavest me; for Mercutio's soul
Is but a little way above our heads,
Staying for thine to keep him company.
Either thou or I, or both, must go with him.
TYBALT: Thou, wretched boy, that didst consort him here,
Shalt with him hence.
ROMEO: This shall determine that.

They fight. Tybalt *falls.*

BENVOLIO: Romeo, away, be gone!
The citizens are up, and Tybalt slain.

[212] climbed or flown to the clouds.
[213] loom or hang over on more days—that is, more trouble may be expected.
[214] considerate gentleness.

ACT III, SC. I — THE TRAGEDY OF ROMEO AND JULIET

    Stand not amazed. The Prince will doom thee death
    If thou art taken. Hence, be gone, away!
ROMEO: O, I am fortune's fool![215]
BENVOLIO: Why dost thou stay?
                                        Exit Romeo.

Enter Citizens.

CITIZEN: Which way ran he that killed Mercutio?
    Tybalt, that murderer, which way ran he?
BENVOLIO: There lies that Tybalt.
CITIZEN: Up, sir, go with me.
    I charge thee in the Prince's name obey.

Enter Prince *with attendants, old* Montague, Capulet, *their* Wives, *and all*.

PRINCE: Where are the vile beginners of this fray?
BENVOLIO: O noble Prince, I can discover all
    The unlucky manage[216] of this fatal brawl.
    There lies the man, slain by young Romeo,
    That slew thy kinsman, brave Mercutio.
CAPULET'S WIFE: Tybalt, my cousin! O my brother's child!
    O Prince! O husband! O, the blood is spilled
    Of my dear kinsman! Prince, as thou art true,
    For blood of ours shed blood of Montague.
    O cousin, cousin!
PRINCE: Benvolio, who began this bloody fray?
BENVOLIO: Tybalt, here slain, whom Romeo's hand did slay.
    Romeo, that spoke him fair, bid him bethink
    How nice[217] the quarrel was, and urged withal
    Your high displeasure. All this—utterèd
    With gentle breath, calm look, knees humbly bowed—
    Could not take truce with the unruly spleen
    Of Tybalt deaf to peace, but that he tilts
    With piercing steel at bold Mercutio's breast;
    Who, all as hot, turns deadly point to point,
    And, with a martial scorn, with one hand beats
    Cold death aside and with the other sends
    It back to Tybalt, whose dexterity
    Retorts it. Romeo he cries aloud,
    'Hold, friends! friends, part!' and swifter than his tongue,

---

[215] Fortune's victim, a victim of fate.

[216] course.

[217] unimportant, trivial.

His agile arm beats down their fatal points,
And 'twixt them rushes; underneath whose arm
An envious thrust from Tybalt hit the life
Of stout Mercutio, and then Tybalt fled;
But by and by comes back to Romeo,
Who had but newly entertained[218] revenge,
And to't they go like lightning; for, ere I
Could draw to part them, was stout Tybalt slain:
And as he fell, did Romeo turn and fly.
This is the truth, or let Benvolio die.

CAPULET'S WIFE: He is a kinsman to the Montague;
Affection makes him false, he speaks not true.
Some twenty of them fought in this black strife,
And all those twenty could but kill one life.
I beg for justice, which thou, Prince, must give.
Romeo slew Tybalt; Romeo must not live.

PRINCE: Romeo slew him; he (*Tybalt*) slew Mercutio.
Who now the price of his dear blood doth owe?

MONTAGUE: Not Romeo, Prince; he was Mercutio's friend;
His fault concludes but what the law should end,
The life of Tybalt.

PRINCE: And for that offense
Immediately we do exile him hence.
I have an interest in your hate's proceeding,
My blood for your rude brawls doth lie a-bleeding;
But I'll amerce[219] you with so strong a fine
That you shall all repent the loss of mine.
I will be deaf to pleading and excuses;
Nor tears nor prayers shall purchase out abuses.
Therefore use none. Let Romeo hence in haste,
Else, when he is found, that hour is his last.
Bear hence this body, and attend our will.
Mercy but murders [in], pardoning those that kill.[220]

Exeunt.

[218] entertained the thought of avenging Mercutio's death.
[219] punish.
[220] In pardoning those that kill we encourage murder with our mercy.

SCENE II [*The Capulet Orchard*]

Enter Juliet *alone.*

JULIET: Gallop apace, you fiery-footed steeds,[221]
Towards Phoebus' lodging! Such a wagoner
As Phaëton[222] would whip you to the west
And bring in cloudy night immediately.
Spread thy close curtain, love-performing night,

[221] horses that draw the chariot of sun-god Phoebus in Greek mythology.
[222] the son of Phoebus who was unable to control the sun-chariot horses.

That runaways' eyes may wink,[223] and Romeo
Leap to these arms untalked of and unseen.
Lovers can see to do their amorous rites
By their own beauties; or, if love be blind,
It best agrees with night. Come, civil night,
Thou sober-suited matron, all in black,
And learn me how to lose a winning match,
Played for a pair of stainless maidenhoods.
Hood[224] my unmanned[225] blood, bating in my cheeks,
With thy black mantle till strange love grow bold,
Think true love acted simple modesty.
Come, night; come, Romeo; come, thou day in night;
For thou wilt lie upon the wings of night
Whiter than new snow upon a raven's back.
Come, gentle night; come, loving, black-browed night;
Give me my Romeo; and, when he shall die,
Take him and cut him out in little stars,
And he will make the face of heaven so fine
That all the world will be in love with night
And pay no worship to the garish sun.
O, I have bought the mansion of a love,
But not possessed it; and though I am sold,
Not yet enjoyed. So tedious is this day
As is the night before some festival
To an impatient child that hath new robes
And may not wear them. O, here comes my nurse,

Enter Nurse, *carrying cords.*

And she brings news; and every tongue that speaks
But Romeo's name speaks heavenly eloquence.
Now, nurse, what news? What hast thou there, the cords
That Romeo bid thee fetch?
NURSE: Ay, ay, the cords.
JULIET: Ay me! what news? Why dost thou wring thy hands?
NURSE: Ah, weraday![226] he's dead, he's dead, he's dead!
We are undone, lady, we are undone!
Alack the day! he's gone, he's killed, he's dead!
JULIET: Can heaven be so envious?
NURSE: Romeo can,

[223] close.
[224] cover.
[225] untamed.

[226] welladay, or "alas."

Though heaven cannot. O Romeo, Romeo!
Who ever would have thought it? Romeo!

JULIET: What devil art thou that dost torment me thus?
This torture should be roared in dismal hell.
Hath Romeo slain himself? Say thou but 'I,'
And that bare vowel 'I' shall poison more
Than the death-darting eye of cockatrice.[227]
I am not I, if there be such an 'I'
Or those eyes' shot that makes the answer 'I.'[228]
If he be slain, say 'I'; or if not, 'no.'
Brief sounds determine of my weal or woe.

NURSE: I saw the wound, I saw it with mine eyes,
(God save the mark![229]) here on his manly breast.
A piteous corse, a bloody piteous corse;
Pale, pale as ashes, all bedaubed in blood,
All in gore-blood.[230] I swounded at the sight.

JULIET: O, break, my heart! poor bankrout,[231] break at once!
To prison, eyes; ne'er look on liberty!
Vile earth, to earth resign;[232] end motion here,
And thou and Romeo press one heavy bier!

NURSE: O Tybalt, Tybalt, the best friend I had!
O courteous Tybalt! honest gentleman!
That ever I should live to see thee dead!

JULIET: What storm is this that blows so contrary?
Is Romeo slaught'red, and is Tybalt dead?
My dearest cousin, and my dearer lord?
Then, dreadful trumpet, sound the general doom!
For who is living, if those two are gone?

NURSE: Tybalt is gone, and Romeo banishèd;
Romeo that killed him, he is banishèd.

JULIET: O God! Did Romeo's hand shed Tybalt's blood?

NURSE: It did, it did! alas the day, it did!

JULIET: O serpent heart, hid with a flow'ring face![233]
Did ever dragon keep so fair a cave?
Beautiful tyrant! fiend angelical!
Dove-feathered raven! wolvish-ravening[234] lamb!
Despisèd substance of divinest show!
Just opposite to what thou justly seem'st—
A damnèd saint, an honorable villain!
O nature, what hadst thou to do in hell
When thou did'st bower the spirit of a fiend
In mortal paradise of such sweet flesh?[235]
Was ever book containing such vile matter

---

[227] the basilisk, the fabled serpent that kills with a glance.

[228] the Nurse's eyes' glance; there is punning here on "I" and "eye."

[229] May God avert the evil!

[230] clotted blood.

[231] bankrupt.

[232] That is, let my body return to earth—may I die!

[233] The serpent that tempted Eve in the Garden of Eden was believed to have worn the head of a girl bedecked with flowers.

[234] wolf-like destroying.

[235] A reference to the serpent in the Garden of Eden—the "mortal paradise."

So fairly bound? O, that deceit should dwell
In such a gorgeous palace!

NURSE: There's no trust,
No faith, no honesty in men; all perjured,
All forsworn, all naught, all dissemblers.
Ah, where's my man? Give me some aqua vitae.[236]
These griefs, these woes, these sorrows make me old.
Shame come to Romeo!

JULIET: Blistered be thy tongue
For such a wish! He was not born to shame.
Upon his brow shame is ashamed to sit;
For 'tis a throne where honor may be crowned
Sole monarch of the universal earth.
O, what a beast was I to chide at him!

NURSE: Will you speak well of him that killed your cousin?

JULIET: Shall I speak ill of him that is my husband?
Ah, poor my lord, what tongue shall smooth thy name
When I, thy three-hours wife, have mangled it?
But wherefore, villain, didst thou kill my cousin?
That villain cousin would have killed my husband.
Back, foolish tears, back to your native spring!
Your tributary drops belong to woe,
Which you, mistaking, offer up to joy.
My husband lives, that Tybalt would have slain;
And Tybalt's dead, that would have slain my husband.
All this is comfort; wherefore weep I then?
Some word there was, worser than Tybalt's death,
That murd'red me. I would forget it fain;
But O, it presses to my memory
Like damnèd guilty deeds to sinners' minds!
'Tybalt is dead, and Romeo—banishèd.'
That 'banishèd,' that one word 'banishèd,'
Hath slain ten thousand Tybalts. Tybalt's death
Was woe enough, if it had ended there;
Or, if sour woe delights in fellowship
And needly will be ranked with other griefs,
Why followèd not, when she said 'Tybalt's dead,'
Thy father, or thy mother, nay, or both,
Which modern[237] lamentation might have moved?
But with a rearward following Tybalt's death,
'Romeo is banishèd'—to speak that word
Is father, mother, Tybalt, Romeo, Juliet,
All slain, all dead. 'Romeo is banishèd'—

---

[236] alcoholic beverage.
[237] conventional, ordinary.

There is no end, no limit, measure, bound,
In that word's death; no words can that woe sound.
Where is my father and my mother, nurse?
NURSE: Weeping and wailing over Tybalt's corse.
Will you go to them? I will bring you thither.
JULIET: Wash they his wounds with tears? Mine shall be spent,
When theirs are dry, for Romeo's banishment.
Take up those cords. Poor ropes, you are beguiled,
Both you and I, for Romeo is exiled.
He made you for a highway to my bed;   [238] know.
But I, a maid, die maiden-widowèd.
Come, cords; come, nurse. I'll to my wedding bed;
And death, not Romeo, take my maidenhead!
NURSE: Hie to your chamber. I'll find Romeo
To comfort you. I wot[238] well where he is.
Hark ye, your Romeo will be here at night.
I'll to him; he is hid at Laurence' cell.
JULIET: O, find him! give this ring to my true knight
And bid him come to take his last farewell.
Exeunt.

SCENE III   [*Friar Laurence's cell*]

Enter Friar Laurence.

FRIAR: Romeo, come forth; come forth, thou fearful man.
Affliction is enamored of thy parts,
And thou art wedded to calamity.

Enter Romeo.

ROMEO: Father, what news? What is the Prince's doom?[239]
What sorrow craves acquaintance at my hand
That I yet know not?
FRIAR: Too familiar
Is my dear son with such sour company.
I bring thee tidings of the Prince's doom.
ROMEO: What less than doomsday is the Prince's doom?
FRIAR: A gentler judgment vanished[240] from his lips—

[239] verdict.
[240] issued from his lips.

Not body's death, but body's banishment.
ROMEO: Ha, banishment? Be merciful, say 'death';
For exile hath more terror in his look,
Much more than death. Do not say 'banishment.'
FRIAR: Hence from Verona art thou banishèd.
Be patient, for the world is broad and wide.
ROMEO: There is no world without (*outside*) Verona walls
But purgatory, torture, hell itself.
Hence banishèd is banished from the world,
And world's exile is death. Then 'banishèd'
Is death mistermed. Calling death 'banishèd,'
Thou cut'st my head off with a golden axe
And smilest upon the stroke that murders me.
FRIAR: O deadly sin! O rude unthankfulness!
Thy fault our law calls death; but the kind Prince,
Taking thy part, hath rushed[241] aside the law,
And turned that black word 'death' to banishment.
This is dear mercy, and thou seest it not.
ROMEO: 'Tis torture, and not mercy. Heaven is here,
Where Juliet lives; and every cat and dog
And little mouse, every unworthy thing,
Live here in heaven and may look on her;
But Romeo may not. More validity,
More honorable state, more courtship[242] lives
In carrion flies than Romeo. They may seize
On the white wonder of dear Juliet's hand
And steal immortal blessing from her lips,
Who, even in pure and vestal modesty,
Still blush, as thinking their own kisses sin;
But Romeo may not, he is banishèd.
Flies may do this but I from this must fly;
They are freemen, but I am banishèd.
And sayest thou yet that exile is not death?
Hadst thou no poison mixed, no sharp-ground knife,
No sudden mean of death, though ne'er so mean,[243]
But 'banishèd' to kill me—'banishèd'?
O friar, the damnèd use that word in hell;
Howling attends it! How hast thou the heart,
Being a divine, a ghostly confessor,
A sin-absolver, and my friend professed,
To mangle me with that word 'banishèd'?
FRIAR: Thou fond[244] mad man, hear me a little speak.
ROMEO: O, thou wilt speak again of banishment.
FRIAR: I'll give thee armor to keep off that word;

---

[241] brushed aside.
[242] privilege or power to court or woo.
[243] lowly.
[244] foolish.

Adversity's sweet milk, philosophy,
To comfort thee, though thou art banishèd.
ROMEO: Yet 'banishèd'? Hang up philosophy!
Unless philosophy can make a Juliet,
Displant a town, reverse a prince's doom,
It helps not, it prevails not. Talk no more.
FRIAR: O, then I see that madmen have no ears.
ROMEO: How should they, when that wise men have no eyes?
FRIAR: Let me dispute with thee of thy estate.
ROMEO: Thou canst not speak of that thou dost not feel.
Wert thou as young as I, Juliet thy love,
An hour but married, Tybalt murderèd,
Doting like me, and like me banishèd,
Then mightst thou speak, then mightst thou tear thy hair,
And fall upon the ground, as I do now,
Taking the measure of an unmade grave.

Enter Nurse; she knocks.

FRIAR: Arise; one knocks. Good Romeo, hide thyself.
ROMEO: Not I; unless the breath of heartsick groans
Mist-like infold me from the search of eyes.

(The knocking continues.)

FRIAR: Hark, how they knock! Who's there? Romeo, arise;
Thou wilt be taken.—Stay awhile!—Stand up;
Run to my study.—By and by!—God's will,
What simpleness is this.—I come, I come!
Who knocks so hard? Whence come you? What's your will?

Enter Nurse.

NURSE: Let me come in, and you shall know my errand.
I come from Lady Juliet.
FRIAR: Welcome then.
NURSE: O holy friar, O, tell me, holy friar,
Where is my lady's lord, where's Romeo?
FRIAR: There on the ground, with his own tears made drunk.
NURSE: O, he is even in my mistress' case,
Just in her case! O woeful sympathy!
Piteous predicament! Even so lies she,

Blubb'ring and weeping, weeping and blubb'ring.
Stand up, stand up! Stand, an you be a man.
For Juliet's sake, for her sake, rise and stand!
Why should you fall into so deep an O?

ROMEO: *(rising)* Nurse—

NURSE: Ah sir! ah sir! Death's the end of all.

ROMEO: Spakest thou of Juliet? How is it with her?
Doth not she think me an old[245] murderer,
Now I have stained the childhood of our joy
With blood removed but little from her own?
Where is she? and how doth she! and what says
My concealed lady to our cancelled love?

NURSE: O, she says nothing, sir, but weeps and weeps;
And now falls on her bed, and then starts up,
And Tybalt calls; and then on Romeo cries,
And then down falls again.

ROMEO: As if that name,
Shot from the deadly level[246] of a gun,
Did murder her; as that name's cursèd hand
Murdered her kinsman. O, tell me, friar, tell me,
In what vile part of this anatomy
Doth my name lodge? *(Drawing his dagger to stab himself)* Tell me, that I may sack
The hateful mansion.

FRIAR: Hold thy desperate hand.
Art thou a man? Thy form cries out thou art;
Thy tears are womanish, thy wild acts denote
The unreasonable fury of a beast.
Unseemly[247] woman in a seeming man!
And ill-beseeming[248] beast in seeming both!
Thou hast amazed me. By my holy order,
I thought thy disposition better tempered.
Hast thou slain Tybalt? Wilt thou slay thyself?
And slay thy lady that in thy life lives,
By doing damnèd hate upon thyself?
Why railest thou on thy birth, the heaven, and earth?
Since birth and heaven and earth, all three do meet
In thee at once; which thou at once wouldst lose.
Fie, fie, thou shamest thy shape, thy love, thy wit,
Which,[249] like a usurer, abound'st in all,
And usest none in that true use indeed
Which should bedeck thy shape, thy love, thy wit.
Thy noble shape is but a form of wax,
Digressing from the valor of a man;
Thy dear love sworn but hollow perjury,

---

[245] an accustomed or hardened murderer.
[246] aim.
[247] disorderly.
[248] inappropriate.
[249] who aboundest in everything.

Killing that love which thou hast vowed to cherish;
Thy wit, that ornament to shape and love,
Misshapen in the conduct of them both,
Like powder[250] in a skilless soldier's flask,
Is set afire by thine own ignorance,
And thou dismemb'red with thine own defense.[251]
What, rouse thee, man! Thy Juliet is alive,
For whose dear sake thou wast but lately dead.
There art thou happy. Tybalt would kill thee,
But thou slewest Tybalt. There art thou happy too.
The law, that threat'ned death, becomes thy friend
And turns it to exile. There art thou happy.
A pack of blessings light upon thy back;
Happiness courts thee in her best array;
But, like a misbehaved and sullen wench,
Thou pout'st upon thy fortune and thy love.
Take heed, take heed, for such die miserable.
Go get thee to thy love, as was decreed,
Ascend her chamber, hence and comfort her.
But look thou stay not till the watch be set,
For then thou canst not pass to Mantua,
Where thou shalt live till we can find a time
To blaze[252] your marriage, reconcile your friends,
Beg pardon of the Prince, and call thee back
With twenty hundred thousand times more joy
Than thou went'st forth in lamentation.
Go before, nurse. Commend me to thy lady,
And bid her hasten all the house to bed,
Which heavy sorrow makes them apt unto.
Romeo is coming.

NURSE: O Lord, I could have stayed here all the night
To hear good counsel. O, what learning is!
My lord, I'll tell my lady you will come.

ROMEO: Do so, and bid my sweet prepared to chide.

NURSE: Here is a ring she bid me give you, sir.
Hie you, make haste, for it grows very late.

ROMEO: How well my comfort is revived by this!

FRIAR: Go hence; good night; and here stands all your state:[253]
Either be gone before the watch be set,
Or by the break of day disguised from hence.
Sojourn in Mantua. I'll find out your man,
And he shall signify from time to time
Every good hap to you that chances here.
Give me thy hand. 'Tis late. Farewell; good night.

ROMEO: But that a joy past joy calls out on me,

[250] gunpowder in the powder horn of an inexperienced soldier.
[251] body torn apart with thine own weapon ("defense").
[252] to proclaim.
[253] situation.

It were a grief so brief to part with thee.
Farewell. *Exeunt.*

SCENE IV   [*A Room in the Capulet House*]

Enter old Capulet, *his* Wife, *and* Paris.

CAPULET: Things have fall'n out, sir, so unluckily
That we have had no time to move[254] our daughter.
Look you, she loved her kinsman Tybalt dearly,
And so did I. Well, we were born to die.
'Tis very late; she'll not come down to-night.
I promise you, but for your company,
I would have been abed an hour ago.
PARIS: These times of woe afford no times to woo.
Madam, good night. Commend me to your daughter.
LADY: I will, and know her mind early to-morrow;
To-night she's mewed up[255] to her heaviness.[256]
CAPULET: Sir Paris, I will make a desperate tender[257]
Of my child's love. I think she will be ruled
In all respects by me; nay more, I doubt it not.
Wife, go you to her ere you go to bed;
Acquaint her here of my son Paris' love
And bid her (mark you me?) on Wednesday next—
But soft! what day is this?
PARIS: Monday, my lord.
CAPULET: Monday! ha, ha! Well, Wednesday is too soon.
A Thursday let it be—a Thursday, tell her,
She shall be married to this noble earl.
Will you be ready? Do you like this haste?
We'll keep no great ado—a friend or two;
For hark you, Tybalt being slain so late,
It may be thought we held him carelessly,
Being our kinsman, if we revel much.
Therefore, we'll have some half a dozen friends,
And there an end. But what say you to Thursday?
PARIS: My lord, I would that Thursday were to-morrow.
CAPULET: Well, get you gone. A Thursday be it then.
Go you to Juliet ere you go to bed;
Prepare her, wife, against[258] this wedding day.
Farewell, my lord.—Light to my chamber, ho!

[254] urge.
[255] shut up.
[256] grief.
[257] bold offer.
[258] for—in expectation of this wedding day.

Afore me,[259] it is so very very late
That we may call it early by and by.
Good night.   *Exeunt.*

[259] an oath—"God before me."

SCENE V   [*The Capulet Orchard*]

Enter Romeo *and* Juliet (*above*) *aloft at the window.*

JULIET: Wilt thou be gone? It is not yet near day.
It was the nightingale, and not the lark,
That pierced the fearful hollow of thine ear.
Nightly she sings on yond pomegranate tree.
Believe me, love, it was the nightingale.
ROMEO: It was the lark, the herald of the morn;
No nightingale. Look, love, what envious streaks
Do lace the severing clouds in yonder East.
Night's candles[260] are burnt out, and jocund day
Stands tiptoe on the misty mountain tops.
I must be gone and live, or stay and die.
JULIET: Yond light is not daylight; I know it, I.
It is some meteor that the sun exhales
To be to thee this night a torchbearer
And light thee on thy way to Mantua.
Therefore stay yet; thou need'st not to be gone.
ROMEO: Let me be ta'en, let me be put to death.
I am content, so thou wilt have it so.
I'll say yon grey is not the morning's eye,
'Tis but the pale reflex of Cynthia's brow;[261]
Nor that is not the lark whose notes do beat
The vaulty heaven so high above our heads.
I have more care to stay than will to go.
Come, death, and welcome! Juliet wills it so.
How is't, my soul? Let's talk; it is not day.
JULIET: It is, it is! Hie hence, be gone, away!
It is the lark that sings so out of tune,
Straining harsh discords and unpleasing sharps.
Some say the lark makes sweet division;[262]
This doth not so, for she divideth us.
Some say the lark and loathèd toad change eyes;
O, now I would they had changed voices too,
Since arm from arm that voice doth us affray,
Hunting thee hence with hunt's-up[263] to the day.
O, now be gone! More light and light it grows.

[260] that is, the stars.
[261] Cynthia, a name for the moon personified as a woman.
[262] music.
[263] song to awaken men going on a hunt.

ROMEO: More light and light—more dark and dark our woes.

Enter the Nurse.

NURSE: Madam!
JULIET: Nurse?
NURSE: Your lady mother is coming to your chamber. The day is broke; be wary, look about. *She goes out.*
JULIET: Then, window, let day in, and let life out.
ROMEO: Farewell, farewell! One kiss, and I'll descend.
He starts to go down.
JULIET: Art thou gone so, love-lord, ay husband-friend?[264]
I must hear from thee every day in the hour,
For in a minute there are many days.
O, by this count I shall be much in years
Ere I again behold my Romeo!
ROMEO: Farewell!
I will omit no opportunity
That may convey my greetings, love, to thee.
JULIET: O, think'st thou we shall ever meet again?
ROMEO: I doubt it not; and all these woes shall serve
For sweet discourses in our times to come.
JULIET: O God, I have an ill-divining[265] soul!
Methinks I see thee, now thou art so low,
As one dead in the bottom of a tomb.
Either my eyesight fails, or thou lookest pale.
ROMEO: And trust me, love, in my eye so do you.
Dry sorrow drinks our blood. Adieu, adieu! *Exit.*
JULIET: O Fortune, Fortune! all men call thee fickle.
If thou art fickle, what dost thou with him
That is renowned for faith? Be fickle, Fortune,
For then I hope thou wilt not keep him long
But send him back.[266]

[264] secret lover.
[265] foreboding.
[266] Here she apparently leaves the window.

Enter the Mother.

LADY: Ho, daughter! are you up?
JULIET: Who is't that calls? It is my lady mother.
Is she not down[267] so late, or up so early?
What unaccustomed cause procures her hither?
LADY: Why, how now, Juliet?
JULIET: Madam, I am not well.

[267] in bed.

LADY: Evermore weeping for your cousin's death?
What, wilt thou wash him from his grave with tears?
And if thou couldst, thou couldst not make him live.
Therefore have done. Some grief shows much of love;
But much of grief shows still some want of wit.
JULIET: Yet let me weep for such a feeling loss.
LADY: So shall you feel the loss, but not the friend
Which you weep for.
JULIET: Feeling so the loss,
I cannot choose but ever weep the friend.
LADY: Well, girl, thou weep'st not so much for his death
As that the villain lives which slaughtered him.
JULIET: What villain, madam?
LADY: That same villain Romeo.
JULIET: (*aside—to herself*) Villain and he be many miles asunder.—
God pardon him! I do, with all my heart;
And yet no man like[268] he doth grieve my heart.
LADY: That is because the traitor murderer lives.
JULIET: Ay, madam, from the reach of these my hands.
Would none but I might venge my cousin's death!
LADY: We will have vengeance for it, fear thou not.
Then weep no more. I'll send to one in Mantua,
Where that same banished runagate[269] doth live,
Shall give him such an unaccustomed dram
That he shall soon keep Tybalt company;
And then I hope thou wilt be satisfied.
JULIET: Indeed I never shall be satisfied
With Romeo till I behold him—dead—
Is my poor heart so for a kinsman vexed.
Madam, if you could find out but a man
To bear a poison, I would temper[270] it;
That Romeo should, upon receipt thereof,
Soon sleep in quiet. O, how my heart abhors
To hear him named and cannot come to him,
To wreak the love I bore my cousin
Upon his body that hath slaughtered him!
LADY: Find thou the means, and I'll find such a man.
But now I'll tell thee joyful tidings, girl.
JULIET: And joy comes well in such a needy time.
What are they, beseech your ladyship?
LADY: Well, well, thou hast a careful father, child;
One who, to put thee from thy heaviness,

---

[268] so much as.
[269] renegade.
[270] mix (and at the same time, mollify or moderate) it.

Hath sorted out a sudden day of joy
That thou expects not nor I looked not for.
JULIET: Madam, in happy time! What day is that?
LADY: Marry, my child, early next Thursday morn
The gallant, young, and noble gentleman,
The County Paris, at Saint Peter's Church,
Shall happily make thee there a joyful bride.
JULIET: Now by Saint Peter's Church, and Peter too,
He shall not make me there a joyful bride!
I wonder at this haste, that I must wed
Ere he that should be husband comes to woo.
I pray you tell my lord and father, madam,
I will not marry yet; and when I do, I swear
It shall be Romeo, whom you know I hate,
Rather than Paris. These are news indeed!
LADY: Here comes your father. Tell him so yourself,
And see how he will take it at your hands.

Enter Capulet *and the* Nurse.

CAPULET: When the sun sets the earth doth drizzle dew,
But for the sunset of my brother's son
It rains downright.
How now? a conduit,[271] girl? What, still in tears?
Evermore show'ring? In one little body
Thou counterfeit'st a bark, a sea, a wind:
For still thy eyes, which I may call the sea,
Do ebb and flow with tears; the bark thy body is,
Sailing in this salt flood; the winds, thy sighs,
Who, raging with thy tears and they with them,
Without a sudden calm will overset
Thy tempest-tossèd body. How now, wife?
Have you delivered to her our decree?
LADY: Ay, sir; but she will none, she gives you thanks.[272]
I would the fool were married to her grave!
CAPULET: Soft! take me with you, take me with you,[273] wife.
How? Will she none? Doth she not give us thanks?
Is she not proud? Doth she not count her blest,
Unworthy as she is, that we have wrought
So worthy a gentleman to be her bride?
JULIET: Not proud you have, but thankful that you have.

[271] a water-pipe.
[272] She says, "Thank you, No!"
[273] Let me understand you.

Proud can I never be of what I hate,
But thankful even for hate that is meant love.
CAPULET: How, how, how, how, chopped-logic? What is this?
'Proud'—and 'I thank you'—and 'I thank you not'—
And yet 'not proud'? Mistress minion you,
Thank me no thankings, nor proud me no prouds,
But fettle[274] your fine joints 'gainst Thursday next
To go with Paris to Saint Peter's Church,
Or I will drag thee on a hurdle[275] thither.
Out, you green-sickness[276] carrion! out, you baggage![277]
You tallow-face![278]
LADY: Fie, fie! what, are you mad?
JULIET: Good father, I beseech you on my knees,
Hear me with patience but to speak a word.
CAPULET: Hang thee, young baggage! disobedient wretch!
I tell thee what—get thee to church a Thursday
Or never after look me in the face.
Speak not, reply not, do not answer me!
My fingers itch. Wife, we scarce thought us blest
That God had lent us but this only child;
But now I see this one is one too much,
And that we have a curse in having her.
Out on her, hilding![279]
NURSE: God in heaven bless her!
You are to blame, my lord, to rate her so.
CAPULET: And why, my Lady Wisdom? Hold your tongue,
Good Prudence. Smatter[280] with your gossips, go!
NURSE: I speak no treason.
CAPULET: O, God-i-god-en![281]
NURSE: May not one speak?
CAPULET: Peace, you mumbling fool!
Utter your gravity o'er a gossip's bowl,
For here we need it not.
LADY: You are too hot.
CAPULET: God's bread! it makes me mad.
Day, night; hour, tide, time; work, play;
Alone, in company; still my care hath been
To have her matched; and having now provided
A gentleman of noble parentage,
Of fair demesnes,[282] youthful, and nobly trained,
Stuffed, as they say, with honorable parts,
Proportioned as one's thought would wish a man—

[274] prepare—'get your legs ready to go to church to be married.'
[275] a sledge that was used to carry criminals to execution.
[276] anemic, thin.
[277] worthless girl.
[278] pale-face.
[279] good-for-nothing.
[280] go chatter.
[281] for God's sake.
[282] domains.

And then to have a wretched puling[283] fool,
A whining mammet,[284] in her fortune's tender,[285]
To answer 'I'll not wed, I cannot love;
I am too young, I pray you pardon me'!
But, an you will not wed, I'll pardon you!
Graze where you will, you shall not house with me.
Look to't, think on't; I do not use to jest.
Thursday is near; lay hand on heart, advise:
An you be mine, I'll give you to my friend;
An you be not, hang, beg, starve, die in the streets,
For, by my soul, I'll ne'er acknowledge thee,
Nor what is mine shall never do thee good.
Trust to't. Bethink you. I'll not be forsworn.   *Exit.*

JULIET: Is there no pity sitting in the clouds
That sees into the bottom of my grief?
O sweet my mother, cast me not away!
Delay this marriage for a month, a week;
Or if you do not, make the bridal bed
In that dim monument where Tybalt lies.

LADY: Talk not to me, for I'll not speak a word.
Do as thou wilt, for I have done with thee.   *Exit.*

JULIET: O God!—O nurse, how shall this be prevented?
My husband is on earth, my faith,[286] in heaven.
How shall that faith return again to earth[287]
Unless that husband send it me from heaven
By leaving earth? Comfort me, counsel me.
Alack, alack, that heaven should practise stratagems
Upon so soft a subject as myself!
What say'st thou? Hast thou not a word of joy?
Some comfort, nurse.

NURSE: Faith, here it is.
Romeo is banished; and all the world to nothing[288]
That he dares ne'er come back to challenge[289] you;
Or if he do, it needs must be by stealth.
Then, since the case so stands as now it doth,
I think it best you married with the County.
O, he's a lovely gentleman!
Romeo's a dishclout[290] to him. An eagle, madam,
Hath not so green, so quick, so fair an eye
As Paris hath. Beshrew my very heart,[291]
I think you are happy in this second match,
For it excels your first; or if it did not,
Your first is dead—or 'twere as good he were
As living here and you no use of him.

---

[283] whining.
[284] doll.
[285] when good fortune — a good opportunity of marriage—offers itself.
[286] my pledge of marriage is now recorded in heaven.
[287] how can I marry again unless my husband dies and makes me a widow.
[288] It is certain.
[289] to claim you.
[290] a dish-cloth.
[291] May a curse fall on me.

JULIET: Speak'st thou from thy heart?
NURSE: And from my soul too; else beshrew them both.
JULIET: Amen!
NURSE: What?
JULIET: Well, thou hast comforted me marvellous much.
  Go in; and tell my lady I am gone,
  Having displeased my father, to Laurence' cell,
  To make confession and to be absolved.
NURSE: Marry, I will; and this is wisely done.
                              She goes out.
JULIET: Ancient damnation![292] O most wicked fiend!
  Is it more sin to wish me thus forsworn,
  Or to dispraise my lord with that same tongue
  Which she hath praised him with above compare
  So many thousand times? Go, counsellor!
  Thou and my bosom henceforth shall be twain.[293]
  I'll to the friar to know his remedy.
  If all else fail, myself have power to die.   *Exit.*

[292] damned old woman.
[293] I'll never confide in you again.

ACT IV   SCENE I

Enter Friar Laurence *and* County (Count) Paris.

FRIAR: On Thursday, sir? The time is very short.
PARIS: My father Capulet will have it so,
  And I am nothing slow to slack his haste.
FRIAR: You say you do not know the lady's mind.
  Uneven is the course; I like it not.
PARIS: Immoderately she weeps for Tybalt's death,
  And therefore have I little talked of love;
  For Venus smiles not in a house of tears.[294]
  Now, sir, her father counts it dangerous
  That she do give her sorrow so much sway,
  And in his wisdom hastes our marriage
  To stop the inundation[295] of her tears,
  Which, too much minded by herself alone,
  May be put from her by society.[296]
  Now do you know the reason of this haste.

[294] One cannot talk of love in the midst of sorrow.
[295] flood.
[296] her grief, which has occupied her too much in solitude, may be set aside by company.

FRIAR: *(to himself—aside)* I would I knew not why
    it should be slowed—
    Look, sir, here comes the lady toward my cell.

Enter Juliet.

PARIS: Happily met, my lady and my wife!
JULIET: That may be, sir, when I may be a wife.
PARIS: That 'may be' must be, love, on Thursday next.
JULIET: What must be shall be.
FRIAR: That's a certain text.
PARIS: Come you to make confession to this father?
JULIET: To answer that, I should confess to you.
PARIS: Do not deny to him that you love me.
JULIET: I will confess to you that I love him.
PARIS: So will ye, I am sure, that you love me.
JULIET: If I do so, it will be of more price,
    Being spoke behind your back, than to your face.
PARIS: Poor soul, thy face is much abused with tears.
JULIET: The tears have got small victory by that,
    For it was bad enough before their spite.
PARIS: Thou wrong'st it more than tears with that
    report.
JULIET: That is no slander, sir, which is a truth;
    And what I spake, I spake it to my face.
PARIS: Thy face is mine, and thou hast sland'red it.
JULIET: It may be so, for it is not mine own.
    Are you at leisure, holy father, now,
    Or shall I come to you at evening mass?
FRIAR: My leisure serves me, pensive daughter, now.
    My lord, we must entreat the time alone.
PARIS: God shield[297] I should disturb devotion!
    Juliet, on Thursday early will I rouse ye.
    Till then, adieu, and keep this holy kiss.   *Exit.*
JULIET: O, shut the door! and when thou hast done
    so,
    Come weep with me—past hope, past cure, past help!
FRIAR: Ah, Juliet, I already know thy grief;
    It strains me past the compass of my wits.[298]
    I hear thou must, and nothing may prorogue it,[299]
    On Thursday next be married to this County.
JULIET: Tell me not, friar, that thou hearest of this,
    Unless thou tell me how I may prevent it.
    If in thy wisdom thou canst give no help,
    Do thou but call my resolution wise

---

[297] forbid.
[298] the limits ("compass") of my understanding ("wits").
[299] postpone it.

And with this knife I'll help it presently.
God joined my heart and Romeo's, thou our hands;
And ere this hand, by thee to Romeo's sealed,
Shall be the label[300] to another deed,
Or my true heart with treacherous revolt
Turn to another, this shall slay them both.
Therefore, out of thy long-experienced time,
Give me some present counsel; or, behold,
'Twixt my extremes[301] and me this bloody knife
Shall play the umpire, arbitrating that
Which the commission of thy years and art[302]
Could to no issue of true honor bring.[303]
Be not so long to speak. I long to die
If what thou speak'st speak not of remedy.

FRIAR: Hold, daughter. I do spy a kind of hope,
Which craves as desperate an execution
As that is desperate which we would prevent.
If, rather than to marry County Paris,
Thou hast the strength of will to slay thyself,
Then is it likely thou wilt undertake
A thing like death to chide[304] away this shame,
That cop'st[305] with death himself to scape from it;
And, if thou darest, I'll give thee remedy.

JULIET: O, bid me leap, rather than marry Paris,
From off the battlements of any tower,
Or walk in thievish ways,[306] or bid me lurk
Where serpents are; chain me with roaring bears,
Or hide me nightly in a charnel house,[307]
O'ercovered quite with dead men's rattling bones,
With reeky[308] shanks and yellow chapless[309] skulls;
Or bid me go into a new-made grave
And hide me with a dead man in his shroud—
Things that, to hear them told, have made me tremble—
And I will do it without fear or doubt,
To live an unstained wife to my sweet love.

FRIAR: Hold, then. Go home, be merry, give consent
To marry Paris. Wednesday is to-morrow.
To-morrow night look that thou lie alone;
Let not the nurse lie with thee in thy chamber.
Take thou this vial, being then in bed,
And this distilling liquor drink thou off;
When presently through all thy veins shall run
A cold and drowsy humor;[310] for no pulse
Shall keep his native progress, but surcease;[311]
No warmth, no breath, shall testify thou livest;

[300] tab of parchment bearing the seal or stamp affixed to a legal document.
[301] desperation ('extremes' of unhappiness).
[302] which thy authority and ability.
[303] could not bring to an honorable result.
[304] drive away.
[305] copests, meets, encounters.
[306] paths infested with thieves.
[307] vault in which dead bodies or the bones of the dead are kept.
[308] ill-smelling.
[309] jawless; lacking the lower jaw, which has dropped off.
[310] a cold and sleep-inducing fluid.
[311] cease; that is, your pulse will not beat as is usual ("native progress") and will stop.

> The roses in thy lips and cheeks shall fade[312]
> To wanny[313] ashes, thy eyes' windows[314] fall
> Like death when he shuts up the day of life;
> Each part, deprived of supple government,[315]
> Shall, stiff and stark and cold, appear like death;
> And in this borrowèd likeness of shrunk death
> Thou shalt continue two-and-forty hours,
> And then awake as from a pleasant sleep.
> Now, when the bridegroom in the morning comes
> To rouse thee from thy bed, there art thou dead.
> Then, as the manner of our country is,
> In my best robes uncoverèd on the bier
> Thou shalt be borne to that same ancient vault
> Where all the kindred of the Capulets lie.
> In the meantime, against thou shalt awake,
> Shall Romeo by my letters know our drift;[316]
> And hither shall he come; and he and I
> Will watch thy waking, and that very night
> Shall Romeo bear thee hence to Mantua.
> And this shall free thee from this present shame,
> If no inconstant toy[317] nor womanish fear
> Abate thy valor in the acting it.
>
> JULIET: Give me, give me! O, tell not me of fear!
> FRIAR: Hold! Get you gone, be strong and prosperous
> In this resolve. I'll send a friar with speed
> To Mantua, with my letters to thy lord.
> JULIET: Love give me strength! and strength shall help afford.
> Farewell, dear father.

[312] the blood ("roses"—red roses) will leave your lips and cheeks.
[313] pale.
[314] eyelids.
[315] deprived of the mobility or flowing energy that determines life.
[316] plan or intention.
[317] notion, whim.

SCENE II   [*The Hall in the Capulet House*]

Enter Father Capulet, Mother, Nurse, *and* Servingmen, *two or three.*

CAPULET: So many guests invite as here are writ.
Sirrah, go hire me twenty cunning cooks.
SERVINGMAN: You shall have none ill, sir; for I'll try if they can lick their fingers.
CAPULET: How canst thou try them so?
SERVINGMAN: Marry, sir, 'tis an ill cook that cannot lick his own fingers. Therefore he that cannot lick his fingers goes not with me.
CAPULET: Go, be gone.   *The* Servingman *departs.*

We shall be much unfurnished for this time.
What, is my daughter gone to Friar Laurence?
NURSE: Ay, forsooth.
CAPULET: Well, he may chance to do some good on her.
A peevish self-willed harlotry[318] it is.

Enter Juliet.

NURSE: See where she comes from shrift with merry look.
CAPULET: How now, my headstrong? Where have you been gadding?
JULIET: Where I have learnt me to repent the sin
Of disobedient opposition
To you and your behests, and am enjoined
By holy Laurence to fall prostrate here
To beg your pardon. Pardon, I beseech you!
Henceforward I am ever ruled by you.
CAPULET: Send for the County. Go tell him of this.
I'll have this knot knit up to-morrow morning.[319]
JULIET: I met the youthful lord at Laurence' cell
And gave him what becomèd love I might,
Not stepping o'er the bounds of modesty.
CAPULET: Why, I am glad on't. This is well. Stand up.
This is as't should be. Let me see the County.
Ay, marry, go, I say, and fetch him hither.
Now, afore God, this reverend holy friar,
All our whole city is much bound[320] to him.
JULIET: Nurse, will you go with me into my closet
To help me sort such needful ornaments
As you think fit to furnish me to-morrow?
MOTHER: No, not till Thursday. There is time enough.
CAPULET: Go, nurse, go with her. We'll to church to-morrow. (Juliet *and the* Nurse *leave the stage.*)
MOTHER: We shall be short in our provision.
'Tis now near night.
CAPULET: Tush, I will stir about,
And all things shall be well, I warrant[321] thee, wife.
Go thou to Juliet, help to deck up her.
I'll not to bed to-night; let me alone.
I'll play the housewife for this once. What, ho!
They are all forth; well, I will walk myself
To County Paris, to prepare up him

---

[318] silly or perverse girl.

[319] Note that Juliet's irritated father now intends to have her marriage one day earlier than had been planned. This makes Juliet's situation more desperate, and her taking the sleeping potion more urgent.

[320] beholden or indebted to him.

[321] I guarantee or assure thee.

Against to-morrow. My heart is wondrous light,
Since this same wayward girl is so reclaimed.
Exeunt Father *and* Mother.

SCENE III [*Juliet's Chamber*]

Enter Juliet *and* Nurse.

[322] prayers.

JULIET: Ay, those attires are best; but, gentle nurse,
I pray thee leave me to myself to-night;
For I have need of many orisons[322]
To move the heavens to smile upon my state,
Which, well thou knowest, is cross and full of sin.

Enter Mother.

MOTHER: What, are you busy, ho? Need you my help?
JULIET: No, madam; we have culled such necessaries
As are behoveful[323] for our state to-morrow.
So please you, let me now be left alone,
And let the nurse this night sit up with you;
For I am sure you have your hands full all
In this so sudden business.
MOTHER: Good night.
Get thee to bed, and rest; for thou hast need.
The Mother *and the* Nurse *leave.*

[323] suitable for our "state"—our station in life—on the occasion of the wedding.
[324] administered.

JULIET: Farewell! God knows when we shall meet again.
I have a faint cold fear thrills through my veins
That almost freezes up the heat of life.
I'll call them back again to comfort me.
Nurse!—What should she do here?
My dismal scene I needs must act alone.
Come, vial.
What if this mixture do not work at all?
Shall I be married then to-morrow morning?
No, no! This shall forbid it. Lie thou there.
(*She lays down a dagger.*)
What if it be a poison which the friar
Subtly hath minist'red[324] to have me dead,
Lest in this marriage he should be dishonored
Because he married me before to Romeo?

I fear it is; and yet methinks it should not,
For he hath still been tried[325] a holy man.
How if, when I am laid into the tomb,
I wake before the time that Romeo
Come to redeem me? There's a fearful point!
Shall I not then be stifled in the vault,
To whose foul mouth no healthsome air breathes in,
And there die strangled ere my Romeo comes?
Or, if I live, is it not very like
The horrible conceit[326] of death and night,
Together with the terror of the place—
As in a vault, an ancient receptacle
Where for this many hundred years the bones
Of all my buried ancestors are packed;
Where bloody Tybalt, yet but green[327] in earth,
Lies fest'ring in his shroud; where, as they say,
At some hours in the night spirits resort—
Alack, alack, is it not like that I,
So early waking—what with loathsome smells,
And shrieks like mandrakes[328] torn out of the earth,
That living mortals, hearing them, run mad—
O, if I wake, shall I not be distraught,[329]
Environèd[330] with all these hideous fears,
And madly play with my forefathers' joints,
And pluck the mangled Tybalt from his shroud,
And, in this rage, with some great kinsman's bone
As with a club dash out my desp'rate brains?
O, look! methinks I see my cousin's ghost
Seeking out Romeo, that did spit his body
Upon a rapier's point. Stay, Tybalt, stay!
Romeo, I come! this do I drink to thee.
    (*She falls upon her bed within the curtains.*)

[325] proved; shown to be a holy man.
[326] conception.
[327] freshly laid in earth.
[328] the sleep-inducing drug mandragora having a forked root and therefore resembling the human figure; it was believed to shriek wildly when pulled out of the earth.
[329] shall I not be driven mad?
[330] surrounded.

SCENE IV   [*The Hall in the Capulet House*]

Enter the Lady of the House *and the* Nurse.

LADY: Hold, take these keys and fetch more spices, nurse.
NURSE: They call for dates and quinces in the pastry.

Enter old Capulet.

CAPULET: Come, stir, stir, stir! The second cock hath crowed,

The curfew bell hath rung, 'tis three o'clock.
Look to the baked meats, good Angelica;
Spare not for cost.
NURSE: Go, you cot-quean,[331] go,
Get you to bed! Faith, you'll be sick to-morrow
For this night's watching.[332]
CAPULET: No, not a whit. What, I have watched ere now
All night for lesser cause, and ne'er been sick.
LADY: Ay, you have been a mouse-hunt[333] in your time;
But I will watch you from such watching now.
Exit Lady *and* Nurse.
CAPULET: A jealous hood,[334] a jealous hood!

[331] male-housewife.
[332] staying awake all night.
[333] a prowler after women.
[334] "A jealous woman!"—the wearer of the hood or cap of jealousy, because Lady Capulet has accused her husband of running after women in his younger years ("in your time").

Enter three or four Servants *with spits and logs and baskets.*

Now, fellow,
What is there?
FIRST FELLOW: Things for the cook, sir; but I know not what.
CAPULET: Make haste, make haste. [*Exit first Fellow.*]
Sirrah, fetch drier logs.
Call Peter; he will show thee where they are.
SECOND FELLOW: I have a head, sir, that will find out logs
And never trouble Peter for the matter.
CAPULET: Mass,[335] and well said; a merry whoreson,[336] ha!
Thou shalt be loggerhead.[337] [*Exit second Servant, with the others.*] Good Father! 'tis day.
The County will be here with music straight,
For so he said he would. *Music.*
I hear him near.
Nurse! Wife! What, ho! What, nurse, I say!

[335] "By the mass!"—an exclamation.
[336] rascal.
[337] blockhead.

Enter the Nurse.

Go waken Juliet; go and trim her up.
I'll go and chat with Paris. Hie, make haste,
Make haste! The bridegroom he is come already:
Make haste, I say. *Exit.*

SCENE V [*Juliet's Chamber*]

NURSE: Mistress! what, mistress! Juliet! Fast,[338] I
   warrant her, she.
Why, lamb! why, lady! Fie, you slug-abed.
Why, love, I say! madam! sweetheart! Why, bride!
What, not a word? You take your pennyworths[339]
   now;
Sleep for a week; for the next night, I warrant,
The County Paris hath set up his rest,[340]
That you shall rest but little. God forgive me!
Marry, and amen. How sound is she asleep!
I needs must wake her. Madam, madam, madam!
Ay, let the County take you in your bed;
He'll fright you up, i' faith. Will it not be?
   She draws aside the curtains of Juliet's *bed*.
What, dressed, and in your clothes, and down[341]
   again?
I must needs wake you. Lady! lady! lady!
Alas, alas! Help, help! my lady 's dead!
O weraday[342] that ever I was born!
Some aqua vitae,[343] ho! My lord! my lady!

[338] fast asleep.
[339] Take your small change, small portion, of sleep now.
[340] set his mind, decided.
[341] back to bed.
[342] alack, alas (welladay).
[343] some alcohol (in order to revive the girl).

Enter the Mother.

MOTHER: What noise is here?
NURSE: O lamentable day!
MOTHER: What is the matter?
NURSE: Look, look! O heavy day!
MOTHER: O me, O me! My child, my only life!
   Revive, look up, or I will die with thee!
   Help, help! Call help.

Enter the Father.

FATHER: For shame, bring Juliet forth; her lord is
   come.
NURSE: She's dead, deceased; she's dead, alack the
   day!
MOTHER: Alack the day, she's dead, she's dead, she's
   dead!
CAPULET: Ha! let me see her. Out alas! she's cold,

Her blood is settled, and her joints are stiff;
Life and these lips have long been separated.
Death lies on her like an untimely frost
Upon the sweetest flower of all the field.
NURSE: O lamentable day!
MOTHER: O woeful time!
CAPULET: Death, that hath ta'en her hence to make me wail,
Ties up my tongue and will not let me speak.

Enter Friar Laurence *and the* County Paris. *with* Musicians.

FRIAR: Come, is the bride ready to go to church?
CAPULET: Ready to go, but never to return.
O son, the night before thy wedding day
Hath Death lain with thy wife. There she lies,
Flower as she was, deflowerèd by him.
Death is my son-in-law, Death is my heir;
My daughter he hath wedded. I will die
And leave him all. Life, living, all is Death's.
PARIS: Have I thought long to see this morning's face,
And doth it give me such a sight as this?
MOTHER: Accursed, unhappy, wretched, hateful day!
Most miserable hour that e'er time saw
In lasting labor[344] of his pilgrimage!
But one, poor one, one poor and loving child,
But one thing to rejoice and solace in,
And cruel Death hath catched it from my sight.
NURSE: O woe! O woeful, woeful, woeful day!
Most lamentable day, most woeful day
That ever, ever, I did yet behold!
O day, O day, O day! O hateful day!
Never was seen so black a day as this.
O woeful day! O woeful day!
PARIS: Beguiled divorcèd, wrongèd, spited, slain!
Most detestable Death, by thee beguiled,
By cruel cruel thee quite overthrown.
O love! O life! not life, but love in death!
CAPULET: Despised, distressèd, hated, martyred, killed!
Uncomfortable time, why cam'st thou now
To murder, murder our solemnity?
O child, O child! my soul, and not my child!
Dead art thou—alack, my child is dead,
And with my child my joys are buried!

---

[344] Time in its continuous workings.

FRIAR: Peace, ho, for shame! Confusion's cure lives not
  In these confusions. Heaven and yourself
  Had part in this fair maid—now heaven hath all,
  And all the better is it for the maid.
  Your part in her[345] you could not keep from death,
  But heaven keeps his part[346] in eternal life.
  The most you sought was her promotion,
  For 'twas your heaven she should be advanced;
  And weep ye now, seeing she is advanced
  Above the clouds, as high as heaven itself?
  O, in this love, you love your child so ill
  That you run mad, seeing that she is well.
  She's not well married that lives married long,
  But she's best married that dies married young.
  Dry up your tears and stick your rosemary[347]
  On this fair corse, and, as the custom is,
  In all her best array bear her to church;
  For though fond nature bids us all lament,
  Yet nature's tears are reason's merriment.[348]
CAPULET: All things that we ordainèd festival
  Turn from their office to black funeral—
  Our instruments to melancholy bells,
  Our wedding cheer to a sad burial feast;
  Our solemn hymns to sullen dirges change;
  Our bridal flowers serve for a buried corse;
  And all things change them to the contrary.
FRIAR: Sir, go you in; and, madam, go with him;
  And go, Sir Paris. Every one prepare
  To follow this fair corse unto her grave.
  The heavens do low'r[349] upon you for some ill;
  Move them no more by crossing their high will.
  They go out, leaving the Nurse *and the* Musicians *on stage.*
FIRST MUSICIAN: Faith, we may put up our pipes and be gone.
NURSE: Honest good fellows, ah, put up, put up!
  For well you know this is a pitiful case.
              The Nurse *leaves.*
FIRST MUSICIAN: Ay, by my troth, the case may be amended.

  Enter Peter.

PETER: Musicians, O, musicians, 'Heart's ease,' 'Heart's ease'!

---

[345] her body—the mortal part in her in contrast to the spiritual part of the girl that came not from the parents but from God ("heaven" in the next line).

[346] her imperishable soul, which belongs to "heaven."

[347] a plant which symbolized "remembrance."

[348] "Reason" does not grieve, but finds a reason for hope; whereas "Nature"—our emotional self—sheds tears.

[349] looks down ("lowers") angrily on you for some sin ("ill") you have committed.

O, an you will have me live, play 'Heart's ease.'

FIRST MUSICIAN: Why 'Heart's ease'?

PETER: O, musicians, because my heart itself plays 'My heart is full of woe.' O, play me some merry dump to comfort me.

FIRST MUSICIAN: Not a dump[350] we! 'Tis no time to play now.

PETER: You will not then?

FIRST MUSICIAN: No.

PETER: I will then give it you soundly.

FIRST MUSICIAN: What will you give us?

PETER: No money, on my faith, but the gleek.[351] I will give you the minstrel.[352]

FIRST MUSICIAN: Then will I give you the serving-creature.

PETER: Then will I lay the serving-creature's dagger on your pate. I will carry no crotchets.[353] I'll re you, I'll fa you. Do you note me?

FIRST MUSICIAN: An you re us and fa us, you note us.

SECOND MUSICIAN: Pray you put up your dagger, and put out your wit.

PETER: Then have at you with my wit! I will dry-beat you with an iron wit, and put up my iron dagger. Answer me like men.
  'When griping grief the heart doth wound,
    And doleful dumps the mind oppress,
  Then music with her silver sound'—
Why 'silver sound'? Why 'music with her silver sound'?
What say you, Simon Catling?[354]

FIRST MUSICIAN: Marry, sir, because silver hath a sweet sound.

PETER: Pretty! What say you, Hugh Rebeck?[355]

SECOND MUSICIAN: I say 'silver sound' because musicians sound for silver.

PETER: Pretty too! What say you, James Soundpost?[356]

THIRD MUSICIAN: Faith, I know not what to say.

PETER: O, I cry you mercy! you are the singer. I will say for you. It is 'music with her silver sound' because musicians have no gold for sounding.
  'Then music with her silver sound
    With speedy help doth lend redress.' (*Exit.*)

FIRST MUSICIAN: What a pestilent knave is this same!

---

[350] "Not even a slow melody ("dump") will we play.

[351] mock.

[352] Peter threatens to insult him by calling him not a musician but a mere "minstrel," whereupon the musician, in the next lines, threatens to insult him in turn by calling him a "serving creature," whereupon Peter threatens to crack him on the head ("pate") with his dagger.

[353] there is punning here because "crotchets" means both quarter-notes and whims. "An" means "If."

[354] Simon "lutestring"—Peter calls the musician a "catstring" because the lutestring was popularly thought to be made from catgut.

[355] a three-stringed fiddle; Peter calls him "Hugh Fiddle."

[356] peg underneath the bridge of a stringed musical instrument.

SECOND MUSICIAN: Hang him, Jack! Come, we'll in
here, tarry for the mourners, and stay dinner.
He leaves with the other musicians.
(*Exit.*)

ACT V   SCENE I   [*A Street in Mantua*]

Enter Romeo.

ROMEO: If I may trust the flattering truth of sleep,
My dreams presage some joyful news at hand.
My bosom's lord[357] sits lightly in his throne,
And all this day an unaccustomed spirit
Lifts me above the ground with cheerful thoughts.
I dreamt my lady came and found me dead
(Strange dream that gives a dead man leave to
    think!)
And breathed such life with kisses in my lips
That I revived and was an emperor.
Ah me! how sweet is love itself possessed,
When but love's shadows[358] are so rich in joy!

Enter Romeo's servant Balthasar.

News from Verona! How now, Balthasar?
Dost thou not bring me letters from the friar?
How doth my lady? Is my father well?
How fares my Juliet? That I ask again,
For nothing can be ill if she be well.
BALTHASAR: Then she is well, and nothing can be ill.
Her body sleeps in Capel's monument,
And her immortal part with angels lives.
I saw her laid low in her kindred's vault
And presently took post[359] to tell it you.
O, pardon me for bringing these ill news,
Since you did leave it for my office, sir.
ROMEO: Is it e'en so? Then I defy you, stars![360]
Thou knowest my lodging. Get me ink and paper
And hire posthorses. I will hence to-night.

[357] that is, the heart.
[358] the phantoms of a dream.

[359] took posthorses.
[360] 'I defy you, Fate'; the stars were popularly believed to determine one's destiny.

BALTHASAR: I do beseech you, sir, have patience.
Your looks are pale and wild and do import
Some misadventure.
ROMEO: Tush, thou art deceived.
Leave me and do the thing I bid thee do.
Hast thou no letters to me from the friar?
BALTHASAR: No, my good lord.
ROMEO: No matter. Get thee gone
And hire those horses. I'll be with thee straight.
(*Exit* Balthasar.)
Well, Juliet, I will lie with thee to-night.
Let's see for means. O mischief, thou art swift
To enter in the thoughts of desperate men!
I do remember an apothecary,
And hereabouts 'a dwells, which late I noted
In tatt'red weeds, with overwhelming brows,
Culling of simples.[361] Meagre were his looks,
Sharp misery had worn him to the bones;
And in his needy shop a tortoise hung,
An alligator stuffed, and other skins
Of ill-shaped fishes; and about his shelves
A beggarly account[362] of empty boxes,
Green earthen pots, bladders, and musty seeds,
Remnants of packthread, and old cakes of roses[363]
Were thinly scatterèd, to make up a show.
Noting this penury, to myself I said,
'An if a man did need a poison now
Whose sale is present death in Mantua,
Here lives a caitiff[364] wretch would sell it him.'
O, this same thought did but forerun my need,
And this same needy man must sell it me.
As I remember, this should be the house.
Being holiday, the beggar's shop is shut.
What, ho! apothecary!
The Apothecary *appears.*
APOTHECARY: Who calls so loud?
ROMEO: Come hither, man. I see that thou art poor.
Hold, there is forty ducats. Let me have
A dram of poison, such soon-speeding gear[365]
As will disperse itself through all the veins
That the life-weary taker may fall dead,
And that the trunk[366] may be discharged of breath
As violently as hasty powder fired
Doth hurry from the fatal cannon's womb.
APOTHECARY: Such mortal drugs I have; but
Mantua's law

[361] medicinal herbs.
[362] a poor array or collection of empty boxes.
[363] cakes of compressed rose petals.
[364] miserable.
[365] stuff.
[366] the body.

Is death to any he[367] that utters them.
ROMEO: Art thou so bare and full of wretchedness
And fearest to die? Famine is in thy cheeks,
Need and oppression starveth in thy eyes,
Contempt and beggary hangs upon thy back:
The world is not thy friend, nor the world's law;
The world affords no law to make thee rich;
Then be not poor, but break it and take this.
APOTHECARY: My poverty but not my will consents.
ROMEO: I pay thy poverty and not thy will.
APOTHECARY: Put this in any liquid thing you will
And drink it off, and if you had the strength
Of twenty men, it would dispatch you straight.
ROMEO: There is thy gold—worse poison to men's souls,
Doing more murder in this loathsome world,
Than these poor compounds that thou mayst not sell.
I sell thee poison; thou hast sold me none.
Farewell. Buy food and get thyself in flesh.
Come, cordial and not poison, go with me
To Juliet's grave; for there must I use thee.
Exeunt.

[367] any man that sells ("utters") them.

SCENE II [*Friar Laurence's Cell*]

Enter Friar John *to* Friar Laurence.

JOHN: Holy Franciscan friar, brother, ho!

Enter Friar Laurence.

LAURENCE: This same should be the voice of Friar John.
Welcome from Mantua. What says Romeo?
Or, if his mind be writ, give me his letter.
JOHN: Going to find a barefoot brother[368] out,
One of our order, to associate me
Here in this city visiting the sick,
And finding him, the searchers of the town,
Suspecting that we both were in a house
Where the infectious pestilence did reign,
Sealed up the doors, and would not let us forth,
So that my speed to Mantua there was stayed.

[368] a friar.

LAURENCE: Who bore my letter, then, to Romeo?
JOHN: I could not send it—here it is again—
Nor get a messenger to bring it thee,
So fearful were they of infection.
LAURENCE: Unhappy fortune! By my brotherhood,[369]
The letter was not nice,[370] but full of charge,[371]
Of dear import; and the neglecting it
May do much danger. Friar John, go hence,
Get me an iron crow[372] and bring it straight
Unto my cell.
JOHN: Brother, I'll go and bring it thee.
Exit.
LAURENCE: Now must I to the monument alone.
Within this three hours will fair Juliet wake.
She will beshrew[373] me much that Romeo
Hath had no notice of these accidents;
But I will write again to Mantua,
And keep her at my cell till Romeo come—
Poor living corse, closed in a dead man's tomb!
Exit.

[369] my friars' order; Laurence is a member of the Franciscan order of friars.
[370] trivial; the letter was not an unimportant one.
[371] full of weight ("charge"), full of important matters.
[372] a crowbar.
[373] blame.

SCENE III [*Churchyard containing the Capulets' family tomb*]

Enter Paris *and his* Page *carrying flowers.*

PARIS: Give me thy torch, boy. Hence, and stand aloof.
Yet put it out, for I would not be seen.
Under yond yew tree lay thee all along,[374]
Holding thy ear close to the hollow ground.
So shall no foot upon the churchyard tread
(Being loose, unfirm, with digging up of graves)
But thou shalt hear it. Whistle then to me,
As signal that thou hearest something approach.
Give me those flowers. Do as I bid thee, go.
PAGE: I am almost afraid to stand alone
Here in the churchyard; yet I will adventure.
He leaves.
PARIS: Sweet flower, with flowers thy bridal bed I strew
O woe! thy canopy is dust and stones
Which with sweet water nightly I will dew;
Or, wanting that, with tears distilled by moans.

[374] lie flat.

The obsequies that I for thee will keep
Nightly shall be to strew thy grave and weep.
                    (*A Whistle is heard from the* Page.)
The boy gives warning something doth approach.
What cursèd foot wanders this way to-night
To cross[375] my obsequies and true love's rite?
What, with a torch? Muffle[376] me, night, awhile.
                                        He retires.

[375] 'to thwart, or interfere with, my rites' for the presumably dead Juliet.

[376] hide.

Enter Romeo, *and* Balthasar, *the servant, with a torch, a mattock (a pickaxe) and a crow of iron (crowbar).*

ROMEO: Give me that mattock and the wrenching
   iron.
   Hold, take this letter. Early in the morning
   See thou deliver it to my lord and father.
   Give me the light. Upon thy life I charge thee,
   Whate'er thou hearest or seest, stand all aloof
   And do not interrupt me in my course.
   Why I descend into this bed of death
   Is partly to behold my lady's face,
   But chiefly to take thence from her dead finger
   A precious ring—a ring that I must use
   In dear[377] employment. Therefore hence, be gone.
   But if thou, jealous, dost return to pry
   In what I farther shall intend to do,
   By heaven, I will tear thee joint by joint
   And strew this hungry churchyard with thy limbs.
   The time and my intents are savage-wild,
   More fierce and more inexorable far
   Than empty tigers or the roaring sea.

[377] important. (The "precious ring" is used by Romeo as an excuse for sending Balthasar away.)

BALTHASAR: I will be gone, sir, and not trouble you.
ROMEO: So shalt thou show me friendship. (*Giving him a purse containing money*) Take thou that.
   Live, and be prosperous; and farewell, good fellow.
BALTHASAR: (*to himself—aside*) For all this same,
   I'll hide me hereabout.
   His look I fear, and his intents I doubt.
                                        (*He leaves.*)
ROMEO: (*forcing the entry to the tomb open*) Thou
   detestable maw, thou womb of death,
   Gorged with the dearest morsel of the earth,
   Thus I enforce thy rotten jaws to open,
   And in despite I'll cram thee with more food.
PARIS: (*appearing out of the darkness*) This is that
   banished haughty Montague

That murd'red my love's cousin—with which grief
It is supposèd the fair creature died—
And here is come to do some villainous shame
To the dead bodies. I will apprehend him.
Stop thy unhallowèd toil, vile Montague!
Can vengeance be pursued further than death?
Condemnèd villain, I do apprehend thee.
Obey, and go with me; for thou must die.

ROMEO: I must indeed; and therefore came I hither.
Good gentle youth, tempt not a desp'rate man.
Fly hence and leave me. Think upon these gone;[378]
Let them affright thee. I beseech thee, youth,
Put not another sin upon my head
By urging me to fury. O, be gone!
By heaven, I love thee better than myself,
For I come hither armed against myself.
Stay not, be gone. Live, and hereafter say
A madman's mercy bid thee run away.

PARIS: I do defy thy conjuration[379]
And apprehend thee for a felon here.

ROMEO: Wilt thou provoke me? Then have at thee, boy! *They strike at each other with their swords.*

PAGE: (*running for help*) O Lord, they fight! I will go call the watch. *Paris falls down.*

PARIS: O, I am slain! If thou be merciful,
Open the tomb, lay me with Juliet. *He dies.*

ROMEO: In faith, I will. Let me peruse this face.
Mercutio's kinsman, noble County Paris!
What said my man when my betossèd[380] soul
Did not attend[381] him as we rode? I think
He told me Paris should have married Juliet.
Said he not so? or did I dream it so?
Or am I mad, hearing him talk of Juliet,
To think it was so? O, give me thy hand,
One writ with me in sour misfortune's book!
I'll bury thee in a triumphant grave.
A grave? O, no, a lanthorn,[382] slaught'red youth,
For here lies Juliet, and her beauty makes
This vault a feasting presence[383] full of light.
Death, lie thou there, by a dead man interred.
He lays Paris *in the tomb.*
How oft when men are at the point of death
Have they been merry! which their keepers[384] call
A lightning before death. O, how may I
Call this a lightning? O my love! my wife!
Death, that hath sucked the honey of thy breath,

---

[378] the dead.
[379] demands, entreaties filled with threats.
[380] troubled.
[381] did not pay attention to him.
[382] a windowed turret or tower room.
[383] chamber, presence-chamber.
[384] jailers.

Hath had no power yet upon thy beauty.
Thou art not conquered. Beauty's ensign[385] yet
Is crimson in thy lips and in thy cheeks,
And death's pale flag is not advancèd there.
Tybalt, liest thou there in thy bloody sheet?
O, what more favor can I do to thee
Than with that hand that cut thy youth in twain
To sunder his that was thine enemy?
Forgive me, cousin! Ah, dear Juliet,
Why art thou yet so fair? Shall I believe
That unsubstantial Death is amorous,
And that the lean abhorrèd monster keeps
Thee here in dark to be his paramour?
For fear of that I still will stay with thee
And never from this pallet of dim night
Depart again. Here, here will I remain
With worms that are thy chambermaids. O, here
Will I set up my everlasting rest
And shake the yoke of inauspicious stars
From this world-wearied flesh. Eyes, look your last!
Arms, take your last embrace! and, lips, O you
The doors of breath, seal with a righteous kiss
A dateless[386] bargain to engrossing[387] death!
Come, bitter conduct; come, unsavory guide!
Thou desperate pilot, now at once run on
The dashing rocks thy seasick weary bark!
Here's to my love! (*He drinks*) O true apothecary!
Thy drugs are quick. Thus with a kiss I die.
     He falls down and dies.

[385] banner.
[386] endless.
[387] all-taking, all-consuming, death.

Enter Friar Laurence, *with lanthorn (lantern), crow, and spade.*

FRIAR: Saint Francis be my speed![388] how oft to-night
 Have my old feet stumbled at graves! Who's there?
BALTHASAR: Here's one, a friend, and one that knows
 you well.
FRIAR: Bliss be upon you! Tell me, good my friend,
 What torch is yond that vainly lends his light
 To grubs and eyeless skulls? As I discern,
 It burneth in the Capels' monument.
BALTHASAR: It doth so, holy sir; and there's my master,
 One that you love.
FRIAR: Who is it?

[388] help.

ACT V, SC. III

BALTHASAR: Romeo.
FRIAR: How long hath he been there?
BALTHASAR: Full half an hour.
FRIAR: Go with me to the vault.
BALTHASAR: I dare not, sir.
  My master knows not but I am gone hence,
  And fearfully did menace me with death
  If I did stay to look on his intents.
FRIAR: Stay then; I'll go alone. Fear comes upon me.
  O, much I fear some ill unthrifty[389] thing.
BALTHASAR: As I did sleep under this yew tree here,
  I dreamt my master and another fought,
  And that my master slew him.
FRIAR: Romeo!
  Alack, alack, what blood is this which stains
  The stony entrance of this sepulchre?
  What mean these masterless and gory swords
  To lie discolored by this place of peace?
                He advances toward the tomb.
  Romeo! O, pale! Who else? What, Paris too?
  And steeped in blood? Ah, what an unkind hour
  Is guilty of this lamentable chance!
  The lady stirs.
JULIET: (*rising*) O comfortable friar! where is my lord?
  I do remember well where I should be,
  And there I am. Where is my Romeo?
FRIAR: I hear some noise. Lady, come from that nest
  O death, contagion, and unnatural sleep.
  A greater power than we can contradict
  Hath thwarted our intents. Come, come away.
  Thy husband in thy bosom there lies dead;
  And Paris too. Come, I'll dispose of thee
  Among a sisterhood of holy nuns.
  Stay not to question, for the watch is coming.
  Come, go, good Juliet. I dare no longer stay.
JULIET: Go, get thee hence, for I will not away.
                      Friar Laurence *leaves.*
  What's here? A cup, closed in my true love's hand?
  Poison, I see, hath been his timeless[390] end.
  O churl! drunk all, and left no friendly drop
  To help me after? I will kiss thy lips.
  Haply[391] some poison yet doth hang on them
  To make me die with a restorative.[392]
  (*Kissing him*) Thy lips are warm!
              A Watchman *appears with the* Page.

---

[389] unprofitable, unfortunate.
[390] untimely.
[391] perhaps.
[392] 'a poison that will restore me to you in death—so that I may join you in death!'

WATCHMAN: Lead, boy. Which way?
JULIET: Yea, noise? Then I'll be brief. O happy[393]
    dagger! *She takes* Romeo's *dagger.*
This is thy sheath; there rest, and let me die.
                  She stabs herself and dies.

[393] 'dagger, that is fortunately on hand.'

Enter the Chief Watchman *and the* Boy *or* Page, *and others.*

BOY (*Page*): This is the place. There, where the torch doth burn.
CHIEF WATCHMAN: The ground is bloody. Search about the churchyard.
Go, some of you; whoe'er you find attach.
         The Watchmen *start their search.*
Pitiful sight! here lies the County slain;
And Juliet bleeding, warm, and newly dead,
Who here hath lain this two days burièd.
Go, tell the Prince; run to the Capulets;
Raise up the Montagues; some others search.
    The Watchmen *disperse to carry out his order.*
We see the ground[394] whereon these woes do lie,
But the true ground of all these piteous woes
We cannot without circumstance descry.[395]

[394] cause and basis ("ground") of all these misfortunes ("woe").
[395] We cannot determine ("descry") without knowing the detailed circumstances or additional details.

Enter Romeo's servant Balthasar *and* Watchmen.

SECOND WATCHMAN: Here's Romeo's man. We found him in the churchyard.
CHIEF WATCHMAN: Hold him in safety till the Prince come hither.

Enter Friar Laurence *and another* Watchman.

THIRD WATCHMAN: Here is a friar that trembles, sighs, and weeps.
We took this mattock and this spade from him
As he was coming from this churchyard side.
CHIEF WATCHMAN: A great suspicion! Stay[396] the friar too.

[396] hold, arrest.

Enter the Prince *and his Attendants.*

PRINCE: What misadventure is so early up,
　　That calls our person from our morning rest?

Enter Capulet *and* Lady Capulet, *and others.*

CAPULET: What should it be, that is so shrieked abroad?
LADY CAPULET: O the people in the street cry 'Romeo,'
　　Some 'Juliet,' and some 'Paris'; and all run,
　　With open outcry, toward our monument.
PRINCE: What fear is this which startles in your ears?
CHIEF WATCHMAN: Sovereign, here lies the County Paris slain;
　　And Romeo dead; and Juliet, dead before,
　　Warm and new killed.
PRINCE: Search, seek, and know how this foul murder comes.
CHIEF WATCHMAN: Here is a friar, and slaughtered Romeo's man,
　　With instruments upon them fit to open
　　These dead men's tombs.
CAPULET: O heavens! O wife, look how our daughter bleeds!
　　This dagger hath mista'en, for, lo, his house[397]
　　Is empty on the back of Montague,
　　And it missheathèd in my daughter's bosom!
LADY CAPULET: O me! this sight of death is as a bell
　　That warns[398] my old age[399] to a sepulchre.

Enter Montague *with Attendants.*

PRINCE: Come, Montague; for thou art early up
　　To see thy son and heir more early down.
MONTAGUE: Alas, my liege, my wife is dead to-night!
　　Grief of my son's exile hath stopped her breath.
　　What further woe conspires against mine age?
PRINCE: Look, and thou shalt see.
MONTAGUE: O thou untaught! what manners is in this,
　　To press before thy father to a grave?
PRINCE: Seal up the mouth of outrage[400] for a while,
　　Till we can clear these ambiguities[401]
　　And know their spring, their head, their true descent;

---

[397] for, behold ("lo"), its sheath ("his house").
[398] summons.
[399] Lady Capulet is not old but feels old now that Juliet is dead.
[400] stifle all outcries for awhile.
[401] these unclear matters.

And then will I be general[402] of your woes
And lead you even to death. Meantime forbear,
And let mischance be slave to patience.[403]
Bring forth the parties of suspicion.

FRIAR: I am the greatest, able to do least,
Yet most suspected, as the time and place
Doth make against me, of this direful murder;
And here I stand, both to impeach and purge[404]
Myself condemnèd and myself excused.

PRINCE: Then say at once what thou dost know in this.

FRIAR: I will be brief, for my short date of breath[405]
Is not so long as is a tedious tale.
Romeo, there dead, was husband to that Juliet;
And she, there dead, that Romeo's faithful wife.
I married them; and their stol'n marriage day
Was Tybalt's doomsday, whose untimely death
Banished the new-made bridegroom from this city;
For whom, and not for Tybalt, Juliet pined.
You, to remove that siege of grief from her,
Betrothed and would have married her perforce
To County Paris. Then comes she to me
And with wild looks bid me devise some mean
To rid her from this second marriage,
Or in my cell there would she kill herself.
Then gave I her, so tutored by my art,
A sleeping potion; which so took effect
As I intended, for it wrought on her
The form of death. Meantime I writ to Romeo
That he should hither come as this[406] dire night
To help to take her from her borrowèd grave,
Being the time the potion's force should cease.
But he which bore my letter, Friar John,
Was stayed by accident, and yesternight
Returned my letter back. Then all alone
At the prefixèd[407] hour of her waking
Came I to take her from her kindred's vault;
Meaning to keep her closely[408] at my cell
Till I conveniently could send to Romeo.
But when I came, some minute ere the time
Of her awakening, here untimely lay
The noble Paris and true Romeo dead.
She wakes; and I entreated her come forth
And bear this work of heaven with patience;
But then a noise did scare me from the tomb,
And she, too desperate, would not go with me,

[402] I will be your leader in lamenting.
[403] 'let your grief over these unfortunate events be controlled by (let it be "slave to") patience.'
[404] 'and accuse myself and free myself from suspicion.'
[405] 'my expectation of life'—and the elderly Friar Laurence does not expect to live much longer.
[406] on this.
[407] the previously fixed.
[408] secretly—'to keep her hidden in my cell.'

But, as it seems, did violence on herself.
All this I know, and to the marriage
Her nurse is privy;[409] and if aught in this
Miscarried by my fault, let my old life
Be sacrificed, some hour before his time,
Unto the rigor of severest law.

PRINCE: We still have known thee for a holy man.
Where's Romeo's man? What can he say in this?

BALTHASAR: I brought my master news of Juliet's death;
And then in post he came from Mantua
To this same place, to this same monument.
This letter he early bid me give his father,
And threat'ned me with death, going in the vault,
If I departed not and left him there.

PRINCE: Give me the letter. I will look on it.
Where is the County's page that raised the watch?
Sirrah, what made[410] your master in this place?

BOY [*Page*]: He came with flowers to strew his lady's grave;
And bid me stand aloof, and so I did.
Anon[411] comes one with light to ope the tomb;
And by and by my master drew[412] on him;
And then I ran away to call the watch.

PRINCE: This letter doth make good the friar's words,
Their course of love, the tidings of her death;
And here he writes that he did buy a poison
Of a poor pothecary, and therewithal
Came to this vault to die, and lie with Juliet.
Where be these enemies? Capulet, Montague,
See what a scourge is laid upon your hate,
That heaven finds means to kill your joys with[413] love.
And I, for winking[414] at your discords too,
Have lost a brace of kinsmen.[415] All are punished.

CAPULET: O brother Montague, give me thy hand
This is my daughter's jointure,[416] for no more
Can I demand.

MONTAGUE: But I can give thee more;
For I will raise her statue in pure gold,
That whiles Verona by that name is known,
There shall no figure at such rate[417] be set
As that of true and faithful Juliet.

CAPULET: As rich shall Romeo's by his lady's lie—
Poor sacrifices of our enmity!

---

[409] shares the secret.

[410] 'what was your master doing in this place, what was his business in this place?'

[411] soon.

[412] 'drew his sword against him.'

[413] by means of love—that is, the love of Romeo and Juliet.

[414] keeping my eyes closed, overlooking your feuds ("discords").

[415] The Prince is referring to his kinsmen Mercutio and Count Paris; he considers himself to have been punished in losing these kinsmen.

[416] marriage portion.

[417] value.

PRINCE: A glooming[418] peace this morning with it
   brings.
The sun for sorrow will not show his head.
Go hence, to have more talk of these sad things;
   Some shall be pardoned, and some punishèd;
For never was a story of more woe
Than this of *Juliet* and her *Romeo*.   *Exeunt.*[419]

[418] clouded.
[419] They all go out.

Finis

QUESTIONS

A. Understanding the Action:

1. What reasons are there for calling *Romeo and Juliet* a lyrical drama? a young man's play? a tragedy? As a tragedy, is it a "tragedy of character" or of "fate"? Do the protagonists possess tragic flaws, or are these flaws attributed to other characters in the play? Which other characters?

2. Does Shakespeare want us to understand that Romeo is destroyed by his lack of moderation or temperance? Explain. Describe Romeo's love for Juliet; is it sinful? morbid? unmanly? Is Romeo a philanderer? Is he a sentimentalist in his love for Juliet as he was in his love for Rosaline?

3. To what degree are Romeo and Juliet responsible for their tragedy? In what respects are they *not* the authors of their own misfortune?

4. How is *Romeo and Juliet* a "romantic" tragedy? Are there any "romantic" assumptions in the play? To what degree does Shakespeare analyze Romeo's passion for Juliet?

5. The action of the play covers less than a week. Why is there such a short span of time? Draw up a time scheme that approximately dates each scene.

6. What chance events are there in the play? What events are the result of the feud? What is the climax of the play? By what simple plot change could a happy ending have been brought about? Would this improve the play? Explain.

7. A dramatist sometimes uses *foreshadowing* to suggest coming events. On what three occasions does Romeo have premonitions of disaster? When does Juliet have such premonitions?

8. *Irony* is another device frequently used by a dramatist. What characters in the play produce by their actions a result that is the exact opposite of what they had expected?

B. Understanding the Characters:

1. In what respects do Romeo and Juliet develop as characters?

2. Mercutio sometimes satirizes particular individuals, sometimes types. Where in the play, and in what terms, does he ridicule (a) Romeo, Benvolio, the Nurse, Tybalt, and Rosaline; (b) courtiers, lawyers, parsons, soldiers, fops, and the French? What part does his sense of humor play in causing his death? What is the motivation of his Queen Mab speech; what does it reveal of his character? Why does he lay a curse "on both your houses"?

3. What is the dramatic function of the Nurse? On what is the relationship of Juliet and the Nurse based? Where does the break between them come? Why?

4. What is the philosophy and character of the Friar? What is his attitude toward the lovers? Why does he secretly marry Romeo and Juliet? If his end is a worthy one, how are his desperate and deceitful plans justified? Why don't his plans for a happy ending work out?

5. What strong indication is there in the play that the head of one of the two rival families is the sort of person who would sustain a feud? Characterize the two men.

6. What is Paris' function in the play? What is his conception of love and marriage? What is your attitude toward him: sympathy, contempt, pity, other? Justify your choice.

7. What is the function of Rosaline in the play?

C. Comparisons:

1. What do *Romeo and Juliet* and *The Barretts of Wimpole Street* have in common? In what respects are they different in characterization, plot, background, dramatic form, and dialogue?

2. Compare the attitude of Creon in *Antigone* toward his son Haemon with that of Capulet toward his daughter Juliet. To what extent are the parents in both plays shown to be responsible for the death of their children? To what extent do you condemn the rashness or impulsiveness of the children for the tragedy of their own lives and their death?

D. Critical Evaluation:

1. Is there any justification for S. N. Butcher's view that the lovers came to ruin because "in their new-found rapture they act in defiance of all external obligations"? Does Shakespeare seem to share this opinion?

2. Discuss the argument that Juliet's tragedy is caused by her lying to her parents and concealing her purposes as she goes to confession under the pretense of piety? Again, does Shakespeare seem to share this opinion?

3. "Most of Shakespeare's lovers in tragedy could with propriety and without much change have been put into comedies." Discuss whether *Romeo and Juliet* bears out this statement.

HENRIK IBSEN (1828-1906)

When in 1879 in the final scene of *A Doll's House*, Nora left her stunned husband and children, the slamming of that door, like the shot fired at Concord Bridge, was "heard round the world" and started a revolution. Ibsen, the father of modern drama, became the central figure of controversy in the world theatre for a generation. Long considered the most important dramatist since Shakespeare by advocates of modern realism, he is still a potent force influencing many of the serious playwrights of the twentieth century.

In the first half of the nineteenth century, the European theatre was the most popular form of entertainment for all classes but catered especially to the tired, middle-class businessman. The plays that dominated the stage consisted, for the most part, of colorful spectacles, sentimental romances, melodramas, French farces, and comic operas. Because in this period nationalism became a powerful force, the historical play, treating heroes of legend or history romantically and reinforcing national patriotism, also became very popular. The few serious plays that were produced flattered the vanity and supported the smug respectability of the typical middle-class audience. It is no wonder then that Nora's defiance of the marriage conventions of the time came as a shattering experience to theatregoers.

Ibsen's plays fall roughly into three classes: romantic and historical drama, from his first play *Catiline*, in 1850, to *Emperor and Galilean* in 1873; realistic, social problem drama, from *Pillars of Society* in 1877 to *Hedda Gabler* in 1890; and symbolist drama, from *The Lady from the Sea* in 1880 to his last work, *When We Dead Awaken*, in 1899.

Ibsen was born in 1828 in the small, provincial seaport of Skien on the southeastern coast of Norway, a town with a mountain background (reflected in his famous poetic drama *Peer Gynt*). When Ibsen was eight years old, his father lost his fortune in a depression. The family moved to a drab farm on the outskirts of Skien. The sensitive, imaginative youngster, embittered by poverty, social ostracism, and lack of sympathy at home, received a very inadequate education at a poor people's school. Lacking financial resources, and receiving no encouragement in his early ambition to become an artist, at the age of fifteen he left his family to become apprenticed to an apothecary in Grimstad, a day's travel by steamer from Skien.

To relieve the drudgery of his job, Ibsen began to read extensively, and joined a radical young group of unconventional patriots who protested in impassioned manifestoes against the militaristic expansionism of Prussia. Failing to pass the entrance examinations to the University of Christiania, he abandoned medicine for journalism. He first wrote for a liberal weekly on public affairs, and then for a revolutionary labor paper. When in the summer of 1851 the government imprisoned the editor, Ibsen gave up journalism and political agitation for playwriting.

His fortunes at last took a turn for the better when in the fall of 1851 Ole Bull, the founder and director of the Bergen Theatre, appointed him to the position of official playwright and stage manager or stage director; Ibsen was also subsidized to study the theatre in Copenhagen and Dresden. The six years he spent at Bergen gave him invaluable theatrical experience. He staged 145 plays from a wide repertory, ranging from Shakespeare to the French and German romantic dramatists of the nineteenth century. He learned all the tricks of the "well-made play" technique of plot fabrication which he later utilized for higher dramatic purposes. He also had an opportunity to develop his own dramatic talents, writing an annual historical play. Most of these poetic nationalistic plays are of little interest today, but they strengthened his reputation.

In 1857 Ibsen left the Bergen Theatre to become the director of the Norwegian Theatre in Christiania. The following year he married Susanna Thoresen, the daughter of a minister, and became the father of one son. The failure of his *Love's Comedy*, a verse satire on conventional love and marriage, published in 1862, and the bankruptcy of the Norwegian Theatre depressed Ibsen. These unhappy events in addition to the spiritual provincialism and political timidity he attributed to the Norwegians exasperated him so much that he went into voluntary exile. For twenty-seven years thereafter—from 1864 to 1891—Ibsen lived abroad, mostly in Italy and Germany.

His epic verse drama *Brand*, written in Rome and published in 1866, ran into four editions before the end of the year. The religious hero of this play is an uncompromising idealist whose motto is "All or nothing." This tragedy, like the work of Kierkegaard, the Danish theologian, attacks superficiality in the practice of the Christian religion. The following year he wrote a humorous fantasy in verse, one of his greatest works, called *Peer Gynt*, whose careless hero, always compromising, refuses to face reality. Then, abandoning verse and turning to contemporary themes, Ibsen wrote two more controversial plays—*The League of Youth* and *The Pillars of Society*—before he shocked all of Europe with *A Doll's House*.

To answer the critics who said that Nora, heroine of *A Doll's House*, should have stayed with her family, Ibsen wrote *Ghosts*, a play that disturbed audiences even more. Mrs. Alving, heroine of *Ghosts*, following the conventional advice of her pastor, returns to her dissipated husband whom she left briefly as an outraged young wife. The play, the first to mention venereal disease in the theatre, shows the appalling consequences of this "moral" decision. Like Walt Whitman earlier in America, on publishing *Leaves of Grass*, and Thomas Hardy later in England, on writing *Jude the Obsure*, Ibsen became an object of vilification in conservative circles. He was denounced by an outraged public as a corrupter of society. His reply was his satirical comedy *An Enemy of the People*.

In the last fifteen years of his dramatic productivity—from 1884 to 1899, Ibsen wrote a series of plays in which the symbolic elements predominate over the realistic. (The powerful psychological drama *Hedda Gabler*, in 1892, is an exception). These plays are *The Wild Duck, Rosmersholm, The Lady from the Sea, The Master Builder, John Gabriel Borkman,* and *When We Dead Awaken*.

In 1891 Ibsen returned to his homeland, where he spent the concluding fifteen years of his life. At Oslo he wrote his last three symbolic plays. Physical and mental infirmities prevented him from writing anything in the final six years of his life. Acclaimed as the leading dramatist of his century, he died on May 23, 1906.

Ibsen's contributions to the development of the drama—both in subject matter and treatment—have been of great importance. Like all significant artists, he created a world of his own and filled it with living three-dimensional characters. After he had outgrown his early romantic attitude, he wisely limited his vision to the society of which he was a part and that he knew so well, the middle class. He was interested not in the working class and not in the aristocracy, but in doctors, lawyers, teachers, architects, pastors. Subordinating outer action to inner action, he penetrated with psychological insight into the lives of these people revealing their emotional conflicts in dramatic terms. By focusing his attention upon the soul in spiritual crisis and by using more or less contemporary conversational prose, he rid the stage of the romantic and melodramatic claptrap of violent action, duels, disguises, and inflated rhetoric.

Like Sophocles and Shakespeare, he made the theatre once more an arena for the presentation of serious ideas instead of just a place of entertainment. Courageously this Norwegian individualist moved into the area of contemporary problems in defiance of nineteenth century conventions or taboos and brought into the theatre ideas on sex, religion, politics, and economics. His interest was centered not only in modern man, but also in the impact of powerful social forces upon the individual. Personal tragedy became social tragedy in his mature plays. As satirist, realist, naturalist, and symbolist, he became the father of the social-problem play, and the drama of ideas.

But Ibsen did more than develop psychological and spiritual portraiture and broaden the subject matter of the stage. He made important innovations in dramatic technique. He constructed his plays carefully, and with almost mathematical exactness he concentrated his attention on the events immediately preceding the crisis in the lives of his characters. The *last* act of other playwrights became his *first*. He returned to the simplicity of the tragic Greek dramatists by approximating very closely the classical unities of time, place, and action. He also made himself the master of so-called *retrospective exposition.* Instead of introducing all his expository material in the early part of the play as Shakespeare did, Ibsen by cleverly revealing it bit by bit throughout the whole course of the drama, showed us the power of the past over the present. The masterly construction of *Ghosts* has often been compared to that of Sophocles' *Oedipus the King*. It is not surprising then to see such outstanding twentieth century dramatists as Bernard Shaw, Arthur Miller, and Tennessee Williams following in the footsteps of the Norwegian master.

INTRODUCTION TO *AN ENEMY OF THE PEOPLE*

For many years Ibsen had pondered the problem of the idealistic individual in conflict with a community united by deep-rooted conventions. He was familiar with de Tocqueville's phrase "the tyranny of the majority," with Kierkegaard's statement, "The mob is falsehood," and John Stuart Mill's warning that the unrestrained majority sometimes endangers individual liberty. Ibsen had supported the belief that being true to oneself is more important to progress than the support of outworn institutions of society. Man's soul should resist sterile formulas and popular catchwords.

In 1872 he had written in a letter to the Danish critic George Brandes, "To me, at any rate, it appears that the lonely man is the strongest" and later that he supported "that minority which leads the van, and pushes on to points which the majority has not yet reached." He added, "I hold that that man is in the right who is most closely in league with the future." But the storm of abuse that descended upon Ibsen with the publication of *Ghosts* was undoubtedly the main reason for his writing *An Enemy of the People.*

Ghosts, a play dealing with "an unmentionable disease," with the problem of euthanasia (mercy-killing), and incest naturally stirred up a hornet's nest. What aroused Ibsen's wrath was the fact that not only the conservatives ("the stagnationists") attacked him as "ungodly, immoral, and subversive," but also the liberals. Although Ibsen, always a meticulous craftsman, usually spent about two years in writing a play, he dashed off *An Enemy of the People* in only nine months. What is remarkable is that he produced not a passionate polemic of self-justification but a well-constructed play filled with psychological penetration, derisive humor, and a many-sided presentation of a complex problem.

The knowledge he had gained of the "well-made" play by staging the plays of Scribe and Sardou now stood him in good stead.

An Enemy of the People opens with a brilliant exposition scene, starts the plot with the inciting force of the arrival of the letter, moves rapidly to an explosive climax, holds our attention in the falling action, and comes to a satisfactory resolution of the conflict in its challenging conclusion.

In creating the character of the rash, exuberant, muddled but courageous Dr. Stockmann, the dramatist made use of reformers he had known, and added some of his own youthful idealism. Himself branded as an enemy of society, Ibsen in the ringing speeches of the heroic doctor answered his detractors. But the dramatist was not blind to the confusion and shortcomings of his hero. The other characters involved in the conflict are also envisioned clearly and portrayed realistically.

That Ibsen had serene control of his dramatic material is evidenced by the humor that radiates from the play. Bursts of laughter like a refreshing breeze sweep through it. Dr. Stockmann's remark on the great rent in his black trousers, "You should never wear your best trousers when you go out to fight for freedom and truth," and his driving out the three rascals, "the devil's messengers," with his brandished umbrella are examples of high comedy that help balance the seriousness of the play.

Like Dr. Stockmann, Ibsen learned that though democratic society moves forward because of the courage, idealism, and honesty of a minority, the support of the masses, who can be enlightened only through a continued process of education, is essential. Selfish, unscrupulous misleaders of humanity must be exposed, and the polluted well springs of society must be purified. When he was compared to Zola, the French naturalistic novelist, Ibsen replied, "Zola descends into the cesspool to take a bath, I to cleanse it."

AN ENEMY OF THE PEOPLE

HENRIK IBSEN

CHARACTERS

DR. THOMAS STOCKMANN, *Medical Officer of the Municipal Baths*
MRS. STOCKMANN, *his wife*
PETRA, *their daughter, a teacher*
EJLIF } *their sons, aged 13 and 10 respectively*
MORTEN
PETER STOCKMANN, *the Doctor's elder brother; Mayor of the Town and Chief Constable and Chairman of the Baths' Committee*
MORTEN KIIL, *a tanner* (MRS. STOCKMANN'S *adoptive father*)
HOVSTAD, *editor of the "People's Messenger"*
BILLING, *sub-editor*
CAPTAIN HORSTER
ASLAKSEN, *a printer*
MEN *of various occupations, women, and a troop of schoolboys—the audience at a public meeting*

The action takes place in a coast town in southern Norway.

ACT I

SCENE: DR. STOCKMANN'S *sitting-room. It is evening. The room is plainly but neatly appointed and furnished. In the right-hand wall are two doors; the farther leads out to the hall, the nearer to the doctor's study. In the left-hand wall, opposite the door leading to the hall, is a door leading to the other rooms occupied by the family. In the middle of the same wall stands the stove, and, further forward, a couch with a looking-glass hanging over it and an oval table in front of it. On the table, a lighted lamp, with a lampshade. At the back of the room, an open door leads to the dining-room.* BILLING *is seen sitting at the dining table, on which a lamp is burning. He has a napkin tucked under his chin, and* MRS. STOCKMANN *is standing by the table handing him a large plateful of roast beef. The other places at the table are empty, and the table somewhat in disorder, a meal having evidently recently been finished.*

MRS. STOCKMANN: You see, if you come an hour late, Mr. Billing, you have to put up with cold meat.

BILLING: (*as he eats*) It is uncommonly good, thank you—remarkably good.

MRS. STOCKMANN: My husband makes such a point of having his meals punctually, you know—

BILLING: That doesn't affect me a bit. Indeed, I almost think I enjoy a meal all the better when I can sit down and eat all by myself and undisturbed.

MRS. STOCKMANN: Oh well, as long as you are enjoying it—. (*Turns to the hall door, listening.*) I expect that is Mr. Hovstad coming too.

BILLING: Very likely.

(PETER STOCKMANN *comes in. He wears an overcoat and his official hat, and carries a stick.*)

PETER STOCKMANN: Good evening, Katherine.

MRS. STOCKMANN: (*coming forward into the sitting-room*) Ah, good evening—is it you? How good of you to come up and see us!

PETER STOCKMANN: I happened to be passing, and so—(*looks into the dining-room.*) But you have company with you, I see.

MRS. STOCKMANN: (*a little embarrassed*) Oh, no—it was quite by chance he came in. (*Hurriedly.*) Won't you come in and have something, too?

PETER STOCKMANN: I! No, thank you. Good gracious—hot meat at night! Not with my digestion.

MRS. STOCKMANN: Oh, but just once in a way—

PETER STOCKMANN: No, no, my dear lady; I stick to my tea and bread and butter. It is much more wholesome in the long run—and a little more economical, too.

MRS. STOCKMANN: (*smiling*) Now you mustn't think that Thomas and I are spendthrifts.

PETER STOCKMANN: Not you, my dear; I would never think that of you. (*Points to the* DOCTOR's *study.*) Is he not at home?

MRS. STOCKMANN: No, he went out for a little turn after supper—he and the boys.

PETER STOCKMANN: I doubt if that is a wise thing to do. (*Listens.*) I fancy I hear him coming now.

MRS. STOCKMANN: No, I don't think it is he. (*A knock is heard at the door.*) Come in! (HOVSTAD *comes in from the hall.*) Oh, it is you, Mr. Hovstad!

HOVSTAD: Yes, I hope you will forgive me, but I was delayed at the printer's. Good evening, Mr. Mayor.

PETER STOCKMANN: (*bowing a little distantly*) Good evening. You have come on business, no doubt.

HOVSTAD: Partly. It's about an article for the paper.

PETER STOCKMANN: So I imagined. I hear my brother has become a prolific contributor to the "People's Messenger."

HOVSTAD: Yes, he is good enough to write in the "People's Messenger" when he has any home truths to tell.

MRS. STOCKMANN: (*to* HOVSTAD) But won't you—? (*Points to the dining-room.*)

PETER STOCKMANN: Quite so, quite so. I don't blame him in the least, as a writer, for addressing himself to the quarters where he will find the readiest sympathy. And, besides that, I personally have no reason to bear any ill will to your paper, Mr. Hovstad.

HOVSTAD: I quite agree with you.

PETER STOCKMANN: Taking one thing with another, there is an excellent spirit of toleration in the town—an admirable municipal spirit. And it all springs from the fact of our having a great common interest to unite us—an interest that is in an equally high degree the concern of every rightminded citizen—

HOVSTAD: The Baths, yes.

PETER STOCKMANN: Exactly—our fine, new, handsome Baths. Mark my words, Mr. Hovstad—the Baths will become the focus of our municipal life! Not a doubt of it!

MRS. STOCKMANN: That is just what Thomas says.

PETER STOCKMANN: Think how extraordinarily the place has developed within the last year or two! Money has been flowing in, and there is some life and some business doing in the town. Houses and landed property are rising in value every day.

HOVSTAD: And unemployment is diminishing.

PETER STOCKMANN: Yes, that is another thing. The burden of the poor-rates has been lightened, to the great relief of the propertied classes; and that relief will be even greater if only we get a really good summer this year, and lots of visitors—plenty of invalids, who will make the Baths talked about.

HOVSTAD: And there is a good prospect of that, I hear.

PETER STOCKMANN: It looks very promising. Enquiries about apartments and that sort of thing are reaching us every day.

HOVSTAD: Well, the doctor's article will come in very suitably.

PETER STOCKMANN: Has he been writing something just lately?

HOVSTAD: This is something he wrote in the winter, a recommendation of the Baths—an account of the excellent sanitary conditions here. But I held the article over, temporarily.

PETER STOCKMANN: Ah,—some little difficulty about it, I suppose?

HOVSTAD: No, not at all; I thought it would be better to wait till the spring, because it is just at this time that people begin to think seriously about their summer quarters.

PETER STOCKMANN: Quite right; you were perfectly right, Mr. Hovstad.

MRS. STOCKMANN: Yes, Thomas is really indefatigable when it is a question of the Baths.

PETER STOCKMANN: Well—remember, he is the Medical Officer to the Baths.

HOVSTAD: Yes, and what is more, they owe their existence to him.

PETER STOCKMANN: To him? Indeed! It is true I have heard from time to time that some people are of that opinion. At the same time I must say I imagined that I took a modest part in the enterprise.

MRS. STOCKMANN: Yes, that is what Thomas is always saying.

HOVSTAD: But who denies it, Mr. Stockmann? You set the thing going and made a practical concern of it; we all know that. I only meant that the idea of it came first from the doctor.

PETER STOCKMANN: Oh, ideas—yes! My brother has had plenty of them in his time—unfortunately. But when it is a question of putting an idea into practical shape, you have to apply to a man of different mettle, Mr. Hovstad. And I certainly should have thought that in this house at least—

MRS. STOCKMANN: My dear Peter—

HOVSTAD: How can you think that—?

MRS. STOCKMANN: Won't you go in and have something, Mr. Hovstad? My husband is sure to be back directly.

HOVSTAD: Thank you, perhaps just a morsel. (*Goes into the dining-room.*)

PETER STOCKMANN: (*lowering his voice a little*) It is a curious thing that these farmers' sons never seem to lose their want of tact.

MRS. STOCKMANN: Surely it is not worth bothering about! Cannot you and Thomas share the credit as brothers?

PETER STOCKMANN: I would have thought so; but apparently some people are not satisfied with a share.

MRS. STOCKMANN: What nonsense! You and Thomas get on so capitally together. (*Listens.*) There he is at last, I think.

(*Goes out and opens the door leading to the hall.*)

DR. STOCKMANN: (*laughing and talking outside*) Look here—here is another guest for you, Katherine. Isn't that jolly? Come in, Captain Horster; hang your coat up on this peg. Ah, you don't wear an overcoat. Just think, Katherine; I met him in the street and could hardly persuade him to come up! (CAPTAIN HORSTER *comes into the room and greets* MRS. STOCKMANN. *He is followed by* DR. STOCKMANN.) Come along in, boys. They are ravenously hungry again, you know. Come along,

Captain Horster; you must have a slice of beef.

(*Pushes* HORSTER *into the dining-room.* EJLIF *and* MORTEN *go in after them.*)

MRS. STOCKMANN: But Thomas, don't you see—?

DR. STOCKMANN: (*turning in the doorway*) Oh, is it you, Peter? (*Shakes hands with him.*) Now that is very delightful.

PETER STOCKMANN: Unfortunately I must go in a moment—

DR. STOCKMANN: Rubbish! There is some toddy just coming in. You haven't forgotten the toddy, Katherine?

MRS. STOCKMANN: Of course not; the water is boiling now.
(*Goes into the dining-room.*)

PETER STOCKMANN: Toddy too!

DR. STOCKMANN: Yes, sit down and we will have it comfortably.

PETER STOCKMANN: Thanks, I never care about an evening's drinking.

DR. STOCKMANN: But this isn't an evening's drinking.

PETER STOCKMANN: It seems to me—. (*Looks towards the dining-room.*) It is extraordinary how they can put away all that food.

DR. STOCKMANN: (*rubbing his hands*) Yes, isn't it splendid to see young people eat? They have always got an appetite, you know! That's as it should be. Lots of food—to build up their strength! They are the people who are going to stir up the fermenting forces of the future, Peter.

PETER STOCKMANN: May I ask what they will find here to "stir up," as you put it?

DR. STOCKMANN: Ah, you must ask the young people that—when the time comes. We shan't be able to see it, of course. That stands to reason—two old fogies, like us—

PETER STOCKMANN: Really, really! I must say that is an extremely odd expression to—

DR. STOCKMANN: Oh, you mustn't take me too literally, Peter. I am so heartily happy and contented, you know. I think it is such an extraordinary piece of good fortune to be in the middle of all this growing, germinating life. It is a splendid time to live in! It is as if a whole new world were being created around one.

PETER STOCKMANN: Do you really think so?

DR. STOCKMANN: Ah, naturally you can't appreciate it as keenly as I. You have lived all your life in these surroundings, and your impressions have got blunted. But I, who have been buried all these years in my little corner up north, almost without ever seeing a stranger who might bring new ideas with him—well, in my case it has just the same effect as if I had been transported into the middle of a crowded city.

PETER STOCKMANN: Oh, a city—!

DR. STOCKMANN: I know, I know; it is all cramped enough here, compared with many other places. But there is life here—there is promise—there are innumerable things to work for and fight for; and that is the main thing. (*Calls.*) Katherine, hasn't the postman been here?

MRS. STOCKMANN: (*from the dining-room*) No.

DR. STOCKMANN: And then to be comfortably off, Peter! That is something one learns to value, when one has been on the brink of starvation, as we have.

PETER STOCKMANN: Oh, surely—

DR. STOCKMANN: Indeed I can assure you we have often been very hard put to it, up there. And now to be able to live like a lord! Today, for instance, we had roast beef for dinner—and, what is more, for supper too. Won't you come and have a little bit? Or let me show it to you, at any rate? Come here—

PETER STOCKMANN: No, no—not for worlds!

DR. STOCKMANN: Well, but just come here then. Do you see, we have got a table-cover?

PETER STOCKMANN: Yes, I noticed it.

DR. STOCKMANN: And we have got a lamp-shade too. Do you see? All out of Katherine's savings! It makes the room so cosy. Don't you think so? Just stand here for a moment—no, no, not there—just here, that's it! Look now, when you get the light on it altogether—I really think it looks very nice, doesn't it?

PETER STOCKMANN: Oh, if you can afford luxuries of this kind—

DR. STOCKMANN: Yes, I can afford it now. Katherine tells me I earn almost as much as we spend.

PETER STOCKMANN: Almost—yes!

DR. STOCKMANN: But a scientific man must live in a little bit of style. I am quite sure an ordinary civil servant spends more in a year than I do.

PETER STOCKMANN: I daresay. A civil servant—a man in a well-paid position—

DR. STOCKMANN: Well, any ordinary merchant, then! A man in that position spends two or three times as much as—

PETER STOCKMANN: It just depends on circumstances.

DR. STOCKMANN: At all events I assure you I don't waste money unprofitably. But I can't find it in my heart to deny myself the pleasure of entertaining my friends. I need that sort of thing, you know. I have lived for so long shut out of it all that it is a necessity of life to me to mix with young, eager, ambitious men, men of liberal and active minds; and that describes every one of those fellows who are enjoying their supper in there. I wish you knew more of Hovstad—

PETER STOCKMANN: By the way, Hovstad was telling me he was going to print another article of yours.

DR. STOCKMANN: An article of mine?

PETER STOCKMANN: Yes, about the Baths. An article you wrote in the winter.

DR. STOCKMANN: Oh, that one! No, I don't intend that to appear just for the present.

PETER STOCKMANN: Why not? It seems to me that this would be the most opportune moment.

DR. STOCKMANN: Yes, very likely—under normal conditions. (*Crosses the room.*)

PETER STOCKMANN: (*following him with his eyes*) Is there anything abnormal about the present conditions?

DR. STOCKMANN: (*standing still*) To tell you the truth, Peter, I can't say just at this moment—at all events not tonight. There may be much that is very abnormal about the present conditions—and it is possible there may be nothing abnormal about them at all. It is quite possible it may be merely my imagination.

PETER STOCKMANN: I must say it all sounds most mysterious. Is there something going on that I am to be kept in ignorance of? I should have imagined that I, as Chairman of the governing body of the Baths—

DR. STOCKMANN: And I should have imagined that I—. Oh, come, don't let us fly out at one another, Peter.

PETER STOCKMANN: Heaven forbid! I am not in the habit of flying out at people, as you call it. But I am entitled to request most emphatically that all arrangements shall be made in a business-like manner, through the proper channels, and shall be dealt with by the legally constituted authorities. I can allow no going behind our backs by any roundabout means.

DR. STOCKMANN: Have I ever at any time tried to go behind your backs?

PETER STOCKMANN: You have an ingrained tendency to take your own way, at all events; and that is almost equally inadmissible in a well-ordered community. The individual ought undoubtedly to acquiesce in subordinating himself to the community—or, to speak more accurately, to the authorities who have the care of the community's welfare.

DR. STOCKMANN: Very likely. But what the deuce has all this got to do with me?

PETER STOCKMANN: That is exactly what you never appear to be willing to learn, my dear Thomas. But, mark my words, some day you will have to suffer for it—sooner or later. Now I have told you. Good-bye.

DR. STOCKMANN: Have you taken leave of your senses? You are on the wrong scent altogether.

PETER STOCKMANN: I am not usually that. You must excuse me now if I—(*calls into the dining-room*). Good night, Katherine. Good night, gentlemen.
(*Goes out.*)

MRS. STOCKMANN: (*coming from the dining-room*) Has he gone?

DR. STOCKMANN: Yes, and in such a bad temper.

MRS. STOCKMANN: But, dear Thomas, what have you been doing to him again?

DR. STOCKMANN: Nothing at all. And, anyhow, he can't oblige me to make my report before the proper time.

MRS. STOCKMANN: What have you got to make a report to him about?

DR. STOCKMANN: Hm! Leave that to me, Katherine.—It is an extraordinary thing that the postman doesn't come.
(HOVSTAD, BILLING, *and* HORSTER *have got up from the table and come into the sitting-room*. EJLIF *and* MORTEN *come in after them.*)

BILLING: (*stretching himself*) Ah!—one feels a new man after a meal like that.

HOVSTAD: The mayor wasn't in a very sweet temper tonight, then.

DR. STOCKMANN: It is his stomach; he has a wretched digestion.

HOVSTAD: I rather think it was us two of the "People's Messenger" that he couldn't digest.

MRS. STOCKMANN: I thought you came out of it pretty well with him.

HOVSTAD: Oh yes; but it isn't anything more than a sort of truce.

BILLING: That is just what it is! That word sums up the situation.

DR. STOCKMANN: We must remember that Peter is a lonely man, poor chap. He has no home comforts of any kind; nothing but everlasting business. And all that infernal weak tea wash that he pours into himself! Now then, my boys, bring chairs up to the table. Aren't we going to have that toddy, Katherine?

MRS. STOCKMANN: (*going into the dining-room*) I am just getting it.

DR. STOCKMANN: Sit down here on the couch beside me, Captain Horster. We so seldom see you—. Please sit down, my friends.

(*They sit down at the table.* MRS. STOCKMANN *brings a tray, with a spirit-lamp, glasses, bottles, etc., upon it.*)

MRS. STOCKMANN: There you are! This is arrack, and this is rum, and this one is the brandy. Now every one must help himself.

DR. STOCKMANN: (*taking a glass*) We will. (*They all mix themselves some toddy.*) And let us have the cigars, Ejlif, you know where the box is. And you, Morten, can fetch my pipe. (*The two boys go into the room on the right.*) I have a suspicion that Ejlif pockets a cigar now and then!—but I take no notice of it. (*Calls out.*) And my smoking-cap too, Morten. Katherine, you can tell him where I left it. Ah, he has got it. (*The boys bring the various things.*) Now, my friends. I stick to my pipe, you know. This one has seen plenty of bad weather with me up north. (*Touches glasses with them.*) Your good health! Ah! it is good to be sitting snug and warm here.

MRS. STOCKMANN: (*who sits knitting*) Do you sail soon, Captain Horster?

HORSTER: I expect to be ready to sail next week.

MRS. STOCKMANN: I suppose you are going to America?

HORSTER: Yes, that is the plan.

MRS. STOCKMANN: Then you won't be able to take part in the coming election.

HORSTER: Is there going to be an election?

BILLING: Didn't you know?

HORSTER: No, I don't mix myself up with those things.

BILLING: But do you not take an interest in public affairs?

HORSTER: No, I don't know anything about politics.

BILLING: All the same, one ought to vote, at any rate.

HORSTER: Even if one doesn't know anything about what is going on?

BILLING: Doesn't know! What do you mean by that? A community is like a ship; every one ought to be prepared to take the helm.

HORSTER: Maybe that is all very well on shore, but on board ship it wouldn't work.

HOVSTAD: It is astonishing how little most sailors care about what goes on on shore.

BILLING: Very extraordinary.

DR. STOCKMANN: Sailors are like birds of passage; they feel equally at home in any latitude. And that is only an additional reason for our being all the more keen, Hovstad. Is there to be anything of public interest in tomorrow's "Messenger"?

HOVSTAD: Nothing about municipal affairs. But the day after to-morrow I was thinking of printing your article—

DR. STOCKMANN: Ah, devil take it—my article! Look here, that must wait a bit.

HOVSTAD: Really? We had just got convenient space for it, and I thought it was just the opportune moment—

DR. STOCKMANN: Yes, yes, very likely you are right; but it must wait all the same. I will explain to you later.

(PETRA *comes in from the hall, in hat and cloak and with a bundle of exercise books under her arm.*)

PETRA: Good evening.

DR. STOCKMANN: Good evening, Petra; come along.

(*Mutual greetings;* PETRA *takes off her things and puts them down on a chair by the door.*)

PETRA: And you have all been sitting here enjoying yourselves, while I have been out slaving!

DR. STOCKMANN: Well, come and enjoy yourself too!

BILLING: May I mix a glass for you?

PETRA: (*coming to the table*) Thanks, I would rather do it; you always mix it too strong. But I forgot, father—I have a letter for you.

(*Goes to the chair where she has laid her things.*)

DR. STOCKMANN: A letter? From whom?

PETRA: (*looking in her coat pocket*) The postman gave it to me just as I was going out—

DR. STOCKMANN: (*getting up and going to her*) And you only give it to me now!

PETRA: I really had no time to run up again. There it is!

DR. STOCKMANN: (*seizing the letter*) Let's see, let's see, child! (*Looks at the address.*) Yes, that's all right!

MRS. STOCKMANN: Is it the one you have been expecting so anxiously, Thomas?

DR. STOCKMANN: Yes, it is. I must go to my room now and—. Where shall I get a light, Katherine? Is there no lamp in my room again?

MRS. STOCKMANN: Yes, your lamp is all ready lit on your desk.

DR. STOCKMANN: Good, good. Excuse me for a moment—.

(*Goes into his study.*)

PETRA: What do you suppose it is, mother?

MRS. STOCKMANN: I don't know; for the last day or two he has always been asking if the postman has not been.

BILLING: Probably some country patient.

PETRA: Poor old dad!—he will overwork himself soon. (*Mixes a glass for herself.*) There, that will taste good!

HOVSTAD: Have you been teaching in the evening school again today?

PETRA: (*sipping from her glass*) Two hours.

BILLING: And four hours of school in the morning—

PETRA: Five hours.

MRS. STOCKMANN: And you have still got exercises to correct, I see.

PETRA: A whole heap, yes.

HORSTER: You are pretty full up with work too, it seems to me.

PETRA: Yes—but that is good. One is so delightfully tired after it.

BILLING: Do you like that?

PETRA: Yes, because one sleeps so well then.

MORTEN: You must be dreadfully wicked, Petra.

PETRA: Wicked?

MORTEN: Yes, because you work so much. Mr. Rörlund says work is a punishment for our sins.

EJLIF: Pooh, what a duffer you are, to believe a thing like that!

MRS. STOCKMANN: Come, come, Ejlif!

BILLING: (*laughing*) That's capital!

HOVSTAD: Don't you want to work as hard as that, Morten?

MORTEN: No, indeed I don't.

HOVSTAD: What do you want to be, then?

MORTEN: I should like best to be a Viking.

EJLIF: You would have to be a pagan then.

MORTEN: Well, I could become a pagan, couldn't I?

BILLING: I agree with you, Morten! My sentiments, exactly.

MRS. STOCKMANN: (*signalling to him*) I am sure that is not true, Mr. Billing.

BILLING: Yes, I swear it is! I am a pagan, and I am proud of it. Believe me, before long we shall all be pagans.

MORTEN: And then shall be allowed to do anything we like?

BILLING: Well, you see, Morten—.

MRS. STOCKMANN: You must go to your room now, boys; I am sure you have some lessons to learn for tomorrow.

EJLIF: I should like so much to stay a little longer—

MRS. STOCKMANN: No, no; away you go, both of you.

(*The boys say good-night and go into the room on the left.*)

HOVSTAD: Do you really think it can do the boys any harm to hear such things?

MRS. STOCKMANN: I don't know, but I don't like it.

PETRA: But you know, mother, I think you really are wrong about it.

MRS. STOCKMANN: Maybe, but I don't like it—not in our own home.

PETRA: There is so much falsehood both at home and at school. At home one must not speak, and at school we have to stand and tell lies to the children.

HORSTER: Tell lies?

PETRA: Yes, don't you suppose we have to teach them all sorts of things that we don't believe?

BILLING: That is perfectly true.

PETRA: If only I had the means I would start a school of my own, and it would be conducted on very different lines.

BILLING: Oh, bother the means—!

HORSTER: Well, if you are thinking of that, Miss Stockmann, I shall be delighted to provide you with a school-room. The great big old house my father left me is standing almost empty; there is an immense dining-room downstairs—

PETRA: (*laughing*) Thank you very

much; but I am afraid nothing will come of it.

HOVSTAD: No, Miss Petra is much more likely to take to journalism, I expect. By the way, have you had time to do anything with that English story you promised to translate for us?

PETRA: No, not yet; but you shall have it in good time.

(DR. STOCKMANN *comes in from his room with an open letter in his hand.*)

DR. STOCKMANN: (*waving the letter*) Well, now the town will have something new to talk about, I can tell you!

BILLING: Something new?

MRS. STOCKMANN: What is this?

DR. STOCKMANN: A great discovery, Katherine.

HOVSTAD: Really?

MRS. STOCKMANN: A discovery of yours?

DR. STOCKMANN: A discovery of mine. (*Walks up and down.*) Just let them come saying, as usual, that it is all fancy and a crazy man's imagination! But they will be careful what they say this time, I can tell you!

PETRA: But, father, tell us what it is.

DR. STOCKMANN: Yes, yes—only give me time, and you shall all know about it. If only I had Peter here now! It just shows how we men can go about forming our judgments, when in reality we are as blind as any moles—

HOVSTAD: What are you driving at, Doctor?

DR. STOCKMANN: (*standing still by the table*) Isn't it the universal opinion that our town is a healthy spot?

HOVSTAD: Certainly.

DR. STOCKMANN: Quite an unusually healthy spot, in fact—a place that deserves to be recommended in the warmest possible manner either for invalids or for people who are well—

MRS. STOCKMANN: Yes, but my dear Thomas—

DR. STOCKMANN: And we have been recommending it and praising it—I have written and written, both in the "Messenger" and in pamphlets—

HOVSTAD: Well, what then?

DR. STOCKMANN: And the Baths—we have called them the "main artery of the town's life-blood," the "nerve-centre of our town," and the devil knows what else—

BILLING: "The town's pulsating heart" was the expression I once used on an important occasion—

DR. STOCKMANN: Quite so. Well, do you know what they really are, these great, splendid, much praised Baths, that have cost so much money—do you know what they are?

HOVSTAD: No, what are they?

MRS. STOCKMANN: Yes, what are they?

DR. STOCKMANN: The whole place is a pesthouse!

PETRA: The Baths, father?

MRS. STOCKMANN: (*at the same time*) Our Baths!

HOVSTAD: But, Doctor—

BILLING: Absolutely incredible!

DR. STOCKMANN: The whole Bath establishment is a whited, poisoned sepulchre, I tell you—the gravest possible danger to the public health! All the nastiness up at Mölledal, all that stinking filth, is infecting the water in the conduit-pipes leading to the reservoir; and the same cursed, filthy poison oozes out on the shore too—

HORSTER: Where the bathing-place is?

DR. STOCKMANN: Just there.

HOVSTAD: How do you come to be so certain of all this, Doctor?

DR. STOCKMANN: I have investigated the matter most conscientiously. For a long time past I have suspected something of the kind. Last year we had some very strange cases of illness among the visitors —typhoid cases, and cases of gastric fever—

MRS. STOCKMANN: Yes, that is quite true.

DR. STOCKMANN: At the time, we supposed the visitors had been infected before they came; but later on, in the winter, I began to have a different opinion; and so I set myself to examine the water, as well as I could.

MRS. STOCKMANN: Then that is what you have been so busy with?

DR. STOCKMANN: Indeed I have been busy, Katherine. But here I had none of the necessary scientific apparatus, so I sent samples, both of the drinking-water and of the sea-water, up to the University, to have an accurate analysis made by a chemist.

HOVSTAD: And have you got that?

DR. STOCKMANN: (showing him the letter) Here it is! It proves the presence of decomposing organic matter in the water—it is full of infusoria. The water is absolutely dangerous to use, either internally or externally.

MRS. STOCKMANN: What a mercy you discovered it in time.

DR. STOCKMANN: You may well say so.

HOVSTAD: And what do you propose to do now, Doctor?

DR. STOCKMANN: To see the matter put right—naturally.

HOVSTAD: Can that be done?

DR. STOCKMANN: It must be done. Otherwise the Baths will be absolutely useless and wasted. But we need not anticipate that; I have a very clear idea what we shall have to do.

MRS. STOCKMANN: But why have you kept this all so secret, dear?

DR. STOCKMANN: Do you suppose I was going to run about the town gossiping about it, before I had absolute proof? No, thank you. I am not such a fool.

PETRA: Still, you might have told us—

DR. STOCKMANN: Not a living soul. But to-morrow you may run round to the old Badger—

MRS. STOCKMANN: Oh, Thomas! Thomas!

DR. STOCKMANN: Well, to your grandfather, then. The old boy will have something to be astonished at! I know he thinks I am cracked—and there are lots of other people think so too, I have noticed. But now these good folks shall see—they shall just see—! (*Walks about, rubbing his hands.*) There will be a nice upset in the town, Katherine; you can't imagine what it will be. All the conduit-pipes will have to be relaid.

HOVSTAD: (*getting up*) All the conduit-pipes—?

DR. STOCKMANN: Yes, of course. The intake is too low down; it will have to be lifted to a position much higher up.

PETRA: Then you were right after all.

DR. STOCKMANN: Ah, you remember, Petra—I wrote opposing the plans before the work was begun. But at that time no one would listen to me. Well, I am going to let them have it, now! Of course I have prepared a report for the Baths Committee; I have had it ready for a week, and was only waiting for this to come. (*Shows the letter.*) Now it shall go off at once. (*Goes into his room and comes back with some papers.*) Look at that! Four closely written sheets!—and the letter shall go with them. Give me a bit of paper, Katherine—something to wrap them up in. That will do! Now give it to—to—(*stamps his foot*)—what the deuce is her name?—give it to the maid, and tell her to take it at once to the Mayor.

(MRS. STOCKMANN *takes the packet and goes out through the dining-room.*)

PETRA: What do you think uncle Peter will say, father?

DR. STOCKMANN: What is there for him to say? I should think he would be very glad that such an important truth has been brought to light.

HOVSTAD: Will you let me print a short note about your discovery in the "Messenger?"

DR. STOCKMANN: I shall be very much obliged if you will.

HOVSTAD: It is very desirable that the public should be informed of it without delay.

DR. STOCKMANN: Certainly.

MRS. STOCKMANN: (*coming back*) She has just gone with it.

BILLING: Upon my soul, Doctor, you are going to be the foremost man in the town!

DR. STOCKMANN: (*walking about happily*) Nonsense! As a matter of fact I have done nothing more than my duty. I have only made a lucky find—that's all. Still, all the same—

BILLING: Hovstad, don't you think the town ought to give Dr. Stockmann some sort of testimonial?

HOVSTAD: I will suggest it, anyway.

BILLING: And I will speak to Aslaksen about it.

DR. STOCKMANN: No, my good friends, don't let us have any of that nonsense. I won't hear of anything of the kind. And if the Baths Committee should think of voting me an increase of salary, I will not accept it. Do you hear, Katherine?— I won't accept it.

MRS. STOCKMANN: You are quite right, Thomas.

PETRA: (*lifting her glass*) Your health, father!

HOVSTAD *and* BILLING: Your health, Doctor! Good health!

HORSTER: (*touches glasses with* DR. STOCKMANN) I hope it will bring you nothing but good luck.

DR. STOCKMANN: Thank you, thank you, my dear fellows! I feel tremendously happy! It is a splendid thing for a man to be able to feel that he has done a service to his native town and to his fellow-citizens. Hurrah, Katherine!

(*He puts his arms round her and whirls her round and round, while she protests with laughing cries. They all laugh, clap their hands and cheer the* DOCTOR. *The boys put their heads in at the door to see what is going on.*)

CURTAIN

ACT II

SCENE: *The same. The door into the dining-room is shut. It is morning.* MRS. STOCKMANN, *with a sealed letter in her hand, comes in from the dining-room, goes to the door of the* DOCTOR'S *study and peeps in.*

MRS. STOCKMANN: Are you in, Thomas?

DR. STOCKMANN: (*from within his room*) Yes, I have just come in. (*Comes into the room.*) What is it?

MRS. STOCKMANN: A letter from your brother.

DR. STOCKMANN: Aha, let us see! (*Opens the letter and reads:*) "I return herewith the manuscript you sent me"— (*reads on in a low murmur*) Hm!—

MRS. STOCKMANN: What does he say?

DR. STOCKMANN: (*putting the papers in his pocket*) Oh, he only writes that he will come up here himself about midday.

MRS. STOCKMANN: Well, try and remember to be at home this time.

DR. STOCKMANN: That will be all right; I have got through all my morning visits.

MRS. STOCKMANN: I am extremely curious to know how he takes it.

DR. STOCKMANN: You will see he won't like it's having been I, and not he, that made the discovery.

MRS. STOCKMANN: Aren't you a little nervous about that?

DR. STOCKMANN: Oh, he really will be pleased enough, you know. But, at the same time, Peter is so confoundedly afraid of anyone's doing any service to the town except himself.

MRS. STOCKMANN: I will tell you what, Thomas—you should be good-natured, and share the credit of this with him. Couldn't you make out that it was he who set you on the scent of this discovery?

DR. STOCKMANN: I am quite willing. If only I can get the thing set right. I— (MORTEN KIIL *puts his head in through the door leading from the hall, looks round in an enquiring manner and chuckles.*)

MORTEN KIIL: (*slyly*) Is it—is it true?

MRS. STOCKMANN: (*going to the door*) Father!—is it you?

DR. STOCKMANN: Ah, Mr. Kiil—good morning, good morning!

MRS. STOCKMANN: But come along in.

MORTEN KIIL: If it is true, I will; if not, I am off.

DR. STOCKMANN: If what is true?

MORTEN KIIL: This tale about the water-supply. Is it true?

DR. STOCKMANN: Certainly it is true. But how did you come to hear it?

MORTEN KIIL: (*coming in*) Petra ran in on her way to the school—

DR. STOCKMANN: Did she?

MORTEN KIIL: Yes; and she declares that—. I thought she was only making a fool of me, but it isn't like Petra to do that.

DR. STOCKMANN: Of course not. How could you imagine such a thing?

MORTEN KIIL: Oh well, it is better never to trust anybody; you may find you have been made a fool of before you know where you are. But it is really true, all the same?

DR. STOCKMANN: You can depend upon it that it is true. Won't you sit down? (*Settles him on the couch.*) Isn't it a real bit of luck for the town—

MORTEN KIIL: (*suppressing his laughter*) A bit of luck for the town?

DR. STOCKMANN: Yes, that I made the discovery in good time.

MORTEN KIIL: (*as before*) Yes, yes, yes!—But I should never have thought you the sort of man to pull your own brother's leg like this!

DR. STOCKMANN: Pull his leg!

MRS. STOCKMANN: Really, father dear—

MORTEN KIIL: (*resting his hands and his chin on the handle of his stick and winking slyly at the* DOCTOR) Let me see, what was the story? Some kind of beast that had got into the water-pipes, wasn't it?

DR. STOCKMANN: Infusoria—yes.

MORTEN KIIL: And a lot of these beasts had got in, according to Petra—a tremendous lot.

DR. STOCKMANN: Certainly; hundreds of thousands of them, probably.

MORTEN KIIL: But no one can see them —isn't that so?

DR. STOCKMANN: Yes; you can't see them.

MORTEN KIIL: (*with a quiet chuckle*) Damme—it's the finest story I have ever heard!

DR. STOCKMANN: What do you mean?

MORTEN KIIL: But you will never get the Mayor to believe a thing like that.

DR. STOCKMANN: We shall see.

MORTEN KIIL: Do you think he will be fool enough to—?

DR. STOCKMANN: I hope the whole town will be fools enough.

MORTEN KIIL: The whole town! Well, it wouldn't be a bad thing. It would just serve them right, and teach them a lesson. They think themselves so much cleverer than we old fellows. They hounded me out of the council; they did, I tell you—they hounded me out. Now they shall pay for it. You pull their legs too, Thomas!

DR. STOCKMANN: Really, I—

MORTEN KIIL: You pull their legs! (*Gets up.*) If you can work it so that the Mayor and his friends all swallow the same bait, I will give ten pounds to a charity—like a shot!

DR. STOCKMANN: That is very kind of you.

MORTEN KIIL: Yes, I haven't got much money to throw away, I can tell you; but if you can work this, I will give five pounds to a charity at Christmas.

(HOVSTAD *comes in by the hall door.*)

HOVSTAD: Good morning! (*Stops.*) Oh, I beg your pardon—

DR. STOCKMANN: Not at all; come in.

MORTEN KIIL: (*with another chuckle.*) Oho!—is he in this too?

HOVSTAD: What do you mean?

DR. STOCKMANN: Certainly he is.

MORTEN KIIL: I might have known it! It must get into the papers. You know how to do it, Thomas! Set your wits to work. Now I must go.

DR. STOCKMANN: Won't you stay a little while?

MORTEN KIIL: No, I must be off now. You keep up this game for all it is worth; you won't repent it, I'm damned if you will!

(*He goes out;* MRS. STOCKMANN *follows him into the hall.*)

DR. STOCKMANN: (*laughing*) Just imagine—the old chap doesn't believe a word of all this about the water-supply.

HOVSTAD: Oh, that was it, then?

DR. STOCKMANN: Yes, that was what we were talking about. Perhaps it is the same thing that brings you here?

HOVSTAD: Yes, it is. Can you spare me a few minutes, Doctor?

DR. STOCKMANN: As long as you like, my dear fellow.

HOVSTAD: Have you heard from the Mayor yet?

DR. STOCKMANN: Not yet. He is coming here later.

HOVSTAD: I have given the matter a great deal of thought since last night.

DR. STOCKMANN: Well?

HOVSTAD: From your point of view, as a doctor and a man of science, this affair of the water-supply is an isolated matter. I mean, you do not realise that it involves a great many other things.

DR. STOCKMANN: How do you mean? —Let us sit down, my dear fellow. No, sit here on the couch. (HOVSTAD *sits down on the couch,* DR. STOCKMANN *on a chair on the other side of the table.*) Now then. You mean that—?

HOVSTAD: You said yesterday that the pollution of the water was due to impurities in the soil.

DR. STOCKMANN: Yes, unquestionably it is due to that poisonous morass up at Mölledal.

HOVSTAD: Begging your pardon, doctor, I fancy it is due to quite another morass altogether.

DR. STOCKMANN: What morass?

HOVSTAD: The morass that the whole life of our town is built on and is rotting in.

DR. STOCKMANN: What the deuce are you driving at, Hovstad?

HOVSTAD: The whole of the town's interests have, little by little, got into the hands of a pack of officials.

DR. STOCKMANN: Oh, come!—they are not all officials.

HOVSTAD: No, but those that are not officials are at any rate the officials' friends and adherents; it is the wealthy folk, the old families in the town, that have got us entirely in their hands.

DR. STOCKMANN: Yes, but after all they are men of ability and knowledge.

HOVSTAD: Did they show any ability or knowledge when they laid the conduit-pipes where they are now?

DR. STOCKMANN: No, of course that was a great piece of stupidity on their part. But that is going to be set right now.

HOVSTAD: Do you think that will be all such plain sailing?

DR. STOCKMANN: Plain sailing or no, it has got to be done, anyway.

HOVSTAD: Yes, provided the press takes up the question.

DR. STOCKMANN: I don't think that will be necessary, my dear fellow; I am certain my brother—

HOVSTAD: Excuse me, doctor; I feel bound to tell you I am inclined to take the matter up.

DR. STOCKMANN: In the paper?

HOVSTAD: Yes. When I took over the "People's Messenger," my idea was to break up this ring of self-opinionated old fossils who had got hold of all the influence.

DR. STOCKMANN: But you know you told me yourself what the result had been; you nearly ruined your paper.

HOVSTAD: Yes, at the time we were obliged to climb down a peg or two, it is quite true, because there was a danger of the whole project of the Baths coming to nothing if they failed us. But now the scheme has been carried through, and we can dispense with these grand gentlemen.

DR. STOCKMANN: Dispense with them, yes; but we owe them a great debt of gratitude.

HOVSTAD: That shall be recognised ungrudgingly. But a journalist of my democratic tendencies cannot let such an opportunity as this slip. The bubble of official infallibility must be pricked. The superstition must be destroyed, like any other.

DR. STOCKMANN: I am whole-heartedly with you in that, Mr. Hovstad; if it is a superstition, away with it!

HOVSTAD: I should be very reluctant to bring the Mayor into it, because he is your brother. But I am sure you will agree with me that truth should be the first consideration.

DR. STOCKMANN: That goes without saying. (*With sudden emphasis.*) Yes, but—but—

HOVSTAD: You must not misjudge me. I am neither more self-interested nor more ambitious than most men.

DR. STOCKMANN: My dear fellow— who suggests anything of the kind?

HOVSTAD: I am of humble origin, as you know; and that has given me opportunities of knowing what is the most crying need in the humbler ranks of life. It is that they should be allowed some part in the direction of public affairs, Doctor. That is what will develop their faculties and intelligence and self-respect—

DR. STOCKMANN: I quite appreciate that.

HOVSTAD: Yes—and in my opinion a journalist incurs a heavy responsibility if he neglects a favorable opportunity of emancipating the masses—the humble and oppressed. I know well enough that in exalted circles I shall be called an agitator, and all that sort of thing; but they may call what they like. If only my conscience doesn't reproach me, then—

DR. STOCKMANN: Quite right! Quite right, Mr. Hovstad. But all the same— devil take it! (*A knock is heard at the door.*) Come in!

(ASLAKSEN *appears at the door. He is poorly but decently dressed, in black, with a slightly crumpled white neckcloth; he wears gloves and has a felt hat in his hand.*)

ASLAKSEN: (*bowing*) Excuse my taking the liberty, Doctor—

DR. STOCKMANN: (*getting up*) Ah, it is you, Aslaksen!

ASLAKSEN: Yes, Doctor.

HOVSTAD: (*standing up*) Is it me you want, Aslaksen?

ASLAKSEN: No; I didn't know I should find you here. No, it was the Doctor I—

DR. STOCKMANN: I am quite at your service. What is it?

ASLAKSEN: Is what I heard from Mr. Billing true, sir—that you mean to improve our water-supply?

DR. STOCKMANN: Yes, for the Baths.

ASLAKSEN: Quite so, I understand. Well, I have come to say that I will back that up by every means in my power.

HOVSTAD: (*to the* DOCTOR) You see!

DR. STOCKMANN: I shall be very grateful to you but—

ASLAKSEN: Because it may be no bad thing to have us small tradesmen at your back. We form, as it were, a compact majority in the town—if we choose. And it is always a good thing to have the majority with you, Doctor.

DR. STOCKMANN: That is undeniably true; but I confess I don't see why such unusual precautions should be necessary in this case. It seems to me that such a plain, straightforward thing—

ASLAKSEN: Oh, it may be very desirable, all the same. I know our local authorities so well; officials are not generally very ready to act on proposals that come from other people. That is why I think it would not be at all amiss if we made a little demonstration.

HOVSTAD: That's right.

DR. STOCKMANN: Demonstration, did you say? What on earth are you going to make a demonstration about?

ASLAKSEN: We shall proceed with the greatest moderation, Doctor. Moderation is always my aim; it is the greatest virtue in a citizen—at least, I think so.

DR. STOCKMANN: It is well known to be a characteristic of yours, Mr. Aslaksen.

ASLAKSEN: Yes, I think I may pride myself on that. And this matter of the water-supply is of the greatest importance to us small tradesmen. The Baths promise to be a regular gold-mine for the town. We shall all make our living out of them, especially those of us who are householders. That is why we will back up the project as strongly as possible. And as I am at present Chairman of the Householders' Association—

DR. STOCKMANN: Yes—?

ASLAKSEN: And, what is more, local secretary of the Temperance Society—you know, sir, I suppose, that I am a worker in the temperance cause?

DR. STOCKMANN: Of course, of course.

ASLAKSEN: Well, you can understand that I come into contact with a great many people. And as I have the reputation of a temperate and law-abiding citizen—like yourself, Doctor—I have a certain influence in the town, a little bit of power, if I may be allowed to say so.

DR. STOCKMANN: I know that quite well, Mr. Aslaksen.

ASLAKSEN: So you see it would be an easy matter for me to set on foot some testimonial, if necessary.

DR. STOCKMANN: A testimonial?

ASLAKSEN: Yes, some kind of address of thanks from the townsmen for your share in a matter of such importance to the community. I need scarcely say that it would have to be drawn up with the greatest regard to moderation, so as not to offend the authorities—who, after all, have the reins in their hands. If we pay strict attention to that, no one can take it amiss, I should think!

HOVSTAD: Well, and even supposing they didn't like it—

ASLAKSEN: No, no, no; there must be no discourtesy to the authorities, Mr. Hovstad. It is no use falling foul of those upon whom our welfare so closely depends. I have done that in my time, and no good ever comes of it. But no one can take exception to a reasonable and frank expression of a citizen's views.

DR. STOCKMANN: (*shaking him by the hand*) I can't tell you, dear Mr. Aslaksen, how extremely pleased I am to find such hearty support among my fellow-citizens. I am delighted—delighted! Now, you will take a small glass of sherry, eh?

ASLAKSEN: No, thank you; I never drink alcohol of that kind.

DR. STOCKMANN: Well, what do you say to a glass of beer, then?

ASLAKSEN: Nor that either, thank you, Doctor. I never drink anything as early as this. I am going into town now to talk this over with one or two householders, and prepare the ground.

DR. STOCKMANN: It is tremendously kind of you, Mr. Aslaksen; but I really cannot understand the necessity for all these precautions. It seems to me that the thing should go of itself.

ASLAKSEN: The authorities are somewhat slow to move, Doctor. Far be it from me to seem to blame them—

HOVSTAD: We are going to stir them up in the paper to-morrow, Aslaksen.

ASLAKSEN: But not violently, I trust, Mr. Hovstad. Proceed with moderation, or you will do nothing with them. You may take my advice; I have gathered my experience in the school of life. Well, I must say good-bye, Doctor. You know now that we small tradesmen are at your back at all events, like a solid wall. You have the compact majority on your side, Doctor.

DR. STOCKMANN: I am very much obliged, dear Mr. Aslaksen. (*Shakes hands with him.*) Good-bye, good-bye.

ASLAKSEN: Are you going my way, towards the printing-office, Mr. Hovstad?

HOVSTAD: I will come later; I have something to settle up first.

ASLAKSEN: Very well.

(*Bows and goes out;* STOCKMANN *follows him into the hall.*)

HOVSTAD: (*as* STOCKMANN *comes in again*) Well, what do you think of that, Doctor? Don't you think it is high time we stirred a little life into all this slackness and vacillation and cowardice?

DR. STOCKMANN: Are you referring to Aslaksen?

HOVSTAD: Yes, I am. He is one of those who are floundering in a bog—decent enough fellow though he may be, otherwise. And most of the people here are in just the same case—seesawing and edging first to one side and then to the other, so overcome with caution and scruple that they never dare to take any decided step.

DR. STOCKMANN: Yes, but Aslaksen seemed to me so thoroughly well-intentioned.

HOVSTAD: There is one thing I esteem higher than that; and that is for a man to be self-reliant and sure of himself.

DR. STOCKMANN: I think you are perfectly right there.

HOVSTAD: That is why I want to seize this opportunity, and try if I cannot manage to put a little virility into these well-intentioned people for once. The idol of Authority must be shattered in this town. This gross and inexcusable blunder about the water-supply must be brought home to the mind of every municipal voter.

DR. STOCKMANN: Very well; if you are of opinion that it is for the good of the community, so be it. But not until I have had a talk with my brother.

HOVSTAD: Anyway, I will get a leading article ready; and if the Mayor refuses to take the matter up—

DR. STOCKMANN: How can you suppose such a thing possible?

HOVSTAD: It is conceivable. And in that case—

DR. STOCKMANN: In that case I promise you—. Look here, in that case you may print my report—every word of it.

HOVSTAD: May I? Have I your word for it?

DR. STOCKMANN: (*giving him the MS.*) Here it is; take it with you. It can do no harm for you to read it through, and you can give it back to me later on.

HOVSTAD: Good, good! That is what I will do. And now good-bye, Doctor.

DR. STOCKMANN: Good-bye, good-bye. You will see everything will run quite smoothly, Mr. Hovstad—quite smoothly.

HOVSTAD: Hm!—we shall see. (*Bows and goes out.*)

DR. STOCKMANN: (*opens the dining-door and looks in*) Katherine! Oh, you are back, Petra?

PETRA: (*coming in*) Yes, I have just come from the school.

MRS. STOCKMANN: (*coming in*) Has he not been here yet?

DR. STOCKMANN: Peter? No. But I have had a long talk with Hovstad. He is quite excited about my discovery. I find it has a much wider bearing than I at first imagined. And he has put his paper at my disposal if necessity should arise.

MRS. STOCKMANN: Do you think it will?

DR. STOCKMANN: Not for a moment. But at all events it makes me feel proud to know that I have the liberal-minded independent press on my side. Yes, and—just imagine—I have had a visit from the Chairman of the Householders' Association!

MRS. STOCKMANN: Oh! What did he want?

DR. STOCKMANN: To offer me his support too. They will support me in a body if it should be necessary. Katherine—do you know what I have got behind me?

MRS. STOCKMANN: Behind you? No, what have you got behind you?

DR. STOCKMANN: The compact majority.

MRS. STOCKMANN: Really? Is that a good thing for you, Thomas?

DR. STOCKMANN: I should think it was a good thing. (*Walks up and down rubbing his hands.*) By Jove, it's a fine thing to feel this bond of brotherhood between onself and one's fellow-citizens!

PETRA: And to be able to do so much that is good and useful, father!

DR. STOCKMANN: And for one's own native town into the bargain, my child!

MRS. STOCKMANN: That was a ring at the bell.

DR. STOCKMANN: It must be he, then. (*A knock is heard at the door.*) Come in!

PETER STOCKMANN: (*comes in from the hall*) Good morning.

DR. STOCKMANN: Glad to see you, Peter!

MRS. STOCKMANN: Good morning, Peter. How are you?

PETER STOCKMANN: So so, thank you. (*To* DR. STOCKMANN.) I received from you yesterday, after office-hours, a report dealing with the condition of the water at the Baths.

DR. STOCKMANN: Yes. Have you read it?

PETER STOCKMANN: Yes, I have.

DR. STOCKMANN: And what have you to say to it?

PETER STOCKMANN: (*with a sidelong glance*) Hm!—

MRS. STOCKMANN: Come along, Petra. (*She and* PETRA *go into the room on the left.*)

PETER STOCKMANN: (*after a pause*) Was it necessary to make all these investigations behind my back?

DR. STOCKMANN: Yes, because until I was absolutely certain about it—

PETER STOCKMANN: Then you mean that you are absolutely certain now?

DR. STOCKMANN: Surely you are convinced of that.

PETER STOCKMANN: Is it your intention to bring this document before the Baths Committee as a sort of official communication?

DR. STOCKMANN: Certainly. Something must be done in the matter—and that quickly.

PETER STOCKMANN: As usual, you employ violent expressions in your report. You say, amongst other things, that what we offer visitors in our Baths is a permanent supply of poison.

DR. STOCKMANN: Well, can you describe it any other way, Peter? Just think—water that is poisonous, whether you drink it or bathe in it! And this we offer to the poor sick folk who come to us trustfully and pay us at an exorbitant rate to be made well again!

PETER STOCKMANN: And your reasoning leads you to this conclusion, that we must build a sewer to draw off the alleged impurities from Mölledal and must re-lay the water-conduits.

DR. STOCKMANN: Yes. Do you see any other way out of it? I don't.

PETER STOCKMANN: I made a pretext this morning to go and see the town engineer, and, as if only half seriously, broached the subject of these proposals as a thing we might perhaps have to take under consideration some time later on.

DR. STOCKMANN: Some time later on!

PETER STOCKMANN: He smiled at what he considered to be my extravagance, naturally. Have you taken the trouble to consider what your proposed alterations would cost? According to the information I obtained, the expenses would probably mount up to fifteen or twenty thousand pounds.

DR. STOCKMANN: Would it cost so much?

PETER STOCKMANN: Yes; and the worst part of it would be that the work would take at least two years.

DR. STOCKMANN: Two years? Two whole years?

PETER STOCKMANN: At least. And what are we to do with the Baths in the meantime? Close them? Indeed we should be obliged to. And do you suppose any one would come near the place after it had got about that the water was dangerous?

DR. STOCKMANN: Yes, but, Peter, that is what it is.

PETER STOCKMANN: And all this at this juncture—just as the Baths are beginning to be known. There are other towns in the neighborhood with qualifications to attract visitors for bathing purposes. Don't you suppose they would immediately strain every nerve to divert the entire stream of strangers to themselves? Unquestionably they would; and then where should we be? We should probably have to abandon the whole thing, which has cost us so much money—and then you would have ruined your native town.

DR. STOCKMANN: I—should have ruined—!

PETER STOCKMANN: It is simply and solely through the Baths that the town has before it any future worth mentioning. You know that just as well as I.

DR. STOCKMANN: But what do you think ought to be done, then?

PETER STOCKMANN: Your report has not convinced me that the condition of the water at the Baths is as bad as you represent it to be.

DR. STOCKMANN: I tell you it is even worse!—or at all events it will be in summer, when the warm weather comes.

PETER STOCKMANN: As I said, I believe you exaggerate the matter considerably. A capable physician ought to know what measures to take—he ought to be capable of preventing injurious influences or of remedying them if they become obviously persistent.

DR. STOCKMANN: Well? What more?

PETER STOCKMANN: The water-supply for the Baths is now an established fact, and in consequence must be treated as such. But probably the Committee, at its discretion, will not be disinclined to consider the question of how far it might be possible to introduce certain improvements consistent with a reasonable expenditure.

DR. STOCKMANN: And do you suppose that I will have anything to do with such a piece of trickery as that?

PETER STOCKMANN: Trickery!!

DR. STOCKMANN: Yes, it would be a trick—a fraud, a lie, a downright crime towards the public, towards the whole community!

PETER STOCKMANN: I have not, as I remarked before, been able to convince myself that there is actually any imminent danger.

DR. STOCKMANN: You have not! It is

impossible that you should not be convinced. I know I have represented the facts absolutely truthfully and fairly. And you know it very well, Peter, only you won't acknowledge it. It was owing to your action that both the Baths and the water-conduits were built where they are; and that is what you won't acknowledge—that damnable blunder of yours. Pooh!—do you suppose I don't see through you?

PETER STOCKMANN: And even if that were true? If I perhaps guard my reputation somewhat anxiously, it is in the interests of the town. Without moral authority I am powerless to direct public affairs as seems, to my judgment, to be best for the common good. And on that account—and for various other reasons, too—it appears to me to be a matter of importance that your report should not be delivered to the Committee. In the interest of the public, you must withhold it. Then, later on, I will raise the question and we will do our best, privately; but nothing of this unfortunate affair—not a single word of it—must come to the ears of the public.

DR. STOCKMANN: I am afraid you will not be able to prevent that now, my dear Peter.

PETER STOCKMANN: It must and shall be prevented.

DR. STOCKMANN: It is no use, I tell you. There are too many people that know about it.

PETER STOCKMANN: That know about it? Who? Surely you don't mean those fellows on the "People's Messenger"?

DR. STOCKMANN: Yes, they know. The liberal-minded independent press is going to see that you do your duty.

PETER STOCKMANN: (*after a short pause*) You are an extraordinarily independent man, Thomas. Have you given no thought to the consequences this may have for yourself?

DR. STOCKMANN: Consequences?—for me?

PETER STOCKMANN: For you and yours, yes.

DR. STOCKMANN: What the deuce do you mean?

PETER STOCKMANN: I believe I have always behaved in a brotherly way to you—have always been ready to oblige or to help you?

DR. STOCKMANN: Yes, you have, and I am grateful to you for it.

PETER STOCKMANN: There is no need. Indeed, to some extent I was forced to do so—for my own sake. I always hoped that, if I helped to improve your financial position, I should be able to keep some check on you.

DR. STOCKMANN: What!! Then it was only for your own sake—!

PETER STOCKMANN: Up to a certain point, yes. It is painful for a man in an official position to have his nearest relative compromising himself time after time.

DR. STOCKMANN: And do you consider that I do that?

PETER STOCKMANN: Yes, unfortunately, you do, without even being aware of it. You have a restless, pugnacious, rebellious disposition. And then there is that disastrous propensity of yours to want to write about every sort of possible and impossible thing. The moment an idea comes into your head, you must needs go and write a newspaper article or a whole pamphlet about it.

DR. STOCKMANN: Well, but is it not the duty of a citizen to let the public share in any new ideas he may have?

PETER STOCKMANN: Oh, the public doesn't require any new ideas. The public is best served by the good, old-established ideas it already has.

DR. STOCKMANN: And that is your honest opinion?

PETER STOCKMANN: Yes, and for once I must talk frankly to you. Hitherto I have tried to avoid doing so, because I know how irritable you are; but now I must tell you the truth, Thomas. You have no conception what an amount of harm you do yourself by your impetuosity. You complain of the authorities, you even complain of the government—you are always pulling them to pieces; you insist that you have been neglected and persecuted. But what else can such a cantankerous man as you expect?

DR. STOCKMANN: What next! Cantankerous, am I?

PETER STOCKMANN: Yes, Thomas, you are an extremely cantankerous man to work with—I know that to my cost. You disregard everything that you ought to have consideration for. You seem completely to forget that it is me you have to thank for your appointment here as medical officer to the Baths—

DR. STOCKMANN: I was entitled to it as a matter of course!—I and nobody else! I was the first person to see that the town could be made into a flourishing watering-place, and I was the only one who saw it at that time. I had to fight single-handed in support of the idea for many years; and I wrote and wrote—

PETER STOCKMANN: Undoubtedly. But things were not ripe for the scheme then—though, of course, you could not judge of that in your out-of-the-way corner up north. But as soon as the opportune moment came I—and the others—took the matter into our hands—

DR. STOCKMANN: Yes, and made this mess of all my beautiful plan. It is pretty obvious now what clever fellows you were!

PETER STOCKMANN: To my mind the whole thing only seems to mean that you are seeking another outlet for your combativeness. You want to pick a quarrel with your superiors—an old habit of yours. You cannot put up with any authority over you. You look askance at anyone who occupies a superior official position; you regard him as a personal enemy, and then any stick is good enough to beat him with. But now I have called your attention to the fact that the town's interests are at stake—and, incidentally, my own too. And therefore I must tell you, Thomas, that you will find me inexorable with regard to what I am about to require you to do.

DR. STOCKMANN: And what is that?

PETER STOCKMANN: As you have been so indiscreet as to speak of this delicate matter to outsiders, despite the fact that you ought to have treated it as entirely official and confidential, it is obviously impossible to hush it up now. All sorts of rumors will get about directly, and everybody who has a grudge against us will take care to embellish these rumors. So it will be necessary for you to refute them publicly.

DR. STOCKMANN: I! How? I don't understand.

PETER STOCKMANN: What we shall expect is that, after making further investigations, you will come to the conclusion that the matter is not by any means as dangerous or as critical as you imagined in the first instance.

DR. STOCKMANN: Oho!—so that is what you expect!

PETER STOCKMANN: And, what is more, we shall expect you to make public profession of your confidence in the Committee and in their readiness to consider fully and conscientiously what steps may be necessary to remedy any possible defects.

DR. STOCKMANN: But you will never be able to do that by patching and tinkering at it—never! Take my word for it, Peter; I mean what I say, as deliberately and emphatically as possible.

PETER STOCKMANN: As an officer under the Committee, you have no right to any individual opinion.

DR. STOCKMANN: (*amazed*) No right?

PETER STOCKMANN: In your official capacity, no. As a private person, it is quite another matter. But as a subordinate member of the staff of the Baths, you have no right to express any opinion which runs contrary to that of your superiors.

DR. STOCKMANN: This is too much! I, a doctor, a man of science, have no right to—!

PETER STOCKMANN: The matter in hand is not simply a scientific one. It is a complicated matter, and has its economic as well as its technical side.

DR. STOCKMANN: I don't care what it is! I intend to be free to express my opinion on any subject under the sun.

PETER STOCKMANN: As you please— but not on any subject concerning the Baths. That we forbid.

DR. STOCKMANN: (*shouting*) You forbid—! You! A pack of—

PETER STOCKMANN: *I* forbid it—I, your chief; and if I forbid it, you have to obey.

DR. STOCKMANN: (*controlling himself*) Peter—if you were not my brother—

PETRA: (*throwing open the door*) Father, you shan't stand this!

MRS. STOCKMANN: (*coming in after her*) Petra, Petra!

PETER STOCKMANN: Oh, so you have been eavesdropping.

MRS. STOCKMANN: You were talking so loud, we couldn't help—

PETRA: Yes, I was listening.

PETER STOCKMANN: Well, after all, I am very glad—

DR. STOCKMANN: (*going up to him*) You were saying something about forbidding and obeying?

PETER STOCKMANN: You obliged me to take that tone with you.

DR. STOCKMANN: And so I am to give myself the lie, publicly?

PETER STOCKMANN: We consider it absolutely necessary that you should make some such public statement as I have asked for.

DR. STOCKMANN: And if I do not—obey?

PETER STOCKMANN: Then we shall publish a statement ourselves to reassure the public.

DR. STOCKMANN: Very well; but in that case I shall use my pen against you. I stick to what I have said; I will show that I am right and that you are wrong. And what will you do then?

PETER STOCKMANN: Then I shall not be able to prevent your being dismissed.

DR. STOCKMANN: What—?

PETRA: Father—dismissed!

MRS. STOCKMANN: Dismissed!

PETER STOCKMANN: Dismissed from the staff of the Baths. I shall be obliged to propose that you shall immediately be given notice, and shall not be allowed any further participation in the Baths' affairs.

DR. STOCKMANN: You would dare to do that!

PETER STOCKMANN: It is you that are playing the daring game.

PETRA: Uncle, that is a shameful way to treat a man like father!

MRS. STOCKMANN: Do hold your tongue, Petra!

PETER STOCKMANN: (*looking at* PETRA) Oh, so we volunteer our opinions already, do we? Of course. (*To* MRS. STOCKMANN.) Katherine, I imagine you are the most sensible person in this house. Use any influence you may have over your husband, and make him see what this will entail for his family as well as—

DR. STOCKMANN: My family is my own concern and nobody else's!

PETER STOCKMANN: —for his own family, as I was saying, as well as for the town he lives in.

DR. STOCKMANN: It is I who have the real good of the town at heart! I want to lay bare the defects that sooner or later must come to the light of day. I will show whether I love my native town.

PETER STOCKMANN: You, who in your blind obstinacy want to cut off the most important source of the town's welfare?

DR. STOCKMANN: The source is poisoned, man! Are you mad? We are making our living by retailing filth and corruption! The whole of our flourishing municipal life derives its sustenance from a lie!

PETER STOCKMANN: All imagination—or something even worse. The man who can throw out such offensive insinuations about his native town must be an enemy of our community.

DR. STOCKMANN: (*going up to him*) Do you dare to—!

MRS. STOCKMANN: (*throwing herself between them*) Thomas!

PETRA: (*catching her father by the arm*) Don't lose your temper, father!

PETER STOCKMANN: I will not expose myself to violence. Now you have had a warning; so reflect on what you owe to yourself and your family. Good-bye.
(*Goes out.*)

DR. STOCKMANN: (*walking up and down*) Am I to put up with such treatment as this? In my own house, Katherine! What do you think of that!

MRS. STOCKMANN: Indeed it is both shameful and absurd, Thomas—

PETRA: If only I could give uncle a piece of my mind—

DR. STOCKMANN: It is my own fault. I ought to have flown out at him long ago!—shown my teeth!—bitten! To hear him call me an enemy to our community! Me! I shall not take that lying down, upon my soul!

MRS. STOCKMANN: But, dear Thomas, your brother has power on his side—

DR. STOCKMANN: Yes, but I have right on mine, I tell you.

MRS. STOCKMANN: Oh yes, right—right. What is the use of having right on your side if you have not got might?

PETRA: Oh, mother!—how can you say such a thing!

DR. STOCKMANN: Do you imagine that in a free country it is no use having right on your side? You are absurd, Katherine. Besides, haven't I got the liberal-minded, independent press to lead the way, and the compact majority behind me? That is might enough, I should think!

MRS. STOCKMANN: But, good heavens, Thomas, you don't mean to—?

DR. STOCKMANN: Don't mean to what?

MRS. STOCKMANN: To set yourself up in opposition to your brother.

DR. STOCKMANN: In God's name, what else do you suppose I should do but take my stand on right and truth?

PETRA: Yes, I was just going to say that.

MRS. STOCKMANN: But it won't do you any earthly good. If they won't do it, they won't.

DR. STOCKMANN: Oho, Katherine! Just give me time, and you will see how I will carry the war into their camp.

MRS. STOCKMANN: Yes, you carry the war into their camp, and you get your dismissal—that is what you will do.

DR. STOCKMANN: In any case I shall have done my duty towards the public—towards the community. I, who am called its enemy!

MRS. STOCKMANN: But towards your family, Thomas? Towards your own home! Do you think that is doing your duty towards those you have to provide for?

PETRA: Ah, don't think always first of us, mother.

MRS. STOCKMANN: Oh, it is easy for you to talk; you are able to shift for yourself, if need be. But remember the boys, Thomas; and think a little, too, of yourself, and of me—

DR. STOCKMANN: I think you are out of your senses, Katherine! If I were to be such a miserable coward as to go on my knees to Peter and his damned crew, do you suppose I should ever know an hour's peace of mind all my life afterwards?

MRS. STOCKMANN: I don't know anything about that; but God preserve us from the peace of mind we shall have all the same, if you go on defying him! You will find yourself again without the means of subsistence, with no income to count upon. I should think we had had enough of that in the old days. Remember that, Thomas; think what that means.

DR. STOCKMANN: (*collecting himself with a struggle and clenching his fists*) And this is what this slavery can bring upon a free, honorable man! Isn't it horrible, Katherine?

MRS. STOCKMANN: Yes, it is sinful to treat you so, it is perfectly true. But, good heavens, one has to put up with so much injustice in this world.—There are the boys, Thomas! Look at them! What is to become of them? Oh, no, no, you can never have the heart—.

(EJLIF *and* MORTEN *have come in while she was speaking, with their school books in their hands.*)

DR. STOCKMANN: The boys—! (*Recovers himself suddenly.*) No, even if the whole world goes to pieces, I will never bow my neck to this yoke! (*Goes towards his room.*)

MRS. STOCKMANN: (*following him*) Thomas—what are you going to do!

DR. STOCKMANN: (*at his door*) I mean to have the right to look my sons in the face when they are grown men.

(*Goes into his room.*)

MRS. STOCKMANN: (*bursting into tears*) God help us all!

PETRA: Father is splendid! He will not give in.

(*The boys look on in amazement;* PETRA *signs to them not to speak.*)

CURTAIN

ACT III

SCENE: *The editorial office of the "People's Messenger." The entrance door is on the left-hand side of the back wall; on the right-hand side is another door with glass panels through which the printing-room can be seen. Another door in the right-hand wall. In the middle of the room is a large table covered with papers, newspapers, and books. In the foreground on the left a window, before which stand a desk and a high stool. There are a couple of easy chairs by the table, and other chairs standing along the wall. The room is dingy and uncomfortable; the furniture is old, the chairs stained and torn. In the printing-room the compositors are seen at work, and a printer is working a handpress.* HOVSTAD *is sitting at the desk, writing.* BILLING *comes in from the right with* DR. STOCKMANN'S *manuscript in his hand.*

BILLING: Well, I must say!

HOVSTAD: (*still writing*) Have you read it through?

BILLING: (*laying the MS. on the desk*) Yes, indeed I have.

HOVSTAD: Don't you think the Doctor hits them pretty hard.

BILLING: Hard? Bless my soul, he's crushing! Every word falls like—how shall I put it?—like the blow of a sledgehammer.

HOVSTAD: Yes, but they are not the people to throw up the sponge at the first blow.

BILLING: That is true; and for that reason we must strike blow upon blow until the whole of this aristocracy tumbles to pieces. As I sat in there reading this, I almost seemed to see a revolution in being.

HOVSTAD: (*turning round*) Hush!— Speak so that Aslaksen cannot hear you.

BILLING: (*lowering his voice*) Aslaksen is a chicken-hearted chap, a coward; there is nothing of the man in him. But this time you will insist on your own way, won't you? You will put the Doctor's article in?

HOVSTAD: Yes, and if the Mayor doesn't like it —

BILLING: That will be the devil of a nuisance.

HOVSTAD: Well, fortunately we can turn the situation to good account, whatever happens. If the Mayor will not fall in with the Doctor's project, he will have all the small tradesmen down on him—the whole of the Householders' Association and the rest of them. And if he does fall in with it, he will fall out with the whole crowd of large shareholders in the Baths, who up to now have been his most valuable supporters—

BILLING: Yes, because they will certainly have to fork out a pretty penny—

HOVSTAD: Yes, you may be sure they will. And in this way the ring will be broken up, you see, and then in every issue of the paper we will enlighten the public on the Mayor's incapability on one point and another, and make it clear that all the positions of trust in the town, the whole control of municipal affairs, ought to be put in the hands of the Liberals.

BILLING: That is perfectly true! I see it coming—I see it coming; we are on the threshold of a revolution!

(*A knock is heard at the door.*)

HOVSTAD: Hush (*Calls out*) Come in! (DR. STOCKMANN *comes in by the street door.* HOVSTAD *goes to meet him.*) Ah, it is you, Doctor! Well?

DR. STOCKMANN: You may set to work and print it, Mr. Hovstad!

HOVSTAD: Has it come to that, then?

BILLING: Hurrah!

DR. STOCKMANN: Yes, print away. Undoubtedly it has come to that. Now they must take what they get. There is going to be a fight in the town, Mr. Billing!

BILLING: War to the knife, I hope! We will get our knives to their throats, Doctor!

DR. STOCKMANN: This article is only a beginning. I have already got four or five more sketched out in my head. Where is Aslaksen?

BILLING: (*calls into the printing-room*) Aslaksen, just come here for a minute!

HOVSTAD: Four or five more articles, did you say? On the same subject?

DR. STOCKMANN: No—far from it, my dear fellow. No, they are about quite another matter. But they all spring from the question of the water-supply and the drainage. One thing leads to another, you know. It is like beginning to pull down an old house, exactly.

BILLING: Upon my soul, it's true; you find you are not done till you have pulled all the old rubbish down.

ASLAKSEN: (*coming in*) Pulled down? You are not thinking of pulling down the Baths surely, Doctor?

HOVSTAD: Far from it; don't be afraid.

DR. STOCKMANN: No, we meant something quite different. Well, what do you think of my article, Mr. Hovstad?

HOVSTAD: I think it is simply a masterpiece—

DR. STOCKMANN: Do you really think so? Well, I am very pleased, very pleased.

HOVSTAD: It is so clear and intelligible. One need have no special knowledge to understand the bearing of it. You will have every enlightened man on your side.

ASLAKSEN: And every prudent man too, I hope?

BILLING: The prudent and the imprudent—almost the whole town.

ASLAKSEN: In that case we may venture to print it.

DR. STOCKMANN: I should think so!

HOVSTAD: We will put it in tomorrow morning.

DR. STOCKMANN: Of course—you must not lose a single day. What I wanted to ask you, Mr. Aslaksen, was if you would supervise the printing of it yourself.

ASLAKSEN: With pleasure.

DR. STOCKMANN: Take care of it as if it were a treasure! No misprints—every word is important. I will look in again a little later; perhaps you will be able to let me see a proof. I can't tell you how eager I am to see it in print, and see it burst upon the public—

BILLING: Burst upon them—yes, like a flash of lightning!

DR. STOCKMANN: —and to have it submitted to the judgment of my intelligent fellow-townsmen. You cannot imagine what I have gone through today. I have been threatened first with one thing and then with another; they have tried to rob me of my most elementary rights as a man—

BILLING: What! Your rights as a man!

DR. STOCKMANN: —they have tried to degrade me, to make a coward of me, to force me to put personal interests before my most sacred convictions—

BILLING: That is too much—I'm damned if it isn't.

HOVSTAD: Oh, you mustn't be surprised at anything from that quarter.

DR. STOCKMANN: Well, they will get the worst of it with me; they may assure themselves of that. I shall consider the "People's Messenger" my sheet-anchor now, and every single day I will bombard them with one article after another, like bomb-shells—

ASLAKSEN: Yes, but—

BILLING: Hurrah!—it is war, it is war!

DR. STOCKMANN: I shall smite them to the ground—I shall crush them—I shall break down all their defences, before the eyes of the honest public! That is what I shall do!

ASLAKSEN: Yes, but in moderation, Doctor—proceed with moderation—

BILLING: Not a bit of it, not a bit of it! Don't spare the dynamite!

DR. STOCKMANN: Because it is not merely a question of water-supply and drains now, you know. No—it is the whole of our social life that we have got to purify and disinfect—

BILLING: Spoken like a deliverer!

DR. STOCKMANN: All the incapables must be turned out, you understand—and that in every walk of life! Endless vistas have opened themselves to my mind's eye today. I cannot see it all quite clearly yet, but I shall in time. Young and vigorous standard-bearers—those are what we need and must seek, my friends; we must have new men in command at all our outposts.

BILLING: Hear, hear!

DR. STOCKMANN: We only need to stand by one another, and it will all be perfectly easy. The revolution will be launched like a ship that runs smoothly off the stocks. Don't you think so?

HOVSTAD: For my part I think we have now a prospect of getting the municipal authority into the hands where it should lie.

ASLAKSEN: And if only we proceed with moderation, I cannot imagine that there will be any risk.

DR. STOCKMANN: Who the devil cares whether there is any risk or not? What I am doing, I am doing in the name of truth and for the sake of my conscience.

HOVSTAD: You are a man who deserves to be supported, Doctor.

ASLAKSEN: Yes, there is no denying that the Doctor is a true friend to the town—a real friend to the community, that he is.

BILLING: Take my word for it, Aslaksen, Dr. Stockmann is a friend of the people.

ASLAKSEN: I fancy the Householders' Association will make use of that expression before long.

DR. STOCKMANN: (*affected, grasps their hands*) Thank you, thank you, my dear staunch friends. It is very refreshing to me to hear you say that; my brother called me something quite different. By Jove, he shall have it back, with interest! But now I must be off to see a poor devil—. I will come back, as I said. Keep a very careful eye on the manuscript, Aslaksen, and don't for worlds leave out any of my notes of exclamation! Rather put one or two more in! Capital, capital! Well, good-bye for the present—good-bye, good-bye!

(*They show him to the door, and bow him out.*)

HOVSTAD: He may prove an invaluably useful man to us.

ASLAKSEN: Yes, so long as he confines himself to this matter of the Baths. But if he goes farther afield, I don't think it would be advisable to follow him.

HOVSTAD: Hm!—that all depends—

BILLING: You are so infernally timid, Aslaksen!

ASLAKSEN: Timid? Yes, when it is a question of the local authorities, I am timid, Mr. Billing; it is a lesson I have learnt in the school of experience, let me tell you. But try me in higher politics, in matters that concern the government itself, and then see if I am timid.

BILLING: No, you aren't, I admit. But this is simply contradicting yourself.

ASLAKSEN: I am a man with a conscience, and that is the whole matter. If you attack the government, you don't do the community any harm, anyway; those fellows pay no attention to attacks, you see—they go on just as they are, in spite of them. But *local* authorities are different; they *can* be turned out, and then perhaps you may get an ignorant lot into office who may do irreparable harm to the householders and everybody else.

HOVSTAD: But what of the education of citizens by self-government—don't you attach any importance to that?

ASLAKSEN: When a man has interests of his own to protect, he cannot think of everything, Mr. Hovstad.

HOVSTAD: Then I hope I shall never have interests of my own to protect!

BILLING: Hear, hear!

ASLAKSEN: (*with a smile*) Hm! (*Points to the desk.*) Mr. Sheriff Stensgaard was your predecessor at that editorial desk.

BILLING: (*spitting*) Bah! That turncoat.

HOVSTAD: I am not a weathercock—and never will be.

ASLAKSEN: A politician should never be too certain of anything, Mr. Hovstad. And as for you, Mr. Billing, I should think it is time for you to be taking in a reef or two in your sails, seeing that you are applying for the post of secretary to the Bench.

BILLING: I—?

HOVSTAD: Are you, Billing?

BILLING: Well, yes—but you must clearly understand I am doing it only to annoy the bigwigs.

ASLAKSEN: Anyhow, it is no business of mine. But if I am to be accused of timidity and of inconsistency in my principles, this is what I want to point out: my political past is an open book. I have never changed, except perhaps to become a little more moderate, you see. My heart is still with the people; but I don't deny that my reason has a certain bias towards the authorities—the local ones, I mean.

(*Goes into the printing-room.*)

BILLING: Oughtn't we to try and get rid of him, Hovstad?

HOVSTAD: Do you know anyone else who will advance the money for our paper and printing bill?

BILLING: It is an infernal nuisance that we don't possess some capital to trade on.

HOVSTAD: (*sitting down at his desk*) Yes, if we only had that, then—

BILLING: Suppose you were to apply to Dr. Stockmann?

HOVSTAD: (*turning over some papers*) What is the use? He has got nothing.

BILLING: No, but he has got a warm man in the background, old Morten Kiil—"the Badger," as they call him.

HOVSTAD: (*writing*) Are you so sure *he* has got anything?

BILLING: Good Lord, of course he has! And some of it must come to the Stockmanns. Most probably he will do something for the children, at all events.

HOVSTAD: (*turning half round*) Are you counting on that?

BILLING: Counting on it? Of course I am not counting on anything.

HOVSTAD: That is right. And I should not count on the secretaryship to the Bench either, if I were you; for I can assure you—you won't get it.

BILLING: Do you think I am not quite aware of that? My object is precisely *not* to get it. A slight of that kind stimulates a man's fighting power—it is like getting a supply of fresh bile—and I am sure one needs that badly enough in a hole-and-corner place like this, where so seldom anything happens to stir one up.

HOVSTAD: (*writing*) Quite so, quite so.

BILLING: Ah, I shall be heard of yet!—Now I shall go and write the appeal to the Householders' Association.
(*Goes into the room on the right.*)

HOVSTAD: (*sitting at his desk, biting his penholder, says slowly*) Hm!—that's it, is it? (*A knock is heard.*) Come in! (PETRA *comes in by the outer door.* HOVSTAD *gets up.*) What, you!—here?

PETRA: Yes, you must forgive me—

HOVSTAD: (*pulling a chair forward*) Won't you sit down?

PETRA: No, thank you; I must go again in a moment.

HOVSTAD: Have you come with a message from your father, by any chance?

PETRA: No, I have come on my own account. (*Takes a book out of her coat pocket.*) Here is the English story.

HOVSTAD: Why have you brought it back?

PETRA: Because I am not going to translate it.

HOVSTAD: But you promised me faithfully—

PETRA: Yes, but then I had not read it. I don't suppose you have read it either?

HOVSTAD: No, you know quite well I don't understand English; but—

PETRA: Quite so. That is why I wanted to tell you that you must find something else. (*Lays the book on the table.*) You can't use this for the "People's Messenger."

HOVSTAD: Why not?

PETRA: Because it conflicts with all your opinions.

HOVSTAD: Oh, for that matter—

PETRA: You don't understand me. The burden of this story is that there is a supernatural power that looks after the so-called good people in this world and makes everything happen for the best in their case—while all the so-called bad people are punished.

HOVSTAD: Well, but that is all right. That is just what our readers want.

PETRA: And are you going to be the one to give it to them? For myself, I do not believe a word of it. You know quite well that things do not happen so in reality.

HOVSTAD: You are perfectly right, but an editor cannot always act as he would prefer. He is often obliged to bow to the wishes of the public in unimportant matters. Politics are the most important thing in life—for a newspaper, anyway; and if I want to carry my public with me on the path that leads to liberty and progress, I must not frighten them away. If they find a moral tale of this sort in the serial at the bottom of the page, they will be all the more ready to read what is printed above it; they feel more secure, as it were.

PETRA: For shame! You would never go and set a snare like that for your readers; you are not a spider!

HOVSTAD: (*smiling*) Thank you for having such a good opinion of me. No; as a matter of fact that is Billing's idea and not mine.

PETRA: Billing's?

HOVSTAD: Yes; anyway he propounded

that theory here one day. And it is Billing who is so anxious to have that story in the paper; I don't know anything about the book.

PETRA: But how can Billing, with his emancipated views—

HOVSTAD: Oh, Billing is a many-sided man. He is applying for the post of secretary to the Bench, too, I hear.

PETRA: I don't believe it, Mr. Hovstad. How could he possibly bring himself to do such a thing?

HOVSTAD: Ah, you must ask him that.

PETRA: I should never have thought it of him.

HOVSTAD: (*looking more closely at her*) No? Does it really surprise you so much?

PETRA: Yes. Or perhaps not altogether. Really, I don't quite know—

HOVSTAD: We journalists are not worth much, Miss Stockmann.

PETRA: Do you really mean that?

HOVSTAD: I think so sometimes.

PETRA: Yes, in the ordinary affairs of everyday life, perhaps; I can understand that. But now, when you have taken a weighty matter in hand—

HOVSTAD: This matter of your father's, you mean?

PETRA: Exactly. It seems to me that now you must feel you are a man worth more than most.

HOVSTAD: Yes, today I do feel something of that sort.

PETRA: Of course you do, don't you? It is a splendid vocation you have chosen —to smooth the way for the march of unappreciated truths and new and courageous lines of thought. If it were nothing more than because you stand fearlessly in the open and take up the cause of an injured man—

HOVSTAD: Especially when that injured man is—ahem!—I don't rightly know how to—

PETRA: When that man is so upright and so honest, you mean?

HOVSTAD: (*more gently*) Especially when he is your father, I meant.

PETRA: (*suddenly checked*) *That?*

HOVSTAD: Yes, Petra—Miss Petra.

PETRA: Is it *that*, that is first and foremost with you? Not the matter itself? Not the truth?—not my father's big generous heart?

HOVSTAD: Certainly—of course—that too.

PETRA: No, thank you; you have betrayed yourself, Mr. Hovstad, and now I shall never trust you again in anything.

HOVSTAD: Can you really take it so amiss in me that it is mostly for your sake—?

PETRA: I am angry with you for not having been honest with my father. You talked to him as if the truth and the good of the community were what lay nearest to your heart. You have made fools of both my father and me. You are not the man you made yourself out to be. And that I shall never forgive you—never!

HOVSTAD: You ought not to speak so bitterly, Miss Petra—least of all now.

PETRA: Why not now, especially?

HOVSTAD: Because your father cannot do without my help.

PETRA: (*looking him up and down*) Are you that sort of man too? For shame!

HOVSTAD: No, no, I am not. This came upon me so unexpectedly—you must believe that.

PETRA: I know what to believe. Goodbye.

ASLAKSEN: (*coming from the printing-room, hurriedly and with an air of mystery*) Damnation, Hovstad!—(*Sees* PETRA.) Oh, this is awkward—

PETRA: There is the book; you must give it to some one else.

(*Goes towards the door.*)

HOVSTAD: (*following her*) But, Miss Stockmann—

PETRA: Good-bye. (*Goes out.*)

ASLAKSEN: I say—Mr. Hovstad—

HOVSTAD: Well, well!—what is it?

ASLAKSEN: The Mayor is outside in the printing-room.

HOVSTAD: The Mayor, did you say?

ASLAKSEN: Yes, he wants to speak to you. He came in by the back door—didn't want to be seen, you understand.

HOVSTAD: What can he want? Wait a bit—I will go myself. (*Goes to the door of the printing-room, opens it, bows and invites* PETER STOCKMANN *in.*) Just see, Aslaksen, that no one—

ASLAKSEN. Quite so.

(*Goes into the printing-room.*)

PETER STOCKMANN. You did not expect to see me here, Mr. Hovstad?

HOVSTAD: No, I confess I did not.

PETER STOCKMANN: (*looking round*) You are very snug in here—very nice indeed.

HOVSTAD: Oh—

PETER STOCKMANN: And here I come, without any notice, to take up your time!

HOVSTAD: By all means, Mr. Mayor. I am at your service. But let me relieve you of your— (*takes* STOCKMANN'S *hat and stick and puts them on a chair.*) Won't you sit down?

PETER STOCKMANN: (*sitting down by the table*) Thank you. (HOVSTAD *sits down.*) I have had an extremely annoying experience today, Mr. Hovstad.

HOVSTAD: Really? Ah well, I expect with all the various business you have to attend to—

PETER STOCKMANN: The Medical Officer of the Baths is responsible for what happened today.

HOVSTAD: Indeed? The Doctor?

PETER STOCKMANN: He has addressed a kind of report to the Baths Committee on the subject of certain supposed defects in the Baths.

HOVSTAD: Has he indeed?

PETER STOCKMANN: Yes—has he not told you? I thought he said—

HOVSTAD: Ah, yes—it is true he did mention something about—

ASLAKSEN: (*coming from the printing-room*) I ought to have that copy—

HOVSTAD: (*angrily*) Ahem!—there it is on the desk.

ASLAKSEN: (*taking it*) Right.

PETER STOCKMANN: But look there—that is the thing I was speaking of!

ASLAKSEN: Yes, that is the Doctor's article, Mr. Mayor.

HOVSTAD: Oh, is *that* what you were speaking about?

PETER STOCKMANN: Yes, that is it. What do you think of it?

HOVSTAD: Oh, I am only a layman—and I have only taken a very cursory glance at it.

PETER STOCKMANN: But you are going to print it?

HOVSTAD: I cannot very well refuse a distinguished man—

ASLAKSEN: I have nothing to do with editing the paper, Mr. Mayor—

PETER STOCKMANN: I understand.

ASLAKSEN: I merely print what is put into my hands.

PETER STOCKMANN: Quite so.

ASLAKSEN: And so I must—

(*Moves off towards the printing-room.*)

PETER STOCKMANN: No, but wait a moment, Mr. Aslaksen. You will allow me, Mr. Hovstad?

HOVSTAD: If you please, Mr. Mayor.

PETER STOCKMANN: You are a discreet and thoughtful man, Mr. Aslaksen.

ASLAKSEN: I am delighted to hear you think so, sir.

PETER STOCKMANN: And a man of very considerable influence.

ASLAKSEN: Chiefly among the small tradesmen, sir.

PETER STOCKMANN: The small taxpayers are the majority—here as everywhere else.

ASLAKSEN: That is true.

PETER STOCKMANN: And I have no doubt you know the general trend of opinion among them, don't you?

ASLAKSEN: Yes, I think I may say I do, Mr. Mayor.

PETER STOCKMANN: Yes. Well, since there is such a praiseworthy spirit of self-sacrifice among the less wealthy citizens of our town—

ASLAKSEN: What?

HOVSTAD: Self-sacrifice?

PETER STOCKMANN: It is pleasing evidence of a public-spirited feeling, extremely pleasing evidence. I might almost say I hardly expected it. But you have a closer knowledge of public opinion than I.

ASLAKSEN: But, Mr. Mayor—

PETER STOCKMANN: And indeed it is no small sacrifice that the town is going to make.

HOVSTAD: The town?

ASLAKSEN: But I don't understand. Is it the Baths—?

PETER STOCKMANN: At a provisional estimate, the alterations that the Medical Officer asserts are desirable will cost somewhere about twenty thousand pounds.

ASLAKSEN: That is a lot of money, but—

PETER STOCKMANN: Of course it will be necessary to raise a municipal loan.

HOVSTAD: (*getting up*) Surely you never mean that the town must pay—?

ASLAKSEN: Do you mean that it must come out of the municipal funds?—out of the ill-filled pockets of the small tradesmen?

PETER STOCKMANN: Well, my dear Mr. Aslaksen, where else is the money to come from?

ASLAKSEN: The gentlemen who own the Baths ought to provide that.

PETER STOCKMANN: The proprietors of the Baths are not in a position to incur any further expense.

ASLAKSEN: Is that absolutely certain, Mr. Mayor?

PETER STOCKMANN: I have satisfied myself that it is so. If the town wants these very extensive alterations, it will have to pay for them.

ASLAKSEN: But, damn it all—I beg your pardon—this is quite another matter, Mr. Hovstad!

HOVSTAD: It is, indeed.

PETER STOCKMANN: The most fatal part of it is that we shall be obliged to shut the Baths for a couple of years.

HOVSTAD: Shut them? Shut them altogether?

ASLAKSEN: For two years?

PETER STOCKMANN: Yes, the work will take as long as that—at least.

ASLAKSEN: I'm damned if we will stand that, Mr. Mayor! What are we householders to live upon in the meantime?

PETER STOCKMANN: Unfortunately, that is an extremely difficult question to answer, Mr. Aslaksen. But what would you have us do? Do you suppose we shall have a single visitor in the town, if we go about proclaiming that our water is polluted, that we are living over a plague spot, that the entire town—

ASLAKSEN: And the whole thing is merely imagination?

PETER STOCKMANN: With the best will in the world, I have not been able to come to any other conclusion.

ASLAKSEN: Well then, I must say it is absolutely unjustifiable of Dr. Stockmann—I beg your pardon, Mr. Mayor—

PETER STOCKMANN: What you say is lamentably true, Mr. Aslaksen. My brother has, unfortunately, always been a headstrong man.

ASLAKSEN: After this, do you mean to give him your support, Mr. Hovstad?

HOVSTAD: Can you suppose for a moment that I—?

PETER STOCKMANN: I have drawn up a short *résumé* of the situation as it appears from a reasonable man's point of view. In it I have indicated how certain possible defects might suitably be remedied without outrunning the resources of the Baths Committee.

HOVSTAD: Have you got it with you, Mr. Mayor?

PETER STOCKMANN: (*fumbling in his pocket*) Yes, I brought it with me in case you should—

ASLAKSEN: Good Lord, there he is!

PETER STOCKMANN: Who? My brother?

HOVSTAD: Where? Where?

ASLAKSEN: He has just gone through the printing-room.

PETER STOCKMANN: How unlucky! I don't want to meet him here, and I had still several things to speak to you about.

HOVSTAD: (*pointing to the door on the right*) Go in there for the present.

PETER STOCKMANN: But—?

HOVSTAD: You will only find Billing in there.

ASLAKSEN: Quick, quick, Mr. Mayor—he is just coming.

PETER STOCKMANN: Yes, very well; but see that you get rid of him quickly. (*Goes out through the door on the right, which* ASLAKSEN *opens for him and shuts after him.*)

HOVSTAD: Pretend to be doing something, Aslaksen.

(*Sits down and writes.* ASLAKSEN *begins foraging among a heap of newspapers that are lying on a chair.*)

DR. STOCKMANN: (*coming in from the printing-room*) Here I am again. (*Puts down his hat and stick.*)

HOVSTAD: (*writing*) Already, Doctor? Hurry up with what we were speaking about, Aslaksen. We are very pressed for time today.

DR. STOCKMANN: (*to* ASLAKSEN) No proof for me to see yet, I hear.

ASLAKSEN: (*without turning round*) You couldn't expect it yet, Doctor.

DR. STOCKMANN: No, no; but I am impatient, as you can understand. I shall not know a moment's peace of mind till I see it in print.

HOVSTAD: Hm!—it will take a good while yet, won't it, Aslaksen?

ASLAKSEN: Yes, I am almost afraid it will.

DR. STOCKMANN: All right, my dear friends; I will come back. I do not mind coming back twice if necessary. A matter of such great importance—the welfare of the town at stake—it is no time to shirk trouble. (*Is just going, but stops and comes back.*) Look here—there is one thing more I want to speak to you about.

HOVSTAD: Excuse me, but could it not wait till some other time?

DR. STOCKMANN: I can tell you in half a dozen words. It is only this. When my article is read tomorrow and it is realized that I have been quietly working the whole winter for the welfare of the town—

HOVSTAD: Yes, but, Doctor—

DR. STOCKMANN: I know what you are going to say. You don't see how on earth it was any more than my duty—my obvious duty as a citizen. Of course it wasn't; I know that as well as you. But my fellow-citizens, you know—! Good Lord, think of all the good souls who think so highly of me—!

ASLAKSEN: Yes, our townsfolk have had a very high opinion of you so far, Doctor.

DR. STOCKMANN: Yes, and that is just why I am afraid they—. Well, this is the point; when this reaches them, especially the poorer classes, and sounds in their ears like a summons to take the town's affairs into their own hands for the future—

HOVSTAD: (*getting up*) Ahem! Doctor, I won't conceal from you the fact—

DR. STOCKMANN: Ah!—I knew there was something in the wind! But I won't hear a word of it. If anything of that sort is being set on foot—

HOVSTAD: Of what sort?

DR. STOCKMANN: Well, whatever it is—whether it is a demonstration in my honor, or a banquet, or a subscription list for some presentation to me—whatever it is, you must promise me solemnly and faithfully to put a stop to it. You too, Mr. Aslaksen; do you understand?

HOVSTAD: You must forgive me, Doctor, but sooner or later we must tell you the plain truth—

(*He is interrupted by the entrance of* MRS. STOCKMANN, *who comes in from the street door.*)

MRS. STOCKMANN: (*seeing her husband*) Just as I thought!

HOVSTAD: (*going towards her*) You too, Mrs. Stockmann?

DR. STOCKMANN: What on earth do *you* want here, Katherine?

MRS. STOCKMANN: I should think you know very well what I want.

HOVSTAD: Won't you sit down? Or perhaps—

MRS. STOCKMANN: No, thank you; don't trouble. And you must not be offended at my coming to fetch my husband; I am the mother of three children, you know.

DR. STOCKMANN: Nonsense!—we know all about that.

MRS. STOCKMANN: Well, one would not give you credit for much thought for your wife and children today; if you had had that, you would not have gone and dragged us all into misfortune.

DR. STOCKMANN: Are you out of your senses, Katherine? Because a man has a wife and children, is he not to be allowed to proclaim the truth—is he not to be allowed to be an actively useful citizen—is he not to be allowed to do a service to his native town?

MRS. STOCKMANN: Yes, Thomas—in reason.

ASLAKSEN: Just what I say. Moderation is everything.

MRS. STOCKMANN: And that is why you wrong us, Mr. Hovstad, in enticing my husband away from his home and making a dupe of him in all this.

HOVSTAD: I certainly am making a dupe of no one—

DR. STOCKMANN: Making a dupe of me! Do you suppose *I* should allow myself to be duped?

MRS. STOCKMANN: It is just what you do. I know quite well you have more brains than anyone in the town, but you are extremely easily duped, Thomas. (*To* HOVSTAD.) Please realize that he loses his post at the Baths if you print what he has written—

ASLAKSEN: What!

HOVSTAD: Look here, Doctor—

DR. STOCKMANN: (*laughing*) Ha—ha!—just let them try! No, no—they will take good care not to. I have got the compact majority behind me, let me tell you!

MRS. STOCKMANN: Yes, that is just the worst of it—your having any such horrid thing behind you.

DR. STOCKMANN: Rubbish, Katherine!—Go home and look after your house and leave me to look after the community. How can you be so afraid, when I am so confident and happy? (*Walks up and down, rubbing his hands.*) Truth and the People will win the fight, you may be certain! I see the whole of the broad-minded middle class marching like a victorious army—! (*Stops beside a chair.*) What the deuce is that lying there?

ASLAKSEN: Good Lord!

HOVSTAD: Ahem!

DR. STOCKMANN: Here we have the topmost pinnacle of authority!

(*Takes the* MAYOR'S *official hat carefully between his finger-tips and holds it up in the air.*)

MRS. STOCKMANN: The Mayor's hat!

DR. STOCKMANN: And here is the staff of office too. How in the name of all that's wonderful—?

HOVSTAD: Well, you see—

DR. STOCKMANN: Oh, I understand. He has been here trying to talk you over. Ha—ha!—he made rather a mistake there! And as soon as he caught sight of me in the printing-room—. (*Bursts out laughing.*) Did he run away, Mr. Aslaksen?

ASLAKSEN: (*hurriedly*) Yes, he ran away, Doctor.

DR. STOCKMANN: Ran away without his stick or his—. Fiddlesticks! Peter doesn't run away and leave his belonging behind him. But what the deuce have you done with him? Ah!—in there, of course. Now you shall see, Katherine.

MRS. STOCKMANN: Thomas—please don't—!

ASLAKSEN: Don't be rash, Doctor.

(DR. STOCKMANN *has put on the* MAYOR'S *hat and taken his stick in his hand. He goes up to the door, opens it and stands with his hand to his hat at the salute.* PETER STOCKMANN *comes in, red with anger.* BILLING *follows him.*)

PETER STOCKMANN: What does this tomfoolery mean?

DR. STOCKMANN: Be respectful, my good Peter. I am the chief authority in the town now. (*Walks up and down.*)

MRS. STOCKMANN: (*almost in tears*) Really, Thomas!

PETER STOCKMANN: (*following him about*) Give me my hat and stick.

DR. STOCKMANN: (*in the same tone as before*) If you are chief constable, let me tell you that I am the Mayor—I am the master of the whole town, please understand!

PETER STOCKMANN: Take off my hat, I tell you. Remember it is part of an official uniform.

DR. STOCKMANN: Pooh! Do you think the newly awakened lion-hearted people are going to be frightened by an official hat? There is going to be a revolution in the town tomorrow, let me tell you. You thought you could turn me out; but now I shall turn you out—turn you out of all your various offices. Do you think I cannot? Listen to me. I have triumphant social forces behind me. Hovstad and Billing will thunder in the "People's Messenger," and Aslaksen will take the field at the head of the whole Householders' Association—

ASLAKSEN: That I won't, Doctor.

DR. STOCKMANN: Of course you will—

PETER STOCKMANN: Ah!—may I ask then if Mr. Hovstad intends to join this agitation?

HOVSTAD: No, Mr. Mayor.

ASLAKSEN: No, Mr. Hovstad is not such a fool as to go and ruin his paper and himself for the sake of an imaginary grievance.

DR. STOCKMANN: (*looking round him*) What does this mean?

HOVSTAD: You have represented your case in a false light, Doctor, and therefore I am unable to give you my support.

BILLING: And after what the Mayor was so kind as to tell me just now, I—

DR. STOCKMANN: A false light! Leave that part of it to me. Only print my article; I am quite capable of defending it.

HOVSTAD: I am not going to print it. I cannot and will not and dare not print it.

DR. STOCKMANN: You dare not? What nonsense!—you are the editor; and an editor controls his paper, I suppose!

ASLAKSEN: No, it is the subscribers, Doctor.

PETER STOCKMANN: Fortunately, yes.

ASLAKSEN: It is public opinion—the enlightened public—householders and people of that kind; they control the newspapers.

DR. STOCKMANN: (*composedly*) And I have all these influences against me?

ASLAKSEN: Yes, you have. It would

mean the absolute ruin of the community if your article were to appear.

DR. STOCKMANN: Indeed.

PETER STOCKMANN: My hat and stick, if you please. (DR. STOCKMANN *takes off the hat and lays it on the table with the stick.* PETER STOCKMANN *takes them up.*) Your authority as mayor has come to an untimely end.

DR. STOCKMANN: We have not got to the end yet. (*To* HOVSTAD.) Then it is quite impossible for you to print my article in the "People's Messenger"?

HOVSTAD: Quite impossible—out of regard for your family as well.

MRS. STOCKMANN: You need not concern yourself about his family, thank you, Mr. Hovstad.

PETER STOCKMANN: (*taking a paper from his pocket*) It will be sufficient, for the guidance of the public, if this appears. It is an official statement. May I trouble you?

HOVSTAD: (*taking the paper*) Certainly; I will see that it is printed.

DR. STOCKMANN: But not mine. Do you imagine that you can silence me and stifle the truth? You will not find it so easy as you suppose. Mr. Aslaksen, kindly take my manuscript at once and print it as a pamphlet—at my expense. I will have four hundred copies—no, five—six hundred.

ASLAKSEN: If you offered me its weight in gold, I could not lend my press for any such purpose, Doctor. It would be flying in the face of public opinion. You will not get it printed anywhere in the town.

DR. STOCKMANN: Then give it back to me.

HOVSTAD: (*giving him the MS.*) Here it is.

DR. STOCKMANN: (*taking his hat and stick*) It shall be made public all the same. I will read it out at a mass meeting of the townspeople. All my fellow-citizens shall hear the voice of truth!

PETER STOCKMANN: You will not find any public body in the town that will give you the use of their hall for such a purpose.

ASLAKSEN: Not a single one, I am certain.

BILLING: No, I'm damned if you will find one.

MRS. STOCKMANN: But this is too shameful! Why should every one turn against you like that?

DR. STOCKMANN: (*angrily*) I will tell you why. It is because all the men in this town are old women—like you; they all think of nothing but their families, and never of the community.

MRS. STOCKMANN: (*putting her arm into his*) Then I will show them that an— an old woman can be a man for once. I am going to stand by you, Thomas!

DR. STOCKMANN: Bravely said, Katherine! It shall be made public—as I am a living soul! If I can't hire a hall, I shall hire a drum, and parade the town with it and read it at every street corner.

PETER STOCKMANN: You are surely not such an arrant fool as that!

DR. STOCKMANN: Yes, I am.

ASLAKSEN: You won't find a single man in the whole town to go with you.

BILLING: No, I'm damned if you will.

MRS. STOCKMANN: Don't give in, Thomas. I will tell the boys to go with you.

DR. STOCKMANN: That is a splendid idea!

MRS. STOCKMANN: Morten will be delighted; and Ejlif will do whatever he does.

DR. STOCKMANN: Yes, and Petra!— and you too, Katherine!

MRS. STOCKMANN: No, I won't do that; but I will stand at the window and watch you, that's what I will do.

DR. STOCKMANN: (*puts his arms round her and kisses her*) Thank you, my dear! Now you and I are going to try a fall, my

fine gentlemen! I am going to see whether a pack of cowards can succeed in gagging a patriot who wants to purify society!
(*He and his wife go out by the street door.*)

PETER STOCKMANN: (*shaking his head seriously*) Now he has sent *her* out of her senses, too.

CURTAIN

ACT IV

SCENE: *A big old-fashioned room in* CAPTAIN HORSTER'S *house. At the back folding-doors, which are standing open, lead to an anteroom. Three windows in the left-hand wall. In the middle of the opposite wall a platform has been erected. On this is a small table with two candles, a water-bottle and glass, and a bell. The room is lit by lamps placed between the windows. In the foreground on the left there is a table with candles and a chair. To the right is a door and some chairs standing near it. The room is nearly filled with a crowd of townspeople of all sorts, a few women and schoolboys being amongst them. People are still streaming in from the back, and the room is soon filled.*

FIRST CITIZEN: (*meeting another*) Hullo, Lamstad! You here too?

SECOND CITIZEN: I go to every public meeting, I do.

THIRD CITIZEN: Brought your whistle too, I expect!

SECOND CITIZEN: I should think so. Haven't you?

THIRD CITIZEN: Rather! And old Evensen said he was going to bring a cow-horn, he did.

SECOND CITIZEN: Good old Evensen! (*Laughter among the crowd.*)

FOURTH CITIZEN: (*coming up to them*) I say, tell me what is going on here tonight.

SECOND CITIZEN: Dr. Stockmann is going to deliver an address attacking the Mayor.

FOURTH CITIZEN: But the Mayor is his brother.

FIRST CITIZEN: That doesn't matter; Dr. Stockmann's not the chap to be afraid.

THIRD CITIZEN: But he is in the wrong; it said so in the "People's Messenger."

SECOND CITIZEN: Yes, I expect he must be in the wrong this time, because neither the Householders' Association nor the Citizens' Club would lend him their hall for his meeting.

FIRST CITIZEN: He couldn't even get the loan of the hall at the Baths.

SECOND CITIZEN: No, I should think not.

A MAN IN ANOTHER PART OF THE CROWD: I say—who are we to back up in this?

ANOTHER MAN, BESIDE HIM: Watch Aslaksen, and do as he does.

BILLING: (*pushing his way through the crowd, with a writing-case under his arm*) Excuse me, gentlemen—do you mind letting me through? I am reporting for the "People's Messenger." Thank you very much!
(*He sits down at the table on the left.*)

A WORKMAN: Who was that?

SECOND WORKMAN: Don't you know him? It's Billing, who writes for Aslaksen's paper.

(CAPTAIN HORSTER *brings in* MRS. STOCKMANN *and* PETRA *through the door on the right.* EJLIF *and* MORTEN *follow them in.*)

HORSTER: I thought you might all sit here; you can slip out easily from here, if things get too lively.

MRS. STOCKMANN: Do you think there will be a disturbance?

HORSTER: One can never tell—with such a crowd. But sit down, and don't be uneasy.

MRS. STOCKMANN: (*sitting down*) It was extremely kind of you to offer my husband the room.

HORSTER: Well, if nobody else would—

PETRA: (*who has sat down beside her mother*) And it was a plucky thing to do, Captain Horster.

HORSTER: Oh, it is not such a great matter as all that.

(HOVSTAD *and* ASLAKSEN *make their way through the crowd.*)

ASLAKSEN: (*going up to* HORSTER) Has the Doctor not come yet?

HORSTER: He is waiting in the next room.

(*Movement in the crowd by the door at the back.*)

HOVSTAD: Look—here comes the Mayor!

BILLING: Yes, I'm damned if he hasn't come after all!

(PETER STOCKMANN *makes his way gradually through the crowd, bows courteously and takes up a position by the wall on the left. Shortly afterwards* DR. STOCKMANN *comes in by the right-hand door. He is dressed in a black frockcoat, with a white tie. There is a little feeble applause, which is hushed down. Silence is obtained.*)

DR. STOCKMANN: (*in an undertone*) How do you feel, Katherine?

MRS. STOCKMANN: All right, thank you. (*Lowering her voice.*) Be sure not to lose your temper, Thomas.

DR. STOCKMANN: Oh, I know how to control myself. (*Looks at his watch, steps onto the platform and bows.*) It is a quarter past—so I will begin.

(*Takes his MS. out of his pocket.*)

ASLAKSEN: I think we ought to elect a chairman first.

DR. STOCKMANN: No, it is quite unnecessary.

SOME OF THE CROWD: Yes—yes!

PETER STOCKMANN: I certainly think, too, that we ought to have a chairman.

DR. STOCKMANN: But I have called this meeting to deliver a lecture, Peter.

PETER STOCKMANN: Dr. Stockmann's lecture may possibly lead to a considerable conflict of opinion.

VOICES IN THE CROWD: A chairman! A chairman!

HOVSTAD: The general wish of the meeting seems to be that a chairman should be elected.

DR. STOCKMANN: (*restraining himself*) Very well—let the meeting have its way.

ASLAKSEN: Will the Mayor be good enough to undertake the task?

THREE MEN: (*clapping their hands*) Bravo! Bravo!

PETER STOCKMANN: For various reasons, which you will easily understand, I must beg to be excused. But fortunately we have amongst us a man who I think will be acceptable to you all. I refer to the President of the Householders' Association, Mr. Aslaksen.

SEVERAL VOICES: Yes—Aslaksen! Bravo! Aslaksen!

(DR. STOCKMANN *takes up his MS. and walks up and down the platform.*)

ASLAKSEN: Since my fellow-citizens choose to entrust me with this duty, I cannot refuse.

(*Loud applause.* ASLAKSEN *mounts the platform.*)

BILLING: (*writing*) "Mr. Aslaksen was elected with enthusiasm."

ASLAKSEN: And now, as I am in this position, I should like to say a few brief words. I am a quiet and peaceable man, who believes in discreet moderation, and —and—in moderate discretion. All my friends can bear witness to that.

SEVERAL VOICES: That's right! That's right, Aslaksen!

ASLAKSEN: I have learnt in the school of life and experience that moderation is the most valuable virtue a citizen can possess—

PETER STOCKMANN: Hear, hear!

ASLAKSEN: —And moreover that discretion and moderation are what enable a man to be of most service to the community. I would therefore suggest to our esteemed fellow-citizen, who has called this meeting, that he should strive to keep strictly within the bounds of moderation.

A MAN BY THE DOOR: Three cheers for the Moderation Society!

A VOICE: Shame!

SEVERAL VOICES: Sh!—Sh!

ASLAKSEN: No interruptions, gentlemen, please! Does anyone wish to make any remarks?

PETER STOCKMANN: Mr. Chairman.

ASLAKSEN: The Mayor will address the meeting.

PETER STOCKMANN: In consideration of the close relationship in which, as you all know, I stand to the present Medical Officer of the Baths, I should have preferred not to speak this evening. But my official position with regard to the Baths and my solicitude for the vital interests of the town compel me to bring forward a motion. I venture to presume that there is not a single one of our citizens present who considers it desirable that unreliable and exaggerated accounts of the sanitary condition of the Baths and the town should be spread abroad.

SEVERAL VOICES: No, no! Certainly not! We protest against it!

PETER STOCKMANN: Therefore I should like to propose that the meeting should not permit the Medical Officer either to read or to comment on his proposed lecture.

DR. STOCKMANN: (*impatiently*) Not permit—! What the devil—!

MRS. STOCKMANN: (*coughing*) Ahem! —ahem!

DR. STOCKMANN: (*collecting himself*) Very well. Go ahead!

PETER STOCKMANN: In my communication to the "People's Messenger," I have put the essential facts before the public in such a way that every fair-minded citizen can easily form his own opinion. From it you will see that the main result of the Medical Officer's proposals—apart from their constituting a vote of censure on the leading men of the town—would be to saddle the taxpayers with an unnecessary expenditure of at least some thousands of pounds.

(*Sounds of disapproval among the audience, and some catcalls.*)

ASLAKSEN: (*ringing his bell*) Silence, please, gentlemen! I beg to support the Mayor's motion. I quite agree with him that there is something behind this agitation started by the Doctor. He talks about the Baths; but it is a revolution he is aiming at—he wants to get the administration of the town put into new hands. No one doubts the honesty of the Doctor's intentions—no one will suggest that there can be any two opinions as to that. I myself am a believer in self-government for the people, provided it does not fall too heavily on the taxpayers. But that would be the case here; and that is why I will see Dr. Stockmann damned—I beg your pardon—before I go with him in the matter. You can pay too dearly for a thing sometimes; that is my opinion.

(*Loud applause on all sides.*)

HOVSTAD: I, too, feel called upon to explain my position. Dr. Stockmann's agitation appeared to be gaining a certain amount of sympathy at first, so I supported it as impartially as I could. But presently we had reason to suspect that we had allowed ourselves to be misled by misrepresentation of the state of affairs—

DR. STOCKMANN: Misrepresentation—!

HOVSTAD: Well, let us say a not entirely trustworthy representation. The Mayor's statement has proved that. I hope no one here has any doubt as to my liberal principles; the attitude of the "People's Messenger" towards important political questions is well known to every one. But the advice of experienced and thoughtful men has convinced me that in purely local matters a newspaper ought to proceed with a certain caution.

ASLAKSEN: I entirely agree with the speaker.

HOVSTAD: And, in the matter before us, it is now an undoubted fact that Dr. Stockmann has public opinion against him. Now, what is an editor's first and most obvious duty, gentlemen? Is it not to work in harmony with his readers? Has he not received a sort of tacit mandate to work persistently and assiduously for the welfare of those whose opinions he represents? Or is it possible I am mistaken in that?

VOICES FROM THE CROWD: No, no! You are quite right!

HOVSTAD: It has cost me a severe struggle to break with a man in whose house I have been lately a frequent guest—a man who till today has been able to pride himself on the undivided goodwill of his fellow-citizens—a man whose only, or at all events whose essential, failing is that he is swayed by his heart rather than his head.

A FEW SCATTERED VOICES: That is true! Bravo, Stockmann!

HOVSTAD: But my duty to the community obliged me to break with him. And there is another consideration that impels me to oppose him, and, as far as possible, to arrest him on the perilous course he has adopted; that is, consideration for his family—

DR. STOCKMANN: Please stick to the water-supply and drainage!

HOVSTAD: —consideration, I repeat, for his wife and his children for whom he has made no provision.

MORTEN: Is that us, mother?

MRS. STOCKMANN: Hush!

ASLAKSEN: I will now put the Mayor's proposition to the vote.

DR. STOCKMANN: There is no necessity! Tonight I have no intention of dealing with all that filth down at the Baths. No; I have something quite different to say to you.

PETER STOCKMANN: (*aside*) What is coming now?

A DRUNKEN MAN: (*by the entrance door*) I am a taxpayer! And therefore I have a right to speak too! And my entire —firm—inconceivable opinion is—

A NUMBER OF VOICES: Be quiet at the back there!

OTHERS: He is drunk! Turn him out! (*They turn him out.*)

DR. STOCKMANN: Am I allowed to speak?

ASLAKSEN: (*ringing his bell*) Dr. Stockmann will address the meeting.

DR. STOCKMANN: I should like to have seen anyone, a few days ago, dare to attempt to silence me as has been done tonight! I would have defended my sacred rights as a man, like a lion! But now it is all one to me; I have something of even weightier importance to say to you.

(*The crowd presses nearer to him,* MORTEN KIIL *conspicuous among them.*)

DR. STOCKMANN: (*continuing*) I have thought and pondered a great deal, these last few days—pondered over such a variety of things that in the end my head seemed too full to hold them—

PETER STOCKMANN: (*with a cough*) Ahem!

DR. STOCKMANN: —but I got them clear in my mind at last, and then I saw the whole situation lucidly. And that is why I am standing here tonight. I have a great revelation to make to you, my fellow-citizens! I will impart to you a discovery of a far wider scope than the trifling matter that our water-supply is poisoned and our medicinal Baths are standing on pestiferous soil.

A NUMBER OF VOICES: (*shouting*) Don't talk about the Baths! We won't hear you! None of that!

DR. STOCKMANN: I have already told you that what I want to speak about is the great discovery I have made lately—the discovery that all the sources of our *moral* life are poisoned and that the whole fabric of our civic community is founded on the pestiferous soil of falsehood.

VOICES OF DISCONCERTED CITIZENS: What is that he says?

PETER STOCKMANN: Such an insinuation—!

ASLAKSEN: (*with his hand on his bell*) I call upon the speaker to moderate his language.

DR. STOCKMANN: I have always loved my native town as a man only can love the home of his youthful days. I was not old when I went away from here; and exile, longing, and memories cast, as it were, an additional halo over both the town and its inhabitants. (*Some clapping and applause.*) And there I stayed, for many years, in a horrible hole far away up north. When I came into contact with some of the people that lived scattered about among the rocks, I often thought it would have been more service to the poor half-starved creatures if a veterinary doctor had been sent up there, instead of a man like me.

(*Murmurs among the crowd.*)

BILLING: (*laying down his pen*) I'm damned if I have ever heard—!

HOVSTAD: It is an insult to a respectable population!

DR. STOCKMANN: Wait a bit! I do not think anyone will charge me with having forgotten my native town up there. I was like one of the eider-ducks brooding on its nest, and what I hatched was—the plans for these Baths. (*Applause and protests.*) And then when fate at last decreed for me the great happiness of coming home again—I assure you, gentlemen, I thought I had nothing more in the world to wish for. Or rather, there was one thing I wished for—eagerly, untiringly, ardently —and that was to be able to be of service to my native town and the good of the community.

PETER STOCKMANN: (*looking at the ceiling*) You chose a strange way of doing it—ahem!

DR. STOCKMANN: And so, with my eyes blinded to the real facts, I revelled in happiness. But yesterday morning—no, to be precise, it was yesterday afternoon—the eyes of my mind were opened wide, and the first thing I realized was the colossal stupidity of the authorities—.

(*Uproar, shouts, and laughter.* MRS. STOCKMANN *coughs persistently.*)

PETER STOCKMANN: Mr. Chairman!

ASLAKSEN: (*ringing his bell*) By virtue of my authority—!

DR. STOCKMANN: It is a petty thing to catch me up on a word, Mr. Aslaksen. What I mean is only that I got scent of the unbelievable piggishness our leading men had been responsible for down at the Baths. I can't stand leading men at any price!—I have had enough of such people in my time. They are like billy-goats in a young plantation; they do mischief everywhere. They stand in a free man's way, whichever way he turns, and what I should like best would be to see them exterminated like any other vermin—. (*Uproar.*)

PETER STOCKMANN: Mr. Chairman, can we allow such expressions to pass?

ASLAKSEN: (*with his hand on his bell*) Doctor—!

DR. STOCKMANN: I cannot understand how it is that I have only now acquired a clear conception of what these gentry are, when I had almost daily before my eyes in this town such an excellent specimen of them—my brother Peter—slow-witted and hidebound in prejudice—.

(*Laughter, uproar, and hisses.* MRS. STOCKMANN *sits coughing assiduously.* ASLAKSEN *rings his bell violently.*)

THE DRUNKEN MAN: (*who has got in again*) Is it me he is talking about? My name's Petersen, all right—but devil take me if I—

ANGRY VOICES: Turn out that drunken man! Turn him out.

(*He is turned out again.*)

PETER STOCKMANN: Who was that person?

FIRST CITIZEN: I don't know who he is, Mr. Mayor.

SECOND CITIZEN: He doesn't belong here.

THIRD CITIZEN: I expect he is a lumberman from over at (*the rest is inaudible.*)

ASLAKSEN: He had obviously had too much beer.—Proceed, Doctor; but please strive to be moderate in your language.

DR. STOCKMANN: Very well, gentlemen, I will say no more about our leading men. And if anyone imagines, from what I have just said, that my object is to attack these people this evening, he is wrong—absolutely wide of the mark. For I cherish the comforting conviction that these parasites—all these venerable relics of a dying school of thought—are most admirably paving the way for their own extinction; they need no doctor's help to hasten their end. Nor is it folk of that kind who constitute the most pressing danger to the community. It is not they who are most instrumental in poisoning the sources of our moral life and infecting the ground on which we stand. It is not they who are the most dangerous enemies of truth and freedom amongst us.

SHOUTS FROM ALL SIDES: Who then? Who is it? Name! Name!

DR. STOCKMANN: You may depend upon it I shall name them! That is precisely the great discovery I made yesterday. (*Raises his voice.*) The most dangerous enemy of truth and freedom amongst us is the compact majority—yes, the damned compact Liberal majority—that is it! Now you know!

(*Tremendous uproar. Most of the crowd are shouting, stamping, and hissing. Some of the older men among them exchange stolen glances and seem to be enjoying themselves.* MRS. STOCKMANN *gets up, looking anxious.* EJLIF *and* MORTEN *advance threateningly upon some schoolboys who are playing pranks.* ASLAKSEN *rings his bell and begs for silence.* HOVSTAD *and* BILLING *both talk at once, but are inaudible. At last quiet is restored.*)

ASLAKSEN: As chairman, I call upon the speaker to withdraw the ill-considered expressions he has just used.

DR. STOCKMANN: Never, Mr. Aslaksen! It is the majority in our community that denies me my freedom and seeks to prevent my speaking the truth.

HOVSTAD: The majority always has right on its side.

BILLING: And truth too, by God!

DR. STOCKMANN: The majority *never* has right on its side. Never, I say! That is one of these social lies against which an independent, intelligent man must wage war. Who constitutes the majority of the population in a country? Is it the clever folk or the stupid? I don't imagine you will dispute the fact that at present the stupid people are in an absolutely overwhelming majority all the world over. But, good Lord!—you can never pretend that it is right that the stupid folk should govern the clever ones! (*Uproar and cries.*) Oh, yes—you can shout me down, I know! but you cannot answer me. The majority has *might* on its side—unfortunately; but *right* it has *not*. I am in the right—I and a few other scattered individuals. The minority is always in the right.

(*Renewed uproar.*)

HOVSTAD: Aha!—so Dr. Stockmann has become an aristocrat since the day before yesterday!

DR. STOCKMANN: I have already said that I don't intend to waste a word on the puny, narrow-chested, short-winded crew whom we are leaving astern. Pulsating life no longer concerns itself with them. I am thinking of the few, the scattered few amongst us, who have absorbed new and vigorous truths. Such men stand, as it were, at the outposts, so far ahead that the compact majority has not yet been able to come up with them; and there they are fighting for truths that are too newly-born into the world of consciousness to have any considerable number of people on their side as yet.

HOVSTAD: So the Doctor is a revolutionary now!

DR. STOCKMANN: Good heavens—of course I am, Mr. Hovstad! I propose to raise a revolution against the lie that the majority has the monopoly of the truth. What sort of truths are they that the majority usually supports? They are truths that are of such advanced age that they are beginning to break up. And if a truth is as old as that, it is also in a fair way to become a lie, gentlemen. (*Laughter and mocking cries.*) Yes, believe me or not, as you like; but truths are by no means as long-lived as Methuselah—as some folk imagine. A normally constituted truth lives, let us say, as a rule seventeen or eighteen, or at most twenty years; seldom longer. But truths as aged as that are always worn frightfully thin, and nevertheless it is only then that the majority recognizes them and recommends them to the community as wholesome moral nourishment. There is no great nutritive value in that sort of fare, I can assure you; and, as a doctor, I ought to know. These "majority truths" are like last year's cured meat—like rancid, tainted ham; and they are the origin of the moral scurvy that is rampant in our communities.

ASLAKSEN: It appears to me that the speaker is wandering a long way from his subject.

PETER STOCKMANN: I quite agree with the Chairman.

DR. STOCKMANN: Have you gone clean out of your senses, Peter? I am sticking as closely to my subject as I can; for my subject is precisely this, that it is the masses, the majority—this infernal compact majority—that poisons the sources of our moral life and infects the ground we stand on.

HOVSTAD: And all this because the great, broad-minded majority of the people is prudent enough to show deference only to well-ascertained and well-approved truths?

DR. STOCKMANN: Ah, my good Mr. Hovstad, don't talk nonsense about well-ascertained truths! The truths of which the masses now approve are the very truths that the fighters at the outposts held to in the days of our grandfathers. We fighters at the outposts nowadays no longer approve of them; and I do not believe there is any other well-ascertained truth except this, that no community can live a healthy life if it is nourished only on such old marrowless truths.

HOVSTAD: But instead of standing there using vague generalities, it would be interesting if you would tell us what these old marrowless truths are, that we are nourished on.

(*Applause from many quarters.*)

DR. STOCKMANN: Oh, I could give you a whole string of such abominations; but to begin with I will confine myself to one well-approved truth, which at bottom is a foul lie, but upon which nevertheless Mr. Hovstad and the "People's Messenger" and all the "Messenger's" supporters are nourished.

HOVSTAD: And that is—?

DR. STOCKMANN: That is, the doctrine you have inherited from your forefathers and proclaim thoughtlessly far and wide—the doctrine that the public, the crowd, the masses are the essential part of the population—that they constitute the People—that the common folk, the ignorant and incomplete element in the community, have the same right to pronounce judgment and to approve, to direct, and to govern, as the isolated, intellectually superior personalities in it.

BILLING: Well, damn me if ever I—

HOVSTAD: (*at the same time, shouting out*) Fellow-citizens, take good note of that!

A NUMBER OF VOICES: (*angrily*) Oho!—we are not the People! Only the superior folks are to govern, are they?

A WORKMAN: Turn the fellow out, for talking such rubbish!

ANOTHER: Out with him!

ANOTHER: (*calling out*) Blow your horn, Evensen!

(*A horn is blown loudly, amidst hisses and an angry uproar.*)

DR. STOCKMANN: (*when the noise has somewhat abated*) Be reasonable! Can't you stand hearing the voice of truth for once? I don't in the least expect you to agree with me all at once; but I must say I did expect Mr. Hovstad to admit I was right, when he had recovered his composure a little. He claims to be a freethinker—

VOICES: (*in murmurs of astonishment*) Freethinker, did he say? Is Hovstad a freethinker?

HOVSTAD: (*shouting*) Prove it, Dr. Stockmann! When have I said so in print?

DR. STOCKMANN: (*reflecting*) No, confound it, you are right!—you have never had the courage to. Well, I won't put you in a hole, Mr. Hovstad. Let us say it is I that am the freethinker, then. I am going to prove to you, scientifically, that the "People's Messenger" leads you by the nose in a shameful manner when it tells you that you—that the common people, the crowd, the masses are the real essence of the People. That is only a newspaper lie, I tell you! The common people are nothing more than the raw material of which a People is made. (*Groans, laughter and uproar.*) Well, isn't that the case? Isn't there an enormous difference between a well-bred and an ill-bred strain of animals? Take, for instance, a common barn-door hen. What sort of eating do you get from a shrivelled-up old scrag of a fowl like that? Not much, do you? And what sort of eggs does it lay? A fairly good crow or a raven can lay pretty nearly as good an egg. But take a well-bred Spanish or Japanese hen, or a good pheasant or a turkey—then you will see the difference. Or take the case of dogs, with whom we humans are on such intimate terms. Think first of an ordinary common cur—I mean one of the horrible, coarsehaired, low-bred curs that do nothing but run about the streets and befoul the walls of the houses. Compare one of these curs with a poodle whose sires for many generations have been bred in a gentleman's house, where they have had the best of food and had the opportunity of hearing soft voices and music. Do you not think that the poodle's brain is developed to quite a different degree from that of the cur? Of course it is. It is puppies of wellbred poodles like that that showmen train to do incredibly clever tricks—things that a common cur could never learn to do even if it stood on its head.

(*Uproar and mocking cries.*)

A CITIZEN: (*calls out*) Are you going to make out we are dogs, now?

ANOTHER CITIZEN: We are not animals, Doctor!

DR. STOCKMANN: Yes, but, bless my soul, we *are*, my friend! It is true we are the finest animals anyone could wish for; but, even amongst us, exceptionally fine animals are rare. There is a tremendous difference between poodle-men and curmen. And the amusing part of it is that Mr. Hovstad quite agrees with me as long as it is a question of four-footed animals—

HOVSTAD: Yes, it is true enough as far as they are concerned.

DR. STOCKMANN: Very well. But as soon as I extend the principle and apply it to two-legged animals, Mr. Hovstad stops short. He no longer dares to think independently, or to pursue his ideas to their logical conclusion; so he turns the whole theory upside down and proclaims in the "People's Messenger" that it is the barn-door hens and street curs that are the finest specimens in the menagerie. But that is always the way, as long as a man retains the traces of common origin and has not worked his way up to intellectual distinction.

HOVSTAD: I lay no claim to any sort of distinction. I am the son of humble countryfolk, and I am proud that the stock I come from is rooted deep among the common people he insults.

VOICES: Bravo, Hovstad! Bravo! Bravo!

DR. STOCKMANN: The kind of common people I mean are not only to be found low down in the social scale; they crawl and swarm all around us—even in the highest social positions. You have only to look at your own fine, distinguished Mayor! My brother Peter is every bit as plebeian as anyone that walks in two shoes— (*Laughter and hisses.*)

PETER STOCKMANN: I protest against personal allusions of this kind.

DR. STOCKMANN: (*imperturbably*) — and that, not because he is, like myself, descended from some old rascal of a pirate from Pomerania or thereabouts—because that is who we are descended from—

PETER STOCKMANN: An absurd legend. I deny it!

DR. STOCKMANN: —but because he thinks what his superiors think and holds the same opinions as they. People who do that are, intellectually speaking, common people; and that is why my magnificent brother Peter is in reality so very far from any distinction—and consequently also so far from being liberal-minded.

PETER STOCKMANN: Mr. Chairman—!

HOVSTAD: So it is only the distinguished men that are liberal-minded in this country? We are learning something quite new! (*Laughter.*)

DR. STOCKMANN: Yes, that is part of my new discovery too. And another part of it is that broad-mindedness is almost precisely the same thing as morality. That is why I maintain that it is absolutely inexcusable in the "People's Messenger" to proclaim, day in and day out, the false doctrine that the masses, the crowd, the compact majority have the monopoly of broad-mindedness and morality—and that vice and corruption and every kind of intellectual depravity are the result of culture, just as all the filth that is draining into our Baths is the result of the tanneries up at Mölledal! (*Uproar and interruptions. DR. STOCKMANN is undisturbed, and goes on, carried away by his ardor, with a smile.*) And yet this same "People's Messenger" can go on preaching that the masses ought to be elevated to higher conditions of life! But, bless my soul, if the "Messenger's" teaching is to be depended upon, this very raising up the masses would mean nothing more or less than setting them straightway upon the paths of depravity! Happily the theory that culture demoralizes is only an old falsehood that our forefathers believed in and we have inherited. No, it is ignorance, poverty, ugly conditions of life that do the devil's work! In a house which does not get aired and swept every day—my wife Katherine maintains that the floor ought to be scrubbed as well, but that is a debatable question—in such a house, let me tell you, people will lose within two or three years the power of thinking or acting in a moral manner. Lack of oxygen weakens the conscience. And there must be a plentiful lack of oxygen in very many houses in this town. I should think, judging from the fact that the whole compact majority can be unconscientious enough to wish to build the town's prosperity on a quagmire of falsehood and deceit.

ASLAKSEN: We cannot allow such a grave accusation to be flung at a citizen community.

A CITIZEN: I move that the Chairman direct the speaker to sit down.

VOICES: (*angrily*) Hear, hear! Quite right! Make him sit down!

DR. STOCKMANN: (*losing his self-con-

trol) Then I will go and shout the truth at every street corner! I will write it in other towns' newspapers! The whole country shall know what is going on here!

HOVSTAD: It almost seems as if Dr. Stockmann's intention were to ruin the town.

DR. STOCKMANN: Yes, my native town is so dear to me that I would rather ruin it than see it flourishing upon a lie.

ASLAKSEN: This is really serious.

(*Uproar and catcalls.* MRS. STOCKMANN *coughs, but to no purpose; her husband does not listen to her any longer.*)

HOVSTAD: (*shouting above the din*) A man must be a public enemy to wish to ruin a whole community!

DR. STOCKMANN: (*with growing fervor*) What does the destruction of a community matter, if it lives on lies! It ought to be razed to the ground, I tell you! All who live by lies ought to be exterminated like vermin! You will end by infecting the whole country; you will bring about such a state of things that the whole country will deserve to be ruined. And if things come to that pass, I shall say from the bottom of my heart: Let the whole country perish, let all these people be exterminated!

VOICES FROM THE CROWD: That is talking like an out-and-out enemy of the people!

BILLING: There sounded the voice of the people, by all that's holy!

THE WHOLE CROWD: (*shouting*) Yes, yes! He is an enemy of the people! He hates his country! He hates his own people!

ASLAKSEN: Both as a citizen and as an individual, I am profoundly disturbed by what we have had to listen to. Dr. Stockmann has shown himself in a light I should never have dreamed of. I am unhappily obliged to subscribe to the opinion which I have just heard my estimable fellow-citizens utter; and I propose that we should give expression to that opinion in a resolution. I propose a resolution as follows: "This meeting declares that it considers Dr. Thomas Stockmann, Medical Officer of the Baths, to be an enemy of the people."

(*A storm of cheers and applause. A number of men surround the* DOCTOR *and hiss him.* MRS. STOCKMANN *and* PETRA *have got up from their seats.* MORTEN *and* EJLIF *are fighting the other schoolboys for hissing; some of their elders separate them.*)

DR. STOCKMANN: (*to the men who are hissing him*) Oh, you fools! I tell you that—

ASLAKSEN: (*ringing his bell*) We cannot hear you now, Doctor. A formal vote is about to be taken; but, out of regard for personal feelings, it shall be by ballot and not verbal. Have you any clean paper, Mr. Billing?

BILLING: I have both blue and white here.

ASLAKSEN: (*going to him*) That will do nicely; we shall get on more quickly that way. Cut it up into small strips—yes, that's it. (*To the meeting*) Blue means no; white means yes. I will come round myself and collect votes.

(PETER STOCKMANN *leaves the hall.* ASLAKSEN *and one or two others go round the room with the slips of paper in their hats.*)

FIRST CITIZEN: (*to* HOVSTAD) I say, what has come to the Doctor? What are we to think of it?

HOVSTAD: Oh, you know how headstrong he is.

SECOND CITIZEN: (*to* BILLING) Billing, you go to their house—have you ever noticed if the fellow drinks?

BILLING: Well, I'm hanged if I know what to say. There are always spirits on the table when you go.

THIRD CITIZEN: I rather think he goes quite off his head sometimes.

FIRST CITIZEN: I wonder if there is any madness in his family?

BILLING: I shouldn't wonder if there were.

FOURTH CITIZEN: No, it is nothing more than sheer malice; he wants to get even with somebody for something or other.

BILLING: Well certainly he suggested a rise in his salary on one occasion lately, and did not get it.

THE CITIZENS: (*together*) Ah!—then it is easy to understand how it is!

THE DRUNKEN MAN: (*who has got amongst the audience again*) I want a blue one, I do! And I want a white one too!

VOICES: It's that drunken chap again! Turn him out!

MORTEN KIIL: (*going up to* DR. STOCKMANN) Well, Stockmann, do you see what these monkey tricks of yours lead to?

DR. STOCKMANN: I have done my duty.

MORTEN KIIL: What was that you said about the tanneries at Mölledal?

DR. STOCKMANN: You heard well enough. I said they were the source of all the filth.

MORTEN KIIL: My tannery too?

DR. STOCKMANN: Unfortunately your tannery is by far the worst.

MORTEN KIIL: Are you going to put that in the papers?

DR. STOCKMANN: I shall conceal nothing.

MORTEN KIIL: That may cost you dear, Stockmann. (*Goes out.*)

A STOUT MAN: (*going up to* CAPTAIN HORSTER, *without taking any notice of the ladies*) Well, Captain, so you lend your house to enemies of the people?

HORSTER: I imagine I can do what I like with my own possessions, Mr. Vik.

THE STOUT MAN: Then you can have no objection to my doing the same with mine.

HORSTER: What do you mean, sir?

THE STOUT MAN: You shall hear from me in the morning.

(*Turns his back on him and moves off.*)

PETRA: Was that not your owner, Captain Horster?

HORSTER: Yes, that was Mr. Vik, the ship-owner.

ASLAKSEN: (*with the voting-papers in his hands, gets up on to the platform and rings his bell*) Gentlemen, allow me to announce the result. By the votes of every one here except one person—

A YOUNG MAN: That is the drunk chap!

ASLAKSEN: By the votes of every one here except a tipsy man, this meeting of citizens declares Dr. Thomas Stockmann to be an enemy of the people. (*Shouts and applause.*) Three cheers for our ancient and honorable citizen community! (*Renewed applause.*) Three cheers for our able and energetic Mayor, who has so loyally suppressed the promptings of family feeling! (*Cheers.*) The meeting is dissolved. (*Gets down.*)

BILLING: Three cheers for the Chairman!

THE WHOLE CROWD: Three cheers for Aslaksen! Hurah!

DR. STOCKMANN: My hat and coat, Petra! Captain, have you room on your ship for passengers to the New World?

HORSTER: For you and yours we will make room, Doctor.

DR. STOCKMANN: (*as* PETRA *helps him into his coat*) Good. Come, Katherine! Come, boys!

MRS. STOCKMANN: (*in an undertone*) Thomas, dear, let us go out by the back way.

DR. STOCKMANN: No back ways for me, Katherine. (*Raising his voice.*) You will hear more of this enemy of the people, before he shakes the dust off his shoes upon you! I am not so forgiving as a certain Person; I do not say: "I forgive you, for ye know not what ye do."

ASLAKSEN: (*shouting*) That is a blasphemous comparison, Dr. Stockmann!

BILLING: It is, by God! It's dreadful for an earnest man to listen to.

A COARSE VOICE: Threatens us now, does he?

OTHER VOICES: (*excitedly*) Let's go and break his windows! Duck him in the fjord!

ANOTHER VOICE: Blow your horn, Evensen! Pip, pip!

(*Horn-blowing, hisses, and wild cries.* DR. STOCKMANN *goes out through the hall with his family,* HORSTER *elbowing a way for them.*)

THE WHOLE CROWD: (*howling after them as they go*) Enemy of the People! Enemy of the People!

BILLING: (*as he puts his papers together*) Well, I'm damned if I go and drink toddy with the Stockmanns tonight!

(*The crowd presses towards the exit. The uproar continues outside; shouts of* "Enemy of the People!" *are heard from without.*)

CURTAIN

ACT V

SCENE: DR. STOCKMANN'S *study. Bookcases and cabinets containing specimens line the walls. At the back is a door leading to the hall; in the foreground on the left, a door leading to the sitting-room. In the right-hand wall are two windows, of which all the panes are broken. The* DOCTOR'S *desk, littered with books and papers, stands in the middle of the room, which is in disorder. It is morning.* DR. STOCKMANN *in dressing-gown, slippers, and a smoking-cap, is bending down and raking with an umbrella under one of the cabinets. After a little while he rakes out a stone.*

DR. STOCKMANN: (*calling through the open sitting-room door*) Katherine, I found another one.

MRS. STOCKMANN: (*from the sitting-room*) Oh, you will find a lot more yet, I expect.

DR. STOCKMANN: (*adding the stone to a heap of others on the table*) I shall treasure these stones as relics. Ejlif and Morten shall look at them every day, and when they are grown up they shall inherit them as heirlooms. (*Rakes about under a bookcase*) Hasn't—what the deuce is her name?—the girl, you know—hasn't she been to fetch the glazier yet?

MRS. STOCKMANN: (*coming in*) Yes, but he said he didn't know if he would be able to come today.

DR. STOCKMANN: You will see he won't dare to come.

MRS. STOCKMANN: Well, that is just what Randine thought—that he didn't dare to, on account of the neighbors. (*Calls into the sitting-room.*) What is it you want, Randine? Give it to me. (*Goes in, and comes out again directly.*) Here is a letter for you, Thomas.

DR. STOCKMANN: Let me see it. (*Opens and reads it.*) Ah!—of course.

MRS. STOCKMANN: Who is it from?

DR. STOCKMANN: From the landlord. Notice to quit.

MRS. STOCKMANN: Is it possible? Such a nice man—

DR. STOCKMANN: (*looking at the letter*) Does not dare do otherwise, he says. Doesn't like doing it, but dare not do otherwise—on account of his fellow-citizens—out of regard for public opinion. Is in a dependent position—dare not offend certain influential men—

MRS. STOCKMANN: There, you see, Thomas!

DR. STOCKMANN: Yes, yes, I see well enough; the whole lot of them in the town are cowards; not a man among them dares do anything for fear of the others. (*Throws the letter onto the table.*) But it doesn't matter to us, Katherine. We are going to sail away to the New World, and—

MRS. STOCKMANN: But, Thomas, are you sure we are well advised to take this step?

DR. STOCKMANN: Are you suggesting that I should stay here, where they have pilloried me as an enemy of the people—branded me—broken my windows! And just look here, Katherine—they have torn a great rent in my black trousers too!

MRS. STOCKMANN: Oh, dear!—and they are the best pair you have got!

DR. STOCKMANN: You should never wear your best trousers when you go out to fight for freedom and truth. It is not that I care so much about the trousers, you know; you can always sew them up again for me. But that the common herd should dare to make this attack on me, as if they were my equals—that is what I cannot, for the life of me, swallow!

MRS. STOCKMANN: There is no doubt they have behaved very ill to you, Thomas; but is that sufficient reason for our leaving our native country for good and all?

DR. STOCKMANN: If we went to another town, do you suppose we should not find the common people just as insolent as they are here? Depend upon it, there is not much to choose between them. Oh, well, let the curs snap—that is not the worst part of it. The worst is that, from one end of this country to the other, every man is the slave of his Party. Although, as far as that goes, I daresay it is not much better in the free West either; the compact majority, and liberal public opinion, and all that infernal old bag of tricks are probably rampant there too. But there things are done on a larger scale, you see. They may kill you, but they won't put you to death by slow torture. They don't squeeze a free man's soul in a vice, as they do here. And, if need be, one can live in solitude. (*Walks up and down.*) If only I knew where there was a virgin forest or a small South Sea island for sale, cheap—

MRS. STOCKMANN: But think of the boys, Thomas.

DR. STOCKMANN: (*standing still*) What a strange woman you are, Katherine! Would you prefer to have the boys grow up in a society like this? You saw for yourself last night that half the population are out of their minds; and if the other half have not lost their senses, it is because they are mere brutes, with no sense to lose.

MRS. STOCKMANN: But, Thomas dear, the imprudent things you said had something to do with it, you know.

DR. STOCKMANN: Well, isn't what I said perfectly true? Don't they turn every idea topsy-turvy? Don't they make a regular hotch-potch of right and wrong? Don't they say that the things I know are true are lies? The craziest part of it all is the fact of these "liberals," men of full age, going about in crowds imagining that they are the broad-minded party! Did you ever hear anything like it, Katherine?

MRS. STOCKMANN: Yes, yes, it's mad enough of them, certainly; but— (PETRA *comes in from the sitting-room.*) Back from school already?

PETRA: Yes. I have been given notice of dismissal.

MRS. STOCKMANN: Dismissal?

DR. STOCKMANN: You too?

PETRA: Mrs. Busk gave me my notice; so I thought it was best to go at once.

DR. STOCKMANN: You were perfectly right, too!

MRS. STOCKMANN: Who would have thought Mrs. Busk was a woman like that?

PETRA: Mrs. Busk isn't a bit like that, mother; I saw quite plainly how it hurt her to do it. But she didn't dare do otherwise, she said; and so I got my notice.

DR. STOCKMANN: (*laughing and rubbing his hands*) She didn't dare do otherwise, either! It's delicious!

MRS. STOCKMANN: Well, after the dreadful scenes last night—

PETRA: It was not only that. Just listen to this, father!

DR. STOCKMANN: Well?

PETRA: Mrs. Busk showed me no less than three letters she received this morning—

DR. STOCKMANN: Anonymous, I suppose?

PETRA: Yes.

DR. STOCKMANN: Yes, because they didn't dare to risk signing their names, Katherine!

PETRA: And two of them were to the effect that a man, who has been our guest here, was declaring last night at the Club that my views on various subjects are extremely emancipated—

DR. STOCKMANN: You did not deny that, I hope?

PETRA: No, you know I wouldn't. Mrs. Busk's own views are tolerably emancipated, when we are alone together; but now that this report about me is being spread, she dare not keep me on any longer.

MRS. STOCKMANN: And some one who had been a guest of ours! That shows you the return you get for your hospitality, Thomas!

DR. STOCKMANN: We won't live in such a disgusting hole any longer. Pack up as quickly as you can, Katherine; the sooner we can get away the better.

MRS. STOCKMANN: Be quiet—I think I hear some one in the hall. See who it is, Petra.

PETRA: (*opening the door*) Oh, it's you, Captain Horster! Do come in.

HORSTER: (*coming in*) Good morning. I thought I would just come in and see how you were.

DR. STOCKMANN: (*shaking his hand*) Thanks—that is really kind of you.

MRS. STOCKMANN: And thank you, too, for helping us through the crowd, Captain Horster.

PETRA: How did you manage to get home again?

HORSTER: Oh, somehow or other. I am fairly strong, and there is more sound than fury about these folk.

DR. STOCKMANN: Yes, isn't their swinish cowardice astonishing? Look here, I will show you something! There are all the stones they have thrown through my windows. Just look at them! I'm hanged if there are more than two decently large bits of hardstone in the whole heap; the rest are nothing but gravel—wretched little things. And yet they stood out there bawling and swearing that they would do me some violence; but as for *doing* anything—you don't see much of that in this town.

HORSTER: Just as well for you this time, Doctor!

DR. STOCKMANN: True enough. But it makes one angry all the same; because if some day it should be a question of a national fight in real earnest, you will see that public opinion will be in favor of taking to one's heels, and the compact majority will turn tail like a flock of sheep, Captain Horster. That is what is so mournful to think of; it gives me so much concern, that—. No, devil take it, it is ridiculous to care about it! They have called me an enemy of the people, so an enemy of the people let me be!

MRS. STOCKMANN: You will never be that, Thomas.

DR. STOCKMANN: Don't swear to that, Katherine. To be called an ugly name may have the same effect as a pin-scratch in the lung. And that hateful name—I can't get quit of it. It is sticking here in the pit of my stomach, eating into me like a corrosive acid. And no magnesia will remove it.

PETRA: Bah!—you should only laugh at them, father.

HORSTER: They will change their minds some day, Doctor.

MRS. STOCKMANN: Yes, Thomas, as sure as you are standing here.

DR. STOCKMANN: Perhaps, when it is too late. Much good may it do them! They may wallow in their filth then and rue the day when they drove a patriot into exile. When do you sail, Captain Horster?

HORSTER: Hm!—that was just what I had come to speak about—

DR. STOCKMANN: Why, has anything gone wrong with the ship?

HORSTER: No; but what has happened is that I am not to sail in it.

PETRA: Do you mean that you have been dismissed from your command?

HORSTER: (*smiling*) Yes, that's just it.

PETRA: You too.

MRS. STOCKMANN: There, you see, Thomas!

DR. STOCKMANN: And that for the truth's sake! Oh, if I had thought such a thing possible—

HORSTER: You mustn't take it to heart; I shall be sure to find a job with some ship-owner or other, elsewhere.

DR. STOCKMANN: And that is this man Vik—a wealthy man, independent of every one and everything—! Shame on him!

HORSTER: He is quite an excellent fellow otherwise; he told me himself he would willingly have kept me on, if only he had dared—

DR. STOCKMANN: But he didn't dare? No, of course not.

HORSTER: It is not such an easy matter, he said, for a party man—

DR. STOCKMANN: The worthy man spoke the truth. A party is like a sausage machine; it mashes up all sorts of heads together into the same mincemeat—fatheads and blockheads, all in one mash!

MRS. STOCKMANN: Come, come, Thomas dear!

PETRA: (*to* HORSTER) If only you had not come home with us, things might not have come to this pass.

HORSTER: I do not regret it.

PETRA: (*holding out her hand to him*) Thank you for that!

HORSTER: (*to* DR. STOCKMANN) And so what I came to say was that if you are determined to go away, I have thought of another plan—

DR. STOCKMANN: That's splendid!—if only we can get away at once.

MRS. STOCKMANN: Hush!—wasn't that some one knocking?

PETRA: That is uncle, surely.

DR. STOCKMANN: Aha! (*Calls out.*) Come in!

MRS. STOCKMANN: Dear Thomas, promise me definitely— (PETER STOCKMANN *comes in from the hall.*)

PETER STOCKMANN: Oh, you are engaged. In that case, I will—

DR. STOCKMANN: No, no, come in.

PETER STOCKMANN: But I wanted to speak to you alone.

MRS. STOCKMANN: We will go into the sitting-room in the meanwhile.

HORSTER: And I will look in again later.

DR. STOCKMANN: No, go in there with them, Captain Horster; I want to hear more about—.

HORSTER: Very well, I will wait, then.

(*He follows* MRS. STOCKMANN *and* PETRA *into the sitting-room.*)

DR. STOCKMANN: I daresay you find it rather draughty here today. Put your hat on.

PETER STOCKMANN: Thank you, if I may. (*Does so.*) I think I caught cold last night; I stood and shivered—

DR. STOCKMANN: Really? I found it warm enough.

PETER STOCKMANN: I regret that it was not in my power to prevent those excesses last night.

DR. STOCKMANN: Have you anything particular to say to me besides that?

PETER STOCKMANN: (*taking a big*

letter from his pocket) I have this document for you, from the Baths Committee.

DR. STOCKMANN: My dismissal?

PETER STOCKMANN: Yes, dating from today. (*Lays the letter on the table.*) It gives us pain to do it; but, to speak frankly, we dared not do otherwise on account of public opinion.

DR. STOCKMANN: (*smiling*) Dared not? I seem to have heard that word before, today.

PETER STOCKMANN: I must beg you to understand your position clearly. For the future you must not count on any practice whatever in the town.

DR. STOCKMANN: Devil take the practice! But why are you so sure of that?

PETER STOCKMANN: The Householders' Association is circulating a list from house to house. All right-minded citizens are being called upon to give up employing you; and I can assure you that not a single head of a family will risk refusing his signature. They simply dare not.

DR. STOCKMANN: No, no; I don't doubt it. But what then?

PETER STOCKMANN: If I might advise you, it would be best to leave the place for a little while—

DR. STOCKMANN: Yes, the propriety of leaving the place *has* occurred to me.

PETER STOCKMANN: Good. And then, when you have had six months to think things over, if, after mature consideration, you can persuade yourself to write a few words of regret, acknowledging your error—

DR. STOCKMANN: I might have my appointment restored to me, do you mean?

PETER STOCKMANN: Perhaps. It is not at all impossible.

DR. STOCKMANN: But what about public opinion, then? Surely you would not dare to do it on account of public feeling.

PETER STOCKMANN: Public opinion is an extremely mutable thing. And, to be quite candid with you, it is a matter of great importance to us to have some admission of that sort from you in writing.

DR. STOCKMANN: Oh, that's what you are after, is it? I will just trouble you to remember what I said to you lately about foxy tricks of that sort!

PETER STOCKMANN: Your position was quite different then. At that time you had reason to suppose you had the whole town at your back—

DR. STOCKMANN: Yes, and now I feel I have the whole town *on* my back—(*flaring up*) I would not do it if I had the devil and his dam on my back—! Never—never, I tell you!

PETER STOCKMANN: A man with a family has no right to behave as you do. You have no right to do it, Thomas.

DR. STOCKMANN: I have no right! There is only one single thing in the world a free man has no right to do. Do you know what that is?

PETER STOCKMANN: No.

DR. STOCKMANN: Of course you don't, but I will tell you. A free man has no right to soil himself with filth; he has no right to behave in a way that would justify his spitting in his own face.

PETER STOCKMANN: This sort of thing sounds extremely plausible, of course; and if there were no other explanation for your obstinacy—. But as it happens there is.

DR. STOCKMANN: What do you mean?

PETER STOCKMANN: You understand very well what I mean. But, as your brother and as a man of discretion, I advise you not to build too much upon expectations and prospects that may so very easily fail you.

DR. STOCKMANN: What in the world is all this about?

PETER STOCKMANN: Do you really ask me to believe that you are ignorant of the terms of Mr. Kiil's will?

DR. STOCKMANN: I know that the small amount he possesses is to go to an institution for indigent old work-people. How does that concern me?

PETER STOCKMANN: In the first place, it is by no means a small amount that is in question. Mr. Kiil is a fairly wealthy man.

DR. STOCKMANN: I had no notion of that!

PETER STOCKMANN: Hm!—hadn't you really? Then I suppose you had no notion, either, that a considerable portion of his wealth will come to your children, you and your wife having a life-income from the capital. Has he never told you so?

DR. STOCKMANN: Never, on my honor! Quite the reverse; he has consistently done nothing but fume at being so unconscionably heavily taxed. But are you perfectly certain of this, Peter?

PETER STOCKMANN: I have it from an absolutely reliable source.

DR. STOCKMANN: Then, thank God, Katherine is provided for—and the children too! I must tell her this at once—(*calls out*) Katherine, Katherine!

PETER STOCKMANN: (*restraining him*) Hush, don't say a word yet!

MRS. STOCKMANN: (*opening the door*) What is the matter?

DR. STOCKMANN: Oh, nothing, nothing; you can go back. (*She shuts the door.* DR. STOCKMANN *walks up and down in his excitement.*) Provided for!—Just think of it, we are all provided for! And for life! What a blessed feeling it is to know one is provided for!

PETER STOCKMANN: Yes, but that is just exactly what you are not. Mr. Kiil can alter his will any day he likes.

DR. STOCKMANN: But he won't do that, my dear Peter. The "Badger" is much too delighted at my attack on you and your wise friends.

PETER STOCKMANN: (*starts and looks intently at him*) Ah, that throws a light on various things.

DR. STOCKMANN: What things?

PETER STOCKMANN: I see that the whole thing was a combined manœuvre on your part and his. These violent, reckless attacks that you have made against the leading men of the town, under the pretense that it was in the name of truth—

DR. STOCKMANN: What about them?

PETER STOCKMANN: I see that they were nothing else than the stipulated price for that vindictive old man's will.

DR. STOCKMANN: (*almost speechless*) Peter—you are the most disgusting plebeian I have ever met in all my life.

PETER STOCKMANN: All is over between us. Your dismissal is irrevocable—we have a weapon against you now. (*Goes out.*)

DR. STOCKMANN: For shame! For shame! (*Calls out.*) Katherine, you must have the floor scrubbed after him! Let—what's her name—devil take it, the girl who has always got soot on her nose—

MRS. STOCKMANN: (*in the sitting-room*) Hush, Thomas, be quiet!

PETRA: (*coming to the door*) Father, grandfather is here, asking if he may speak to you alone.

DR. STOCKMANN: Certainly he may. (*Going to the door.*) Come in, Mr. Kiil. (MORTEN KIIL *comes in.* DR. STOCKMANN *shuts the door after him.*) What can I do for you? Won't you sit down?

MORTEN KIIL: I won't sit. (*Looks around.*) You look very comfortable here today, Thomas.

DR. STOCKMANN: Yes, don't we?

MORTEN KIIL: Very comfortable—plenty of fresh air. I should think you have got enough today of that oxygen you were talking about yesterday. Your conscience must be in splendid order today, I should think.

DR. STOCKMANN: It is.

MORTEN KIIL: So I should think. (*Taps his chest.*) Do you know what I have got here?

DR. STOCKMANN: A good conscience, too, I hope.

MORTEN KIIL: Bah!—No, it is something better than that.

(*He takes a thick pocket-book from his breast-pocket, opens it, and displays a packet of papers.*)

DR. STOCKMANN: (*looking at him in astonishment*) Shares in the Baths?

MORTEN KIIL: They were not difficult to get today.

DR. STOCKMANN: And you have been buying—?

MORTEN KIIL: As many as I could pay for.

DR. STOCKMANN: But, my dear Mr. Kiil—consider the state of the Baths' affairs!

MORTEN KIIL: If you behave like a reasonable man, you can soon set the Baths on their feet again.

DR. STOCKMANN: Well, you can see for yourself that I have done all I can, but—. They are all mad in this town!

MORTEN KIIL: You said yesterday that the worst of this pollution came from my tannery. If that is true, then my grandfather and my father before me, and I myself, for many years past, have been poisoning the town like three destroying angels. Do you think I am going to sit quiet under that reproach?

DR. STOCKMANN: Unfortunately, I am afraid you will have to.

MORTEN KIIL: No, thank you. I am jealous of my name and reputation. They call me "the Badger," I am told. A badger is a kind of pig, I believe; but I am not going to give them the right to call me that. I mean to live and die a clean man.

DR. STOCKMANN: And how are you going to set about it?

MORTEN KIIL: You shall cleanse me, Thomas.

DR. STOCKMANN: I!

MORTEN KIIL: Do you know what money I have bought these shares with? No, of course you can't know—but I will tell you. It is the money that Katherine and Petra and the boys will have when I am gone. Because I have been able to save a little bit after all, you know.

DR. STOCKMANN: (*flaring up*) And you have gone and taken Katherine's money for *this*!

MORTEN KIIL: Yes, the whole of the money is invested in the Baths now. And now I just want to see whether you are quite stark, staring mad, Thomas! If you still make out that these animals and other nasty things of that sort come from my tannery, it will be exactly as if you were to flay broad strips of skin from Katherine's body, and Petra's, and the boys'; and no decent man would do that—unless he were mad.

DR. STOCKMANN: (*walking up and down*) Yes, but I *am* mad; I *am* mad!

MORTEN KIIL: You cannot be so absurdly mad as all that, when it is a question of your wife and children.

DR. STOCKMANN: (*standing still in front of him*) Why couldn't you consult me about it, before you went and bought all that trash?

MORTEN KIIL: What is done cannot be undone.

DR. STOCKMANN: (*walks about uneasily*) If only I were not so certain about it—! But I am absolutely convinced that I am right.

MORTEN KIIL: (*weighing the pocket-book in his hand*) If you stick to your mad idea, this won't be worth much, you know. (*Puts the pocket-book in his pocket.*)

DR. STOCKMANN: But, hang it all! it might be possible for science to discover some prophylactic, I should think—or some antidote of some kind—

MORTEN KIIL: To kill these animals, do you mean?

DR. STOCKMANN: Yes, or to make them innocuous.

MORTEN KIIL: Couldn't you try some rat's-bane?

DR. STOCKMANN: Don't talk nonsense! They all say it is only imagination, you know. Well, let it go at that! Let them have their own way about it! Haven't the ignorant, narrow-minded curs reviled me as an enemy of the people?—and haven't they been ready to tear the clothes off my back too?

MORTEN KIIL: And broken all your windows to pieces!

DR. STOCKMANN: And then there is my duty to my family. I must talk it over with Katherine; she is great on those things.

MORTEN KIIL: That is right; be guided by a reasonable woman's advice.

DR. STOCKMANN: (*advancing towards him*) To think you could do such a preposterous thing! Risking Katherine's money in this way, and putting me in such a horribly painful dilemma! When I look at you, I think I see the devil himself—.

MORTEN KIIL: Then I had better go. But I must have an answer from you before two o'clock—yes or no. If it is no, the shares go to a charity, and that this very day.

DR. STOCKMANN: And what does Katherine get?

MORTEN KIIL: Not a halfpenny. (*The door leading to the hall opens, and* HOVSTAD *and* ASLAKSEN *make their appearance.*) Look at those two!

DR. STOCKMANN: (*staring at them*) What the devil!—have *you* actually the face to come into my house?

HOVSTAD: Certainly.

ASLAKSEN: We have something to say to you, you see.

MORTEN KIIL: (*in a whisper*) Yes or no—before two o'clock.

ASLAKSEN: (*glancing at* HOVSTAD) Aha! (MORTEN KIIL *goes out.*)

DR. STOCKMANN: Well, what do you want with me? Be brief.

HOVSTAD: I can quite understand that you are annoyed with us for our attitude at the meeting yesterday—

DR. STOCKMANN: Attitude, do you call it? Yes, it was a charming attitude! I call it weak, womanish—damnably shameful!

HOVSTAD: Call it what you like; we could not do otherwise.

DR. STOCKMANN: You *dared* not do otherwise—isn't that it?

HOVSTAD: Well, if you like to put it that way.

ASLAKSEN: But why did you not let us have word of it beforehand?—just a hint to Mr. Hovstad or to me?

DR. STOCKMANN: A hint? Of what?

ASLAKSEN: Of what was behind it all.

DR. STOCKMANN: I don't understand you in the least.

ASLAKSEN: (*with a confidential nod*) Oh, yes, you do, Dr. Stockmann.

HOVSTAD: It is no good making a mystery of it any longer.

DR. STOCKMANN: (*looking first at one of them and then at the other*) What the devil do you both mean?

ASLAKSEN: May I ask if your father-in-law is not going round the town buying up all the shares in the Baths?

DR. STOCKMANN: Yes, he has been buying Baths' shares today; but—

ASLAKSEN: It would have been more prudent to get some one else to do it—some one less nearly related to you.

HOVSTAD: And you should not have let your name appear in the affair. There was no need for anyone to know that the attack on the Baths came from you. You ought to have consulted me, Dr. Stockmann.

DR. STOCKMANN: (*looks in front of him; then a light seems to dawn on him and he says in amazement:*) Are such things conceivable? Are such things possible?

ASLAKSEN: (*with a smile*) Evidently they are. But it is better to use a little finesse, you know.

HOVSTAD: And it is much better to have several persons in a thing of that sort, because the responsibility of each individual is lessened, when there are others with him.

DR. STOCKMANN: (*composedly*) Come to the point, gentlemen. What do you want?

ASLAKSEN: Perhaps Mr. Hovstad had better—

HOVSTAD: No, you tell him, Aslaksen.

ASLAKSEN: Well, the fact is that, now we know the bearings of the whole affair, we think we might venture to put the "People's Messenger" at your disposal.

DR. STOCKMANN: Do you dare do that now? What about public opinion? Are you not afraid of a storm breaking upon our heads?

HOVSTAD: We will try to weather it.

ASLAKSEN: And you must be ready to go off quickly on a new tack, Doctor. As soon as your invective has done its work—

DR. STOCKMANN: Do you mean, as soon as my father-in-law and I have got hold of the shares at a low figure?

HOVSTAD: Your reasons for wishing to get the control of the Baths are mainly scientific, I take it.

DR. STOCKMANN: Of course; it was for scientific reasons that I persuaded the old "Badger" to stand in with me in the matter. So we will tinker at the conduit-pipes a little, and dig up a little bit of the shore, and it shan't cost the town a sixpence. That will be all right—eh?

HOVSTAD: I think so—if you have the "People's Messenger" behind you.

ASLAKSEN: The Press is a power in a free community, Doctor.

DR. STOCKMANN: Quite so. And so is public opinion. And you, Mr. Aslaksen— I suppose you will be answerable for the Householders' Association?

ASLAKSEN: Yes, and for the Temperance Society. You may rely on that.

DR. STOCKMANN: But, gentlemen—I really am ashamed to ask the question— but, what return do you—?

HOVSTAD: We should prefer to help you without any return whatever, believe me. But the "People's Messenger" is in rather a shaky condition; it doesn't go really well; and I should be very unwilling to suspend the paper now, when there is so much work to do here in the political way.

DR. STOCKMANN: Quite so; that would be a great trial to such a friend of the people as you are. (*Flares up.*) But I am an enemy of the people, remember! (*Walks about the room.*) Where have I put my stick? Where the devil is my stick?

HOVSTAD: What's that?

ASLAKSEN: Surely you never mean—?

DR. STOCKMANN: (*standing still*) And suppose I don't give you a single penny of all I get out of it? Money is not very easy to get out of us rich folk, please to remember!

HOVSTAD: And you please to remember that this affair of the shares can be represented in two ways!

DR. STOCKMANN: Yes, and you are just the man to do it. If I don't come to the rescue of the "People's Messenger," you will certainly take an evil view of the affair; you will hunt me down, I can well imagine—pursue me—try to throttle me as a dog does a hare.

HOVSTAD: It is a natural law; every animal must fight for its own livelihood.

ASLAKSEN: And get its food where it can, you know.

DR. STOCKMANN: (*walking about the room*) Then you go and look for yours in the gutter, because I am going to show you which is the strongest animal of us three! (*Finds an umbrella and brandishes it above his head.*) Ah, now—!

HOVSTAD: You are surely not going to use violence!

ASLAKSEN: Take care what you are doing with that umbrella.

DR. STOCKMANN: Out of the window with you, Mr. Hovstad!

HOVSTAD: (*edging to the door*) Are you quite mad?

DR. STOCKMANN: Out of the window, Mr. Aslaksen! Jump, I tell you! You will have to do it, sooner or later.

ASLAKSEN: (*running round the writing-table*) Moderation, Doctor—I am a delicate man—I can stand so little—(*calls out.*) Help, help!

(MRS. STOCKMANN, PETRA, *and* HORSTER *come in from the sitting-room.*)

MRS. STOCKMANN: Good gracious, Thomas! What is happening?

DR. STOCKMANN: (*brandishing the umbrella*) Jump out, I tell you! Out into the gutter!

HOVSTAD: An assault on an unoffending man! I call you to witness, Captain Horster.

(*Hurries out through the hall.*)

ASLAKSEN: (*irresolutely*) If only I knew the way about here—.

(*Steals out through the sitting-room.*)

MRS. STOCKMANN: (*holding her husband back*) Control yourself, Thomas!

DR. STOCKMANN: (*throwing down the umbrella*) Upon my soul, they have escaped after all.

MRS. STOCKMANN: What did they want you to do?

DR. STOCKMANN: I will tell you later on; I have something else to think about now. (*Goes to the table and writes something on a calling-card.*) Look there, Katherine; what is written there?

MRS. STOCKMANN: Three big No's; what does that mean?

DR. STOCKMANN: I will tell you that too, later on. (*Holds out the card to* PETRA.) There, Petra; tell sooty-face to run over to the "Badger's" with that, as quickly as she can. Hurry up!

(PETRA *takes the card and goes out to the hall.*)

DR. STOCKMANN: Well, I think I have had a visit from every one of the devil's messengers today! But now I am going to sharpen my pen till they can feel its point; I shall dip it in venom and gall; I shall hurl my ink-pot at their heads!

MRS. STOCKMANN: Yes, but we are going away, you know, Thomas.

(PETRA *comes back.*)

DR. STOCKMANN: Well?

PETRA: She has gone with it.

DR. STOCKMANN: Good.—Going away, did you say? No, I'll be hanged if we are going away! We are going to stay where we are, Katherine!

PETRA: Stay here?

MRS. STOCKMANN: Here, in the town?

DR. STOCKMANN: Yes, here. This is the field of battle—this is where the fight will be. This is where I shall triumph! As soon as I have had my trousers sewn up I shall go out and look for another house. We must have a roof over our heads for the winter.

HORSTER: That you shall have in my house.

DR. STOCKMANN: Can I?

HORSTER: Yes, quite well. I have plenty of room, and I am almost never at home.

MRS. STOCKMANN: How good of you, Captain Horster!

PETRA: Thank you!

DR. STOCKMANN: (*grasping his hand*) Thank you, thank you! That is one trouble over! Now I can set to work in earnest at once. There is an endless amount of things to look through here, Katherine! Luckily I shall have all my time at my disposal, because I have been dismissed from the Baths, you know.

MRS. STOCKMANN: (*with a sigh*) Oh, yes, I expected that.

DR. STOCKMANN: And they want to take my practice away from me, too. Let them! I have got the poor people to fall back upon, anyway—those that don't pay anything; and, after all, they need me most, too. But, by Jove, they will have to listen to me; I shall preach to them in season and out of season, as it says somewhere.

MRS. STOCKMANN: But, dear Thomas, I should have thought events had showed you what use it is to preach.

DR. STOCKMANN: You are really ridiculous, Katherine. Do you want me to let myself be beaten off the field by public opinion and the compact majority and all that devilry? No, thank you! And what I want to do is so simple and clear and straightforward. I only want to drum into the heads of these curs the fact that the liberals are the most insidious enemies of freedom—that party programmes strangle every young and vigorous truth—that considerations of expediency turn morality and justice upside down—and that they will end by making life here unbearable. Don't you think, Captain Horster, that I ought to be able to make people understand that?

HORSTER: Very likely; I don't know much about such things myself.

DR. STOCKMANN: Well, look here—I will explain! It is the party leaders that must be exterminated. A party leader is like a wolf, you see—like a voracious wolf. He requires a certain number of smaller victims to prey upon every year, if he is to live. Just look at Hovstad and Aslaksen! How many smaller victims have they not put an end to—or at any rate maimed and mangled until they are fit for nothing except to be householders or subscribers to the "People's Messenger"! (*Sits down on the edge of the table.*) Come here, Katherine—look how beautifully the sun shines today! And this lovely spring air I am drinking in!

MRS. STOCKMANN: Yes, if only we could live on sunshine and spring air, Thomas.

DR. STOCKMANN: Oh, you will have to pinch and save a bit—then we shall get along. That gives me very little concern. What is much worse is that I know of no one who is liberal-minded and high-minded enough to venture to take up my work after me.

PETRA: Don't think about that, father; you have plenty of time before you.—Hullo, here are the boys already!

(EJLIF *and* MORTEN *come in from the sitting-room.*)

MRS. STOCKMANN: Have you got a holiday?

MORTEN: No; but we were fighting with the other boys between lessons—

EJLIF: That isn't true; it was the other boys were fighting with us.

MORTEN: Well, and then Mr. Rörlund said we had better stay at home for a day or two.

DR. STOCKMANN: (*snapping his fingers and getting up from the table*) I have it! I have it, by Jove! You shall never set foot in the school again!

THE BOYS: No more school!

MRS. STOCKMANN: But, Thomas—

DR. STOCKMANN: Never, I say. I will educate you myself; that is to say, you shan't learn a blessed thing—

MORTEN: *Hooray!*

DR. STOCKMANN: —but I will make liberal-minded and high-minded men of you. You must help me with that, Petra.

PETRA: Yes, father, you may be sure I will.

DR. STOCKMANN: And my school shall be in the room where they insulted me and called me an enemy of the people. But we are too few as we are; I must have at least twelve boys to begin with.

MRS. STOCKMANN: You will certainly never get them in this town.

DR. STOCKMANN: We shall. (*To the boys.*) Don't you know any street urchins —regular ragamuffins—?

MORTEN: Yes, father, I know lots!

DR. STOCKMANN: That's capital! Bring me some specimens of them. I am going to experiment with curs, just for once; there may be some exceptional heads amongst them.

MORTEN: And what are we going to do, when you have made liberal-minded and high-minded men of us?

DR. STOCKMANN: Then you shall drive all the wolves out of the country, my boys! (EJLIF *looks rather doubtful about it;* MORTEN *jumps about crying "Hurrah!"*)

MRS. STOCKMANN: Let us hope it won't be the wolves that will drive you out of the country, Thomas.

DR. STOCKMANN: Are you out of your mind, Katherine? Drive me out! Now—when I am the strongest man in the town!

MRS. STOCKMANN: The strongest—now?

DR. STOCKMANN: Yes, and I will go so far as to say that now I am the strongest man in the whole world.

MORTEN: I say!

DR. STOCKMANN: (*lowering his voice*) Hush! You mustn't say anything about it yet, but I have made a great discovery.

MRS. STOCKMANN: Another one?

DR. STOCKMANN: Yes. (*Gathers them round him, and says confidentially:*) It is this, let me tell you—that the strongest man in the world is he who stands most alone.

MRS. STOCKMANN: (*smiling and shaking her head*) Oh, Thomas, Thomas!

PETRA: (*encouragingly, as she grasps her father's hands*) Father!

CURTAIN

QUESTIONS

A. Understanding the Action:

Good exposition in a play must, in an artistic and interesting way, provide the audience with necessary information about the characters, background, and events. It must establish the tone of the play (i.e., put the audience in the right mood), suggest the central situation, and create suspense.

1. In many of his plays Ibsen introduces antecedent action not only in the exposition but throughout the play. Does he here? How successfully does he solve the difficult problem of exposition in Act I?

2. In Act II, what three individuals support Dr. Stockmann? For what motives?

3. Who are Dr. Stockmann's opponents and what are their various motives in opposing him?

4. What dramatic reversal (peripetia) takes place in Act III? How is it brought about?

5. What is the climax of the play? How does Ibsen sustain interest after the climax?

6. Discuss the theatrical effectiveness of the curtain scenes (i.e., the tableau at the end of each act). How do they add to the dramatic power of the play?

7. In Act V, what three temptations does Dr. Stockmann resist?

8. Though the play deals with serious issues, what satire do you find in it? What irony? What humor?

9. What are the various types of conflicts in the play?

10. Is the conclusion a satisfactory resolution of the conflict? Explain.

11. What arguments would you advance for calling *An Enemy of the People* a "realistic" drama?

B. Understanding the Characters:

1. What admirable traits does Dr. Stockmann possess? What weaknesses? Is he a static or dynamic character (i.e., does he change in the course of the play and how)?

2. What contrasts of character are there in the play?

3. In the quarrel between the two brothers in Act II, is Dr. Stockmann entirely in the right? Does Ibsen give Peter a good case? With whom do you sympathize and why?

4. Describe the relationship between Dr. Stockmann and his father-in-law.

5. What types of citizens is Ibsen satirizing in the beginning of Act I?

6. Show wherein Ibsen's treatment of character in the play is well-balanced. How

is it realistic; how is it cynical? What is his criticism of the conservative faction? What is his criticism of the liberal faction?

7. What function do the following characters serve: Petra; the "Badger"; Captain Horster; the drunkard at the meeting?

C. *Understanding the Approach:*

1. Discuss whether this play is an attack on democracy, on the entrenched forces of evil, or on bureaucracy.

2. Is the theme of the play a simple conflict between truth and falsehood, or the conflict between good and evil? Explain.

3. Does Dr. Stockmann believe that an intellectual elite should rule society? Explain your agreement or disagreement with him.

4. When Dr. Stockmann proclaims to his fellow citizens that "the majority never has right on its side . . . the minority is always right," is he uttering absolute truths or half-truths? Justify your answer.

5. Dr. Stockmann stated elsewhere, "All who live by lies ought to be exterminated like vermin." What does this statement show you about the speaker? Has he the makings of a dictator, in your opinion?

D. *Comparisons:*

Both Antigone and Dr. Stockmann are heroic individuals defending noble ideals at great personal sacrifice.

1. What emotions aroused in an audience witnessing Antigone's ordeal are likely to be missing in an audience watching Dr. Stockmann's?

2. Contrast the family life of the Stockmanns with that of the Barretts; contrast with the family life of the Wingfields in *The Glass Menagerie.*

3. Compare Ibsen's treatment of the aroused "mass man" at the public meeting with similar scenes in literature. Examples are the description of the crowd at the funeral oration by Mark Antony in Shakespeare's *Julius Caesar,* or the description of Colonel Sherburne's denunciation of the lynch mob in Mark Twain's *Huckleberry Finn.*

E. *Critical Evaluation:*

1. Dr. Stockmann has been called by some critics a stubborn, muddleheaded idealist who would ruin a community; by others, an uncompromising hero in the vanguard of progress, a saviour of his people. What do you think is Ibsen's final view? What is your own view? Why?

2. It has been said of Ibsen that in this play he "sought to explore the nature of the complex social order in order to determine what limits are placed upon the individual who would apply the ideal standard in social matters." In the specific context of the play, what does this statement mean? How might this statement be a definition of the theme of *An Enemy of the People?*

LORD DUNSANY (1878-1957)

The author of *A Night at an Inn* was one of the Irish playwrights who gave the Irish drama world-wide fame during the early decades of the twentieth century. Lord Dunsany was born in London of a distinguished family on July 27, 1878, and was educated at Eton and Sandhurst. He was a soldier and a sportsman in the old British tradition, and he won a considerable reputation as the writer of romantic and fantastic tales. He published his autobiography, *Patches of Sunlight*, in 1938 and collected his ideas on the art of the theatre in a book published under the title of *Donellan Lectures 1943*. However, he is best known as a dramatist of rare imagination and love of the world of mystery and magic.

Lord Dunsany began to establish a reputation as a playwright in his thirty-first year with his short poetic play *The Glittering Gate* produced by William Butler Yeats at the Abbey Theatre of Dublin in 1909. He achieved further distinction in 1911 with a beautiful one-act symbolical drama, *King Argemines and the Unknown Warrior*. Another fantastic work, *The Gods of the Mountain*, became successful in 1911. It was followed in 1916 by *The Queen's Enemies*, a macabre play in which an ancient Egyptian Queen gives a sumptuous feast in a great hall and then drowns all her guests by flooding it with the waters of the Nile River. Dunsany attracted attention in the theatre with his fantastic, yet ironic style, and his inventive playwriting through the early years of the third decade of our century, especially with *If*, and *The Silk Hat*, in 1921.

INTRODUCTION TO *A NIGHT AT AN INN*

Dunsany's work was greatly favored for a time by amateur groups in England and the United States. His highly original melodrama *A Night at an Inn* opened on August 2, 1919, and was immediately acclaimed as a small masterpiece.

It attracted attention equally with its action, atmosphere, suspense, and imagination. It was turned into an opera under the title of *The Ruby*, which had its first production in 1955 at the University of Indiana at Bloomington, Indiana.

A NIGHT AT AN INN

LORD DUNSANY

CHARACTERS

A. E. SCOTT-FORTESCUE (THE TOFF) *a dilapidated gentleman*
WILLIAM JONES (BILL)
ALBERT THOMAS
JACOB SMITH (SNIGGERS)

} *Merchant Sailors*

1ST PRIEST OF KLESH
2ND PRIEST OF KLESH
3RD PRIEST OF KLESH
KLESH

[*The Curtain rises on a room in an inn.*]

SNIGGERS *and* BILL *are talking.* THE TOFF *is reading a paper.* ALBERT *sits a little apart.*

SNIGGERS: What's the idea, I wonder?

BILL: I don't know.

SNIGGERS: And how much longer will he keep us here?

BILL: We've been here three days.

SNIGGERS: And 'aven't seen a soul.

BILL: And a pretty penny it cost us when he rented the pub.

SNIGGERS: 'Ow long did 'e rent the pub for?

BILL: You never know with him.

SNIGGERS: It's lonely enough.

BILL: 'Ow long did you rent the pub for, Toffy?

(THE TOFF *continues to read a sporting paper; he takes no notice of what is said.*)

SNIGGERS: 'E's *such* a toff.

BILL: Yet 'e's clever, no mistake.

SNIGGERS: Those clever ones are the beggars to make a muddle. Their plans are clever enough, but they don't work, and then they make a mess of things much worse than you or me.

BILL: Ah.

SNIGGERS: I don't like this place.

BILL: Why not?

SNIGGERS: I don't like the looks of it.

BILL: He's keeping us here because here those niggers can't find us. The three heathen priests what was looking for us so. But we want to go and sell our ruby soon.

ALBERT: There's no sense in it.

BILL: Why not, Albert?

ALBERT: Because I gave those black devils the slip in Hull.

BILL: You give 'em the slip, Albert?

ALBERT: The slip, all three of them. The fellows with the gold spots on their foreheads. I had the ruby then and I give them the slip in Hull.

BILL: How did you do it, Albert?

ALBERT: I had the ruby and they were following me....

BILL: Who told them you had the ruby? You didn't show it?

ALBERT: No.... But they kind of know.

SNIGGERS: They kind of know, Albert?

ALBERT: Yes, they know if you've got it. Well, they sort of mouched after me, and I tells a policeman, and he says, Oh, they were only three poor niggers and they wouldn't hurt me. Ugh! When I thought of what they did in Malta to poor old Jim.

BILL: Yes and to George in Bombay before we started.

SNIGGERS: Ugh!

BILL: Why didn't you give 'em in charge?

ALBERT: What about the ruby, Bill?

BILL: Ah!

ALBERT: Well, I did better than that. I walks up and down through Hull. I walks slow enough. And then I turns a corner and I runs. I never sees a corner but I turns it. But sometimes I let a corner pass just to fool them. I twists about like a hare. Then I sits down and waits. No priests.

SNIGGERS: What?

ALBERT: No heathen black devils with gold spots on their face. I give 'em the slip.

BILL: Well done, Albert.

SNIGGERS: (*after a sigh of content*) Why didn't you tell us?

ALBERT: 'Cause 'e won't let you speak. 'E's got 'is plans and 'e thinks we're silly folk. Things must be done 'is way. And all the time I've give 'em the slip. Might 'ave 'ad one o' them crooked knives in him before now but for me who give 'em the slip in Hull.

BILL: Well done, Albert.

SNIGGERS: Do you hear that, Toffy? Albert has give 'em the slip.

THE TOFF: Yes, I hear.

SNIGGERS: Well, what do you say to that?

THE TOFF: Oh... Well done, Albert.

ALBERT: And what a' you going to do?

THE TOFF: Going to wait.

ALBERT: Don't seem to know what 'e's waiting for.

SNIGGERS: It's a nasty place.

ALBERT: It's getting silly, Bill. Our money's gone and we want to sell the ruby. Let's get on to a town.

BILL: But 'e won't come.

ALBERT: Then we'll leave him.

SNIGGERS: We'll be all right if we keep away from Hull.

ALBERT: We'll go to London.

BILL: But 'e must 'ave 'is share.

SNIGGERS: All right. Only let's go. (*To* THE TOFF) We're going, do you hear? Give us the ruby.

THE TOFF: Certainly. (*He gives them a ruby from his waist-coat pocket, it is the size of a small hen's egg*) (*He goes on reading his paper.*)

ALBERT: Come on, Sniggers.

(*Exeunt* ALBERT *and* SNIGGERS.)

BILL: Good-bye, old man. We'll give you your fair share, but there's nothing to do here, no girls, no halls, and we must sell the ruby.

THE TOFF: I'm not a fool, Bill.

BILL: No, no, of course not. Of course you ain't, and you've helped us a lot. Good-bye. You'll say good-bye.

THE TOFF: Oh, yes. Good-bye. (*Still reads paper. Exit* BILL.)

(THE TOFF *puts a revolver on the table beside him and goes on with his paper.*)

SNIGGERS: (*out of breath*) We've come back, Toffy.

THE TOFF: So you have.

ALBERT: Toffy—how did they get here?

THE TOFF: They walked, of course.

ALBERT: But it's eighty miles.

SNIGGERS: Did you know they were here, Toffy?

THE TOFF: Expected them about now.

ALBERT: Eighty miles.

BILL: Toffy, old man—what are we to do?

THE TOFF: Ask Albert.

BILL: If they can do things like this there's no one can save us but you, Toffy —I always knew you were a clever one. We won't be fools any more. We'll obey you, Toffy.

THE TOFF: You're brave enough and strong enough. There isn't many that would steal a ruby eye out of an idol's head, and such an idol as that was to look at, and on such a night. You're brave enough, Bill. But you're all three of you fools. Jim would have none of my plans and where's Jim? And George. What did they do to him?

SNIGGERS: Don't, Toffy!

THE TOFF: Well, then, your strength is no use to you. You want cleverness; or they'll have you the way that they had George and Jim.

ALL: Ugh!

THE TOFF: These black priests would follow you round the world in circles. Year after year, till they got their idol's eye. And if we died with it they'd follow our grandchildren. That fool thinks he can escape men like that by running round three streets in the town of Hull.

ALBERT: God's truth, *you* 'aven't escaped them, because they're 'ere.

THE TOFF: So I supposed.

ALBERT: You *supposed*?

THE TOFF: Yes, I believe there's no announcement in the society papers. But I took this country seat especially to receive them. There's plenty of room if you dig, it is pleasantly situated, and, what is most important, it is in a very quiet neighborhood. So I am at home to them this afternoon.

BILL: Well, you're a deep one.

THE TOFF: And remember you've only my wits between you and death, and don't put your futile plans against those of an educated gentleman.

ALBERT: If you're a gentleman why don't you go about among gentlemen instead of the likes of us?

THE TOFF: Because I was too clever for them as I am too clever for you.

ALBERT: Too clever for them?

THE TOFF: I never lost a game of cards in my life.

BILL: You never lost a game!

THE TOFF: Not when there was money on it.

BILL: Well, well.

THE TOFF: Have a game of poker?

ALL: No thanks.

THE TOFF: Then do as you're told.

BILL: All right, Toffy.

SNIGGERS: I saw something just then. Hadn't we better draw the curtains?

THE TOFF: No.

SNIGGERS: What?

THE TOFF: Don't draw the curtains.

SNIGGERS: Oh, all right.

BILL: But, Toffy, they can see us. One doesn't let the enemy do that. I don't see why....

THE TOFF: No, of course you don't.

BILL: Oh, all right, Toffy.

(*All begin to pull out revolvers.*)

THE TOFF: (*putting his own away*) No revolvers, please.

ALBERT: Why not?

THE TOFF: Because I don't want any noise at my party. We might get guests that hadn't been invited. *Knives* are a different matter.

(*All draw knives.* THE TOFF *signs to them not to draw them yet.* THE TOFF *has already taken back his ruby.*)

BILL: I think they're coming, Toffy.

THE TOFF: Not yet.

ALBERT: When will they come?

THE TOFF: When I am quite ready to receive them. Not before.

SNIGGERS: I should like to get this over.

THE TOFF: Should you? Then we'll have them now.

SNIGGERS: Now?

THE TOFF: Yes. Listen to me. You shall do as you see me do. You will all pretend to go out. I'll show you how. I've got the ruby. When they see me alone they will come for their idol's eye.

BILL: How can they tell like this which of us has it?

THE TOFF: I confess I don't know, but they seem to.

SNIGGERS: What will you do when they come in?

THE TOFF: I shall do nothing.

SNIGGERS: What?

THE TOFF: They will creep up behind me. Then my friends, Sniggers and Bill and Albert, who gave them the slip, will do what they can.

BILL: All right, Toffy. Trust us.

THE TOFF: If you're a little slow you will see enacted the cheerful spectacle that accompanied the demise of Jim.

SNIGGERS: Don't, Toffy. We'll be there all right.

THE TOFF: Very well. Now watch me. (*He goes past the windows to the inner door Right; he opens it inwards, and then under cover of the open door he slips down on his knee and closes it, remaining on the inside, appearing to have gone out. He signs to the others who understand. Then he appears to re-enter in the same manner.*)

THE TOFF: Now, I shall sit with my back to the door. You go out one by one so far as our friends can make out. Crouch very low, to be on the safe side. They mustn't see you through the window.

(BILL *makes his sham exit.*)

THE TOFF: Remember, no revolvers. The police are, I believe, proverbially inquisitive.

(*The other two follow* BILL. *All three are now crouching inside the door Right.* THE TOFF *puts the ruby beside him on the table. He lights a cigarette.*)

(*The door in back opens so slowly that you can hardly say at what moment it began.* THE TOFF *picks up his paper.*)

(*A* NATIVE *of India wriggles along the floor ever so slowly, seeking cover from chairs. He moves Left where* THE TOFF *is. The three sailors are Right.* SNIGGERS *and* ALBERT *lean forward.* BILL'S *arm keeps them back. An arm-chair had better conceal them from the Indian. The black* PRIEST *nears* THE TOFF.)

(BILL *watches to see if any more are coming. Then he leaps forward alone (he has taken his boots off) and knifes the* PRIEST.)

(*The* PRIEST *tries to shout, but* BILL'S *left hand is over his mouth.*)

(THE TOFF *continues to read his sporting paper. He never looks round.*)

BILL: (*sotto voce*) There's only one, Toffy. What shall we do?

THE TOFF: (*without turning his head*) Only one?

BILL: Yes.

THE TOFF: Wait a moment. Let me think. (*Still apparently absorbed in his paper.*) Ah, yes. You go back, Bill. We must attract another guest. Now are you ready?

BILL: Yes.

THE TOFF: All right. You shall now see my demise at my Yorkshire residence. You must receive guests for me. (*He leaps up in full view of the window, flings up both arms and falls on to the floor near the dead* PRIEST.) Now be ready. (*His eyes close.*)

(*There is a long pause. Again the door opens, very, very slowly. Another* PRIEST *creeps in. He has three golden spots upon his forehead. He looks round, then he creeps up to his companion and turns him over and looks inside each of his clenched hands. Then he looks at the recumbent* TOFF. *Then he creeps towards him.* BILL *slips after him and knifes him like the other with his left hand over his mouth.*)

BILL: (*sotto voce*) We've only got two, Toffy.

THE TOFF: Still another.

BILL: What'll we do?

THE TOFF: (*sitting up*) Hum.

BILL: This is the best way, much.

THE TOFF: Out of the question. Never play the same game twice.

BILL: Why not, Toffy?

THE TOFF: Doesn't work if you do.

BILL: Well?

THE TOFF: I have it, Albert. You will now walk into the room. I showed you how to do it.

ALBERT: Yes.

THE TOFF: Just run over here and have a fight at this window with these two men.

ALBERT: But they're—

THE TOFF: Yes, they're dead, my perspicuous Albert. But Bill and I are going to resuscitate them—. Come on.

(BILL *picks up a body under the arms.*)

THE TOFF: That's right, Bill. (*Does the same.*) Come and help us, Sniggers— (SNIGGERS *comes.*) Keep low, keep low. Wave their arms about, Sniggers. Don't show yourself. Now, Albert, over you go. Our Albert is slain. Back you get, Bill. Back Sniggers. Still Albert. Mustn't move when he comes. Not a muscle.

(A FACE *appears at the window and stays for some time. Then the door opens and looking craftily round, the third* PRIEST *enters. He looks at his companion's bodies and turns round. He suspects something.*

He takes up one of the knives and with a knife in each hand he puts his back to the wall. He looks to the left and right.)

THE TOFF: Come on, Bill.

(*The* PRIEST *rushes to the door.* THE TOFF *knifes the last* PRIEST *from behind.*)

THE TOFF: A good day's work, my friends.

BILL: Well done, Toffy. Oh, you are a deep one.

ALBERT: A deep one if ever there was one.

SNIGGERS: There ain't any more, Bill, are there?

THE TOFF: No more in the world, my friend.

BILL: Aye, that's all there are. There were only three in the temple. Three priests and their beastly idol.

ALBERT: What is it worth, Toffy? Is it worth a thousand pounds?

THE TOFF: It's worth all they've got in the shop. Worth just whatever we like to ask for it.

ALBERT: Then we're millionaires now.

THE TOFF: Yes, and what is more important, we no longer have any heirs.

BILL: We'll have to sell it now.

ALBERT: That won't be easy. It's a pity it isn't small and we had half a dozen. Hadn't the idol any other on him?

BILL: No, he was green jade all over and only had this one eye. He had it in the middle of his forehead, and was a long sight uglier than anything else in the world.

SNIGGERS: I'm sure we ought all to be very grateful to Toffy.

BILL: And indeed we ought.

ALBERT: If it hadn't 'ave been for him—

BILL: Yes, if it hadn't a been for old Toffy.

SNIGGERS: He's a deep one.

THE TOFF: Well you see I just have a knack of foreseeing things.

SNIGGERS: I should think you did.

BILL: Why, I don't suppose anything happens that our Toff doesn't foresee. Does it, Toffy?

THE TOFF: Well, I don't think it does, Bill. I don't think it often does.

BILL: Life is no more than just a game of cards to our old Toff.

THE TOFF: Well, we've taken these fellows' trick.

SNIGGERS: (*going to the window*) It wouldn't do for anyone to see them.

THE TOFF: Oh, nobody will come this way. We're all alone on a moor.

BILL: Where will we put them?

THE TOFF: Bury them in the cellar, but there's no hurry.

BILL: And what then, Toffy?

THE TOFF: Why, then we'll go to London and upset the ruby business. We have really come through this job very nicely.

BILL: I think the first thing that we ought to do is to give a little supper to old Toffy. We'll bury these fellows tonight.

ALBERT: Yes, let's.

SNIGGERS: The very thing.

BILL: And we'll all drink his health.

ALBERT: Good old Toffy.

SNIGGERS: He ought to have been a general or a premier.

(*They get bottles from cupboard, etc.*)

THE TOFF: Well, we've earned our bit of a supper.

(*They sit down.*)

BILL: (*glass in hand*) Here's to old Toffy who guessed everything.

ALBERT and SNIGGERS: Good old Toffy.

BILL: Toffy who saved our lives and made our fortunes.

ALBERT and SNIGGERS: Hear. Hear.

THE TOFF: And here's to Bill who saved me twice tonight.

BILL: Couldn't have done it but for your cleverness, Toffy.

SNIGGERS: Hear, hear. Hear, hear.

ALBERT: He foresees everything.

BILL: A speech, Toffy. A speech from our general.

ALL: Yes, a speech.

SNIGGERS: A speech.

THE TOFF: Well, get me some water. This whiskey's too much for my head, and I must keep it clear till our friends are safe in the cellar.

BILL: Water. Yes, of course. Get him some water, Sniggers.

SNIGGERS: We don't use water here. Where shall I get it?

BILL: Outside in the garden.

(*Exit* SNIGGERS.)

ALBERT: Here's to fortune.

(*They all drink.*)

BILL: Here's to Albert Thomas, Esquire. (*He drinks.*)

THE TOFF: Albert Thomas, Esquire. (*He drinks.*)

ALBERT: And William Jones, Esquire.

THE TOFF: William Jones, Esquire. (THE TOFF and ALBERT *drink.*)

(*Re-enter* SNIGGERS *terrified.*)

THE TOFF: Hullo, here's Jacob Smith, Esquire, J.P., alias Sniggers, back again.

SNIGGERS: Toffy, I've been a thinking about my share in that ruby. I don't want it, Toffy, I don't want it.

THE TOFF: Nonsense, Sniggers, nonsense.

SNIGGERS: You shall have it, Toffy, you shall have it yourself, only say Sniggers has no share in this 'ere ruby. Say it, Toffy, say it.

BILL: Want to turn informer, Sniggers?

SNIGGERS: No, no. Only I don't want the ruby, Toffy. . . .

THE TOFF: No more nonsense, Sniggers, we're all in together in this, if one hangs we all hang; but they won't outwit me. Besides, it's not a hanging affair, they had their knives.

SNIGGERS: Toffy, Toffy, I always treated you fair, Toffy. I was always one to say, give Toffy a chance. Take back my share, Toffy.

THE TOFF: What's the matter? What are you driving at?

SNIGGERS: Take it back, Toffy.

THE TOFF: Answer me, what are you up to?

SNIGGERS: I don't want my share any more.

BILL: Have you seen the police? (ALBERT *pulls out his knife.*)

THE TOFF: No, no knives, Albert.

ALBERT: What then?

THE TOFF: The honest truth in open court, barring the ruby. We were attacked.

SNIGGERS: There's no police.

THE TOFF: Well, then, what's the matter?

BILL: Out with it.

SNIGGERS: I swear to God . . .

ALBERT: Well?

THE TOFF: Don't interrupt.

SNIGGERS: I swear I saw something *what I didn't like.*

THE TOFF: What you didn't like?

SNIGGERS: (*in tears*) O Toffy, Toffy, take it back. Take my share. Say you take it.

THE TOFF: What has he seen?

(*Dead silence only broken by* SNIGGERS' *sobs. Then stony steps are heard.*)

(*Enter a hideous* IDOL. *It is blind and gropes its way. It gropes its way to the ruby and picks it up and screws it into a socket in the forehead.*)

(SNIGGERS *still weeps softly, the rest stare in horror. The* IDOL *steps out not groping. Its steps move off then stop.*)

THE TOFF: Oh, great heavens!

ALBERT: (*in a childish, plaintive voice*) What is it, Toffy?

BILL: Albert, it is that obscene idol (*in a whisper*) come from India.

ALBERT: It is gone.

BILL: It has taken its eye.

SNIGGERS: We are saved.

OFF, A VOICE: (*with outlandish accent*) Meestaire William Jones, Able Seaman.

(THE TOFF *has never spoken, never moved. He only gazes stupidly in horror.*)

BILL: Albert, Albert, what is this? (*He rises and walks out. One moan is heard.* SNIGGERS *goes to window. He falls back sickly.*)

ALBERT: (*in a whisper*) What has happened?

SNIGGERS: I have seen it. I have seen it. Oh, I have seen it. (*He returns to table.*)

THE TOFF: (*laying his hand very gently on* SNIGGERS' *arm, speaking softly and winningly*) What was it, Sniggers?

SNIGGERS: I have seen it.

ALBERT: What?

SNIGGERS: Oh . . .

VOICE: Meestaire Albert Thomas, Able Seaman.

ALBERT: Must I go, Toffy? Toffy, must I go?

SNIGGERS: (*clutching him*) Don't move.

ALBERT: (*going*) Toffy, Toffy. (*Exit.*)

VOICE: Meestaire Jacob Smith, Able Seaman.

SNIGGERS: I can't go, Toffy. I can't go. I can't do it. (*He goes.*)

VOICE: Meestaire Arnold Everett Scott-Fortescue, late Esquire, Able Seaman.

THE TOFF: I did not foresee it. (*Exit.*)

CURTAIN

QUESTIONS

A. Understanding the Action:

A melodrama is characterized by sensational incidents and violent appeals to the emotions, as well as to an elementary moral sense—when goodness is rewarded and evil is punished. Its primary purpose is to give the audience thrills.

1. Why is *A Night at an Inn* considered a melodrama rather than a tragedy?
2. Is there any marked realism in the play? Where?
3. Describe the oriental element in *A Night at an Inn* and how it is employed in the play.
4. How does the author employ contrasts of background, content, and tone?
5. What is the macabre element in the play, and how does it contribute to the effectiveness of the melodrama?
6. Is there "poetic justice" in the play and does it contribute to the melodramatic effect?
7. What is the major element of suspense in the play?
8. What details of the dramatic action impress you as especially ingenious, novel, or effective?
9. What details of stage business contribute to the excitement of the action?
10. What is the major reversal—the so-called *peripeteia*—of the action? What is its effect on the play? Does it deepen your understanding of character or human nature?
11. Does the action develop or support any particular idea, argument, principle? If not, what is the effect of the action?

Allardyce Nicoll, the English dramatic critic, states, "Melodrama regularly varies its scenes of stirring action with buffoonery of a farcical kind."

12. Is this true of *A Night at an Inn?*

B. Understanding the Characters:

1. Is there any differentiation of character parts in the play or are the characters merely left undefined and undifferentiated?
2. How much character-analysis does this play need?

C. Comparisons:

1. In what way does the essential action of this play differ from the action in a) *Romeo and Juliet?* b) in *An Enemy of the People?*
2. In what different ways or to what degree is suspense employed in *An Enemy of the People*, and *A Night at an Inn?*

BIOGRAPHY AND AUTOBIOGRAPHY

"Biography" is the term for an account of some individual's life. It may cover an entire life or only some selected episodes in a life. In either case, "biography" signifies something other than a humdrum collection of facts and figures; it re-creates the characteristics, the experiences, and the thoughts and feelings of its subject; it brings the individual to life again. Biographies, as a rule, also contain explicit or implicit evaluations of their subject's personality and career.

There has never been a time when the theatre lacked biographical material. Even the primitive stages of ancient Egypt and Greece were concerned with an individual's life—the life of the Egyptian corn-god Osiris and his Greek equivalent Dionysus, who was also celebrated as the god of wine and ecstasy and the divine patron of the theatre. Episodes, strung together as a sort of Passion Play, constituted a pattern that followed the life-cycle of nature; the god is born, he waxes strong and proves beneficial to man, he comes into conflict with a powerful enemy (Winter, Darkness, Death, the Titans, and so on), he dies, and he is magically restored to life like the earth's vegetation. All these episodes, amounting to the complete Passion Play, or only a few especially vivid episodes were recited, danced or mimed, or completely dramatized and supplied with dialogue. An example of complete dramatization of a single episode is the fifth century B.C. Athenian playwright Euripides' tragedy the *Bacchae*, in which Dionysus cruelly punishes King Pentheus for having tried to stamp out the worship of Dionysus.

Mythical and legendary heroes, the latter considered more or less historical and "real," followed the gods into the theatre. Plays based on their lives or on portions of their lives are the first important biographical dramas. Some of the world's greatest tragedies were, in fact, written about the heroes and heroines of the Trojan War and other adventures celebrated in early Greek epics such as the *Iliad* and the *Odyssey*. In the section on tragedy in the present book we encounter Antigone, heroic daughter of ill-fated Oedipus, legendary king of Thebes. During the Renaissance and the time of Shakespeare, during the age of Louis XIV in seventeenth century France, and ever since then, legendary and historical figures (Tamburlaine, Edward II, Lear, Hamlet, Macbeth, Antony and Cleopatra, the biblical Esther, and many other characters) have occupied the center of the stage. Each country has been fascinated with its own national heroes and heroines. English and American playwrights have been partial to such historical figures as Becket (Tennyson's *Becket* and T. S. Eliot's *Murder in the Cathedral*), Sir Thomas More (Robert Bolt's *A Man for All Seasons*), Queen Elizabeth (Maxwell Anderson's *Elizabeth the Queen*), Queen Victoria (Laurence Housman's *Victoria*

Regina), Abraham Lincoln (Robert Sherwood's *Abe Lincoln in Illinois*), and T. E. Lawrence (Terence Rattigan's *Ross*).

In the case of many of these subjects, the historical interest is primary and the biographical interests secondary. This is true of Henry IV and his son Prince Hal in Shakespeare's play *Henry IV*. We do not therefore, call *Henry IV* a biographical but a "history" or "chronicle" play. We apply these terms, too, to a number of other works by Shakespeare and other playwrights.

But where the author of a play concentrates on an historical character's private life, the term biographical drama is appropriate. Admittedly, there are borderline cases, but the largely unpolitical episodes of *Queen Victoria* and *Abe Lincoln in Illinois* make these plays "biographies" rather than historical chronicles. Also, if the leading characters had an essentially nonpolitical career, the play dealing with them is likely to prove a "biography" rather than a "history" even if the individual in question became well known. This is most likely to be the case when the characters are authors, composers, physicians, and other creative individuals rather than political figures whose activities set armies into motion, affected elections, and produced international complications. In their case, it is possible to deal, to a large extent, with *private* life, and psychological complications. Thus there have been plays in English about the poets Byron, Shelley, and Keats, the scientists Galileo and Pasteur, the actors Booth and Kean, the composers Wagner and Grieg, and so on.

It is worth noting, moreover, that biographical drama marks a modern development in the drama, for the artist is a fairly new arrival in the theatre. He does not play an important role in the drama until the last century. The rise of democracy gave the private man (as contrasted with royalty and the ruling-class nobility) social status, and the early nineteenth-century romantic movement turned the artist into a dramatic hero. Biographical drama concerned with an artist or even with an historically important commoner such as Joan of Arc (Schiller's *Maid of Orleans*, Shaw's *Saint Joan*, Anderson's *Joan of Lorraine*, and Anouilh's *The Lark* all deal with this peasant heroine) is a modern development. The main characteristics are well exemplified in *The Barretts of Wimpole Street*. Here the characters are the two English poets, Elizabeth Barrett and Robert Browning, and the complications are domestic and psychological. The central conflict takes place in a middle class household and concerns a tyrannically possessive Victorian father and an invalid spinster verging on middle age.

It is only a step from biographical to autobiographical drama. In autobiographical drama the author may or may not make any marked identification of the characters, but it is apparent that his main concern is with his own life and that of his close relatives and friends. Such was the case of Eugene O'Neill when he wrote his celebrated family drama *Long Day's Journey into Night*. (This play is autobiographical, even though O'Neill gave more attention to his parents and elder brother than to himself; and also because family tensions were conditioning him to become a dramatist of tragically twisted characters.) The author of an autobiographical drama is content, as a rule, to present himself as a sensitive human being who suffers, observes, and acts in private situations.

While there are no absolute criteria for an autobiographical drama, it is normally recognized by the extremely personal nature of the characterizations and complications. It evokes a sense of intimacy and authenticity. This is true of John Van Druten's *I Remember Mama*, although the subject is not the playwright but Kathryn Forbes, the author of the book, *Mama's Bank Account*, which John Van Druten turned into a play. Tennessee Williams' *The Glass Menagerie* (page 268), is perhaps the best available example of the creative utilization of autobiographical material. It is doubtful that any of the significant episodes actually occurred as set down in the play. *The Glass Menagerie* is a *re-creation* of personal experience. It is idle, perhaps even impertinent, to inquire whether the writer has provided accurate portraits of all or any of the characters. It is important only that *The Glass Menagerie* "feels" intimately real—that it seems to come right out of the author's personal experience, and that one of the characters cannot be other than a projection—a "persona" or mask—of the playwright himself as a troubled adolescent boy who feels trapped in his household and place of employment. Moreover, the author adopts the "first-person" narrative technique; in the prologue and epilogue, at the beginning and at the conclusion of the play, he makes it clear to the audience that he is remembering his own life. At the same time, the fact that he is "remembering" the life he presents—he calls *The Glass Menagerie* a "memory play"—reminds the playgoer that the author does not guarantee literal accuracy.

Autobiographical and approximations of autobiographical drama (O'Neill's *Ah, Wilderness* and Carson McCullers' *The Member of the Wedding* are well known examples of such approximations) are also modern developments in the theatre. We are apt to encounter in autobiography the mixed type of drama (it has been called variously "comedy-drama," "tragi-comedy," "serious-drama" and *"drame"*) which comprises much of our modern realistic playwriting. Biographical drama, when it deals with some heroic figures such as Sir Thomas More, may achieve the noble estate of tragedy. But the author of an autobiographical drama would lay himself open to a serious charge of vanity and pretentiousness if he inflated himself into a heroic figure of tragedy. At the same time, it is not to be expected that a playwright would want to make himself the subject of satiric comedy.

Autobiographical drama tends to be "modern" in the special sense of taking a close look at ourselves and providing a realistic yet sympathetic view of the trials of ordinary life.

RUDOLF BESIER (1878-1942)

The British dramatist Rudolf Besier's fame rests entirely on a single play, *The Barretts of Wimpole Street*, which was virtually the last play he wrote before declining into obscurity so far as the theatre is concerned. Born in Java, of Dutch descent, in 1878 he was educated at Elizabeth College, Guernsey, and at the famous German university Heidelberg. After practicing journalism for a while, he turned to writing plays. Among those which reached the stage were *The Virgin Goddess* in 1906, *Lady Patricia*, a successful vehicle for the famous American actress Mrs. Fiske, in 1911, and *A Run for His Money* in 1916. He also collaborated with H. G. Wells in dramatizing the latter's novel *Kipps*, and with the novelist Hugh Walpole in dramatizing *Robin's Father*. In 1930 came *The Barretts of Wimpole Street*, the appealing Victorian romance of the poets Elizabeth Barrett and Robert Browning, which was especially successful in the United States in a production starring the romantic actor Brian Aherne and Katharine Cornell, who came to be considered one of the leading actresses of the American stage.

Besier died in London on June 15, 1942 without having affected the course of the theatre either in England or the United States. But his biographical drama which was also filmed successfully with Norma Shearer and Fredric March in the main roles, has held the stage ever since 1930 and remains one of the most successful plays based on well-known characters whose story is personal and yet universal —as universal as the family, illness and recovery, young love and the difficulties it may encounter, hope, and trust are universal. The emotional reality of the play is not limited to the period, about a century ago, in which the two young poets lived; but their lives are complicated, their problems aggravated, and their reactions colored by the age in which they experienced their ageless little human drama.

A little information about the principals of the play may be helpful to the student, who should bear in mind that they were better known to older generations including the one to which the play was first presented in 1930.

A NOTE ON THE BROWNINGS

The love affair of the Brownings is the most famous romance in literary history. When on September 12, 1846, Miss Elizabeth Barrett secretly married Robert Browning in Marylebone Church, she was already famous as a Victorian "poetess"; he had only a few devoted readers. When Wordsworth died in 1850, she was Tennyson's only rival for the poet-laureateship of England. Today we recognize Robert Browning as a major poet and his wife as a minor one.

Browning was born in a suburb of London on May 7, 1812. His father, an official of the Bank of England, had a deep love for literature and art. He owned a large, valuable library which his two children, Robert and his sister, used extensively. Browning's mother was a deeply religious woman who loved music. Robert received little formal schooling; most of his education came from private tutors and his own intellectual curiosity. By mastering Greek, Latin, modern languages, and gaining a formidable knowledge of music, history, and art, he made himself the most learned English poet. However, he was not by any means just a pedantic bookworm. He possessed an amazing zest for life as revealed in the wide range of his poetry and in his skill in fencing, boxing, riding, and dancing. All his life he was a cheerful, gregarious "diner-outer." (Tennyson prophesied Browning would die in his dress suit.)

Although Browning devoted his whole life to poetry, he never won enough popularity to earn a living from it. Not a single copy of his first poem, *Pauline* (1833), was bought by the public. His next work, a philosophical play, *Paracelsus*, did almost as poorly. When he issued in 1840 his *Sordello*, a difficult poem in six books, he obtained a lifelong reputation for obscurity. The first line of the poem reads, "Who will, may hear Sordello's story told" and the last, "who would has heard Sordello's story told." Tennyson, his Victorian poetic rival, commented that he understood only the first and last lines of *Sordello*, and they were both lies. Browning continued his self-education by traveling to Russia and Italy. He then wrote a series of plays which also failed to win popular favor.

From John Kenyon, Elizabeth Barrett's cousin, Browning had heard of the famous poetess and had read her work avidly. When he found his name mentioned in one of her sentimental ballads *Lady Geraldine's Courtship*, he wrote her an enthusiastic letter on January 10, 1845, declaring, "I love your verses with all my heart . . . and I love you too." After four months of this wooing by correspondence (according to Bernard Shaw the best method), Browning was finally granted permission to meet her.

Elizabeth Barrett, the eldest of eleven children, was living at 50 Wimpole Street in a gloomy house which she described as a prison turned inside out. Because of a spine injury sustained in her childhood and because of her weak lungs, she was virtually an invalid prisoner in her room. Her temperamental father, ruling his three daughters and eight sons with an iron will and intense possessiveness, considered any thought of their marrying as "unfilial treachery." Though Elizabeth Barrett and Robert Browning were supremely happy in their marriage, her father never forgave her; her letters remained unopened. Even the birth of their son later in Italy failed to reconcile him.

In their fifteen years of marriage, Elizabeth and Robert were not separated for a single day. She declared a woman needed only three things to be happy—Life, Love, Italy—and she had all three. Her deep love is expressed in her finest work, *Sonnets from the Portuguese*. She died in Browning's arms on June 29, 1861.

He left Florence and came back to England to supervise the education of his son. He continued to publish many volumes of poetry, including *The Ring and the Book*, a remarkable psychological study of an old Italian murder case as seen through the minds of different characters. His reputation began to grow both in England and America; in 1882 Oxford conferred an honorary degree upon him. He retains his fame today as the author of "dramatic monologues," poems in which he does not comment directly on anyone or anything, but allows some character to reveal himself by his statements to someone, or by his inner thoughts. An example of this is Browning's famous poem, *My Last Duchess*.

Browning died in Venice on December 12, 1889.

INTRODUCTION TO *THE BARRETTS OF WIMPOLE STREET*

The *Barretts of Wimpole Street* like *Romeo and Juliet,* dealing with first love and a romantic elopement, has been a popular play enjoyed by young and old. During World War II when Katharine Cornell played it in army camps, it was a tremendous success. The reasons for its popularity are not hard to find.

Besier has successfully solved the two chief problems in handling his material: first, avoiding a sentimental treatment of the famous love affair of the two poets; and second, bringing to life on the stage two characters so well known in literary history. Through a careful choice of dramatic incidents and the use of effective, realistic dialogue, he has universalized for us one of the great real-life love stories of all time.

But Besier has not only molded his material into an exciting plot full of suspense; he has enriched the play by placing his characters in an accurate Victorian setting and has given us a picture of the manners of that age. We learn from Bevan, "Mr. Tennyson always writes like a gentleman" and from Bella we hear about the religious conflicts in the English Church brought about by the Oxford Movement. The therapeutic effects of drinking porter,[1] the sternness and infallibility of parents, the position of the army man in an imperialist nation—these and other characteristics of the Victorian era are unobtrusively delineated.

As the title suggests, the play deals not only with the two poets but with a family. It is a psychological study of the strained relations between a parent and his children, some acquiescent, some rebellious. Finally, the charming comic scenes and characters serve as a contrast to the underlying seriousness of the conflict between an obsessed Victorian father and his offspring, and prepare us for the final triumph of the lovers as they flee to their beloved Italy.

---

[1] A heavy, dark-brown beer made with malt browned by drying at a high temperature. (Short for porter's ale, originally brewed for porters.)

THE BARRETTS OF WIMPOLE STREET

RUDOLF BESIER

CHARACTERS

DOCTOR CHAMBERS

ELIZABETH BARRETT MOULTON-BARRETT

WILSON

HENRIETTA MOULTON-BARRETT

ARABEL MOULTON-BARRETT

OCTAVIUS MOULTON-BARRETT

SEPTIMUS MOULTON-BARRETT

ALFRED MOULTON-BARRETT

CHARLES MOULTON-BARRETT

HENRY MOULTON-BARRETT

GEORGE MOULTON-BARRETT

EDWARD MOULTON-BARRETT

BELLA HEDLEY

HENRY BEVAN

ROBERT BROWNING

DOCTOR FORD-WATERLOW

CAPTAIN SURTEES COOK

FLUSH

ACT I

Porter in a Tankard

(ELIZABETH BARRETT'S *bed-sitting-room at Number 50, Wimpole Street, London. A window overlooking the street at the back. A door on the left. Fireplace on the right.*) *It is best to give a description of the room in Elizabeth's own words from a letter to a friend:*

"... *The bed like a sofa and no bed: the large table placed out in the room, towards the wardrobe end of it; the sofa rolled where a sofa should be rolled—opposite the armchair: the drawers crowned with a coronal of shelves (of paper, deal, and crimson merino) to carry my books; the washing-table opposite turned into a cabinet with another coronal of shelves; and Chaucer's and Homer's busts on guard over their two departments of English and Greek poetry; three more busts consecrate the wardrobe. ... In the window is fixed a deep box full of soil, where are springing up my scarlet-runners, nasturtiums, and convolvuluses, although they were disturbed a few days ago by the revolutionary insertion among them of a great ivy root with trailing branches so long and wide that the top tendrils were fastened to Henrietta's window of the higher storey, while the lower ones cover all my panes. ..."*

It is evening; blinds and curtains are drawn; the fire glows dully; lamplight.

(ELIZABETH *lies on her sofa, her feet covered with a couvre-pieds. Seated beside her is* DOCTOR CHAMBERS, *an elderly, white-whiskered man. He is feeling her pulse, watch in hand.* FLUSH—*Elizabeth's dog—lies asleep in his basket. On the table is a tray with the remains of a meal, and a pewter tankard.*)

CHAMBERS: (*dropping her wrist and pocketing his watch*) Hm—yes. It's this increasingly low vitality of yours that worries me. No life in you—none. . . . What are we going to do about it?

ELIZABETH: (*lightly*) Well, Doctor, if you shut a person up in one room for years on end, you can't very well expect to find her bursting with life and vigour! Why not prescribe something really exciting for a change?

CHAMBERS: Exciting, eh?

ELIZABETH: A gallop three times round the Park every morning—dumb-bell exercises—a course of calisthenics—a long sea voyage . . .

CHAMBERS: How I wish I could, my dear!

ELIZABETH: It's funny to think of it now—but you know, Doctor, as a child I was a regular tomboy!

CHAMBERS: Yes, I've heard all about that—and, mentally, you're a tomboy still! To tell you the truth, Miss Ba— oh forgive me, my dear Miss Elizabeth, that quaint nickname of yours slipped out unawares! I'm always hearing it from your brothers and sisters. . . .

ELIZABETH: (*smiling*) Oh, please . . .

CHAMBERS: To tell you the truth, I'm not sure that brain of yours isn't altogether too active. The trouble with you is that you never will do anything in moderation—not even playing the invalid! Seriously, aren't we, perhaps, overdoing our studies?

ELIZABETH: Of course not.

CHAMBERS: Still hard at Greek?

ELIZABETH: Oh, not more than two or three hours a day.

CHAMBERS: Hm. Are you engaged on any literary work at the moment?

ELIZABETH: Only a few articles for the *Athenæum* and other papers.

CHAMBERS: The *Athenæum*—dear, dear! . . . Now why not give all these heavy labours a rest, and turn your mind to something light and easy for a change? . . . Poetry! You're not neglecting your poetry, I hope?

ELIZABETH: Meaning something—light and easy! (*Laughs*) Oh, Doctor, I must remember to tell that to Mr. Robert Browning when I see him tomorrow!

CHAMBERS: Robert Browning? A brother bard, eh?

ELIZABETH: Don't tell me you've never heard of him!

CHAMBERS: Well, my dear, poetry isn't much in my line, you know.

ELIZABETH: That's evident! All the same, read Mr. Browning's "Sordello"—and then come back and tell me that poetry's—light and easy!

CHAMBERS: I'll make a note of it. . . . Well, well, I suppose we mustn't rob you of your mental exercises if they keep you contented.

ELIZABETH: Contented! Oh, Doctor, I shudder to think what my life would be like if I hadn't a turn for scribbling and study!

CHAMBERS: Hm, yes. Quite so. Yes. . . . And this isn't the liveliest house for any one to live in—let alone an invalid.

ELIZABETH: No, I suppose not. . . . I wish dear Papa were a happier man! It would make such a world of difference to all of us. . . .

CHAMBERS: Happier, eh? It's no business of mine, but when a man has good health, plenty of money, and a jolly family of boys and girls, I can't see why he should make life a burden to himself and others! . . . It's amazing—incredible, and—well, as I said, it's no concern of mine. But you *are*, my dear—and a very worrying concern, too! Of course, the winter has been abominable, and these spring months are always trying. The fact is you oughtn't to live in England at all. Italy's the place for you.

ELIZABETH: Italy! Oh, Doctor, what a heavenly dream!

CHAMBERS: Yes—and must remain a dream, I fear. . . . But if only I could prescribe some sort of change for you—something—anything—to get you out of these dismal surroundings for a time. . . . Tell me now, Miss Elizabeth, have you ventured on your feet at all lately?

ELIZABETH: No, hardly at all. I rather lost my nerve after that fall I had last Christmas.

CHAMBERS: I remember.

ELIZABETH: Papa, as you know, or one of my brothers, carries me from my bed to the sofa in the morning, and back to bed again at night. Sometimes, when I'm feeling venturesome, my maid supports me across the room.

CHAMBERS: Feeling venturesome at the moment?

ELIZABETH: Not particularly. . . .

CHAMBERS: All the same, I think we'll try a step or two. (*Rising, he takes both of her hands*) Quietly now—slowly—there's no hurry. (*With his assistance she gets on to her feet*) There we are. (*She sways a little. He supports her*) Feeling giddy, eh?

ELIZABETH: A little. . . .

CHAMBERS: Close your eyes and lean against me. It will pass in a minute. . . . Better?

ELIZABETH: Yes. . . . Oh, yes. . . .

CHAMBERS: Take your time now, and step carefully. Don't be nervous; I won't let go your hands. . . . (*She takes a couple of faltering steps, he walking backwards, holding her hands*) No—don't look at the floor. Look straight ahead. . . . That's first rate—that's fine—splendid—splendid. . . . (*After taking half a dozen steps she falters and sways.*)

ELIZABETH: Oh, Doctor! . . .

(*He quickly catches her in his arms and carries her back to the sofa.*)

CHAMBERS: Feeling faint?

ELIZABETH: No, no, I'm all right. . . . I—I am really. . . . It's only my knees—they don't seem able to—to support me.

CHAMBERS: Well, if they can't do that, they're a pretty useless pair! Why, there's no more to you than to a five-year-old! . . . How's the appetite? Just peck at your food, I suppose?

ELIZABETH: I always try to eat what I'm given. But I'm never very hungry. (*With sudden animation*) Doctor, that reminds me! Do you remember Papa suggesting to you that a kind of beer—called porter—might do me good?

CHAMBERS: Yes—and an excellent suggestion too!

ELIZABETH: Oh, but forgive me, it was nothing of the kind! I have to drink it twice a day out of a pewter tankard—and my life, in consequence, has become one long misery!

CHAMBERS: God bless my soul!

ELIZABETH: I am not exaggerating—*one long misery!*

CHAMBERS: But, my dear child, quite apart from its invaluable blood-making properties, porter is generally considered a most palatable beverage. There's nothing I enjoy more than a pint of porter with my steak or chops at breakfast.

ELIZABETH: (*in a shocked whisper*) With your breakfast! . . . All I can say is that to me porter is entirely horrible. . . . Horrible to look at, more horrible to smell, and most horrible to drink. Surely something one abominates so intensely can't possibly do one any good! It's no use *my* appealing to Papa—especially as the dreadful idea originated with him. But if *you*, dear, dear Doctor Chambers, were to suggest to him that something else—anything—I don't mind what it is—might be equally efficacious . . .

CHAMBERS: (*laughing*) You poor little lady! But of course I will!

ELIZABETH: Oh, thank you a thousand times!

CHAMBERS: What do you say to a couple of glasses of hot milk as a substitute?

ELIZABETH: I dislike milk—but I'll drink it all day long, if only you'll rescue me from porter! (*A knock at the door*) Come in. (WILSON, ELIZABETH'S *maid, enters. She is a fine, capable-looking girl in the middle twenties*) Yes, Wilson?

WILSON: Begging your pardon, Miss, but (*turning to the* DOCTOR) the Master wishes most particularly to see you before you leave, sir.

CHAMBERS: Of course, of course.... (*Looks at his watch*) And high time I were off! Is your Master in his study?

WILSON: Yes, sir.

CHAMBERS: Well, good-bye, Miss Elizabeth, good-bye. (*Takes her hand.*)

ELIZABETH: Good-bye, Doctor. (*In a low voice*) And you won't forget?

CHAMBERS: Eh?

ELIZABETH: (*spelling the word*) P-O-R-T-E-R.

CHAMBERS: (*laughing*) I'll speak to him about it now.

ELIZABETH: Oh, thank you! thank you!

CHAMBERS: (*still laughing*) Good night. (*To* WILSON, *as he goes to the door*) You needn't see me downstairs, I know my way.

WILSON: Thank you, sir. (DOCTOR CHAMBERS *goes out*) I'm just going to post your letters, Miss Ba. Shall I take Flush with me?

ELIZABETH: (*excitedly*) Quick, Wilson—away with it! (*Points at the tankard of porter.*)

WILSON: (*bewildered*) What, Miss?...

ELIZABETH: I hadn't the courage to drink it at dinner. I was putting off the dreadful moment as long as I could....

WILSON: Your porter, Miss?

ELIZABETH: And now dear Doctor Chambers tells me I needn't drink it any longer. Take it away! Quick! Quick! And never mention the word porter to me again!

WILSON: Lor', Miss! Very good, Miss. But since you haven't had your porter, won't you—

ELIZABETH: (*covering her ears*) I told you never to mention the word again! Take it away! Please! Please!

WILSON: Very good, Miss Ba. Come, Flush. (*She picks up the dog and puts him out of the room; then returns for the tray, with a rather concerned glance at* ELIZABETH, *who starts laughing.* HENRIETTA *enters suddenly. She is a beautiful, high-spirited, blooming girl.*)

HENRIETTA: What are you laughing at, Ba?

ELIZABETH: Wilson thinks I've gone mad.

WILSON: Mad, Miss? What things you do say!

ELIZABETH: (*still laughing*) Will you, or won't you, take away that—that black beer?

WILSON: Very good, Miss. (WILSON *goes out.*)

HENRIETTA: I don't know why you're laughing, Ba, and you needn't tell me. Only don't stop! I'll tickle you if you think you can't keep it up without being helped!... Oh, dinner was awful!

ELIZABETH: But, Henrietta—

HENRIETTA: Awful! Awful!

ELIZABETH: Was Papa—

HENRIETTA: Yes, he was. It was awful. He was in one of his moods—the worst kind. The nagging mood is bad enough, the shouting mood is worse—but don't you think the *dumb* mood is the worst of all?

ELIZABETH: Yes, perhaps, but —

HENRIETTA: I don't believe there were more than a dozen remarks all through dinner—and most of them were frozen off at the tips! Papa would just turn his glassy eyes on the speaker.... You know? For the last twenty minutes or so the only sound in the room was the discreet clatter of knives and forks. Directly dinner was over he ordered his port to be taken to the study

ELIZABETH: —and, thank Heaven! he followed it almost at once.

ELIZABETH: Doctor Chambers is with him now.

HENRIETTA: Oh, Ba, I do hope, for all our sakes, his report of you isn't *too* good.

ELIZABETH: But, Henrietta . . .

HENRIETTA: (*all sudden contrition, kneeling at the sofa and putting her arms around* ELIZABETH) Forgive me, dearest! It was odious of me to say that! You know I didn't mean it, don't you? Nothing in the whole world matters to me if only you get better. You know that, don't you?

ELIZABETH: Of course I do, you silly child. But what you said makes Papa an inhuman monster. And that's wickedly untrue. In his own way—he cares for all his children.

HENRIETTA: In his own way . . . ! No, dear, what I meant was that good news of any kind would be certain to aggravate him in his present mood. I don't know why it should, but it does. (*With sudden anxiety*) Ba, Doctor Chambers isn't dissatisfied with you? You're not worse?

ELIZABETH: No, no, dear; I am just the same—neither better nor worse. . . . (ARABEL *enters. She is a tall, dark, serious woman.*)

ARABEL: Oh, you're here, Henrietta! I've been looking for you everywhere. Papa has just sent you this note from his study.

HENRIETTA: Me? Oh dear! When he starts sending out notes from his study look out for squalls! (*Opens the note and reads*) "I have heard this morning that your Aunt and Uncle Hedley, and your Cousin Bella, have arrived in London earlier than was expected. They are staying at Fenton's Hotel. Your Cousin Bella and her fiancé, Mr. Bevan, propose to call on you tomorrow at 3 o'clock. You and Arabel will, of course, be here to receive them, and if Elizabeth is well enough, you will bring them upstairs to see her. I have written to invite your Uncle and Aunt and Cousin to dinner next Thursday.—Papa." Well!

ARABEL: I understand now why Papa seemed so—so displeased at dinner.

HENRIETTA: Vile-tempered you mean.

ARABEL: Is it necessary always to use the ugliest word?

HENRIETTA: Yes, Arabel—when you're describing the ugliest thing. Oh, but Papa is quite impossible! He got that letter from the Hedleys at breakfast. Why couldn't he have spoken then? Why couldn't he have spoken at dinner? Heaven knows he had opportunity enough!

ARABEL: I'm afraid he was too displeased.

HENRIETTA: (*with a grimace*) Displeased. . . . Oh, of course, we all know that he hates being ordinarily polite to any one—and now he's simply bound to show some kind of hospitality to the Hedleys! No wonder he was—*displeased.*

ELIZABETH: Are you quite fair, dear? Papa seldom objects to us receiving our friends here.

HENRIETTA: For a cup of tea and a bun—and so long as the house is clear of them before he's back from the City! Has *any* one of us *ever* been allowed to ask *any* one to dinner? Or even to luncheon? But that's an old story! What enrages me is that I was expecting a friend tomorrow at three—and now I shall have to put him off somehow.

ARABEL: (*archly*) Why?

HENRIETTA: Why what?

ARABEL: (*as before*) Why must you put your friend off? Bella and her *fiancé* won't eat—your friend.

HENRIETTA: (*angrily*) What—what business is that of yours?

ARABEL: (*dismayed*) But, Henrietta—

HENRIETTA: I hate people prying into my affairs! . . . (*She goes quickly out of the room, slamming the door behind her.*)

ARABEL: (*distressed*) Oh, dear! Oh, dear! What can be the matter with her tonight? Usually she quite enjoys being quizzed about Captain Surtees Cook.

ELIZABETH: Perhaps she may have begun to take his attentions seriously.

ARABEL: Oh, Ba, I hope not! You remember when young Mr. Palfrey wanted to marry her two years ago—those dreadful scenes with Papa?

ELIZABETH: I should rather forget them.

ARABEL: Oh, why can't Henrietta realise that if there's one thing Papa will never, *never* permit, it's a marriage in the family? It doesn't worry *me* at all, as gentlemen never attracted me in that way. Nor you, dear . . .

ELIZABETH: (*with a laugh*) Me!

ARABEL: Of course, my poor darling, today anything of that kind is quite out of the question—Papa or no Papa. But even when you were younger and stronger, I don't ever remember your having had . . . little affairs with gentlemen.

ELIZABETH: (*whimsically*) Perhaps the gentlemen never gave me the chance.

ARABEL: Oh, but you were quite pretty as a young girl.

ELIZABETH: What is Captain Surtees Cook like? Is he nice?

ARABEL: Yes, I think so. Yes, quite nice. But he never says much. He just sits and looks at Henrietta.

ELIZABETH: She's very lovely. . . .

ARABEL: But Papa would never countenance any kind of understanding between them. Captain Cook would be forbidden the house at the least mention of such a thing—and it's dreadful to think what would happen to Henrietta! Even if he came offering her a coronet, instead of being an officer with a small allowance in addition to his pay, it would make no difference. You know that as well as I do.

ELIZABETH: Poor Henrietta. . . .

(HENRIETTA *reënters. She goes quickly up to* ARABEL *and kisses her.*)

HENRIETTA: I'm sorry.

ARABEL: Oh, my dear, I never meant to annoy you.

HENRIETTA: You didn't—you *displeased* me! (*With a laugh*) Oh, I'm Papa's daughter all right!

ELIZABETH: When Bella and her *fiancé* call tomorrow, Arabel will bring them up here to see me—and you can entertain Captain Cook in the drawing-room.

(ARABEL *looks distressed.*)

HENRIETTA: What a thing it is to be a genius! You darling! (*Embraces* ELIZABETH.)

ELIZABETH: But I must have the room to myself at half-past three, as Mr. Robert Browning is calling then.

HENRIETTA: (*excitedly*) No!

ARABEL: But I thought—

HENRIETTA: Of course, I know you've been corresponding with Mr. Browning for months as I've posted any number of your letters to him. But then you write to so many literary people whom you absolutely refuse to see, and—

ARABEL: Has Papa given his permission?

ELIZABETH: Of course.

HENRIETTA: But why—why have you made an exception of Mr. Browning? I've heard he's wonderfully handsome, but—

ELIZABETH: (*laughing*) Oh, Henrietta, you're incorrigible!

ARABEL: I know he's been most anxious to call. Mr. Kenyon told me so.

HENRIETTA: But you said yourself, only a short time ago, that you didn't intend to receive him!

ELIZABETH: I didn't—and I don't particularly want to now.

HENRIETTA: But why?

ELIZABETH: (*lightly*) Because, my dear, at heart I'm as vain as a peacock! . . . You see, when people admire my work they are quite likely to picture the poetess as stately and beautiful as her verses. At least, that's what I always tell myself. . . . And it's dreadfully humiliating to disillusion them!

HENRIETTA: Don't be silly, Ba. You're very interesting and picturesque.

ELIZABETH: (*laughing*) Isn't that how guidebooks usually describe a ruin?

HENRIETTA: Oh, Ba, I didn't mean—

ELIZABETH: Of course not, dear! . . . As a matter of fact, Mr. Browning has been so insistent that, out of sheer weariness, I've given way. But I don't want an audience to witness the tragedy of his disillusionment! So mind, Arabel—Bella and her Mr. Bevan must have left the room before he arrives. (*A knock at the door*) Come in. (OCTAVIUS BARRETT *enters. He is about eighteen, and he stammers slightly*) Come in, Occy.

OCTAVIUS: I've j-just come to see how you are, and to wish you g-good-night. (*Bends down and kisses her*) Doctor satisfied?

ELIZABETH: Oh, yes, I think so.

HENRIETTA: (*handing* OCTAVIUS *Barrett's note*). Read that, Octavius.

ARABEL: (*while* OCTAVIUS *reads*) Oh, dear! I quite forgot that I was to attend a lecture on the Chinese Wesleyan Mission at Exeter Hall tomorrow afternoon!

OCTAVIUS: Well, you can't attend it. (*Flourishes* BARRETT'S *letter*) This is undoubtedly a Royal D-decree!

HENRIETTA: (*dramatically*) Given at Our study at 50, Wimpole Street, on this 19th day of May, 1845. God save Papa!

ARABEL: (*reprovingly*) Henrietta dear! (*A knock at the door.*)

ELIZABETH: Come in (SEPTIMUS BARRETT *enters. He is a year older than* OCTAVIUS. *Like* OCTAVIUS *and the other Barrett brothers who subsequently appear, he is in evening dress*) Well, Septimus?

SEPTIMUS: How are you, Ba? (*Kisses her*) I hope the Doctor is satisfied with you?

ELIZABETH: Oh, yes, I think so.

OCTAVIUS: I say, Septimus, the Hedleys are d-dining here in force next Thursday.

SEPTIMUS: Bai Jove! Not really? (*A knock at the door.*)

ELIZABETH: Come in. (ALFRED BARRETT *enters. He is older than* SEPTIMUS) Come in, Alfred.

ALFRED: And how's our dear Ba tonight? I hope the Doctor was happy about you?

ELIZABETH: Oh, yes, I think so. (*A knock at the door*) Come in. (CHARLES BARRETT *enters. He is somewhat older than* ALFRED) Come in, Charles.

CHARLES: How are you feeling tonight, Ba? (*Kisses her*) I hope Doctor Chambers' report was good?

ELIZABETH: Oh, yes, I think so. (*A knock at the door*) Come in. (HENRY BARRETT *enters. He is slightly older than* CHARLES) Come in, Henry.

HENRY: Well, Ba? How are you, my dear? (*Kisses her*) Was the Doctor pleased with his patient?

ELIZABETH: Oh, yes, I think so.

HENRY: That's good. I must say I think you are looking a little better. What d'you say, Charles?

CHARLES: Eh?

HENRY: Looking better, don't you know. More herself, what? (*A knock at the door.*)

ELIZABETH: Come in. (GEORGE BARRETT *enters. He is slightly older than* HENRY) Come in, George.

GEORGE: Well, and how's Ba tonight? (*Kisses her*) The Doctor's just been, hasn't he? I'm afraid he wasn't too pleased with you.

ELIZABETH: Oh, yes, I think so. . . . I mean—why?

GEORGE: You're not looking so well. Is she, Henry?

HENRY: On the contrary, I think she's looking considerably better. So does Charles. Don't you, Charles?

CHARLES: Eh?

OCTAVIUS: I say, George, the Hedleys

have arrived unexpectedly in town. Bella and her swain are c-calling on the girls tomorrow afternoon. And on Thursday she and her parents are d-dining here in state.

ALFRED, HENRY, SEPTIMUS: (*simultaneously*) Dining here!

GEORGE: Well, I hope they'll enjoy their dinner as much as we did tonight!

HENRY: You have met this Mr. Bevan, haven't you?

GEORGE: I have.

HENRY: What is he like?

GEORGE: Pompous ass. But warm—a very warm man. Ten thousand pounds a year, if he has a penny.

HENRIETTA: No!

GEORGE: And ten thousand more when his grandmother dies.

ARABEL: Oh!

HENRIETTA: It's grossly unfair! What has Bella done to deserve such luck?

OCTAVIUS: George say's he a p-pompous ass.

HENRIETTA: Oh, that's jealousy! No man with ten thousand a year can be (*imitating his stammer*) a—p-p-p-p-pompous ass!

GEORGE: I think it's just possible that you'll all be interested to hear that Papa is going to Plymouth on business next week, and—

(*Excited exclamations from all except* ELIZABETH.)

HENRIETTA: Go on, George, go on! And—?

GEORGE: And that he's not expected to return—for at least a fortnight. (*Murmurs of satisfaction and smiling faces.*)

HENRIETTA: Oh, George! (*She flings her arms round his neck*) How wonderful! How glorious! Do you polk, George?

GEORGE: Don't be childish.

HENRIETTA: Well, I polk! (*She dances the polka round the room, humming a polka measure. The others look on amused.* OCTAVIUS *claps his hands. The door is opened quietly and* EDWARD MOULTON-BARRETT *enters. He is a well-set-up handsome man of sixty.*)

ELIZABETH: Papa . . . (*An uneasy silence falls.* HENRIETTA, *in the middle of the room, stops dead.* BARRETT *stands for a moment just beyond the threshold, looking before him with a perfectly expressionless face*) Good evening, Papa. . . .

(*Without replying,* BARRETT *crosses the room and takes his stand with his back to the fireplace. A pause. No one moves.*)

BARRETT: (*in a cold, measured voice*) I am most displeased. (*A pause*) It is quite in order that you should visit your sister of an evening and have a few quiet words with her. But I think I have pointed out, not once, but several times, that, in her very precarious state of health, it is inadvisable for more than three of you to be in her room at the same time. My wishes in this matter have been disregarded—as usual. (*A pause*) You all know very well that your sister must avoid any kind of excitement. Absolute quiet is essential, especially before she retires for the night. And yet I find you romping around her like a lot of disorderly children. . . . I am gravely displeased. (HENRIETTA *gives a nervous little giggle*) I am not aware that I have said anything amusing, Henrietta?

HENRIETTA: I—I beg your pardon, Papa.

BARRETT: And may I ask what you were doing as I came into the room?

HENRIETTA: I was showing Ba how to polk.

BARRETT: To . . . polk?

HENRIETTA: How to dance the polka.

BARRETT: I see.

(*A pause*)

OCTAVIUS: (*nervously*) Well, B-Ba, I think I'll say g-good-night, and—

BARRETT: I should be grateful if you would kindly allow me to finish speaking.

OCTAVIUS: Sorry, sir. I—I thought you'd d-done.

BARRETT: (*with frigid anger*) Are you being insolent, sir?

OCTAVIUS: N-no indeed, sir—I assure you, I—

BARRETT: Very well. Now—

ELIZABETH: (*quickly, nervously*) As I am really the cause of your displeasure, Papa, I ought to tell you that I like nothing better than a—a little noise occasionally. (*A slight pause*) It—it's delightful having all the family here together—and can't possibly do me any harm. . . .

BARRETT: Perhaps you will forgive my saying, Elizabeth, that you are not the best judge of what is good or bad for you. . . . And that brings me to what I came here to speak to you about. Doctor Chambers told me just now that you had persuaded him to allow you to discontinue drinking porter with your meals.

ELIZABETH: It needed very little persuasion, Papa. I said I detested porter, and he agreed at once that I should take milk instead.

BARRETT: I questioned him closely as to the comparative strength-giving values of porter and milk, and he was forced to admit that porter came decidedly first.

ELIZABETH: That may be, Papa. But when you dislike a thing to loathing, I don't see how it can do you any good.

BARRETT: I said just now that you are not the best judge of what is good or bad for you, my child. May I add that self-discipline is always beneficial, and self-indulgence invariably harmful?

ELIZABETH: If you think my drinking milk shows reckless self-indulgence, Papa, you're quite wrong. I dislike it only less than porter.

BARRETT: Your likes and dislikes are quite beside the point in a case like this.

ELIZABETH: But, Papa—

BARRETT: Believe me, Elizabeth, I have nothing but your welfare at heart when I warn you that if you decide to discontinue drinking porter, you will incur my grave displeasure.

ELIZABETH: (*indignantly*) But — but when Doctor Chambers himself—

BARRETT: I have told you what Doctor Chambers said.

ELIZABETH: Yes, but—

BARRETT: Did you drink your porter at dinner?

ELIZABETH: No.

BARRETT: Then I hope you will do so before you go to bed.

ELIZABETH: No, Papa, that's really asking too much! I—I can't drink the horrible stuff in cold blood.

BARRETT: Very well. Of course, I have no means of coercing you. You are no longer a child. But I intend to give your better nature every chance of asserting itself. A tankard of porter will be left at your bedside. And I hope that tomorrow you will be able to tell me that—you have obeyed your Father.

ELIZABETH: I am sorry, Papa—but I sha'n't drink it.

BARRETT: (*to* HENRIETTA) Go down to the kitchen and fetch a tankard of porter.

HENRIETTA: No.

BARRETT: I beg your pardon?

HENRIETTA: (*her voice trembling with anger and agitation*) It's—it's sheer cruelty. You know how Ba hates the stuff. The Doctor has let her off. You're just torturing her because you—you like torturing.

BARRETT: I have told you to fetch a tankard of porter from the kitchen.

HENRIETTA: I won't do it.

BARRETT: Must I ask you a third time? (*Suddenly shouting*) Obey me this instant!

ELIZABETH: (*sharply*) Papa . . . Go and fetch it, Henrietta! Go at once! I can't stand this. . . .

HENRIETTA: No, I—

ELIZABETH: Please—please . . .

(*After a moment's indecision,* HENRIETTA *turns and goes out.*)

BARRETT: (*quietly, after a pause*) You had all better say good night to your sister.

ARABEL: (*in a whisper*) Good night, dearest. (*She kisses* ELIZABETH *on the cheek.*)

ELIZABETH: (*receiving the kiss impassively*) Good night.

(ARABEL *leaves the room. Then each of the brothers in turn goes to* ELIZABETH *and kisses her cheek.*)

GEORGE: Good night, Ba.

ELIZABETH: Good night.

(GEORGE *goes out.*)

ALFRED: Good night, Ba.

ELIZABETH: Good night.

(ALFRED *goes out.*)

HENRY: Good night, Ba.

ELIZABETH: Good night.

(HENRY *goes out.*)

CHARLES: Good night, Ba.

ELIZABETH: Good night.

(CHARLES *goes out.*)

SEPTIMUS: Good night, Ba.

ELIZABETH: Good night.

(SEPTIMUS *goes out.*)

OCTAVIUS: G-good night, Ba.

ELIZABETH: Good night.

(OCTAVIUS *goes out.* BARRETT, *standing before the fireplace, and* ELIZABETH, *on her sofa, look before them with expressionless faces. A pause.* HENRIETTA *enters with a tankard on a small tray. She stands a little beyond the threshold, glaring at her father and breathing quickly.*)

ELIZABETH: Give it to me, please.

(HENRIETTA *goes to her.* ELIZABETH *takes the tankard and is putting it to her lips, when* BARRETT *suddenly, but quietly, intervenes.*)

BARRETT: No. (*Putting* HENRIETTA *aside, he takes the tankard from* ELIZABETH. *To* HENRIETTA) You may go.

HENRIETTA: Good night, Ba darling. (*She moves forward to* ELIZABETH, *but* BARRETT *waves her back.*)

BARRETT: You may go.

ELIZABETH: Good night.

(HENRIETTA, *with a defiant look at her father, goes out.* BARRETT *puts the tankard on the mantelpiece; then goes to the sofa and stands looking down at* ELIZABETH. *She stares up at him with wide, fearful eyes.*)

BARRETT: (*in a gentle voice*) Elizabeth.

ELIZABETH: (*in a whisper*) Yes?

BARRETT: (*placing his hand on her head and bending it slightly back*) Why do you look at me like that, child? . . . Are you frightened?

ELIZABETH: (*as before*) No.

BARRETT: You're trembling. . . . Why?

ELIZABETH: I—I don't know.

BARRETT: You're not frightened of me? (ELIZABETH *is about to speak—he goes on quickly*) No, no. You mustn't say it. I couldn't bear to think that. (*He seats himself on the side of the sofa and takes her hands*) You're everything in the world to me—you know that. Without you I should be quite alone—you know that too. And you—if you love me, you can't be afraid of me. For love casts out fear. . . . You love me, my darling? You love your father?

ELIZABETH: (*in a whisper*) Yes.

BARRETT: (*eagerly*) And you'll prove your love by doing as I wish?

ELIZABETH: I don't understand. I was going to drink—

BARRETT: (*quickly*) Yes—out of fear, not love. Listen, dear. I told you just now that if you disobeyed me you would incur my displeasure. I take that back. I shall never, in any way, reproach you. You shall never know by deed or word, or hint, of mine how much you have grieved and wounded your father by refusing to do the little thing he asked. . . .

ELIZABETH: Oh, please, please, don't say any more. It's all so petty and sordid. Please give me the tankard.

BARRETT: (*rising*) You are acting of your own free will, and not—

ELIZABETH: Oh, Papa, let us get this over and forget it! I can't forgive myself for having made the whole house miserable over a tankard of porter.

(*He gives her the tankard. She drinks the porter straight off.* BARRETT *places the tank-*

ard back on the mantelpiece; then returns to the sofa and looks yearningly down at ELIZABETH.)

BARRETT: You're not feeling worse to-night, my darling?

ELIZABETH: (listlessly) No, Papa.

BARRETT: Just tired?

ELIZABETH: Yes . . . just tired.

BARRETT: I'd better leave you now. . . . Shall I say a little prayer with you before I go?

ELIZABETH: Please, Papa.

(BARRETT *kneels down beside the sofa, clasps his hands, lifts his face, and shuts his eyes.* ELIZABETH *clasps her hands, but keeps her eyes wide open.*)

BARRETT: Almighty and merciful God, hear me, I beseech Thee, and grant my humble prayer. In Thine inscrutable wisdom Thou hast seen good to lay on Thy daughter Elizabeth grievous and heavy afflictions. For years she hath languished in sickness; and for years, unless in Thy mercy Thou take her to Thyself, she may languish on. Give her to realise the blessed word that Thou chastisest those whom Thou lovest. Give her to bear her sufferings in patience. Give her to fix her heart and soul on Thee and on that Heavenly Eternity which may at any moment open out before her. Take her into Thy loving care tonight; purge her mind of all bitter and selfish and unkind thoughts; guard her and comfort her. These things I beseech Thee for the sake of Thy dear Son, Jesus Christ. Amen.

ELIZABETH: Amen.

BARRETT: (*rising to his feet, and kissing her forehead*) Good night, my child.

ELIZABETH: (*receiving his kiss impassively*) Good night, Papa. (BARRETT *goes out.* ELIZABETH *lies motionless, staring before her for a moment or two. A knock at the door*) Come in.

(WILSON *enters, carrying* FLUSH.)

WILSON: (*putting* FLUSH *in his basket*) Are you ready for your bed now, Miss Ba?

ELIZABETH: Oh, Wilson, I'm so tired—tired—tired of it all. . . . Will it never end?

WILSON: End, Miss?

ELIZABETH: This long, long, grey death in life.

WILSON: Oh, Miss Ba, you shouldn't say such things!

ELIZABETH: No, I suppose I shouldn't. . . . . Did Flush enjoy his run?

WILSON: Oh, yes, Miss. (*A short pause.*)

ELIZABETH: Is it a fine night, Wilson?

WILSON: Yes, Miss, and quite warm, and there's such a lovely moon.

ELIZABETH: (*eagerly*) A moon! Oh, do you think I can see it from here?

WILSON: I don't know, I'm sure.

ELIZABETH: Draw back the curtains and raise the blind.

(WILSON *does so; and moonlight, tempered by the lamplight, streams on* ELIZABETH'S *face.*)

WILSON: There you are, Miss! The moon's right above the chimleys. You can see it lovely!

ELIZABETH: (*dreamily*) Yes. . . . Yes. . . . Please put out the lamp and leave me for a little. I don't want to go to bed quite yet.

WILSON: Very well, Miss Ba. (WILSON *extinguishes the lamp and goes out.* ELIZABETH *is bathed in strong moonlight. She stares, for a while, with wide eyes at the moon. Then her quickened breathing becomes audible, and her whole body is shaken with sobs. She turns over on her side and buries her face in her arms. The only sound is her strangled weeping as the scene closes.*)

ACT II

Mr. Robert Browning

(*The afternoon of the following day. The curtains are drawn aside, the blinds are up, and sunshine pours into the room. On a little table near Elizabeth's sofa is a tray, with an untouched sweet on it.*)

ACT II   THE BARRETTS OF WIMPOLE STREET

(ELIZABETH *lies on the sofa, her couvre-pieds over her feet. She is reading a small book with intense absorption; now and again running her fingers through her ringlets or tossing them back from her face.* FLUSH *lies in his basket.*)

ELIZABETH: (*with puzzled emphasis*):
"With flowers in completeness,
All petals, no prickles,
Delicious as trickles
Of wine poured at mass-time."
(*A knock at the door.* ELIZABETH, *absorbed, takes no notice. She repeats, clutching her forehead*)
"All petals, no prickles,
Delicious as trickles—"
(*The knock repeated*)
"Of wine—"
Come in. . . . (WILSON *enters*) Oh, yes, Wilson . . . I'm quite ready for lunch.

WILSON: (*stolidly*) You've had your lunch, Miss Ba.

ELIZABETH: Oh, yes, of course. . . . And I enjoyed it very much!

WILSON: You only picked at the fish, Miss Ba. An' I took away the best part of that nice chop. An' I see you haven't touched the pudding—cornflour blammonge too, with raspberry jam.

ELIZABETH: (*wonderingly regarding the tray*) Oh. . . . Anyhow, it's too late now. . . . (*She once more plunges into her book.* WILSON *carries out the tray and reënters immediately, shutting the door after her.*)

WILSON: (*going to the mantelpiece and measuring out some medicine into a medicine glass*) And now, Miss Ba, if you're all nice and comfortable, I'll take Flush out for his airing. (ELIZABETH, *absorbed in her reading, takes no notice.* WILSON *holds the glass of medicine towards her*) Your physic, Miss Ba.

ELIZABETH: (*taking the glass, with her eyes still fixed on her book*) Thank you. (*With the glass in her hand she continues reading.*)

WILSON: (*going to the window*) I think, p'raps, I'd better pull down the blind a bit. Too much sun isn't good for you, Miss. . . . (*She half draws down the blind.*)

ELIZABETH: (*holding out the untouched glass, her eyes still on the book*) Thank you. . . .

WILSON: You haven't drunk it yet, Miss.

ELIZABETH: Oh. . . . (*She swallows the medicine and, with a little grimace, hands the glass back to* WILSON) Please open the door, Wilson. I am expecting visitors this afternoon, and I want the room to be quite fresh for them. How I wish we could open the window!

WILSON: (*shocked*) Open the window, Miss Ba!

ELIZABETH: (*with a sigh*) Yes, I know it's strictly forbidden. . . . Well, open the door *wide*.

WILSON: I'd best cover you well up first of all. (*Fetches a rug*) Visitors, Miss Ba? . . .

ELIZABETH: (*while* WILSON *covers her up to her chin*) Yes, my cousin, Miss Bella Hedley. I haven't seen her since she was a child—such a lovely slip of a child! And now she's just become engaged.

WILSON: Indeed, Miss. And is she bringing her young gentleman with her?

ELIZABETH: Yes. (WILSON *opens the door*) And Mr. Robert Browning is calling later.

WILSON: Indeed, Miss? The gentleman who's always sending you such lovely boukeys?

ELIZABETH: Yes.
(*Starts reading again.*)

WILSON: Sure you don't feel a draught, Miss Ba?

ELIZABETH: (*without looking up*) Quite, thanks.

WILSON: Hadn't you better keep your arms covered? These spring days the air is that treacherous.

ELIZABETH: (*to herself, with despair-*

ing emphasis) No—it's quite beyond me! I give it up!

WILSON: Beg pardon?

ELIZABETH: (*speaking intensely*) Wilson.

WILSON: Yes, Miss.

ELIZABETH: (*as before*) Have you noticed anything—*strange* in me today?

WILSON: Strange, Miss?

ELIZABETH: Yes, strange. I mean—dull-witted — thick-headed — stupid — idiotic. . . .

WILSON: Lor'! No! P'raps a bit absent-minded like—but that isn't anything for you to worry about, Miss Ba.

ELIZABETH: Then you don't think I'm going—*mad*?

WILSON: Mercy on us! Mad!

ELIZABETH: Very well. But now, listen carefully and tell me what you make of this: (*She reads*)
"And after, for pastime,
If June be refulgent
With flowers in completeness,
All petals, no prickles,
Delicious as trickles
Of wine poured at mass-time,—
And choose one indulgent
To redness and sweetness:
Or if, with experience of man and of spider,
June used by June-lightning, the strong insect-ridder,
To stop the fresh film work,—why June will consider."
Well?

WILSON: (*enthusiastically*) I call that just lovely, Miss Ba!

ELIZABETH: But do you know what it means?

WILSON: Oh, no, Miss.

ELIZABETH: Does it convey *anything* at *all* to your mind?

WILSON: Oh, no, Miss.

ELIZABETH: (*with a sigh of relief*) Thank Heaven for that!

WILSON: But then po'try never does, Miss. Leastways, not real po'try, like what you make.

ELIZABETH: (*laughing*) But *I* didn't write that! It's by Mr. Browning.

WILSON: He must be a clever gentleman!

ELIZABETH: Oh, yes! He's all that! (WILSON *has picked up* FLUSH) Well, Flush dear, are you going to behave nicely today? (*She holds out her arms for the dog and* WILSON *gives it to her*) I shall ask Wilson for a full report when she gets home. (*To* WILSON) Where are you taking him to?

WILSON: Well, Miss, being so fine, I thought of a little walk in the Park.

ELIZABETH: Oh, yes. And mind you notice the flowers! I shall want to hear all about them. The laburnum is over, of course. But there ought to be still some pink May, and tulips, and wall-flowers. And perhaps some early roses. . . . Oh, Flush, I'd give almost anything to be going with you instead of Wilson!

OCTAVIUS: (*outside*) May I c-come in?

ELIZABETH: Occy, dear! (OCTAVIUS *enters.* ELIZABETH *gives* FLUSH *to* WILSON) What on earth are you doing at home at this time of the day?

(WILSON *goes out, carrying* FLUSH.)

OCTAVIUS: Papa's b-bright idea. Suggested I should take a half-holiday to help you feed and entertain the l-lovebirds.

ELIZABETH: (*laughing*) But why? Henrietta and Arabel are socially quite competent. So am I.

OCTAVIUS: But you labour under the d-disadvantage of being all the same sex. Papa appears to think that at least one male B-Barrett ought to show up. He seems fully determined to do the p-polite thing by the Hedleys. And when Papa is fully d-determined on a thing, that thing is done. Or am I wrong?

ELIZABETH: (*sighing*) No—that thing is done. . . . But now—I want you to be diplomatic. Captain Surtees Cook is calling at the same time as Bella and Mr. Bevan. He's coming to see Henrietta. . . .

OCTAVIUS: Is he, by Jove! And won't the gallant fella rejoice when he finds Henrietta chaperoned f-four times over!

ELIZABETH: I've arranged for Arabel to bring Bella and Mr. Bevan up here to see me. *You* must come with them.

OCTAVIUS: Must I indeed? And why?

ELIZABETH: So that Henrietta may have Captain Cook to herself for a little while.

OCTAVIUS: Oh. Ah. Yes. Quite so. I see. . . . And you d-don't look in the least ashamed of yourself!

ELIZABETH: I'm not.

OCTAVIUS: But does it occur to you, my dear Ba, that we may be doing Henrietta an uncommonly b-bad turn by encouraging this b-budding romance?

ELIZABETH: Yes. But I think we ought to chance that. . . . (*He looks at her questioningly*) Occy, when you six boys wished me good night yesterday, a queer thought came into my mind. You weren't alive at all—just automata.

OCTAVIUS: By Jove!

ELIZABETH: Like automata, you get up at half-past seven every morning. Like automata, you eat your breakfasts. Like automata, you go to work. Like automata, you return home. You dine like automata. You go to bed like automata.

OCTAVIUS: But I say—

ELIZABETH: And though she works on different lines, Arabel is as automatic. You all seem to me to have cut out of life everything that makes life worth living—excitement, adventure, change, conflict, frivolity, love. . . .

OCTAVIUS: *We* haven't cut 'em out, my dear! That operation was performed by dear P-Papa.

ELIZABETH: I know, but—

OCTAVIUS: Oh, I admit we're a pretty spineless lot! But what would you? We're none of us particularly g-gifted—and we're all of us wholly dependent on Papa, and must obey, or be broken. You're not c-counselling sedition?

ELIZABETH: No—but not resignation. Keep your souls alive. What frightens me is that you may become content with a life which isn't life at all. You're going that way—all of you—except Henrietta.

OCTAVIUS: And what does she get by t-trying to be herself? More kicks than ha'pence!

ELIZABETH: Yes—but being kicked keeps one alive. So don't let us do anything, just for the sake of peace and quiet, to hinder her little romance. Even if it should come to grief.

OCTAVIUS: It will.

ELIZABETH: Grief is better than stagnation.

OCTAVIUS: All very f-fine, my dear Ba —but what about you?

ELIZABETH: Me?

OCTAVIUS: Yes, you. We may all, with the possible exception of young Henrietta, be drifting with the stream. But I don't notice that you make much of a struggle against it? Where did that p-porter finally g-get to last night?

ELIZABETH: (*with a dreary little laugh*) Oh, but I don't count! I am quite out of it. You have your lives before you. My life is over.

OCTAVIUS: Rubbish!

(HENRIETTA *enters.*)

HENRIETTA: Why, Occy, what are you doing here?

OCTAVIUS: Papa's n-notion. He somehow got wind that Surtees Cook was p-prowling around this afternoon and sent me home to head the f-feller off.

ELIZABETH: Occy!

HENRIETTA: (*in breathless consternation*) How did he hear? He couldn't have heard—(*to* ELIZABETH) unless you, or Arabel—

ELIZABETH: Occy, you idiot! No, dear—

OCTAVIUS: Sorry! My little joke, you know. . . .

HENRIETTA: (*hotly*) I hate you!

OCTAVIUS: Quite right, too. (*Puts his arm around her*) I repeat, I'm sorry. You may s-slap me if you like.

HENRIETTA: (*half mollified*) I've a good mind to.

OCTAVIUS: (*sitting down and drawing her on to his knee*) No, my che-ild, it's like this. His Majesty sent me home to represent His Majesty at the reception. I don't intend to leave Bella's side—not even when she and her beloved come up here to embrace Ba. Meanwhile you'll amuse Cook—j-just as you're amusing me now. (*Kisses her*) In fact, we may take this as a l-little rehearsal.

HENRIETTA: (*jumping up from his knee*) Occy! how can you be so vulgar! (*She listens*) What's that? (*Runs to the window*) Oh, Ba, they've arrived! And in state! The Bevan family barouche, powdered footman and all! (OCTAVIUS *joins her at the window*) Look at Bella! What a gown! What a bonnet! Lovely! Oh, and Mr. Bevan's whiskers! (*Gestures round her chin*) Aren't you green with envy, Occy?

OCTAVIUS: Positively verdant.

HENRIETTA: (*pushing* OCTAVIUS *to the door*) Go and help Arabel receive them. Off with you! Quick! I'll wait here till Captain Cook arrives. I'm going to let him in. And then you and Arabel can bring Bella and Mr. Bevan up here.

OCTAVIUS: All c-cut and dried, what? But l-look here—

HENRIETTA: Go along with you! (*Pushes him out of the room and shuts the door. Then runs again to the window and looks eagerly down into the street*) What's the time?

ELIZABETH: (*smiling*) Five minutes past three.

HENRIETTA: *Past* three?

ELIZABETH: Past three.

HENRIETTA: I don't understand. . . . He said *three*. . . . (*With sudden anxiety*) Ba! Today *is* Thursday, isn't it?

ELIZABETH: Yes, dear.

HENRIETTA: (*with a sigh of relief*) Oh . . . (*turns again to the window*) I wish he were able to come in his uniform. That would take the curl out of Mr. Bevan's whiskers! (ELIZABETH *laughs*) Oh, there he comes! (*She runs out of the room, leaving the door open.*)

ELIZABETH: Please shut the door. (*But* HENRIETTA *has gone*. ELIZABETH *smilingly shrugs her shoulders, picks up her book and starts reading. After a moment one hears voices outside; then approaching footsteps.* OCTAVIUS *reënters.*)

OCTAVIUS: Are you ready to receive them?

ELIZABETH: Yes, quite. What are they like, Occy?

OCTAVIUS: Oh, *she's* a dream of l-loveliness! And *he*—isn't. (*He goes out. A pause. The voices grow nearer. Then* BELLA HEDLEY *flutters in. She is an exquisitely pretty, exquisitely turned-out little creature, voluble, affected, sentimental, with a constitutional inability to pronounce her r's. She is followed by* ARABEL, MR. HENRY BEVAN, *and* OCTAVIUS. MR. BEVAN *is a model of deportment, inwardly and outwardly. He affects a magnificent Kruger beard, and his voice and manner are as beautifully rounded as his legs.*)

BELLA: (*ecstatically*) Cousin Elizabeth!

ELIZABETH: (*stretching out her hand*) Bella, dear. . . .

BELLA: Ba! (*Drops on her knees at the sofa and embraces* ELIZABETH) Deawest Ba! After all these years! . . . But oh, my poor, poor Ba, how sadly you've changed! So pale, so fwagile, so etheweal!

ELIZABETH: And you, Bella, are even lovelier than you promised to be as a child.

BELLA: Flattewer! (*She kisses* ELIZABETH's *hand, and still holding the hand, rises to her feet*) You hear that, Ha'wy? This is my dear, dear Ha'wy. Mr. Bevan—Miss Elizabeth Ba'wett.

BEVAN: (*bowing*) Delighted, Miss Barrett, charmed....

BELLA: (*stretching out her free hand to* BEVAN. *He takes it*) No, no, Ha'wy, you must take her hand.... (*Tenderly to* ELIZABETH) Such a little hand! So fwail! So spiwitual!

BEVAN: (*taking* ELIZABETH'S *hand and bowing over it*) And the hand that penned so much that is noble and eloquent!... I am honoured, Miss Barrett.

ELIZABETH: Thank you. And may I congratulate you?—both of you? I hope you will be very happy.

BEVAN: Thank you, Miss Barrett. I am indeed a fortunate man!

BELLA: Dear Ha'wy. Dear Ba.

ELIZABETH: But won't you sit down? (BELLA, ARABEL, *and* BEVAN *seat themselves*. OCTAVIUS *stands near the window*.)

BELLA: I adore your poems, Ba—especially when dear Ha'wy weads them! He wead me "Lady Gewaldine's Courtship" the day after we became engaged. He weads so beautifully! And he *too* adores your poems —which ought to please you, as he is dweadfully cwitical!

BEVAN: Oh, come, come, my pet!

BELLA: Oh, but Ha'wy, you are! He doesn't quite approve of even Mr. Alfwed Tennyson's poems.

ELIZABETH: Really, Mr. Bevan?

BEVAN: I have nothing against them as poetry, no, indeed. Mr. Tennyson always writes like a gentleman. What grieves me, Miss Barrett, is that his attitude towards sacred matters is all too often an attitude tinged with doubt.

ARABEL: How sad....

BEVAN: Sad indeed, Miss Arabel! and I grieve to say a very prevalent attitude among the younger men of today. Loss of faith, lack of reverence, and a spirit of mockery, seem to be growing apace. Of course, I am not alluding to Mr. Tennyson when I say this. His work is always reverent even when expressing doubt. Now your poems, my dear Miss Barrett, show no touch anywhere of these modern tendencies. There's not a line in one of them that I would disapprove of even dear Bella reading.

ELIZABETH: That—that's very satisfactory....

BELLA: Dear Ha'wy is so fwightfully earnest!

BEVAN: Oh, come, come, my pet....

OCTAVIUS: I say, Mr. B-Bevan, you've not yet met my father, have you?

BEVAN: No, that pleasure is yet to come.

OCTAVIUS: I think you and he would g-get on famously together!

BEVAN: Indeed?

BELLA: Oh, yes! for dear Uncle Edward is fwightfully earnest as well! Mamma has often told me so.... But there is one matter on which they are bound to differ. Like Mamma and Papa, dear Uncle Edward is a stwict Nonconformist, Ha'wy.

BEVAN: (*sadly*) Ah, ah, indeed....

ELIZABETH: Then you are a member of the Church of England, Mr. Bevan?

BEVAN: I am indeed, Miss Barrett. Like Bella, I was brought up in Dissent. But Oxford changed all that. A dear friend of mine persuaded me to attend the services at St. Mary's, where Doctor Newman preaches, you know; and to study Pusey's works.... Two years ago I was received into the Church.

ARABEL: (*in a scared voice*) Pusey... Doctor Pusey.... But, Mr. Bevan, you're not—you're not—

BELLA: Oh, but he is, dear Awabel, and so am I! We're both Puseyites! Of course, dear Mamma and Papa were fwightfully distwessed about it at first, and feared my change of faith was entirely due to dear Ha'wy's influence. But in weality, I had long felt a lack of *something* in Nonconformity.

... Don't you think it lacks *something*, dear Ba? Don't you feel it's a form of worship less suited to people in our walk of life than to the lower orders?

ELIZABETH: (*with a quickly suppressed little laugh*) No, I—I can't say it ever struck me quite like that.... But now tell me, dear, when is the wedding to be? Or am I being indiscreet?

BEVAN: Not at all, dear Miss Barrett, not at all. We—

BELLA: (*excitedly*) Oh, that weminds me! Where's dear Henwietta? . . . The wedding? Early in August. (*Looks round the room*) Where's Henwietta?

OCTAVIUS: At the moment she's d-downstairs entertaining a friend.

BELLA: Oh, I wanted to ask her—A fwiend? Not that tall gentleman we passed in the hall?

ELIZABETH: Yes, Captain Surtees Cook.

BELLA: Oh, in the Army? How thwilling! I thought his ca'wiage was militawy! So he's a fwiend of dear Henwietta?

ELIZABETH: Yes. . . . You wanted to ask Henrietta something?

BELLA: Oh, yes! Oh, Ba, I do so want her to be one of my bwidesmaids! Do you think— (HENRIETTA *enters. She is visibly distraite.* BELLA *jumps to her feet*) Henwietta! (*Taking both her hands*) Henwietta darling, I was just saying— Oh, you must be one of my bwidesmaids! you simply must!

HENRIETTA: Bridesmaids? Oh, yes—at your wedding. I should love to, Bella. It's sweet of you to ask me. And of course I will—if Papa— But I'm sure he won't mind. . . .

BELLA: Mind? Uncle Edward? Why should he mind?

HENRIETTA: No, no, I'm sure it will be all right. I don't see how he could possibly object.

BELLA: Object? But I don't understand! . . . Isn't she funny, Ba? You're only asked to be a bwidesmaid, darling—not a bwide!

HENRIETTA: Yes, I know, but— Oh, it's so hard to explain. . . .

BEVAN: (*gravely helpful*) Perhaps Mr. Barrett looks on bridesmaids as frivolous irrelevancies at so solemn a sacrament as marriage . . . ?

HENRIETTA: No, no, Mr. Bevan. It's not that. It's—(*the words suddenly rush out*) It's simply that nothing—nothing at all in this house must happen without Papa's sanction. You know he once owned slaves in Jamaica. And as slavery has been abolished there, he carries it on in England. I'm quite serious. We are all his slaves here.

ARABEL: Henrietta!

(BEVAN *and* BELLA *look astonished and embarrassed.*)

HENRIETTA: Well, aren't we? Aren't we, Occy? Aren't we, Ba? We can't move hand or foot without his permission. We've got to obey his least whim and fall in with his moods—and they're as changeable as the weather! We haven't a soul of our own, not one of us . . . ! I tell you, Bella, it's more than likely that he'll refuse to let me be your bridesmaid, for no rhyme or reason —except that he's out of temper!

OCTAVIUS: I say, what about t-tea?

ARABEL: (*rising quickly*) Oh, yes, yes!

HENRIETTA: Tea is quite ready. I'm sorry—I—I forgot to tell you.

OCTAVIUS: Good Heavens, let's h-hurry or Captain Cook will have swallowed it all! (*Crosses to the door and opens it.*)

HENRIETTA: He's gone. . . . (*She moves to the window and stands there, her face half averted.*)

BELLA: A *wivederci*, deawest Ba! (*Kisses her*) It's been so lovely seeing you! May I come soon again? And next time I shall want you all to myself—without Ha'wy, I mean.

ELIZABETH: Come whenever you like, dear.

BEVAN: But why must I be excluded?

BELLA: Because I've heaps and heaps to tell dear Ba about a certain big, big man who might easily gwow conceited if he heard me!

BEVAN: Oh, come, come, my pet.

(BELLA *takes* ARABEL'S *arm.* BEVAN *bows over* ELIZABETH'S *hand*) Good-bay, dear Miss Barrett.

ELIZABETH: Good-bye. It was nice of you to come and see me.

BEVAN: Not at all. I have long been looking forward to the honour of meeting you. Good-bay.

(BELLA, *her arm still in* ARABEL'S, *kisses her hand to* ELIZABETH.)

BELLA: *Au wevoir*, darling!

ELIZABETH: *Auf wiedersehen.*

(BELLA *and* ARABEL *go out.*)

BEVAN: (*turning and bowing at the door*) Good-bay.

ELIZABETH: Good-bye.

(BEVAN *goes out.* OCTAVIUS, *turning at the door, bows to* ELIZABETH, *in imitation of* BEVAN, *and follows him.* ELIZABETH *smiles, and glances at* HENRIETTA, *who still stands with averted face at the window; then she takes up a book and starts reading. A pause. Suddenly* HENRIETTA *turns on her.*)

HENRIETTA: (*vehemently*) Well, why don't you say something?

ELIZABETH: (*coldly*) What do you want me to say?

HENRIETTA: Nothing. . . . Oh, Ba, don't scold me! (*Goes to* ELIZABETH, *and sits on the floor beside her sofa*) I know I deserve it. I have been dreadful. But I couldn't help it. I'm so miserable.

ELIZABETH: (*quickly*) Miserable, dear?

HENRIETTA: Yes—and so—so wildly happy! . . . Ba dear, may I tell you about it? I oughtn't to, I know. Because if it should ever come to anything, and Papa asks if you had any idea of what was going on, you'll have to lie—which you hate doing —or admit that you knew. And then he'd vent half his rage on you for not warning him in time.

ELIZABETH: Never mind, dear. Go on.

HENRIETTA: Surtees has just asked me to marry him.

ELIZABETH: Oh, Henrietta! But—

HENRIETTA: And, of course, I accepted him—and said that I couldn't. And I had to tell him that we must never see each other again. When he calls here tomorrow, we shall have to—

ELIZABETH: You're not talking sense, child. What really *has* happened?

HENRIETTA: I don't know . . . except that we both love each other terribly. . . . Oh, Ba, what *are* we to do? Surtees has only just enough money to keep himself decently. And, of course, I haven't a penny of my own. If only I had your four hundred a year, I might defy Papa and leave the house and marry Surtees tomorrow!

ELIZABETH: And what earthly good is that money to me? I'd give it to you, and how gladly—

HENRIETTA: I know you would, darling! But that's utterly impossible! Just think what your life would be like if Papa knew that you had made it possible for me to marry! No. But isn't it a cruel irony that the only one of the family with the means to be free and happy hasn't any use for it? (*With sudden urgency*) Ba dear, is there anything—anything at all—to be said for Papa's attitude towards marriage? Can it possibly be wrong to want a man's love desperately—and—and to long for babies of my own?

ELIZABETH: No. . . . But who am I to answer a question like that? Love and babies are so utterly remote from my life.

HENRIETTA: Yes, I know, dear. You're a woman apart. But love and babies are natural to an ordinary girl like me. And what's natural can't be wrong.

ELIZABETH: No. . . . And yet the holiest men and women renounced these things.

HENRIETTA: I daresay. But I'm not holy. And come to that, neither is Papa —not by any means! Didn't he marry, and — (*A knock at the door.*)

ELIZABETH: Come in.

(WILSON *enters.*)

WILSON: Mr. Robert Browning has called, Miss.

ELIZABETH: (*breathlessly*) Mr.—Mr. Browning . . . ?

WILSON: Yes, Miss.

HENRIETTA: Then I'd better be off!

ELIZABETH: (*agitated, quickly*) No—no, stay here. I can't see him. I—I don't feel up to it. I can't—

HENRIETTA: But Ba, what on earth is the matter? You told me yesterday—

ELIZABETH: I know. I know. But I really don't feel that I can see him now. (*To* WILSON) Tell Mr. Browning I am very sorry but I am not well enough to receive him.

HENRIETTA: But that's not true, Ba! You can't send him away like that, dear. It would be too rude and unkind after having asked him to call, and all the efforts he has made to get here. (*To* WILSON) Where is Mr. Browning?

WILSON: I showed him into the library, Miss.

ELIZABETH: But I—I'd much—much rather not see him. . . .

HENRIETTA: Oh, fudge! You're not a silly schoolgirl! I'll bring him up myself. Mr. Kenyon says he's wonderfully romantic-looking, and quite the dandy. (HENRIETTA *goes out*)

ELIZABETH: Is—is my hair tidy?

WILSON: Yes, Miss Ba.

ELIZABETH: Oh, please arrange the *couvre-pieds*. . . . (WILSON *arranges the couvre-pieds*) Thank you. . . . And, Wilson —no. . . . Thank you, that will do. . . .

WILSON: Yes, Miss.

(*She goes out.*)

(ELIZABETH, *obviously in a state of strained nerves, awaits the coming of* ROBERT BROWNING. *A pause.* HENRIETTA *enters.*)

HENRIETTA: Mr. Robert Browning.

(ROBERT BROWNING *enters. He is a dark, handsome man in the middle thirties, faultlessly, perhaps even a trifle foppishly, dressed. Over his shoulder he wears a cape fastened with a chain at the throat. He carries his high hat, lemon-coloured gloves, and clouded cane. Browning's manner is sincere and ardent; his speech rapid, voluble, and emphasised by free gestures.* HENRIETTA *goes out.*)

BROWNING: (*pausing for a moment a few steps beyond the threshold*) Miss Barrett?

ELIZABETH: (*stretching out her hand*) How-do-you-do, Mr. Browning?

BROWNING: (*quickly lays aside his hat, cane and gloves, and crossing to the sofa, takes her hand in both of his*) Dear Miss Barrett—at last! (*Raises her hand to his lips*) At last!

ELIZABETH: (*still all nerves, and rather overcome by the ardour and unconventionality of his manner*) I—I've had to put off the pleasure of meeting you much longer than I wished. . . .

BROWNING: (*still holding her hand*) Would you ever have received me if I hadn't been so tiresomely insistent?

ELIZABETH: As you know from my letters, I've not been at all well during the winter, and I— (*Realising that her hand is still in his, she gently withdraws it*) But won't you take off your cape?

BROWNING: Thank you. (*Unfastens his cape and lays it aside.*)

ELIZABETH: I—I hope you don't find the room very close, Mr. Browning?

BROWNING: No, no. . . .

ELIZABETH: My doctor obliges me to live in what I am afraid must be to you a—a hot-house temperature. . . .

BROWNING: (*who has thrown a quick glance round the room*) Wonderful! You may think, Miss Barrett, that this is the first time I've been here. You're quite wrong, you know!

ELIZABETH: But—

BROWNING: Quite wrong. I have seen

this room more times than I can remember. It's as familiar to me as my own little study at home! Before I came in, I knew just how your books were arranged, just how that tendril of ivy slanted across the window panes—and those busts of Homer and Chaucer are quite old friends, and have looked down on me often before!

ELIZABETH: (*smilingly protesting*) No, really—!

BROWNING: But I could never make out who the other fellows were on the top of the wardrobe, and—

ELIZABETH: (*laughing, and now quite at her ease*) Oh, come, Mr. Browning! I know that dear Mr. Kenyon is never tired of talking about his friends; but I can't believe that he described my poor little room to you in detail!

BROWNING: (*seating himself beside her*) I dragged all the details I possibly could out of him—and my imagination supplied the rest. Directly after I had read your brave and lovely verses I was greedy for anything and everything I could get about you.

ELIZABETH: (*smilingly*) You frighten me, Mr. Browning!

BROWNING: Why?

ELIZABETH: Well, you know how Mr. Kenyon's enthusiasms run away with his tongue? He and I are the dearest of friends. What he told you about poor me I quite blush to imagine!

BROWNING: You mean, Miss Barrett, about you—you *yourself?*

ELIZABETH: I feel it would be hopeless for me to try to live up to his description.

BROWNING: He never told me anything about you—personally—which had the slightest interest for me.

ELIZABETH: (*puzzled*) Oh?

BROWNING: Everything he could give me about your surroundings and the circumstances of your life I snatched at with avidity. But all he said about *you* was quite beside the point, because I knew it already —and better than Mr. Kenyon, old friend of yours though he is!

ELIZABETH: But—Oh, Mr. Browning, do my poor writings give me so hopelessly away?

BROWNING: Hopelessly — utterly — entirely to *me*! . . . I can't speak for the rest of the world.

ELIZABETH: (*smilingly*) You frighten me again!

BROWNING: No!

ELIZABETH: But you do! For I'm afraid it would be quite useless my ever trying to play-act with you!

BROWNING: Quite useless!

ELIZABETH: I shall always have to be —just myself?

BROWNING: Always.

ELIZABETH: Oh . . .(*quickly*) And you too, Mr. Browning?

BROWNING: Always—just myself! (*He stretches out his hand; she takes it with a smile. Then, with a sudden laugh*) But really, you know, Miss Barrett, I sha'n't be able to take much credit for that! Being myself comes to me as easily as breathing. It's play-acting I can't manage—and the hot water I've got into in consequence... ! If life's to run smoothly we should all be mummers. Well, I can't mum!

ELIZABETH: Yes, I can well believe that now I know you. But isn't it extraordinary? When you are *writing* you never do anything else but—play-act.

BROWNING: I know—

ELIZABETH: You have never been yourself in any one of your poems. It's always somebody else speaking through you.

BROWNING: Yes. And shall I tell you why? I am a very modest man. (*Quickly, after a slight pause*) I am really!

ELIZABETH: (*with suppressed amusement*) I didn't question it, Mr. Browning.

BROWNING: So modest, I fully realise that if I wrote about myself—my hopes and fears, hates and loves, and the rest of it— my poems would be intolerably dull.

ELIZABETH: (*laughingly, vivaciously*) Well—since we are pledged to nothing but the truth, I won't contradict that—until I know you better!

BROWNING: (*with a laugh*) Bravo!

ELIZABETH: (*ardently*) Oh, but those poems with their glad and great-hearted acceptance of life—you can't imagine what they mean to me! Here am I shut in by four walls, the view of Wimpole Street my only glimpse of the world. And they troop into the room and round my sofa, those wonderful people of yours out of every age and country, and all so tingling with life! life! life! No, you'll never begin to realise how much I owe you!

BROWNING: (*with emotion*) You—you really mean that?

ELIZABETH: Why, why, Mr. Browning—

BROWNING: But of course you do, or you wouldn't say it! And you'll believe me when I tell you that what you have said makes up to me a thousand times over for all the cold-shouldering I've had from the public?

ELIZABETH: (*fiercely*) Oh, it infuriates me! Why can we never know an eagle for an eagle until it has spread its wings and flown away from us for good? Sometimes —I detest the British public!

BROWNING: (*lightly*) Oh, no, no! Dear old British public! At least it gives us generously the jolly pastime of abusing it! And mind you, Miss Barrett, I've an uneasy feeling that my style is largely to blame for my unpopularity.

ELIZABETH: (*a little too eagerly*) Oh, surely not!

BROWNING: Didn't we agree never to play-act with each other?

ELIZABETH: (*with a laugh*) Touché! Well, perhaps, there *are* passages in your work a little invol—I mean a little too— too profound for the general reader.

BROWNING: Oh, no! it's not what I say, but how I say it.

ELIZABETH: Oh, but—

BROWNING: And yet to me it's all simple and easy as the rule of three! And to you?

ELIZABETH: Well . . . not *quite* always. Sometimes there *are* passages. . . . (*She picks up a book*) I have marked one or two in your "Sordello" which rather puzzle me. Here, for instance . . .

(*She opens the book and hands it to him.*)

BROWNING: (*taking the book*) Oh, "Sordello!" Somebody once called it "a horror of great darkness!" I've done my best to forget it. However— (*He reads the passage to himself, smiling. The smile fades; he passes his hand over his brow and reads it again. She watches him, covertly smiling. He mutters*) Extraordinary. . . . But—but a passage torn from its context. . . . (*He rises and goes to the window, as though to get more light on the subject, and reads the passage a third time.* ELIZABETH *has some difficulty in suppressing her amusement. He turns to her with an expression of humorous chagrin.*)

ELIZABETH: Well? . . .

BROWNING: Well, Miss Barrett—when that passage was written only God and Robert Browning understood it. Now only God understands it. (*She laughs, and he joins in*) What do you say—shall we lighten this great darkness by pitching it on the fire?

ELIZABETH: (*indignantly*) No, indeed! We shall do nothing of the kind! Please give me back the book. (*He does so*) Such passages are only spots on the sun. I love "Sordello."

BROWNING: (*eagerly*) You would! Of course you would! And shall I tell you why? Because it's a *colossal failure*.

ELIZABETH: If by a failure you mean an attempt—yes! you're right! That's just why "Sordello" appeals to my very heart. I too am always making colossal attempts— and always failing.

BROWNING: Isn't one such failure worth a hundred small successes?

ELIZABETH: Oh, a thousand and more!

BROWNING: (*eagerly*) You think so too? But, of course, I knew that! . . . Miss Barrett, you smiled when I told you that Kenyon had no need to describe you because I knew you through and through already. And what you have just said about success and failure proves to me finally how right I was. All Kenyon did was to fill in the background. I—I had painted the portrait—with the true soul of you, ardent and lovely, looking out of it.

ELIZABETH: Ardent and lovely! And you think you know me! (*With a bitter smile*) Oh, Mr. Browning—too often impatient and rebellious. . . .

BROWNING: Well, what of it? I've no love for perfect patience under affliction. My portrait is the portrait of a woman, not a saint. Who has more right to be impatient and rebellious than you?

ELIZABETH: Did Mr. Kenyon paint my background with a very gloomy brush?

BROWNING: Old Rembrandt would have envied him!

ELIZABETH: (*smilingly*) Poor dear Mr. Kenyon! He is more Royalist than the Queen herself! I assure you my afflictions worry him a great deal more than they worry me. . . . I suppose he told you that I am a—a dying woman?

BROWNING: We are all of us—dying.

ELIZABETH: And that our family life was one of unrelieved gloom?

BROWNING: Yes, he hinted at something of the sort.

ELIZABETH: He really shouldn't say such things! Frankly now, Mr. Browning, do you find me such a very pitiable object?

BROWNING: I find you, as I expected to find you, full of courage and gaiety. . . . And yet, in spite of what you say, I'm not at all sure that Kenyon's colours were too sombre.

ELIZABETH: But—

BROWNING: (*eagerly interrupting*) No, no, listen to me. Those colours are not yet dry. They must be scraped off! The whole background must be repainted! . . . And if only you'll allow it—I must have a hand in that splendid work.

ELIZABETH: But, Mr. Browning—

BROWNING: (*carried away*) No, listen! I'll dip my brush into the sunrise and the sunset and the rainbow! You say my verses have helped you—they're nothing. It's I—I who am going to help you now! We have come together at last—and I don't intend to let you go again.

ELIZABETH: But—

BROWNING: No, listen. Give me your hands. (*Bends forward and takes them*) I've more life than is good for one man—it seethes and races in me. Up to now I've spent a little of all that surplus energy in creating imaginary men and women. But there's still so much that I've no use for but to give! Mayn't I give it to you? Don't you feel new life tingling and prickling up your fingers and arms right into your heart and brain?

ELIZABETH: (*rather frightened and shaken*) Oh, please . . . Mr. Browning, please let go my hands. . . .

(*He opens his hands; but she still leaves hers lying on his palms for a moment. Then she withdraws them, and clasping her cheeks, looks at him with wide, disturbed eyes.*)

BROWNING: (*softly*) Well?

ELIZABETH: (*a little shakily, with forced lightness*). You—you are really rather an overwhelming person, and in sober truth, I'm—

BROWNING: No—don't tell me again that you are afraid of me! You're not. It's life you're afraid of—and that shouldn't be.

ELIZABETH: Life?

BROWNING: Yes.

ELIZABETH: Well, when life becomes a series of electric shocks!

BROWNING: (*smiling*) Was it as bad as all that?

ELIZABETH: (*smiling*) Indeed, yes! Do you affect other people in the same way?

BROWNING: They've often told me so.

ELIZABETH: (*lightly*) No wonder I hesitated about meeting you, much as I wanted to! Something of your disturbing vitality must have come to me from your letters and poems.... You'll laugh at me, Mr. Browning, but do you know we very nearly didn't meet today after all! When my maid told me you had arrived I was so panic-stricken that I all but sent down a message that I was too unwell to receive you. And it was a big effort to pull myself together, and behave like a sensible woman, when you came into the room!

BROWNING: I think I must have been quite as nervous as you at that moment.

ELIZABETH: You, Mr. Browning!

BROWNING: Yes—and I'm anything but a nervous man as a rule. But that moment was the climax of my life—up to now.... Miss Barrett, do you remember the first letter I wrote to you?

ELIZABETH: Yes, indeed! It was a wonderful letter.

BROWNING: You may have thought I dashed it off in a fit of white-hot enthusiasm over your poems. I didn't. I weighed every word of every sentence. And of one sentence in particular—this sentence: "*I love your books with all my heart—and I love you too.*" You remember?

ELIZABETH: (*lightly*) Yes — and I thought it charmingly impulsive of you!

BROWNING: (*almost with irritation*) But I tell you there was nothing impulsive about it. That sentence was as deeply felt and anxiously thought over as any sentence I've ever written.

ELIZABETH: I hope I have many readers like you! It's wonderful to think I may have good friends all the world over whom I have never seen or heard of.

BROWNING: I am not speaking of friendship, but of love. (ELIZABETH *is about to make a smiling rejoinder*) No, it's quite useless your trying to put aside the word with a smile and a jest. I said love—and I mean love—

ELIZABETH: But really, Mr. Browning, I must ask you—

BROWNING: (*swiftly interrupting her*) I'm neither mad nor morbidly impressionable—I'm as sane and level-headed as any man alive. Yet all these months, since first I read your poems, I've been haunted by you. And today you are the centre of my life.

ELIZABETH: (*very gravely*) If I were to take you seriously, Mr. Browning, it would, of course, mean the quick finish of a friendship which promises to be very pleasant to both of us.

BROWNING: Why?

ELIZABETH: You know very well that love—in the sense you, apparently, use the word—has no place, and can have no place, in my life.

BROWNING: Why?

ELIZABETH: For many reasons—but let this suffice. As I told you before, I am a dying woman.

BROWNING: (*passionately*) I refuse to believe it! For if that were so, God would be callous, and I *know* that He's compassionate—and life would be dark and evil, and I *know* that it's good. You must never say such a thing again. I forbid you to.

ELIZABETH: Forbid, Mr. Browning? ...

BROWNING: Yes—forbid. Isn't it only fair that if you forbid me to speak of you as I feel, and I accept your orders, as I must, that I should be allowed a little forbidding as well?

ELIZABETH: Yes, but—

BROWNING: (*breaking in with sudden gaiety*) Dear Miss Barrett, what a splendid beginning to our friendship! We have known each other a bare half hour and yet we've talked intimately of art and life and death and love, and we've ordered each other about, and we've almost quarrelled! Could anything be happier and more promising? ... With your permission, I'm going now. Mr. Kenyon impressed upon me to make my first visit as short as possible, as strangers tire you. Not that I'm a stranger! —still I can see that you are tired. . . . When may I call again?

ELIZABETH: (*a little dazed*) I don't quite know . . . I—

BROWNING: Will next Wednesday suit you?

ELIZABETH: (*as before*) Yes, I—I think so. But perhaps it would be better—

BROWNING: Next Wednesday then.

ELIZABETH: But—

BROWNING: At half-past three again?

ELIZABETH: Yes—but I—

BROWNING: (*bowing over her hand*) Au revoir then.

ELIZABETH: Good-bye.

BROWNING: (*gently masterful, retaining her hand*) Au revoir.

ELIZABETH: (*a little breathlessly, after a slight pause*) Au revoir.

BROWNING: Thank you.

(*He kisses her hand, turns and picks up his hat and cape, etc., and goes out*)

(*The moment after the door has closed behind him* ELIZABETH *sits up and clasps her face with both her hands. Then she slips off the sofa and unsteadily gets on to her feet. With the help of the table and the chairs, she manages to cross the room to the window. Grasping the curtain to support herself, she stands looking down into the street after the departing* BROWNING, *her face as alive with excitement and joy as though she were a young girl. And the scene slowly closes.*)

ACT III

Robert

(*Some three months later.*)

(DOCTOR CHAMBERS *stands by the fireplace.* DOCTOR FORD-WATERLOW *sits on the sofa. He is a sharp-featured, sharp-tongued old man. Both* DOCTORS *are intently watching* ELIZABETH *as she walks with firm and sure tread across the room to the window and back again.* FLUSH *lies on the sofa.*)

FORD-WATERLOW: Once again, if you please. (ELIZABETH *walks across the room again*) My dear Miss Barrett, I congratulate you. Now sit down. (*She sits close to him, and he feels her pulse while talking*) When exactly was it you last called me in for consultation, Doctor Chambers.

CHAMBERS: Three months ago almost to a day.

FORD-WATERLOW: Yes, yes—and your patient was in a very low condition at the time. Well, you've done wonders, Doctor.

CHAMBERS: Oh, mine was just the ordinary spade-work. Honesty compels me to give most of the credit to another.

FORD-WATERLOW: Eh?

CHAMBERS: The real healer is no one but Miss Barrett herself.

ELIZABETH: But, Doctor . . . !

CHAMBERS: I mean it, my dear, I mean it. Three months ago you seemed more than a little inclined to let life and the world slip through your pretty fingers. Then slowly the change began. Oh, believe me, I was watching you like a lynx! Life and the world became more and more worth grasping. The wish to live is better than a dozen physicians—as I think even my distinguished friend will admit.

FORD-WATERLOW: The wish to live . . . Hm, yes. . . . And you are able to get about and take the air occasionally nowadays?

ELIZABETH: Oh, yes, Doctor. I have visited some of my friends, and been for several delightful drives round the Park. The only bother is getting up and down stairs. I'm inclined to lose my head going down, and I'm not yet able to undertake the upward journey.

FORD-WATERLOW: Quite so. Quite so.

CHAMBERS: (*smilingly*) Fortunately it doesn't need a very strong man to carry you.

ELIZABETH: Oh, but that's where you're wrong! (*To* FORD-WATERLOW) You have no idea how I am putting on weight!

FORD-WATERLOW: Is that so indeed?

CHAMBERS: (*solemnly*) So much so, that I have seriously thought of docking Miss Barrett's porter—a beverage, I may say, of which she is inordinately fond.

ELIZABETH: (*laughing*) I wonder you're not ashamed to mention that subject, Doctor Chambers!

FORD-WATERLOW: Well now, about the future, Miss Barrett. I fully agree with Doctor Chambers that another winter in London must, if possible, be avoided. If you continue picking up strength as you are doing, I see no reason against your travelling South by October, say.

ELIZABETH: (*with barely controlled eagerness*). Travelling . . . South? . . .

FORD-WATERLOW: To the Riviera, or, better still, to Italy.

ELIZABETH: (*breathlessly*) Italy . . . ! Oh, Doctor, do you really mean it?

FORD-WATERLOW: Why not? You could travel there by easy stages. I have been given to understand that you have set your heart on Italy, and that there are no—er—practical difficulties in the way of your going there.

ELIZABETH: If by practical, you mean financial—none at all. I have my own little income, and—

FORD-WATERLOW: Quite so, quite so.

CHAMBERS: I've taken the liberty to tell Doctor Ford-Waterlow of the only real difficulty in the way of your wintering abroad, and he is quite prepared to deal with—him.

FORD-WATERLOW: Quite—and drastically.

ELIZABETH: (*quickly*) Oh, I am sure that won't be necessary! Papa may not raise any kind of objection. It depends how he is feeling at the time, and—

FORD-WATERLOW: (*testily*) Fiddlesticks, my dear young lady! Mr. Barrett's feelings are neither here nor there. All that matters is his daughter's health and happiness, as I intend to make clear to him. Quite clear.

ELIZABETH: Oh, you mustn't think that Papa isn't kindness and generosity itself. But gentlemen have their moods. . . . Italy! Oh, it's hard to take in even the bare possibility of going there! My promised land, Doctor, which I never thought to see otherwise than in dreams!

FORD-WATERLOW: (*rising*) Well, well, let us hope realisation won't bring disillusion along with it! A grossly overrated country to my mind. Nothing but heaps of rubbish, dust, flies, stenches, and beggars! Good-bye, my dear Miss Barrett. No, please don't get up. (*Takes her hand*) I'm delighted with your improvement. Delighted. And now for a little talk with your father. Good-bye.

ELIZABETH: Good-bye, Doctor.

CHAMBERS: Good-bye, Miss Elizabeth.

ELIZABETH: Good-bye. (*Both* DOCTORS *go out.* ELIZABETH *clasps her cheeks and whispers*) Italy—Italy—Italy. . . . (*She picks up* FLUSH) And you're coming with us, too, Flushy! We'll see Rome together, Florence, Venice, Vesuvius—(ARABEL *enters.* ELIZABETH *puts* FLUSH *down and jumps to her feet*) Arabel! (*Embracing* ARABEL *impetuously*) It's all but settled, my dear! I'm to go to Italy! He says that I shall be quite fit to travel by October! . . . Rome! Florence! Venice! Vesuvius! Raphael! Dante! "Sordello"! . . . Oh, I don't know what I'm saying—I'm quite off my head with excitement!

ARABEL: How wonderful for you! I'm so glad! . . . And you think Papa will consent?

ELIZABETH: But of course he will! Both the Doctors are putting it before him as strongly as they can. Oh, surely he'd never have the heart to refuse when he realises all this Italian trip means to me. . . .

ARABEL: (*without conviction*) No, dear, no. . . .

ELIZABETH: Have you seen him this afternoon?

ARABEL: Yes.

ELIZABETH: (*quickly*) What was he like?

ARABEL: (*eagerly*) Oh, quite sunny! He called me "Puss"—and he never does that when he's in one of his moods. And afterwards, when Bella came in, he was really merry.

ELIZABETH: Thank Heaven for that!

ARABEL: Which reminds me, dear—Bella has brought the gown Henrietta is to wear as bridesmaid. They want you to see it. They're trying it on now. . . .

ELIZABETH: Oh, I should love to! (*She pulls the bell rope*) I want badly some distraction to help me over the suspense of waiting for Papa's decision. . . .

ARABEL: Somehow I feel, Ba, that it wasn't altogether wise of you to keep this Italian plan secret from Papa, and then spring it suddenly on him.

ELIZABETH: Yes, I know, but—(*A knock at the door*) Come in. (WILSON *enters*) Please tell Miss Hedley and Miss Henrietta I shall be delighted to see them now.

WILSON: Yes, Miss.

ELIZABETH: Oh, and take Flush out. He gets so excited when there are several people in the room. (WILSON *picks up* FLUSH *and goes out with him*) It was Doctor Chambers himself who advised me to say nothing to Papa until *both doctors* were satisfied that I was absolutely fit to travel. I quite agreed with him at the time. But now—oh, Arabel, I'm not so sure now! I'm so afraid Papa may think— (*Voices and laughter outside*) Don't say anything about this to them. . . . (ARABEL *nods*.)

BELLA: (*outside*) May we come in?

ELIZABETH: (*rising*) Come in, dear. (BELLA *flutters in, followed by* HENRIETTA, *shy but radiant, in her bridesmaid's array*) Bella dear!

BELLA: (*embracing* ELIZABETH) Darling, darling! Oh, but you weally shouldn't get up to weceive little me!

ARABEL: (*contemplating* HENRIETTA) How perfectly lovely!

ELIZABETH: Delicious!

BELLA: Yes, isn't it? Isn't she, I should say! Dear Henwietta will be quite the pwettiest of my bwidesmaids. Indeed, I'm afwaid she'll dwaw all eyes from the little bwide! At any wate, all the gentlemen's! . . . But, darling Ba, you weally mustn't stand about like this! (*Leads her to the sofa*.)

ELIZABETH: But I'm as well able to stand as anyone nowadays.

BELLA: (*as* ELIZABETH *submits to be laid on the sofa*) No, no . . . ! One has only to see your dear face, so twanspawent and spiwitual, to know how near you are to Heaven. You always have a look in your eyes, darling, as though you alweady saw the angels!

HENRIETTA: She's looking at me, Bella —and I'm no angel!

BELLA: No, I'm afwaid you're not. . . . But you're vewy, vewy beautiful! . . . And fancy, Ba, if I hadn't spoken to Uncle Edward myself, I should never have had her for my bwidesmaid!

ELIZABETH: Yes, my dear, you certainly have a way with you.

HENRIETTA: *Spoken* to Papa! I like that! Why, you sat on his knee and stroked his whiskers.

ARABEL: (*reprovingly*) Henrietta dear! (ELIZABETH *laughs*.)

BELLA: And why not? Isn't he my Uncle? . . . Besides that, I think he's most fwightfully thwilling! I adore that stern and gloomy type of gentleman. It's so exciting to coax and manage them. And so easy —if you know how! And I weally think I do. . . . But what I can't understand is his extwaordinawy attitude towards love and ma'wiage, and all that. It isn't as if he were in any way a mis—mis—oh, what's the howwid word?

ELIZABETH: Misogynist?

BELLA: Yes, and—

HENRIETTA: Well, *I* should describe him as the king of misogynists!

BELLA: But he *isn't,* I tell you.

HENRIETTA: How do *you* know?

BELLA: Never mind. But I *do* know. . . . Besides, didn't he mawwy himself—and, what's more, have eleven childwen? . . . (*An uncomfortable silence*) Oh, have I said anything—vewy dweadful?

ARABEL: No, dear—but, perhaps, not quite nice. When God sends us children it's not for us to enquire how and why. . . .

BELLA: I'm so sowwy! I didn't mean to be i'wevewent. . . . But I *do* find dear Uncle Edward's attitude extwaordinawy—and so useless! For in spite of it—and wight under his nose—and all unknown to him—his whole house is litewally seething with womance!

ARABEL: Bella!

HENRIETTA: (*sharply*) What on earth do you mean?

BELLA: *You* ought to know, darling.

HENRIETTA: I?

BELLA: (*enthusiastically*) I think Captain Surtees Cook is quite fwightfully thwilling! The way he looks at you, dear—and looks—and looks—and looks! . . . If he ever looked at *me* like that my knees would twemble so that I shouldn't be able to stand, and I'd get the loveliest shivers down my back!

ARABEL: Really, Bella!

HENRIETTA: (*vexed and embarrassed*) I've never met any one who was able to pack more sheer nonsense into a couple of sentences than you.

BELLA: Haven't you, darling? . . . And then, there's George! *You* may not believe it, but *I'm* absolutely certain he has a thwilling understanding with your little cousin Lizzie. . . . And you weally mean to tell me that Charles and Miss what's-her-name are just mere fwiends? As for poor Occy—well, I don't mind telling you, in confidence, that my dear, dear Ha'wy is fwightfully jealous of him. . . .

ARABEL: Mr. Bevan jealous of Occy! But why?

BELLA: Why indeed? Aren't gentlemen silly?

ELIZABETH: (*laughing*) What an extraordinary girl you are, Bella!

BELLA: Oh, I'm a fwightfully observant little thing! F'winstance, though you hardly ever mention his name, I know that Mr. Wobert Bwowning comes here to see you at least once evewy week. And at other times he sends you flowers. And he often bwings little cakes for dear Flush. . . . Flush! Oh, wouldn't it be fwightfully intewesting if only dear Flush could speak!

ARABEL: Good gracious, why?

ELIZABETH: (*coldly*) But not so interesting as if Bella were occasionally silent.

BELLA: *Touché*, darling! I know I'm a dweadful little wattle—but you don't weally mind my quizzing you, do you?

ELIZABETH: Not in the least.

BELLA: (*to* ARABEL) You see, dear Flush is the only witness of all that goes on at Ba's weekly *tête-à-tête* with the handsomest poet in England. He—Flush, I mean—ought to know a wonderful lot about poetwy by this time! For when two poets are gathered together they talk about whymes and whythms all the time? Or don't they? . . . I'm fwightfully ignowant.

ELIZABETH: Oh, no, my dear! On the contrary—you're "fwightfully" knowing.

BELLA: Me?

HENRIETTA: I hope to goodness you won't chatter any of this outrageous nonsense in front of Papa.

BELLA: Nonsense, is it? Well, I've my own little opinion about that! . . . But, of course, I won't bweathe a word of it to Uncle Edward. I'm all on the side of womance, and the path of twue love, and all that. . . .

ARABEL: (*solemnly*) Bella, I regret to say it, but I think you are one of the few girls I know who would have benefited entirely under Papa's system of upbringing. (ELIZABETH *and* HENRIETTA *laugh*.)

BELLA: Ooh . . . what a thwilling thought! He was always fwightfully stwickt, wasn't he? Did he whip you when you were naughty? How fwightfully exciting to be whipped by Uncle Edward!

(*A knock at the door. The* BARRETT SISTERS *are on the alert at once.*)

ELIZABETH: Come in.

(BARRETT *enters.* BELLA *jumps to her feet with a little scream and runs up to him.*)

BELLA: Oh, Uncle Edward! (*She thrusts her hand through his arm and snuggles against him*) Uncle dear, if I had been your little girl instead of Papa's would you have been te'wibly severe with me? . . . You wouldn't, would you? Or would you?

BARRETT: Would—wouldn't—would—would? Are you trying to pose me with some silly riddle?

BELLA: (*drawing him into the room*) No, no, no. Sit down. (*Pushes him into a chair and perches herself on his knee*) It's like this— But why that gloomy fwown, Uncle Edward? . . . (*She passes her fingers lightly over his forehead*) There—there—all gone! (BARRETT *has slipped his arm round her waist*) Awabel says it would have done me all the good in the world to have been bwought up by you. She thinks I'm a spoilt, fwivolous little baggage, and—

ARABEL: Bella! I never said anything of the sort!

BELLA: I know you didn't. But you *do*! (*Points to* HENRIETTA *and* ELIZABETH) And *you* do. And *you* do. . . . But *you* don't, Uncle, do you?

ARABEL: Really, Bella—

BARRETT: (*speaking to* BELLA, *but at the others*) If my children were as bright and open and affectionate as you are I should be a much happier man.

BELLA: Oh, you mustn't say such things, or they'll hate me . . . !

BARRETT: (*drawing her close. The two seem to be quite withdrawn from the others and oblivious of them*) And you're a distractingly lovely little creature. . . .

BELLA: Anything w'ong in that?

BARRETT: I didn't say so. . . .

BELLA: Then why do you look at me so fiercely? Do you want to eat me up?

BARRETT: What's that scent you have on you?

BELLA: Scent? Me? (*Giggling and snuggling up to him*) Don't you like it?

BARRETT: I abominate scent as a rule—but yours is different.

BELLA: Nice?

BARRETT: It's very delicate and subtle. . . . Still, I should prefer you not to use it.

BELLA: Why?

BARRETT: Never mind. (*Gently but audibly smacks her thigh.*)

BELLA: Ooh—that hurts!

BARRETT: Nonsense.

BELLA: (*triumphantly*) But I never use scent! I haven't a dwop on me. I think it's ho'wid and common! (*With her arms round his neck*) Oh, Uncle, you're a darling! You've called me bwight and open and affectionate, distwactingly lovely and fwagwant all within a few minutes! You may kiss me!

(BARRETT *kisses her twice so roughly on the mouth that she gives a little cry. Then he pushes her abruptly off his knee and gets to his feet. She looks a little frightened.*)

BARRETT: (*brusquely*) There, there, child, run away now. I want to speak to Ba. (*To the others*) You can go too.

(*He crosses to the window and stands looking out, with his back to the room.*)

BELLA: (*in a rather injured voice*) Good-bye, Uncle.

BARRETT: (*without turning*) Good-bye.

BELLA: Good-bye, Ba.

(*With a little toss of her head, she goes out.*)

ELIZABETH: Good-bye.

(HENRIETTA *and* ARABEL *go out. A pause.* ELIZABETH *looks with nervous expectancy at her father, who still stands at the window with his back to the room.*)

BARRETT: (*without turning*) When is the wedding?

ELIZABETH: The wedding? Oh, Bella's . . . On the twenty-seventh.

BARRETT: (*turning, and speaking half to himself*) Good. Less than a fortnight. . . . We are not likely to see much of her till then. And afterwards—well, she'll be living in the country most of the year.

ELIZABETH: But I thought you were so fond of her, Papa.

BARRETT: (*sharply*) Fond of her? Why not? Isn't she my niece? . . . But she's a disturbing influence in the house. To see your brothers following her about with their eyes—especially Octavius. . . . Faugh! the room is still full of her! I shall be glad when she's gone. But I don't want to talk about Bella. Your doctors have just left me.

ELIZABETH: (*expectantly*) Yes, Papa . . . ?

BARRETT: (*with forced heartiness*) Their report is excellent. Astonishing. I'm more than gratified. I'm delighted. . . . Of course, my poor child, it's unlikely that you will ever be a normal woman. Even Chambers—optimistic fool though he is—was forced to admit that. . . . By the way, who *is* this Doctor Ford-Waterlow?

ELIZABETH: I've been told he is one of the cleverest physicians in London.

BARRETT: Really? . . . Well, he needs some amazing qualities to counterbalance his execrable manners. But even this medical phenomenon is unable to account for the sudden improvement in your health. Puts it down to Chambers' ministrations—which is, of course, arrant nonsense.

ELIZABETH: Perhaps the wonderful weather we've been having has most to do with it. I always thrive in warmth and sunshine.

BARRETT: Rubbish. Last summer was sweltering, and you have never been worse than then. No, to my mind, there is only One whom we have to thank—though this Doctor what's-his-name was pleased to sneer when I mentioned—Him.

ELIZABETH: Him?

BARRETT: I mean Almighty God. . . . It amazes me, Elizabeth, that you, on whom this miracle of recovery has been worked, should ascribe it to mere earthly agencies. Haven't I knelt here night after night and implored our all-loving Father to have compassion on His child? . . . It amazes me. It grieves me unspeakably. That is all I have to say for the present.

(*He turns to the door.*)

ELIZABETH: Papa.

BARRETT: Well?

ELIZABETH: Didn't Doctor Ford-Waterlow speak to you about—about next winter?

BARRETT: Doctor Ford-Waterlow talked, if I may say so, a great deal of nonsense. (*He turns to go.*)

ELIZABETH: But Papa—

BARRETT: (*testily*) What is it?

ELIZABETH: Didn't he tell you that I should avoid spending next winter in England?

BARRETT: Well?

ELIZABETH: And that he thinks I shall be fit to travel to Italy in October, if you—

BARRETT: So! It's out at last! And how long has this precious plot been hatching, may I ask?

ELIZABETH: It's now several weeks since Doctor Chambers first mentioned Italy as a real possibility.

BARRETT: I see. And do your brothers and sisters know anything of this delightful project?

ELIZABETH: I believe I mentioned it to them.

BARRETT: You believe you mentioned it to them. And Mr. Kenyon, and Mr. Horne, and the Hedleys, and that charlatan Browning—all your friends and relations in short—you've discussed your plans with the lot of them, I suppose?

ELIZABETH: Oh, Papa, what does it matter? My only reason—

BARRETT: Matter? Not in the least! It's nothing at all that I alone should be shut out of my favourite daughter's confidence, treated like a cipher—ignored—insulted—

ELIZABETH: Insulted?

BARRETT: Grossly insulted. When that fellow, Ford-Waterlow, sprung your carefully prepared mine on me and I naturally expressed my astonishment and displeasure, he became extremely offensive, and—

ELIZABETH: Believe me, Papa, my one reason for not worrying you with this Italian idea before was—

BARRETT: The fear that I should nip it in the bud at once. Exactly. I quite understand.

ELIZABETH: But—

BARRETT: No. I beg you to spare me explanations and excuses. The whole miserable business is abundantly clear. I am cut to the heart that *you*—the only one of my children whom I trusted implicitly—should be capable of such underhand conduct.

ELIZABETH: No—no—

BARRETT: If returning health must bring with it such sad change of character I shall be driven to wish that you were once more lying helpless on that sofa. There is nothing more to be said.

(*He turns to the door.*)

ELIZABETH: (*with restrained anger*) But there is more to be said, and I must beg you to listen to me, Papa. How many years have I lain here? Five? Six? It's hard to remember—as each year has been like ten. And all that time I've had nothing to look forward to, or hope for, but death.

BARRETT: Death . . . ?

ELIZABETH: Yes, death. I was born with a large capacity for happiness—you remember me as a young girl?—and when life brought me little happiness and much pain, I was often impatient for the end, and—

BARRETT: (*outraged*) Elizabeth! I'm shocked that—

ELIZABETH: (*swiftly*) And now this miracle has happened! Day by day I am better able to take and enjoy such good things as every one has a right to—able to meet my friends, to breathe the open air and feel the sun, and see grass and flowers growing under the sky. . . . When Doctor Chambers first spoke to me of Italy I put the idea from me—it seemed too impossibly wonderful! But as I grew stronger, it came over me, like a revelation, that Italy wasn't an impossibility at all, that nothing really stood in the way of my going, that I had every right to go.

BARRETT: Right?

ELIZABETH: Yes! every right—if only I could get your consent. So I set about consulting my friends, meeting all obstacles, settling every detail, so as to have a perfectly arranged plan to put before you after the doctors had given you their opinion. In my eagerness I may have acted stupidly, mistakenly, tactlessly. But to call my conduct underhand and deceitful is more than unkind. It's unjust. It's cruel.

BARRETT: (*more in sorrow than in anger*) Self! Self! Self! No thought, no consideration, for any one but yourself, or for anything but your pleasure.

ELIZABETH: (*passionately*) But Papa—

BARRETT: (*with a silencing gesture*) Didn't it even once occur to you that all through those long, dark months you proposed to enjoy yourself in Italy, your father would be left here utterly alone?

ELIZABETH: Alone?

BARRETT: Utterly alone. . . . Your brothers and sisters might as well be shadows for all the companionship they afford me. And you—oh, my child, don't think that I haven't noticed that you too, now that you are stronger and no longer wholly dependent on me, are slowly drawing away from your father. . . .

ELIZABETH: It's not true!

BARRETT: It is true—and, in your heart, you know it's true.

ELIZABETH: No!

BARRETT: New life, new interests, new pleasures, new friends—and, little by little, I am being pushed into the background—

I who used to be your whole world, I who love you—who love you—

ELIZABETH: But Papa—

BARRETT: (*with a silencing gesture*) No. There is nothing more to be said. (*He crosses to the window, looks out, then turns*) You want my consent for this—Italian jaunt. I shall neither give it nor withhold it. To give it would be against my conscience as encouraging selfishness and self-indulgence. To withhold it would be a futile gesture. You are your own mistress. Even if I refused to pay your expenses, you have ample means of your own to carry out your intentions. You are at liberty to do as you wish. . . . And if you go, I hope you will sometimes spare a thought for your father. Think of him at night stealing into this room which once held all he loved. Think of him kneeling alone by the empty sofa and imploring the Good Shepherd to— (*A knock at the door*) Eh . . . ?

ELIZABETH: (*with a start, her hand going to her heart*) Oh. . . .

BARRETT: (*testily*) Who's that? Come in.

(WILSON *enters.*)

WILSON: If you please, Mr. Browning has called.

BARRETT: (*under his breath*) That fellow again. . . .

WILSON: I showed Mr. Browning into the drawing-room, Miss, seeing as you were engaged.

ELIZABETH: Would you like to meet Mr. Browning, Papa?

BARRETT: Certainly not. I should have thought you knew by this time that I never inflict myself on any of my children's friends. (*To* WILSON) You may show Mr. Browning up.

WILSON: Very good, sir.

(*She goes out.*)

BARRETT: Mr. Browning appears to consider this his second home.

ELIZABETH: I have not seen him since last Wednesday.

BARRETT: Indeed.

(*He goes out.*)

(ELIZABETH *sits quite still, breathing quickly, her eyes fixed on the door.* WILSON *enters.*)

WILSON: Mr. Browning.

(BROWNING *enters and* ELIZABETH *rises to receive him.*)

(WILSON *goes out.*)

BROWNING: (*taking her hands*) Oh, but how splendid! This is the fourth time you've received me—standing!

ELIZABETH: (*her whole manner has changed: she is all sparkle and life*) If ever I receive you from my sofa again you may put it down to my bad manners and nothing else!

BROWNING: I will, with all my heart, I will! And now, tell me quickly. I've been dithering with suspense all day. You've seen them? What do they say?

ELIZABETH: Doctor Ford-Waterlow was quite taken out of his grumpy self with astonished delight at my improvement.

BROWNING: (*delightedly*) Say that again!

ELIZABETH: Oh, must I? The whole sentence?

BROWNING: I should like to see it in letters of fire burning at me from each of these four walls! This is the best moment I've had since I got your note giving me permission to call on you! How many years ago was that?

ELIZABETH: Three months.

BROWNING: Absurd! We've always been friends! I've known you a lifetime and over! So, he was quite taken out of his grumpy self with astonished delight, was he? Splendid! Of course, *I* never once doubted that you would turn the corner some day. The world isn't rich enough to afford the waste of such a life as yours! But even *I* little dreamt recovery would be so rapid. And Italy? Are both Doctors agreed about your wintering there?

ELIZABETH: (*with a note of reserve in her voice*) Yes.

BROWNING: And when do they think you'll be fit for travelling?

ELIZABETH: The middle of October—unless there's a relapse.

BROWNING: Relapse? There isn't such a word! October! Extraordinary! For you know, October suits my own plans to perfection.

ELIZABETH: *Your* plans?

BROWNING: Don't you remember my telling you that I had thought of wintering in Italy myself? Well now I am quite decided. You see, I have practically made up my mind to remodel "Sordello." I should never be able to grapple with the task satisfactorily in England. Impossible to get the Italian atmosphere in a land of drizzle and fog! May I call on you often in Italy? Where do you intend to stay? (ELIZABETH *laughs*) Why are you laughing?

ELIZABETH: In Italy I'm afraid you'll need seven-league boots—when you call on me!

BROWNING: What do you mean?

ELIZABETH: I shall be at 50, Wimpole Street next winter.

BROWNING: Here?

ELIZABETH: Yes.

BROWNING: But didn't you tell me that both doctors—

ELIZABETH: Doctors may propose; but the decision rests—elsewhere.

BROWNING: Your father?

ELIZABETH: Yes.

BROWNING: He—he has vetoed the plan?

ELIZABETH: No—not exactly. But I am quite sure that he—that it will be impossible for me to go.

BROWNING: But—didn't the doctors make it clear to him that this move of yours may mean all the difference between —life and death?

ELIZABETH: I believe Doctor Ford-Waterlow spoke very forcibly.

BROWNING: Then, in Heaven's name—

ELIZABETH: (*quickly, nervously*) Oh, it's rather hard to explain to someone who doesn't know all the circumstances. . . . You see, Papa is very devoted to me, and—

BROWNING: Devoted? . . .

ELIZABETH: Very devoted to me—and depends a lot on my companionship. He hasn't many points of contact with my brothers and sisters. If I were away for six months, he—

BROWNING: (*visibly and audibly putting restraint on himself*) Miss Barrett—may I speak plainly?

ELIZABETH: (*nervously*) Oh, do you think you'd better? I know—more or less —how you feel about this. But you don't quite understand the situation. How should you?

BROWNING: Very well. Then I'll say nothing. . . . (*His control suddenly gives way: his words pour out in a furious torrent*) You tell me I don't understand. You are quite right. I don't. You tell me he is devoted to you. I don't understand a devotion that demands favours as if they were rights, demands duty and respect and obedience and love, demands all and takes all, and gives nothing in return—I don't understand a devotion that spends itself in petty tyrannies and gross bullying—I don't understand a devotion that grudges you any ray of light and glimpse of happiness, and doesn't even stop at risking your life to gratify its colossal selfishness! Devotion! Give me good, sound, honest hatred rather than devotion like that?

ELIZABETH: Mr. Browning—I must ask you—

BROWNING: Forgive me—but I won't be silent any longer! Even before I met you, I knew that sickness wasn't the only shadow on your life. And all these months —though you never once breathed a syllable of complaint—I felt that other shadow deepening, and I've stood by, and looked on, and said nothing. Who was I to step in between you and the man nature, as an ugly jest, chose for your father? A mere friend! I might find you tired and sick after hateful scenes I could picture only too vividly—and I must pretend to know nothing, see nothing, feel nothing. Well! I've done with pretence from today on! I refuse any longer to let myself be gagged and handcuffed! It's not just your comfort and happiness which are at stake now. It's your very life. And I forbid you to play with your life. And I have the right to forbid you.

ELIZABETH: (*desperately*) No—no—no . . . Oh, please don't say any more!

BROWNING: (*with compelling ardour*) The right. And you won't deny it—you're too utterly candid and true. At our first meeting you forbade me to speak of love—there was to be nothing more than friendship between us. I obeyed you. But I knew well enough—we both knew—that I was to be much more than just your friend. Even before I passed that door, and our eyes first met across the room, I loved you—and I've gone on loving you—and I love you now more than words can tell—and I shall love you to the end, and beyond. You know that? You've always known?

ELIZABETH: (*brokenly*) Yes—yes—I've always known. . . . And now for pity's sake—for pity's sake—leave me.

BROWNING: (*seizing both her hands*) No.

ELIZABETH: Oh, please . . . please . . . let me go. Leave me. We must never see each other again.

BROWNING: I shall never let you go. I shall never leave you. (*He draws her into his arms*) Elizabeth . . . Elizabeth . . .

ELIZABETH: (*struggling feebly in his embrace*) No—no. . . . Oh, Robert, have mercy on me. . . .

BROWNING: Elizabeth, my darling. . . . (*He kisses her; and at the touch of his lips, her arms go round his neck.*)

ELIZABETH: Oh, Robert, I love you—I love you—I love you.

(*They kiss each other again. Then she sinks into a chair, and he kneels beside her, holding her hands.*)

BROWNING: And yet you ask me to take my marching orders and go out of your life?

ELIZABETH: Yes, Robert, for what have I to give you? I have so little of all that love asks for. I have no beauty, and no health, and I'm no longer young. . . .

BROWNING: I love you.

ELIZABETH: (*with restrained spiritual passion*) I should have refused to see you again after our first meeting. For I loved you then, though I would have denied it—even to myself. . . . Oh, Robert, I think Eve must have felt as I did when her first dawn broke over Paradise—the terror, the wonder, the glory of it! I had no strength to put up any kind of resistance except the pitiful pretence of mere friendship. I was helpless, I was paralysed, with happiness I had never dreamt it was possible to feel. . . . That's my only excuse—and God knows I need one!—for not having sent you away from me at once.

BROWNING: I love you.

ELIZABETH: My life had reached its lowest ebb. I was worn out, and hope was dead. Then you came. . . . Robert, do you know what you have done for me? I could have laughed when Doctor Chambers said that I had healed myself by wanting to live. He was right! Oh, he was right! But he little knew what lay behind his words! I wanted to live—eagerly, desperately, passionately—and only because life meant you—you—and the sight of your face, and the sound of your voice, and the touch of your hand. Oh, and so much more than that! Because of you the air once more was sweet to breathe, and all the world was good and green again.

BROWNING: (*kissing her hands*) And with those words singing in my ears, I'm to turn my back on you and go?

ELIZABETH: But, Robert, can't you—can't you see how impossible—

BROWNING: I've never yet turned my back on a friend or an enemy. Am I likely to turn it on you?

ELIZABETH: But how is it all to end? What have we to look forward to? And how—

BROWNING: I love you—and I want you for my wife.

ELIZABETH: Robert, I can't marry you. How can I when—

BROWNING: Not today or tomorrow. Not this year, perhaps, or next. Perhaps not for years to come—

ELIZABETH: I may never be able to marry you.

BROWNING: What then? If you remain to the last beyond my reach, I shall die proud and happy in having spent a lifetime fighting to gain the richest prize a man was ever offered.

ELIZABETH: No—no! Oh, Robert, put aside your dream of me—and look on me as I am. I love you too well to let you waste your manhood pursuing the pale ghost of a woman.

BROWNING: Do you think I'm a boy to be swept off my feet by an impulse? Or a sentimental dreamer blind to reality? There's no man alive who sees things as they are with clearer eyes than I do, and has his feet more firmly planted on the earth. And I tell you, in all soberness, that my need of you is as urgent as your need of me. If your weakness asks my strength for support, my abundant strength cries out for your weakness to complete my life and myself.

ELIZABETH: (*after a pause*) Robert, have you thought what your position here would be like if you went on seeing me after today?

BROWNING: Yes.

ELIZABETH: (*quickly*) We should have to keep our love secret from every one lest a whisper of it get to my father's ears.

BROWNING: I know.

ELIZABETH: If he had the least suspicion that you were more than a friend, the door would be slammed in your face, my letters supervised, and my life made unbearable.

BROWNING: I know.

ELIZABETH: And you, my dear—you're as frank and open as the day—how would you enjoy coming here under false pretences, and all the deceits, subterfuges, intrigues we'd be forced to use?

BROWNING: (*with an exultant laugh*) I shall *detest* it—I shall *hate* it with all my heart and soul. And I thank God for that!

ELIZABETH: But Robert—

BROWNING: For it's splendid and right that I should suffer some discomfort, at least, for such a reward as you! The immortal garland was never run for without dust and heat!

ELIZABETH: (*bitterly*) Immortal! Oh, Robert, fading, if not already faded! (*He is about to protest*) No, don't speak! don't speak! . . . (*She rises and goes to the window and looks, with unseeing eyes, into the street. After a moment she turns to him*) Robert, if we were to say good-bye today, we should have nothing but beautiful memories of each other to last to the end of our lives. We should be unhappy: but there are many kinds of unhappiness. Ours would be the unhappiness of those who have put love away from them for the sake of love. There would be no disillusion in it, or bitterness or remorse.

BROWNING: (*in a low, tense voice*) Is it *you* who are speaking?

ELIZABETH: What do you mean?

BROWNING: I don't know you. I thought yours was the courage that dared the uttermost, careless of defeat. Here's life —*life*—offering us the best that life can give, and you dare not grasp at it for fear it will turn to dust in your hand! We're to dream away the rest of our lives in tepid sadness rather than risk utter disaster for utter happiness. I don't know you. I never thought you were a coward!

ELIZABETH: (*proudly, indignantly*) A coward? I? (*With a sudden change of voice*) Yes, I'm a coward, Robert—a coward through and through. . . . But it's not for myself that I'm afraid.

BROWNING: (*going swiftly up to her and taking her in his arms*) I know that, my darling.

ELIZABETH: What's another disaster, great or small, to me who have known little but disaster all my life? But you're a fighter —and you were born for victory and triumph. If disaster came to you through me—

BROWNING: Yes, a fighter. But I'm sick of fighting alone. I need a comrade-at-arms to fight beside me—and—

ELIZABETH: Not one already wounded in the battle. . . .

BROWNING: Wounded—but undefeated, undaunted, unbroken.

ELIZABETH: Yes, but—

BROWNING: What finer comrade could a man ask for?

ELIZABETH: But Robert—

BROWNING: No.

ELIZABETH: But Robert—

BROWNING: No.

(*And he kisses the protest from her lips as the scene closes.*)

ACT IV

Henrietta

(*Some weeks later.*)

(ARABEL *enters, carrying* FLUSH. *She is in outdoor clothes and has her bonnet on.*)

ARABEL: (*standing in the open doorway and speaking*) You had really better let Wilson help you up the last few stairs, Ba.

ELIZABETH: (*outside*) No! No, Wilson, don't touch me!

ARABEL: But, my dear . . .

(ELIZABETH *enters, bonneted and in outdoor clothes. She is breathless but triumphant.* WILSON *follows at her heels.*)

ELIZABETH: There! All the way up, and without one pause or help of any kind! And I feel splendid—just a little out of breath, that's all. . . . (*She sways a little on her feet. Both* WILSON *and* ARABEL *stretch out hands to support her*) No, don't touch me! I'm perfectly all right. . . . (*She walks to the sofa and sits down, and takes her bonnet and gloves off during the following*) Now wasn't that a glorious triumph? And you know, Wilson, I got out of the carriage and walked quite—two miles in the Park!

WILSON: Lor', Miss!

ARABEL: Ba, *dear* . . . !

ELIZABETH: Well, one mile then. Anyhow, that's what I'm going to tell Doctor Chambers.

ARABEL: *Really*, Ba . . . !

ELIZABETH: Oh, my dear, Flush has muddied your gown disgracefully! What a filthy state you're in, Flushy! . . . You had better take him, Wilson, and get Jenny to bathe him. He's not been properly washed for ages.

WILSON: (*taking* FLUSH *from* ARABEL) Very good, Miss Ba.

(WILSON *goes out carrying* FLUSH.)

ELIZABETH: (*pointing to a little heap of letters*) Oh, the post has come. Please give me those letters, dear.

ARABEL: (*handing her the letters*) Why, that's Mr. Browning's handwriting! I'm sorry, I couldn't help seeing it, Ba. But aren't you expecting him this afternoon?

ELIZABETH: (*absently*) Yes. . . . (*She tears open the letter and reads it, smiling to herself*) Yes, dear, he should be here very soon now. . . . This was just to wish me good night.

ARABEL: To wish you good night . . . ?

ELIZABETH: Yes, it was written yesterday evening.

ARABEL: Oh. . . .

ELIZABETH: (*turning over the letters*) Mr. Haydon—Miss Martineau—Mr. Horne —Oh! . . . (*A sharp change coming into her voice*) This is from Papa.

ARABEL: (*anxiously*) From Papa! But he's returning today. . . .

ELIZABETH: Perhaps he's been detained. . . .

(*She opens the letter.*)

ARABEL: (*hopefully*) Oh, do you think so?

ELIZABETH: (*she quickly scans the letter; then in a voice of consternation*) Oh! . . . Oh, Arabel! . . .

ARABEL: What is it, dear?

ELIZABETH: We're leaving.

ARABEL: Leaving?

ELIZABETH: Yes—leaving this house. Leaving London. Listen—

(*A knock at the door and* HENRIETTA's *voice.*)

HENRIETTA: (*outside*) May I come in, Ba?

ELIZABETH: Come in, dear. (*In a hurried whisper to* ARABEL) Don't speak of this yet. . . .

(HENRIETTA *enters.*)

HENRIETTA: (*in great excitement*) Oh, Ba, you must see him at once! You positively must!

ELIZABETH: Him . . . ?

HENRIETTA: He's in his full regimentals. He's just been to St. James' to receive —or whatever you call it—his adjutancy— or something—from Queen Victoria herself. He's wonderful! He's gorgeous! May I bring him up here for you to look at?

ELIZABETH: But—

HENRIETTA: Papa need never know. Oh, Ba, do let me! You've never seen him yet—it's high time you met—and you couldn't see him to better advantage than now! . . . I'm talking of Captain Cook, you know.

ELIZABETH: Yes, so I've gathered. But I can't see him now, dear. I'm expecting Mr. Browning any minute.

HENRIETTA: (*crestfallen but resigned*) Oh . . . then of course it's impossible. . . . But I tell you what, Ba! I'll try to keep him until Mr. Browning goes. I don't think he'll mind. (*She hurries to the door, and throws over her shoulder*) You can keep your poet here as long as you like.

(*She goes out.*)

ELIZABETH: (*with a short laugh that ends in a sigh*) Yes, she had best make the most of her soldier while she can, poor darling. She is not likely to see much of him in the future.

(*She takes up* BARRETT's *letter.*)

ARABEL: Oh, Ba, tell me quickly. . . .

ELIZABETH: He writes from Dorking. (*She reads*) "This is to let you know that we shall be leaving London on Monday, the 22nd of this month. I have taken a furnished house at Bookham, in Surrey, some twenty miles from London and six miles from Leatherhead, the nearest railway station. Whether we shall eventually make it our permanent home I have not yet decided. At any rate, we shall spend the winter there. You will benefit by the country air and the complete seclusion of your new surroundings. I have felt for some time now that your present feverishly restless mode of life in London will, if continued, affect you harmfully both physically and morally. I am writing this letter so that you may inform your brothers and sisters of my decision and tell them that I decline absolutely to discuss it when I return home tomorrow." —That's today.—"The matter is finally settled, and you and they will make such preparations as are needful for the move."

ARABEL: Oh, Ba! . . .

ELIZABETH: (*bitterly*) That's not quite all. He finishes up with a characteristic touch of humour.

ARABEL: Humour?

ELIZABETH: Yes. He signs himself— "Your loving Papa."

ARABEL: The twenty-second. That gives us barely a fortnight longer here.

ELIZABETH: (*stormily*) My "feverishly restless mode of life"!—a few drives, a few calls on my friends, a few visitors. . . . I wonder he doesn't describe me as a recklessly dissipated woman! He made my going to Italy impossible. And now I am to be cut off any little pleasures I have begun to find here.

(*She crumbles up the letter and tosses it into the grate.*)

ARABEL: I know, dear, I understand—and I'm very sorry for you. . . . The change won't hit me so hardly. My only ties in London are my Mission work and district visiting. But you and Henrietta—
(*She hesitates.*)

ELIZABETH: Well?

ARABEL: (*with sudden earnestness*) Oh, Ba, don't be angry with me if I tell you that this move may, in the long run, be a blessing in disguise for you.

ELIZABETH: A blessing in disguise! I seem to have been brought up on that pious *cliché*! What do you mean?

ARABEL: We all pretend to be ignorant of each other's affairs in this house—except poor Henrietta's. It's safer so. And yet we know—we all know—that you and Mr. Browning—

ELIZABETH: Well?

ARABEL: Oh, Ba, one has only to look at your face when you're expecting him—and again after he has left you. . . .

ELIZABETH: (*proudly*) I love him and he loves me. What of it? Haven't I as much right to love and be loved as any other woman?

ARABEL: Oh, yes, dear—but how is it all to end? So long as Papa's alive none of us will ever be able to marry with his consent—and to marry without it is unthinkable. And, in your case it isn't only a question of Papa's consent. . . . Of course it's—it's wonderful how much stronger and better you are—you walked upstairs splendidly just now. . . . But—but—

ELIZABETH: But even if I can manage to walk up a few steps it doesn't mean that I shall ever be fit to marry—is that what you're trying to say?

ARABEL: Oh, Ba, darling, it's because I love you so dearly, and don't want you to suffer, that I'm forcing myself to speak. I know very little about gentlemen—except that they all want to marry the ladies they fall in love with. I—I don't know Mr. Browning at all—but— But even great poets want to settle down in time, and have a home of their own, and a wife, and—and little ones. . . . It would be so dreadful if—

ELIZABETH: (*springing to her feet*) Oh, be quiet! be quiet! Do you suppose I haven't thought of all that a thousand times already?

(*She goes to the window and looks out.*)

ARABEL: I am sorry. . . . I—I didn't mean to interfere. All I want is to save you any— (*She notices that* ELIZABETH *is no longer listening, but is waving her hand to some one in the street, her face transformed with joy*) Oh . . .

(*She rises and slips softly out of the room, unnoticed by* ELIZABETH.)

ELIZABETH: (*turning*) Mr. Browning has just— (*Realises the empty room*) Oh. . . . (*Her eyes light on* BARRETT'S *crumpled letter in the grate. She picks it up and smooths it out, her face emptied of joy. She puts it on the mantelpiece. A knock at the door*) Come in.

(BROWNING *enters. They look at each other in silence for a moment; then he goes up to her and takes her in his arms.*)

BROWNING: My love.

ELIZABETH: Robert. . . .

(*They kiss.*)

BROWNING: (*holding her at arm's length*) You look tired, sweetheart. What have you been doing today?

ELIZABETH: (*with forced lightness*) I went for a drive—and a walk in the Park. And afterwards I ran all the way upstairs—without help, and without one stop.

BROWNING: Oh, but you know—! Of course, dearest, it's a splendid feat, and I'm proud of you! . . . Come and sit down. (*Leads her to the sofa, and they sit down*) Now, aren't you being a trifle too ambitious?

ELIZABETH: I don't think so. . . . I'm feeling wonderfully well. . . .

BROWNING: Look at me. (*She looks at him*) What's the matter, Ba?

ELIZABETH: Nothing. . . .

BROWNING: Has your father returned?

ELIZABETH: No. We expect him today.

BROWNING: (*taking her face in his hands*) Those talking eyes of yours give you hopelessly away. Something has gone wrong. What is it? You must tell me.

ELIZABETH: Read that letter on the mantelpiece, Robert.

BROWNING: (*goes to the mantelpiece and takes* BARRETT's *letter*) From your father?

ELIZABETH: Yes. (*He reads the letter; then looks at her with a strange smile on his face*) Well?

BROWNING: (*still smiling*) I think, by the look of it, you crumpled up this letter furiously in your little hand—and I'm quite sure you pitched it into the grate.

ELIZABETH: Yes, I did. But—

BROWNING: Why?

ELIZABETH: Oh, Robert, don't you see what this means to us?

BROWNING: Yes—and perhaps better than you do.

ELIZABETH: Better than I? Oh, you mustn't deceive yourself! You think this move will make little difference to us. You think you'll be able to ride over from London and see me almost as often as we see each other here. But you're wrong! you're wrong! You don't know Papa as I do. He's grown jealous of my life here, my pleasures and my friends—and I'm slowly and surely to be parted from them. I've felt this coming for some time now. Oh, Robert, it will soon be made impossible for me to see you at all. . . .

BROWNING: This precious letter may mean all that. But it means a great deal more that you haven't as yet been able to grasp.

ELIZABETH: A great deal more . . . ?

BROWNING: It means that you will be in Italy before the month is out.

ELIZABETH: (*in a whisper*) Italy . . . ?

BROWNING: Yes— and with me.

ELIZABETH: Robert . . .

BROWNING: It means that we must be married at once.

ELIZABETH: (*standing up*) Do you know what you're saying?

BROWNING: Yes, I know what I am saying. And I repeat it. We must be married at once. (*He goes up to her*) My darling, listen to me—

(*He is about to take her hands.*)

ELIZABETH: (*starting back*) No! Don't touch me! What you say is madness! . . . I can't marry you—I can never marry you.

BROWNING: (*with a sudden blaze of passion*) You can, and you shall! You'll marry me if I have to carry you out of this house and up to the altar! (*Controlling himself*) Do you seriously imagine I'm going to allow myself to be elbowed out of your life now? And just to satisfy the selfish jealousy of a man whom I no longer believe to be sane? You ought to know me better by this time—

ELIZABETH: (*quickly breaking in*) Oh, Robert, it's not only Papa who stands between us. It's I—it's I . . .

BROWNING: We've gone into that a hundred times already, and—

ELIZABETH: Yes, and now we must go into it once again, and frankly, for the last time.

BROWNING: But—

ELIZABETH: (*silencing him with a gesture*) Robert, it's no use deceiving ourselves. However much stronger I may become, I shall always remain an invalid. You tell me that you want me sick or well —and it's wonderful of you to say that, and I know you believe it. . . . But I— Robert, I'm not generous enough—I'm too proud, if you like—to accept what I feel through and through, in spite of anything you say, to be a sacrifice of your life and your manhood. As your wife I should be haunted day and night by thoughts of all the glorious things you would have enjoyed but for me—freedom, ease, adventure, and passionate love I—I could never really satisfy. . . .

BROWNING: No—no—listen—

ELIZABETH: (*with all her soul in her voice*) Oh, Robert, I should be haunted by the ghosts of your unborn children. . . . When I read that letter my world seemed to fall to pieces. . . . But now I thank God that it came while we're still free, and have the strength to shake hands and say good-bye. . . .

(*She stretches out her hand.*)

BROWNING: (*with a complete change of manner, ignoring her hand, and speaking in a quiet, matter-of-fact voice*) On the whole I think this will be our best plan of campaign. The family leave here on the—(*he consults the letter*)—on the twenty-second. So we have barely a fortnight to get everything done in. You told me last week that Mr. Hedley had invited your sisters to picnic in Richmond Park next Saturday. So the house will be conveniently empty. We'll meet at Mary-le-Bone Church and be married quietly some time in the morning. I'll see about a licence at once, and interview the Vicar.

ELIZABETH: (*who has been staring at him with bewilderment and fear*) Robert—

BROWNING: (*as before*) It would be madness to leave England on the same day. You'll need all the rest and quiet you can get before the journey. So, directly after we are married, I think you had better return here and take things very easily for a day or two. You'll have six days if we leave on Saturday week. Now— (*He takes a paper out of his pocket.*)

ELIZABETH: Oh, stop! I can't listen to you!

BROWNING: (*as before, consulting the paper*) For some time now I've kept careful note of the sailings from Southampton in case of just such an emergency as this.

The Packet leaves the Royal Pier on Saturdays at nine o'clock. We must catch the five o'clock express at Vauxhall. It arrives at Southampton at eight.

ELIZABETH: Oh... (*She laughs wildly, the laugh changing into sobs.* BROWNING *takes her into his arms and draws her down beside him on the sofa. Her sobs gradually subside. She says brokenly*) And—and I always believed Papa was the most overbearing man in the world. . . .

BROWNING: (*smiling*) And yet you've known me for some time now!

ELIZABETH: But I mustn't give way, Robert—I mustn't—I daren't. . . .

BROWNING: There's one other thing, my darling, of the utmost importance that we must settle at once. You can't possibly travel without a maid. Wilson must have a pretty shrewd idea of our relations. You say she is entirely devoted to you. But do you think she will be willing to come abroad with us?

ELIZABETH: (*after a pause, in a low voice*) Robert . . . have you ever thought that my strength may break down on the journey?

BROWNING: Yes.

ELIZABETH: Suppose I were to—to die on your hands?

BROWNING: (*softly, after slight pause*) Are you afraid, Ba?

ELIZABETH: (*proudly, indignantly*) Afraid? I? You know that I am not afraid! You know that I would sooner die with you beside me than live a hundred lives without you. . . . But—but how would *you* feel if I were to die like that? And what would the world say of you?

BROWNING: (*quietly*) I should be branded as little better than a murderer. And what I should feel I—I leave you to imagine.

ELIZABETH: And yet you ask me to come with you?

BROWNING: Yes. I am prepared to risk your life—and much more than mine —to get you out of this dreadful house into the sunshine, and to have you for my wife.

ELIZABETH: You love me like that?

BROWNING: I love you like that.

(*A long pause.*)

ELIZABETH: Robert . . . will you—will you give me a little time?

BROWNING: Time is short, my dear.

ELIZABETH: Yes, I know. But I must have a little time. I can't decide now. I daren't. . . . I feel something *must* happen soon to show me definitely the way. . . . Give me a few hours. Before I sleep tonight I'll write and tell you my decision. . . . Please, Robert.

BROWNING: You promise me that?

ELIZABETH: I promise.

BROWNING: Very well.

ELIZABETH: Thank you.

BROWNING: Shall I go now?

ELIZABETH: Please. . . . (*He kneels and takes both her hands and presses them passionately to his lips. She receives the caress passively. He rises and leaves the room in silence. She sits motionless, staring before her. A pause. Then a light knock at the door. Another pause. Then a louder knock.* ELIZABETH *starts out of her thoughts*) Come in.

(HENRIETTA *enters.*)

HENRIETTA: I saw Mr. Browning going down the stairs. . . . May I bring him in?

ELIZABETH: Him?

HENRIETTA: He's standing on the landing outside. . . . (*She gives* ELIZABETH *a little shake*) Wake up, Ba! I'm talking of Surtees.

ELIZABETH: Oh, yes, of course. . . . But won't some other time do as well?

HENRIETTA: No! No! I told you he was in uniform. You promised to see him, Ba!

ELIZABETH: (*with a sigh*) Very well, dear. . . .

(HENRIETTA *kisses* ELIZABETH *impulsively; then goes to the door and opens it.*)

HENRIETTA: (*speaking into the passage*) Come in, Surtees. (CAPTAIN SURTEES COOK *enters: a huge, handsome, whiskered, frank-faced man. He is arrayed in the full splendour of his "regimentals" and carries his headgear under his arm*) Captain Surtees Cook, Ba.—My sister, Elizabeth.

(ELIZABETH *has risen to receive him.* COOK *clicks his heels together and bows stiffly.*)

COOK: Your servant, Miss Barrett.

ELIZABETH: (*offering him her hand*) How-do-you-do?

COOK: (*taking her hand and bowing over it*) Greatly honoured, 'pon my word I am, Miss Barrett. Understand not every one received here.

HENRIETTA: No indeed, Surtees! With the exception of the family, very few gentlemen have ever been allowed in Ba's room.

COOK: Twice honoured in one day, y'know. First by Her Majesty; now by you, Miss Barrett. Can't think what I've done to deserve it.

ELIZABETH: Oh, I had forgotten! You've just come from the Palace. I have never seen the Queen. What is she like?

COOK: Very little lady, Ma'am; but royal, every inch of her.

HENRIETTA: Surtees, you haven't got your sword on!

COOK: Not etiquette, as I told you, to wear it indoors.

HENRIETTA: Oh, bother etiquette! I want Ba to see you in full war-paint. Where did you leave it?

COOK: In the hall.

HENRIETTA: I'll fetch it. (*Runs to the door.*)

COOK: No, but really—Miss Barrett doesn't want—

(HENRIETTA *goes out.*)

ELIZABETH: But indeed I do, Captain Cook! I don't think I've ever seen an officer in . . . full war-paint before, except at reviews and ceremonies—and that was years ago.

COOK: Indeed? (*After a short pause*) Er—Miss Barrett . . .

ELIZABETH: Yes?

COOK: Miss Barrett . . .

ELIZABETH: (*encouragingly*) Yes, Captain Cook?

COOK: I say, Miss Barrett. . . .

ELIZABETH: You want to tell me something about Henrietta?

COOK: (*eagerly*) Just so, Miss Barrett, just so. Exactly. You know, Miss Barrett—you know— (*He is unable to go on.*)

ELIZABETH: (*very kindly*) Yes, Captain Cook, I know. And though I'm quite powerless to help, believe me, you have my heartfelt sympathy. (*She gives him her hand.*)

COOK: (*taking it in both of his*) Thank you. Thank you. More than I deserve. Thank you, Miss Barrett. Never was such a girl, y'know—Henrietta, I mean. Dunno what I've done to deserve—

(HENRIETTA *enters with the sword.* ELIZABETH *and* COOK *are still holding hands.*)

HENRIETTA: Oh, yes, I thought he'd seize the opportunity to tell you something while I was out of the room. Did he really manage to get it out?

ELIZABETH: (*smiling*) Perhaps, not quite. Did you, Captain Cook?

COOK: Well—ah—y'know. . . . Still, like most ladies—quick in the uptake. . . .

ELIZABETH: Yes, I understood. (*Kissing* HENRIETTA) My dear, how I wish I could do something for you both!

HENRIETTA: Well, you can't, favourite daughter though you are! Nobody can. (*She sits down with the sword across her lap*) Surtees wants to ask Papa for my hand and all that—quite like the conventional suitor. I can't get it into his poor head that such things are simply not possible at 50, Wimpole Street.

ELIZABETH: (*earnestly*) Oh, believe me, Captain Cook, it would be more than useless! You would be peremptorily ordered out of the house—and I don't know what would happen to Henrietta!

COOK: Quite aware that I'm not much of a match, Miss Barrett. Poor man, y'know. Little else than my pay. Still, quite respectable and all that. Decent family and all that. Should be more than willing, if necessary, to throw up soldiering and take to some money-making business, but—

HENRIETTA: And a fine mess you'd make of it, my poor dear!

COOK: Well, I'm not so sure about that. Admit, of course, that soldiering's my special job. Haven't the brain for much else, I'm afraid. Still, you never know what a fella can't do with a prize like Henrietta to reward his efforts. What d'you say, Miss Barrett?

HENRIETTA: Oh, Ba, can *you* make him understand? I can't!

ELIZABETH: (*very impressively*) Captain Cook, if you were a Prince of Eldorado and came here courting, with a pedigree of lineal descent from some signory in the Moon in one hand, and a ticket of good behaviour from the nearest Independent Chapel in the other—even then, Papa would show you the door! *Now* do you understand?

COOK: Can't say I do.

HENRIETTA: Well, anyhow, you're not to speak to Papa, and I forbid you to give up soldiering. Now that I've seen you in your glory, do you suppose I should ever take you without your uniform? Get up. I want to buckle on your sword.

COOK: Aw, I say— (*Stands up, smiling rather sheepishly.*)

HENRIETTA: (*getting to work*) Ba thinks poets are the flower of manhood—a certain poet, at any rate. I mean to show her that she's mistaken. . . .

COOK: I say, you've got it wrong. Sword hangs from the left hip, y'know.

HENRIETTA: Why?

COOK: Well—

(BARRETT *enters, and taking in the scene with a look of amazement, his face immediately hardens into a mould of freezing displeasure. Both* GIRLS *stare at him in consternation.* COOK *stands rigid.*)

ELIZABETH: Papa.... You're—you're home earlier than I expected, Papa.

BARRETT: I don't think I have the privilege of this gentleman's acquaintance.

HENRIETTA: Captain Cook, may I introduce my father? Papa—Captain Surtees Cook.

COOK: Your servant, sir.

(BOTH MEN *bow stiffly.*)

HENRIETTA: (*after a short pause*) Captain Cook is a great friend of George and Occy.

BARRETT: Indeed? (*To* COOK) My sons are very rarely at home at this time of the day.

COOK: Fact is—just passing the house—thought I'd look in on the off chance, y'know, sir—finding one of them in and all that....

BARRETT: I see.

ELIZABETH: (*breaking a pause*) Captain Cook has just come from Buckingham Palace ... and Henrietta thought I should like to see him in all the splendour of his regimentals.

BARRETT: Indeed. (*Takes out his watch and looks at it.*)

COOK: Nothing much to look at, of course—but ladies like a bit of colour, and er— By Jove, must be getting late!

BARRETT: (*pocketing his watch*) It's nineteen-and-a-half minutes past five.

COOK: By Jove! High time I were moving.... (BARRETT *pulls the bell rope twice*) Good-bye, Miss Barrett.

ELIZABETH: Good-bye, Captain Cook. (*She gives him her hand.* BARRETT *crosses to the door and holds it open.*)

COOK: Good-bye, Miss Henrietta.

HENRIETTA: I'll see you out.

(COOK *moves to the door, followed by* HENRIETTA.)

COOK: (*to* BARRETT) Your servant, sir.

(BARRETT *returns his bow in silence.* COOK *goes out and* HENRIETTA *is about to follow.* BARRETT *stays her with a gesture.*)

HENRIETTA: I am seeing Captain Cook to the door.

BARRETT: The servant will attend to that. (*He closes the door, and, in silence, crosses to the fireplace and takes up his stand in front of it. When he speaks he looks straight before him*) Your list of gentlemen visitors appears to be lengthening, Elizabeth.

ELIZABETH: This is the first time I have had the pleasure of meeting Captain Cook.

BARRETT: Indeed. But I infer, from what I saw as I came into the room, that Henrietta's acquaintance is of somewhat longer standing? Or am I mistaken?

HENRIETTA: I have known Captain Cook for some time now.

BARRETT: Ah. And since when has it been your custom to buckle on his accoutrements?

HENRIETTA: I have never seen him in uniform before.

BARRETT: And I think it improbable that you will see him in uniform, or in mufti, very frequently in the future.

HENRIETTA: (*in a strained voice*) Why?

BARRETT: (*ignoring the question*) Again I may be mistaken, but I was under the impression, Elizabeth, that notice should be given me before strangers visited you here.

ELIZABETH: One can hardly describe a friend of George and Occy as a stranger, Papa.

HENRIETTA: Is Captain Cook to be

forbidden the house because I helped him on with his sword?

BARRETT: (*to* ELIZABETH, *ignoring* HENRIETTA) You received my letter?

ELIZABETH: Yes, Papa.

BARRETT: What has just happened fully confirms me in the wisdom of my decision. This house is fast becoming a *rendezvous* for half London. I have neither time nor inclination to find out whether all the persons visiting here are desirable acquaintances for my children. Fortunately our new home is so far from town that your London friends are not likely to trouble us—at least, during the winter.

HENRIETTA: (*blankly*) Our new home? . . .

BARRETT: (*to* ELIZABETH) You have not told your sisters?

ELIZABETH: Arabel knows.

HENRIETTA: I don't understand. Are we—are we leaving Wimpole Street?

BARRETT: (*without looking at* HENRIETTA) I have taken a house at Bookham, in Surrey. And we move in on the twenty-second.

HENRIETTA: Why?

BARRETT: I am not in the habit of accounting for my actions to any one—least of all, to my children.

HENRIETTA: But one thing I have a right to ask you, Papa. If Captain Cook is to be forbidden to visit us, is it because you found him here in Ba's room and saw me fastening on his sword?

BARRETT: (*after a slight pause, looking fixedly at her*) I understood you to say that Captain Cook is George's friend and Occy's.

HENRIETTA: Yes . . . and my friend too.

BARRETT: Ah.

HENRIETTA: Yes, and since it was I who suggested his seeing Ba, and I who asked him to show me how to buckle on his sword, it's unjust to penalise him for—

ELIZABETH: (*warningly*) Henrietta . . .

BARRETT: (*to* HENRIETTA *in a sharp low voice*) Come here.

HENRIETTA: (*she takes a few steps towards him, and speaks, a little breathlessly*) Yes, Papa . . . ?

BARRETT: (*looks at her steadily under lowered brows for a moment, then points to the floor at his feet*) Come here. (*She goes right up to him, breathing quickly and fearfully. He keeps his eyes fixed on her face. Then in a low, ominous voice*) What is this fellow to you?

HENRIETTA: I—I've told you. . . . He's a friend of ours.

BARRETT: What is he to *you*?

HENRIETTA: A—a friend. . . .

BARRETT: Is that all?

HENRIETTA: Yes.

BARRETT: (*suddenly grasping her wrist, his voice like the crack of a whip*) You liar!

ELIZABETH: (*sharply*) Papa!

HENRIETTA: (*gaspingly*) Let me go!

BARRETT: (*tightening his grip*) What's this man to you? Answer me. (*She tries to free herself and cries out*) Answer me.

HENRIETTA: Oh, Papa . . . please . . .

BARRETT: Answer me.

HENRIETTA: Oh, don't . . . don't . . .

BARRETT: Answer me.

HENRIETTA: (*in a strangled voice*) He's—he's—oh, Papa, I love him—

BARRETT: Ah . . . (*between his teeth, seizing her other wrist and forcing her to her knees*) ah—you—you—you— (*She gives a cry of pain.*)

ELIZABETH: (*seizing* BARRETT'S *arm*) Let her go, Papa! I won't have it! Let her go at once!

(BARRETT *flings* HENRIETTA *off. She collapses in a heap on the floor, sobbing, her face buried in her hands.*)

BARRETT: (*turning on* ELIZABETH) And you—you knew of this—filthiness?

ELIZABETH: I've known for some time that Henrietta loved Captain Cook, and I've given her all my sympathy.

BARRETT: You dare to tell me—

ELIZABETH: Yes. And I would have given her my help as well, if I had had it to give.

BARRETT: I'll deal with you later. (*To* HENRIETTA) Get up.

HENRIETTA: (*suddenly clasping his knees and speaking in a voice of passionate entreaty*) Oh, Papa, please listen to me—please. I—I'm not a bad girl—I swear to you I'm not. I know I've deceived you—and I'm sorry—I'm sorry. . . . But I couldn't help it. I—I love him—we love each other—and if you'd known you would have turned him from the house. . . . Oh, can't you understand—won't you try to understand? . . . He's poor—we don't expect to be married yet—but he's a good man—and it can't be wrong to love him. Other women love—why must I be forbidden? I want love—I can't live without love. Remember how you loved Mamma and how she loved you—and—and you'll understand and pity me. . . .

BARRETT: (*inexorably*) Get up.

HENRIETTA: Have pity on me, Papa. . . .

BARRETT: Get up. (*He forcibly loosens her hold of his knees, and she staggers to her feet*) Sit there. (*He points to a chair. She drops into it, and sits listlessly with drooped head*) How long has this been going on? (HENRIETTA *says nothing*) Do you hear me? How long have you been carrying on with this fellow?

HENRIETTA: I—I've known him a little over a year.

BARRETT: And you've been with him often?

HENRIETTA: Yes.

BARRETT: Alone?

HENRIETTA: Yes.

BARRETT: Where?

HENRIETTA: We—I—I've met him in the Park, and—and—

BARRETT: And—here?

HENRIETTA: Yes.

BARRETT: Here. And alone? (HENRIETTA *is silent*) Have you met him in this house alone?

HENRIETTA: Yes.

BARRETT: So! Furtive unchastity under my own roof—and abetted by one whom I believed to be wholly chaste and good. . . .

HENRIETTA: No—no—

ELIZABETH: (*fiercely*) How dare you, Papa!

BARRETT: Silence! (*To* HENRIETTA, *his voice hard and cold as ice*) Now attend to me. Something like this happened a year or two ago, and I thought I had crushed the devil in you then. I was wrong. It needed sterner measures than I had the courage to use. . . . So now, unless I have your solemn word that you will neither see nor in any way communicate with this man again, you leave my house at once, as you are, with nothing but the clothes you have on. In which case, you will be your own mistress, and can go to perdition any way you please. But of this you may be certain. Once outside my doors you will never again be admitted, on any pretext whatever, so long as I live. I think by this time you have learnt that it's not my habit to make idle threats, and that I never go back on my word. Very well. You have your choice. Take it.

HENRIETTA: (*after an agonised mental struggle*) Is it nothing to you that I—that I shall hate you for this to the end of my life?

BARRETT: Less than nothing.

HENRIETTA: But—but I must let Captain Cook know that—

BARRETT: I will deal with Captain Cook.

HENRIETTA: (*desperately*) But Papa—

BARRETT: Will you give me your word neither to see nor to communicate with this man again?

HENRIETTA: (*after a pause, in a dead voice*) I—I have no choice.

BARRETT: Give me your Bible, Elizabeth.

ELIZABETH: Why?

BARRETT: I am not prepared to accept your sister's bare promise. But I think even she would hesitate to break an oath made with her hand resting on the Word of God. Give me your Bible.

ELIZABETH: My Bible belonged to Mamma. I can't have it used for such a purpose.

BARRETT: Give me your Bible.

ELIZABETH: No.

BARRETT: You refuse?

ELIZABETH: Yes.

(BARRETT *pulls the bell rope. A pause. No one speaks or moves.* WILSON *enters.*)

BARRETT: I want you to go to my bedroom and fetch my Bible. Are your hands clean?

WILSON: (*looking at her hands*) My hands, sir?

BARRETT: Are they clean?

WILSON: (*with a touch of asperity*) Yes, sir. I've just been helping to bathe Flush.

BARRETT: You will find the Bible on the table beside my bed.

WILSON: Very good, sir.

(*She goes out. All three are silent and motionless until she returns.* WILSON *re-enters with* BARRETT's *Bible. She gives it to him and goes out.*)

BARRETT: (*to* HENRIETTA, *placing the Bible reverently on the table*) Come here. (HENRIETTA *rises and goes to the table*) Place your hand upon the Book. (*She does so*) Repeat after me: "I give you my solemn word that I will neither see, nor have any communication with, Captain Cook again."

HENRIETTA: (*in a toneless voice*) I give you my solemn word that I will neither see, nor have any communication with, Captain Cook again.

BARRETT: You will now go to your room and remain there until you have my permission to leave it. (*Without a word, but with her head held high,* HENRIETTA *goes out.... After a pause*) Have you anything to say to me, Elizabeth?

ELIZABETH: No.

BARRETT: Then I must leave you under my extreme displeasure. I shall not see you again, I can have nothing to do with you, until God has softened your heart, and you repent of your wickedness, and ask for His forgiveness, and ... mine. (*He takes his Bible and goes out. The moment he has closed the door* ELIZABETH *gets up and pulls the bell rope. She does so with an air of decision. A pause.* WILSON *enters.*)

ELIZABETH: Shut the door, please. (*Impulsively*) Wilson, are you my friend?

WILSON: (*bewildered*) Your ... friend, Miss?

ELIZABETH: Yes, my friend. I am in dire need of friendship and help at the moment.

WILSON: I—I don't quite understand, Miss Ba.... But I'm that fond of you— I'd do anything to help you.

ELIZABETH: You would? And I know I can trust you?

WILSON: Yes, indeed, Miss.

ELIZABETH: Wilson, next Saturday, I am going to marry Mr. Browning.

WILSON: (*with a gasp*) Marry ... !

ELIZABETH: Hush.... Yes. Of course nobody in this house knows—and nobody must know.

WILSON: Lor', Miss, I should just think not indeed!

ELIZABETH: We're to be married secretly at Mary-le-Bone Church. Will you come with me?

WILSON: Me, Miss? Yes, Miss—and gladly.

ELIZABETH: Directly afterwards I shall return here for a few days, and—

WILSON: (*in boundless amazement*) Here! With Mr. Browning . . . !

ELIZABETH: (*with an hysterical laugh*) No—no—no! Just alone with you. . . . Then, on the following Saturday, I shall join Mr. Browning, and we're going abroad. . . . We're going to Italy. . . . Will you come with us?

WILSON: (*in a whisper*) To Italy . . . ?

ELIZABETH: Yes. . . . Will you come with me?

WILSON: Well, Miss, I can't see as how I can help myself. Not that I hold with foreign parts—I don't. But husband or no husband, you'd never get to Italy alive without me.

ELIZABETH: Then you'll come? Then you'll come! Oh, I am so glad! I'll tell Mr. Browning—I'm writing to him now. And I shall want you to take the letter to the post at once. Go and put on your things—I'll have finished by the time you're ready.

WILSON: Yes, Miss.

(WILSON *goes out, and* ELIZABETH *takes pen and paper and starts writing rapidly as the scene closes.*)

ACT V   SCENE I [*Papa*]

(ELIZABETH *is kneeling beside* FLUSH *and fastening a lead on to his collar. She pats his head abstractedly, rises, and picks up a little heap of letters in their envelopes from the table, runs through them and places them on the mantelpiece. Then, with a shuddering sigh, she walks to the window, clasping and unclasping her hands in agitation. After standing at the window for a moment, she sighs again and returns to the mantelpiece, picks up the letters and replaces them one by one on the table. Her cloak and bonnet and gloves, etc., are on the bed.*)

(WILSON *hurries into the room with two travelling rugs on her arm.*)

WILSON: Oh, Miss Ba, I'm that sorry! In my flurry to get the luggage off to the railway station yesterday I clean forgot to pack these rugs. And there was heaps of room in the carpetbag.

ELIZABETH: Never mind.

WILSON: (*placing the rugs across the back of a chair*) I do hope we haven't forgotten nothing else.

ELIZABETH: And if we have it won't matter much. Mr. Browning insisted that we should travel as lightly as possible. We shall be able to get all we need in Paris.

WILSON: Lor', Miss, it don't seem possible we'll be in Paris tomorrow!

ELIZABETH: No. . . . (*She consults her watch*) Oh, how the time crawls! We've still an hour and a half of this dreadful waiting. . . . You're sure, Wilson, they quite understood at the livery stables exactly when, and where, the cab was to meet us?

WILSON: Oh, yes, Miss, I was most particular to see that the young man took it all down—the cab to be at the corner of Wimpole Street at ha'-past three punctual. It won't take us more than ten minutes to get to Hodgson's Library—and then Mr. Browning will have us in his charge. (*Her voice drops to a warm confidential tone*) Your husband, Miss Ba, dear . . .

ELIZABETH: Oh, hush! hush! Don't breathe that word here.

WILSON: But, Miss Ba—

ELIZABETH: I'm foolishly nervous, but I can't help it. The very walls seem to be listening. There is no one in the house, I know, except Miss Henrietta—and she should have gone out by now. Still—

WILSON: Miss Henrietta was putting on her bonnet as I came along the passage.

ELIZABETH: Oh, Wilson, it's impossible to believe that in little more than an hour I shall have left this room, never, in all likelihood, to see it again. . . .

WILSON: And glad you'll be to see the last of it, I'm sure, Miss Ba.

ELIZABETH: Yes—and no. . . . I've been very miserable here, and very happy. . . . Oh, I wish it were time to go! This waiting is killing me!

WILSON: Have you finished writing your letters, Miss?

ELIZABETH: (*almost hysterically*) Yes. Yes. I've written to them all to tell them what I've done and to wish them good-bye. I've just been reading over my letter to Mr. Barrett to see if there was something I could add—something—anything. But I can't think—I can't think.

WILSON: Least said, soonest mended, Miss. (*With a chuckling laugh*) Oh, Miss Ba, I know I shouldn't say such things—but there's a lot I'd give to be here tonight when the Master reads your letter and knows you've been a married lady for almost a week. . . .

ELIZABETH: (*quickly*) Don't, Wilson, don't! The very thought terrifies me! I can see his face—I can hear his voice. . . . Thank God, we shall be miles and miles away. . . . (*She looks at her watch*) An hour and twenty minutes still. Will time never pass?

WILSON: (*after a pause*) Why don't you write some po'try, Miss?

ELIZABETH: (*dumbfounded*) Poetry?

WILSON: Yes, Miss. That 'ud make the time pass nicely, I'm sure.

(ELIZABETH *breaks into rather hysterical laughter.* HENRIETTA *enters in her shawl and bonnet. She has a letter in her hand.* ELIZABETH *abruptly stops laughing and looks at her with frightened eyes.*)

ELIZABETH: (*hastily turning her letters on to their faces*) I—I thought you had gone out.

HENRIETTA: Wilson, I want to speak to Miss Ba.

WILSON: Yes, Miss. (*She goes out.*)

HENRIETTA: I was just going when I ran into a messenger at the door. He brought this letter. It's for you.

ELIZABETH: (*anxiously, reaching out her hand*) For me?

HENRIETTA: (*retaining the letter*) Yes. But it's in—in *his* handwriting.

ELIZABETH: Captain Cook's?

HENRIETTA: Yes.

ELIZABETH: Open it, dear.

HENRIETTA: (*tears open the letter and reads*) "Dear Miss Barrett, I know I am doing very wrong in drawing you once again into my, and Henrietta's, affairs. But the matter is so urgent I am sure you will forgive me. My regiment has been ordered to Somerset at short notice—and I must positively see Henrietta before I go. If I wrote to her direct, my letter would certainly be read by Mr. Barrett. I understand he opens all her correspondence. Hence my trespass on your kindness. Will you please give Henrietta the enclosed letter, and believe me your grateful and obedient servant, Surtees Cook." . . . Somerset . . . (*She drops the letter, opens the enclosure and reads it eagerly.* ELIZABETH *picks up the letter and tears it into little pieces*) What is the time?

ELIZABETH: A quarter past two.

HENRIETTA: (*in a low, tense voice*) You remember Papa threatened to turn me out of the house unless I swore on the Bible not to write to or see Surtees?

ELIZABETH: Yes.

HENRIETTA: (*defiantly*) Well, I'm going to break that "Bible oath" today.

ELIZABETH: (*quietly*) Are you, dear?

HENRIETTA: (*more defiantly still*) Yes —and I shall glory in breaking it! Surtees says he'll be at—never mind where!—between four and six—the only free time he has—*every* day until he leaves next Wednesday. We shall all have left here on Monday: so I must meet him either today or tomorrow. I shall meet him *both* days. And if Papa asks me where I have been—I shall go out of my way to lie to him as often and as grossly as I can.

ELIZABETH: (*quietly*) I see. Why do you tell me all this?

HENRIETTA: (*belligerently*) Because I want you to say that I'm a wicked, deceitful, perjured, *loose* woman, so that I can fling the words back in your face! (*Suddenly throws her arms round* ELIZABETH) Oh, Ba, darling, forgive me! I'm not myself these days. I am all love and hate—and I don't know which is the worse torture. . . .

ELIZABETH: (*with passionate tenderness*) My dear, my dear, you think I don't understand! Oh, but I do! I do! And I feel for you and pity you with all my heart! . . . I can do nothing to help you. I daren't even advise you. . . . But never lose hope—never lose courage—never— (WILSON *flashes into the room. She is in a state of uncontrolled agitation.*)

WILSON: (*gaspingly*) Oh, Miss Ba—Miss Ba . . . !

(*Both sisters stare at her,* HENRIETTA *astonished,* ELIZABETH *in terror.*)

ELIZABETH: What is it, Wilson? (*To* HENRIETTA) Shut the door.

WILSON: The Master, Miss! He—he's just come in. . . .

ELIZABETH: (*in a whisper*) Papa. . . .

WILSON: Yes—just this minute. . . . He must 'ave 'eard—some one must have told him—

ELIZABETH: Be quiet.

HENRIETTA: (*who has been looking in bewilderment from one to the other*) But Ba, what on earth is the matter,

ELIZABETH: Nothing. Nothing. It's—it's only that Papa hasn't been to see me for ten days now—ever since—you remember—? And—and scenes of forgiveness are always trying. . . . (*To* WILSON, *sharply*) Put away my hat and cloak. Quick. (WILSON *does so.*)

HENRIETTA: I don't believe that's all. You're as white as a sheet. What did Wilson mean? Ba, is there anything I can—

ELIZABETH: (*softly, intensely*) No, no, no! Don't speak—don't ask me anything. . . . You know nothing—you understand? —nothing—nothing.

HENRIETTA: But—

ELIZABETH: No. (*To* WILSON) Those rugs . . . (WILSON *picks them up. There is a knock at the door.* WILSON *gasps.* ELIZABETH *speaks in a whisper*) come in. (*She clears her throat, then louder*) Come in. (BARRETT *enters. They are all standing in tense attitudes.* ELIZABETH *commands her voice*) You're home early, Papa. . . .

(BARRETT, *without replying, looks at each of the three in turn; then crosses to the fireplace.* WILSON, *obviously terror-stricken, slips out of the room, the rugs over her arm.*)

BARRETT: (*to* ELIZABETH) What's the matter with that girl?

ELIZABETH: Wilson?

BARRETT: Yes. . . . And with you?

ELIZABETH: Nothing, Papa. . . .

BARRETT: (*after staring broodingly at her for a moment, he turns to* HENRIETTA) Where have you been?

HENRIETTA: Nowhere.

BARRETT: Where are you going?

HENRIETTA: To tea with Aunt Hedley.

BARRETT: Is that the truth?

HENRIETTA: Yes.

BARRETT: You remember your oath?

HENRIETTA: Yes.

BARRETT: Have you kept it?

HENRIETTA: Yes.

BARRETT: Are you going to keep it?

HENRIETTA: Yes.

BARRETT: (*after staring at her for a moment*) I want to speak to your sister. You can go. (*Without a glance at either of them,* HENRIETTA *goes out.* ELIZABETH *sits perfectly still, waiting.* BARRETT *walks to the window; then turns and goes up to her*) Do you know why I am back so early?

ELIZABETH: (*in a whisper*) No, Papa.

BARRETT: (*in a low, intense voice*) Because I could bear it no longer.... It's ten days since last I saw you....

ELIZABETH: Am I to blame for that, Papa?

BARRETT: (*with restrained fury*) You dare to ask me such a question? Weren't you a party in your sister's shameless conduct? Haven't you encouraged her? Haven't you helped her? Haven't you defended her? And did you expect to go scot-free of my displeasure? (*Stopping himself with a violent gesture*) I've not come to speak about that—but to put it behind me—to forget it—to forget it.... I wonder, my child, have you been half so miserable these last ten days as your father?

ELIZABETH: Miserable, Papa?

BARRETT: Do you suppose I'm happy when I'm bitterly estranged from all I love in the world? Do you know that night after night I had to call up all my will power to hold me from coming here to forgive you?

ELIZABETH: Papa—

BARRETT: All my will power, I tell you—all my sense of duty and right and justice.... But today I could bear it no longer. The want of your face and your voice became a torment. I had to come. I am not so strong as they think me. I had to come. And I despise myself for coming —despise myself—hate myself....

ELIZABETH: No—no! (*Suddenly rises and puts her hands on his shoulders*) Oh, Papa, can't you see, won't you ever see, that strength may be weakness, and your sense of justice and right and duty all mistaken and wrong?

BARRETT: (*hoarsely, taking her hands from his shoulders*) Mistaken and wrong? What do you mean?... (*Quickly stopping her from speaking*) No, be silent. Don't answer me.... Mistaken and wrong? You don't know what you're saying.

ELIZABETH: If you'll only listen to me, Papa, I—

BARRETT: No.

ELIZABETH: But, Papa—

BARRETT: No. (*He moves to the window and stands there, his face half averted from her. A pause. He turns*) If there were even a vestige of truth in what you say, my whole life would be a hideous mockery. For always—through all misfortunes and miseries—I've been upheld by knowing, beyond a doubt, what was right, and doing it unflinchingly, however bitter the consequences.... And bitter they've been—how bitter, only God knows! It's been my heavy cross that those whom I was given to guide and rule have always fought against the right that I knew to be the right—and was in duty bound to impose upon them.... Even you. Even your mother.

ELIZABETH: (*in a whisper*) My mother?

BARRETT: Yes, your mother.... But not at first.... You—you, my eldest child, were born of love and only love.... But the others—long before they came the rift had begun to open between your mother and me. Not that she ever opposed me—never once. Or put into words what she felt. She was silent and dutiful and obedient. But love died out—and fear took its place—fear....

ELIZABETH: (*sharply*) No! No!

BARRETT: And all because I saw the right—and did it.

ELIZABETH: (*in a low voice, staring before her*) Oh ... oh, dear God, what she must have suffered.

BARRETT: She?—She?... And what of me? What of me?

ELIZABETH: You?... Oh, Papa, then you—you still loved her—after her love for you had died?

BARRETT: (*in a muffled voice, looking aside*) Love?... What's love?... She was my wife. . . . You—you don't understand. . . .

ELIZABETH: (*in a horrified whisper*) And all those children . . . born in fear. . . . Oh, it's horrible—it's horrible—it's horrible. . . .(*With a shuddering sob, she covers her face with her hands.*)

BARRETT: (*aghast and embarrassed*) Ba, my dear—don't—don't . . . I—I shouldn't have spoken—I shouldn't have told you all that. . . . Forget it, child. . . . (*He goes up to her*) Take your hands from your face. . . . (*He gently touches her wrists. She starts away from him, looking at him with wide, frightened eyes*) Don't look at me like that. (*In a low, thick voice, averting his eyes*) You don't understand. How should you? You know nothing of the brutal tyranny of—passion, and how even the strongest and best are driven by it to hell. Would you have abetted your sister in her—

ELIZABETH: (*fiercely*) Henrietta's love —how dare you speak of it in the same breath as—

BARRETT: (*brutally*) Her *love*? *You* ignorant little fool! What do *you* know of love? Love! The lust of the eye—the lowest urge of the body—

ELIZABETH: (*springing to her feet*) I won't listen to you!

BARRETT: (*seizing her wrist and forcing her back to her seat*) You must—you shall! It's time a little reality were brought into your dream of life. Do you suppose I should have guarded my house like a dragon from this so-called love if I hadn't known, from my own life, all it entails of cruelty and loathing and degradation and remorse? . . . (*He pulls himself together*) With the help of God, and through years of tormenting abstinence, I strangled it in myself. And so long as I have breath in my body, I'll keep it away from those I was given to protect and care for. You understand me?

ELIZABETH: (*in a low voice, looking him full in the face*) Yes—I understand you . . . I understand you. . . .

BARRETT: Very well. (*A pause.* ELIZABETH *sits quite still, looking before her. When he speaks again his voice has changed*) This has been a hateful necessity. I had to speak—plainly—lest your very innocence should smirch the purity I am utterly resolved to maintain in my home. . . . And because I feel that you acted in innocence and ignorance, I—I forgive you freely, my child. . . . We must turn over this ugly page—and forget what was on it. . . . (*He takes her hand*) You're—cold as ice. . . . Why are you trembling?

ELIZABETH: (*drawing her hand from his*) I shall never forget what you have said.

BARRETT: Never forget—but—And yet, perhaps that's as well. . . . (*With sudden urgency*) But, for God's sake, my darling, don't let this raise any further barrier between us! I've told you how all these past months I've seemed to feel you slipping little by little away from me. . . . Your love is all I have left to me in the world.

ELIZABETH: You had Mamma's love once. You might have had the love of all your children.

BARRETT: Yes, if I'd played the coward's part, and taken the easier way, and shirked my duty. I'd rather be hated by the whole world than gain love like that.

ELIZABETH: (*in a broken voice*) Oh, Papa, you—you don't know how I pity you. . . .

BARRETT: (*roughly*) Pity? I don't want your pity. . . . But if I should ever lose you or your love— (*He seizes her unwilling hands*) My darling, next week we shall have left this house, and I hope we shall never return here. I've grown to loathe it. In our new home we shall draw close to each other again. There will be little to distract you in the country— nothing and no one to come between us. (*He draws her stiffening form into his arms*) My child, my darling, you want me to be happy. The only happiness I shall ever know is all yours to give or take. You must look up to me, and depend on me, and lean on me. You must share your thoughts with me, your hopes, your fears, your prayers. I want all your heart and all your soul.... (*He holds her passionately close; she leans away from him, her face drawn with fear and pain.*)

ELIZABETH: (*sobbingly*) I can't bear it— I can't bear any more.... Let me go. Papa—please let me go....
(*He loosens his embrace, and she falls away from him, her arm covering her face. He rises and bends over her.*)

BARRETT: Forgive me, dear. I've said too much. I was carried away. I'll leave you now.

ELIZABETH: (*in a whisper*) Please ...

BARRETT: Shall I see you again tonight?

ELIZABETH: (*as before*) Not tonight.

BARRETT: I shall pray for you.

ELIZABETH: (*half to herself*) Pray for me? ... Tonight.... (*She turns and looks up at him*) Yes, pray for me tonight—if you will.... (*He kisses her forehead gently, and goes out. She sits for a moment looking before her, and then, with frightened eyes, round the room. She whispers*) I must go at once—I must go —I must go.... (*She gets up quickly, and fetches her cloak and bonnet from the wardrobe.* WILSON *enters, stealthily and hurriedly, the rugs on her arm.*)

WILSON: He's gone to the study.

ELIZABETH: (*putting on her bonnet*) We must go. Now. At once.

WILSON: But, Miss Ba—

ELIZABETH: At once. Help me on with my cloak.

WILSON: (*doing so*) But the cab won't be there yet—not for an hour. Besides—

ELIZABETH: Then we must walk about the streets. I can't stay here any longer. I'm frightened. I'm frightened. Fetch your cloak and bonnet.

WILSON: Walk about the streets, Miss? You can't—you can't. Besides—the Master's at home. He may see us leaving. For God's sake, Miss—

ELIZABETH: Where did I put those letters? Ah, here.... (*Spreading them out on the table*) Fetch your cloak and bonnet. Quick.

WILSON: But if he saw us leaving—

ELIZABETH: We must chance that.

WILSON: But, Miss Ba—

ELIZABETH: He can't stop me. I don't belong to him any more. I belong to my husband. Papa can kill me. But he can't stop me.

WILSON: I daren't, Miss, I daren't.

ELIZABETH: Then I must go alone.

WILSON: You can't do that.

ELIZABETH: (*with compelling earnestness*) Wilson, things have passed between my father and me which force me to leave this house at once. Until today I didn't realise quite how unforgivably I have been driven to deceive him. Until today— I've never really known him. He's not like other men. He's—dreadfully different.... I—I can't say any more.... If you want to draw back you need never reproach yourself. This, after all, is no affair of yours. But I must go now.

WILSON: I'll fetch my cloak and bonnet at once, Miss. (ELIZABETH *puts her arm round* WILSON'S *neck and kisses her*) Oh, Miss Ba ... (WILSON *goes out quickly.* ELIZABETH *spreads the letters on the table. Then, from a ribbon on which it is hung, she draws her wedding ring from her bosom. She slips it on to her finger; looks at it for a moment; then pulls on her gloves.* WILSON *reënters, softly and quickly, in cloak and bonnet.*)

ELIZABETH: I am quite ready. You take the rugs, Wilson. I had better carry Flush.

WILSON: (*breathlessly*) Yes, Miss.

ELIZABETH: And now slip downstairs and see whether the study door is shut.

WILSON: Yes, Miss.

(WILSON *goes out, leaving the door open.* ELIZABETH *picks up* FLUSH, *and stands with him under her arm, and looks round the room with an indescribable expression on her face.* WILSON *reënters.*)

WILSON: (*in a whisper*) The door's shut—and all's quiet.

ELIZABETH: Very well. (*She passes out, and* WILSON *follows, closing the door softly after her. For a moment the room stands empty. Then the scene slowly closes.*)

SCENE II

(*The curtain rises on the still empty room. An hour or two has elapsed. The sky, seen through the window, is full of colour from the afterglow. A pause.* ARABEL *enters.*)

ARABEL: (*on entering*) Ba, dear, I want— (*She realises the room's emptiness and stares bewildered around her. Her eyes light on the letters* ELIZABETH *has left. Leaving the door open, she goes to the table and looks at them. She picks up a letter, and whispers, visibly agitated*) For me.... What can it mean...? (*She tears open the letter, and reads it with little gasping exclamations*) Oh...! No, no ...! Married...! No...! Oh... Oh...!

(*She looks up from the letter, her face transformed with terror and excitement; then suddenly sits back on the sofa and goes into shrieks and peals of hysterical laughter. The noise is appalling. After a moment there are voices, and steps outside, and* GEORGE, CHARLES, *and* OCTAVIUS *enter almost simultaneously.* GEORGE *is dressed for dinner; but the other two have not yet finished their toilet.*)

GEORGE: Arabel!

CHARLES: For God's sake!

GEORGE: Arabel! What on earth—

OCTAVIUS: High-strikes! B-by Jove!

(ARABEL *laughs on.*)

GEORGE: (*taking one of her hands and slapping it*) Stop that, Arabel! Stop it at once!

ARABEL: (*half gasping, half shrieking*) Married—gone—married—gone— (*She goes into another wild peal of laughter.*)

GEORGE: Be quiet! (*Slaps her hand again*) Fetch some water some one . . .

OCTAVIUS: Eau-de-Cologne . . .

(ALFRED, SEPTIMUS, *and* HENRY, *two of them dressed, the other without coat and collar, enter hurriedly.*)

ALFRED: What's the matter?

HENRY: Is Ba ill? Arabel!

ARABEL: (*gaspingly*) She's married— she's gone—married—gone . . . (HENRIETTA *enters in her cloak and bonnet. She stands for a moment, wide-eyed, taking in the scene*) Married and gone—Married and gone. . . .

(*She moans and sobs. Realization begins to dawn on the brothers.*)

CHARLES: What does she mean? Where's Ba?

SEPTIMUS: Married and gone—she's mad!

GEORGE: (*taking* ARABEL *by the shoulder*) Arabel—what do you mean?

OCTAVIUS: Married . . . !

(HENRIETTA *suddenly pushes them aside, seizes* ARABEL *by the shoulders and vigorously shakes her.*)

HENRIETTA: Arabel! Arabel! Pull yourself together at once! . . . Where's Ba? . . . Answer me! . . . Where's Ba?

ARABEL: (*gaspingly*) She—she's m-m-married Mr. Robert Browning. . . .

HENRIETTA: (*in a whisper*) Married! (*Consternation among the brothers and amazed exclamations:* — "Married!"— "Married!"—"It can't be true!"—"Robert Browning!"—"Good God!" . . .)

HENRIETTA: (*to* ARABEL, *who is still sobbing*) Where is she?

ARABEL: She—she's gone. . . . Those letters— She's written to—to all of us. . . . She—she's gone. . . . (OCTAVIUS *has pounced on the letters.*)

OCTAVIUS: F-for you. (*Hands a letter to* HENRIETTA. *She tears it open and reads*) George—Henry—Alfred—Septimus—Charles.

(*He hands them each a letter which is quickly torn open and read with muttered exclamations:*—"*Good God!*"—"*Impossible!*"—"*Married!*"—"*A week ago—*")

GEORGE: Yes, she was married last Saturday.

OCTAVIUS: (*holding up a letter*) And this letter is for P-papa.

(*A frightened silence falls on them. Only* HENRIETTA *looks before her with an inscrutable smile on her face.*)

ARABEL: (*in a shuddering whisper*) P-P-papa....

SEPTIMUS: Is he in?

GEORGE: Dressing for dinner.

OCTAVIUS: What's to be d-done?

HENRY: Some one must give him Ba's letter.

HENRIETTA: (*in a clear voice*) Let me. I should love to.

ARABEL: (*in a terrified whisper*) Oh, hush—hush...

(*She points tremblingly to the door. They all hold their breath. In the pause one hears the sound of approaching footsteps. Then* BARRETT, *in evening dress, appears on the threshold. He looks at his assembled family in stern amazement. No one stirs.*)

BARRETT: What is the meaning of this? (*No one stirs or replies*) Who was making that hideous noise just now? (*No one stirs or replies*) Why are you gentlemen half-dressed? (*No one stirs or replies. A pause. Then sharply*) Where is Elizabeth? (*A silence. He passes into the room. With a stifled cry,* ARABEL *rises and clings on to* HENRIETTA'S *arm*) Do you hear me?... (*To* HENRIETTA) Where is your sister?

HENRIETTA: (*freeing herself from* ARABEL *and picking up the letter*) She left you this letter.

BARRETT: (*without touching it, in a low voice, his face becoming a mask*) Left me.... What do you mean?

HENRIETTA: She left letters for all of us. This is yours.

(*His eyes fixed on her face, he slowly takes the letter from her. He is about to open it when she suddenly seizes his arm.... Passionately, entreatingly*) You must forgive her, Papa—you must forgive her—not for her sake—but for yours! I thought I hated you, but I don't. I pity you—I pity you.... And if you've any pity for yourself—forgive her....

(*He looks at her steadily for a moment; then puts her away from him. He opens and reads the letter. Nothing but his quickened breathing betrays the fury of emotions seething in him. His face, when at last he raises it from the letter, is a white mask. He stands motionless, staring before him and mechanically folding and refolding the letter. He turns and walks to the window, and his gait somehow gives the impression that he is blind. He throws open the window and stands in front of it with his back to the room and his hands clasped behind him, grasping the letter. The movement of his shoulders shows that he is breathing quickly and heavily. No one stirs.*)

BARRETT: (*half to himself, turning from the window*) Yes—yes.... Her dog.... (*A smile of indescribable ugliness flickers across his face*) Yes—I'll have her dog.... Octavius.

OCTAVIUS: Sir?

BARRETT: Her dog must be destroyed. At once.

HENRIETTA: But—

BARRETT: (*slightly raising his voice*) You will take it to the vet—tonight.... You understand me?... Tonight. (*A pause*) You understand me?

OCTAVIUS: (*desperately*) I really d-don't see what the p-poor little beast has d-done to—

BARRETT: (*ominously*) You understand me?

HENRIETTA: (*vainly trying to control the triumph in her voice*) In her letter to me Ba writes that she has taken Flush with her. . . .

(*A silence.* BARRETT *stands perfectly still, staring straight before him and mechanically tearing* ELIZABETH's *letter into little pieces, which drop to his feet.*)

CURTAIN

QUESTIONS

A. Understanding the action:

A dramatist has always had great difficulty in portraying a genius realistically.

1. Has Besier succeeded in the first meeting of Elizabeth and Browning in Act II and in their mutual declaration of love in Act III? Why or why not?
2. What conflicts are there in the play? Which are outer? Which characters have inner conflicts?
3. How does Besier maintain suspense in the play?
4. What are the functions of the Bella-Bevan and Henrietta-Cook love affairs in the play?
5. What part do letters play in the action?
6. Why does Elizabeth refuse to let her father use her Bible?
7. What incident finally causes Elizabeth to consent to marry Browning?
8. What part does Flush play?

B. Understanding the characters:

1. What differences are there in the attitudes of the three sisters toward their father?
2. What is Barrett's religion? What use does he make of it? What is Browning's? How is it suggested in the play?
3. What does Elizabeth mean when she refers to her father in Act V Scene I, "Until to-day—I've never really known him. He's not like other men. He's—dreadfully different. . ." Is Barrett insane? neurotic? obsessed? sadistic? or what?
4. What does Henrietta mean when she says her father once owned slaves in Jamaica, and as slavery has been abolished there, he carries it on in England?
5. What type of comic character is Bevan? Bella? Would she fit in *The School for Scandal?*
6. What is the significance of the scene between Barrett and Bella in Act II?
7. In the quarrel between Barrett and Elizabeth about the trip to Italy who is the selfish one? Explain.
8. What is Barrett's opinion of Browning? Browning's of Barrett?
9. To what type of poems is Elizabeth referring when she says to Browning: "You have never been yourself in any one of your poems. It's always somebody else speaking through you"?

C. Understanding the approach:

1. Near the end of Act III Elizabeth says to Browning, "You're a fighter—and you were born for victory and triumph." What does Browning say about this in his poem *Prospice* written shortly after his wife's death?
2. Poets are usually thought to be impractical. Was Browning? Does he possess the characteristics you associate with a typical poet? Explain.
3. What is Wilson's conception of poetry as revealed by her remark to the jittery Elizabeth in Act V, "Why don't you write some po'try, Miss? . . . That 'ud make the time pass nicely, I'm sure"?
4. How does the relation of parents to children in America today differ from that portrayed in this play?
5. When Barrett says to Elizabeth, "You must look up to me, and depend on me, and lean on me. You must share your thoughts with me, your hopes, your fears, your prayers. I want all your heart and all your soul . . .", is this deep parental love or destructive possessiveness?

D. Comparisons:

1. Compare Creon (in *Antigone*), Old Capulet (in *Romeo and Juliet*) and Barrett as fathers.
2. To get a more personal view of the Brownings read some of Elizabeth's *Sonnets from the Portuguese* and Browning's *One Word More.*

TENNESSEE WILLIAMS (1914-   )

Tennessee Williams, like Byron, awoke one morning and found himself famous. ("I was snatched out of virtual oblivion, and thrust into sudden prominence.") When on December 26, 1944, *The Glass Menagerie* opened in Chicago, perceptive critics at once recognized that a new and important playwright had appeared on the American scene. But his rise to fame was a slow, laborious climb with many setbacks.

A child of the "Gothic South" of Faulkner, Williams was born in Columbus, Mississippi, the second of three children. Because his father, a traveling salesman for a shoe company, was often away from home, the family lived with his maternal grandfather, an Episcopal rector. The happiness of his childhood was disturbed by two incidents which left deep psychological scars on the sensitive boy. In a fit of petulance he called their affectionate Negro nurse Ozzie a derogatory name; she left the house, never to return. For many years a feeling of guilt haunted him. Then an attack of diphtheria injured his heart so that he was confined to his room for a whole year. Reading and fantasies stimulated the imagination of the solitary boy ("I still beguile myself with fantasies at night"), but insomnia and hypochondria became his lifelong enemies.

When he was thirteen, the family moved from Mississippi—"a dark wide spacious land that you can breathe in"—to St. Louis into a "perpetually dim little apartment in a wilderness of identical brick and concrete structures." His sister, to whom he was closely attached, found it difficult to adjust to the ugliness of urban life with its glaring differences between the rich and the poor. His sister's room faced a narrow sunless area that he named Death Valley, for every night stray dogs cornered stray cats and tore them to pieces. By painting the furniture white, hanging white curtains, and collecting little glass animals, brother and sister tried to disperse some of the gloom of their surroundings and conquer their anxieties.

For two years he attended the University of Missouri, wrote some poetry, and won some prizes. The depression forced him to leave and go to work in a shoe company. ("The job was designed for insanity," he wrote later. "It was a living death.") After work he wrote unsaleable short stories and poetry. This double toil and frustration broke down his health, and he convalesced at the home of his grandparents. For a year he continued his education at Washington University in St. Louis and completed it at the University of Iowa, receiving his B.A. in 1938 as a drama major. During this period he wrote two plays, produced by The Mummers of St. Louis. One was fairly successful; the other, a complete failure.

Opposing his father's wish to reinstate him in the shoe factory and finding home unendurable, the restless youth for the next five years (like O'Neill, Sherwood Anderson, and Vachel Lindsay) became "that common American phenomenon, a rootless, wandering writer." A bellhop in New Orleans, a teletypist in Jacksonville, a feather picker on a pigeon ranch in California, an usher in a New York movie theatre, a reciter of racy verses in Greenwich Village dives—he traveled cross country, meanwhile writing more stories, poems, and one-act plays. Four short pieces, *American Blues*, dealing with victims of the depression, won a one-hundred-dollar prize competition from the Group Theatre and attracted the attention of the New York agent, Audrey Wood. In

January, 1940, two associates of the Theatre Guild, Theresa Helburn and John Gassner, gave him a scholarship to their advanced playwright's seminar where he wrote *Battle of Angels*. Produced by the Theatre Guild in Boston, the play proved to be a failure. It reappeared in revised form about a dozen years later under the title of *Orpheus Descending*.

Added to this professional humiliation were his rejection by the draft board as 4F and a series of four operations on his left eye for a cataract. Destitute, he again turned to the hand-to-mouth existence of a Bohemian. In 1943 events took a turn for the better. Awards from the American Academy, the Rockefeller Fellowship, and a six-months' Hollywood contract gave him the opportunity to write *The Glass Menagerie*. The remarkable performances of Laurette Taylor as the mother and Julie Haydon as the daughter made this play one of the highest achievements of the twentieth-century American theatre. It had a run of 561 performances and won the Drama Critics Award.

Even more successful was *A Streetcar Named Desire* in 1947. This play, performed by Vivien Leigh in England and by Jessica Tandy and Marlon Brando in America, won the Pulitzer Prize and many other awards. Other plays of Tennessee Williams that gave him an international reputation are *Summer and Smoke, The Rose Tattoo, Camino Real, Sweet Bird of Youth, Cat on a Hot Tin Roof*, and *The Night of the Iguana*. He also published some poetry, a volume of one-act plays, two volumes of short stories, and a novel, *The Roman Spring of Mrs. Stone*, which was presented as a film with Vivien Leigh in the leading role in 1961.

Tennessee Williams defined the central thread of meaning in his work in these words: "For me the dominating premise has been the need for understanding and tenderness and fortitude among individuals trapped by circumstance." His plays whether realistic or naturalistic express this philosophy of determinism by showing us neurotic characters driven by passions and forces they can neither understand nor control. These blighted souls are sensitive romantics who cannot adjust to the harsh realities of a brutal world. They are pitiful targets for "the slings and arrows of outrageous fortune," suffering from alienation and frustration, and in extreme cases driven to madness and death. What redeems Williams' portrayal of this sordid world is his brilliant, poetic dialogue, his deep compassion, his artistic sincerity, and his psychological understanding of human weaknesses.

With the exception of *The Glass Menagerie*, Williams' plays certainly reveal a shocking morbidity. Does this expression of human depravity stem from the dramatist's urge to exorcise private demons obsessing man's primitive nature or is it a faithful reflection of a twentieth-century world filled with anxieties and neuroses bred by unparalleled violence? This question has been frequently debated. One thing is evident: Mr. Williams has tried to express his reaction to the world as he sees it. His work is the product of a sensitive mind recoiling in horror before what strikes him as a banal, mechanical civilization (his portrayal of urban living in St. Louis and New Orleans reminds us of the swarming ant-heap city of Baudelaire), a civilization that, in his opinion, warps, frustrates, and finally destroys those who strive for the attainment of beauty, joy and happiness.

The two most important literary influences upon him—for the better or the worse—have been D. H. Lawrence and Anton Chekhov. From the first he acquired an obsessive interest in the part sex plays in human lives and from the second, a regard for the spiritual significance of trivial events and the importance of mood in a play. From Chekhov he appears to have derived his concern with "the tragedy of incomprehension"—that is, with the inability of people to understand one another.

INTRODUCTION TO *THE GLASS MENAGERIE*

The Glass Menagerie is a "memory play" in which the dramatist tries to come to terms with his troubled youth and to understand his own rebellion against his family. In this moving drama, Tom Wingfield, a sensitive man, constricted by poverty, drabness, and misunderstanding, takes flight into the reality of experience in the contemporary world.

The problem of the artist in using autobiographical material is not only to give it organic form and effective expression, but to place enough distance between himself and his earlier subjective experiences so that he may view them objectively.

In *The Glass Menagerie*, Williams, by his poetic imagination, careful selection of realistic details, and skillful use of theatrical techniques communicates the pathos of one American family leading "lives of quiet desperation." He shows us, as his Narrator says, "truth in the pleasant disguise of illusion."

By placing the pathetic Wingfield story in the larger framework of war and social upheaval, Williams reveals not the triviality but the universal nature of human hopes and frustrations, and of the destruction of romantic illusions by cruel reality.

In this play, Williams shows us in truly poetic fashion the great that lies in the little, the importance of the trivial. The microscope is as important an instrument of truth as the telescope. For though "nowadays the world is lit by lightning," rust still destroys more lives than bombardments. Tom, the sensitive and intelligent Narrator, is an objective observer and commentator, and, through time moving backward, also a subjective participator in the action of the play.

In this episodic play of seven carefully drawn vignettes, the dramatist has brought his four characters to life by his brilliant use of realistic dialogue. Amanda is the sentimental mother living in a dream world of Southern gentility perfumed by jonquils; Laura is the abnormally shy daughter as fragile as her glass collection; Tom is the trapped poet who rebels; "the gentleman caller" is the success-seeker who comes briefly into the Wingfield home from the bustling competitive world of a Dale Carnegie America. All these characters are honestly portrayed by the artistry of a poetic realist who has gained complete mastery over his material.

THE GLASS MENAGERIE

TENNESSEE WILLIAMS

CHARACTERS

AMANDA WINGFIELD, *the mother*　　TOM WINGFIELD, *her son*
LAURA WINGFIELD, *her daughter*　　JIM O'CONNOR, *the gentleman caller*

Scene: AN ALLEY IN ST. LOUIS

PART I. Preparation for a Gentleman Caller.
PART II. The Gentleman calls.
TIME: Now and the Past.

SCENE I

The Wingfield apartment is in the rear of the building, one of those vast hive-like conglomerations of cellular living-units that flower as warty growths in overcrowded urban centers of lower middle-class population and are symptomatic of the impulse of this largest and fundamentally enslaved section of American society to avoid fluidity and differentiation and to exist and function as one interfused mass of automatism.

The apartment faces an alley and is entered by a fire-escape, a structure whose name is a touch of accidental poetic truth, for all of these huge buildings are always burning with the slow and implacable fires of human desperation. The fire-escape is included in the set—that is, the landing of it and steps descending from it.

The scene is memory and is therefore nonrealistic. Memory takes a lot of poetic license. It omits some details; others are exaggerated, according to the emotional value of the articles it touches, for memory is seated predominantly in the heart. The interior is therefore rather dim and poetic.

At the rise of the curtain, the audience is faced with the dark, grim rear wall of the Wingfield tenement. This building, which runs parallel to the footlights, is flanked on both sides by dark, narrow alleys which run into murky canyons of tangled clotheslines, garbage cans and the sinister lattice-work of neighboring fire-escapes. It is up and down these side alleys that exterior entrances and exits are made, during the play. At the end of TOM's opening commentary, the dark tenement wall slowly reveals (by means of a transparency) the interior of the ground floor Wingfield apartment.

Downstage is the living room, which also serves as a sleeping room for LAURA, the sofa unfolding to make her bed. Upstage, center, and divided by a wide arch or second proscenium with transparent faded portieres (or second curtain), is the dining room. In an old-fashioned what-not in the living room are seen scores of transparent glass animals. A blown-up photograph of the father hangs on the wall of the living room, facing the audience, to the left of the archway. It is the face of a very handsome young man in a doughboy's First World War cap. He is gallantly smiling, ineluctably smiling, as if to say, "I will be smiling forever."

The audience hears and sees the opening scene in the dining room through both the transparent fourth wall of the building and the transparent gauze portieres of the dining-room arch. It is during this revealing scene that the fourth wall slowly ascends, out of sight. This transparent exterior wall is not brought down again until the very end of the play, during TOM's final speech.

The narrator is an undisguised convention of the play. He takes whatever license with dramatic convention as is convenient to his purposes.

TOM *enters dressed as a merchant sailor from alley, stage left, and strolls across the front of the stage to the fire-escape. There he stops and lights a cigarette. He addresses the audience.*

TOM: Yes, I have tricks in my pocket, I have things up my sleeve. But I am the opposite of a stage magician. He gives you illusion that has the appearance of truth. I give you truth in the pleasant disguise of illusion. To begin with, I turn back time. I reverse it to that quaint period, the thirties, when the huge middle class of America was matriculating in a school for the blind. Their eyes had failed them, or they had failed their eyes, and so they were having their fingers pressed forcibly down on the fiery Braille alphabet of a dissolving economy. In Spain there was revolution. Here there was only shouting and confusion. In Spain there was Guernica. Here there were disturbances of labor, sometimes pretty violent, in otherwise peaceful cities such as Chicago, Cleveland, Saint Louis . . . This is the social background of the play.

(MUSIC.)

(*Curtain.*)

The play is memory. Being a memory play, it is dimly lighted, it is sentimental, it is not realistic. In memory everything seems to happen to music. That explains the fiddle in the wings. I am the narrator of the play, and also a character in it. The other characters are my mother, Amanda, my sister, Laura, and a gentleman caller who appears in the final scenes. He is the most realistic character in the play, being an emissary from a world of reality that we were somehow set apart from. But since I have a poet's weakness for symbols, I am using this character also as a symbol; he is the long delayed but always expected something that we live for. There is a fifth character in the play who doesn't appear except in this larger-than-life photograph over the mantel. This is our father who left us a long time ago. He was a telephone man who fell in love with long distances; he gave up his job with the telephone company and skipped the light fantastic out of town . . . The last we heard of him was a picture post-card from Mazatlan, on the Pacific coast of Mexico, containing a message of two words— "Hello—Good-bye!" and no address. I think the rest of the play will explain itself. . . .

(AMANDA'S *voice becomes audible through the portieres.*)

(LEGEND ON SCREEN: "OÙ SONT LES NEIGES.")

(*He divides the portieres and enters the upstage area.*)

(AMANDA *and* LAURA *are seated at a drop-leaf table. Eating is indicated by gestures without food or utensils.* AMANDA *faces the audience.* TOM *and* LAURA *are seated in profile.*)

(*The interior has lit up softly and through

the scrim we see AMANDA and LAURA seated at the table in the upstage area.)

AMANDA: (calling) Tom?

TOM: Yes, Mother.

AMANDA: We can't say grace until you come to the table!

TOM: Coming, Mother. (*He bows slightly and withdraws, reappearing a few moments later in his place at the table.*)

AMANDA: (*to her son*) Honey, don't push with your *fingers*. If you have to push with something, the thing to push with is a crust of bread. And chew—chew! Animals have sections in their stomachs which enable them to digest food without mastication, but human beings are supposed to chew their food before they swallow it down. Eat food leisurely, son, and really enjoy it. A well-cooked meal has lots of delicate flavors that have to be held in the mouth for appreciation. So chew your food and give your salivary glands a chance to function!

(TOM *deliberately lays his imaginary fork down and pushes his chair back from the table.*)

TOM: I haven't enjoyed one bite of this dinner because of your constant directions on how to eat it. It's you that make me rush through meals with your hawk-like attention to every bite I take. Sickening—spoils my appetite—all this discussion of animals' secretion—salivary glands—mastication!

AMANDA: (*lightly*) Temperament like a Metropolitan star! (*He rises and crosses downstage.*) You're not excused from the table.

TOM: I'm getting a cigarette.

AMANDA: You smoke too much.
(LAURA *rises.*)

LAURA: I'll bring in the blanc mange. (*He remains standing with his cigarette by the portieres during the following.*)

AMANDA: (*rising*) No, sister, no, sister—you be the lady this time and I'll be the darky.

LAURA: I'm already up.

AMANDA: Resume your seat, little sister—I want you to stay fresh and pretty—for gentlemen callers!

LAURA: I'm not expecting any gentlemen callers.

AMANDA: (*crossing out to kitchenette. Airily*) Sometimes they come when they are least expected! Why, I remember one Sunday afternoon in Blue Mountain—(*Enters kitchenette.*)

TOM: I know what's coming!

LAURA: Yes. But let her tell it.

TOM: Again?

LAURA: She loves to tell it.

(AMANDA *returns with bowl of dessert.*)

AMANDA: One Sunday afternoon in Blue Mountain—your mother received—*seventeen!*—gentlemen callers! Why, sometimes there weren't chairs enough to accommodate them all. We had to send the servant over to bring in folding chairs from the parish house.

TOM: (*remaining at portieres*) How did you entertain those gentlemen callers?

AMANDA: I understood the art of conversation!

TOM: I bet you could talk.

AMANDA: Girls in those days *knew* how to talk, I can tell you.

TOM: Yes?

(IMAGE: AMANDA AS A GIRL ON A PORCH, GREETING CALLERS.)

AMANDA: They knew how to entertain their gentlemen callers. It wasn't enough for a girl to be possessed of a pretty face and a graceful figure—although I wasn't slighted in either respect. She also needed to have a nimble wit and a tongue to meet all occasions.

TOM: What did you talk about?

AMANDA: Things of importance going on in the world! Never anything coarse or common or vulgar. (*She addresses* TOM *as though he were seated in the vacant chair at the table though he remains by portieres. He plays this scene as though he held the book.*) My callers were gentlemen—all! Among my callers were some of the most prominent young planters of the Mississippi Delta—planters and sons of planters!

(TOM *motions for music and a spot of light on* AMANDA.)

(*Her eyes lift, her face glows, her voice becomes rich and elegiac.*)

(SCREEN LEGEND: "OU SONT LES NEIGES.") There was young Champ Laughlin who later became vice-president of the Delta Planters Bank. Hadley Stevenson who was drowned in Moon Lake and left his widow one hundred and fifty thousand in Government bonds. There were the Cutrere brothers, Wesley and Bates. Bates was one of my bright particular beaux! He got in a quarrel with that wild Wainwright boy. They shot it out on the floor of Moon Lake Casino. Bates was shot through the stomach. Died in the ambulance on his way to Memphis. His widow was also well-provided for, came into eight or ten thousand acres, that's all. She married him on the rebound—never loved her—carried my picture on him the night he died! And there was that boy that every girl in the Delta had set her cap for! That beautiful, brilliant young Fitzhugh boy from Greene County!

TOM: What did he leave his widow?

AMANDA: He never married! Gracious, you talk as though all of my old admirers had turned up their toes to the daisies!

TOM: Isn't this the first you've mentioned that still survives?

AMANDA: That Fitzhugh boy went North and made a fortune—came to be known as the Wolf of Wall Street! He had the Midas touch, whatever he touched turned to gold! And I could have been Mrs. Duncan J. Fitzhugh, mind you! But —I picked your *father*!

LAURA: (*rising*) Mother, let me clear the table.

AMANDA: No, dear, you go in front and study your typewriter chart. Or practice your shorthand a little. Stay fresh and pretty!—It's almost time for our gentlemen callers to start ariving. (*She flounces girlishly toward the kitchenette.*) How many do you supose we're going to entertain this afternoon?

(TOM *throws down the paper and jumps up with a groan.*)

LAURA: (*alone in the dining room*) I don't believe we're going to receive any, Mother.

AMANDA: (*reappearing, airily*) What? No one—not one? You must be joking! (LAURA *nervously echoes her laugh. She slips in a fugitive manner through the half-open portieres and draws them gently behind her. A shaft of very clear light is thrown on her face against the faded tapestry of the curtains.* MUSIC: "THE GLASS MENAGERIE" UNDER FAINTLY. *Lightly:*) Not one gentleman caller? It can't be true! There must be a flood, there must have been a tornado!

LAURA: It isn't a flood, it's not a tornado, Mother. I'm just not popular like you were in Blue Mountain. . . . (TOM *utters another groan.* LAURA *glances at him with a faint apologetic smile. Her voice catching a little.*) Mother's afraid I'm going to be an old maid.

THE SCENE DIMS OUT WITH "GLASS MENAGERIE" MUSIC.

SCENE II

(LEGEND ON SCREEN: "LAURA, HAVEN'T YOU EVER LIKED SOME BOY?")

(*On the dark stage the screen is lighted with the image of blue roses.*

Gradually LAURA'S *figure becomes apparent and the screen goes out.*

The music subsides.

LAURA *is seated in the delicate ivory chair at the small claw-foot table.*

She wears a dress of soft violet material

for a kimono—her hair tied back from her forehead with a ribbon.

She is washing and polishing her collection of glass.

AMANDA *appears on the fire-escape steps. At the sound of her ascent,* LAURA *catches her breath, thrusts the bowl of ornaments away and seats herself stiffly before the diagram of the typewriter keyboard as though it held her spellbound. Something has happened to* AMANDA. *It is written in her face as she climbs to the landing: a look that is grim and hopeless and a little absurd.*

She has on one of those cheap or imitation velvety-looking cloth coats with imitation fur collar. Her hat is five or six years old, one of those dreadful cloche hats that were worn in the late twenties and she is clasping an enormous black patent-leather pocketbook with nickel clasps and initials. This is her full-dress outfit, the one she usually wears to the D.A.R.

Before entering she looks through the door.

She purses her lips, opens her eyes wide, rolls them upward and shakes her head.

Then she slowly lets herself in the door. Seeing her mother's expression LAURA *touches her lips with a nervous gesture.)*

LAURA: Hello, Mother, I was— (*She makes a nervous gesture toward the chart on the wall.* AMANDA *leans against the shut door and stares at* LAURA *with a martyred look.*)

AMANDA: Deception? Deception? (*She slowly removes her hat and gloves, continuing the sweet suffering stare. She lets the hat and gloves fall on the floor—a bit of acting.*)

LAURA: (*shakily*) How was the D.A.R. meeting? (AMANDA *slowly opens her purse and removes a dainty white handkerchief which she shakes out delicately and delicately touches to her lips and nostrils.*) Didn't you go to the D.A.R. meeting, Mother?

AMANDA: (*faintly, almost inaudibly*) —No.—No. (*Then more forcibly:*) I did not have the strength—to go to the D.A.R. In fact, I did not have the courage! I wanted to find a hole in the ground and hide myself in it forever! (*She crosses slowly to the wall and removes the diagram of the typewriter keyboard. She holds it in front of her for a second, staring at it sweetly and sorrowfully—then bites her lips and tears it in two pieces.*)

LAURA: (*faintly*) Why did you do that, Mother? (AMANDA *repeats the same procedure with the chart of the* Gregg *Alphabet.*) Why are you—

AMANDA: Why? Why? How old are you, Laura?

LAURA: Mother, you know my age.

AMANDA: I thought that you were an adult; it seems that I was mistaken. (*She crosses slowly to the sofa and sinks down and stares at* LAURA.)

LAURA: Please don't stare at me, Mother.

(AMANDA *closes her eyes and lowers her head. Count ten.*)

AMANDA: What are we going to do, what is going to become of us, what is the future?

(*Count ten.*)

LAURA: Has something happened, Mother? (AMANDA *draws a long breath and takes out the handkerchief again. Dabbing process.*) Mother, has—something happened?

AMANDA: I'll be all right in a minute. I'm just bewildered—(*Count five*)—by life....

LAURA: Mother, I wish that you would tell me what's happened!

AMANDA: As you know, I was supposed to be inducted into my office at the D.A.R. this afternoon. (IMAGE ON SCREEN: A SWARM OF TYPEWRITERS.) But I stopped off at Rubicam's Business College to speak to your teachers about your having a cold and ask them what progress they thought you were making down there.

LAURA: Oh....

AMANDA: I went to the typing instructor and introduced myself as your mother. She didn't know who you were. Wingfield, she said. We don't have any such student enrolled at the school! I assured her she did, that you had been going to classes since early in January. "I wonder," she said, "if you could be talking about that terribly shy little girl who dropped out of school after only a few days' attendance?" "No," I said, "Laura, my daughter has been going to school every day for the past six weeks!" "Excuse me," she said. She took the attendance book out and there was your name, unmistakably printed, and all the dates you were absent until they decided that you had dropped out of school. I still said, "No, there must have been some mistake! There must have been some mix-up in the records!" And she said, "No—I remember her perfectly now. Her hands shook so that she couldn't hit the right keys! The first time we gave a speed-test, she broke down completely—was sick at the stomach and almost had to be carried into the wash-room! After that morning she never showed up any more. We phoned the house but never got any answer—while I was working at Famous and Barr, I suppose, demonstrating those— Oh!" I felt so weak I could barely keep on my feet! I had to sit down while they got me a glass of water! Fifty dollars' tuition, all of our plans—my hopes and ambitions for you —just gone up the spout, just gone up the spout like that. (LAURA *draws a long breath and gets awkwardly to her feet. She crosses to the victrola and winds it up.*) What are you doing?

LAURA: Oh! (*She releases the handle and returns to her seat.*)

AMANDA: Laura, where have you been going when you've gone out pretending that you were going to business college?

LAURA: I've just been going out walking.

AMANDA: That's not true.

LAURA: It is. I just went walking.

AMANDA: Walking? Walking? In winter? Deliberately courting pneumonia in that light coat? Where did you walk to, Laura?

LAURA: All sorts of places—mostly in the park.

AMANDA: Even after you'd started catching that cold?

LAURA: It was the lesser of two evils, Mother. (IMAGE ON SCREEN: WINTER SCENE IN PARK.) I couldn't go back up. I—threw up—on the floor!

AMANDA: From half past seven till after five every day you mean to tell me you walked around in the park, because you wanted to make me think that you were still going to Rubicam's Business College?

LAURA: It wasn't as bad as it sounds. I went inside places to get warmed up.

AMANDA: Inside where?

LAURA: I went in the art museum and the bird-houses at the Zoo. I visited the penguins every day! Sometimes I did without lunch and went to the movies. Lately I've been spending most of my afternoons in the Jewel-box, that big glass house where they raise the tropical flowers.

AMANDA: You did all this to deceive me, just for deception? (LAURA *looks down.*) Why?

LAURA: Mother, when you're disappointed, you get that awful suffering look on your face, like the picture of Jesus' mother in the museum!

AMANDA: Hush!

LAURA: I couldn't face it.

(*Pause. A whisper of strings.*)

(LEGEND ON SCREEN: "THE CRUST OF HUMILITY.")

AMANDA: (*hopelessly fingering the huge pocketbook*) So what are we going to do the rest of our lives? Stay home and watch the parades go by? Amuse ourselves with the glass menagerie, darling?

Eternally play those worn-out phonograph records your father left as a painful reminder of him? We won't have a business career—we've given that up because it gave us nervous indigestion! (*Laughs wearily.*) What is there left but dependency all our lives? I know so well what becomes of unmarried women who aren't prepared to occupy a position. I've seen such pitiful cases in the South—barely tolerated spinsters living upon the grudging patronage of sister's husband or brother's wife!—stuck away in some little mouse-trap of a room—encouraged by one in-law to visit another—little birdlike women without any nest—eating the crust of humility all their life! Is that the future that we've mapped out for ourselves? I swear it's the only alternative I can think of! It isn't a very pleasant alternative, is it? Of course—some girls *do* marry. (LAURA *twists her hands nervously.*) Haven't you ever liked some boy?

LAURA: Yes. I liked one once. (*Rises.*) I came across his picture a while ago.

AMANDA: (*with some interest*) He gave you his picture?

LAURA: No, it's in the yearbook.

AMANDA: (*disappointed*) Oh—a high-school boy.

(SCREEN IMAGE: JIM AS HIGH-SCHOOL HERO BEARING A SILVER CUP.)

LAURA: Yes. His name was Jim. (LAURA *lifts the heavy annual from the claw-foot table.*) Here he is in *The Pirates of Penzance*.

LAURA: The operetta the senior class put on. He had a wonderful voice and we sat across the aisle from each other Mondays, Wednesdays and Fridays in the Aud. Here he is with the silver cup for debating! See his grin?

AMANDA: (*absently*) He must have had a jolly disposition.

LAURA: He used to call me— Blue Roses.

(IMAGE ON SCREEN: BLUE ROSES.)

AMANDA: Why did he call you such a name as that?

LAURA: When I had that attack of pleurosis—he asked me what was the matter when I came back. I said pleurosis—he thought that I said Blue Roses! So that's what he always called me after that. Whenever he saw me, he'd holler, "Hello, Blue Roses!" I didn't care for the girl that he went out with. Emily Meisenbach. Emily was the best-dressed girl at Soldan. She never struck me, though, as being sincere . . . It says in the Personal Section —they're engaged. That's—six years ago! They must be married by now.

AMANDA: Girls that aren't cut out for business careers usually wind up married to some nice man. (*Gets up with a spark of revival.*) Sister, that's what you'll do! (LAURA *utters a startled, doubtful laugh. She reaches quickly for a piece of glass.*)

LAURA: But, Mother—

AMANDA: Yes? (*Crossing to photograph.*)

LAURA: (*in a tone of frightened apology*) I'm—crippled!

(IMAGE: SCREEN.)

AMANDA: Nonsense! Laura, I've told you never, never to use that word. Why, you're not crippled, you just have a little defect—hardly noticeable, even! When people have some slight disadvantage like that, they cultivate other things to make up for it—develop charm—and vivacity —and—*charm!* That's all you have to do! (*She turns again to the photograph.*) One thing your father had *plenty of*—was *charm!*

(TOM *motions to the fiddle in the wings.*)

THE SCENE FADES OUT WITH MUSIC

SCENE III

(LEGEND ON SCREEN: "AFTER THE FIASCO—")

(TOM *speaks from the fire-escape landing.*)

TOM: After the fiasco at Rubicam's Business College, the idea of getting a gentleman caller for Laura began to play a more important part in Mother's calculations. It became an obsession. Like some archetype of the universal unconscious, the image of the gentleman caller haunted our small apartment. . . . (IMAGE ON SCREEN: YOUNG MAN AT DOOR WITH FLOWERS.) An evening at home rarely passed without some allusion to this image, this spectre, this hope. . . . Even when he wasn't mentioned, his presence hung in Mother's preoccupied look and in my sister's frightened, apologetic manner—hung like a sentence passed upon the Wingfields! Mother was a woman of action as well as words. She began to take logical steps in the planned direction. Late that winter and in the early spring—realizing that extra money would be needed to properly feather the nest and plume the bird—she conducted a vigorous campaign on the telephone, roping in subscribers to one of those magazines for matrons called *The Homemaker's Companion,* the type of journal that features the serialized sublimations of ladies of letters who think in terms of delicate cuplike breasts, slim, tapering waists, rich, creamy thighs, eyes like wood-smoke in autumn, fingers that soothe and caress like strains of music, bodies as powerful as Etruscan sculpture.

(SCREEN IMAGES: GLAMOR MAGAZINE COVER.)

(AMANDA *enters with phone on long extension cord. She is spotted in the dim stage.*)

AMANDA: Ida Scott? This is Amanda Wingfield! We *missed* you at the D.A.R. last Monday! I said to myself: She's probably suffering with that sinus condition! How is that sinus condition? Horrors! Heaven have mercy!— You're a Christian martyr, yes, that's what you are, a Christian martyr! Well, I just now happened to notice that your subscription to the *Companion's* about to expire! Yes, it expires with the next issue, honey!—just when that wonderful new serial by Bessie Mae Hopper is getting off to such an exciting start. Oh, honey, it's something that you can't miss! You remember how *Gone With the Wind* took everybody by storm? You simply couldn't go out if you hadn't read it. All everybody *talked* was Scarlett O'Hara. Well, this is a book that critics already compare to *Gone With the Wind.* It's the *Gone With the Wind* of the post-World War generation!— What?— Burning?— Oh, honey, don't let them burn, go take a look in the oven and I'll hold the wire! Heavens—I think she's hung up!

DIM OUT

(LEGEND ON SCREEN: "YOU THINK I'M IN LOVE WITH CONTINENTAL SHOEMAKERS?") (*Before the stage is lighted, the violent voices of* TOM *and* AMANDA *are heard.*) (*They are quarreling behind the portieres. In front of them stands* LAURA *with clenched hands and panicky expression.*) (*A clear pool of light on her figure throughout this scene.*)

TOM: What in Christ's name am I—

AMANDA: (*shrilly*) Don't you use that—

TOM: Supposed to do!

AMANDA: Expression! Not in my—

TOM: Ohhh!

AMANDA: Presence! Have you gone out of your senses?

TOM: I have, that's true, *driven* out!

AMANDA: What is the matter with you, you—big—big—IDIOT!

TOM: Look—I've got *no thing,* no single thing—

AMANDA: Lower your voice!

TOM: In my life here that I can call my OWN! Everything is—

AMANDA: Stop that shouting!

TOM: Yesterday you confiscated my books! You had the nerve to—

AMANDA: I took that horrible novel back to the library—yes! That hideous book by that insane Mr. Lawrence. (TOM *laughs wildly.*) I cannot control the output of diseased minds or people who cater to them—(TOM *laughs still more wildly.*) BUT I WON'T ALLOW SUCH FILTH BROUGHT INTO MY HOUSE! No, no, no, no, no!

TOM: House, house! Who pays rent on it, who makes a slave of himself to—

AMANDA: (*fairly screeching*) Don't you DARE to—

TOM: No, no, *I* mustn't say things! *I've* got to just—

AMANDA: Let me tell you—

TOM: I don't want to hear any more! (*He tears the portieres open. The upstage area is lit with a turgid smoky red glow.*) (AMANDA's *hair is in metal curlers and she wears a very old bathrobe, much too large for her slight figure, a relic of the faithless Mr. Wingfield.*)

(*An upright typewriter and a wild disarray of manuscripts is on the drop-leaf table. The quarrel was probably precipitated by* AMANDA's *interruption of his creative labor. A chair lying overthrown on the floor.*)

(*Their gesticulating shadows are cast on the ceiling by the fiery glow.*)

AMANDA: You *will* hear more, you—

TOM: No, I won't hear more, I'm going out!

AMANDA: You come right back in—

TOM: Out, out out! Because I'm—

AMANDA: Come back here, Tom Wingfield! I'm not through talking to you!

TOM: Oh, go—

LAURA: (*desperately*)—Tom!

AMANDA: You're going to listen, and no more insolence from you! I'm at the end of my patience! (*He comes back toward her.*)

TOM: What do you think I'm at? Aren't I suppose to have any patience to reach the end of, Mother? I know, I know. It seems unimportant to you, what I'm *doing*—what I *want* to do—having a little *difference* between them! You don't think that—

AMANDA: I think you've been doing things that you're ashamed of. That's why you act like this. I don't believe that you go every night to the movies. Nobody goes to the movies night after night. Nobody in their right minds goes to the movies as often as you pretend to. People don't go to the movies at nearly midnight, and movies don't let out at two A.M. Come in stumbling. Muttering to yourself like a maniac! You get three hours' sleep and then go to work. Oh, I can picture the way you're doing down there. Moping, doping, because you're in no condition.

TOM: (*wildly*) No, I'm in no condition!

AMANDA: What right have you got to jeopardize your job? Jeopardize the security of us all? How do you think we'd manage if you were—

TOM: Listen! You think I'm crazy about the *warehouse*? (*He bends fiercely toward her slight figure.*) You think I'm in love with the Continental Shoemakers? You think I want to spend fifty-five *years* down there in that—*celotex interior!* with —*fluorescent—tubes!* Look! I'd rather somebody picked up a crowbar and battered out my brains—than go back mornings! I *go!* Every time you come in yelling that God damn *"Rise and Shine!" "Rise and Shine!"* I say to myself, "How *lucky dead* people are!" But I get up. I *go!* For sixty-five dollars a month I give up all that I dream of doing and being *ever!* And you say self—*self's* all I ever think of. Why, listen, if self is what I thought of, Mother, I'd be where he is—GONE! (*Pointing to father's picture.*) As far as the system of transportation reaches! (*He starts past her. She grabs his arm.*) Don't grab at me, Mother!

AMANDA: Where are you going?

TOM: I'm going to the *movies!*

AMANDA: I don't believe that lie!

TOM: (*crouching toward her, over-*

towering her tiny figure. She backs away, gasping) I'm going to opium dens! Yes, opium dens, dens of vice and criminals' hang-outs, Mother. I've joined the Hogan gang, I'm a hired assassin, I carry a tommy-gun in a violin case! I run a string of cat-houses in the Valley! They call me Killer, Killer Wingfield, I'm leading a double-life, a simple, honest warehouse worker by day, by night, a dynamic *czar* of the *underworld, Mother.* I go to gambling casinos, I spin away fortunes on the roulette table! I wear a patch over one eye and a false mustache, sometimes I put on green whiskers. On those occasions they call me—*El Diablo!* Oh, I could tell you things to make you sleepless! My enemies plan to dynamite this place. They're going to blow us all sky-high some night! I'll be glad, very happy, and so will you! You'll go up, up on a broomstick, over Blue Mountain with seventeen gentlemen callers! You ugly—babbling old—witch.... (*He goes through a series of violent, clumsy movements, seizing his overcoat, lunging to the door, pulling it fiercely open. The women watch him, aghast. His arm catches in the sleeve of the coat as he struggles to pull it on. For a moment he is pinioned by the bulky garment. With an outraged groan he tears the coat off again, splitting the shoulder of it, and hurls it across the room. It strikes against the shelf of* LAURA'S *glass collection, there is a tinkle of shattering glass.* LAURA *cries out as if wounded.*)

(MUSIC LEGEND: "THE GLASS MENAGERIE.")

LAURA: (*shrilly*) My glass!—menagerie.... (*She covers her face and turns away.*)

(*But* AMANDA *is still stunned and stupefied by the "ugly witch" so that she barely notices this occurrence. Now she recovers her speech.*)

AMANDA: (*in an awful voice*) I won't speak to you—until you apologize! (*She crosses through portieres and draws them together behind her.* TOM *is left with* LAURA. LAURA *clings weakly to the mantel with her face averted.* TOM *stares at her stupidly for a moment. Then he crosses to shelf. Drops awkwardly on his knees to collect the fallen glass, glancing at* LAURA *as if he would speak but couldn't.*)

"The Glass Menagerie" steals in as

THE SCENE DIMS OUT

SCENE IV

(*The interior is dark. Faint light in the alley.*

A deep-voiced bell in a church is tolling the hour of five as the scene commences.

TOM *appears at the top of the alley. After each solemn boom of the bell in the tower, he shakes a little noise-maker or rattle as if to express the tiny spasm of man in contrast to the sustained power and dignity of the Almighty. This and the unsteadiness of his advance make it evident that he has been drinking.*

As he climbs the few steps to the fire-escape landing light steals up inside. LAURA *appears in night-dress, observing* TOM'S *empty bed in the front room.*

TOM *fishes in his pockets for door-key, removing a motley assortment of articles in the search, including a perfect shower of movie-ticket stubs and an empty bottle. At last he finds the key, but just as he is about to insert it, it slips from his fingers. He strikes a match and crouches below the door.*)

TOM: (*bitterly*) One crack—and it falls through!

(LAURA *opens the door.*)

LAURA: Tom! Tom, what are you doing?

TOM: Looking for a door-key.

LAURA: Where have you been all this time?

TOM: I have been to the movies.

LAURA: All this time at the movies?

TOM: There was a very long program. There was a Garbo picture and a Mickey Mouse and a travelogue and a news-reel and a preview of coming attractions. And there was an organ solo and a collection for the milk-fund—simultaneously—which ended up in a terrible fight between a fat lady and an usher!

LAURA: (*innocently*) Did you have to stay through everything?

TOM: Of course! And, oh, I forgot! There was a big stage show! The headliner on this stage show was Malvolio the Magician. He performed wonderful tricks, many of them, such as pouring water back and forth between pitchers. First it turned to wine and then it turned to beer and then it turned to whiskey. I know it was whiskey it finally turned into because he needed somebody to come up out of the audience to help him, and I came up—both shows! It was Kentucky Straight Bourbon. A very generous fellow, he gave souvenirs. (*He pulls from his back pocket a shimmering rainbow-colored scarf.*) He gave me this. This is his magic scarf. You can have it, Laura. You wave it over a canary cage and you get a bowl of gold-fish. You wave it over the gold-fish bowl and they fly away canaries. . . . But the wonderfullest trick of all was the coffin trick. We nailed him into a coffin and he got out of the coffin without removing one nail. (*He has come inside.*) There is a trick that would come in handy for me—get me out of this 2 by 4 situation! (*Flops onto bed and starts removing shoes.*)

LAURA: Tom—Shhh!

TOM: What're you shushing me for?

LAURA: You'll wake up Mother.

TOM: Goody, goody! Pay 'er back for all those "Rise an' Shines." (*Lies down, groaning.*) You know it don't take much intelligence to get yourself into a nailed-up coffin, Laura. But who in hell ever got himself out of one without removing one nail?

(*As if in answer, the father's grinning photograph lights up.*)

SCENE DIMS OUT

(*Immediately following: The church bell is heard striking six. At the sixth stroke the alarm clock goes off in* AMANDA'S *room, and after a few moments we hear her calling: "Rise and Shine! Rise and Shine! Laura, go tell your brother to rise and shine!"*)

TOM: (*Sitting up slowly*) I'll rise—but I won't shine.

(*The light increases.*)

AMANDA: Laura, tell your brother his coffee is ready.

(LAURA *slips into front room.*)

LAURA: Tom, it's nearly seven. Don't make Mother nervous. (*He stares at her stupidly. Beseechingly.*) Tom, speak to Mother this morning. Make up with her, apologize, speak to her!

TOM: She won't to me. It's her that started not speaking.

LAURA: If you just say you're sorry she'll start speaking.

TOM: Her not speaking—is that such a tragedy?

LAURA: Please—please!

AMANDA: (*calling from kitchenette*) Laura, are you going to do what I asked you to do, or do I have to get dressed and go out myself?

LAURA: Going, going—soon as I get on my coat! (*She pulls on a shapeless felt hat with nervous, jerky movement, pleadingly glancing at* TOM. *Rushes awkwardly for coat. The coat is one of* AMANDA'S, *inaccurately made-over, the sleeves too short for* LAURA) Butter and what else?

AMANDA: (*entering upstage*) Just butter. Tell them to charge it.

LAURA: Mother, they make such faces when I do that.

AMANDA: Sticks and stones can break our bones, but the expression on Mr.

Garfinkel's face won't harm us! Tell your brother his coffee is getting cold.

LAURA: (*at door*) Do what I asked you, will you, will you, Tom?

(*He looks sullenly away.*)

AMANDA: Laura, go now or just don't go at all!

LAURA: (*rushing out*) Going—going! (*A second later she cries out.* TOM *springs up and crosses to door.* AMANDA *rushes anxiously in.* TOM *opens the door.*)

TOM: Laura?

LAURA: I'm all right. I slipped, but I'm all right.

AMANDA: (*peering anxiously after her*) If anyone breaks a leg on those fire-escape steps, the landlord ought to be sued for every cent he possesses! (*She shuts door. Remembers she isn't speaking and returns to other room.*)

(*As* TOM *enters listlessly for his coffee, she turns her back to him and stands rigidly facing the window on the gloomy gray vault of the areaway. Its light on her face with its aged but childish features is cruelly sharp, satirical as a Daumier print.*)

(MUSIC UNDER SCENE: "AVE MARIA.")

(TOM *glances sheepishly but sullenly at her averted figure and slumps at the table. The coffee is scalding hot; he sips it and gasps and spits it back in the cup. At his gasp,* AMANDA *catches her breath and half turns. Then catches herself and turns back to window.*)

(TOM *blows on his coffee, glancing sidewise at his mother. She clears her throat.* TOM *clears his. He starts to rise. Sinks back down again, scratches his head, clears his throat again,* AMANDA *coughs.* TOM *raises his cup in both hands to blow on it, his eyes staring over the rim of it at his mother for several moments. Then he slowly sets the cups down and awkwardly and hesitantly rises from the chair.*)

TOM: (*hoarsely*) Mother. I—I apologize. Mother. (AMANDA *draws a quick, shuddering breath. Her face works grotesquely. She breaks into childlike tears.*) I'm sorry for what I said, for everything that I said, I didn't mean it.

AMANDA: (*sobbingly*) My devotion has made me a witch and so I make myself hateful to my children!

TOM: *No,* you *don't.*

AMANDA: I worry so much, don't sleep, it makes me nervous!

TOM: (*gently*) I understand that.

AMANDA: I've had to put up a solitary battle all these years. But you're my right-hand bower! Don't fall down, don't fail!

TOM: (*gently*) I try, Mother.

AMANDA: (*with great enthusiasm*) Try and you will SUCCEED! (*The notion makes her breathless.*) Why, you—you're just *full* of natural endowments! Both of my children—they're *unusual* children! Don't you think I know it? I'm so—*proud!* Happy and—feel I've—so much to be thankful for but— Promise me one thing, son!

TOM: What, Mother?

AMANDA: Promise, son, you'll—never be a drunkard!

TOM: (*turns to her grinning*) I will never be a drunkard, Mother.

AMANDA: That's what frightened me so, that you'd be drinking! Eat a bowl of Purina!

TOM: Just coffee, Mother.

AMANDA: Shredded wheat biscuit?

TOM: No. No, Mother, just coffee.

AMANDA: You can't put in a day's work on an empty stomach. You've got ten minutes—don't gulp! Drinking too-hot liquids makes cancer of the stomach. . . . Put cream in.

TOM: No, thank you.

AMANDA: To cool it.

TOM: No! No, thank you, I want it black.

AMANDA: I know, but it's not good for

you. We have to do all that we can to build ourselves up. In these trying times we live in, all that we have to cling to is —each other.... That's why it's so important to— Tom, I— I sent out your sister so I could discuss something with you. If you hadn't spoken I would have spoken to you. (*Sits down.*)

TOM: (*gently*) What is it, Mother, that you want to discuss?

AMANDA: *Laura!*

(TOM *puts his cup down slowly.*)

(LEGEND ON SCREEN: "LAURA.")

(MUSIC: "THE GLASS MENAGERIE.")

TOM: —Oh.—Laura...

AMANDA: (*touching his sleeve*) You know how Laura is. So quiet but—still water runs deep! She notices things and I think she—broods about them. (TOM *looks up.*) A few days ago I came in and she was crying.

TOM: What about?

AMANDA: You.

TOM: Me?

AMANDA: She has an idea that you're not happy here.

TOM: What gave her that idea?

AMANDA: What gives her any idea? However, you do act strangely. I—I'm not criticizing, understand *that!* I know your ambitions do not lie in the warehouse, that like everybody in the whole wide world—you've had to—make sacrifices, but—Tom—Tom—life's not easy, it calls for—Spartan endurance! There's so many things in my heart that I cannot describe to you! I've never told you but I—*loved* your father....

TOM: (*gently*) I know that, Mother.

AMANDA: And you—when I see you taking after his ways! Staying out late—and—well, you *had* been drinking the night you were in that—terrifying condition! Laura says that you hate the apartment and that you go out nights to get away from it! Is that true, Tom?

TOM: No. You say there's so much in your heart that you can't describe to me. That's true of me, too. There's so much in my heart that I can't describe to *you!* So let's respect each other's—

AMANDA: But, why—*why*, Tom—are you always so *restless?* Where do you *go* to, nights?

TOM: I—go to the movies.

AMANDA: Why do you go to the movies so much, Tom?

TOM: I go to the movies because—I like adventure. Adventure is something I don't have much of at work, so I go to the movies.

AMANDA: But, Tom, you go to the movies *entirely* too *much!*

TOM: I like a lot of adventure.

(AMANDA *looks baffled, then hurt. As the familiar inquisition resumes he becomes hard and impatient again.* AMANDA *slips back into her querulous attitude toward him.*)

(IMAGE ON SCREEN: SAILING VESSEL WITH JOLLY ROGER.)

AMANDA: Most young men find adventure in their careers.

TOM: Then most young men are not employed in a warehouse.

AMANDA: The world is full of young men employed in warehouses and offices and factories.

TOM: Do all of them find adventure in their careers?

AMANDA: They do or they do without it! Not everybody has a craze for adventure.

TOM: Man is by instinct a lover, a hunter, a fighter, and none of those instincts are given much play at the warehouse!

AMANDA: Man is by instinct! Don't quote instinct to me! Instinct is something that people have got away from! It belongs to animals! Christian adults don't want it!

TOM: What do Christian adults want, then, Mother?

AMANDA: Superior things! Things of

the mind and the spirit! Only animals have to satisfy instincts! Surely your aims are somewhat higher than theirs! Than monkeys—pigs—

TOM: I reckon they're not.

AMANDA: You're joking. However, that isn't what I wanted to discuss.

TOM: (*rising*) I haven't much time.

AMANDA: (*pushing his shoulders*) Sit down.

TOM: You want me to punch in red at the warehouse, Mother?

AMANDA: You have five minutes. I want to talk about Laura.

(LEGEND ON SCREEN: "PLANS AND PROVISIONS.")

TOM: All right! What about Laura?

AMANDA: We have to be making plans and provisions for her. She's older than you, two years, and nothing has happened. She just drifts along doing nothing. It frightens me terribly how she just drifts along.

TOM: I guess she's the type that people call home girls.

AMANDA: There's no such type, and if there is, it's a pity! That is unless the home is hers, with a husband!

TOM: What?

AMANDA: Oh, I can see the handwriting on the wall as plain as I see the nose in front of my face! It's terrifying! More and more you remind me of your father! He was out all hours without explanation —Then *left! Good-bye!* And me with the bag to hold. I saw that letter you got from the Merchant Marine. I know what you're dreaming of. I'm not standing here blindfolded. Very well, then. Then *do* it! But not till there's somebody to take your place.

TOM: What do you mean?

AMANDA: I mean that as soon as Laura has got somebody to take care of her, married, a home of her own, independent —why, then you'll be free to go wherever you please, on land, on sea, whichever way the wind blows you! But until that time you've got to look out for your sister. I don't say me because I'm old and don't matter! I say for your sister because she's young and dependent. I put her in business college—a dismal failure! Frightened her so it made her sick to her stomach. I took her over to the Young People's League at the church. Another fiasco. She spoke to nobody, nobody spoke to her. Now all she does is fool with those pieces of glass and play those worn-out records. What kind of a life is that for a girl to lead?

TOM: What can I do about it?

AMANDA: Overcome selfishness! Self, self, self is all that you ever think of! (TOM *springs up and crosses to get his coat. It is ugly and bulky. He pulls on a cap with earmuffs.*) Where is your muffler? Put your wool muffler on! (*He snatches it angrily from the closet and tosses it around his neck and pulls both ends tight.*) Tom! I haven't said what I had in mind to ask you.

TOM: I'm too late to—

AMANDA: (*catching his arm—very importunately. Then shyly*) Down at the warehouse, aren't there some—nice young men?

TOM: No!

AMANDA: There *must be*—some . . .

TOM: Mother—

(*Tom makes a protesting gesture.*)

AMANDA: Find out one that's clean-living—doesn't drink and—ask him out for sister!

TOM: What?

AMANDA: For *sister!* To *meet!* Get *acquainted!*

TOM: (*stamping to door*) Oh, my go-osh!

AMANDA: Will you? (*He opens door. Imploringly.*) Will you? (*He starts down.*) Will you? *Will* you, dear?

TOM: (*calling back*) Yes!

(AMANDA *closes the door hesitantly and*

with a troubled but faintly hopeful expression.)

(SCREEN IMAGE: GLAMOR MAGAZINE COVER.)

(Spot AMANDA at phone.)

AMANDA: Ella Cartwright? This is Amanda Wingfield! How are you, honey? How is that kidney condition? *Horrors!* You're a Christian martyr, yes, honey, that's what you are, a Christian martyr! Well, I just happened to notice in my little red book that your subscription to the *Companion* has just run out! I knew that you wouldn't want to miss out on the wonderful serial starting in this new issue. It's by Bessie Mae Hopper, the first thing she's written since *Honeymoon for Three*. Wasn't that a strange and interesting story? Well, this one is even lovelier, I believe. It has a sophisticated, society background. It's all about the horsey set on Long Island!

FADE OUT

SCENE V

(LEGEND ON SCREEN: "ANNUNCIATION." *Fade in with music.*)

(*It is early dusk of a spring evening. Supper has just been finished in the Wingfield apartment.* AMANDA *and* LAURA *in light colored dresses are removing dishes from the table, in the upstage area, which is shadowy, their movements formalized almost as a dance or ritual, their moving forms as pale and silent as moths.*)

(TOM, *in white shirt and trousers, rises from the table and crosses toward the fire-escape.*)

AMANDA: (*as he passes her*) Son, will you do me a favor?

TOM: What?

AMANDA: Comb your hair! You look so pretty when your hair is combed!

(TOM *slouches on sofa with evening paper. Enormous caption "Franco Triumphs."*) There is only one respect in which I would like you to emulate your father.

TOM: What respect is that?

AMANDA: The care he always took of his appearance. He never allowed himself to look untidy. (*He throws down the paper and crosses to fire-escape.*) Where are you going?

TOM: I'm going out to smoke.

AMANDA: You smoke too much. A pack a day at fifteen cents a pack. How much would that amount to in a month? Thirty times fifteen is how much, Tom? Figure it out and you will be astounded at what you could save. Enough to give you a night-school course in accounting at Washington U! Just think what a wonderful thing that would be for you, son!

(TOM *is unmoved by the thought.*)

TOM: I'd rather smoke. (*He steps out on landing, letting the screen door slam.*)

AMANDA: (*sharply*) I know! That's the tragedy of it. . . . (*Alone, she turns to look at her husband's picture.*)

(DANCE MUSIC: "ALL THE WORLD IS WAITING FOR THE SUNRISE!")

TOM: (*to the audience*) Across the alley from us was the Paradise Dance Hall. On evenings in spring the windows and doors were open and the music came outdoors. Sometimes the lights were turned out except for a large glass sphere that hung from the ceiling. It would turn slowly about and filter the dusk with delicate rainbow colors. Then the orchestra played a waltz or a tango, something that had a slow and sensuous rhythm. Couples would come outside, to the relative privacy of the alley. You could see them kissing behind ash-pits and telephone poles. This was the compensation for lives that passed like mine, without any change or adventure. Adventure and change were imminent in this year. They were waiting around the corner for all these kids. Suspended in the mist over Berchtesgaden, caught in the folds of Chamberlain's umbrella—In Spain there was Guernica! But here there was only hot swing music and liquor, dance halls, bars, and movies, and sex that hung in the gloom like a chandelier and flooded the world with brief, deceptive rainbows. . . . All the world was waiting for bombardments!

(AMANDA *turns from the picture and comes outside.*)

AMANDA: (*sighing*) A fire-escape landing's a poor excuse for a porch. (*She spreads a newspaper on a step and sits down, gracefully and demurely as if she were settling into a swing on a Mississippi veranda.*) What are you looking at?

TOM: The moon.

AMANDA: Is there a moon this evening?

TOM: It's rising over Garfinkel's Delicatessen.

AMANDA: So it is! A little silver slipper of a moon. Have you made a wish on it yet?

TOM: Um-hum.

AMANDA: What did you wish for?

TOM: That's a secret.

AMANDA: A secret, huh? Well, I won't tell mine either. I will be just as mysterious as you.

TOM: I bet I can guess what yours is.

AMANDA: Is my head so transparent?

TOM: You're not a sphinx.

AMANDA: No, I don't have secrets. I'll tell you what I wished for on the moon. Success and happiness for my precious children! I wish for that whenever there's a moon, and when there isn't a moon, I wish for it, too.

TOM: I thought perhaps you wished for a gentleman caller.

AMANDA: Why do you say that?

TOM: Don't you remember asking me to fetch one?

AMANDA: I remember suggesting that it would be nice for your sister if you brought home some nice young man from the warehouse. I think that I've made that suggestion more than once.

TOM: Yes, you have made it repeatedly.

AMANDA: Well?

TOM: We are going to have one.

AMANDA: *What?*

TOM: A gentleman caller!

(THE ANNUNCIATION IS CELEBRATED WITH MUSIC.)

(AMANDA *rises.*)

(IMAGE ON SCREEN: CALLER WITH BOUQUET.)

AMANDA: You mean you have asked some nice young man to come over?

TOM: Yep. I've asked him to dinner.

AMANDA: You really did?

TOM: I did!

AMANDA: You did, and did he—accept?

TOM: He did!

AMANDA: Well, well—well, well! That's —lovely!

TOM: I thought that you would be pleased.

AMANDA: It's definite, then?

TOM: Very definite.

AMANDA: Soon?

TOM: Very soon.

AMANDA: For heaven's sake, stop putting on and tell me some things, will you?

TOM: What things do you want me to tell you?

AMANDA: *Naturally* I would like to know when he's *coming!*

TOM: He's coming tomorrow.

AMANDA: *Tomorrow?*

TOM: Yep. Tomorrow.

AMANDA: But, Tom!

TOM: Yes, Mother?

AMANDA: Tomorrow gives me no time!

TOM: Time for what?

AMANDA: Preparations! Why didn't

you phone me at once, as soon as you asked him, the minute that he accepted? Then, don't you see, I could have been getting ready!

TOM: You don't have to make any fuss.

AMANDA: Oh, Tom, Tom, Tom, of course I have to make a fuss! I want things nice, not sloppy! Not thrown together. I'll certainly have to do some fast thinking, won't I?

TOM: I don't see why you have to think at all.

AMANDA: You just don't know. We can't have a gentleman caller in a pig-sty! All my wedding silver has to be polished, the monogrammed table linen ought to be laundered! The windows have to be washed and fresh curtains put up. And how about clothes? We have to *wear* something, don't we?

TOM: Mother, this boy is no one to make a fuss over!

AMANDA: Do you realize he's the first young man we've introduced to your sister? It's terrible, dreadful, disgraceful that poor little sister has never received a single gentleman caller! Tom, come inside! (*She opens the screen door.*)

TOM: What for?

AMANDA: I want to ask you some things.

TOM: If you're going to make such a fuss, I'll call it off, I'll tell him not to come!

AMANDA: You certainly won't do anything of the kind. Nothing offends people worse than broken engagements. It simply means I'll have to work like a Turk! We won't be brilliant, but we will pass inspection. Come on inside. (TOM *follows, groaning.*) Sit down.

TOM: Any particular place you would like me to sit?

AMANDA: Thank heavens I've got that new sofa! I'm also making payments on a floor lamp I'll have sent out! And put the chintz covers on, they'll brighten things up! Of course I'd hoped to have these walls re-papered.... What is the young man's name?

TOM: His name is O'Connor.

AMANDA: That, of course, means fish —tomorrow is Friday! I'll have that salmon loaf—with Durkee's dressing! What does he do? He works at the warehouse?

TOM: Of course! How else would I—

AMANDA: Tom, he—doesn't drink?

TOM: Why do you ask me that?

AMANDA: Your father *did!*

TOM: Don't get started on that!

AMANDA: He *does* drink, then?

TOM: Not that I know of!

AMANDA: Make sure, be certain! The last thing I want for my daughter's a boy who drinks!

TOM: Aren't you being a little bit premature? Mr. O'Connor has not yet appeared on the scene!

AMANDA: But will tomorrow. To meet your sister, and what do I know about his character? Nothing! Old maids are better off than wives of drunkards!

TOM: Oh, my God!

AMANDA: Be still!

TOM: (*leaning forward to whisper*) Lots of fellows meet girls whom they don't marry!

AMANDA: Oh, talk sensibly, Tom—and don't be sarcastic! (*She has gotten a hairbrush.*)

TOM: What are you doing?

AMANDA: I'm brushing that cow-lick down! What is this young man's position at the warehouse?

TOM: (*submitting grimly to the brush and the interrogation*) This young man's position is that of a shipping clerk, Mother.

AMANDA: Sounds to me like a fairly responsible job, the sort of a job *you* would be in if you just had more *get-up*. What is his salary? Have you any idea?

TOM: I would judge it to be approximately eight-five dollars a month.

AMANDA: Well—not princely, but—

TOM: Twenty more than I make.

AMANDA: Yes, how well I know! But for a family man, eight-five dollars a month is not much more than you can just get by on. . . .

TOM: Yes, but Mr. O'Connor is not a family man.

AMANDA: He might be, mightn't he? Some time in the future?

TOM: I see. Plans and provisions.

AMANDA: You are the only young man that I know of who ignores the fact that the future becomes the present, the present the past, and the past turns into everlasting regret if you don't plan for it!

TOM: I will think that over and see what I can make of it.

AMANDA: Don't be supercilious with your mother! Tell me some more about this—what do you call him?

TOM: James D. O'Connor. The D. is for Delaney.

AMANDA: Irish on *both* sides! *Gracious!* And doesn't drink?

TOM: Shall I call him up and ask him right this minute?

AMANDA: The only way to find out about those things is to make discreet inquiries at the proper moment. When I was a girl in Blue Mountain and it was suspected that a young man drank, the girl whose attentions he had been receiving, if any girl *was*, would sometimes speak to the minister of his church, or rather her father would if her father was living, and sort of feel him out on the young man's character. That is the way such things are discreetly handled to keep a young woman from making a tragic mistake!

TOM: Then how did you happen to make a tragic mistake?

AMANDA: That innocent look of your father's had everyone fooled! He *smiled*— the world was *enchanted!* No girl can do worse than put herself at the mercy of a handsome appearance! I hope that Mr. O'Connor is not too good-looking.

TOM: No, he's not too good-looking. He's covered with freckles and hasn't too much of a nose.

AMANDA: He's not right-down homely, though?

TOM: Not right-down homely. Just medium homely, I'd say.

AMANDA: Character's what to look for in a man.

TOM: That's what I've always said, Mother.

AMANDA: You've never said anything of the kind and I suspect you would never give it a thought.

TOM: Don't be so suspicious of me.

AMANDA: At least I hope he's the type that's up and coming.

TOM: I think he really goes in for self-improvement.

AMANDA: What reason have you to think so?

TOM: He goes to night school.

AMANDA: (*beaming*) Splendid! What does he do, I mean study?

TOM: Radio engineering and public speaking!

AMANDA: Then he has visions of being advanced in the world! Any young man who studies public speaking is aiming to have an executive job some day! And radio engineering? A thing for the future! Both of these facts are very illuminating. Those are the sort of things that a mother should know concerning any young man who comes to call on her daughter. Seriously or—not.

TOM: One little warning. He doesn't know about Laura. I didn't let on that we had dark ulterior motives. I just said, why don't you come and have dinner with us? He said okay and that was the whole conversation.

AMANDA: I bet it was! You're eloquent

as an oyster. However, he'll know about Laura when he gets here. When he sees how lovely and sweet and pretty she is, he'll thank his lucky stars he was asked to dinner.

TOM: Mother, you mustn't expect too much of Laura.

AMANDA: What do you mean?

TOM: Laura seems all those things to you and me because she's ours and we love her. We don't even notice she's crippled any more.

AMANDA: Don't say crippled! You know that I never allow that word to be used!

TOM: But face facts, Mother. She is and—that's not all—

AMANDA: What do you mean "not all"?

TOM: Laura is very different from other girls.

AMANDA: I think the difference is all to her advantage.

TOM: Not quite all—in the eyes of others—strangers—she's terribly shy and lives in a world of her own and those things make her seem a little peculiar to people outside the house.

AMANDA: Don't say peculiar.

TOM: Face the facts. She is.

(THE DANCE-HALL MUSIC CHANGES TO A TANGO THAT HAS A MINOR AND SOMEWHAT OMINOUS TONE.)

AMANDA: In what way is she peculiar —may I ask?

TOM: (*gently*) She lives in a world of her own—a world of—little glass ornaments, Mother.... (*Gets up.* AMANDA *remains holding brush, looking at him, troubled.*) She plays old phonograph records and—that's about all— (*He glances at himself in the mirror and crosses to door.*)

AMANDA: (*sharply*) Where are you going?

TOM: I'm going to the movies. (*Out screen door.*)

AMANDA: Not to the movies, every night to the movies! (*Follows quickly to screen door.*) I don't believe you always go to the movies! (*He is gone.* AMANDA *looks worriedly after him for a moment. Then vitality and optimism return and she turns from the door. Crossing to portieres.*) Laura! Laura! (LAURA *answers from kitchenette.*)

LAURA: Yes, Mother.

AMANDA: Let those dishes go and come in front! (LAURA *appears with dish towel. Gaily.*) Laura, come here and make a wish on the moon!

LAURA: (*entering*) Moon—moon?

AMANDA: A little silver slipper of a moon. Look over your left shoulder, Laura, and make a wish! (LAURA *looks faintly puzzled as if called out of sleep.* AMANDA *seizes her shoulders and turns her at an angle by the door.*) No! Now, darling, *wish!*

LAURA: What shall I wish for, Mother?

AMANDA: (*her voice trembling and her eyes suddenly filling with tears*) Happiness! Good Fortune!

(*The violin rises and the stage dims out.*)

SCENE VI

(IMAGE ON SCREEN: HIGH SCHOOL HERO.)

TOM: And so the following evening I brought Jim home to dinner. I had known Jim slightly in high school. In high school Jim was a hero. He had tremendous Irish good nature and vitality with the scrubbed and polished look of white chinaware. He seemed to move in a continual spotlight. He was a star in basketball, captain of the debating club, president of the senior class and the glee club and he sang the male lead in the annual light operas. He was always running or bounding, never just walking. He seemed always at the point of defeating the law of gravity. He was shooting with such velocity through his adolescence that you would logically expect him to arrive at nothing short of the White House by the time he was thirty. But Jim apparently ran into more interference after his graduation from Soldan. His speed had definitely slowed. Six years after he left high school he was holding a job that wasn't much better than mine.

(IMAGE ON SCREEN: CLERK.)

He was the only one at the warehouse with whom I was on friendly terms. I was valuable to him as someone who could remember his former glory, who had seen him win basketball games and the silver cup in debating. He knew of my secret practice of retiring to a cabinet of the washroom to work on poems when business was slack in the warehouse. He called me Shakespeare. And while the other boys in the warehouse regarded me with suspicious hostility, Jim took a humorous attitude toward me. Gradually his attitude affected the others, their hostility wore off and they also began to smile at me as people smile at an oddly fashioned dog who trots across their path at some distance.

I knew that Jim and Laura had known each other at Soldan, and I have heard Laura speak admiringly of his voice. I didn't know if Jim remembered her or not. In high school Laura had been as unobtrusive as Jim had been astonishing. If he did remember Laura, it was not as my sister, for when I asked him to dinner, he grinned and said, "You know, Shakespeare, I never thought of you as having folks!"

He was about to discover that I did. . . . (*Light up stage.*)

(LEGEND ON SCREEN: "THE ACCENT OF A COMING FOOT.")

(*Friday evening. It is about five o'clock of a late spring evening which comes "scattering poems in the sky."*)

(*A delicate lemony light is in the Wingfield apartment.*)

(AMANDA *has worked like a Turk in preparation for the gentleman caller. The results are astonishing. The new floor lamp with its rose-silk shade is in place, a colored paper lantern conceals the broken light fixture in the ceiling, new billowing white curtains are at the windows, chintz covers are on chairs and sofa, a pair of new sofa pillows make their initial appearance.*)

(*Open boxes and tissue paper are scattered on the floor.*)

(LAURA *stands in the middle with lifted arms while* AMANDA *crouches before her, adjusting the hem of the new dress, devout and ritualistic. The dress is colored and designed by memory. The arrangement of* LAURA's *hair is changed; it is softer and more becoming. A fragile, unearthly prettiness has come out in* LAURA: *she is like a piece of translucent glass touched by light, given a momentary radiance, not actual, not lasting.*)

AMANDA: (*impatiently*) Why are you trembling?

LAURA: Mother, you've made me so nervous!

AMANDA: How have I made you nervous?

LAURA: By all this fuss! You make it seem so important!

AMANDA: I don't understand you, Laura. You couldn't be satisfied with just sitting home, and yet whenever I try to arrange something for you, you seem to resist it. (*She gets up.*) Now take a look at yourself. No, wait! Wait just a moment—I have an idea!

LAURA: What is it now?

(AMANDA *produces two powder puffs which she wraps in handkerchiefs and stuffs in* LAURA's *bosom.*)

LAURA: Mother, what are you doing?

AMANDA: They call them "Gay Deceivers"!

LAURA: I won't wear them!

AMANDA: You will!

LAURA: Why should I?

AMANDA: Because, to be painfully honest, your chest is flat.

LAURA: You make it seem like we were setting a trap.

AMANDA: All pretty girls are a trap, a pretty trap, and men expect them to be. (LEGEND ON SCREEN: "A PRETTY TRAP.") Now look at yourself, young lady. This is the prettiest you will ever be! I've got to fix myself now! You're going to be surprised by your mother's appearance! (*She crosses through portieres, humming gaily.*) (LAURA *moves slowly to the long mirror and stares solemnly at herself.*)

(*A wind blows the white curtains inward in a slow, graceful motion and with a faint, sorrowful sighing.*)

AMANDA: (*off stage*) It isn't dark enough yet. (*She turns slowly before the mirror with a troubled look.*)

(LEGEND ON SCREEN: "THIS IS MY SISTER: CELEBRATE HER WITH STRINGS!" MUSIC.)

AMANDA: (*laughing offstage*) I'm going to show you something. I'm going to make a spectacular appearance!

LAURA: What is it, Mother?

AMANDA: Possess your soul in patience—you will see! Something I've resurrected from that old trunk! Styles haven't changed so terribly much after all.... (*She parts the portieres.*) Now just look at your mother! (*She wears a girlish frock of yellowed voile with a blue silk sash. She carries a bunch of jonquils—the legend of her youth is nearly revived. Feverishly*) This is the dress in which I led the cotillion. Won the cakewalk twice at Sunset Hill, wore one spring to the Governor's ball in Jackson! See how I sashayed around the ballroom, Laura? (*She raises her skirt and does a mincing step around the room.*) I wore it on Sundays for my gentlemen callers! I had it on the day I met your father—I had malaria fever all that spring. The change of climate from East Tennessee to the Delta—weakened resistance—I had a little temperature all the time—not enough to be serious—just enough to make me restless and giddy! Invitations poured in—parties all over the Delta!—"Stay in bed," said Mother, "you have fever!"—but I just wouldn't.—I took quinine but kept on going, going!—Evenings, dances!—Afternoons, long, long rides! Picnics—lovely!—So lovely, that country in May.—All lacy with dogwood, literally flooded with jonquils!—That was the spring I had the craze for jonquils. Jonquils became an absolute obsession. Mother said, "Honey, there's no more room for jonquils." And still I kept on bringing in more jonquils. Whenever, wherever I saw them, I'd say, "Stop! Stop! I see jonquils!" I made the young men help me gather the jonquils! It was a joke, Amanda and her jonquils! Finally there were no more vases to hold them, every available space was filled with jonquils. No vases to hold them? All right, I'll hold them myself! And then I—(*She stops in front of the picture.* MUSIC.) met your father! Malaria fever and jonquils and then—this—boy.... (*She switches on the rose-colored lamp.*) I hope they get here before it starts to rain. (*She crosses upstage and places the jonquils in bowl on table.*) I gave your brother a little extra change so he and Mr. O'Connor could take the service car home.

LAURA: (*with altered look*) What did you say his name was?

AMANDA: O'Connor.

LAURA: What is his first name?

AMANDA: I don't remember. Oh, yes, I do. It was—Jim!

(LAURA *sways slightly and catches hold of a chair.*)

(LEGEND ON SCREEN: "NOT JIM!")

LAURA: (*faintly*) Not—Jim!

AMANDA: Yes, that was it, it was Jim! I've never known a Jim that wasn't nice! (MUSIC: OMINOUS.)

LAURA: Are you sure his name is Jim O'Connor?

AMANDA: Yes. Why?

LAURA: Is he the one that Tom used to know in high school?

AMANDA: He didn't say so. I think he just got to know him at the warehouse.

LAURA: There was a Jim O'Connor we both knew in high school—(*Then, with effort.*) If that is the one that Tom is bringing to dinner—you'll have to excuse me, I won't come to the table.

AMANDA: What sort of nonsense is this?

LAURA: You asked me once if I'd ever liked a boy. Don't you remember I showed you this boy's picture?

AMANDA: You mean the boy you showed me in the yearbook?

LAURA: Yes, that boy.

AMANDA: Laura, Laura, were you in love with that boy?

LAURA: I don't know, Mother. All I know is I couldn't sit at the table if it was him!

AMANDA: It won't be him! It isn't the least bit likely. But whether it is or not, you will come to the table. You will not be excused.

LAURA: I'll have to be, Mother.

AMANDA: I don't intend to humor your silliness, Laura. I've had too much from you and your brother, both! So just sit down and compose yourself till they come. Tom has forgotten his key so you'll have to let them in, when they arrive.

LAURA: (*panicky*) Oh, Mother—*you* answer the door!

AMANDA: (*lightly*) I'll be in the kitchen—busy!

LAURA: Oh, Mother, please answer the door, don't make me do it!

AMANDA: (*crossing into kitchenette*) I've got to fix the dressing for the salmon. Fuss, fuss—silliness!—over a gentleman caller!

(*Door swings shut.* LAURA *is left alone.*)
(LEGEND ON SCREEN: "TERROR!")
(*She utters a low moan and turns off the lamp—sits stiffly on the edge of the sofa, knotting her fingers together.*)
(LEGEND ON SCREEN: "THE OPENING OF A DOOR!")
(TOM *and* JIM *appear on the fire-escape steps and climb to landing. Hearing their approach,* LAURA *rises with a panicky gesture. She retreats to the portieres.*)
(*The doorbell.* LAURA *catches her breath and touches her throat. Low drums.*)

AMANDA: (*calling*) Laura, sweetheart! The door!

(LAURA *stares at it without moving.*)

JIM: I think we just beat the rain.

TOM: Uh-huh. (*He rings again, nervously.* JIM *whistles and fishes for a cigarette.*)

AMANDA: (*very, very gaily*) Laura, that is your brother and Mr. O'Connor! Will you let them in, darling?

(LAURA *crosses toward kitchenette door.*)

LAURA: (*breathlessly*) Mother—you go to the door!

(AMANDA *steps out of kitchenette and stares furiously at* LAURA. *She points imperiously at the door.*)

LAURA: Please, please!

AMANDA: (*in a fierce whisper*) What is the matter with you, you silly thing?

LAURA: (*desperately*) Please, you answer it, *please!*

AMANDA: I told you I wasn't going to humor you, Laura. Why have you chosen this moment to lose your mind?

LAURA: Please, please, please, you go!

AMANDA: You'll have to go to the door because I can't!

LAURA: (*despairingly*) I can't either!

AMANDA: *Why?*

LAURA: I'm *sick!*

AMANDA: I'm sick, too—of your nonsense! Why can't you and your brother be normal people? Fantastic whims and behavior! (TOM *gives a long ring.*) Preposterous goings on! Can you give me one reason—(*Calls out lyrically:*) COMING! JUST ONE SECOND!—why you should be afraid to open a door? Now you answer it, Laura!

LAURA: Oh, oh, oh . . . (*She returns through the portieres. Darts to the victrola and winds it frantically and turns it on.*)

AMANDA: Laura Wingfield, you march right to that door!

LAURA: Yes—yes, Mother!

(*A faraway, scratchy rendition of "Dardanella" softens the air and gives her strength to move through it. She slips to the door and draws it cautiously open.*) (TOM *enters with the caller,* JIM O'CONNOR.)

TOM: Laura, this is Jim. Jim, this is my sister, Laura.

JIM: (*stepping inside*) I didn't know that Shakespeare had a sister!

LAURA: (*retreating stiff and trembling from the door*) How—how do you do?

JIM: (*heartily extending his hand*) Okay!

(LAURA *touches it hesitantly with hers.*)

JIM: Your hand's *cold*, Laura!

LAURA: Yes, well—I've been playing the victrola. . . .

JIM: Must have been playing classical music on it! You ought to play a little hot swing music to warm you up!

LAURA: Excuse me—I haven't finished playing the victrola. . . .

(*She turns awkwardly and hurries into the front room. She pauses a second by the victrola. Then catches her breath and darts through the portieres like a frightened deer.*)

JIM: (*grinning*) What was the matter?

TOM: Oh—with Laura? Laura is—terribly shy.

JIM: Shy, huh? It's unusual to meet a shy girl nowadays. I don't believe you ever mentioned you had a sister.

TOM: Well, now you know. I have one. Here is the *Post Dispatch.* You want a piece of it?

JIM: Uh-huh.

TOM: What piece? The comics?

JIM: Sports! (*Glances at it.*) Ole Dizzy Dean is on his bad behavior.

TOM: (*with disinterest*) Yeah? (*Lights cigarette and crosses back to fire-escape door.*)

JIM: Where are *you* going?

TOM: I'm going out on the terrace.

JIM: (*goes after him*) You know, Shakespeare—I'm going to sell you a bill of goods!

TOM: What goods?

JIM: A course I'm taking.

TOM: Huh?

JIM: In public speaking! You and me, we're not the warehouse type.

TOM: Thanks—that's good news. But what has public speaking got to do with it?

JIM: It fits you for—executive positions!

TOM: Awww.

JIM: I tell you it's done a helluva lot for me.

(IMAGE ON SCREEN: EXECUTIVE AT DESK.)

TOM: In what respect?

JIM: In every! Ask yourself what is the difference between you an' me and men in the office down front? Brains?—No!—Ability?—No! Then what? Just one little thing—

TOM: What is that one little thing?

JIM: Primarily it amounts to—social poise! Being able to square up to people and hold your own on any social level!

AMANDA: (*off stage*) Tom?

TOM: Yes, Mother?

AMANDA: Is that you and Mr. O'Connor?

TOM: Yes, Mother.

AMANDA: Well, you just make yourselves comfortable in there.

TOM: Yes, Mother.

AMANDA: Ask Mr. O'Connor if he would like to wash his hands.

JIM: Aw, no—no—thank you—I took care of that at the warehouse. Tom—

TOM: Yes?

JIM: Mr. Mendoza was speaking to me about you.

TOM: Favorably?

JIM: What do you think?

TOM: Well—

JIM: You're going to be out of a job if you don't wake up.

TOM: I am waking up—

JIM: You show no signs.

TOM: The signs are interior.

(IMAGE ON SCREEN: THE SAILING VESSEL WITH JOLLY ROGER AGAIN.)

TOM: I'm planning to change. (*He leans over the rail speaking with quiet exhilaration. The incandescent marquees and signs of the first-run movie houses light his face from across the alley. He looks like a voyager.*) I'm right at the point of committing myself to a future that doesn't include the warehouse and Mr. Mendoza or even a night-school course in public speaking.

JIM: What are you gassing about?

TOM: I'm tired of the movies.

JIM: Movies!

TOM: Yes, movies! Look at them— (*A wave toward the marvels of Grand Avenue.*) All of those glamorous people— having adventures—hogging it all, gobbling the whole thing up! You know what happens? People go to the *movies* instead of *moving!* Hollywood characters are supposed to have all the adventures for everybody in America, while everybody in America sits in a dark room and watches them have them! Yes, until there's a war. That's when adventure becomes available to the masses! *Everyone's* dish, not only Gable's! Then the people in the dark room come out of the dark room to have some adventures themselves—Goody, goody!—It's our turn now, to go to the South Sea Island—to make a safari—to be exotic, far-off!—But I'm not patient. I don't want to wait till then. I'm tired of the *movies* and I am *about* to *move!*

JIM: (*incredulously*) Move?

TOM: Yes.

JIM: When?

TOM: Soon!

JIM: Where? Where?

(THEME THREE MUSIC SEEMS TO ANSWER THE QUESTION, WHILE TOM THINKS IT OVER. HE SEARCHES AMONG HIS POCKETS.)

TOM: I'm starting to boil inside. I know I seem dreamy, but inside—well, I'm boiling! Whenever I pick up a shoe, I shudder a little thinking how short life is and what I am doing!—Whatever that means, I know it doesn't mean shoes— except as something to wear on a traveler's feet! (*Finds paper.*) Look—

JIM: What?

TOM: I'm a member.

JIM: (*reading*) The Union of Merchant Seamen.

TOM: I paid my dues this month, instead of the light bill.

JIM: You will regret it when they turn the lights off.

TOM: I won't be here.

JIM: How about your mother?

TOM: I'm like my father. The bastard son of a bastard! See how he grins? And he's been absent going on sixteen years!

JIM: You're just talking, you drip. How does your mother feel about it?

TOM: Shhh!—Here comes Mother! Mother is not acquainted with my plans!

AMANDA: (*enters portieres*) Where are you all?

TOM: On the terrace, Mother.

(*They start inside. She advances to them.* TOM *is distinctly shocked at her appearance. Even* JIM *blinks a little. He is making his first contact with girlish Southern vivacity and in spite of the night-school course in public speaking is somewhat thrown off the beam by the unexpected outlay of social charm.*)

(*Certain responses are attempted by* JIM *but are swept aside by* AMANDA'S *gay laughter and chatter.* TOM *is embarrassed but after the first shock* JIM *reacts very warmly. Grins and chuckles, is altogether won over.*)

(IMAGE ON SCREEN: AMANDA AS A GIRL.)

AMANDA: (*coyly smiling, shaking her girlish ringlets*) Well, well, well, so this is Mr. O'Connor. Introductions entirely unnecessary. I've heard so much about you from my boy. I finally said to him, Tom—good gracious!—why don't you bring this paragon to supper? I'd like to meet this nice young man at the warehouse!—Instead of just hearing him sing your praises so much! I don't know why my son is so standoffish—that's not Southern behavior! Let's sit down and—I think we could stand a little more air in here! Tom, leave the door open. I felt a nice fresh breeze a moment ago. Where has it gone to? Mmm, so warm already! And not quite summer, even. We're going to burn up when summer really gets started. However, we're having—we're having a very light supper. I think light things are better fo' this time of year. The same as light clothes are. Light clothes an' light food are what warm weather calls fo'. You know our blood gets so thick during th' winter—it takes a while fo' us to *adjust ou'selves!*—when the season changes . . . It's come so quick this year. I wasn't prepared. All of a sudden—heavens! Already summer!—I ran to the trunk an' pulled out this light dress— Terribly old! Historical almost! But feels so good—so good an' co-ol, y'know. . . .

TOM: Mother—

AMANDA: Yes, honey?

TOM: How about—supper?

AMANDA: Honey, you go ask Sister if supper is ready! You know that Sister is in full charge of supper! Tell her you hungry boys are waiting for it. (*To* JIM.) Have you met Laura?

JIM: She—

AMANDA: Let you in? Oh, good, you've met already! It's rare for a girl as sweet an' pretty as Laura to be domestic! But Laura is, thank heavens, not only pretty but also very domestic. I'm not at all. I never was a bit. I never could make a thing but angel-food cake. Well, in the South we had so many servants. Gone, gone, gone. All vestige of gracious living! Gone completely! I wasn't prepared for what the future brought me. All of my gentlemen callers were sons of planters and so of course I assumed that I would be married to one and raise my family on a large piece of land with plenty of servants. But man proposes—and woman accepts the proposal!—To vary that old, old saying a little bit—I married no planter! I married a man who worked for the telephone company!—That gallantly smiling gentleman over there! (*Points to the picture.*) A telephone man who—fell in love with long-distance!—Now he travels and I don't even know where!— But what am I going on for about my—tribulations? Tell me yours—I hope you don't have any! Tom?

TOM: (*returning*) Yes, Mother?

AMANDA: Is supper nearly ready?

TOM: It looks to me like supper is on the table.

AMANDA: Let me look— (*She rises prettily and looks through portieres.*) Oh, lovely!— But where is Sister?

TOM: Laura is not feeling well and she

says that she thinks she'd better not come to the table.

AMANDA: What?—Nonsense!—Laura? Oh, Laura!

LAURA: (*off stage, faintly*) Yes, Mother.

AMANDA: You really must come to the table. We won't be seated until you come to the table! Come in, Mr. O'Connor. You sit over there, and I'll— Laura? Laura Wingfield! You're keeping us waiting, honey! We can't say grace until you come to the table!

(*The back door is pushed weakly open and* LAURA *comes in. She is obviously quite faint, her lips trembling, her eyes wide and staring. She moves unsteadily toward the table.*)

(LEGEND ON SCREEN: "TERROR!")

(*Outside a summer storm is coming abruptly. The white curtains billow inward at the windows and there is a sorrowful murmur and deep blue dusk.*)

(LAURA *suddenly stumbles—she catches at a chair with a faint moan.*)

TOM: Laura!

AMANDA: Laura! (*There is a clap of thunder.*) (LEGEND ON SCREEN: "AH!") (*Despairingly.*) Why, Laura, you are *sick*, darling! Tom, help your sister into the living room, dear! Sit in the living room, Laura—rest on the sofa. Well! (*To the gentleman caller.*) Standing over the hot stove made her ill!—I told her that it was just too warm this evening, but—(TOM *comes back in.* LAURA *is on the sofa.*) Is Laura all right now?

TOM: Yes.

AMANDA: What *is* that? Rain? A nice cool rain has come up! (*She gives the gentleman caller a frightened look.*) I think we may—have grace—now . . . (TOM *looks at her stupidly.*) Tom, honey —you say grace!

TOM: Oh . . . "For these and all thy mercies—" (*They bow their heads,* AMANDA *stealing a nervous glance at* JIM. *In the living room* LAURA, *stretched on the sofa, clenches her hand to her lips, to hold back a shuddering sob.*) God's Holy Name be praised—

THE SCENE DIMS OUT

SCENE VII

(LEGEND ON SCREEN: A SOUVENIR.)

(*Half an hour later. Dinner is just being finished in the upstage area which is concealed by the drawn portieres.*

As the curtain rises LAURA *is still huddled upon the sofa, her feet drawn under her, her head resting on a pale blue pillow, her eyes wide and mysteriously watchful. The new floor lamp with its shade of rose-colored silk gives a soft, becoming light to her face, bringing out the fragile, unearthly prettiness which usually escapes attention. There is a steady murmur of rain, but it is slackening and stops soon after the scene begins; the air outside becomes pale and luminous as the moon breaks out.*

A moment after the curtain rises, the lights in both rooms flicker and go out.)

JIM: Hey, there, Mr. Light Bulb!

(AMANDA *laughs nervously.*)

(LEGEND ON SCREEN: "SUSPENSION OF A PUBLIC SERVICE.")

AMANDA: Where was Moses when the lights went out? Ha-ha. Do you know the answer to that one, Mr. O'Connor?

JIM: No, Ma'am, what's the answer?

AMANDA: In the dark! (JIM *laughs appreciably.*) Everybody sit still. I'll light the candles. Isn't it lucky we have them on the table? Where's a match? Which of you gentlemen can provide a match?

JIM: Here.

AMANDA: Thank you, sir.

JIM: Not at all, Ma'am!

AMANDA: I guess the fuse has burnt out. Mr. O'Connor, can you tell a burnt-out fuse? I know I can't and Tom is a total loss when it comes to mechanics. (SOUND: GETTING UP: VOICES RECEDE A LITTLE TO KITCHENETTE.) Oh, be careful you don't bump into something. We don't want our gentleman caller to break his neck. Now wouldn't that be a fine howdy-do?

JIM: Ha-ha! Where is the fuse-box?

AMANDA: Right here next to the stove. Can you see anything?

JIM: Just a minute.

AMANDA: Isn't electricity a mysterious thing? Wasn't it Benjamin Franklin who tied a key to a kite? We live in such a mysterious universe, don't we? Some people say that science clears up all the mysteries for us. In my opinion it only creates more! Have you found it yet?

JIM: No, Ma'am. All these fuses look okay to me.

AMANDA: Tom!

TOM: Yes, Mother?

AMANDA: That light bill I gave you several days ago. The one I told you we got the notices about?

TOM: Oh.—Yeah.

(LEGEND ON SCREEN: "HA!")

AMANDA: You didn't neglect to pay it by any chance?

TOM: Why, I—

AMANDA: Didn't! I might have known it!

JIM: Shakespeare probably wrote a poem on that light bill, Mrs. Wingfield.

AMANDA: I might have known better than to trust him with it! There's such a high price for negligence in this world!

JIM: Maybe the poem will win a ten-dollar prize.

AMANDA: We'll just have to spend the remainder of the evening in the nineteenth century, before Mr. Edison made the Mazda lamp!

JIM: Candlelight is my favorite kind of light.

AMANDA: That shows you're romantic! But that's no excuse for Tom. Well, we got through dinner. Very considerate of them to let us get through dinner before they plunged us into everlasting darkness, wasn't it, Mr. O'Connor?

JIM: Ha-ha!

AMANDA: Tom, as a penalty for your carelessness you can help me with the dishes.

JIM: Let me give you a hand.

AMANDA: Indeed you will not!

JIM: I ought to be good for something.

AMANDA: Good for something? (*Her tone is rhapsodic.*) *You?* Why, Mr. O'Connor, nobody, *nobody's* given me this much entertainment in years—as you have!

JIM: Aw, now, Mrs. Wingfield!

AMANDA: I'm not exaggerating, not one bit! But Sister is all by her lonesome. You go keep her company in the parlor! I'll give you this lovely old candelabrum that used to be on the altar at the church of the Heavenly Rest. It was melted a little out of shape when the church burnt down. Lightning struck it one spring. Gypsy Jones was holding a revival at the time and he intimated that the church was destroyed because the Episcopalians gave card parties.

JIM: Ha-ha.

AMANDA: And how about you coaxing Sister to drink a little wine? I think it would be good for her! Can you carry both at once?

JIM: Sure. I'm Superman!

AMANDA: Now, Thomas, get into this apron!

(*The door of kitchenette swings closed on* AMANDA's *gay laughter; the flickering light approaches the portieres.*)

(LAURA *sits up nervously as he enters. Her speech at first is low and breathless from the almost intolerable strain of being alone with a stranger.)*

(LEGEND ON SCREEN: "I DON'T SUPPOSE YOU REMEMBER ME AT ALL!")

(In her first speeches in this scene, before JIM'S *warmth overcomes her paralyzing shyness,* LAURA'S *voice is thin and breathless as though she has just run up a steep flight of stairs.)*

*(*JIM'S *attitude is gently humorous. In playing this scene it should be stressed that while the incident is apparently unimportant, it is to* LAURA *the climax of her secret life.)*

JIM: Hello, there, Laura.

LAURA: *(faintly)* Hello. *(She clears her throat.)*

JIM: How are you feeling now? Better?

LAURA: Yes. Yes, thank you.

JIM: This is for you. A little dandelion wine. *(He extends it toward her with extravagant gallantry.)*

LAURA: Thank you.

JIM: Drink it—but don't get drunk! *(He laughs heartily.* LAURA *takes the glass uncertainly; laughs shyly.)* Where shall I set the candles?

LAURA: Oh—oh, anywhere . . .

JIM: How about here on the floor? Any objections?

LAURA: No.

JIM: I'll spread a newspaper under to catch the drippings. I like to sit on the floor. Mind if I do?

LAURA: Oh, no.

JIM: Give me a pillow?

LAURA: What?

JIM: A pillow!

LAURA: Oh . . . *(Hands him one quickly.)*

JIM: How about you? Don't you like to sit on the floor?

LAURA: Oh—yes.

JIM: Why don't you, then?

LAURA: I—will.

JIM: Take a pillow! (LAURA *does. Sits on the other side of the candelabrum.* JIM *crosses his legs and smiles engagingly at her.)* I can't hardly see you sitting way over there.

LAURA: I can—see you.

JIM: I know, but that's not fair, I'm in the limelight. (LAURA *moves her pillow closer.)* Good! Now I can see you! Comfortable?

LAURA: Yes.

JIM: So am I. Comfortable as a cow. Will you have some gum?

LAURA: No, thank you.

JIM: I think that I will indulge, with your permission. *(Musingly unwraps it and holds it up.)* Think of the fortune made by the guy that invented the first piece of chewing gum. Amazing, huh? The Wrigley Building is one of the sights of Chicago.—I saw it summer before last when I went up to the Century of Progress. Did you take in the Century of Progress?

LAURA: No, I didn't.

JIM: Well, it was quite a wonderful exposition. What impressed me most was the Hall of Science. Gives you an idea of what the future will be in America, even more wonderful than the present time is! *(Pause. Smiling at her.)* Your brother tells me you're shy. Is that right, Laura?

LAURA: I—don't know.

JIM: I judge you to be an old-fashioned type of girl. Well, I think that's a pretty good type to be. Hope you don't think I'm being too personal—do you?

LAURA: *(hastily, out of embarrassment)* I believe I *will* take a piece of gum, if you—don't mind. *(Clearing her throat.)* Mr. O'Connor, have you—kept up with your singing?

JIM: Singing? Me?

LAURA: Yes. I remember what a beautiful voice you had.

JIM: When did you hear me sing?

(Voice off stage in the pause.)

VOICE (*off stage*).
> O blow, ye winds, heigh-ho,
> A-roving I will go!
>   I'm off to my love
>   With a boxing glove—
> Ten thousand miles away!

JIM: You say you've heard me sing?

LAURA: Oh, yes! Yes, very often . . . I—don't suppose you remember me—at all?

JIM: (*smiling doubtfully*) You know I have an idea I've seen you before. I had that idea soon as you opened the door. It seemed almost like I was about to remember your name. But the name that I started to call you—wasn't a name! And so I stopped myself before I said it.

LAURA: Wasn't it—Blue Roses?

JIM: (*springs up. Grinning*) Blue Roses! My gosh, yes—Blue Roses! That's what I had on my tongue when you opened the door! Isn't it funny what tricks your memory plays? I didn't connect you with high school somehow or other. But that's where it was; it was high school. I didn't even know you were Shakespeare's sister! Gosh, I'm sorry.

LAURA: I didn't expect you to. You—barely knew me!

JIM: But we did have a speaking acquaintance, huh?

LAURA: Yes, we—spoke to each other.

JIM: When did you recognize me?

LAURA: Oh, right away!

JIM: Soon as I came in the door?

LAURA: When I heard your name I thought it was probably you. I knew that Tom used to know you a little in high school. So when you came in the door—Well, then I was—sure.

JIM: Why didn't you *say* something, then?

LAURA: (*breathlessly*) I didn't know what to say, I was—too surprised!

JIM: For goodness' sake! You know, this sure is funny!

LAURA: Yes! Yes, isn't it, though . . .

JIM: Didn't we have a class in something together?

LAURA: Yes, we did.

JIM: What class was that?

LAURA: It was—singing—Chorus!

JIM: Aw!

LAURA: I sat across the aisle from you in the Aud.

JIM: Aw.

LAURA: Mondays, Wednesdays and Fridays.

JIM: Now I remember—you always came in late.

LAURA: Yes, it was so hard for me, getting upstairs. I had that brace on my leg—it clumped so loud!

JIM: I never heard any clumping.

LAURA: (*wincing at the recollection*) To me it sounded like—thunder!

JIM: Well, well, well, I never even noticed.

LAURA: And everybody was seated before I came in. I had to walk in front of all those people. My seat was in the back row. I had to go clumping all the way up the aisle with everyone watching!

JIM: You shouldn't have been self-conscious.

LAURA: I know, but I was. It was always such a relief when the singing started.

JIM: Aw, yes, I've placed you now! I used to call you Blue Roses. How was it that I got started calling you that?

LAURA: I was out of school a little while with pleurosis. When I came back you asked me what was the matter. I said I had pleurosis—you thought I said Blue Roses. That's what you always called me after that!

JIM: I hope you didn't mind.

LAURA: Oh, no—I liked it. You see, I wasn't acquainted with many—people. . . .

JIM: As I remember you sort of stuck by yourself.

LAURA: I—I—never had much luck at—making friends.

JIM: I don't see why you wouldn't.

LAURA: Well, I—started out badly.

JIM: You mean being—

LAURA: Yes, it sort of—stood between me—

JIM: You shouldn't have let it!

LAURA: I know, but it did, and—

JIM: You were shy with people!

LAURA: I tried not to be but never could—

JIM: Overcome it?

LAURA: No, I—I never could!

JIM: I guess being shy is something you have to work out of kind of gradually.

LAURA: (*sorrowfully*) Yes—I guess it—

JIM: Takes time!

LAURA: Yes—

JIM: People are not so dreadful when you know them. That's what you have to remember! And everybody has problems, not just you, but practically everybody has got some problems. You think of yourself as having the only problems, as being the only one who is disappointed. But just look around you and you will see lots of people as disappointed as you are. For instance, I hoped when I was going to high school that I would be further along at this time, six years later, than I am now— You remember that wonderful write-up I had in *The Torch?*

LAURA: Yes! (*She rises and crosses to table.*)

JIM: It said I was bound to succeed in anything I went into! (LAURA *returns with the annual.*) Holy Jeez! *The Torch!* (*He accepts it reverently. They smile across it with mutual wonder.* LAURA *crouches beside him and they begin to turn through it.* LAURA'S *shyness is dissolving in his warmth.*)

LAURA: Here you are in *Pirates of Penzance!*

JIM: (*wistfully*) I sang the baritone lead in that operetta.

LAURA: (*rapidly*) So—*beautifully!*

JIM: (*protesting*) Aw—

LAURA: Yes, yes—beautifully—beautifully!

JIM: You heard me?

LAURA: All three times!

JIM: No!

LAURA: Yes!

JIM: All three performances?

LAURA: (*looking down*) Yes.

JIM: Why?

LAURA: I—wanted to ask you to—autograph my program.

JIM: Why didn't you ask me to?

LAURA: You were always surrounded by your own friends so much that I never had a chance to.

JIM: You should have just—

LAURA: Well, I—thought you might think I was—

JIM: Thought I might think you was—what?

LAURA: Oh—

JIM: (*with reflective relish*) I was beleaguered by females in those days.

LAURA: You were terribly popular!

JIM: Yeah—

LAURA: You had such a—friendly way—

JIM: I was spoiled in high school.

LAURA: Everybody—liked you!

JIM: Including you?

LAURA: I—yes, I—I did, too— (*She gently closes the book in her lap.*)

JIM: Well, well, well!—Give me that program, Laura. (*She hands it to him. He signs it with a flourish.*) There you are—better late than never!

LAURA: Oh, I—what a—surprise!

JIM: My signature isn't worth very much right now. But some day—maybe—it will increase in value! Being disappointed is one thing and being discouraged is something else. I am disappointed but I am not discouraged. I'm twenty-three years old. How old are you?

LAURA: I'll be twenty-four in June.

JIM: That's not old age!

LAURA: No, but—

JIM: You finished high school?

LAURA: (*with difficulty*) I didn't go back.

JIM: You mean you dropped out?

LAURA: I made bad grades in my final examinations. (*She rises and replaces the book and the program. Her voice strained.*) How is—Emily Meisenbach getting along?

JIM: Oh, that kraut-head!

LAURA: Why do you call her that?

JIM: That's what she was.

LAURA: You're not still—going with her?

JIM: I never see her.

LAURA: It said in the Personal Section that you were—engaged!

JIM: I know, but I wasn't impressed by that—propaganda!

LAURA: It wasn't—the truth?

JIM: Only in Emily's optimistic opinion!

LAURA: Oh—

(LEGEND. "WHAT HAVE YOU DONE SINCE HIGH SCHOOL?")

(JIM *lights a cigarette and leans indolently back on his elbows smiling at* LAURA *with a warmth and charm which lights her inwardly with altar candles. She remains by the table and turns in her hands a piece of glass to cover her tumult.*)

JIM: (*after several reflective puffs on a cigarette*) What have you done since high school? (*She seems not to hear him.*) Huh? (LAURA *looks up.*) I said what have you done since high school, Laura?

LAURA: Nothing much.

JIM: You must have been doing something these six long years.

LAURA: Yes.

JIM: Well, then, such as what?

LAURA: I took a business course at business college—

JIM: How did that work out?

LAURA: Well, not very—well—I had to drop out, it gave me—indigestion—

(JIM *laughs gently.*)

JIM: What are you doing now?

LAURA: I don't do anything—much. Oh, please don't think I sit around doing nothing! My glass collection takes up a good deal of time. Glass is something you have to take good care of.

JIM: What did you say—about glass?

LAURA: Collection I said—I have one— (*She clears her throat and turns away again, acutely shy.*)

JIM: (*abruptly*) You know what I judge to be the trouble with you? Inferiority complex! Know what that is? That's what they call it when someone low-rates himself? I understand it because I had it, too. Although my case was not so aggravated as yours seems to be. I had it until I took up public speaking, developed my voice, and learned that I had an aptitude for science. Before that time I never thought of myself as being outstanding in any way whatsoever! Now I've never made a regular study of it, but I have a friend who says I can analyze people better than doctors that make a profession of it. I don't claim that to be necessarily true, but I can sure guess a person's psychology, Laura! (*Takes out his gum.*) Excuse me, Laura. I always take it out when the flavor is gone. I'll use this scrap of paper to wrap it in. I know how it is to get it stuck on a shoe. Yep—that's what I judge to be your principal trouble. A lack of confidence in yourself as a person. You don't have the proper amount of faith in yourself. I'm basing that fact on a number of your remarks and also on certain observations I've made. For instance that clumping you thought was so awful in high school. You say that you even dreaded to walk into class. You see what you did? You dropped out of school, you gave up an education because of a clump, which as far as I know was practically nonexistent! A little physical defect is what you have. Hardly noticeable even! Magnified thousands of times by imagination! You know what my strong advice to you is? Think of yourself as *superior* in some way!

LAURA: In what way would I think?

JIM: Why, man alive, Laura! Just look about you a little. What do you see? A world full of common people! All of 'em born and all of 'em going to die! Which of them has one-tenth of your good points! Or mine! Or anyone else's, as far as that goes— Gosh! Everybody excels in some one thing. Some in many! (*Unconsciously glances at himself in the mirror.*) All you've got to do is discover in *what!* Take me, for instance. (*He adjusts his tie at the mirror.*) My interest happens to lie in electro-dynamics. I'm taking a course in radio engineering at night school, Laura, on top of a fairly responsible job at the warehouse. I'm taking that course and studying public speaking.

LAURA: Ohhhh.

JIM: Because I believe in the future of television! (*Turning back to her.*) I wish to be ready to go up right along with it. Therefore I'm planning to get in on the ground floor. In fact I've already made the right connections and all that remains is for the industry itself to get under way! Full steam— (*His eyes are starry.*) Knowledge—Zzzzzp! Money—Zzzzzp!— Power! That's the cycle democracy is built on! (*His attitude is convincingly dynamic.* LAURA *stares at him, even her shyness eclipsed in her absolute wonder. He suddenly grins.*) I guess you think I think a lot of myself!

LAURA: No—o-o-o, I—

JIM: Now how about you? Isn't there something you take more interest in than anything else?

LAURA: Well, I do—as I said—have my—glass collection—

(*A peal of girlish laughter from the kitchen.*)

JIM: I'm not right sure I know what you're talking about. What kind of glass is it?

LAURA: Little articles of it, they're ornaments mostly! Most of them are little animals made out of glass, the tiniest little animals in the world. Mother calls them a glass menagerie! Here's an example of one, if you'd like to see it! This one is one of the oldest. It's nearly thirteen. (MUSIC: "THE GLASS MENAGERIE.") (*He stretches out his hand.*) Oh, be careful— if you breathe, it breaks!

JIM: I'd better not take it. I'm pretty clumsy with things.

LAURA: Go on, I trust you with him! (*Places it in his palm.*) There now— you're holding him gently! Hold him over the light, he loves the light! You see how the light shines through him?

JIM: It sure does shine!

LAURA: I shouldn't be partial, but he is my favorite one.

JIM: What kind of a thing is this one supposed to be?

LAURA: Haven't you noticed the single horn on his forehead?

JIM: A unicorn, huh?

LAURA: Mmm-hmmm!

JIM: Unicorns, aren't they extinct in the modern world?

LAURA: I know!

JIM: Poor little fellow, he must feel sort of lonesome.

LAURA: (*smiling*) Well, if he does he doesn't complain about it. He stays on a shelf with some horses that don't have horns and all of them seem to get along nicely together.

JIM: How do you know?

LAURA: (*lightly*) I haven't heard any arguments among them!

JIM: (*grinning*) No arguments, huh? Well, that's a pretty good sign! Where shall I set him?

LAURA: Put him on the table. They all like a change of scenery once in a while!

JIM: (*stretching*) Well, well, well, well— Look how big my shadow is when I stretch!

LAURA: Oh, oh, yes—it stretches across the ceiling!

JIM: (*crossing to door*) I think it's stopped raining. (*Opens fire-escape door.*) Where does the music come from?

LAURA: From the Paradise Dance Hall across the alley.

JIM: How about cutting the rug a little, Miss Wingfield?

LAURA: Oh, I—

JIM: Or is your program filled up? Let me have a look at it. (*Grasps imaginary card.*) Why, every dance is taken! I'll just have to scratch some out. (WALTZ MUSIC: "LA GOLONDRINA") Ahhh, a waltz! (*He executes some sweeping turns by himself then holds his arms toward* LAURA.)

LAURA: (*breathlessly*) I—can't dance!

JIM: There you go, that inferiority stuff!

LAURA: I've never danced in my life!

JIM: Come on, try!

LAURA: Oh, but I'd step on you!

JIM: I'm not made out of glass.

LAURA: How—how—how do we start?

JIM: Just leave it to me. You hold your arms out a little.

LAURA: Like this?

JIM: A little bit higher. Right. Now don't tighten up, that's the main thing about it—relax.

LAURA: (*laughing breathlessly*) It's hard not to.

JIM: Okay.

LAURA: I'm afraid you can't budge me.

JIM: What do you bet I can't? (*He swings her into motion.*)

LAURA: Goodness, yes, you can!

JIM: Let yourself go, now, Laura, just let yourself go.

LAURA: I'm—

JIM: Come on!

LAURA: Trying!

JIM: Not so stiff— Easy does it!

LAURA: I know but I'm—

JIM: Loosen th' backbone! There now, that's a lot better.

LAURA: Am I?

JIM: Lots, lots better! (*He moves her about the room in a clumsy waltz.*)

LAURA: Oh, my!

JIM: Ha-ha!

LAURA: Oh, my goodness!

JIM: Ha-ha-ha! (*They suddenly bump into the table.* JIM *stops.*) What did we hit on?

LAURA: Table.

JIM: Did something fall off it? I think—

LAURA: Yes.

JIM: I hope that it wasn't the little glass horse with the horn!

LAURA: Yes.

JIM: Aw, aw, aw. Is it broken?

LAURA: Now it is just like all the other horses.

JIM: It's lost its—

LAURA: Horn! It doesn't matter. Maybe it's a blessing in disguise.

JIM: You'll never forgive me. I bet that that was your favorite piece of glass.

LAURA: I don't have favorites much. It's no tragedy, Freckles. Glass breaks so easily. No matter how careful you are. The traffic jars the shelves and things fall off them.

JIM: Still I'm awfully sorry that I was the cause.

LAURA: (*smiling*) I'll just imagine he had an operation. The horn was removed to make him feel less—freakish! (*They both laugh.*) Now he will feel more at

JIM: Ha-ha, that's very funny! (*Suddenly serious.*) I'm glad to see that you have a sense of humor. You know—you're —well—very different! Surprisingly different from anyone else I know! (*His voice becomes soft and hesitant with a genuine feeling.*) Do you mind me telling you that? (LAURA *is abashed beyond speech.*) I mean it in a nice way . . . (LAURA *nods shyly, looking away.*) You make me feel sort of—I don't know how to put it! I'm usually pretty good at expressing things, but— This is something that I don't know how to say! (LAURA *touches her throat and clears it—turns the broken unicorn in her hands.*) (*Even softer.*) Has anyone ever told you that you were pretty? (PAUSE: MUSIC.) (LAURA *looks up slowly, with wonder, and shakes her head.*) Well, you are! In a very different way from anyone else. And all the nicer because of the difference, too. (*His voice becomes low and husky.* LAURA *turns away, nearly faint with the novelty of her emotions.*) I wish that you were my sister. I'd teach you to have some confidence in yourself. The different people are not like other people, but being different is nothing to be ashamed of. Because other people are not such wonderful people. They're one hundred times one thousand. You're one times one! They walk all over the earth. You just stay here. They're common as—weeds, but—you—well, you're —Blue Roses!

(IMAGE ON SCREEN: BLUE ROSES.)

(MUSIC CHANGES.)

LAURA: But blue is wrong for— roses . . .

JIM: It's right for you— You're —pretty!

LAURA: In what respect am I pretty?

JIM: In all respects—believe me! Your eyes—your hair—are pretty! Your hands are pretty! (*He catches hold of her hand.*) You think I'm making this up because I'm invited to dinner and have to be nice. Oh, I could do that! I could put on an act for you, Laura, and say lots of things without being very sincere. But this time I am. I'm talking to you sincerely. I happened to notice you had this inferiority complex that keeps you from feeling comfortable with people. Somebody needs to build your confidence up and make you proud instead of shy and turning away and—blushing— Somebody ought to— Ought to—*kiss* you, Laura! (*His hand slips slowly up her arm to her shoulder.*) (MUSIC SWELLS TUMULTUOUSLY.) (*He suddenly turns her about and kisses her on the lips.*) (*When he releases her* LAURA *sinks on the sofa with a bright, dazed look.*) (JIM *backs away and fishes in his pocket for a cigarette.*) (LEGEND ON SCREEN: "SOUVENIR.") Stumble-john! (*He lights the cigarette, avoiding her look.*) (*There is a peal of girlish laughter from* AMANDA *in the kitchen.*) (LAURA *slowly raises and opens her hand. It still contains the little broken glass animal. She looks at it with a tender, bewildered expression.*) Stumble-john! I shouldn't have done that— That was way off the beam. You don't smoke, do you? (*She looks up, smiling, not hearing the question.*) (*He sits beside her a little gingerly. She looks at him speechlessly— waiting.*) (*He coughs decorously and moves a little farther aside as he considers the situation and senses her feelings, dimly, with perturbation.*) (*Gently.*) Would you—care for a—mint? (*She doesn't seem to hear him but her look grows brighter even.*) Peppermint—Life Saver? My pocket's a regular drug store —wherever I go . . . (*He pops a mint in his mouth. Then gulps and decides to make a clean breast of it. He speaks slowly and gingerly.*) Laura, you know, if I had a sister like you, I'd do the same thing as Tom. I'd bring out fellows and—introduce her to them. The right type of boys of a type to—appreciate her. Only—well—he made a mistake about me. Maybe I've got no call to be saying this. That may not have been the idea in having me over. But what if it was? There's nothing wrong about that. The only trouble is that in my case—I'm not in a situation to—do the right thing. I can't take down your number and say I'll phone. I can't call up next week and—ask for a date. I thought I had better explain the situation in case you misunderstood it and—hurt your feelings. . . . (*Pause.*) (*Slowly, very slowly,* LAURA's *look changes, her eyes returning slowly from his to the ornament in her palm.*) (AMANDA *utters another gay laugh in the kitchen.*)

LAURA: (*faintly*) You—won't—call again?

JIM: No, Laura, I can't. (*He rises from the sofa.*) As I was just explaining, I've—got strings on me, Laura, I've—been going steady! I go out all the time with a girl named Betty. She's a home-girl like you, and Catholic, and Irish, and in a great many ways we—get along fine. I met her last summer on a moonlight boat trip up the river to Alton, on the *Majestic.* Well—right away from the start it was—love! (LEGEND ON SCREEN: LOVE!) (LAURA *sways slightly forward and grips the arm of the sofa. He fails to notice, now enrapt in his own comfortable being.*) Being in love has made a new man of me! (*Leaning stiffly forward, clutching the arm of the sofa,* LAURA *struggles visibly with her storm. But* JIM *is oblivious, she is a long way off.*) The power of love is really pretty tremendous! Love is something that —changes the whole world, Laura! (*The storm abates a little and* LAURA *leans back. He notices her again.*) It happened that Betty's aunt took sick, she got a wire and had to go to Centralia. So Tom—when he asked me to dinner—I naturally just accepted the invitation, not knowing that you—that he—that I— (*He stops awkwardly.*) Huh—I'm a stumble-john! (*He flops back on the sofa.*) (*The holy candles in the altar of* LAURA's *face have been snuffed out. There is a look of almost infinite desolation.*) (JIM *glances at her uneasily.*) I wish that you would—say something. (*She bites her lip which was trembling and then bravely smiles. She opens her hand again on the broken glass ornament. Then she gently takes his hand and raises it level with her own. She carefully places the unicorn in the palm of his hand, then pushes his fingers closed upon it.*) What are you—doing that for? You want me to have him?—Laura? (*She nods.*) What for?

LAURA: A—souvenir . . .

(*She rises unsteadily and crouches beside the victrola to wind it up.*)

(LEGEND ON SCREEN: "THINGS HAVE A WAY OF TURNING OUT SO BADLY!")

(OR IMAGE ON SCREEN: "GENTLEMAN CALLER WAVING GOOD-BYE!—GAILY.")

(*At this moment* AMANDA *rushes brightly back in the front room. She bears a pitcher of fruit punch in an old-fashioned cut-glass pitcher and a plate of macaroons. The plate has a gold border and poppies painted on it.*)

AMANDA: Well, well, well! Isn't the air delightful after the shower? I've made you children a little liquid refreshment. (*Turns gaily to the gentleman caller.*) Jim, do you know that song about lemonade?

"Lemonade, lemonade
   Made in the shade and stirred
     with a spade—
  Good enough for any old maid!"

JIM: (*uneasily*) Ha-ha! No—I never heard it.

AMANDA: Why, Laura! You look so serious!

JIM: We were having a serious conversation.

AMANDA: Good! Now you're better acquainted!

JIM: (*uncertainly*) Ha-ha! Yes.

AMANDA: You modern young people are much more serious-minded than my generation. I was so gay as a girl!

JIM: You haven't changed, Mrs. Wingfield.

AMANDA: Tonight I'm rejuvenated! The gaiety of the occasion, Mr. O'Connor! (*She tosses her head with a peal of laughter. Spills lemonade.*) Oooo! I'm baptizing myself!

JIM: Here—let me—

AMANDA: (*setting the pitcher down*) There now. I discovered we had some maraschino cherries. I dumped them in, juice and all!

JIM: You shouldn't have gone to that trouble, Mrs. Wingfield.

AMANDA: Trouble, trouble? Why it was loads of fun! Didn't you hear me cutting up in the kitchen? I bet your ears were burning! I told Tom how outdone with him I was for keeping you to himself so long a time! He should have brought you over much, much sooner! Well, now that you've found your way, I want you to be a very frequent caller! Not just occasional but all the time. Oh, we're going to have a lot of gay times together! I see them coming! Mmm, just breathe that air! So fresh, and the moon's so pretty! I'll skip back out—I know where my place is when young folks are having a—serious conversation!

JIM: Oh, don't go out, Mrs. Wingfield. The fact of the matter is I've got to be going.

AMANDA: Going, now? You're joking! Why, it's only the shank of the evening, Mr. O'Connor!

JIM: Well, you know how it is.

AMANDA: You mean you're a young workingman and have to keep workingmen's hours. We'll let you off early tonight. But only on the condition that next time you stay later. What's the best night for you? Isn't Saturday night the best night for you workingmen?

JIM: I have a couple of time-clocks to punch, Mrs. Wingfield. One at morning, another one at night!

AMANDA: My, but you *are* ambitious! You work at night, too?

JIM: No, Ma'am, not work but— Betty! (*He crosses deliberately to pick up his hat. The band at the Paradise Dance Hall goes into a tender waltz.*)

AMANDA: Betty? Betty? Who's—Betty! (*There is an ominous cracking sound in the sky.*)

JIM: Oh, just a girl. The girl I go steady with! (*He smiles charmingly. The sky falls.*)

(LEGEND ON SCREEN: "THE SKY FALLS.")

AMANDA: (*a long-drawn exhalation*) Ohhhh . . . Is it a serious romance, Mr. O'Connor?

JIM: We're going to be married the second Sunday in June.

AMANDA: Ohhhh—how nice! Tom didn't mention that you were engaged to be married.

JIM: The cat's not out of the bag at the warehouse yet. You know how they are. They call you Romeo and stuff like that. (*He stops at the oval mirror to put on his hat. He carefully shapes the brim and the crown to give a discreetly dashing effect.*) It's been a wonderful evening, Mrs. Wingfield. I guess this is what they mean by Southern hospitality.

AMANDA: It really wasn't anything at all.

JIM: I hope it don't seem like I'm rushing off. But I promised Betty I'd pick her up at the Wabash depot, an' by the time I get my jalopy down there her train'll be in. Some women are pretty upset if you keep 'em waiting.

AMANDA: Yes, I know— The tyranny of women! (*Extends her hand.*) Goodbye, Mr. O'Connor. I wish you luck—and happiness—and success! All three of them, and so does Laura!— Don't you, Laura?

LAURA: Yes!

JIM: (*taking her hand*) Good-bye, Laura. I'm certainly going to treasure that souvenir. And don't you forget the good advice I gave you. (*Raises his voice to a cheery shout.*) So long, Shakespeare! Thanks again, ladies— Good night! (*He grins and ducks jauntily out.*)

(*Still bravely grimacing,* AMANDA *closes the door on the gentleman caller. Then she turns back to the room with a puzzled expression. She and* LAURA *don't dare to face each other.* LAURA *crouches beside the victrola to wind it.*)

AMANDA: (*faintly*) Things have a way of turning out so badly. I don't believe that I would play the victrola. Well, well —well— Our gentleman caller was engaged to be married! Tom!

TOM: (*from back*) Yes, Mother?

AMANDA: Come in here a minute. I want to tell you something awfully funny.

TOM: (*enters with macaroon and a glass of the lemonade*) Has the gentleman caller gotten away already?

AMANDA: The gentleman caller has made an early departure. What a wonderful joke you played on us!

TOM: How do you mean?

AMANDA: You didn't mention that he was engaged to be married.

TOM: Jim? Engaged?

AMANDA: That's what he just informed us.

TOM: I'll be jiggered! I didn't know about that.

AMANDA: That seems very peculiar.

TOM: What's peculiar about it?

AMANDA: Didn't you call him your best friend down at the warehouse?

TOM: He is, but how did I know?

AMANDA: It seems extremely peculiar that you wouldn't know your best friend was going to be married!

TOM: The warehouse is where I work, not where I know things about people!

AMANDA: You don't know things anywhere! You live in a dream; you manufacture illusions! (*He crosses to door.*) Where are you going?

TOM: I'm going to the movies.

AMANDA: That's right, now that you've had us make such fools of ourselves. The effort, the preparations, all the expense! The new floor lamp, the rug, the clothes for Laura! All for what? To entertain some other girl's fiancé! Go to the movies, go! Don't think about us, a mother deserted, an unmarried sister who's crippled and has no job! Don't let anything interfere with your selfish pleasure! Just go, go, go—to the movies!

TOM: All right, I will! The more you shout about my selfishness to me the quicker I'll go, and I won't go to the movies!

AMANDA: Go, then! Then go to the moon—you selfish dreamer!

(TOM *smashes his glass on the floor. He plunges out on the fire-escape, slamming the door.* LAURA *screams—cut by door.*)

(*Dance-hall music up.* TOM *goes to the rail and grips it desperately, lifting his face in the chill white moonlight penetrating the narrow abyss of the alley.*)

(LEGEND ON SCREEN: "AND SO GOODBYE . . .")

(TOM'S *closing speech is timed with the interior pantomime. The interior scene is played as though viewed through soundproof glass.* AMANDA *appears to be making a comforting speech to* LAURA *who is huddled upon the sofa. Now that we cannot hear the mother's speech, her silliness is gone and she has dignity and tragic beauty.* LAURA'S *dark hair hides her face until at the end of the speech she lifts it to smile at her mother.* AMANDA'S *gestures are slow and graceful, almost dancelike, as she comforts the daughter. At the end of her speech she glances a moment at the father's picture—then withdraws through the portieres. At close of* TOM'S *speech,* LAURA *blows out the candles, ending the play.*)

TOM: I didn't go to the moon, I went much further—for time is the longest distance between two places— Not long after that I was fired for writing a poem on the lid of a shoe-box. I left Saint Louis. I descended the steps of this fire-escape for a last time and followed, from then on, in my father's footsteps, attempting to find in motion what was lost in space—I traveled around a great deal. The cities swept about me like dead leaves, leaves that were brightly colored but torn away from the branches. I would have stopped, but I was pursued by something. It always came upon me unawares, taking me altogether by surprise. Perhaps it was a familiar bit of music. Perhaps it was only a piece of transparent glass— Perhaps I am walking along a street at night, in some strange city, before I have found companions. I pass the lighted window of a shop where perfume is sold. The window is filled with pieces of colored glass, tiny transparent bottles in delicate colors, like bits of a shattered rainbow. Then all at once my sister touches my shoulder. I turn around and look into her eyes . . . Oh, Laura, Laura, I tried to leave you behind me, but I am more faithful than I intended to be! I reach for a cigarette, I cross the street, I run into the movies or a bar, I buy a drink, I speak to the nearest stranger—anything that can blow your candles out!

(LAURA *bends over the candles*)—for nowadays the world is lit by lightning! Blow out your candles, Laura—and so good-bye. . . .

(*She blows the candles out.*)

THE SCENE DISSOLVES

QUESTIONS

A. Understanding the Action:

1. Why did Tennessee Williams construct his play in seven scenes instead of using the conventional pattern of three, four, or five acts?
2. Are the theatrical devices that he uses (musical themes, gauze curtains, etc.) superficial devices external to the play or necessary to its structure? Explain your answer.
3. What is the difference between the speeches of Tom the narrator and Tom the participant in content and tone or style?
4. What is the climax of the play?
5. How would you classify this play? Realistic? Romantic? Poetic? or what?
6. "Memory takes a lot of poetic license." How much has the dramatist taken in this play?
7. What is the dramatic significance of the blown-up photograph of the father?

B. Understanding the Characters:

1. Tennessee Williams tells us that there is endurance and heroism as well as foolishness and cruelty in Amanda. Find some examples of each.
2. He says "her life is paranoia." What does this mean? Is he giving us a clinical study of an abnormal personality, or is Amanda in some respects fairly typical of mothers to be found in many homes?
3. Why has Laura lost contact with the world of reality? Is she a tragic or pathetic figure?
4. What makes Tom unhappy in the world he exists in? Why does he attend so many movies? Would you justify or condemn his flight? Does he harbor feelings of guilt? How does he resemble his father?
5. Williams calls Jim O'Connor "a nice, ordinary, young man." What aspects of contemporary American life are presented in Jim's training, ambition, and values? Are they satirized? Justify your opinion. How does Jim differ from Tom?

C. Understanding the Approach:

1. Tennessee Williams has said, "My chief aim in playwriting is the creation of character. I have always had a deep feeling for the mystery in life, and essentially my plays have been efforts to explore the beauty and meaning in the confusion of living." In this play has he succeeded in his aim? Justify your opinion.
2. Tennessee Williams' dialogue has been highly praised. In the last scene of *A Streetcar Named Desire*, Blanche DuBois says to the doctor who is taking her to a mental institution, "Whoever you are—I have always depended on the kindness of strangers." This poignant sentence is a summation of her life and character. Can

you find in *The Glass Menagerie* statements that are similarly expressive of character?

3. In the plays of Sheridan and Shaw almost all the characters talk cleverly; Shakespeare, on the other hand, sharply differentiates his characters by their speech. What do you think of the dialogue in this play? Are the people characterized by their manner of talking?

4. In the dialogue find examples of Williams' use of symbolism.

D. *Comparisons:*

1. How would you compare Laura and Shakespeare's Juliet in their ability to face reality? Compare Laura and Agnes (in *The Apollo of Bellac*).

2. Compare the flight from a family in this play and in *The Barretts of Wimpole Street*. Is your sympathy as strong for Tom as it is for Elizabeth? Why or why not? How does Tom himself judge his flight?

ALLEGORY AND FANTASY

Playwrights have not hesitated to depart from realistic characterization and plot in order to throw some special light on reality or to create a world of the imagination with which to fascinate the playgoer while instructing or stimulating him.

When playwrights have intended to drive a lesson home directly they have concentrated on events and characters that serve the moral so zealously that the plays have been called "moralities." When the "morality play," moreover, has used abstract characters representing virtues, vices, and other qualities or general concepts (such as Death, Wisdom, the Flesh, the World, and so on), it has been called an allegory.

This type of composition was widespread during the Middle Ages, and it has continued to appear since then not only in plays but in poems (such as Edmund Spenser's long narrative poem *The Faërie Queene*, written in Shakespeare's times) and in prose fiction, such as John Bunyan's *The Pilgrim's Progress*, the famous religious work that influenced many men in England and America, including Abraham Lincoln and Bernard Shaw. Modern allegorical plays have also made a strong impression at one time or another. Perhaps the best known of these have been the Belgian author Maurice Maeterlinck's *The Blue Bird*, produced at the beginning of the century—in 1908; the Russian playwright Leonid Andreyev's *The Life of Man*; and the American playwright Philip Barry's *Here Come the Clowns*.

Fantasy is too familiar a term to require definition. A fantastic play may involve a completely fanciful action such as the fairy (Oberon and Titania) plot of *A Midsummer Night's Dream*. It may, however, include realistically presented characters, actions, and environments, imaginatively used, or combined with fanciful events and characters involving magic, ghosts, and supernatural beings. A good example is the play included in this section, Percy MacKaye's *The Scarecrow*, an imaginative treatment of life and superstition in Puritan New England.

As we familiarize ourselves with dramatic literature throughout the world, however, we are bound to encounter a virtually countless number of plays that are fantasies wholly or in part. The world's theatre indeed would have been much poorer without such plays as *Prometheus Bound* (Aeschylus), *Alcestis* (Euripides), *The Birds* (Aristophanes) from classic Greece of the fifth century B.C., or *Dr. Faustus* (Marlowe), *The Tempest* (Shakespeare), *Faust* (Goethe), *Liliom* (Molnar), *Six Characters in Search of an Author* (Pirandello), *The Dybbuk* (S. Ansky), *On Borrowed Time* (Paul Osborn), and *Peter Pan* (James M. Barrie) since Shakespeare's times.

Many and various have been the uses of fantasy. Fantasy has been used playfully, philosophically, moralistically, and politically as a way of enriching our appreciation or enlarging our understanding of human experience.

INTRODUCTION TO *EVERYMAN*

The author of *Everyman* is anonymous. The play was written toward the end of the fifteenth century, but was probably drawn from an earlier source. The author or adapter of *Everyman* was obviously steeped in the tradition of medieval literature, art, and religion which described life on earth as preparation for a life of eternal bliss or suffering.

The morality plays were a late type of medieval religious drama. The story was designed to impart moral instruction to the public. In order to make the lesson broad enough, the situations were presented in general terms and the characters generalized to such a degree that they became abstractions or so-called allegorical figures. The action of the fully developed morality plays or moral allegories consisted of several episodes. The only surviving complete allegory in English, *The Castle of Perseverance*, included: 1) the battle between the Virtues and the Vices for Man's soul, 2) the summons of Death, requiring Man to examine his conduct and consider the state of his soul, 3) a debate between Body and Soul, and 4) a discussion of the Heavenly Graces.

Everyman, the best of the morality plays, is much more unified than such a string of episodes. Unlike *The Castle of Perseverance*, it is a single episode. Its theme is strictly the Summoning of Man —"*Every Man.*" Especially interesting is the structure of the play; the action is conceived as a journey or "pilgrimage" that Everyman must take. He requests "Fellowship," "Kindred," "Goods," "Good Deeds" (who cannot follow him until he has confessed his guilt), "Knowledge," "Strength," "Discretion," and "Beauty" to accompany him as he takes his final journey to the grave. *Everyman* is unique among the moral allegories of the Middle Ages and it has none of the laborious preachment and crude farcicality of other medieval morality plays. The interest never flags, the mood is never disturbed, and the lesson is never flat or heavy in this short masterpiece, originally written in Middle English but modernized here for the student. It is not surprising that an Austrian poet, Hugo von Hofmannsthal, was able to recast the play successfully in Germany in 1920 for a famous stage production by Max Reinhardt which became an annual summer festival event in Salzburg, Austria.

EVERYMAN

A MODERNIZED VERSION BY JOHN GASSNER

CHARACTERS

EVERYMAN
GOD: ADONAI
DEATH
MESSENGER
FELLOWSHIP
COUSIN
KINDRED
GOODS
GOOD-DEEDS

STRENGTH
DISCRETION
FIVE-WITS
BEAUTY
KNOWLEDGE
CONFESSION
ANGEL
DOCTOR

Here Beginneth a Treatise How the High Father of Heaven Sendeth Death to Summon All Creatures to Come and Give Account of Their Lives in This World and Is in the Manner of a Moral Play.[1]

PROLOGUE

MESSENGER: I pray you all give your audience,
And hear this matter with reverence,
By figure a moral play—
The *Summoning of Everyman* called it is,
That of our lives and ending shows
How transitory we be all our day.
This matter is wondrous precious,
But the intent of it is more gracious,
And sweet to bear away.
The story saith,—Man, in the beginning,
Look well, and take good heed to the ending,
Be you never so gay!
Ye think sin in the beginning full sweet,
Which in the end causeth the soul to weep,
When the body lieth in clay.
Here shall you see how Fellowship and Jollity,

[1] moral play: a morality play, an allegorical drama that conveys a moral lesson.

And Strength, Pleasure, and Beauty,
Will fade from thee as flower in May.
For ye shall hear how our heaven's king
Calleth Everyman to a general reckoning.
Give audience, and hear what he doth say.
(God *appears and speaks*)

GOD: I perceive here in my majesty,
How that all creatures be to me unkind,[2]
Living without dread in worldly prosperity.
Of spiritual sight the people be so blind,
Drowned in sin, they know me not for their God;
In worldly riches is all their mind,
They fear not my righteousness, the sharp rod;
My law that I showed, when I for them died,
They clean forget, and shedding of my blood red;
I hung between two, it cannot be denied;
To get them life I suffered to be dead;
I healed their feet, with thorns hurt was my head—
I could do no more than I did truly,
And now I see the people do clean forsake me.
They use the seven deadly sins damnable;
And pride, covetousness,[3] wrath, and lechery,
Now in the world be made commendable;
And thus they leave of angels the heavenly company;
Every man liveth so after his own pleasure,
And yet of their life they be nothing sure.
I see the more that I them forbear
The worse they be from year to year;
All that liveth impaireth[4] fast,
Therefore I will in all the haste
Have a reckoning of Everyman's person
For if I leave the people thus alone
In their life and wicked tempests,
Verily they will become much worse than beasts;
For now one would by envy another eat up;
Charity they all do clean forget.
I hoped well that every man
In my glory should make his mansion,
And thereto I had them all elect;
But now I see, like traitors abject,
They thank me not for the pleasure that I to them meant,
Nor yet for their being that I them have lent;
I proffered the people great multitude of mercy,
And few there be that ask it earnestly:
They be so cumbered with worldly riches,

---

[2] ungrateful.
[3] greed, desire for possessions.
[4] deteriorates.

That needs on them I must do justice,
On Everyman living without fear.
Where art thou, Death, thou mighty messenger?
    (*Enter* Death)
DEATH: Almighty God, I am here at Thy will,
Thy commandment to fulfil.
GOD: Go thou to Everyman,
And show him in my name
A pilgrimage he must on him take,
Which he in no wise may escape;
And that he bring with him a sure reckoning
Without delay or any tarrying.
    (God *withdraws*)
DEATH: Lord, I will in the world go, run over all,
And cruelly search out both great and small;
Every man I will beset that liveth beastly
Out of God's law, and dreadeth not folly.
He that loveth riches I will strike with my dart,
His sight to blind, and from heaven will him part,
Except that Alms be his good friend,
In hell for to dwell, world without end.
Lo, yonder I see Everyman walking;
Full little he thinketh on my coming.
His mind is on fleshly lusts and his treasure,
And great pain it shall cause him to endure
Before the Lord, heaven's King.
Everyman, stand still! whither art thou going
Thus gaily? Hast thou thy maker forgot?
    (*Enter* Everyman)
EVERYMAN: Why askest thou?
Wouldest thou know?
DEATH: Yea, sir, I will show you.
In great haste I am sent to thee
From God out of his majesty.
EVERYMAN: What, sent to me?
DEATH: Yea, certainly.
Though thou have forgot him here,
He thinketh on thee in his heavenly sphere,
As, ere[5] we depart, thou shalt know.
EVERYMAN: What desireth God of me?
DEATH: That shall I show thee;
A reckoning he will needs have
Without a longer respite.
EVERYMAN: To give a reckoning longer leisure I crave;
This blind[6] matter troubleth my wit.

[5] before.
[6] obscure.

DEATH: On thee thou must take a long journey.
　Therefore thy book of accounts with thee bring;
　For to return thou canst not any way,
　And look thou be sure of thy reckoning:
　For before God thou shalt answer, and show
　Thy many bad deeds and good but a few;
　How thou hast spent thy life, and in what wise,
　Before the Great Lord of Paradise.
　Make preparation that we be on the way,
　For know thou well thou shalt make none thy attorney.
EVERYMAN: Full unready I am such reckoning to give,
　I know thee not. What messenger art thou?
DEATH: I am Death, that no man dreadeth,
　That every man arrests and no man spareth;
　For it is God's commandment
　That all to me should be obedient.
EVERYMAN: O Death, thou comest when I had thee least in mind;
　In thy power it lieth me to save,
　Yet of my goods will I give thee, if ye will be kind,
　Yea, a thousand pound shalt thou have
　To defer this matter till another day!
DEATH: Everyman, it may not be by no way;
　I set not[7] by gold, silver, nor riches,
　Nor by pope, emperor, king, duke, nor princes,
　For if I would receive gifts great,
　All the world I might get;
　But my custom is clean contrary.
　I give thee no respite. Come hence, do not tarry!
EVERYMAN: Alas, shall I have no longer respite?
　I may say Death giveth no warning.
　To think on thee it maketh my heart sick,
　For all unready is my book of reckoning.
　But twelve year if I might have abiding,
　My counting book I would make so clear
　That my reckoning I should not need to fear.
　Wherefore, Death, I pray thee, for God's mercy,
　Spare me till I be provided of remedy.
DEATH: Thee availeth not to cry, weep, and pray,
　But haste thee lightly that thou go on the journey,
　And prove thy friends if thou can.
　For, know thou well, the time abideth no man,
　And in the world each living creature
　For Adam's sin must die by way of nature.
EVERYMAN: Death, if I should this pilgrimage take,

---

[7] care not for gold, etc.

And my reckoning surely make,
Show me, for Saint Charity,
Should I not return here shortly?

DEATH: No, Everyman. If thou be once *there*
Thou mayest nevermore come here,
Trust me verily.

EVERYMAN: O Gracious God, in the high seat celestial,
Have mercy on me in this my need;
Shall I have no company from this vale terrestrial[8]
Of mine acquaintance the way me to lead?

DEATH: Yea, if any be so hardy
That would go with thee and bear thee company.
Hasten that thou be gone to God's magnificence
Thy reckoning to give before his presence.
What, thinkest thou thy life is given thee
And thy worldly goods also?

EVERYMAN: I had thought so, verily.

DEATH: Nay, nay, it was but *lent* thee!
For as soon as thou dost go
Another awhile shall have it and then go therefro[9]
Even as thou hast done.
Everyman, thou art mad. Thou hast thy wits—all five
Yet here on earth will not amend thy life,
For suddenly do I come.

EVERYMAN: O wretched caitiff, whither shall I flee,
That I might escape this endless sorrow!
Now, gentle Death, spare me till to-morrow,
That I may amend me[10]
With good advisement.

DEATH: Nay, thereto I will not consent,
Nor no man will I respite,
But to the heart suddenly I shall smite
Without any advisement.[11]
And now out of thy sight I will me hie.
See thou make thee ready shortly,
For thou mayst say this is the day
That no man living may escape away.
(Death *withdraws*)

EVERYMAN: Alas, I may well weep with sighs deep.
Now have I no manner of company
To help me in my journey, and me to keep.[12]
And also my account is full unready!
What shall I do now for to excuse me?
I would to God I had never been begot!
To my soul a full great profit it would be.

[8] from this earthly place (valley).
[9] therefrom.
[10] improve myself.
[11] without allowing time for reflection.
[12] to guard or protect.

For now I fear pains huge and hot.
The time passeth. Lord, help that all wrought![13]
For though I mourn it availeth nought.
The day passeth, and is almost gone.
I know not well what is to be done.
To whom were I best my complaint to make?
What if I to Fellowship thereof spake,
And showed him of this sudden chance?
For in him is all mine affiance,
We have in the world so many a day
Been good friends in sport and play.
I see him yonder, certainly—
I trust that he will bear me company.
Therefore to him will I speak to ease my sorrow.
   (Fellowship *enters*)
Well met, good Fellowship, and good morrow!

FELLOWSHIP: Everyman, good morrow by this day.
Sir, why lookest thou so piteously?
If any thing be amiss, I pray thee, me say,
That I may help to remedy.

EVERYMAN: Yea, good Fellowship, yea,
I am in great jeopardy.

FELLOWSHIP: My true friend, show to me your mind;
I will not forsake thee, unto my life's end,
In the way of good company.

EVERYMAN: That was well spoken, and lovingly.

FELLOWSHIP: Sir, I must needs know your heaviness—
I have pity to see you in any distress.
If any have wronged you ye shall revenged be,
Though I on the ground be slain for thee,
Though that I know before that I should die.

EVERYMAN: Verily, Fellowship, gramercy.

FELLOWSHIP: Tush! by thy thanks I set not a straw.
Show me your grief and say no more.

EVERYMAN: If I my heart should to you break,
And then you to turn your mind from me
And would not comfort me when you hear me speak,
Then should I ten times sorrier be.

FELLOWSHIP: Sir, I say as I will do indeed.

EVERYMAN: Then be you a good friend at need—
I have found you true here before.

FELLOWSHIP: And so ye shall evermore.
For, in faith, if thou go to Hell,
I will not forsake thee by the way!

---

[13] that made everything.

EVERYMAN: Ye speak like a good friend, I believe
   you well.
   I shall repay it, if I may.
FELLOWSHIP: I speak of no repayment, by this day.
   For he that will say and nothing do
   Is not worthy with good company to go.
   Therefore show me the grief of your mind,
   As to your friend most loving and kind.
EVERYMAN: I shall show you how it is:
   Commanded I am to go a journey,
   A long way, hard and dangerous,
   And give a strict account without delay
   Before the high judge Adonai.[14]
   Wherefore I pray you, bear me company,
   As ye have promised, in this journey.
FELLOWSHIP: This is matter indeed! Promise is duty,
   But, if I should take such a voyage on me,
   I know it well, it should be to my pain.
   Also it maketh me afeard, for certain.
   But let us take counsel here as well as we can,
   For thy words would cow a strong man.
EVERYMAN: Why, ye said, if I had need,
   Ye would me never forsake, quick nor dead,
   Though it were to Hell truly.
FELLOWSHIP: So I said, certainly,
   But from such pleasures set me aside, thee sooth to
      say!
   And also, if we took such a journey,
   When should we come again?
EVERYMAN: Nay, never again till the day of doom.
FELLOWSHIP: In faith, then I will not come there!
   Who hath thee these tidings brought?
EVERYMAN: Indeed, Death was with me here.
FELLOWSHIP: Now, by God that all hath bought,[15]
   If Death were the messenger,
   For no man living here to-day
   Would I go that loathsome journey—
   Nay, nor for the father that begat me!
EVERYMAN: Ye promised otherwise, pardie.[16]
FELLOWSHIP: I know well I did say so truly.
   And yet if thou wilt eat, and drink, and make good
      cheer,
   Or seek together women's lusty company,
   I would not forsake you while the day is clear,[17]
   Trust me verily!

[14] Adonai: In Hebrew, God or The Lord.
[15] redeemed.
[16] by God (*par Dieu*, in French).
[17] until—until the dawn; the reference here is to dissipating all night.

EVERYMAN: Yea, thereto ye would be ready—
To go to mirth, solace, and play
Your mind you would sooner apply
Than to bear me company in my long journey.
FELLOWSHIP: Now, in good faith, I will not that way.
But if thou wilt murder, or any man kill,
In that I will help thee with a good will!
EVERYMAN: O that is a simple advice indeed!
Gentle fellow, help me in my necessity—
We have loved long, and now I need,
And now, gentle Fellowship, remember me.
FELLOWSHIP: Whether ye have loved me or no,
By Saint John, I will not with thee go.
EVERYMAN: Yet I pray thee, take the labor and do so much for me
To keep me company, for Saint Charity,
And comfort me till I come beyond the town.
FELLOWSHIP: Nay, though thou wouldst give me a new gown
I would not a foot with thee go.
But if thou hadst tarried I would not have left thee so.
And so now, God speed thee in thy journey,
For from thee I will depart as fast as I may.
EVERYMAN: Whither away, Fellowship? will you forsake me?
FELLOWSHIP: Yea, by my fay, to God I commend thee!
EVERYMAN: Farewell, good Fellowship, for thee my heart is sore.
Adieu for ever, I shall see thee no more.
FELLOWSHIP: In faith, Everyman, farewell now at the end;
From you I will remember that parting is mourning.
(*Exit* Fellowship)
EVERYMAN: Alack then! shall we thus part indeed?
Our Lady, help him who has no more comfort:
Lo, Fellowship forsaketh me in my most need:
For help in this world whither shall I resort?
Fellowship heretofore with me would merry make,
And now little sorrow for me doth he take.
It is said, in prosperity men friends may find
Which in adversity be full unkind.
Now whither for succor shall I flee,
Since that Fellowship hath forsaken me?
To my kinsmen I will truly,

JOHN GASSNER

Praying them to help me in my necessity.
I believe that they will do so,
For "kind will creep where it can not go."[18]
I will go try, for yonder I see them go.
Where be ye now, my friends and kinsmen?
   (Kindred *and* Cousin *appear*)

KINDRED: Here be we now at your commandment.
Cousin, I pray you show us your intent
In any wise, and do not spare.

COUSIN: Yea, Everyman, and to us declare
If ye be disposed to go anywhere,
For know you well we will live and die together.

KINDRED: In wealth and woe we will with you hold,
For with a kinsman's aid a man may be bold.

EVERYMAN: Gramercy,[19] my friends and kinsmen kind.
Now shall I show you the grief of my mind.
I was commanded by a messenger,
That is an High King's chief officer.
He bade me go a pilgrimage to my pain,
And I know well I shall never come again.
Also I must give a reckoning straight,
For I have a great enemy who lies in wait,
And intendeth me to hinder.

KINDRED: What account is that which ye must render?
That would I know.

EVERYMAN: Of all my works I must show
How I have lived and my days spent.
Also of ill deeds that I have used
In my time since life was me lent,
And of all virtues that I have refused.
Therefore I pray you go thither with me,
To help to make my account, for Saint Charity.

COUSIN: What, to go thither? Is that the matter?
Nay, Everyman, I had rather fast on bread and water
All this five year and more.

EVERYMAN: Alas, that ever I was born!
For now shall I never be merry
If you forsake me.

KINDRED: Ah, sir, what, be ye a merry man?
Take good heart to you, and make no moan.
But one thing I warn you, by Saint Anne:
If ye are counting on me, ye shall go alone.

EVERYMAN: My Cousin, will you not with me go?

COUSIN: No, by our Lady, I have the cramp in my toe.

[18] Kinship will exert itself to help a relative.
[19] "God give you mercy"—a form of saying "Thank you."

Wait not for me, for, so God me speed,
I will forsake you in your utmost need.
KINDRED: It availeth not us to entice.
You shall have my maid with all my heart;
She loveth to go to feasts, there to be nice,
And to dance, and abroad to start.
I will give her leave to help you in that journey
If you and she will agree.
EVERYMAN: Now show me the true meaning of your mind—
Will you go with me, or abide behind?
KINDRED: Abide behind? Yea, that I will, if I may!
Therefore farewell until another day.
EVERYMAN: How should I be merry or glad?
For fair promises men to me make,
But when I have most need they me forsake.
I am deceived, alas—that maketh me sad.
COUSIN: Everyman, farewell now,
For verily I will not go with you.
Also of mine own an unready reckoning
I have to account; therefore I make tarrying.
Now, God keep thee, for now I go.
  (*Exit* Kindred *and* Cousin)
EVERYMAN: Ah, Jesus, is all come hereto?
Lo, fair words make fools fain.
They promise and nothing will do certain.
My kinsmen promised me faithfully
For to abide with me steadfastly,
And now fast away do they flee.
Even so Fellowship promised me.
What friend were best for me to provide?
I lose my time here longer to abide.
Yet in my mind a thing there is—
All my life I have loved Riches;
If that my Goods now help me might,
It would make my heart full light.
I will speak to him in this distress.—
Where art thou, my Goods and Riches?
GOODS: Who calleth me? Everyman, what haste thou hast!
I lie here in corners, trussed and piled so high,
And in chests I am locked so fast,
Also sacked in bags, thou mayst see with thine eye,
I cannot stir; in packs low I lie.
What would ye have, quickly to me say.

EVERYMAN: Come hither, Goods, in all the haste thou may,
  For of counsel I must desire thee.
GOODS: Sir, if ye in the world have trouble or adversity,
  That can I help you to remedy shortly.
EVERYMAN: It is another disease that grieveth me.
  In this world it is not, I tell thee so.
  I am sent for another way to go,
  To give a straight account general
  Before the highest Jupiter of all.
  And all my life I have had joy and pleasure in thee.
  Therefore I pray thee go with me,
  For, peradventure, thou mayst before God Almighty
  My reckoning help to clean and purify.
  For it is said ever us among,
  That money maketh all right that is wrong.
GOODS: Nay, Everyman, I sing another song,
  I follow no man in such voyages.
  For if I went with thee
  Thou shouldst fare much the worse for me.
  For because on me thou did bend thy mind,
  Thy reckoning I have made blotted and blind,
  That thine account thou canst not make truly—
  And that hast thou for the love of me.
EVERYMAN: That would grieve me full sore,
  When I should come to that fearful answer.
  Up, let us go thither together.
GOODS: Nay, not so, I am too brittle, I may not endure.
  I will follow no man one foot, be ye sure.
EVERYMAN: Alas, I have loved thee, and had great pleasure
  All my life-days on goods and treasure.
GOODS: That is to thy damnation without ending;
  For love of me is contrary to the love everlasting.
  But if thou hadst loved me moderately,
  And to the poor given part of me,
  Then shouldst thou not in this dolor be,
  Nor in this great sorrow and care.
EVERYMAN: Lo, now was I deceived ere I was aware,
  And all I may blame my misusing of time.
GOODS: What, thinkest thou that I am thine?
EVERYMAN: I had supposed so.
GOODS: Nay, Everyman, I say no.
  But for a while was I lent thee,

A season thou hast had me in prosperity.
My condition it is a man's soul to kill—
If I save one, a thousand I do spill.
Thinkest thou that I will follow thee?
Nay, not from this world verily.

EVERYMAN: I had thought otherwise.

GOODS: Therefore to thy soul Goods is a thief;
For when thou art dead, this is my game
Another to deceive in ways the same,
As I have done thee, and all to his soul's grief.

EVERYMAN: O false Goods, cursed thou be!
Thou traitor to God, that hast deceived me,
And snatched me in thy snare.

GOODS: Marry, thou hast brought thyself to despair,
Whereof I am glad—
I must needs laugh; I cannot be sad.

EVERYMAN: Ah, Goods, thou hast had long my heart-felt love;
I gave thee that which should be the Lord's above.
But wilt thou not go with me indeed?
I pray thee truth to say.

GOODS: No, so God me speed,
Therefore farewell, and have thou good day.
(*Exit* Goods)

EVERYMAN: O, to whom shall I make my moan
For to go with me in that heavy journey?
First Fellowship said he would with me be gone;
His words were very pleasant and gay,
But afterward he left me alone.
Then spake I to my kinsmen all in despair,
And they also gave me words fair.
They lacked no fair speaking,
But they forsook me in the ending.
Then went I to my Goods that I loved best,
In hope to have comfort, but there had I least.
For my Goods sharply did me tell
That he bringeth many into Hell.
Then of myself I was ashamed,
And so I am worthy to be blamed,
Thus may I well myself hate.
Of whom shall I now counsel take?
I think that I shall never speed
Till that I go to my Good-Deed,
But, alas, she is so weak,
That she can neither walk nor speak.

Yet will I venture on her now.—
My Good-Deeds, where be you?
  (*Enter* Good-Deeds)
GOOD-DEEDS: Here I lie cold in the ground.
  Thy sins have me so sore bound
  That I cannot stir.
EVERYMAN: O, Good-Deeds, I stand in fear;
  I must pray you for counsel,
  For help now would come right well.
GOOD-DEEDS: Everyman, I have understanding
  That you be summoned account to make
  Before Messias, of Jerusalem the King.[20]
  If you walk by me that journey with you I will take.
EVERYMAN: Therefore I come to you, my moan to make—
  I pray you, that ye will go with me.
GOOD-DEEDS: I would full fain, but I cannot stand, verily.
EVERYMAN: Why, did anything you befall?
GOOD-DEEDS: Yea, sir, and I may thank you for all;
  If ye had perfectly cheered me,
  Your book of accounts now full ready would be.
  Look, the books of your works and deeds, ay—
  Oh, see how they under your feet lie,
  Unto your soul's heaviness.
EVERYMAN: Our Lord Jesus, help me!
  For one letter here I cannot see.
GOOD-DEEDS: There is a blind reckoning in time of distress!
EVERYMAN: Good-Deeds, I pray you, help me in this need,
  Or else I am for ever damned indeed.
  Therefore help me to make reckoning
  Before the Redeemer of everything.
  That king is, and was, and ever shall.
GOOD-DEEDS: Everyman, I am sorry for your fall,
  And gladly would I help you, if I were able.
EVERYMAN: Good-Deeds, your counsel I pray you give me.
GOOD-DEEDS: That shall I do verily.
  Though that on my feet I may not go,
  I have a sister that shall with you also,
  Called Knowledge, which shall with you abide,
  To help you to make that dreadful reckoning.
  (*Enter* Knowledge)

[20] The Messiah (literally "the Anointed" in Hebrew); in Christianity, Jesus Christ.

KNOWLEDGE: Everyman, I will go with thee, and be thy guide,
In utmost need to go by thy side.
EVERYMAN: In good condition I am now in every thing,
And am wholly content with this good thing.
Thanked be God, my Creator!
GOOD-DEEDS: And when he hath brought thee there
Where thou shalt heal thee of thy smart,[21]
Then go you with your reckoning and your Good-Deeds together
For to make you joyful at heart
Before the blessed Trinity.
EVERYMAN: My Good-Deeds, gramercy;
I am well content, certainly,
With your words so sweet.
KNOWLEDGE: Now go we together lovingly,
To Confession, that cleansing river.
EVERYMAN: For joy I weep. I would we were there!
But, I pray you, give me cognition[22]
Where dwelleth that holy man, Confession.
KNOWLEDGE: In the house of salvation.[23]
We shall find him in that place
That shall comfort us by God's grace.
    (Confession *appears*)
Lo, this is Confession; kneel down and ask mercy,
For he is in good esteem with God Almighty.
EVERYMAN: O glorious fountain that all uncleanness doth clarify,
Wash from me the spots of vices unclean,
That on me no sin may be seen.
I come with Knowledge for my redemption,
Repent with hearty and full contrition.
For I am commanded a pilgrimage to take,
And straight accounts before God to make.
Now, I pray you, Shrift,[24] mother of Salvation,
Help my Good-Deeds; hear my piteous exclamation!
CONFESSION: I know your sorrow well, Everyman.
Because with Knowledge ye come to me,
I will comfort you as well as I can,
And a precious jewel I will give thee,
Called penance, avoider of adversity.
Therewith shall thy body chastised be,
With abstinence and perseverance in God's service.
Here shalt thou receive that scourge of me

---

[21] pain.
[22] information.
[23] in the Church.
[24] Confession.

Which is penance strong that you must endure,
To remember thy Saviour was scourged for thee
With sharp scourges, and suffered it patiently.
So must thou, ere thou escape that painful pilgrimage;
Knowledge, guard him in this voyage,
And by that time Good-Deeds will be with thee!
And in any wise, make sure of mercy,
For your time approaches if you would saved be.
Ask God mercy, and He will grant truly;
When with the scourge of penance man doth himself bind
The oil of forgiveness then shall he find.

EVERYMAN: Thanked be God for his gracious work!
For now I will my penance begin.
This hath rejoiced and lighted my heart
Though the scourge be painful and hard within.

KNOWLEDGE: Everyman, look that ye your penance fulfil,
Whatever pain it to you be,
And Knowledge shall give you counsel at will
How your accounts ye shall make clearly.

EVERYMAN: O eternal God, O heavenly figure,
O way of righteousness, O goodly vision,
Which descended down in a virgin pure
Because He would Everyman redeem,
Which Adam forfeited by his disobedience.
O blessed Godhead, elect and divine,
Forgive my grievous offence,
Here I cry Thee mercy in this presence.
O soul's treasure, O ransomer and redeemer
Of all the world, hope and leader,
Mirror of joy, and founder of mercy,
Which illumineth heaven and earth thereby,
Hear my clamorous complaint, though it late be,
Receive my prayers. Unworthy in this heavy life
Though I be, a sinner most abominable,
Yet let my name be written in Moses' table;[25]
O Mary, pray to the Maker of everything,
To help me at my ending,
And save me from the power of my enemy,
For Death assaileth me strongly.
And, Lady, that I may by means of thy prayer
Of your Son's glory be the partaker,
By the pity of his Passion I it crave,
I beseech you, help my soul to save.—

[25] Moses' tables of the Law. One of these tablets symbolized penance in the Middle Ages.

Knowledge, give me the scourge of penance,
My flesh therewith shall give a quittance.
I will now begin, if God give me grace.
KNOWLEDGE: Everyman, God give you time and space.
Thus I bequeath you into the hands of our Saviour,
Thus may you make your reckoning sure.
EVERYMAN: In the name of the blessed Trinity,
My body sore punished shall be.
Take this body for the sin of the flesh!
(*He scourges himself*)
Thou that delightest to go gay and fresh
And in the way of damnation didst me bring,
Now suffer therefore these strokes and punishing.
Now of penance I will wade the water clear,
To save me from Purgatory, that sharp fire.
(Good-Deeds, *rising from the ground, joins them*)
GOOD-DEEDS: I thank God, now I can walk and go,
And am delivered of my sickness and woe.
Therefore with Everyman I will go, and not spare—
His good works I will help him to declare.
KNOWLEDGE: Now, Everyman, be merry and glad.
Your Good-Deeds cometh now, ye may not be sad.
Now is your Good-Deeds whole and sound,
Going upright upon the ground.
EVERYMAN: My heart is light, and shall be evermore,
Now I will smite faster than I did before.
GOOD-DEEDS: Everyman, pilgrim, my special friend,
Blessed be thou without end.
For thee is prepared the eternal glory.
Ye have me made whole and sound,
Therefore I will bide by thee in every round.[26]
EVERYMAN: Welcome, my Good-Deeds! Now I hear thy voice,
I weep for very sweetness of love.
KNOWLEDGE: Be no more sad, but ever rejoice,
God seeth thy living from his throne aloft.
Put on this garment which is so soft—
Wet with your tears it is.
Or else before God you may it miss,
When you to your journey's end shall come.
EVERYMAN: Gentle Knowledge, what is its name?
KNOWLEDGE: It is a garment of sorrow:
From pain it will release you;
Contrition it is
That getteth forgiveness;

---

[26] "in every round"—in every trial.

It pleaseth God passing well.
GOOD-DEEDS: Everyman, will you wear it for your weal?[27]

(Everyman *puts on the robe*)

EVERYMAN: Now blessed be Jesu, Mary's Son!
For now have I on true contrition.
And let us go now without tarrying.
Good-Deeds, have we clear our reckoning?
GOOD-DEEDS: Yea, indeed I have it here.
EVERYMAN: Then I trust we need not fear;
Now, friends, let us not part in twain.
KNOWLEDGE: Nay, Everyman, that will we not, certain.
GOOD-DEEDS: Yet must thou lead with thee
Three persons of great might.
EVERYMAN: Who should they be?
GOOD-DEEDS: Discretion and Strength are they hight,[28]
And thy Beauty too may not remain behind.
KNOWLEDGE: Also you must call to mind
Your Five-Wits[29] as for your counselors.
GOOD-DEEDS: You must have them ready at all hours.
EVERYMAN: How shall I get them hither?
KNOWLEDGE: You must call them all together,
And they will hear you incontinent.[30]
EVERYMAN: My friends, come hither and be present,
Discretion, Strength, my Five-Wits, and Beauty.

(Discretion, Strength, Five-Wits *and* Beauty *enter*)

BEAUTY: Here at your will we be all ready.
What will ye that we should do?
GOOD-DEEDS: That ye would with Everyman go,
And help him in his pilgrimage.
Consider, will ye go with him or not on that voyage?
STRENGTH: We will bring him all thither,
To his help and comfort, ye may believe me.
DISCRETION: So will we go with him all together.
EVERYMAN: Almighty God, praised mayest thou be.
I give thee laud that I have hither brought
Strength, Discretion, Beauty, and Five-Wits; now I lack nought!
And my Good-Deeds, with Knowledge clear,
All stay in my company at my will here;
I desire no more for my business.
STRENGTH: And I, Strength, will stand by you in distress,
Though thou wouldest in battle fight on the ground.

[27] salvation.
[28] called.
[29] The Five Senses.
[30] immediately.

FIVE-WITS: And though it were through the world round,
We will not depart for sweet nor sour.
BEAUTY: No more will I until death's hour,
Whatsoever thereof befall.
DISCRETION: Everyman, advise you first of all,
Go with a good advisement and deliberation.
We all give you virtuous monition
That all shall be well.
EVERYMAN: My friends, hearken what I will tell.
I pray God reward you in his heavenly sphere.
Now hearken, all that be here,
For I will make my testament
Here before every one present.
In alms half my goods I will give with my hands twain
In the way of charity, with good intent,
And the other half, my flesh, shall remain
In quiet, to be returned where it ought to be.
This I do in despite of the fiend of hell,
To be quit of his peril
Today and ever after this day.
KNOWLEDGE: Everyman, hearken what I say.
Go to priesthood, I advise,
And receive of him in every wise
The holy sacrament and ointment together,
Then shortly see ye turn again hither:
We will all await you here.
FIVE-WITS: Yea, Everyman, haste you that ye ready be.
There is no emperor, king, duke, nor baron,
That of God hath commission,
As hath the least priest in the world's design.
For of the blessed sacraments pure and benign,
He beareth the keys and thereof hath the care
For man's redemption that is ever there;
Which God for our soul's medicine
Gave us out of his heart with great pain.
Here in this transitory life, for thee and me,
The blessed sacraments seven there be,
Baptism, confirmation, with priesthood good,
And the sacrament of God's precious flesh and blood,
Marriage, the holy extreme unction, and penance;
These seven be good to have in remembrance,
Gracious sacraments of high divinity.

EVERYMAN: Fain would I receive that holy body
And meekly to my spiritual father I will go.
FIVE-WITS: Everyman, that is the best that ye can do.
God will you to salvation bring,
For priesthood exceedeth all other thing.
To us Holy Scripture they do teach,
And convert man from his sin heaven to reach;
God hath to them more power given,
Than to any angel that is in heaven.
With five words[31] he may consecrate
God's body in flesh and blood to make,
And holdeth his maker between his hands,
The priest bindeth and unbindeth all bands,
Both in earth and in heaven,
He ministers all the sacraments seven.—
Though we kissed thy feet thou wert worthy,
Thou art surgeon that cureth sin deadly.
No remedy we find that is good
But only under priesthood.—
Everyman, God gave priests that dignity,
And setteth them in his stead among us to be—
Therefore be they above angels in degree.
(Everyman *departs to receive the last Sacraments*)
KNOWLEDGE: If priests be good it is so surely!
But when Jesus hanged on the cross with great smart
There he *gave*, out of his blessed heart,
The same sacrament in great torment:
He *sold* them not to us, that Lord Omnipotent!
Therefore Saint Peter, the apostle, doth say
That Jesu's curse have all they
Who God their Saviour do buy or sell,
Or if they any money do take or tell.[32]
Sinful priests have to sinners bad example been.
Their children sit by other men's fires, I have seen;
And some priests haunt women's company
With unclean life, in search of lechery:
These be with sin made blind.
FIVE-WITS: I trust to God no such may we find.
Therefore let us priesthood honor,
And follow their doctrine for our souls' succor.
We be their sheep, and they shepherds be
By whom we all are kept in surety.
Peace, for yonder I see Everyman come,
Who hath made true satisfaction.

---

[31] The words, in the Latin, are: "*Hoc est enim corpus meum*"—For this is my body.

[32] count out.

GOOD-DEEDS: Methinketh it is he indeed.
(*Everyman returns*)
EVERYMAN: Now Jesu all our labor speed,
I have received the sacrament for my redemption,
And then mine extreme unction.
Blessed be all they that counseled me to take it!
And now, friends, let us go without longer respite,
I thank God that ye have tarried so long.
Now set each of you on this cross your hand,
And shortly follow me.
I go before where I would be, God be our guide!
STRENGTH: Everyman, we will not from you go,
Till ye have gone this voyage long.
DISCRETION: I, Discretion, will bide by you also.
KNOWLEDGE: And though this pilgrimage be never so hard,
I will never part from you, too.
EVERYMAN: I will stand as secure with thee
As ever I stood with Judas Maccabee.[33]
(*They approach the grave*)
EVERYMAN: Alas, I am so faint I may not stand,
My limbs under me do fold.
Friends, let us not turn again to this land,
Not for all the world's gold,
For into this cave must I creep
And turn to the earth and there sleep.
BEAUTY: What, into this grave? Alas!
EVERYMAN: Yea, there shall you be consumed, all shall pass!
BEAUTY: What more! Should I smother here?
EVERYMAN: Yea, by my faith, and never more appear.
In this world live no more we shall,
But in heaven before the highest lord of all.
BEAUTY: I cross out my vow; adieu by Saint John!
I doff my cap as low as my lap and am gone.
EVERYMAN: What, Beauty, whither will ye?
BEAUTY: Peace, I am deaf! I look not behind me,
Not if thou would give me all the gold in thy chest.
(*Beauty departs*)
EVERYMAN: Alas, in whom may I trust?
Beauty fast away doth hie—
She promised with me to live and die.
STRENGTH: Everyman, I will thee also forsake and deny.
Thy game pleases me not at all.

---

[33] Judas Maccabæus, the leader of the successful revolt of the Jews against the Syrians, who tried to impose pagan worship on the Hebrew people.

EVERYMAN: Why, then ye will forsake me all?
  Sweet Strength, tarry a little space.
STRENGTH: Nay, sir, by the rood of grace
  I will hasten from thee first
  Though thou weep till thy heart burst.
EVERYMAN: Ye would ever bide by me, ye said.
STRENGTH: I have you far enough conveyed.
  Ye be old enough, I understand,
  Your pilgrimage to take on hand;
  I regret I hither came.
EVERYMAN: Strength, you to displease I am to blame;
  Will you break a promise that is a debt?
STRENGTH: In faith, I care not.
  Thou art but a fool to complain,
  You spend your speech and waste your brain—
  Go thrust thee into the ground!
EVERYMAN: I had thought surer to have you found.
    (*Exit* Strength)
  He that trusteth in his Strength
  She deceiveth him at the length.
  Both Strength and Beauty have forsaken me,
  Yet they promised me fair and lovingly.
DISCRETION: Everyman, I will after Strength be gone,
  As for me, I too will leave you alone.
EVERYMAN: Why, Discretion, will ye forsake me?
DISCRETION: Yea, in faith, I will go from thee,
  For when Strength goeth before
  I follow after evermore.
EVERYMAN: Yet, I pray thee, for the love of Trinity,
  Look in my grave once piteously.
DISCRETION: Nay, so near the grave will I not come.
  Farewell, every one!
    (*Exit* Discretion)
EVERYMAN: O all things faileth, save God alone;
  Beauty, Strength, and Discretion;
  For when Death bloweth his blast
  They all run from me full fast.
FIVE-WITS: Everyman, my leave now of thee I take;
  I will follow the other, for here I thee forsake.
EVERYMAN: Alas! then may I wail and weep,
  For I took you for my best friend.
FIVE-WITS: I will not longer thee keep.
  Now farewell, and there an end.
    (*Exit* Five-Wits)
EVERYMAN: O Jesu, help, all have forsaken me!

GOOD-DEEDS: Nay, Everyman, I will bide with thee,
   I will not forsake thee indeed,
   Thou shalt find me a good friend at need.
EVERYMAN: Gramercy, Good-Deeds, now may I true friends see.
   They have forsaken me every one.
   I loved them better than my Good-Deeds alone.
   Knowledge, will ye forsake me also?
KNOWLEDGE: Yea, Everyman, when ye to death do go,
   But not yet for no manner of danger.
EVERYMAN: Gramercy, Knowledge, with all my heart.
KNOWLEDGE: Nay, yet I will not from hence depart,
   Till I see what of thee shall become.
EVERYMAN: Methink, alas, that I must be gone,
   To make my reckoning and debts to pay,
   For I see my time is nigh spent away.
   Take example, all ye that this do hear or see,
   How they that I loved best do forsake me,
   Except my Good-Deeds that bideth truly!
GOOD-DEEDS: All earthly things are but vanity:
   Beauty, Strength, and Discretion, do man forsake,
   Foolish friends and kinsmen, that fair spake,
   All flee save Good-Deeds, and that am I.
EVERYMAN: Have mercy on me, God most mighty;
   And stand by me, thou Mother and Maid, holy Mary.
GOOD-DEEDS: Fear not, I will speak for thee.
EVERYMAN: Here I cry God mercy.
GOOD-DEEDS: Shorten our end, diminish our pain.
   Let us go and never come again.
EVERYMAN: Into Thy hands, Lord, my soul I commend.
   Receive it, Lord, that it be not lost!
   As thou me boughtest, so me defend,
   And save me from the fiend's boast,
   That I may appear with that blessed host
   That shall be saved at the day of doom.
   In manus tuas—of Might's utmost
   Forever—*commendo spiritum meum.*[34]
      (Everyman *and* Good-Deeds *enter the grave*)
KNOWLEDGE: Now hath he suffered what we all shall endure,
   But Good-Deeds shall make all sure.
   Now hath he made ending—
   Methinketh that I hear angels sing
   And make great joy and melody,

---

[34] Into Thy hands, most Mighty One forever, I commend my spirit.

Where Everyman's soul received shall be.
    (*An* Angel *appears*)
ANGEL: Come, excellent elect spouse[35] to Jesu!
    Hereabove thou shalt go
    Because of thy singular virtue.—
    Now the soul is taken from the body so,
    Thy reckoning is crystal-clear.
    Now shalt thou into the heavenly sphere,
    Unto which all ye shall come
    That live well before the day of doom.

Epilogue

(*Enter* Doctor[36])

DOCTOR: This moral men may have in mind:
    Ye hearers, take it of worth, old and young,
    And forsake Pride, for he deceiveth you in the end,
    And remember Beauty, Five-Wits, Strength, and Discretion,
    They all at the last do Everyman forsake,
    Only his Good-Deeds there doth he take.
    But beware, if *they* be small
    Before God, *man hath no help at all;*
    No excuse may there be for Everyman.
    Alas, how shall he fare then?
    For after death amends may no man make,
    For then mercy and pity him forsake.
    If his reckoning be not clear when he come,
    God will say—*ite maledicti in ignem æternum.*[37]
    And he that hath his account whole and sound,
    High in heaven he shall be crowned,
    Unto which place God bring us all thither
    That we may live body and soul together.
    Thereto help blessed Trinity.
    Amen, say ye, for Saint Charity.
    Thus endeth this moral play of Everyman.

---

[35] Everyman's soul, which is about to be united with God, is now called "elect spouse"—that is, the Bride of God.

[36] Doctor: Teacher.

[37] "Depart from me, ye cursed, into everlasting fire" (The Gospel according to St. Matthew XXV:41).

QUESTIONS

A. *Understanding the Action:*

1. What is Everyman's problem? What is the chief source of his anguish? What is his chief error?
2. What is the state of Everyman's soul?
3. Who fails him? Why?
4. Who stands by him? Why?
5. What are we to learn from Everyman's experience?

B. *Understanding the Characters:*

1. How does Everyman's character develop in the course of the play? What changes occur?
2. All the characters are allegorical, i.e. each character personifies an abstract quality. Describe how you visualize each of the characters. What makes the characters different from one another?

3. What is God's role in the play? What is Death's role?

4. If Everyman is the "hero," who is the "villain"? Explain your answer.

C. Understanding the Approach:

1. What is the central theme . . . not the moral, but the theme, or "spine" of the play?

2. What are some of the universal aspects of this play? Discuss why you think so.

3. What is the moral or ethical basis of the play?

4. What dramatic elements are present in the play? Explain the effectiveness of the play's climax.

D. Comparisons:

1. How are the characters in *Antigone* and *Everyman* similar? What differences are there?

2. In the plays *Antigone* and *The Summoning of Everyman* there is a "force" beyond the reach of the leading characters. Explain what the force is.

PERCY MACKAYE (1875-1956)

Percy MacKaye, the son of an important pioneer in theatrical art as well as successful playwright of the 1880's, was for many years in the vanguard of American playwriting. He was overshadowed by a number of later American dramatists such as Eugene O'Neill, Maxwell Anderson, and Elmer Rice after 1920, but even today he can be remembered with respect as one of the few who preferred to serve the cause of imaginative, as opposed to commonplace, drama in the American theatre. In *The Scarecrow*, moreover, he succeeded in combining a love of fantasy with an interest in social realities that made the play vigorously "modern" rather than fancifully romantic like other early twentieth-century poetic plays in Europe and America. It is not surprising, then, that *The Scarecrow* should have been successfully revived in our own day.

Born of earnest New England parents in 1875, Percy MacKaye went to Harvard University in due time. After graduation from the college in 1897, he spent two years abroad, studying at the University of Leipzig in Germany, and then settled down to four years of teaching in New York City. But this son of a theatrical family (even the mother became a playwright and turned out a successful dramatization of the famous English novel *Pride and Prejudice*) wrote plays and choral poems even before entering Harvard. He soon became a prolific writer of verse and of spectacular pageants or "masques," as well as of volumes of poetry, essays, and recollections. He published about a hundred books and had about twenty-five plays produced professionally. His first professionally produced play was the biographical drama *Jeanne d'Arc*, written in 1905, and the famous acting couple Sothern and Marlowe scored a great success with this Joan of Arc play. He experimented with a tragedy of fate *Sappho and Phaon* in 1907; with a romantic fantasy, *A Thousand Years Ago*, in 1913; and with a satire, *Anti-Matrimony*, in which he showed young people being drawn to various absurdities by following the plays of Ibsen and Shaw. His most ambitious dramatic project was a tetralogy, *The Mystery of Hamlet*, consisting of four full-length verse dramas.

MacKaye died at the age of 81, on August 31, 1956.

INTRODUCTION TO *THE SCARECROW*

Percy MacKaye's most distinguished and long-lasting contribution is *The Scarecrow*, which he started to write in 1903 with material drawn from a short story, *Feathertop*, by the great American novelist Nathaniel Hawthorne. Professor Arthur Hobson Quinn, the noted historian of the American drama, justly praised MacKaye for his achievement, writing that "what raises *The Scarecrow* above the usual play of the period is the powerful employment of the fantastic . . . , kindling the rather abstract creations of Hawthorne into life." Professor Quinn also rightly observed how this play, which could have deteriorated into mere supernaturalism, attains tragic force and elevation at the end. Ravensbane, the animated scarecrow hero of the play, "died a man, and the tragedy of the defeated soul leaves us not with a sense of futility, but with the exaltation that comes when we have witnessed a struggle that has been worth while."[1]

The Scarecrow was first staged by the Harvard Dramatic Club, at Cambridge, Massachusetts, on December 8, 1909 and received its first professional production in the United States in 1911 with the famous German actor Emmanuel Reicher (1849-1924) playing the part of Ravensbane for two seasons.

A German version was successfully produced in Berlin by Max Reinhardt.

[1] Arthur Hobson Quinn, *A History of the American Drama*, New York, 1927, 1936, vol. 2, pp. 32-34.

THE SCARECROW

A Tragedy of the Ludicrous

PERCY MacKAYE

CHARACTERS

JUSTICE GILEAD MERTON
GOODY RICKBY (*"Blacksmith Bess"*)
LORD RAVENSBANE (*"Marquis of Oxford, Baron of Wittenberg, Elector of Worms, and Count of Cordova"*), *their hypothetical son*
DICKON, *a Yankee improvisation of the Prince of Darkness (Satan)*
RACHEL MERTON, *niece of the Justice*
MISTRESS CYNTHIA MERTON, *sister of the Justice*

RICHARD TALBOT, *Esquire, betrothed to Rachel*
SIR CHARLES REDDINGTON, *Lieutenant-Governor*
MISTRESS REDDINGTON } *his daughters*
AMELIA REDDINGTON
CAPTAIN BUGBY, *the Governor's Secretary*
MINISTER DODGE
MISTRESS DODGE, *his wife*
REV. MASTER RAND, *of Harvard College*
REV. MASTER TODD, *of Harvard College*
MICAH, *a servant of the Justice*

Time: LATE SEVENTEENTH CENTURY   Place: A TOWN IN MASSACHUSETTS

ACT I

(*The interior of a blacksmith shop. Right center, a forge. Left, a loft, from which are hanging dried cornstalks, hay, and the yellow ears of cattle-corn. Back center, a wide double door, closed when the curtain rises. Through this door—when later it is opened—is visible a New England landscape in the late springtime: a distant wood; stone walls, high elms, a well sweep; and, in the near foreground, a ploughed field, from which the green shoots of early corn are just appearing. The blackened walls of the shop are covered with a miscellaneous collection of old iron, horseshoes, cart-wheels, etc., the usual appurtenances of a smithy. In the right-hand corner, however, is an array of things quite out of keeping with the shop proper; musical instruments, puppets, tall clocks, and fantastical junk. Conspicuous amongst these articles is a large standing mirror, framed grotesquely in old gold and curtained by a dull stuff, embroidered with peaked caps and crescent moons.*)

(*Just before the scene opens, a hammer is heard ringing briskly upon steel. As the curtain rises there is discovered, standing at the anvil in the flickering light of a bright flame from the forge, a woman —powerful, ruddy, proud with a certain* masterful beauty, white-haired (*as though prematurely*), bare-armed to the elbows, clad in a dark skirt (*above her ankles*), a loose blouse, open at the throat; a leathern apron and a workman's cap. The woman is GOODY RICKBY. *On the anvil she is shaping a piece of iron. Beside her stands a framework of iron formed like the ribs and backbone of a man. For a few moments she continues to ply her hammer, amid a shower of sparks, till suddenly the flame on the forge dies down.*)

GOODY RICKBY: Dickon! More flame.

A VOICE: (*above her*) Yea, Goody.

(*The flame in the forge spurts up high and suddenly.*)

GOODY RICKBY: Nay, not so fierce.

THE VOICE: (*at her side*) Votre pardon, madame.[1]

(*The flame subsides.*)

Is that better?

GOODY RICKBY: That will do.

(*With her tongs, she thrusts the iron into the flame; it turns white-hot.*)

Quick work; nothing like brimstone for the smithy trade.

(*At the anvil, she begins to weld the iron rib onto the framework.*)

There, my beauty! We'll make a stout set of ribs for you. I'll see to it this year that I have a scarecrow can outstand all the nor'easters that blow. I've no notion to lose my corn-crop this summer.

(*Outside, the faint cawings of crows are heard. Putting down her tongs and hammer,* GOODY RICKBY *strides to the double door, and flinging it wide open, lets in the gray light of dawn. She looks out over the fields and shakes her fist.*)

So ye're up before me and the sun, are ye? (*Squinting against the light.*)

There's one! Nay, two. Aha!
          One for sorrow,
          Two for mirth—

Good! This time we'll have the laugh on our side.

(*She returns to the forge, where again the fire has died out.*)

Dickon! Fire! Come, come, where be thy wits?

THE VOICE: (*sleepily from the forge*) 'Tis early, dame.

GOODY RICKBY: The more need— (*Takes up her tongs.*)

THE VOICE: (*screams*) Ow!

GOODY RICKBY: Ha! Have I got thee? (*From the blackness of the forge she pulls out with her tongs, by the right ear, the figure of a devil, horned and tailed. In general aspect, though he resembles a medieval familiar demon, yet the suggestions of a goatish beard, a shrewdly humorous smile, and (when he speaks) the slightest of nasal drawls, remotely simulate a species of Yankee rustic.* GOODY RICKBY *substitutes her fingers for the tongs.*) Now, Dickon!

DICKON: *Deus!*[2] I haven't been nabbed like that since St. Dunstan[3] tweaked my nose. Well, sweet Goody?

GOODY RICKBY: The bellows!

DICKON: (*going slowly to the forge*) Why, 'tis hardly dawn yet. Honest folks are still abed. It makes a long day.

GOODY RICKBY: (*working, while* DICKON *plies the bellows*) Aye, for your black pets, the crows, to work in. That's why we must be at it early. You heard 'em. We must have this scarecrow of ours out in the field at his post before sunrise. Here, I've made the frame strong, so as to stand the weather; *you* must make the body lifelike so as to fool the crows. This year, we must make 'em think it's a real human crittur.

DICKON: To fool the philosophers is my specialty, but the crows—hm!

GOODY RICKBY: Pooh! That staggers thee!

DICKON: Madame Rickby, prod not the quick of my genius. I am Phidias,[4] I am Raphael,[5] I am the Lord God!—You shall see—

(*Demands with a gesture.*)

Yonder broom-stick.

GOODY RICKBY: *(fetching him a broom from the corner)* Good boy!

DICKON: *(straddling the handle)* Ha, ha! gee up! my Salem mare.

(Then, pseudo-philosophically.)

A broomstick—that's for imagination!

(He begins to construct the scarecrow, while GOODY RICKBY, *assisting, brings the constructive parts from various nooks and corners.)*

We are all pretty artists, to be sure, Bessie. Phidias, he sculptures the gods; Raphael, he paints the angels; the Lord God, he creates Adam; and Dickon—fetch me the poker—aha! Dickon! What doth Dickon? He nullifies 'em all; he endows the Scarecrow![6] A poker; here's his conscience. There's two fine legs to walk on,—imagination and conscience. Yonder flails now! The ideal—the *beau idéal*,[7] dame—that's what we artists seek. The apotheosis[8] of scarecrows! And pray, what's a scarecrow? Why, the antithesis[9] of Adam.—"Let there be candles!" quoth the Lord God, sitting in the dark. "Let there be candle-extinguishers," saith Dickon. "I am made in the image of my maker," quoth Adam.[10] "Look at yourself in the glass," saith Goodman Scarecrow. *(Taking two implements from* GOODY RICKBY.*)*

Fine! fine! here are flails—one for wit, t'other for satire. *Sapristi!*[11] with two such arms, my lad, how thou wilt work thy way in the world!

GOODY RICKBY: You talk as if you were making a real mortal, Dickon.

DICKON: To fool a crow, Goody, I must fashion a crittur[12] that will first deceive a man.

GOODY RICKBY: He'll scarce do that without a head.

(Pointing to the loft.)

What think ye of yonder Jack-o'-lantern? 'Twas made last Hallowe'en.

DICKON: Rare, my Psyche![13] We shall collaborate. Here!

(Running up the ladder, he tosses down a yellow hollowed pumpkin to GOODY RICKBY, *who catches it. Then rummaging forth an armful of cornstalks, ears, tassels, dried squashes, gourds, beets, etc., he descends and throws them in a heap on the floor.)*

Whist! *(as he drops them.)* Gourd, carrot, turnip, beet:—the anatomy.[14]

GOODY RICKBY: *(placing the pumpkin on the shoulders)* Look!

DICKON: *O Johannes Baptista!*[15] What wouldst thou have given for such a head! I helped Salome[16] to cut his off, dame, and it looked not half so appetizing on her charger. Tut! Copernicus[17] wore once such a pumpkin, but it is rotten. Look at his golden smile! Hail, Phœbus Apollo![18]

GOODY RICKBY: 'Tis the finest scarecrow in town.

DICKON: Nay, poor soul, 'tis but a skeleton yet. He must have a man's heart in him.

(Picking a big red beet from among the cornstalks, he places it under the left side of the ribs.)

Hush! Dost thou hear it *beat?*

GOODY RICKBY: Thou merry rogue!

DICKON: Now for the lungs of him.

(Snatching a small pair of bellows from a peg on the wall.)

That's for eloquence! He'll preach the black knaves[19] a sermon on theft. And now—

(Here, with GOODY RICKBY'S *help, he stuffs the framework with the gourds, corn, etc., from the loft, weaving the husks about the legs and arms.)*

Here goes for digestion and inherited instincts! More corn, Goody. Now he'll fight for his own flesh and blood!

GOODY RICKBY: *(laughing)* Dickon, I am proud of thee.

DICKON: Wait till you see his peruke.[20]

(Seizing a feather duster made of crow's feathers.)

Voici![21] Scalps of the enemy!

(Pulling them apart, he arranges the

feathers on the pumpkin, like a gentleman's wig.)

A rare conqueror!

GOODY RICKBY: Oh, you beauty!

DICKON: And now a bit of comfort for dark days and stormy nights.

(*Taking a piece of corn-cob with the kernels on it,* DICKON *makes a pipe, which he puts into the scarecrow's mouth.*)

So! There, Goody! I tell thee, with yonder brand-new coat and breeches of mine —those there in my cupboard!—we'll make him a lad to be proud of.

(*Taking the clothes, which* GOODY RICKBY *brings—a pair of fine scarlet breeches and a gold-embroidered coat with ruffles of lace—he puts them upon the scarecrow. Then, eying it like a connoisseur,*[22] *makes a few finishing touches.*)

Why, dame, he'll be a son to thee.

GOODY RICKBY: A son? Aye, if I had but a son!

DICKON: Why, here you have him. (*To the scarecrow.*) Thou wilt scare the crows off thy mother's cornfield—won't my pretty? And send 'em all over t'other side the wall to her dear neighbor's, the Justice Gilead Merton's.

GOODY RICKBY: Justice Merton! Nay, if they'd only peck his eyes out, instead of his corn.

DICKON: (*grinning*) Yet the Justice was a dear friend of "Blacksmith Bess."[23]

GOODY RICKBY: Aye, "Blacksmith Bess"! If I hadn't had a good stout arm when he cast me off with the babe, I might have starved for all his worship cared.

DICKON: True, Bessie; 'twas a scurvy trick he played on thee—and on me, that took such pains to bring you together— to steal a young maid's heart—

GOODY RICKBY: And then toss it away like a bad penny to the gutter![24] And the child—to die! (*Lifting her hammer in rage.*) Ha! If I could get the worshipful Justice Gilead into my power again—

(*Drops the hammer sullenly on the anvil.*) But no! I shall beat my life away on this anvil, whilst my justice[25] clinks his gold, and drinks his port to a fat old age. Justice! Ha—justice of God!

DICKON: Whilst, dame! Talk of angels and hear the rustle of their relatives.

GOODY RICKBY: (*turning, watches outside a girl's figure approaching*) His niece —Rachel Merton! What can she want so early? Nay, I mind me; 'twas the mirror. She's a maid after our own hearts, boy,— no Sabbath-go-to-meeting airs about *her!* She hath read the books of the *magi*[26] from cover to cover, and paid me good guineas for 'em, though her uncle knows naught on't. Besides, she's in love, Dickon.

DICKON: (*indicating the scarecrow*) Ah? With *him*? Is it a rendezvous?[27]

GOODY RICKBY: (*with a laugh*) Pff! Begone!

DICKON: (*shakes his finger at the scarecrow*) Thou naughty rogue!

(*Then, still smiling slyly, with his head placed confidentially next to the scarecrow's ear, as if whispering, and with his hand pointing to the maiden outside,* DICKON *fades away into air.* RACHEL *enters, nervous and hesitant.* GOODY RICKBY *makes her a curtsy, which she acknowledges by a nod, half absent-minded.*)

GOODY RICKBY: Mistress Rachel Merton—so early! I hope your uncle, our worshipful Justice, is not ill?

RACHEL: No, my uncle is quite well. The early morning suits me best for a walk. You are—quite alone?

GOODY RICKBY: Quite alone, mistress. (*Bitterly.*) Oh, folks don't call on Goody Rickby—except on business.

RACHEL: (*absently, looking round in the dim shop*) Yes—you must be busy. Is it—is it here?

GOODY RICKBY: You mean the—

RACHEL: (*starting back, with a cry*) Ah! who's that?

GOODY RICKBY: (*chuckling*) Fear not,

mistress, 'tis nothing but a scarecrow. I'm going to put him in my cornfield yonder. The crows are so pesky this year.

RACHEL: (*draws her skirts away with a shiver*) How loathsome!

GOODY RICKBY: (*vastly pleased*) He'll do.

RACHEL: Ah, here!—This is *the* mirror?

GOODY RICKBY: Yea, mistress, and a wonderful glass it is, as I told you. I wouldn't sell it to most comers, but seeing how you and Master Talbot—

RACHEL: Yes; that will do.

GOODY RICKBY: You see, if the town folks guessed what it was, well— You've heard tell of the gibbets[28] on Salem Hill? There's not many in New England like you, Mistress Rachel. You know enough to approve some miracles—outside the Scriptures.

RACHEL: You are quite sure the glass will do all you say? It—never fails?

GOODY RICKBY: Ah, now, mistress, how could it? 'Tis the glass of truth—(*insinuatingly*)—the glass of true lovers. It shows folks just as they are; no shams, no varnish. If a wolf should dress himself in a white sheep's wool, this glass would reflect the black beast inside it.

RACHEL: (*with awe*) The black beast! But what of the sins of the soul, Goody? Vanity, hypocrisy, and—and inconstancy? Will it surely reveal them?

GOODY RICKBY: I have told you, my young lady. If it does not as I say, bring it back and get your money again. Oh, trust me, sweeting, an old dame hath eyes in her heart yet. If your lover be false, this glass shall pluck his fine feathers!

RACHEL: (*with aloofness*) 'Tis no question of that. I wish the glass to—to amuse me.

GOODY RICKBY: (*laughing*) Why, then, try it on some of your neighbors.

RACHEL: You ask a large price for it.

GOODY RICKBY: (*shrugs*) I run risks. Besides, where will you get another?

RACHEL: That is true. Here, I will buy it. That is the sum you mentioned, I believe?

(*She hands a purse to* GOODY RICKBY, *who opens it and counts over some coins.*)

GOODY RICKBY: Let see; let see.

RACHEL: Well?

GOODY RICKBY: Good: 'tis good. Folks call me a witch, mistress. Well—harkee—a witch's word is as good as a justice's gold. The glass is yours—with my blessing.

RACHEL: Spare yourself that, dame. But the glass: how am I to get it? How will you send it to me—quietly?

GOODY RICKBY: Trust me for that. I've a willing lad that helps me with such errands; a neighbor o' mine. (*Calls.*) Ebenezer!

RACHEL: (*startled*) What! is he here?

GOODY RICKBY: In the hayloft. The boy's an orphan; he sleeps there o' times. Ebenezer!

(*A raw, disheveled country* BOY *appears in the loft, slides down the ladder, and shuffles up sleepily.*)

THE BOY: Evenin'.

RACHEL: (*drawing* GOODY RICKBY *aside*) You understand; I desire no comment about this purchase.

GOODY RICKBY: Nor I, mistress, be sure.

RACHEL: Is he—?

GOODY RICKBY: (*tapping her forehead significantly*) Trust his wits who hath no wit; he's mum.

RACHEL: Oh!

THE BOY: (*gaping*) Job?

GOODY RICKBY: Yea, rumple-head! His job this morning is to bear yonder glass to the house of Justice Merton—the big one on the hill; to the side door. Mind, no gabbing. Doth he catch?[29]

THE BOY: (*nodding and grinning*) 'E swallows.

RACHEL: But is the boy strong enough?

GOODY RICKBY: Him? (*Pointing to the anvil.*) Ebenezer!
(*The boy spits on his palms, takes hold of the anvil, lifts it, drops it again, sits on it, and grins at the door, just as* RICHARD TALBOT *appears there, from outside.*)

RACHEL: Gracious!

GOODY RICKBY: Trust him. He'll carry the glass for you.

RACHEL: I will return home at once, then. Let him go quietly to the side door, and wait for me. Good-morning.
(*Turning, she confronts* RICHARD.)

RICHARD: Good-morning.

RACHEL: Richard!—Squire Talbot, you—you are abroad early.

RICHARD: As early as Mistress Rachel. Is it pardonable? I caught sight of you walking in this direction, so I thought it wise to follow, lest—
(*Looks hard at* GOODY RICKBY.)

RACHEL: Very kind. Thanks. We can return together. (*To* GOODY RICKBY.) You will make sure that I receive the—the article.

GOODY RICKBY: Trust me, mistress.
(*She curtsies to* RICHARD.)

RICHARD: (*bluntly, looking from one to the other*) What article?
(RACHEL *ignores the question and starts to go out.* RICHARD *frowns at* GOODY RICKBY, *who stammers.*)

GOODY RICKBY: Begging your pardon, sir?

RICHARD: What article? I said. (*After a short, embarrassed pause, more sternly.*) Well?

GOODY RICKBY: Oh, the article! Yonder old glass, to be sure, sir. A quaint piece, your honor.

RICHARD: Rachel, you haven't come here at sunrise to buy—that thing?

RACHEL: Verily, "that thing," and at sunrise. A pretty time for a pretty purchase. Are you coming?

RICHARD: (*in a low voice*) More witchcraft nonsense? Do you realize this is serious?

RACHEL: Oh, of course. You know I am desperately mystical,[30] so pray let us not discuss it. Good-bye.

RICHARD: Rachel, just a moment. If you want a mirror, you shall have the prettiest one in New England. Or I will import you one from London. Only—I beg of you—don't buy stolen goods.

GOODY RICKBY: Stolen goods?

RACHEL: (*aside to* RICHARD) Don't! don't!

RICHARD: (*to* GOODY RICKBY) Can you account for this mirror—how you came by it?

GOODY RICKBY: I'll show ye! I'll show ye! Stolen—ha!

RICHARD: Come, old swindler, keep your mirror, and give this lady back her money.

GOODY RICKBY: I'll damn ye both, I will!—Stolen!

RACHEL: (*imploringly*) Will you come?

RICHARD: Look you, old Rickby; this is not the first time. Charm all the broomsticks in town, if you like; bewitch all the tables and saucepans and mirrors you please; but gull no more money out of young girls. Mind you! We're not so enterprising in this town as at Salem;[31] but —*it may come to it!* So look sharp! I'm not blind to what's going on here.

GOODY RICKBY: Not blind, Master Puritan? Oho! You can see through all my counterfeits,[32] can ye? So! you would scrape all the wonder out'n[33] the world, as I've scraped all the meat out'n my punkin-head[34] yonder! Aha! wait and see! Afore sundown, I'll send ye a nut to crack, shall make your orthodox[35] jaws ache. Your servant, Master Deuteronomy![36]

RICHARD: (*to* RACHEL, *who has seized his arm*) We'll go.
(*Exeunt* RICHARD *and* RACHEL.)

GOODY RICKBY: (*calls shrilly after*

them) Trot away, pretty team; toss your heads. I'll unhitch ye and take off your blinders.

THE SLOUCHING BOY: (*capering and grimacing in front of the mirror, shrieks with laughter*) Ohoho!

GOODY RICKBY: (*returning, she mutters savagely*) "Stolen goods!" (*Screams.*) Dickon! Stop laughing.

THE BOY: Oh Lord! O Lord!

GOODY RICKBY: What tickles thy mirth now?

THE BOY: For to think that the soul of an orphan innocent, what lives in a hayloft, should wear horns.

(*On looking into the mirror, the spectator perceives therein that the reflection of the slouching boy is the horned demon figure of* DICKON, *who performs the same antics in pantomime within the glass as the boy does without.*)

GOODY RICKBY: Yea; 'tis a wise devil that knows his own face in the glass. But hark now! thou must find me a rival for this cock-squire,—dost hear? A rival, that shall steal away the heart of his Mistress Rachel.

DICKON: And take her to church?

GOODY RICKBY: To church or to hell. All's one.

DICKON: A rival! (*Pointing at the glass.*) How would *he* serve—in there? Dear Ebenezer! Fancy the deacons in the vestry, Goody, and her uncle, the Justice, when they saw him escorting the bride to the altar, with his tail round her waist.

GOODY RICKBY: Tut, tut! Think it over in earnest, and meantime take her the glass. Wait, we'd best fold it up small, so as not to attract notice on the road.

(DICKON, *who has already drawn the curtains over the glass, grasps one side of the large frame,* GOODY RICKBY *the other.*) Now! (*Pushing their shoulders against the two sides, the frame disappears and* DICKON *holds in his hand a mirror about a foot square, of the same design.*) So! Be off! And mind, a rival for Richard!

DICKON:
For Richard a rival,
Dear Goody Rickby
Wants Dickon's connival:[37]
Lord! What can the trick be?

(*To the scarecrow.*) By-by, Sonny; take care of thy mother.

(DICKON *slouches out with the glass, whistling.*)

GOODY RICKBY: Mother! Yea, if only I had a son—the Justice Merton's and mine! If the brat had but lived now to remind him of those merry days, which he has forgotten. Zooks, wouldn't I put a spoke in his wheel![38] But no such luck for me! No such luck!

(*As she goes to the forge, the stout figure of a man appears in the doorway behind her. Under one arm he carries a large book, in the other hand a gold-headed cane. He hesitates, embarrassed.*)

THE MAN: Permit me, madam.

GOODY RICKBY: (*turning*) Ah, him! —Justice Merton!

JUSTICE MERTON: (*removing his hat, steps over the sill, and lays his great book on the table; then with a supercilious*[39] *look, he puts his hat firmly on again*) Permit me, dame.

GOODY RICKBY: You!

(*With confused, affected hauteur,*[40] *the* JUSTICE *shifts from foot to foot, flourishing his cane. As he speaks,* GOODY RICKBY, *with a shrewd, painful expression, draws slowly backward toward the door, left, which opens into the inner room. Reaching it, she opens it part way, stands facing him, and listens.*)

JUSTICE MERTON: I have had the honor —permit me—to entertain suspicions; to rise early, to follow my niece, to meet just now Squire Talbot; to hear his remarks concerning—hem!—you, dame! to call here—permit me—to express myself and inquire—

GOODY RICKBY: Concerning your waistcoat?
(*Turning quickly, she snatches an article of apparel which hangs on the inner side of the door, and holds it up.*)
JUSTICE MERTON: (*starting, crimson*) Woman!
GOODY RICKBY: You left it behind—the last time.
JUSTICE MERTON: I have not the honor to remember—
GOODY RICKBY: The one I embroidered?
JUSTICE MERTON: 'Tis a matter of—
GOODY RICKBY: Of some two-and-twenty years. (*Stretching out the narrow width of the waistcoat.*) Will you try it on now, dearie?
JUSTICE MERTON: Unconscionable![41] Un-un-unconscionable witch!
GOODY RICKBY: Witchling[42]—thou used to say.
JUSTICE MERTON: Pah! pah! I forget myself. Pride, permit me, goeth before a fall. As a magistrate, Rickby, I have already borne with you long! The last straw, however, breaks the camel's back.
GOODY RICKBY: Poor camel!
JUSTICE MERTON: You have soiled, you have smirched, the virgin reputation of my niece. You have inveigled her into notions of witchcraft; already the neighbors are beginning to talk. 'Tis a long lane which hath no turning, saith the Lord. Permit me—as a witch, thou art judged. Thou shalt hang.
A VOICE: (*behind him*) And me, too?
JUSTICE MERTON: (*turns about and stares*) I beg pardon.
THE VOICE: (*in front of him*) Not at all.
JUSTICE MERTON: Did—did somebody speak?
THE VOICE: Don't you recognize my voice? *Still and small*, you know. If you will kindly let me out, we can chat.
JUSTICE MERTON: (*turning fiercely on* GOODY RICKBY) These are thy sorceries.[43]
But I fear them not. The righteous man walketh with God. (*Going to the book which lies on the table.*) Satan, I ban thee! I will read from the Holy Scriptures!
(*Unclasping the Bible, he flings open the ponderous covers.*—DICKON *steps forth in smoke.*)
DICKON: Thanks; it was stuffy in there.
JUSTICE MERTON: (*clasping his hands*) Dickon!
DICKON: (*moving a step nearer on the table*) Hullo, Gilly! Hullo, Bess!
JUSTICE MERTON: Dickon! No! No!
DICKON: Do ye mind Auld Lang Syne—the chorus that night, Gilly? (*Sings.*)
  Gil-ead, Gil-ead, Gil-ead Merton,
    He was a silly head, silly head, Certain,
    When he forgot to steal a bed-Curtain.
Encore,[44] now!
JUSTICE MERTON: No, no, be merciful! I will not harm her; she shall not hang; I swear it, I swear it! (DICKON *disappears.*) I swear—ah! Is he gone? Witchcraft! Witchcraft! I have witnessed it. 'Tis proved on thee, slut. I swear it: thou shall hang. (*Exit wildly.*)
GOODY RICKBY: Ay, Gilead! I shall hang *on!* Ahaha! Dickon, thou angel! Ah, Satan! Satan! For a son now!
DICKON: (*reappearing*) *Videlicet*,[45] in law—a bastard. *N' est ce pas?*[46]
GOODY RICKBY: Yea, in law and in justice, I should 'a' had one now. Worse luck that he died.
DICKON: One-and-twenty years ago? (GOODY RICKBY *nods.*) Good; he should be of age now. One-and-twenty—a pretty age, too, for a rival. Haha!—For arrival?—Marry, he shall arrive, then; arrive and marry and inherit his patrimony[47]—all on his birthday! Come, to work!
GOODY RICKBY: What rant is this?
DICKON: Yet, Dickon, it pains me to perform such an anachronism.[48] All this mediævalism[49] in Massachusetts!—These

old-fashioned flames and alchemic[50] accompaniments, when I've tried so hard to be a native American product; it jars. But *che vuole!*[51] I'm naturally middle-aged. I haven't been really myself, let me think, —since 1492![52]

GOODY RICKBY: What art thou mooning about?

DICKON: (*still impenetrable*) There was my old friend in Germany, Dr. Johann Faustus;[53] he was nigh such a bag of old rubbish when I made him over. Ain't it trite! No, you can't teach an old dog like me new tricks. Still, a scarecrow! that's decidedly local color.[54] Come, then; a Yankee masterpiece!

(*Seizing* GOODY RICKBY *by the arm, and placing her before the scarecrow, he makes a bow and wave of introduction.*)

Behold, madam, your son—illegitimate; the future affianced[55] of Mistress Rachel Merton, the heir-elect, through matrimony,[56] of Merton House,—Gilead Merton second: Lord Ravensbane![57] Your lordship—your mother.

GOODY RICKBY: Dickon! Can you do it?

DICKON: I can—try.

GOODY RICKBY: You will create him for me?—(*wickedly*)—and for Gilead!

DICKON: I will—for a kiss.

GOODY RICKBY: (*about to embrace him*) Dickon!

DICKON: (*dodging her*) Later. Now, the waistcoat.

GOODY RICKBY: (*handing it*) Rare! rare! He shall go wooing in't—like his father.

DICKON: (*shifting the scarecrow's gold-trimmed coat, slips on the embroidered waistcoat and replaces the coat*) Stand still, Jack! So, my macaroni.[58] *Perfecto!*[59] Stay—a walking-stick!

GOODY RICKBY: (*wrenching a spoke out of an old rickety wheel*) Here: the spoke for Gilead. He used to take me to drive in the chaise[60] it came out of.

DICKON: (*placing the spoke as a cane, in the scarecrow's sleeve, views him with satisfaction*) Sic![61] There, Jacky! *Filius fit non nascitur.*[62]—Sam Hill! My Latin is stale. "In the beginning, was the—gourd!"[63] Of these thy modest ingredients may thy spirit smack!

(*Making various mystic passes with his hands,* DICKON *intones, now deep and solemn, now with fanciful shrill rapidity, this incantation.*[64])

    Flail, flip:
    Broom, sweep;
       Sic itur![65]
    Cornstalk
    And turnip, talk!
       Turn crittur!

    Pulse, beet;
    Gourd, eat;
       Ave[66] Hellas!
    Poker and punkin,
    Stir the old junk in;
       Breathe, bellows!

    Corn-cob,
    And crow's feather,
    End the job;
Jumble the rest o' the rubbish together;
    Dovetail and tune 'em
    E pluribus unum![67]

(*The scarecrow remains stock still.*)

The devil! Have I lost the hang of it? Ah! Hullo! He's dropped his pipe. What's a dandy without his 'baccy![68]

(*Picking the pipe up, he shows it to* GOODY RICKBY, *pointing into the pipe-bowl.*)

'Tis my own brand, Goody; brimstone. Without it he'd be naught but a scarecrow. (*Restoring the corn-cob pipe to the scarecrow's mouth.*)

'Tis the life and breath of him. So; hand me yon hazel switch, Goody. (*Waving it.*) Presto!

    Brighten, coal.
    I' the dusk between us!
    Whiten, soul!
    Propinquat Venus![69]

(*A whiff of smoke puffs from the scarecrow's pipe.*)

Sic! Sic! Jacobus!⁷⁰ (*Another whiff.*) Bravo!

(*The whiffs grow more rapid and the thing trembles.*)

GOODY RICKBY: Puff! puff, manny, for thy life!

DICKON: *Fiat, fœtus!*⁷¹—Huzza! *Noch einmal!*⁷² Go it! (*Clouds of smoke issue from the pipe, half fill the shop, and envelop the creature, who staggers.*)

GOODY RICKBY: See! See his eyes!

DICKON: (*beckoning with one finger*) *Veni, fili! Veni!*⁷³ Take'ee first step, *bambino!* Toddle!

(*The* SCARECROW *makes a stiff lurch forward and falls sidewise against the anvil, propped half-reclining against which he leans rigid, emitting fainter puffs of smoke in gasps.*)

GOODY RICKBY: (*screams*) Have a care! He's fallen.

DICKON: Well done, Punkin Jack! Thou shalt be knighted for that! (*Striking him on the shoulder with the hazel rod.*) Rise, Lord Ravensbane!

(*The* SCARECROW *totters to his feet, and makes a forlorn rectilinear salutation.*)

GOODY RICKBY: Look! He bows.—He flaps his flails at thee. He smiles like a tik-doo-loo-roo!

DICKON: (*with a profound reverence, backing away*) Will his reverence deign to follow his tutor?

(*With hitches and jerks, the* SCARECROW *follows* DICKON.)

GOODY RICKBY: O Lord! Lord! the style o' the broomstick!

DICKON: (*holding ready a high-backed chair*) Will his lordship be seated and rest himself?

(*Awkwardly the* SCARECROW *half falls into the chair; his head sinks sideways, and his pipe falls out.* DICKON *snatches it up instantly and restores it to his mouth.*)

Puff! Puff, *puer*;⁷⁴ 'tis thy life.

(*The* SCARECROW *puffs again.*)

Is his lordship's tobacco refreshing?

GOODY RICKBY: Look, now! The red color in his cheeks. The beet-juice is pumping, oho!

DICKON: (*offering his arm*) Your lordship will deign to receive an audience? (*The* SCARECROW *takes his arm and rises.*) The Marchioness of Rickby, your lady mother, entreats leave to present herself.

GOODY RICKBY: (*curtsying low*) My son!

DICKON: (*holding the pipe, and waving the hazel rod*) *Dicite!*⁷⁵ Speak!

(*The* SCARECROW, *blowing out his last mouthful of smoke, opens his mouth, gasps, gurgles, and is silent.*)

*In principio erat verbum!*⁷⁶ Accost thy mother!

(*The* SCARECROW, *clutching at his side in a struggle for coherence, fixes a pathetic look of pain on* GOODY RICKBY.)

THE SCARECROW: Mother!

GOODY RICKBY: (*with a scream of hysterical laughter, seizes both* DICKON'S *hands and dances him about the forge*) O Beelzebub!⁷⁷ I shall die!

DICKON: Thou hast thy son.

(DICKON *whispers in the* SCARECROW'S *ear, shakes his finger, and exit.*)

GOODY RICKBY: He called me "mother." Again, boy, again.

THE SCARECROW: From the bottom of my heart—mother.

GOODY RICKBY: "The bottom of his heart!"—Nay, thou killest me.

THE SCARECROW: Permit me, madam!

GOODY RICKBY: Gilead! Gilead himself! Waistcoat, "permit me," and all: thy father over again, I tell thee.

THE SCARECROW: (*with a slight stammer*) It gives me—I assure you—lady—the deepest happiness.

GOODY RICKBY: Just so the old hypocrite spoke when I said I'd have him. But thou hast a sweeter deference,[78] my son. (Reënter DICKON; he is dressed all in black, save for a white stock[79]—a suit of plain elegance.)

DICKON: Now, my lord, your tutor is ready.

THE SCARECROW: (to GOODY RICKBY) I have the honor—permit me—to wish you—good-morning.

(Bows and takes a step after DICKON, who, taking a three-cornered cocked hat from a peg, goes toward the door.)

GOODY RICKBY: Whoa! Whoa, Jack! Whither away?

DICKON: (presenting the hat) Deign to reply, sir.

THE SCARECROW: I go—with my tutor—Master Dickonson—to pay my respects—to his worship—the Justice—Merton—to solicit—the hand—of his daughter—the fair Mistress—Rachel. (With another bow.) Permit me.

GOODY RICKBY: Permit ye? God speed ye! Thou must teach him his tricks, Dickon.

DICKON: Trust me, Goody. Between here and Justice Merton's, I will play the mother-hen, and I promise thee, our bantling[80] shall be as stuffed with compliments as a callow[81] chick with caterpillars. (As he throws open the big doors, the cawing of crows is heard again.) Hark! your lordship's retainers[82] acclaim you on your birthday. They bid you welcome to your majority. Listen! "Long live Lord Ravensbane! Caw!"

GOODY RICKBY: Look! Count 'em Dickon.

> One for sorrow,
> Two for mirth,
> Three for a wedding,
> Four for a birth—

Four on 'em! So! Good luck on thy birthday! And see! There's three on 'em flying into the Justice's field.

—Flight o' the crows
Tells how the wind blows!—

A wedding! Get ye gone. Wed the girl, and sting the Justice. Bless ye, my son!

THE SCARECROW: (with a profound reverence) Mother—believe me—to be—your ladyship's—most devoted—and obedient—son.

DICKON: (prompting him aloud) Ravensbane.

THE SCARECROW: (donning his hat, lifts his head in hauteur,[83] shakes his lace ruffle over his hand, turns his shoulder, nods slightly, and speaks for the first time with complete mastery of his voice) Hm! Ravensbane!

(With one hand in the arm of DICKON, the other twirling his cane (the converted chaise-spoke), wreathed in halos of smoke from his pipe, the fantastical figure hitches elegantly forth into the daylight, amid louder acclamations of the crows.)

ACT II

(The same morning. JUSTICE MERTON'S parlor, furnished and designed in the style of the early colonial period. On the right wall hangs a portrait of the JUSTICE as a young man; on the left wall, an old-fashioned looking-glass. At the right of the room stands the glass of truth, draped—as in the blacksmith shop—with the strange, embroidered curtain.)

(In front of it are discovered RACHEL and RICHARD; RACHEL is about to draw the curtain.)

RACHEL: Now! Are you willing?

RICHARD: So you suspect me of dark, villainous practices?

RACHEL: No, no, foolish Dick.

RICHARD: Still, I am to be tested; is that it?

RACHEL: That's it.

RICHARD: As your true lover.

RACHEL: Well, yes.

RICHARD: Why, of course, then, I consent. A true lover always consents to the follies of his lady-love.

RACHEL: Thank you, Dick; I trust the glass will sustain your character.[84] Now; when I draw the curtain—

RICHARD: (*staying her hand*) What if I be false?

RACHEL: Then, sir, the glass will reflect you as the subtle fox that you are.

RICHARD: And you—as the goose?[85]

RACHEL: Very likely. Ah! but, Richard dear, we mustn't laugh. It may prove very serious. You do not guess—you do not dream all the mysteries—

RICHARD: (*shaking his head, with a grave smile*) You pluck at too many mysteries. Remember our first mother Eve!

RACHEL: But this is the glass of truth; and Goody Rickby told me—

RICHARD: Rickby, forsooth!

RACHEL: Nay, come; let's have it over. (*She draws the curtain, covers her eyes, steps back by* RICHARD'S *side, looks at the glass, and gives a joyous cry.*)
Ah, there you are, dear! There we are, both of us—just as we have always seemed to each other, true. 'Tis proved. Isn't it wonderful?

RICHARD: Miraculous! That a mirror bought in a blacksmith shop, before sunrise, for twenty pounds, should prove to be actually—a mirror!

RACHEL: Richard, I'm so happy.

(*Enter* JUSTICE MERTON *and* MISTRESS[86] MERTON.)

RICHARD: (*embracing her*) Happy, art thou, sweet goose? Why, then, God bless Goody Rickby.

JUSTICE MERTON: Strange words from you, Squire Talbot.

(RACHEL *and* RICHARD *part quickly;* RACHEL *draws the curtain over the mirror;* RICHARD *stands stiffly.*)

RICHARD: Justice Merton! Why, sir, the old witch is more innocent, perhaps, than I represented her.

JUSTICE MERTON: A witch, believe me, is never innocent.

(*Taking their hands, he brings them together and kisses* RACHEL *on the forehead.*)
Permit me, young lovers. I was once young myself, young and amorous.

MISTRESS MERTON: (*in a low voice*) Verily![87]

JUSTICE MERTON: My fair niece, my worthy young man, beware of witchcraft.

MISTRESS MERTON: And Goody Rickby, too, brother?

JUSTICE MERTON: That woman shall answer for her deeds. She is proscribed.[88]

RACHEL: Proscribed? Why is that?

MISTRESS MERTON: (*examining the mirror*) What is this?

JUSTICE MERTON: She shall hang.

RACHEL: Uncle, no! Not merely because of my purchase this morning.

JUSTICE MERTON: Your purchase?

MISTRESS MERTON: (*pointing to the mirror*) That, I suppose.

JUSTICE MERTON: What! you purchased that mirror of her? You brought it here?

RACHEL: No, the boy brought it; I found it here when I returned.

JUSTICE MERTON: What! From her shop? From her infamous den, into my parlor! (*To* MISTRESS MERTON.) Call the servant. (*Himself calling.*) Micah! Away with it! Micah!

RACHEL: Uncle Gilead, I bought—

JUSTICE MERTON: Micah, I say! Where is the man?

RACHEL: Listen, uncle. I bought it with my own money.

JUSTICE MERTON: Thine own money! Wilt have the neighbors gossip? Wilt have

me, thyself, my house, suspected of complicity[89] with witches?
(*Enter* MICAH.)
Micah, take this away.

MICAH: Yes, sir; but, sir—
JUSTICE MERTON: Out of my house!
MICAH: There be visitors.
JUSTICE MERTON: Away with—
MISTRESS MERTON: (*touching his arm*) Gilead!
MICAH: Visitors, sir; gentry.[90]
JUSTICE MERTON: Ah!
MICAH: Shall I show them in, sir?
JUSTICE MERTON: Visitors! In the morning? Who are they?
MICAH: Strangers, sir. I should judge they be very high gentry; lords, sir.
ALL: Lords!
MICAH: At least, one on 'em, sir. The other—the dark gentleman—told me they left their horses at the inn, sir.
MISTRESS MERTON: Hark!
(*The faces of all wear suddenly a startled expression.*)
Where is that unearthly sound?
JUSTICE MERTON: (*listening*) Is it in the cellar?
MICAH: 'Tis just the dog howling, madam. When he spied the gentry he turned tail and run below.[91]
MISTRESS MERTON: Oh, the dog!
JUSTICE MERTON: Show the gentlemen here, Micah. Don't keep them waiting.
(*Exit* MICAH.)
A lord! (*To* RACHEL.) We shall talk of this matter later.—A lord!
(*Turning to the small glass on the wall, he arranges his peruke and attire.*)
RACHEL: (*to* RICHARD) What a fortunate interruption! But, dear Dick! I wish we needn't meet these strangers now.
RICHARD: Would you really rather we were alone together?
(*They chat aside, absorbed in each other.*)
JUSTICE MERTON: Think of it, Cynthia, a lord!

MISTRESS MERTON: (*dusting the furniture hastily with her handkerchief*) And such dust!
RACHEL: (*to* RICHARD) You know, dear, we need only be introduced, and then we can steal away together.
(*Reënter* MICAH.)
MICAH: (*announcing*) Lord Ravensbane: Marquis of Oxford, Baron of Wittenberg, Elector of Worms, and Count of Cordova; Master Dickonson.
(*Enter* RAVENSBANE *and* DICKON.)
JUSTICE MERTON: Gentlemen, permit me, you are excessively welcome. I am deeply gratified to meet—
DICKON: Lord Ravensbane, of the Rookeries,[92] Somersetshire.
JUSTICE MERTON: Lord Ravensbane—his lordship's most truly honored.
RAVENSBANE: Truly honored.
JUSTICE MERTON: (*turning to* DICKON) His lordship's—?
DICKON: Tutor.
JUSTICE MERTON: (*checking his effusiveness*) Ah, so!
DICKON: Justice Merton, I believe.
JUSTICE MERTON: Of Merton House. —May I present—permit me, your lordship—my sister, Mistress Merton.
RAVENSBANE: Mistress Merton.
JUSTICE MERTON: And my—and my— (*under his breath*)—Rachel! (RACHEL *remains with a bored expression behind* RICHARD.)—My young neighbor, Squire Talbot, Squire Richard Talbot of—of—
RICHARD: Of nowhere, sir.
RAVENSBANE: (*Nods*) Nowhere.
JUSTICE MERTON: And permit me, Lord Ravensbane, my niece—Mistress Rachel Merton.
RAVENSBANE: (*Bows low*) Mistress Rachel Merton.
RACHEL: (*Curtsies*) Lord Ravensbane.
(*As they raise their heads, their eyes meet and are fascinated.* DICKON *just then takes* RAVENSBANE'S *pipe and fills it.*)

RAVENSBANE: Mistress Rachel!

RACHEL: Your lordship!

(DICKON *returns the pipe.*)

MISTRESS MERTON: A pipe! Gilead!—in the parlor!

(JUSTICE MERTON *frowns silence.*)

JUSTICE MERTON: Your lordship—ahem!—has just arrived in town?

DICKON: From London, via New Amsterdam.[93]

RICHARD: (*aside*) Is he staring at *you*? Are you ill, Rachel?

RACHEL: (*indifferently*) What?

JUSTICE MERTON: Lord Ravensbane honors my humble roof.

DICKON: (*touches* RAVENSBANE'S *arm*) Your lordship—"roof."

RAVENSBANE: (*starting, turns to* MERTON) Nay, sir, the roof of my father's oldest friend bestows generous hospitality upon his only son.

JUSTICE MERTON: Only son—ah, yes! Your father—

RAVENSBANE: My father, I trust, sir, has never forgotten the intimate companionship, the touching devotion, the unceasing solicitude for his happiness which you, sir, manifested to him in the days of his youth.

JUSTICE MERTON: Really, your lordship, the—the slight favors which—hem! some years ago, I was privileged to show your illustrious father—

RAVENSBANE: Permit me!—Because, however, of his present infirmities—for I regret to say that my father is suffering a temporary aberration of mind—[94]

JUSTICE MERTON: You distress me!

RAVENSBANE: My lady mother has charged me with a double mission here in New England. On my quitting my home, sir, to explore the wideness and the mystery of this world, my mother bade me to be sure to call upon his worship, the Justice Merton; and deliver to him, first, my father's remembrances; and secondly, my mother's epistle.[95]

DICKON: (*handing to* JUSTICE MERTON *a sealed document*) Her ladyship's letter, sir.

JUSTICE MERTON: (*examining the seal with awe, speaks aside to* MISTRESS MERTON) Cynthia!—a crested seal!

DICKON: His lordship's crest, sir: rooks[96] rampant.

JUSTICE MERTON: (*embarrassed, breaks the seal*) Permit me.

RACHEL: (*looking at* RAVENSBANE) Have you noticed his bearing, Richard: what personal distinction! What inbred nobility! Every inch a true lord!

RICHARD: He may be a lord, my dear, but he walks like a broomstick.[97]

RACHEL: How dare you!

(*Turns abruptly away; as she does so, a fold of her gown catches in a chair.*)

RAVENSBANE: Mistress Rachel—permit me.

(*Stooping, he extricates the fold of her gown.*)

RACHEL: Oh, thank you.

(*They go aside together.*)

JUSTICE MERTON: (*to* DICKON, *glancing up from the letter*) I am astonished —overpowered!

RICHARD: (*to* MISTRESS MERTON) So Lord Ravensbane and his family are old friends of yours?

MISTRESS MERTON: (*monosyllabically*) I never heard the name before, Richard.

RAVENSBANE: (*to* RACHEL, *taking her hand after a whisper from* DICKON) Believe me, sweet lady, it will give me the deepest pleasure.

RACHEL: Can you really tell fortunes?

RAVENSBANE: More than that; I can bestow them.

(RAVENSBANE *leads* RACHEL *off, left, into an adjoining room, the door of which remains open.* RICHARD *follows them.* MISTRESS MERTON *follows him, murmuring,* "RICHARD!" DICKON *stands where he can watch them in the room off scene, while he speaks to the* JUSTICE.)

JUSTICE MERTON: (to DICKON, glancing up from the letter) I am astonished—overpowered! But is her ladyship really serious? An offer of marriage!

DICKON: Pray read it again, sir.

JUSTICE MERTON: (reads) "To the Worshipful, the Justice Gilead Merton, Merton House.

"My Honorable Friend and Benefactor:

"With these brief lines I commend to you our son"—*our* son![98]

DICKON. She speaks likewise for his young lordship's father, sir.

JUSTICE MERTON: Ah! of course. (Reads.) "In a strange land, I entrust him to you as to a father."[99] Honored, believe me! "I have only to add my earnest hope that the natural gifts, graces, and inherited fortune"—ah—!

DICKON: Twenty thousand pounds—on his father's demise.[100]

JUSTICE MERTON: Ah!—"fortune of this young scion[101] of nobility will so propitiate the heart of your niece, Mistress Rachel Merton, as to cause her to accept his proffered hand in matrimony";—but—but—but Squire Talbot is betrothed to—well, well, we shall see;—"in matrimony, and thus cement the early bonds of interest and affection between your honored self and his lordship's father; not to mention, dear sir, your worship's ever grateful and obedient admirer,
"ELIZABETH,
"Marchioness of R."
Of R! of R! Will you believe me, my dear sir, so long is it since my travels in England—I visited at so many—hem! noble estates—permit me, it is so awkward, but—

DICKON: (with his peculiar intonation of Act I) Not at all.

RAVENSBANE: (calls from the adjoining room) Dickon, my pipe!

(DICKON glides away.)

JUSTICE MERTON: (starting in perturbation. To DICKON) Permit me, one moment; I did not catch your name.[102]

DICKON: My name? Dickonson.

JUSTICE MERTON: (with a gasp of relief) Ah, Dickonson! Thank you. I mistook the word.

DICKON: A compound, your worship. (With a malignant smile.) Dickon- (then, jerking his thumb toward the next room) son! (Bowing.) Both at your service.

JUSTICE MERTON: Is he—he there?

DICKON: Bessie's brat; yes; it didn't die, after all, poor suckling! Dickon weaned it. Saved it for balm of Gilead.[103] Raised it for joyful home-coming. Prodigal's return! Twenty-first birthday! Happy son! Happy father!

JUSTICE MERTON: My—son!

DICKON: Felicitations!

JUSTICE MERTON: (faintly) What—what do you want?

DICKON: Only the happiness of your dear ones—the union of these young hearts and hands.

JUSTICE MERTON: What! he will dare—an illegitimate—

DICKON: Fie, fie, Gilly! Why, the brat is a lord now.

JUSTICE MERTON: Oh, the disgrace! Spare me that, Dickon. And she is innocent; she is already betrothed.

DICKON: Twiddle-twaddle! 'Tis a brilliant match; besides, her ladyship's heart is set upon it.

JUSTICE MERTON: Her ladyship—?

DICKON: The Marchioness of Rickby.[104]

JUSTICE MERTON: (glowering) Rickby!—I had forgotten.

DICKON: Her ladyship has never forgotten. So, you see, your worship's alternatives are most simple. Alternative one: advance his lordship's suit with your niece as speedily as possible, and save all scandal. Alternative two: impede his lordship's suit, and—

JUSTICE MERTON: Don't, Dickon! don't reveal the truth; not disgrace now![105]

DICKON: Good; we are agreed, then?

JUSTICE MERTON: I have no choice.

DICKON: (*cheerfully*) Why, true; we ignored that, didn't we?

MISTRESS MERTON: (*reëntering*) This young lord—Why, Gilead, are you ill?

JUSTICE MERTON: (*with a great effort, commands himself*) Not in the least.

MISTRESS MERTON: Rachel's deportment, my dear brother—I tell you, they are fortune-telling!

JUSTICE MERTON: Tush! Tush!

MISTRESS MERTON: Tush? "Tush" to me? Tush!

(*She goes out, right.*)

(RAVENSBANE *and* RACHEL *reënter from the adjoining room followed shortly by* RICHARD.)

RACHEL: I am really at a loss. Your lordship's hand is so very peculiar.

RAVENSBANE: Ah! Peculiar.

RACHEL: This, now, is the line of life.

RAVENSBANE: Of life, yes?

RACHEL: But it begins so abruptly, and see! it breaks off and ends nowhere. And just so here with this line—the line of—love.

RAVENSBANE: Of love. So; it breaks?

RACHEL: Yes.

RAVENSBANE: Ah, then, that must be the *heart* line.

RACHEL: Why, Lord Ravensbane, your pulse. Really, if I am cruel, you are quite heartless. I declare I can't feel your heart beat at all.

RAVENSBANE: Ah, mistress, that is because I have just lost it.

RACHEL: (*archly*) Where?

RAVENSBANE: (*faintly*) Dickon, my pipe!

RACHEL: Alas! my lord, are you ill?

DICKON: (*restoring the lighted pipe to* RAVENSBANE, *speaks aside*) Pardon me, sweet young lady, I must confide to you that his lordship's heart is peculiarly responsive to his emotions. When he feels very ardently, it quite stops. Hence the use of his pipe.

RACHEL: Oh; Is smoking, then, necessary for his heart?

DICKON: Absolutely—to equilibrate the valvular palpitations.[106] Without his pipe—should his lordship experience, for instance—the emotion of love—he might die.[107]

RACHEL: You alarm me!

DICKON: But this is for you only, Mistress Rachel. We may confide in you?

RACHEL: Oh, utterly, sir.

DICKON: His lordship, you know, is so sensitive.

RAVENSBANE: (*to* RACHEL) You have given it back to me. Why did not you keep it?

RACHEL: What, my lord?

RAVENSBANE: My heart.

RICHARD: Intolerable! Do you approve of *this*, sir? Are Lord Ravensbane's credentials satisfactory?

JUSTICE MERTON: Eminently, eminently.

RICHARD: Ah! So her ladyship's letter is—

JUSTICE MERTON: Charming; charming. (*To* RAVENSBANE.) Your lordship will, I trust, make my house your home.

RAVENSBANE: My home, sir.

RACHEL: (*to* DICKON, *who has spoken to her*) Really? (*To* JUSTICE MERTON.) Why, uncle, what is this Master Dickonson tells us?

JUSTICE MERTON: What! What! he has revealed—

RACHEL: Yes, indeed.

JUSTICE MERTON: Rachel! Rachel!

RACHEL: (*laughingly to* RAVENSBANE) My uncle is doubtless astonished to find you so grown.

RAVENSBANE: (*laughingly to* JUSTICE MERTON) I am doubtless astonished, sir, to be so grown.

JUSTICE MERTON: (*to* DICKON) You have—

DICKON: Merely remarked, sir, that your worship had often dandled his lordship—as an infant.[108]

JUSTICE MERTON: (*smiling lugubriously*) Quite so—as an infant merely.

RACHEL: How interesting! Then you must have seen his lordship's home in England.

JUSTICE MERTON: As you say.

RACHEL: (*to* RAVENSBANE) Do describe it to us. We are so isolated here from the grand world. Do you know, I always imagine England to be an enchanted isle, like one of the old Hesperides,[109] teeming with fruits of solid gold.

RAVENSBANE: Ah, yes! my mother raises them.

RACHEL: Fruits of gold?

RAVENSBANE: Round like the rising sun. She calls them—ah! punkins.[110]

MISTRESS MERTON: "Punkins"!

JUSTICE MERTON: (*aside, grinding his teeth*) Scoundrel! Scroundrel!

RACHEL: (*laughing*) Your lordship pokes fun at us.

DICKON: His lordship is an artist in words, mistress. I have noticed that in whatever country he is traveling, he tinges his vocabulary with the local idiom. His lordship means, of course, not pumpkins, but pomegranates.

RACHEL: We forgive him. But, your lordship, please be serious and describe to us your hall.

RAVENSBANE: Quite serious: the hall. Yes, yes; in the middle burns a great fire—on a black—ah! a black altar.

DICKON: A Druidical heirloom.[111] His lordship's mother collects antiques.

RACHEL: How fascinating!

RAVENSBANE: Fascinating! On the walls hang pieces of iron.

DICKON: Trophies of Saxon warfare.[112]

RAVENSBANE: And rusty horseshoes.

GENERAL MURMURS: Horseshoes!

DICKON: Presents from the German Emperor. They were worn by the steeds of Charlemagne.[113]

RAVENSBANE: Quite so; and broken cart-wheels.

DICKON: Relics of British chariots.[114]

RACHEL: How mediæval it must be! (*To* JUSTICE MERTON.) And to think you never described it to us!

MISTRESS MERTON: True, brother; you have been singularly reticent.

JUSTICE MERTON: Permit me; it is impossible to report all one sees on one's travels.

MISTRESS MERTON: Evidently.

RACHEL: But surely your lordship's mother has other diversions besides collecting antiques. I have heard that in England ladies followed the hounds; and sometimes—(*looking at her aunt and lowering her voice*)—they even dance.

RAVENSBANE: Dance—ah, yes; my lady mother dances about the—altar; she swings high a hammer.[115]

DICKON: Your lordship, your lordship! Pray, sir, check this vein of poetry. Lord Ravensbane symbolizes as a hammer and altar a golf-stick and tee—a Scottish game, which her ladyship plays on her Highland estates.

RICHARD: (*to* MISTRESS MERTON) What do you think of this?

MISTRESS MERTON: (*with a scandalized look toward her brother*) He said to me "tush."

RICHARD: (*to* JUSTICE MERTON, *indicating* DICKON) Who is this magpie?

JUSTICE MERTON: (*hisses in fury*) Satan!

RICHARD: I beg pardon!

JUSTICE MERTON: Satan, sir,—makes you jealous.[116]

RICHARD: (*bows stiffly*) Good-morning. (*Walking up to* RAVENSBANE.) Lord

Ravensbane, I have a rustic colonial question to ask. Is it the latest fashion to smoke incessantly in ladies' parlors, or is it—mediæval?

DICKON: His lordship's health, sir, necessitates—

RICHARD: I addressed his lordship.

RAVENSBANE: In the matter of fashions, sir—

(*Hands his pipe to be refilled.*)

My pipe, Dickon!

(*While* DICKON *holds his pipe—somewhat longer than usual—*RAVENSBANE, *with his mouth open as if about to speak, relapses into a vacant stare.*[117])

RICHARD: Well?

DICKON: (*as he lights the pipe for* RAVENSBANE, *speaks suavely and low as if not to be overheard by him*) Pardon me. The fact is, my young pupil is sensitive; the wound from his latest duel is not quite healed; you observe a slight lameness, an occasional—absence of mind.

RACHEL: A wound—in a real duel?

DICKON: (*aside*) You, mistress, know the *true* reason—his lordship's heart.

RICHARD: (*to* RAVENSBANE, *who is still staring vacantly into space*) Well, well, your lordship. (RAVENSBANE *pays no attention.*) You were saying—? (DICKON *returns the pipe*)—in the matter of fashions, sir—?

RAVENSBANE: (*regaining slowly a look of intelligence, draws himself up with affronted hauteur*) Permit me! (*Puffs several wreaths of smoke into the air.*) I *am* the fashions.

RICHARD: (*going*) Insufferable!

(*He pauses at the door.*)

MISTRESS MERTON: (*to* JUSTICE MERTON) Well—what do you think of that?

JUSTICE MERTON: Spoken like King Charles himself.[118]

MISTRESS MERTON: Brother! brother! is there nothing wrong here?

(*Going out, she passes* DICKON, *starts at a look which he gives her, and goes out, quite flustered. Following her,* JUSTICE MERTON *is stopped by* DICKON, *and led off left by him.*)

RACHEL: (*to* RAVENSBANE) I—object to the smoke? Why, I think it is charming.

RICHARD: (*who has returned from the door, speaks in a low, constrained voice*) Rachel!

RACHEL: Oh!—you?

RICHARD: You take quickly to European fashions.

RACHEL: Yes? To what one in particular?

RICHARD: Two; smoking and flirtation.

RACHEL: Jealous?

RICHARD: Of an idiot? I hope not. Manners differ, however. Your confidences to his lordship have evidently not included—your relation to me.

RACHEL: Oh, our relations!

RICHARD: Of course, since you wish him to continue in ignorance—

RACHEL: Not at all. He shall know at once. Lord Ravensbane!

RAVENSBANE: Fair mistress!

RICHARD: Rachel, stop! I did not mean—

RACHEL: (*to* RAVENSBANE) My uncle did not introduce to you with sufficient elaboration this gentleman. Will you allow me to do so now?

RAVENSBANE: I adore Mistress Rachel's elaborations.

RACHEL: Lord Ravensbane, I beg to present Squire Talbot, my *betrothed*.

RAVENSBANE: Betrothed! Is it—(*noticing* RICHARD'S *frown*)—is it pleasant?

RACHEL: (*to* RICHARD) Are you satisfied?

RICHARD: (*trembling with feeling*) *More* than satisfied.

(*Exit.*)

RAVENSBANE: (*looking after him*) Ah! Betrothed is *not* pleasant.

RACHEL: Not always.

RAVENSBANE: (*anxiously*) Mistress Rachel is not pleased?

RACHEL: (*biting her lip, looks after* RICHARD) With him.

RAVENSBANE: Mistress Rachel will smile again?

RACHEL: Soon.

RAVENSBANE: (*ardent*) Ah! What can Lord Ravensbane do to make her smile? See! will you puff my pipe? It is very pleasant.

(*Offering the pipe.*)

RACHEL: (*smiling*) Shall I try?

(*Takes hold of it mischievously.*)

(*Enter* JUSTICE MERTON *and* DICKON, *left.*)

JUSTICE MERTON: (*in a great voice*) Rachel!

RACHEL: Why, uncle!

JUSTICE MERTON: (*speaks suavely to* RAVENSBANE) Permit me, your lordship —Rachel, will you kindly withdraw for a few moments; I desire to confer with Lord Ravensbane concerning his mother's—her ladyship's letter—(*obsequiously to* DICKON)—that is, if you think, sir, that your noble pupil is not too fatigued.

DICKON: Not at all; I think his lordship will listen to you with much pleasure.

RAVENSBANE: (*bowing to* JUSTICE MERTON, *but looking at* RACHEL) With much pleasure.

DICKON: And in the meantime, if Mistress Rachel will allow me, I will assist her in writing those invitations which your worship desires to send in her name.

JUSTICE MERTON: Invitations—from my niece?

DICKON: To his Excellency, the Lieutenant-Governor; to your friends, the Reverend Masters at Harvard College, etc., etc.; in brief, to all your worship's select social acquaintance in the vicinity—to meet his lordship. It was so thoughtful of you to suggest it, sir, and believe me, his lordship appreciates your courtesy in arranging the reception in his honor for this afternoon.

RACHEL: (*to* JUSTICE MERTON) This afternoon! Are we really to give his lordship a reception? And will it be here, uncle?

DICKON: (*looking at him narrowly*) Your worship said *here*, I believe?

JUSTICE MERTON: Quite so, sir; quite so, quite so.

DICKON: Permit me to act as your scribe, Mistress Rachel.

RACHEL: With pleasure. (*With a curtsy to* RAVENSBANE.) Till we meet again!

(*Exit, right.*)

DICKON: (*aside to* JUSTICE MERTON) I advise nothing rash, Gilly; the brat has a weak heart.[119] (*Aside, as he passes* RAVENSBANE.) Remember, Jack! Puff! Puff!

RAVENSBANE: (*staring at the door*) She is gone.

JUSTICE MERTON: Impostor! You, at least, shall not play the lord and master to my face.

RAVENSBANE: Quite—gone!

JUSTICE MERTON: I know with whom I have to deal. If I be any judge of my own flesh and blood—permit me—you shall quail before me.

RAVENSBANE: (*dejectedly*) She did not smile—(*Joyously.*) She smiled!

JUSTICE MERTON: Affected rogue! I know thee. I know thy feigned pauses, thy assumed vagaries. Speak; how much do you want?

RAVENSBANE: (*ecstatically*) Ah! Mistress Rachel!

JUSTICE MERTON: Her! Scoundrel, if thou dost name her again, my innocent— my sweet maid! If thou dost—thou godless spawn of temptation—mark you, I will put an end—

(*Reaching for a pistol that rests in a rack on the wall,—the intervening form of*

DICKON *suddenly appears, pockets the pistol, and exits.*)

DICKON: I beg pardon; I forgot something.

JUSTICE MERTON: (*sinking into a chair*) God, Thou art just![120]
(*He holds his head in his hands and weeps.*)

RAVENSBANE: (*for the first time, since* RACHEL's *departure, observing* MERTON) Permit me, sir, are you ill?

JUSTICE MERTON: (*recoiling*) What art thou!

RAVENSBANE: (*monotonously*) I am Lord Ravensbane: Marquis of Oxford, Baron of Wittenberg, Elector of Worms, and—(*As* JUSTICE MERTON *covers his face again.*) Shall I call Dickon? (*Walking quickly toward the door, calls.*) DICKON!

JUSTICE MERTON: (*starting up*) No, do not call him. Tell me: I hate thee not; thou wast innocent. Tell me!—I thought thou hadst died as a babe.—Where has Dickon, our tyrant, kept thee these twenty years?

RAVENSBANE: (*with gentle courtesy*) Master Dickonson is my tutor.

JUSTICE MERTON: And why has thy mother—Ah, I know well; I deserve all. But yet, it must not be published now! I am a justice now, an honored citizen—and my young niece—Thy mother will not demand so much.

RAVENSBANE: My mother is the Marchioness of Rickby.

JUSTICE MERTON: Yes, yes; 'twas well planned, a clever trick. 'Twas skillful of her. But surely thy mother gave thee commands to—

RAVENSBANE: My mother gave me her blessing.

JUSTICE MERTON: Ah, 'tis well, then. Young man, my son, I too will give thee my blessing, if thou wilt but go—go instantly—go with half my fortune—but leave me my honor—and my Rachel?

RAVENSBANE: Rachel? Rachel is yours? No, no, Mistress Rachel is mine. We are ours.

JUSTICE MERTON: (*pleadingly*) Consider the disgrace—you, an illegitimate—and she—oh, think what thou art!

RAVENSBANE: (*monotonously, puffing smoke at the end*) I am Lord Ravensbane: Marquis of Oxford, Baron of Wittenberg, Elector of Worms, and Count—[121]

JUSTICE MERTON: (*wrenching the pipe from* RAVENSBANE's *hand and lips*) Devil's child! Boor! Buffoon! (*Flinging the pipe away.*) I will stand thy insults no longer. If thou hast no heart—

RAVENSBANE: (*putting his hand to his side, staggers*) Ah! my heart!

JUSTICE MERTON: Hypocrite! Thou canst not fool me. I am thy father.

RAVENSBANE: (*faintly, stretches out his hand to him for support*) Father!

JUSTICE MERTON: Stand away. Thou mayst break thy heart and mine and the devil's, but thou shalt not break Rachel's.

RAVENSBANE: (*faintly*) Mistress Rachel is mine—

(*He staggers again, and falls, half reclining, upon a chair. More faintly he speaks, beginning to change expression.*) Her eyes are mine; her smiles are mine. (*His eyes close.*)

JUSTICE MERTON: Good God! Can it be—his heart? (*With agitated swiftness, he feels and listens at* RAVENSBANE's *side.*) Not a motion; not a sound! Yea, God, Thou art good! 'Tis his heart. He is—ah! he is my son. Judge Almighty, if he should die now; may I not be still a moment more and make sure.[122] No, no, my son—he is changing. (*Calls.*) Help! Help! Rachel! Master Dickonson! Help! Richard! Cynthia! Come hither!

(*Enter* DICKON *and* RACHEL.)

RACHEL: Uncle!

JUSTICE MERTON: Bring wine. Lord Ravensbane has fainted.

RACHEL: Oh! (*Turning swiftly to go.*) Micah, wine.

DICKON: (*detaining her*) Stay! His pipe! Where is his lordship's pipe?

RACHEL: Oh, terrible!

(*Enter, at different doors,* MISTRESS MERTON *and* RICHARD.)

MISTRESS MERTON: What's the matter?

JUSTICE MERTON: (*to* RACHEL) He threw it away. He is worse. Bring the wine.

MISTRESS MERTON: Look! How strange he appears!

RACHEL: (*searching distractedly*) The pipe! His lordship's pipe! It is lost, Master Dickonson.

DICKON: (*stooping, as if searching, with his back turned, having picked up the pipe, is filling and lighting it*) It must be found. This is a heart attack, my friends; his lordship's life depends on the nicotine.

(*Deftly he places the pipe in* RACHEL'S *way.*)

RACHEL: Thank God! Here it is.

(*Carrying it to the prostrate form of* RAVENSBANE, *she lifts his head and is about to put the pipe in his mouth.*) Shall I—shall I put it in?

RICHARD: No! not you.

RACHEL: Sir!

RICHARD: Let his tutor perform that office.

RACHEL: (*lifting* LORD RAVENSBANE'S *head again*) My lord!

RICHARD *and* JUSTICE MERTON: (*together*) Rachel!

DICKON: Pardon me, Mistress Rachel—give the pipe at once. Only a token of true affection can revive his lordship now.

RICHARD: (*as* RACHEL *puts the pipe to* RAVENSBANE'S *lips*) I forbid it, Rachel.

RACHEL: (*watching only* RAVENSBANE) My lord—my lord!

MISTRESS MERTON: Give him air; unbutton his coat.

(RACHEL *unbuttons* RAVENSBANE'S *coat, revealing the embroidered waistcoat.*) Ah, Heavens! What do I see?

JUSTICE MERTON: (*looks, blanches, and signs silence to* MISTRESS MERTON) Cynthia![123]

MISTRESS MERTON: (*aside to* JUSTICE MERTON, *with deep tensity*) That waistcoat! that waistcoat! Brother, hast thou never seen it before?

JUSTICE MERTON: Never, my sister.

DICKON: See! He puffs—he revives. He is coming to himself.

RACHEL: (*as* RAVENSBANE *rises to his feet*) At last!

DICKON: Look! he is restored.

RACHEL: God be thanked!

DICKON: My lord, Mistress Rachel has saved your life.

RAVENSBANE: (*taking* RACHEL'S *hand*) Mistress Rachel is mine; we are ours.

RICHARD: Dare to repeat that.

RAVENSBANE: (*looking at* RACHEL) Her eyes are mine.

RICHARD: (*flinging his glove in his face*) And that, sir, is yours.

RACHEL: Richard!

RICHARD: I believe such is the proper fashion in England. If your lordship's last dueling wound is sufficiently healed, perhaps you will deign a reply.

RACHEL: Richard! Your lordship!

RAVENSBANE: (*stoops, picks up the glove, pockets it, bows to* RACHEL, *and steps close to* RICHARD) Permit me!

(*He blows a puff of smoke full in* RICHARD'S *face.*)

ACT III

The same day. Late afternoon. The same as Act II.

RAVENSBANE *and* DICKON *discovered at table, on which are lying two flails.* RAVENSBANE *is dressed in a costume which, composed of silk and jewels, subtly ap-*

proximates in design to that of his original grosser composition. So artfully, however, is this contrived that, to one ignorant of his origin, his dress would appear to be merely an odd personal whimsy; whereas, to one initiated, it would stamp him grotesquely as the apotheosis of scarecrows.

DICKON *is sitting in a pedagogical attitude;* RAVENSBANE *stands near him, making a profound bow in the opposite direction.*

RAVENSBANE: Believe me, ladies, with the true sincerity of the heart.

DICKON: Inflection a little more lachrymose,[124] please: "The *true* sincerity of the *heart*."

RAVENSBANE: Believe me, ladies, with the *true* sincerity of the *heart*.

DICKON: Prettily, prettily! Next!

RAVENSBANE: (*changing his mien, as if addressing another person*) Verily, sir, as that prince of poets, the immortal Virgil, has remarked:—

"Adeo in teneris consuescere multum est."[125]

DICKON: Basta![126] The next.

RAVENSBANE: (*with another change to courtly manner*) Trust me, your Excellency, I will inform his Majesty of your courtesy.

DICKON: "His Majesty" more emphatic. Remember! You must impress all of the guests this afternoon. But continue, Cobby, dear; the retort now to the challenge!

RAVENSBANE: (*with a superb air*) The second, I believe.

DICKON: Quite so, my lord.

RAVENSBANE: Sir! the local person whom you represent has done himself the honor of submitting to me a challenge to mortal combat. Sir! Since the remotest times of my feudal ancestors, in such affairs of honor, choice of weapons has ever been the—

DICKON: Prerogative!

RAVENSBANE: Prerogative of the challenged. Sir! This right of etiquette must be observed. Nevertheless, believe me, I have no selfish desire that my superior—

DICKON: Attainments!

RAVENSBANE: Attainments in this art should assume advantage over my challenger's ignorance. I have, therefore, chosen those combative utensils[127] most appropriate both to his own humble origin and to local tradition. Permit me, sir, to reveal my choice. (*Pointing grandly to the table.*) There are my weapons![128]

DICKON: Delicious! O thou exquisite flower of love! How thy natal composites[129] have burst in bloom!—The pumpkin in thee to a golden collarette; thy mop of crow's wings to these raven locks; thy broomstick to a lordly limp; thy corn-silk to these pale-tinted tassels. Verily in the gallery of scarecrows, thou art the Apollo Belvedere![130]

RAVENSBANE: Mistress Rachel—I may see her now?

DICKON: Romeo! Romeo! Was ever such an amorous puppet show!

RAVENSBANE: Mistress Rachel!

DICKON: Wait; let me think! Thou art wound up now, my pretty apparatus, for at least six-and-thirty hours. The wooden angel Gabriel that trumpets the hours on the big clock in Venice is not a more punctual manikin[131] than thou with my speeches. Thou shouldst run, therefore,—

RAVENSBANE: (*frowning darkly at* DICKON) Stop talking; permit me! A tutor should know his place.

DICKON: (*rubbing his hands*) Nay, your lordship is beyond comparison.

RAVENSBANE: (*in a terrible voice*) She will come? I shall see her?

(*Enter* MICAH.)

MICAH: Pardon, my lord.

RAVENSBANE: (*turning joyfully to* MICAH) Is it she?

MICAH: Captain Bugby, my lord, the Governor's secretary.

DICKON: Good. Squire Talbot's second. Show him in.

RAVENSBANE: (*flinging despairingly into a chair*) Ah! ah!

MICAH: (*lifting the flails from the table*) Beg pardon, sir; shall I remove—

DICKON: Drop them; go.

MICAH: But, sir—

DICKON: Go, thou slave! (*Exit* MICAH.)

(DICKON *hands* RAVENSBANE *a book.*)
Here, my lord; read. You must be found reading.

RAVENSBANE: (*in childlike despair*) She will not come! I shall not see her! (*Throwing the book into the fireplace.*) She does not come!

DICKON: Fie, fie, Jack; thou must not be breaking thy Dickon's apron-strings with a will of thine own. Come!

RAVENSBANE: Mistress Rachel.

DICKON: Be good, boy, and thou shalt see her soon.

(*Enter* CAPTAIN BUGBY.)
Your lordship was saying—Oh! Captain Bugby?

CAPTAIN BUGBY: (*nervous and awed*) Captain Bugby, sir, ah! at Lord Ravensbane's service—ah!

DICKON: I am Master Dickonson, his lordship's tutor.

CAPTAIN BUGBY: Happy, sir.

DICKON: (*to* RAVENSBANE) My lord, this gentleman waits upon you from Squire Talbot. (*To* CAPTAIN BUGBY.) In regard to the challenge of this morning, I presume?

CAPTAIN BUGBY: The affair, ah! the affair of this morning, sir!

RAVENSBANE: (*with his former superb air—to* CAPTAIN BUGBY) The second, I believe?

CAPTAIN BUGBY: Quite so, my lord.

RAVENSBANE: Sir! the local person whom you represent has done himself the honor of submitting to me a challenge to mortal combat. Sir! Since the remotest times of my feudal ancestors, in such affairs of honor, choice of weapons has ever been the pre-pre- (DICKON *looks at him intensely.*) prerogative of the challenged. Sir! this right of etiquette must be observed.

CAPTAIN BUGBY: Indeed, yes, my lord.

DICKON: Pray do not interrupt. (*To* RAVENSBANE.) Your lordship "observed."

RAVENSBANE: —observed. Nevertheless, believe me, I have no selfish desire that my superior a-a-at-attainments in this art should assume advantage over my challenger's ignorance. I have, therefore, chosen these combative utensils most appropriate both to his own humble origin and to local tradition. Permit me, sir, to reveal my choice. (*Pointing to the table.*) There are my weapons!

CAPTAIN BUGBY: (*looking, bewildered*) These, my lord?

RAVENSBANE: Those.

CAPTAIN BUGBY: But these are—are flails.

RAVENSBANE: Flails.

CAPTAIN BUGBY: Flails, by lord?— Do I understand that your lordship and Squire Talbot—

RAVENSBANE: Flails.

CAPTAIN BUGBY: But your lordship— flails!

(DICKON's *intense glance focusses on* RAVENSBANE's *face with the faintest of smiles.*)

RAVENSBANE: My adversary should be deft in their use. He has doubtless wielded them frequently on his barn floor.

CAPTAIN BUGBY: Ahaha! I understand now. Your lordship—ah! is a wit. Haha! Flails!

DICKON: His lordship's satire is poignant.[132]

CAPTAIN BUGBY: Indeed, sir, so keen that I must apologize for laughing at my principal's expense. But— (*soberly to*

RAVENSBANE)—my lord, if you will deign to speak one moment, seriously—

RAVENSBANE: Seriously?

CAPTAIN BUGBY: I will take pleasure in informing Squire Talbot—ah! as to your *real* preference for—

RAVENSBANE: For flails, sir. I have, permit me, nothing further to say. Flails are final.

(*Turns away haughtily.*)

CAPTAIN BUGBY: Eh! What! Must I really report—?

DICKON: Lord Ravensbane's will is inflexible.

CAPTAIN BUGBY: And his wit, sir, incomparable, I am sorry for the Squire, but 'twill be the greatest joke in years. Ah! will you tell me—is it—(*indicating* RAVENSBANE'S *smoking*)—is it the latest fashion?

DICKON: Lord Ravensbane is always the latest.

CAPTAIN BUGBY: Obliged servant, sir. Aha! Such a joke as—O Lord! flails!

(*Exit.*)

DICKON: (*gayly to* RAVENSBANE) Bravo, my pumpky dear! That squelches the jealous betrothed. Now nothing remains but for you to continue to dazzle the enamored Rachel, and so present yourself to the Justice as a pseudo-son-nephew-in-law.

RAVENSBANE: I may go to Mistress Rachel?

DICKON: She will come to you. She is reading now a poem from you, which I left on her dressing-table.

RAVENSBANE: She is reading a poem from me?

DICKON: With your pardon, my lord, I penned it for you. I am something of a poetaster.[133] Indeed, I flatter myself that I have dictated some of the finest lines in literature.[134]

RAVENSBANE: Dickon! She will come?

DICKON: She comes!

(*Enter* RACHEL, *reading from a piece of paper.*)

(DICKON *draws* RAVENSBANE *back.*)

RACHEL: (*reads*) "To Mistress R—, enchantress:—

"If faith in witchcraft be a sin,
Alas! what peril he is in
Who plights his faith and love in thee,
Sweetest maid of sorcery.

"If witchcraft be a whirling brain,
A roving eye, a heart of pain,
Whose wound no thread of fate can stitch,
How hast thou conjured, cruel witch—[135]

With the brain, eye, heart, and total mortal residue of thine enamored.
"JACK LANTHORNE,
"(LORD R—.)"

(DICKON *goes out.*)

RACHEL: "To Mistress R—, enchantress:" R! It *must* be. R— must mean—

RAVENSBANE: (*with passionate deference*) Rachel!

RACHEL: Ah! How you surprised me, my lord.

RAVENSBANE: You are come again; you are come again.

RACHEL: Has anything happened? Oh, my lord, I have been in such terror. Promise me that there shall be—no—duel!

RAVENSBANE: No duel.

RACHEL: Oh, I am so gratefully happy!

RAVENSBANE: I know I am only a thing to make Mistress Rachel happy. Ah! look at me once more. When you look at me, I live.

RACHEL: It is strange, indeed, my lord, how the familiar world, the daylight, the heavens themselves have changed since your arrival.

RAVENSBANE: This is the world; this is the light; this is the heavens themselves. Mistress Rachel is looking at me.

RACHEL: For me, it is less strange, perhaps. I never saw a real lord before.

But you, my lord, must have seen so many, many girls in the great world.

RAVENSBANE: No, no; never.

RACHEL: No other girls before to-day, my lord!

RAVENSBANE: Before to-day? I do not know; I do not care. I was not here. To-day I was born—in your eyes. Ah! my brain whirls!

RACHEL: (*smiling*)
"If witchcraft be a whirling brain,
A roving eye, a heart of pain,—"
(*In a whisper.*) My lord, do you really believe in witchcraft?

RAVENSBANE: With all my heart.

RACHEL: And approve of it?

RAVENSBANE: With all my soul.

RACHEL: So do I—that is, innocent witchcraft; not to harm anybody, you know, but just to feel all the dark mystery and the trembling excitement—the way you feel when you blow out your candle all alone in your bedroom and watch the little smoke fade away in the moonshine.

RAVENSBANE: Fade away in the moonshine!

RACHEL: Oh, but we mustn't speak of it. In a town like this, all such mysticism is considered damnable. But your lordship understands and approves? I am so glad! Have you read the *Philosophical Considerations* of Glanville, the *Saducismus Triumphatus*, and the *Presignifications of Dreams?* What kind of witchcraft, my lord, do you believe in?

RAVENSBANE: In all yours.

RACHEL: Nay, your lordship must not take me for a real witch. I can only tell fortunes, you know—like this morning.

RAVENSBANE: I know; you told how my heart would break.

RACHEL: Oh, that's palmistry,[136] and that isn't always certain. But the surest way to prophesy—do you know what it is?

RAVENSBANE: Tell me.

RACHEL: To count the crows. Do you know how?
One for sorrow—

RAVENSBANE: Ha, yes! —
Two for mirth!

RACHEL: Three for a wedding—

RAVENSBANE: Four for a birth—

RACHEL: And five for the happiest thing on earth!

RAVENSBANE: Mistress Rachel, come! Let us go and count five crows.

RACHEL: (*delightedly*) Why, my lord, how did *you* ever learn it? I got it from an old goody[137] here in town—a real witchwife. If you will promise not to tell a secret, I will show you.—But you must promise!

RAVENSBANE: I promise.

RACHEL: Come, then. I will show you a real piece of witchcraft that I bought from her this morning—the glass of truth. There! Behind that curtain. If you look in, you will see— But come; I will show you. (*They put their hands on the cords of the curtain.*) Just pull that string, and —ah!

DICKON: (*stepping out through the curtain*) My lord, your pipe.

RACHEL: Master Dickonson, how you frightened me!

DICKON: So excessively sorry!

RACHEL: But how did you—?

DICKON: I believe you were showing his lordship—

RACHEL: (*turning hurriedly away*) Oh, nothing; nothing at all.

RAVENSBANE: (*sternly to* DICKON) Why do you come?

DICKON: (*handing back* RAVENSBANE's *pipe filled*) Allow me. (*Aside.*) 'Tis high time you came to the point, Jack; 'tis near your lordship's reception. Woo and win, boy; woo and win.

RAVENSBANE: (*haughtily*) Leave me.

DICKON: Your lordship's humble, very humble.[138]

(*Exit.*)

RACHEL: *(shivering)* My dear lord, why do you keep this man?

RAVENSBANE: I—keep this man?[139]

RACHEL: Pardon my rudeness—I cannot endure him.

RAVENSBANE: You do not like him? Ah, then, I do not like him also. We will send him away—you and I.

RACHEL: You, my lord, of course; but I—

RAVENSBANE: You will be Dickon! You will be with me always and light my pipe. And I will live for you, and fight for you, and kill your betrothed!

RACHEL: *(drawing away)* No, no!

RAVENSBANE: Ah! but your eyes say "yes." Mistress Rachel leaves me; but Rachel in her eyes remains. Is it not so?

RACHEL: What can I say, my lord! It is true that since my eyes met yours, a new passion has entered into my soul. I have felt—but 'tis so impertinent, my lord, so absurd in me, a mere girl, and you a nobleman of power—yet I have felt it irresistibly, my dear lord,—a longing to help you. I am so sorry for you—so sorry for you! I pity you deeply.—Forgive me; forgive me, my lord!

RAVENSBANE: It is enough.

RACHEL: Indeed, indeed, 'tis so rude of me,—'tis so unreasonable.

RAVENSBANE: It is enough. I grow—I grow—I grow! I am a plant; you give it rain and sun. I am a flower; you give it light and dew; I am a soul, you give it love and speech. I grow. Toward you—toward you I grow!

RACHEL: My lord, I do not understand it, how so poor and mere a girl as I can have helped you. Yet I do believe it is so; for I feel it so. What can I do for you?

RAVENSBANE: Be mine. Let me be yours.

RACHEL: But, my lord—do I love you?

RAVENSBANE: What is "I love you"? Is it a kiss, a sigh, an embrace? Ah! then, you do not love me.—"I love you": is it to nourish, to nestle, to lift up, to smile upon, to make greater—a worm? Ah! then, you love me.

(Enter RICHARD *at left back, unobserved.)*

RACHEL: Do not speak so of yourself, my lord; nor exalt me so falsely.

RAVENSBANE: Be mine.

RACHEL: A great glory has descended upon this day.

RAVENSBANE: Be mine.

RACHEL: Could I but be sure that this glory is love—Oh, *then!*

(Turns toward RAVENSBANE.*)*

RICHARD: *(stepping between them)* It is *not* love; it is witchcraft.

RACHEL: Who are you?—Richard?

RICHARD: You have, indeed, forgotten me? Would to God, Rachel, I could forget you.

RAVENSBANE: Ah, permit me, sir—

RICHARD: Silence! *(To* RACHEL.*)* Against my will, I am a convert to your own mysticism; for nothing less than damnable illusion could so instantly wean your heart from me to—this. I do not pretend to understand it; but that it is witchcraft I am convinced; and I will save you from it.

RACHEL: Go; please go.

RAVENSBANE: Permit me, sir; you have not replied yet to flails!

RICHARD: Permit me, sir. *(Taking something from his coat.)* My answer is—bare cob! *(Holding out a shelled corncob.)* Thresh this, sir, for your antagonist. 'Tis the only one worthy of your lordship.

(Tosses it contemptuously toward him.)

RAVENSBANE: Upon my honor, as a man—

RICHARD: As a *man*, forsooth! Were you, indeed, a man, Lord Ravensbane, I would have accepted your weapons, and flailed you out of New England. But it is not my custom to chastise runagates[140] from asylums, or to banter further words with a natural[141] and a ninny.

RACHEL: Squire Talbot! Will you leave my uncle's house?

RAVENSBANE: One moment, mistress:—I did not wholly catch the import of this gentleman's speech, but I fancy I have insulted him by my reply to his challenge. One insult may perhaps be remedied by another. Sir, permit me to call *you* a ninny, and to offer you—(*drawing his sword and offering it*)—swords.

RICHARD: Thanks; I reject the offer.

RAVENSBANE: (*turning away despondently*) He rejects it. Well!

RACHEL: (*to* RICHARD) And *now* will you leave?

RICHARD: At once. But one word more. Rachel—Rachel, have you forgotten this morning and the Glass of Truth?

RACHEL: (*coldly*) No.

RICHARD: Call it a fancy now if you will. I scoffed at it; yes. Yet *you* believed it. I loved you truly, you said. Well, have I changed?

RACHEL: Yes.

RICHARD: Will you test me again—in the glass?

RACHEL: No. Go; leave us.

RICHARD: I will go. I have still a word with your aunt.

RAVENSBANE: (*to* RICHARD) I beg your pardon, sir. You said just now that had I been a man—

RICHARD: I say, Lord Ravensbane, that the straight fiber of a true man never warps the love of a woman. As for yourself, you have my contempt and pity. Pray to God, sir, pray to God to make you a man.

(*Exit, right.*)

RACHEL: Oh! it is intolerable! (*To* RAVENSBANE.) My dear lord, I do believe in my heart that I love you, and if so, I will with gratitude be your wife. But, my lord, strange glamors, strange darknesses reel, and bewilder my mind. I must be alone; I must think and decide. Will you give me this tassel?

RAVENSBANE: (*unfastening a silk tassel from his coat and giving it to her*) Oh, take it.

RACHEL: If I decide that I love you, that I will be your wife—I will wear it this afternoon at the reception. Good-bye. (*Exit, right.*)

RAVENSBANE: Mistress Rachel!— (*He is left alone. As he looks about gropingly, and raises his arms in vague prayer,* DICKON *appears from the right and watches him, with a smile.*) God, are you here? Dear God, I pray to you—make me a man!

(*Exit, left.*)

DICKON: Poor Jacky! Thou shouldst 'a' prayed to t'other one.[142]

(*Enter, right,* JUSTICE MERTON.)

JUSTICE MERTON: (*to* DICKON) Will you not listen? Will you not listen!

DICKON: Such a delightful room!

JUSTICE MERTON: Are you merciless?

DICKON: And such a living portrait of your Worship! The waistcoat is so beautifully executed.

JUSTICE MERTON: If I pay him ten thousand pounds—

(*Enter, right,* MISTRESS MERTON, *who goes toward the table. Enter, left,* MICAH.)

MISTRESS MERTON: Flails! Flails in the parlor!

MICAH: The minister and his wife have turned into the gate, madam.

MISTRESS MERTON: The guests! Is it so late?

MICAH: Four o'clock, madam.

MISTRESS MERTON: Remove these things at once.

MICAH: Yes, madam.

(*He lifts them, and starts for the door where he pauses to look back and speak.*) Madam, in all my past years of service at Merton House, I never waited upon a lord till to-day. Madam, in all my future years of service at Merton House, I trust I may never wait upon a lord again.

MISTRESS MERTON: Micah, mind the knocker.

MICAH: Yes, madame.
(*Exit, at left back. Sounds of a brass knocker outside.*)

MISTRESS MERTON: Rachel! Rachel!
(*Exit, left.*)

JUSTICE MERTON: (*to* DICKON) So you are contented with nothing less than the sacrifice of my niece!

(*Enter* MICAH.)

MICAH: Minister Dodge, your Worship; and Mistress Dodge.
(*Exit.*)

(*Enter the* MINISTER *and his* WIFE.)

JUSTICE MERTON: (*stepping forward to receive them*) Believe me, this is a great privilege.—Madam!

MINISTER DODGE: (*taking his hand*) The privilege is ours, Justice; to enter a righteous man's house is to stand, as it were, on God's threshold.

JUSTICE MERTON: (*nervously*) Amen, amen. Permit me—ah! Lord Ravensbane, my young guest of honor, will be here directly—permit me to present his lordship's tutor, Master Dickonson; the Reverend Master Dodge, Mistress Dodge.

MINISTER DODGE: (*offering his hand*) Master Dickonson, sir—

DICKON: (*barely touching the minister's fingers, bows charmingly to his wife*) Madam, of all professions in the world, your husband's most allures me.

MISTRESS DODGE: 'Tis a worthy one, sir.

DICKON: Ah! Mistress Dodge, and so arduous—especially for a minister's wife. (*He leads her to a chair.*)

MISTRESS DODGE: (*accepting the chair*) Thank you.

MINISTER DODGE: Lord Ravensbane comes from abroad?

JUSTICE MERTON: From London.

MINISTER DODGE: An old friend of yours, I understand.

JUSTICE MERTON: From London, yes. Did I say from London? Quite so; from London.

(*Enter* MICAH.)

MICAH: Captain Bugby, the Governor's secretary.
(*Exit.*)

(*Enter* CAPTAIN BUGBY. *He walks with a slight lameness, and holds daintily in his hand a pipe, from which he puffs with dandy*[143] *deliberation.*)

CAPTAIN BUGBY: Justice Merton, your very humble servant.

JUSTICE MERTON: Believe me, Captain Bugby.

CAPTAIN BUGBY: (*profusely*) Ah, Master Dickonson! my dear friend Master Dickonson—this is indeed—ah! How is his lordship since—aha! but discretion! Mistress Dodge—her servant! Ah! yes—(*indicating his pipe with a smile of satisfaction*)—the latest, I assure you; the very latest from London. Ask Master Dickonson.

MINISTER DODGE: (*looking at* CAPTAIN BUGBY) These will hatch out in the springtime.

CAPTAIN BUGBY: (*confidentially to* DICKON) But really, my good friend, may not I venture to inquire how his lordship —ah! has been in health since the—ah! since—

DICKON: (*impressively*) Oh! quite, quite!

(*Enter* MISTRESS MERTON: *she joins* JUSTICE MERTON *and* MINISTER DODGE.)

CAPTAIN BUGBY: You know, I informed Squire Talbot of his lordship's epigrammatic retort[144]—his retort of—shh! hahaha! Oh, that reply was a stiletto;[145] 'twas sharper than a swordthrust, I assure you. To have conceived it—'twas inspiration; but to have expressed it—oh! 'twas genius. Hush! "Flails!" Oh! It sticks me now in the ribs. I shall die with concealing it.

MINISTER DODGE: (*to* MISTRESS MERTON) 'Tis true, mistress; but if there were more like your brother in the parish, the conscience of the community would be clearer.

(*Enter* MICAH.)

MICAH: The Reverend Master Rand of Harvard College; the Reverend Master Todd of Harvard College.

(*Exit.*)

(*Enter two elderly, straight-backed divines.*[146])

JUSTICE MERTON: (*greeting them*) Permit me, gentlemen; this is fortunate—before your return to Cambridge.

(*He conducts them to* MISTRESS MERTON *and* MINISTER DODGE, *center. Seated left,* DICKON *is ingratiating himself with* MISTRESS DODGE; CAPTAIN BUGBY, *laughed at by both parties, is received by neither.*)

CAPTAIN BUGBY: (*puffing smoke toward the ceiling*) Really, I cannot understand what keeps his Excellency, the Lieutenant-Governor, so long. He has two such charming daughters, Master Dickonson—

DICKON: (*to* MISTRESS DODGE) Yes, yes; such suspicious women with their charms are an insult to the virtuous ladies of the parish.

CAPTAIN BUGBY: How, sir!

MISTRESS DODGE: And to think that she should actually shoe horses herself!

CAPTAIN BUGBY: (*piqued, walks another way*) Well!

REV. MASTER RAND: (*to* JUSTICE MERTON) It would not be countenanced in the college yard, sir.

REV. MASTER TODD: A pipe! Nay, *mores inhibitae!*[147]

JUSTICE MERTON: 'Tis most unfortunate, gentlemen; but I understand 'tis the new vogue in London.

(*Enter* MICAH.)

MICAH: His Excellency, Sir Charles Reddington, Lieutenant-Governor; the Mistress Reddingtons.

CAPTAIN BUGBY: At last!

MISTRESS MERTON: (*aside*) Micah.

(MICAH *goes to her.*)

(*Enter* SIR CHARLES, MISTRESS REDDINGTON, *and* AMELIA REDDINGTON.)

JUSTICE MERTON: Your Excellency, this is, indeed, a distinguished honor.

SIR CHARLES: (*shaking hands*) Fine weather, Merton. Where's your young lord?

THE TWO GIRLS: (*curtsying*) Justice Merton, Mistress Merton.

(MICAH *goes out.*)

CAPTAIN BUGBY: Oh, my dear Mistress Reddington! Charming Mistress Amelia! You are so very late, but you shall hear—hush!

MISTRESS REDDINGTON: (*noticing his pipe*) Why, what is this, Captain?

CAPTAIN BUGBY: Oh, the latest, I assure you, the very latest. Wait till you see his lordship.

AMELIA: What! isn't he here? (*Laughing.*) La, Captain! Do look at the man!

CAPTAIN BUGBY: Oh, he's coming directly. Quite the mode—what?

(*He talks to them aside, where they titter.*)

SIR CHARLES: (*to* DICKON) What say? Traveling for his health?

DICKON: Partially, your Excellency; but my young pupil and master is a singularly affectionate nature.

THE TWO GIRLS: (*to* CAPTAIN BUGBY) What! flails—really!

(*They burst into laughter among themselves.*)

DICKON: He has journeyed here to Massachusetts peculiarly to pay this visit to Justice Merton—his father's dearest friend.

SIR CHARLES: Ah! knew him abroad, eh?

DICKON: In Rome, your Excellency.

MISTRESS DODGE: (*to* JUSTICE MERTON) Why, I thought it was in London.

JUSTICE MERTON: London, true, quite

so; we made a trip together to Lisbon—ah! Rome.

DICKON: Paris, was it not, sir?[148]

JUSTICE MERTON: (*in great distress*) Paris, Paris, very true; I am—I am—sometimes I am—

(*Enter* MICAH, *right.*)

MICAH: (*announces*) Lord Ravensbane.

(*Enter right,* RAVENSBANE *with* RACHEL.)

JUSTICE MERTON: (*with a gasp of relief*) Ah! his lordship is arrived.

(*Murmurs of "his lordship" and a flutter among the girls and* CAPTAIN BUGBY.)

CAPTAIN BUGBY: Look!—Now!

JUSTICE MERTON: Welcome, my lord! (*To* SIR CHARLES.) Your Excellency, let me introduce—permit me—

RAVENSBANE: Permit me; (*addressing her*) Mistress Rachel!—Mistress Rachel will introduce—

RACHEL: (*curtsying*) Sir Charles, allow me to present my friend, Lord Ravensbane.

MISTRESS REDDINGTON: (*aside to* AMELIA) Her *friend*—did you hear?

SIR CHARLES: Mistress Rachel, I see you are as pretty as ever. Lord Ravensbane, your hand, sir.

RAVENSBANE: Trust me, your Excellency, I will inform his Majesty of your courtesy.

CAPTAIN BUGBY: (*watching* RAVENSBANE *with chagrin*) On my life! he's lost his limp.[149]

RAVENSBANE: (*apart to* RACHEL) You said: "A great glory has descended upon this day."

RACHEL: (*shyly*) My lord!

RAVENSBANE: Be sure—O mistress, be sure—that this glory is love.

SIR CHARLES: My daughters, Fanny and Amelia—Lord Ravensbane.

THE TWO GIRLS: (*curtsying*) Your lordship!

SIR CHARLES: Good girls, but silly.

THE TWO GIRLS: Papa!

RAVENSBANE: Believe me, ladies, with the *true* sincerity of the *heart.*

MISTRESS REDDINGTON: Isn't he perfection!

CAPTAIN BUGBY: What said I?

AMELIA: (*giggling*) I can't help thinking of flails.

SIR CHARLES: (*in a loud whisper aside to* JUSTICE MERTON) Is it congratulations for your niece?

JUSTICE MERTON: Not—precisely.

DICKON: (*to* JUSTICE MERTON) Your worship—a word.

(*Leads him aside.*)

RAVENSBANE: (*whom* RACHEL *continues to introduce to the guests, to* MASTER RAND) Verily, sir, as that prince of poets, the immortal Virgil, has remarked: "Adeo in teneris consuescere multum est."[150]

REV. MASTER TODD: His lordship is evidently a university man.

REV. MASTER RAND: Evidently most accomplished.

JUSTICE MERTON: (*aside to* DICKON) A song! Why, it is beyond all bounds of custom and decorum.

DICKON: Believe me, there is no such flatterer to win the maiden heart as music.

JUSTICE MERTON: And here; in this presence! Never!

DICKON: Nevertheless, it will amuse me vastly, and you will announce it.

JUSTICE MERTON: (*with hesitant embarrassment, which he seeks to conceal*) Your Excellency and friends, I have great pleasure in announcing his lordship's condescension in consenting to regale our present company—with a song.

SEVERAL VOICES: (*in various degrees of amazement and curiosity*) A song!

MISTRESS MERTON: Gilead! What is this?

JUSTICE MERTON: The selection is a German ballad—a particular favorite at the court of Prussia, where his lordship last rendered it. His tutor has made a translation which is entitled—

DICKON: "The Prognostication[151] of the Crows."

ALL: Crows!

JUSTICE MERTON: And I am requested to remind you that in the ancient heathen mythology of Germany, the crow or raven, was the fateful bird of the god Woden.[152]

CAPTAIN BUGBY: How prodigiously novel!

MINISTER DODGE: (*frowning*) Unparalleled!

SIR CHARLES: A ballad! Come now, that sounds like old England again. Let's have it. Will his lordship sing without music?

JUSTICE MERTON: Master Dickonson, hem! has been—persuaded—to accompany his lordship on the spinet.

AMELIA: How delightful!

REV. MASTER RAND: (*aside to* TODD) Shall we remain?

REV. MASTER TODD: We must.

RAVENSBANE: (*to* RACHEL) My tassel, dear mistress; you do not wear it?

RACHEL: My heart still wavers, my lord. But whilst you sing, I will decide.

RAVENSBANE: Whilst I sing? My fate, then, is waiting at the end of a song?

RACHEL: At the end of a song.

DICKON: (*calling to* RAVENSBANE) Your lordship!

RAVENSBANE: (*starting, turns to the company*) Permit me.

(DICKON *sits, facing left, at the spinet. At first, his fingers in playing give sound only to the soft tinkling notes of that ancient instrument; but gradually, strange notes and harmonies of an aerial orchestra mingle with, and at length drown, the spinet. The final chorus is produced solely by fantastic symphonic cawings, as of countless crows, in harsh but musical accord. During the song* RICHARD *enters.* DICKON'S *music, however, does not cease but fills the intervals between the verses. To his accompaniment, amid the whispered and gradually increasing wonder, resentment, and dismay of the assembled guests,* RAVENSBANE, *with his eyes fixed upon* RACHEL, *sings.*)

Baron von Rabentod[153] arose;
    (The golden sun was rising)
Before him flew a flock of crows:
    Sing heigh! Sing heigh! Sing heigh!
    Sing—

"Ill speed, ill speed thee, baron-wight;[154]
    Ill speed thy palfrey[155] pawing!
Blithe is the morn but black the night
    That hears a raven's cawing."

(*Chorus*)
Caw! Caw! Caw!

MISTRESS DODGE: (*whispers to her husband*) Did you hear them?

MINISTER DODGE: Hush!

AMELIA: (*sotto voce*) What *can* it be?

CAPTAIN BUGBY: Oh, the latest, be sure.

DICKON: You note, my friends, the accompanying harmonies; they are an intrinsic part of the ballad, and may not be omitted.

RAVENSBANE: (*Sings*)
The baron recked[156] not a pin;
    (For the golden sun was rising)
He rode to woo, he rode to win;
    Sing heigh! Sing heigh! Sing heigh!
    Sing—

He rode into his prince's hall
    Through knights and damsels flow'ry:
"Thy daughter, prince, I bid thee call;
    I claim her hand and dowry."

(*Enter* RICHARD. MISTRESS MERTON *seizes his arm nervously.*)

SIR CHARLES: (*to* CAPTAIN BUGBY.) This gentleman's playing is rather ventriloquistical.[157]

CAPTAIN BUGBY: Quite, as it were.

REV. MASTER TODD: This smells unholy.

REV. MASTER RAND: (*to* TODD) Shall we leave?

RAVENSBANE: (*Sings*)
"What cock is this, with crest so high,
  That crows with such a pother?"
"Baron von Rabentod am I;
  Methinks we know each other."

"Now welcome, welcome, dear guest of mine,
  So long why didst thou tarry?
Now, for the sake of auld lang syne,
  My daughter thou shalt marry."

AMELIA: (*to* BUGBY) And he kept right on smoking![158]

MINISTER DODGE: (*who, with* RAND *and* TODD, *has risen uneasily*) This smacks of witchcraft.

RAVENSBANE: (*Sings*)
The bride is brought, the priest as well;
  (The golden sun was passing)
They stood beside the altar rail;
  Sing ah! Sing ah! Sing ah! Sing—

"Woman, with this ring I thee wed."
What makes his voice so awing?
The baron by the bride is dead:
  Outside the crows were cawing.

(*Chorus, which grows tumultuous, seeming to fill the room with the invisible birds.*)
Caw! Caw! Caw!

(*The guests rise in confusion.* DICKON *still plays delightedly, and the strange music continues.*)

MINISTER DODGE: This is no longer godly.—Justice Merton! Justice Merton, sir!

RAVENSBANE: (*to* RACHEL, *who holds his tassel in her hand*) Ah! and you have my tassel!

RACHEL: See! I will wear it now. You yourself shall fasten it.

RAVENSBANE: Rachel! Mistress!

RACHEL: My dear lord!

(*As* RAVENSBANE *is placing the silken tassel on* RACHEL'S *breast to fasten it there,* RICHARD, *by the mirror, takes hold of the curtain strings.*)

RICHARD: I told you—witchcraft, like murder will out! Lovers! Behold yourselves!

(*He pulls the curtain back.*)

RACHEL: (*looking into the glass, screams and turns her gaze fearfully upon* RAVENSBANE) Ah! Do not look!

DICKON: (*who, having turned round from the spinet, has leaped forward, now turns back again, biting his finger*) Too late!

(*In the glass are reflected the figures of* RACHEL *and* RAVENSBANE—RACHEL *just as she herself appears, but* RAVENSBANE *in his essential form of a scarecrow, in every movement reflecting* RAVENSBANE'S *motions. The thing in the glass is about to pin a wisp of corn-silk on the mirrored breast of the maiden.*)

RAVENSBANE: What is there?

RACHEL: (*looking again, starts away from* RAVENSBANE) Leave me! Leave me!—Richard!

(*She faints in* RICHARD'S *arms.*)

RAVENSBANE: Fear not, mistress, I will kill the thing.

(*Drawing his sword, he rushes at the glass. Within, the scarecrow, with a drawn wheel-spoke, approaches him at equal speed. They come face to face and recoil.*) Ah! ah! Fear'st thou me? What are thou? Why, 'tis a glass. Thou mockest me? Look, look, mistress, it mocks me! O God, no, no! Take it away. Dear God, do not look!—It is I!

ALL: (*rushing to the doors*) Witchcraft! Witchcraft!

(*As* RAVENSBANE *stands frantically confronting his abject reflection, struck in a like posture of despair, the curtain falls.*)

ACT IV

The same. Night. The moon, shining in broadly at the window, discovers RAVENSBANE *alone, prostrate before the mirror. Raised on one arm to a half-sitting posture, he gazes fixedly at the vaguely seen image of the scarecrow prostrate in the glass.*

RAVENSBANE: All have left me—but not thou. Rachel has left me; her eyes have turned away from me; she is gone. All that I loved, all that loved me, have left me. A thousand ages—a thousand ages ago, they went away; and thou and I have gazed upon each other's desertedness. Speak! and be pitiful! If thou art I, inscrutable image, if thou dost feel these pangs thine own, show them self-mercy; speak! What art thou? What am I? Why are we here? How comes it that we feel and guess and suffer? Nay, though thou answer not these doubts, yet mock them, mock them aloud, even as there, monstrous, thou counterfeitest mine actions. Speak, abject enigma![159]—Speak, poor shadow, thou—
(*Recoiling wildly.*)
Stand back, inanity![160] Thrust not thy mawkish face in pity toward me. Ape and idiot! Scarecrow!—to console me! Haha! —A flail and broomstick! a cob, a gourd and pumpkin, to fuse and sublimate themselves into a mage-philosopher,[161] who discourseth metaphysics[162] to itself—itself, God! Dost Thou hear? Itself! For even such am I—I whom Thou madest to love Rachel. Why, God—haha! dost Thou dwell in this thing? Is it Thou that peerest forth *at* me—*from* me? Why, hark then; Thou shalt listen, and answer—if Thou canst. Between the rise and setting of a sun, I have walked in this world of Thine. I have been thrilled with wonder; I have been calmed with knowledge; I have trembled with joy and passion. Power, beauty, love have ravished me. Infinity itself, like a dream, has blazed before me with the certitude of prophecy; and I have cried, "This world, the heavens, time itself, are mine to conquer," and I have thrust forth mine arm to wear Thy shield forever—and lo! for my shield Thou reachest me—a mirror, and whisperest: "Know thyself! Thou art—a scarecrow: a tinkling clod, a rigmarole of dust, a lump of ordure, contemptible, superfluous, "inane!" Haha! Hahaha! And with such scarecrows Thou dost people a planet! O ludicrous! Monstrous! Ludicrous! At least, I thank Thee, God! at least this breathing bathos[163] can laugh at itself. Thou hast vouchsafed to me, Spirit, —hahaha!—to know myself. Mine, mine is the consummation of man[164]—even self-contempt! (*Pointing in the glass with an agony of derision.*) Scarecrow! Scarecrow! Scarecrow!

THE IMAGE IN THE GLASS: (*more and more faintly*) Scarecrow! Scarecrow! Scarecrow!

(RAVENSBANE *throws himself prone upon the floor, beneath the window, sobbing. There is a pause of silence, and the moon shines brighter.—Slowly then* RAVENSBANE, *getting to his knees, looks out into the night.*)

RAVENSBANE: What face are you, high up through the twinkling leaves? Do you not, like all the rest, turn, aghast, your eyes away from me—me, abject enormity,[165] groveling at your feet? Gracious being, do you not fear—despise me? O white peace of the world, beneath your gaze the clouds glow silver, and the herded cattle, slumbering far afield, crouch—beautiful. The slough[166] shines lustrous as a bridal veil. Beautiful face, you are Rachel's, and you have changed the world. Nothing is mean, but you have made it miraculous; nothing is loathsome, nothing ludicrous, but you have converted it to loveliness, that even this shadow of a mockery myself, cast by your light, gives me the dear assurance I am a man. Rachel, mistress, mother, out of my suffering you have brought forth my soul. I am saved!

THE IMAGE IN THE GLASS: A very pretty sophistry.[167]

(*The moonlight grows dimmer, as at the passing of a cloud.*)

RAVENSBANE: Ah! what voice has snatched you from me?

THE IMAGE: A most poetified pumpkin!

RAVENSBANE: Thing! dost thou speak at last? My soul abhors thee.

THE IMAGE: I *am* thy soul.

RAVENSBANE: Thou liest.

THE IMAGE: Our daddy Dickon and our mother Rickby begot and conceived us at sunrise, in a Jack-o'-lantern.

RAVENSBANE: Thou liest, torturing illusion. Thou art but a phantom in a glass.

THE IMAGE: Why, very true. So art thou. *We* are a pretty phantom in a glass.

RAVENSBANE: It is a lie. I am no longer thou. I feel it; *I am a man.*

THE IMAGE:
And prithee, what's a man? Man's but a mirror,
Wherein the imps and angels play charades,
Make faces, mope, and pull each other's hair—
Till crack! the sly urchin Death shivers the glass,
And the bare coffin boards show underneath.

RAVENSBANE: Yea! if it be so, thou coggery![168] if both of us be indeed but illusions, why, now let us end together. But if it be not so, then let *me* for evermore be free of thee. Now is the test—the glass!

(*Springing to the fireplace, he seizes an iron crosspiece from the andirons.*)

I'll play your urchin Death and shatter it. Let's see what shall survive!

(*He rushes to strike the glass with the iron.* DICKON *steps out of the mirror, closing the curtain.*)

DICKON: I wouldn't, really!

RAVENSBANE: Dickon! dear Dickon! is it you?

DICKON: Yes, Jacky! it's dear Dickon, and I really wouldn't.

RAVENSBANE: Wouldn't what, Dickon?

DICKON: Sweep the cobwebs off the sky with thine aspiring broomstick.[169] When a man questions fate, 'tis bad digestion. When a scarecrow does it, 'tis bad taste.

RAVENSBANE: At last, *you* will tell me the truth, Dickon! And I, then—that thing?

DICKON: You mustn't be so skeptical. Of course you're that thing.

RAVENSBANE: Ah me despicable! Rachel, why didst thou ever look upon me?

DICKON: I fear, cobby, thou hast never studied woman's heart and hero-worship.[170] Take thyself now. I remarked to Goody Bess, thy mother, this morning, as I was chucking her thy pate from the hayloft,[171] that thou wouldst make a Mark Antony or an Alexander before night.[172]

RAVENSBANE: Cease! cease! in pity's name. You do not know the agony of being ridiculous.

DICKON: Nay, Jacky, *all mortals are ridiculous*. Like you, they were rummaged out of the muck;[173] and like you, they shall return to the dunghill. I advise 'em, like you, to enjoy the interim, and smoke.

RAVENSBANE: This pipe, this ludicrous pipe that I forever set to my lips and puff! Why must I, Dickon? Why?

DICKON: To avoid extinction—merely. You see, 'tis just as your fellow in there (*pointing to the glass*) explained. You yourself are the subtlest of mirrors, polished out of pumpkin and pipe-smoke. Into this mirror the fair Mistress Rachel has projected[174] her lovely image, and thus provided you with what men call a soul.

RAVENSBANE: Ah! then, I have a soul—the truth of me? Mistress Rachel has indeed made me a man?

DICKON: Don't flatter thyself, cobby. Break thy pipe, and whiff—soul, Mistress Rachel, man, truth, and this pretty world itself, go up in the last smoke.

RAVENSBANE: No, no! not Mistress Rachel.

DICKON: Mistress Rachel exists for your lordship merely in your lordship's pipebowl.[175]

RAVENSBANE: Wretched, niggling caricature that I am! All is lost to me—lost!

DICKON: "Paradise Lost" again! Always blaming it on me.[176] There's that gaunt fellow in England has lately wrote a parody on me when I was in the apple business.[177]

RAVENSBANE: (*falling on his knees and bowing his head*) O God! I am so contemptible!

(*Enter, at door back,* GOODY RICKBY; *her blacksmith garb is hidden under a dingy black mantle with peaked hood.*)

DICKON: Good verse, too, for a parody!

(*Ruminating, raises one arm rhetorically above* RAVENSBANE.)

—"Farewell, happy fields
Where joy forever dwells! Hail, horrors; hail,
Infernal world! and thou, profoundest hell,
Receive thy new possessor."

GOODY RICKBY: (*seizing his arm*) Dickon!

DICKON: Hullo! You, Bess!

GOODY RICKBY: There's not a minute to lose. Justice Merton and the neighbors have ended their conference at Minister Dodge's, and are returning here.

DICKON: Well, let 'em come. We're ready.

GOODY RICKBY: But thou toldst me they had discovered—

DICKON: A scarecrow in a mirror. Well? The glass is bewitched; that's all.

GOODY RICKBY: All? Witchcraft is hanging—that's all! And the mirror was bought of me—of me, the witch. Wilt thou be my hangman, Dickon?

DICKON: Wilt thou give me a kiss, Goody? When did ever thy Dickon desert thee?

GOODY RICKBY: But how, boy, wilt thou—

DICKON: Trust me, and thy son. When the Justice's niece is thy daughter-in-law, all will be safe. For the Justice will cherish his niece's family.

GOODY RICKBY: But when he knows—

DICKON: But he shall not know. How can he? When the glass is denounced as a fraud, how will he, or any person, ever know that we made this fellow out of rubbish? Who, forsooth, but a poet—or a devil—*would* believe it? You mustn't credit men with our imaginations, my dear.

GOODY RICKBY: Then thou wilt pull me through this safe?

DICKON: As I adore thee—and my own reputation.[178]

GOODY RICKBY: (*at the window*) I see their lanterns down the road.

DICKON: Stay, marchioness[179]—his lordship! My lord—your lady mother.

GOODY RICKBY: (*curtsying, laughs shrilly*) Your servant—my son!
(*About to depart.*)

RAVENSBANE: Ye lie! both of you!—I was born of Rachel.[180]

DICKON: Tut, tut, Jacky; you mustn't mix up mothers and prospective wives at your age. It's fatal.

GOODY RICKBY: (*excitedly*) They're coming!
(*Exit.*)

DICKON: (*calling after her*) Fear not; I'll overtake thee.

RAVENSBANE: She is coming; Rachel is coming, and I may not look upon her!

DICKON: Eh? Why not?

RAVENSBANE: I am a monster.

DICKON: Fie! fie! Thou shalt have her.

RAVENSBANE: Have her, Dickon?

DICKON: For lover and wife.

RAVENSBANE: For wife?

DICKON: For wife and all. Thou hast but to obey.

RAVENSBANE: Ah? who will do this for me?

DICKON: I!

RAVENSBANE: Dickon! Wilt make me a man—a man and worthy of her?

DICKON: Fiddlededee! I make over no masterpieces. Thy mistress shall be Cinderella, and drive to her palace with her gilded pumpkin.[181]

RAVENSBANE: It is the end.

DICKON: What! You'll not?

RAVENSBANE: Never.

DICKON: Harkee, manikin. Hast thou learned to suffer?

RAVENSBANE: (*wringing his hands*) O God!

DICKON: *I* taught thee. Shall I teach thee further?

RAVENSBANE: Thou canst not.

DICKON: Cannot—ha! What if I should teach Rachel, too?

RAVENSBANE: Rachel!—Ah! now I know thee.

DICKON: (*bowing*) Flattered.[182]

RAVENSBANE: Devil! Thou wouldst not torment Rachel?

DICKON: Not if my lord—

RAVENSBANE: Speak! What must I do?

DICKON: *Not* speak. Be silent, my lord, and acquiesce in all I say.

RAVENSBANE: I will be silent.

DICKON: And acquiesce?

RAVENSBANE: I will be silent.[183]

(*Enter* MINISTER DODGE, *accompanied by* SIR CHARLES REDDINGTON, CAPTAIN BUGBY, *the* REVEREND MASTERS RAND *and* TODD, *and followed by* JUSTICE MERTON, RICHARD, MISTRESS MERTON, *and* RACHEL. RICHARD *and* RACHEL *stand somewhat apart,* RACHEL *drawing close to* RICHARD *and hiding her face. All wear their outer wraps, and two or three hold lanterns, which, save*[184] *the moon, throw the only light upon the scene. All enter solemn and silent.*)

MINISTER DODGE: Lord, be Thou present with us, in this unholy spot.

SEVERAL MEN'S VOICES: Amen.

DICKON: Friends! Have you seized her?

MINISTER DODGE: Stand from us.

DICKON: Sir, the witch! Surely you did not let her escape?

ALL: The witch!

DICKON: A dame in a peaked hood. She has but now fled the house. She called herself—Goody Rickby.

ALL: Goody Rickby!

MISTRESS MERTON: She here!

DICKON: Yea, mistress, and hath confessed all the damnable art, by which all of us have lately been so terrorized.

JUSTICE MERTON: What confessed she?

MINISTER DODGE: What said she?

DICKON: This: It appeareth that, for some time past, she hath cherished revengeful thoughts against our honored host, Justice Merton.

MINISTER DODGE: Yea, he hath often righteously condemned her!

DICKON: Precisely! So, in revenge, she bewitched yonder mirror, and this very morning unlawfully inveigled this sweet young lady into purchasing it.[185]

SIR CHARLES: Mistress Rachel!

MINISTER DODGE: (*to* RACHEL) Didst thou purchase that glass?

RACHEL: (*in a low voice*) Yes.

MINISTER DODGE: From Goody Rickby?

RACHEL: Yes. (*Clinging to* RICHARD.) O Richard!

MINISTER DODGE: But the image; what was the damnable image in the glass?

DICKON: A familiar devil of hers—a sly imp, who wears to mortal eyes the shape of a scarecrow. It seems she commanded this devil to reveal himself in the glass as my lord's own image, that thus she might wreck Justice Merton's family felicity.[186]

MINISTER DODGE: Infamous!

DICKON: Indeed, sir, it was this very devil whom but now she stole here to consult withal, when she encountered me, attendant here upon my poor prostrate lord, and—held by the wrath in my eye—confessed it all.

SIR CHARLES: Thunder and brimstone! Where is this accursed hag?

DICKON: Alas—gone, gone! If you had but stopped her.

MINISTER DODGE: I know her den—the blacksmith shop. Let us seize her there!

SIR CHARLES: (starting) Which way?

MINISTER DODGE: To the left.

SIR CHARLES: Go on, there.

MINISTER DODGE: My honored friends, come with us. Heaven shield, with her guilt, the innocent!

(Exeunt all but RICHARD, RACHEL, DICKON and RAVENSBANE.)

DICKON: So, then, dear friends, this strange incident is happily elucidated. Bygones, therefore, be bygones. The future brightens—with orange-blossoms. Hymen[187] and Felicity stand with us here ready to unite two amorous and bashful lovers. His lordship is reticent; yet to you alone, of all beautiful ladies, Mistress Rachel—

RAVENSBANE: (in a mighty voice) Silence!

DICKON: My lord would—

RAVENSBANE: Silence! Dare not to speak to her!

DICKON: (biting his lip) My babe is weaned.[188]

(He steps back, and disappears, left, in the dimness.)

RACHEL: (still at RICHARD's side) Oh, my lord, if I have made you suffer—

RICHARD: (appealingly) Rachel!

RAVENSBANE: (approaching her, raises one arm to screen his face) Gracious lady! let fall your eyes; look not upon me. If I dare now speak once more to you, 'tis because I would have you know—Oh, forgive me!—that I love you.

RICHARD: Sir! This lady has renewed her promise to be my wife.

RAVENSBANE: Your wife, or not, I love her.

RICHARD: Zounds!

RAVENSBANE: Forbear, and hear me! For one wonderful day I have gazed upon this, your world. A million forms—of trees, of stones, of stars, of men, of common things—have swum like motes before my eyes; but one alone was wholly beautiful. That form was Rachel: to her alone I was not ludicrous; to her I also was beautiful. Therefore, I love her.

RICHARD: Sir!

RAVENSBANE: You talk to me of mothers, mistresses, lovers, and wives and sisters, and you say men love these. What is love? The night and day of the world—the *all* of life, the all which must include both you and me and God, of whom you dream. Well, then, I love you, Rachel. What shall prevent me? Mistress, mother, wife—thou art all to me!

RICHARD: My lord, I can only reply for Mistress Rachel, that you speak like one who does not understand this world.[189]

RAVENSBANE: O God! Sir, and do you? If so, tell me—tell me before it be too late—why, in this world, such a thing as *I* can love and talk of love. Why, in this world, a true man and woman, like you and your betrothed, can look upon this counterfeit and be deceived.

RACHEL and RICHARD: Counterfeit?

RAVENSBANE: Me—on me—the ignominy[190] of the earth, the laughing-stock of the angels!

RACHEL: Are you not Lord Ravensbane?

RAVENSBANE: No, I am *not* Lord Ravensbane. I am a nobleman of husks, bewitched from a pumpkin. I am Lord Scarecrow!

RACHEL: Ah me, the image in the glass was true?

RAVENSBANE: Yes, true. It is the glass of truth—Thank God for you, dear.

DICKON: (*his face only reappearing in the mirror, speaks low*) Remember! if you dare—Rachel shall suffer for it.

RAVENSBANE: You lie. She is above your power.

DICKON: Still, thou darest not—

RAVENSBANE: Fool, I dare. (RAVENSBANE *turns to* RACHEL. *While he speaks,* DICKON'S *face slowly fades and disappears.*) Mistress, this pipe is I. This intermittent smoke holds, in its nebula,[191] Venus, Mars, the world. If I should break it—Chaos and the dark! And this of me that now stands up will sink jumbled upon the floor—a scarecrow. See! I break it. (*He breaks the pipe in his hands, and flings the pieces to the ground; then turns, agonized, to* RACHEL.) Oh, Rachel, could I have been a man—!

(*He sways, staggering.*)

RACHEL: Richard! Richard! Support him.

(*She draws the curtain of the mirror, just opposite which* RAVENSBANE *has sunk upon the floor. At her cry, he starts up faintly and gazes at his reflection, which is seen to be a normal image of himself.*[192])

RAVENSBANE: Who is it?

RACHEL: Yourself, my lord—'tis the glass of truth.

RAVENSBANE: (*his face lighting with an exalted joy, starts to his feet, erect, before the glass*) A man! (*He falls back into the arms of the two lovers.*) Rachel! (*He dies.*)

RICHARD: (*bending over him*) Dead!

RACHEL: (*with an exalted look*) But a man![193]

CURTAIN

NOTES

1. Your pardon, madame.
2. God!
3. Archbishop of Canterbury and statesman, 10th Cent., A.D.
4. Greek sculptor, 4th Cent., B.C.
5. Italian painter, 16th Cent., A.D.
6. Gives life to a useless thing.
7. Ideal good.
8. Raised to the rank of a "God of Scarecrows."
9. The "direct opposite of Adam."
10. Name of the first man, founder of the human race.
11. An oath.
12. Dialect: creature, esp. some kind of animal.
13. Greek Mythology: beautiful girl loved by Eros or Cupid; also, soul.
14. Structure of an animal or plant; the various parts.
15. German: "Oh John The Baptist!"
16. Herod Antipas, Salome's stepfather, was so entranced with the girl's dancing that he offered her a reward "unto the half of my kingdom." She asked for the head of John the Baptist on a platter (Matt. xiv).
17. Polish astronomer, 16th Cent., A.D.
18. God of manly beauty.
19. Scoundrels, robbers, etc.
20. Wig worn by men, 17th-18th Cent.
21. French: "Look here."
22. French: One who knows; a specialist; an expert.
23. Goody Rickby's nickname.
24. Throw useless things in gutter.
25. A local officer having jurisdiction to try minor cases, administer oaths, solemnize marriages, etc.
26. Wise men of ancient Persia reported to have had supernatural powers.
27. French: meeting.
28. Gallows with projecting arm from which criminals were hanged.
29. Understand.
30. Very much interested in the occult: magic: witchcraft.
31. "We don't make as much of magic and witchcraft in this town as at Salem . . ." etc. Line has double meaning: Salem was scene for supposed witchcraft, and actual witchcraft trials in 1692. ". . . it may come to it!" is therefore a threat at possibility of a trial in the near future.
32. Things falsely made.

33. Out of.
34. Refers to the scarecrow's head: a pumpkin head.
35. Christian. Also a pun on *orthodox* and *jaws*, meant as an insult.
36. One of the biblical books. Deuteronomy contains the second statement of the Mosaic law. *"Master Deuteronomy!"* Another insult: "Master Lawmaker."
37. Help, in the sense of scheming, plotting in an underhanded way.
38. ". . . spoke in his wheel!" refers to spoiling someone's plan.
39. Haughty, disdainful, contemptuous expression.
40. French: a look of "high pride." Similar to 39.
41. Not guided by conscience: unscrupulous.
42. Little witch. Probably used in an endearing way when the two were younger.
43. Works of magic and witchcraft.
44. French: still, yet, besides. Usually said after a performance to show approval, and thus get an additional performance.
45. Latin: namely. Usually written *viz.*
46. French: isn't that so?
47. An estate inherited from one's father or ancestors.
48. A thing placed out of its proper time.
49. Spirit and practices of the Middle Ages.
50. Medieval chemistry; also any magical power or process of transmuting.
51. Italian: "But what can you expect!"
52. Dickon is not only referring to Columbus' discovery of America, but to Torquemada, leader of the Inquisition under King Ferdinand and Queen Isabella of Spain. Torquemada's name has become a synonym for a cruel persecutor. Dickon of course wants us to think he was behind all this!
53. According to legend a famous German alchemist who sold his soul to the devil in exchange for youth and everlasting life. Story was used by Marlowe, later by Goethe.
54. A thing from the region originating it.
55. One who is betrothed, or pledged to be married.
56. The head of the household through marriage.
57. The raven has for centuries been considered a bird of ill omen . . . a bad luck creature. "Bane" refers to a thing that ruins or spoils, and brings destruction and death. "Ravensbane" is a name meant to combine all these evil qualities.
58. A double pun since macaroni refers not only to food made from hollow farinaceous tubes, but also to an English dandy of the 18th Century who affected foreign ways. Ravensbane is at once fodder for cattle as well as a fancifully dressed dandy resembling a man.
59. Italian: Perfect; magnificent; wonderful.
60. A one-horse, two-wheeled carriage with a hood.
61. Latin: So. Used parenthetically to show that something has been copied from the original.
62. Latin: "A son is made not born." Paraphrase on the poet Horace's statement: "A poet is born not made."
63. Pun on: "In the beginning was the word." The first words of The Gospel of St. John The Evangelist in the New Testament.
64. Chanting of words supposed to have magical power.
65. Latin: "So it goes!"; possibly "So be it," in the sense that the scarecrow is the things Dickon is enumerating while trying to give it life.
66. Latin: Hail, praise, worship.
67. Latin: "One from many" in the sense that from many different parts comes unity, or completeness. The separate parts of man equal the whole man. Irony is added to the scene since "E pluribus unum" is the motto of the United States of America.
68. Possibly a triple pun: tobacco; back, in the sense of "backbone"; and Bacchae, the female attendants of Bacchus, God of wine, drunkenness and wild orgies. When pronounced as "baccy" all as well as any one of the three meanings are possible, and bear out the truth of Dickon's statement.
69. Latin: "Venus approaches." This is probably used in the sense that Venus (who not only is the ancient goddess of love and beauty according to early Roman legend), is also the goddess of gardens and spring; and thus represents the beginning of the life cycle for the plant kingdom.
70. Latin: "So! So! Jacobus!" The word Jacobus could translate as either "Jacob," or "James." According to the Hebrew, Ya'aqōb refers to one who takes by the heel, a supplanter (Genesis 25:26, 27:36); reference here is to one thing taking the place of another: an inanimate thing turning into a living thing. Another example of Dickon's way of saying one thing, and meaning several.
71. Latin: "Let there be a living thing"; also could translate as "Let it be alive."
72. German: "Yet once more!" or "Again."
73. Latin: "Come, son! Come!" (. . . *bambino*: Italian for little child, baby.)
74. Latin: "boy."
75. Latin: "speak!"

76. Latin: "In the beginning was the word." Bible: first words of the Gospel of St. John The Evangelist.
77. Bible: name for the prince of the devils. In Milton's *Paradise Lost*, one of the fallen angels, second only to Satan himself.
78. Submission to another's will.
79. A collar or band fitting around the neck. Dickon therefore looks somewhat like a Puritan minister. This is consistent with the dual quality of his character.
80. Brat.
81. Featherless; unfledged.
82. Usually an old servant of an ancient household; one who has served the household for many years.
83. Disdainfully proud, arrogant, supercilious.
84. The glass will show him as he really is. If Richard is a false lover, the glass will reveal him as such; but if he is true to Rachel he will be shown to be true not only to her but to himself as well. The image could therefore be various degrees of ugliness or beauty for whoever gazes into the mirror.
85. Traditionally the fox has been sly and cunning, and the goose obvious and stupid. Here the lovers are teasing one another about the qualities they may see in the mirror when they look into it.
86. Miss Merton, sister of Justice Merton.
87. "Truly." In other words: "That's a fact."
88. To be condemned to death, and have one's property confiscated, a procedure common for those found guilty of witchcraft in early American Colonial times.
89. Suspected of being an accomplice in an unlawful act or crime. Such a person might be a witch's helper, or one who is learning the art of witchcraft.
90. Wellborn people; members of the upper middle class; also the Nobility: Lords, Dukes, Earls, etc.
91. The dog has sensed the coming of something supernatural, and is frightened. This reference in the play tends to heighten the suspense, and make a dramatic entrance for Lord Ravensbane (the scarecrow) and his servant (Dickon).
92. Possible triple meaning here: a colony of rooks (European crows); a colony of swindlers and other similar evildoers; and a colony of pieces as in chess (rooks—sometimes called castles). These pieces have the ability to move any number of spaces forward, backward, or sidewise. The name "Rookeries" is therefore a grisly joke, a play on the meaning of words Dickon is using instead of saying "Hell" which is what he really means. Somersetshire is an ancient southwestern county of England. Taunton castle and Wells were scenes for the "bloody assizes" held by Judge George Jeffreys in late 1685 in Somersetshire, and these trials were probably somewhat similar in nature to the Salem trials in the same century. In short, Dickon is disguising the fact that he is present wherever and whenever any evil thing is done.
93. A former Dutch town on Manhattan island: the capital of New Netherland; renamed New York by the British, 1664.
94. Loss of memory; a mind wandering from the truth; temporary forgetfulness.
95. Letter.
96. Rooks refers to three possibilities: crows, swindlers, and the castles of a chess set. Rampant refers to the figure or figures shown on an heraldic crest (similar to figures on a shield). The design could therefore include the various rooks in profile on a shield, all of which would be part of the seal. However, it is unlikely that an audience would see the seal on the document. But the words would be heard, and these in turn are a pun since "rampant" also means violent in action; furious; raging.
97. Richard comes close to guessing the true nature of Lord Ravensbane.
98. Justice Merton knows about having a daughter out of wedlock (i.e., Rachel, his "niece"), but it comes as a shock to him to be confronted with the possibility of having a son under the same circumstances. However, Dickon's line: "She speaks likewise for his young lordship's father, sir," has, as usual, a double meaning. Justice Merton realizes that no one else can know of his youthful mistake with Goody Rickby (even though this assumption on his part is false since Dickon knows about it), and therefore he feels safe with his knowledge, but guilty nevertheless. One of the purposes of this scene is to show how Dickon can torment one who has a guilty conscience.
99. The irony of the scene continues, especially with: ". . . I entrust him to you *as to a father.*" Merton is and is not a father at the same time. He responds to the paradox by being "honored," although an insult is intended.
100. Death.
101. A descendant; also a shoot or twig; especially one for grafting or planting; a cutting from the main plant. Pun here is that Ravensbane is a bundle of plant cuttings: corn stalks, grass, and straw, etc.
102. Justice Merton not only has a bad conscience, but he probably thinks his hear-

ing is going bad also. He has not guessed as yet that Dickonson is really his old enemy Dickon in disguise.
103. Pun here is: "Gilead" is Justice Merton's given name: his first name; and "balm" refers to anything that heals, soothes, or relieves pain. However, Dickon is being sarcastic and cruel here, and the opposite is the truth: "Saved it for the torture of Gilead." A third aspect to this pun is that balm of Gilead is an oleoresin that Dickon would use in his practice of alchemy and black magic.
104. A "marchioness" is the widow of a marquis, who in turn is a nobleman ranking next below a duke. The reason for giving Goody Rickby this title might be as follows: Satan is the "Prince of Darkness"; and Dickon is the duke. Those under Dickon have various ranks, and in this case the marquis is Justice Gilead Merton, and his former sweetheart, Goody Rickby, is now the marchioness. Thus a hierarchy of evil would seem to exist as an opposite aspect of a hierarchy of good.
105. Justice Merton fears that the secret of his illicit love affair will become known. As a leader in the community his career would probably be finished. Not wanting to take a chance on being exposed for his misdeed, Justice Merton is forced to agree to whatever Dickon suggests.
106. Dickon is using "fancy" words to say: to make Ravenbane's heart beat evenly. Dickon is "pulling her leg" here . . . having a bit of sport at Rachel's expense since she is so innocent.
107. His heart would stop beating because he would be in love . . . just the opposite of what usually happens. Of course Dickon is playing another one of his jokes since Ravensbane is an inanimate thing already and is not capable of life or death in the human sense at all.
108. Dickon says that Justice Merton bounced Ravensbane on his knee, and pampered him as a child. Justice Merton thinks his secret has been disclosed, and he is about to say something that might incriminate himself, but Dickon covers Merton's near disclosure with a lie that gets Merton out of the situation.
109. Greek mythology: nymphs and a serpent were supposed to protect a garden of golden apples, the wedding gift of Gaea to Hera, at the western end of the world.
110. Pumpkins.
111. A family possession passed on from generation to generation, and in this case one dating back to the time of the Druids (one of an order of priests or ministers of religion among the ancient Celts of Gaul, Britain, and Ireland). In Irish and Welsh legend Druids appear as magicians and soothsayers. It is probably in this sense that the term is being used here in order to heighten the mood and feeling of mystery and magic the playwright constantly tries to present.
112. The Anglo-Saxons conquered and occupied certain parts of south Britain in the fifth and sixth centuries, and the name was extended to the entire Old English people and language before the Norman Conquest.
113. Charlemagne (742-814), king of the Franks (768), and emperor of the West (800), son of Pepin. He and his heroic knights are the subject of many a *chanson de geste* (song of heroic deeds) of which the *Song of Roland* is the most famous.
114. The Romans occupied Britain for many years, and relics of their chariots are referred to here.
115. Ravensbane indicates here that his mother is a blacksmith without actually using the word. The scene disguises the actual surroundings of the smithy with false references to the noble estate Ravensbane pretends to come from. The altar mentioned here is of course a blacksmith's anvil.
116. ". . . makes you jealous" is Merton's way of covering up the disclosure that the devil is present, and thus turns his own slip of the tongue into an accusation that Richard is jealous of Rachel's interest in Ravensbane.
117. Ravensbane's pipe provides him with the breath of life: fire and brimstone, which is an appropriate concoction for a creation of the devil. When Ravensbane doesn't get his pipe he tends to revert to what he is: a lifeless scarecrow.
118. Charles II, king of England (1660-85); in other words, spoken in a gallant way.
119. If Ravensbane should get too excited, then his heart would stop.
120. Justice Merton may have been contemplating either shooting Ravensbane or possibly himself. When Dickon removes the pistol, Merton feels thankful that he was unable to take any action . . . that he was saved from doing more evil.
121. Ravensbane automatically lists the titles Dickon has taught him to say.
122. Without his pipe Ravensbane is helpless. In this scene Justice Merton has snatched Ravensbane's pipe away, and is about to let him "die," but then changes his mind. Although Merton has sinned in the past, and is being made to pay for his faults, he does not choose to commit murder even to a creation of the devil. Merton therefore

123. Merton speaks sharply to his sister, Cynthia Merton, simply by exclaiming her name. He thus indicates that he wants her to keep silent.
124. Sad, as though with tears.
125. "So strong is habit in tender years." Virgil, *Georgics*, Book II, line 272 (Translated by H. R. Fairclough, *Loeb Classical Library*). Another possible translation might be: "It is so important in the case of young tender things (especially plants and vines), to be trained well."
126. Italian: "Enough!"
127. Tools for fighting; weapons.
128. A flail is an instrument for threshing grain by hand, consisting of a staff or handle to one end of which is attached a freely swinging stick or bar. During the Middle Ages a similar implement was used as a weapon of war.
129. Various parts that made up Ravensbane at his birth.
130. Apollo: god who brings back sunshine in spring, who sends plagues, and who founds states and colonies; also the god of music and poetry; had gift of knowing the future. The *Apollo Belvedere* refers to a statue of the god in the Vatican.
131. Model of a person; a dummy; a little man.
132. Distressing to one's feelings.
133. A writer of indifferent verse; an inferior poet. "Inferior" only in the sense that Satan himself is more accomplished.
134. Dickon claims to have inspired many writers. He has spoken to them as they worked.
135. Mistress R— could be either Rickby or Rachel. The ambiguity is intentional, and Dickon knows Rachel will think the poem is meant for her, in which case the reference to "cruel witch" would not be taken as an insult, but as a lover's complaint.
136. Reading one's fortune according to the lines in one's hand.
137. Wife.
138. It was considered sophisticated to shorten such sayings as "your humble servant." But this statement is also a pun because Ravensbane is in fact "humble."
139. Rachel makes an unintentional joke. The point is Ravensbane isn't keeping Dickon. Just the reverse is true.
140. It was the custom to beat persons who ran away from penal institutions.
141. An idiot.
142. Should have prayed to Satan.
143. Fine; first rate; in this sense puffs with pleasure and enjoyment.
144. Reply. A sharp, quick answer or comment.
145. A dagger.
146. Two clergymen.
147. Latin: Forbidden custom.
148. Dickon needles Justice Merton, and makes him appear like a fool.
149. As Ravensbane becomes more and more like a human being his various "scarecrow" characteristics disappear. This would account for his not limping any more as Captain Bugby has just noticed. Bugby is annoyed about this because he has been imitating Ravensbane, thinking the scarecrow's gestures fashionable.
150. See note 125.
151. Telling of the future.
152. The chief English heathen god, identical with the Scandinavian Odin. It is from this name that we get "Wednesday" (Woden's day).
153. German: *Raben:* raven, plus *tod:* death; or *Ravensbane.*
154. Strong and brave; valiant; also active; nimble or swift.
155. A riding horse as distinguished from a war horse.
156. Cared; heeded.
157. Sir Charles means Dickon's music seems to be coming from some place other than the immediate room.
158. Ravensbane needs his pipe to "stay alive." However, in this scene the use of the pipe adds to the fantastic element of the play and helps create a weird atmosphere.
159. "Despicable, humiliating riddle!"
160. Thing without sense.
161. Magician-philosopher.
162. That branch of philosophy which treats of first principles, including the sciences of being (ontology), and of the origin and structure of the universe (cosmology).
163. A ludicrous descent from an elevated to a commonplace position; also in this sense the lowest possible thing.
164. Perfection; fulfillment.
165. Despicable atrocity; a monstrous freak.
166. The soft muddy ground.
167. A false, tricky argument.
168. One who loads dice; a cheat. In this sense to indicate that The Image is loading the argument, and is using deceptive means to win its points, as a cheat would do in a dice game.
169. By this Dickon means Ravensbane should not try to fight the devil's work in God's world.
170. Here Dickon is trying to make Rachel's love seem untrue. He suggests that Rachel will love any hero, and that she is fickle.
171. Ravensbane's head (his pate) was made

from a pumpkin that Dickon found in Goody Rickby's hayloft.
172. Mark Antony: a great soldier and noble prince who was enthralled by the beauty of Cleopatra, Queen of Egypt. Story is subject of Shakespeare's historical tragedy, *Antony and Cleopatra*. Second reference is to Alexander the Great, the world conqueror, and founder of the city of Alexandria, Egypt. Both Mark Antony and Alexander the Great were famous heroes, and in using these two as examples Dickon is therefore "proving" to Ravensbane that Rachel's love is false because she sees him as a hero and not as a man. Ravensbane knows he is neither hero nor man, and that Dickon's jibes are making him suffer. The paradox here is that the degree of Ravensbane's suffering marks how much he is *becoming* a man, despite Dickon's campaign against him.
173. Mud; slime and ooze. Some say that the first life on earth started in the primordial ooze of warm salty oceans many millions of years ago. Dickon characteristically points out in a negative way the humble origin of life rather than the miracle of its occurrence at all.
174. Dickon intimates that Rachel's spirit has radiated from her to the mirror, and there some of it has been reflected to Ravensbane. What Dickon is describing is the spirit that love provides for all those who experience it.
175. A reminder that Ravensbane is nothing without his pipe.
176. Dickon pretends to have his feelings hurt by being reminded of Satan's fall from God's grace when Satan led a revolt of angels against God and was banished forever from heaven. (See John Milton's *Paradise Lost*.)
177. Reference is to John Milton and his epic poem, *Paradise Lost*, which describes, along with Satan's fall, the temptation of Eve in The Garden of Eden, the banishment of Adam and Eve from the Garden for tasting the forbidden fruit of the Tree of Knowledge: an apple; and other biblical scenes.
178. Dickon hopes that he will succeed. His reputation and standing as a devil will suffer if he does not accomplish what he wants done. People won't have "faith" in him if he should fail.
179. Widow of a marquis. See note 104.
180. Ravensbane claims he was not alive prior to receiving Rachel's spirit and her love. Without love he was a dead thing and therefore never was born. With love he claims to be alive from the moment he experienced it, and he was born by the person who first gave him love, and by no other.
181. Dickon is referring to Ravensbane as a "gilded pumpkin," i.e., a pumpkin that has been coated with gold, gold leaf, or gold-colored substance. Gilded also refers to being made red, as with blood . . . possibly blushing.
182. As Ravensbane becomes more and more conscious in the process of becoming a man, he also becomes more aware of what is evil, and of the one who creates it. Dickon is pleased to think that Ravensbane knows a devil when he sees one.
183. Ravensbane agrees only to being silent, and not to further submission to Dickon's will. Had he agreed to both of Dickon's demands, Rachel might have been tortured also. In agreeing only to silence Ravensbane protects his loved one, but seals his own doom. This act of courage, along with his love which made it possible for him to be courageous, earns Ravensbane the thing he wants most: to be a man.
184. With the exception of.
185. Dickon knows he is fighting a losing battle, and in a final devilish attempt tries to get Rachel into trouble by suggesting the facts to Minister Dodge in such a way that Dodge will think Rachel a witch. She might then be hanged for witchcraft.
186. Happiness; good fortune.
187. Greek mythology: god of marriage, represented as a young man carrying a torch and a veil.
188. Pun here: *wean* means not only to break away from a habit (especially small children and animals from mothers' milk), but also *wee ane:* Scottish for little child. Thus Ravensbane is free from Dickon's influence, and is a person in his own right.
189. Richard reaffirms the point Dickon has already made: Ravensbane is a child. We don't expect children to understand the world, but their feelings about it are often more truthful than some adults' feelings. (The child is father of the man . . . see Wordsworth's "My Heart Leaps Up.")
190. Disgrace
191. Latin: mist; vapor; cloud.
192 When he sees himself as he is, he is a man.
193. Ravensbane has been experiencing an awakening to life throughout the play. When he sees himself he does not recognize what he has become. Rachel, whose love helped give Ravensbane a soul and life, and who helped give him "birth" as

the result of sharing her own self with Ravensbane in the magic mirror of truth, now helps the former scarecrow to *identify himself as a man.* His last word is the name of the one he thanks for the miracle: Rachel; and Rachel's closing line identifies the miracle in response to Richard's observation that the scarecrow is dead. Thus in two lines, and in only four words, the essence of the miracle, and the essence of the paradox that the situation presents, brings the play to a close, letting readers and audience alike wonder about the true nature of man, and the truth of life.

QUESTIONS

A. *Understanding the Action:*

The action of the play is not complicated, occurring as it does in a single day and in two places only, the forge and Justice Merton's parlor. To understand the plot, consider the following questions.

1. Explain why Percy MacKaye gave *The Scarecrow* the subtitle of "A Tragedy of the Ludicrous." What are the possible meanings for the word "ludicrous" as used in the play?

2. What is Goody Rickby's purpose in sending the scarecrow to torment Justice Merton?

3. How does Dickon persuade Justice Merton to accept the unpleasant situation?

4. At what point did Ravensbane begin to slip from Dickon's power? Why did this happen?

5. What is the importance of the mirror at the beginning and at the end of the play?

B. *Understanding the Characters:*

Some of the characters in the play are entirely human; others are obviously not, although they display at times human characteristics. The balance between human and nonhuman plays an essential part in the development of the play. Consider the following questions.

1. Who, or what, is Dickon? What evidence is there in his statements of his being what he is?

2. What aspects of Rachel's personality help influence the plot? (What is the nature of her infatuation with Ravensbane?)

3. How does Richard's attitude toward himself and toward Rachel change from the beginning of the play to the end? In what ways is he consistent in his actions?

4. Ravensbane becomes a man at the very end of the play. What brought this change? What is the significance of this change; that is, what might the playwright be saying, in general, about the process of becoming a man?

5. Describe Goody Rickby's motivation and her relation with Dickon.

6. Explain what Dickon impudently implies when, having composed a poem to Rachel for Lord Ravensbane, he says "Indeed, my lord, I flatter myself that I have dictated some of the finest lines in literature."

C. *Understanding the Approach:*

In literature that is called fantasy the characters, often highly imaginative ones, move through a series of unreal events that take place in an unlikely setting. The reader or observer is asked to suspend his disbelief in the impossible or supernatural long enough to partake in these events.

One aspect of fantasy that makes this suspension of disbelief easier, however, is that not too much is demanded of the observer. Thus, a play about dragons on the far side of the moon might be so totally unbelievable, despite its momentary interest or amusing side, that it would fail to have the impact of a play such as *The Scarecrow.* Along with the many fantastic elements it contains, *The Scarecrow* offers much that is recognizable and familiar, making the task easier. For example, the setting of *The Scarecrow* is a historical place and time, 17th century New England of the Salem witch trials.

1. Explain how the use of this time and setting adds to the effect of the play.

2. What are the realistic actions and character portrayals that add to the sense of verisimilitude, of having the appearance of truth?

The author makes much use of the technique of irony in this play. Irony is a statement made in which the real attitude of the speaker is just the opposite of what he has said. For example, through Act III, during the reception, Justice Merton's remarks are frequently ironic, as in his reply of "Amen" to the minister's remark about standing on "God's threshold," (page 361). Or, a situation may be ironic, as indeed the whole situation of Ravensbane pretending to be the son of a dear friend of Justice Merton, while Justice Merton is led to believe he himself is the father of Ravensbane, the scarecrow.

1. Find other ironic statements and explain their irony.

2. What is ironic about the choice of flails as weapons for the duel?

3. Irony is often very apparent, included for the sake of humor alone. What is the humorous irony of some of the names, such as Gilead for Justice Merton, or Ravensbane and "Jack Lanthorne" for the scarecrow?

D. Comparisons:

Both *A Night at an Inn* and *The Scarecrow* have fantastic elements. In what way does the use of fantasy in these plays differ? Consider the essential difference between the idol and the scarecrow. Why is *The Scarecrow* not a melodrama if *A Night at an Inn* is?

COMEDY AND FARCE

Man has been called the only animal capable of laughter. This makes it possible for him to create and enjoy comedy. It argues an ability to detach himself from his own or some other individual's personality, to exercise judgment and see things in perspective. Man has also been called a reasoning animal, and reason, too, plays an important role in the discriminating laughter produced by virtually all forms of comedy except the lowliest horseplay and farce. Comedy is therefore not only pleasure-giving but frequently enlightening, stimulating, and provocative. It is also a therapeutic procedure. Thus, a "sense of humor" is often recommended to us for its curative powers. Although humor is neither the solution to all our problems nor the solvent for all our tensions and misfortunes, comedy often serves to purge us of fears and resentments.

Comedy, moreover, has often been used to protest against human vanities, follies, and abuses. A powerful weapon in the arsenal of comedy has been ridicule or satire. It has been often employed to correct error provided that the nature and the result of our follies have not been so disastrous as to require sterner measures, such as police action. Bernard Shaw reminded his playgoers that if he sometimes made them feel like fools, he managed by the same action to cure them of their folly, just as a dentist cures a toothache by pulling out the offending tooth. If the mistakes of tragic characters can fill us with pity, fear, wonder, and, at times, even admiration, the mistakes of comic characters can only arouse our laughter. Should this prove not to be the case, it may be that the comedy is not "simple" and "pure" but complex and mixed with pathos as in a Chekhov play (see *The Harmful Effects of Smoking*, page 504) or that changes wrought by time have made it difficult to laugh at individuals who were once regarded as objects of laughter.

Comedy, of course, can often be enjoyed for its own sake, for its liveliness and zest for life, but this does not mean that it cannot be corrective at the same time. A good example of fun combined with criticism is the very first play in our section of comedy, Molière's famous little social satire The Pretentious Ladies (*Les Précieuses ridicules*, page 384).

The range of comedy is very wide; it is decidedly wider than the range of tragedy, perhaps because there are more ways of our being ridiculous than tragic, and perhaps also because comedy is more dependent than tragedy on the influence of environment; there are many environments, manners and fashions, and tastes change frequently. Many comedies, in fact, become outmoded not because they are poor pieces of work, but because they make many topical allusions, and we cannot, of course, find them amusing if we do not understand them or if our taste in humor has changed. Shakespeare's contemporaries, for example, thought that the insane were legitimate subjects for humor, and well-bred gallants enjoyed observing and baiting poor helpless lunatics. At least some of these gentlemen apparently had enough good taste in other respects to admire the poetic and dramatic art of Shakespeare.

Often the world of the comic playwright is a joyous experience. The dramatic action concludes happily for the hero and heroine while injurious characters are ridiculed, defeated, and variously punished, though rarely with great severity. Sometimes this happy world bustles with physical activity and light-hearted intrigue. The comedian's horizon is usually darkened by nothing more distressing than silly misunderstandings, mistaken identities, easily pricked vanities, and no less easily exploded pretensions. Fortune in the world of comedy usually favors the good or the brave; marriages between the young are favored and are consummated despite opposition from one source or another; misunderstandings are cleared up and differences of opinion ironed out.

In this world, too, ridicule is essentially unhurtful and the playwright is so genial or carefree that he never strikes the characters with the lash of satire. Nonsense, instead of offending him, entertains him, and he often cultivates nonsense for the pleasure and sense of freedom from the demands of reality that he can provide for himself and his public. Exuberance is cherished and promoted, as in the old fertility rites from which comedy appears to have arisen; life is affirmed and given freedom to assert itself.

When this type of entertainment is least restrained, when it moves most freely from one amusing situation to another without concern for credibility, we have *farce*. In farce we concentrate not on characters or character-conditioned events, but on freely invented situations. And the action is usually as rapid as it is extravagant, giving playgoers as little opportunity as possible to ask whether the plot possesses probability. The fun, moreover, is broad and loud so that we shall not miss a joke or an amusing turn of events.

The lowest form of farce is horseplay or slapstick. The highest form may be sparked by wit and intelligence, enriched with telling points or epigrams and clearly aimed at foolish notions, absence of intelligence, or lack of truth. Oscar Wilde's *The Importance of Being Earnest* is the most brilliantly written farce of this order. If the entertaining play includes reasonably credible, though extravagant, character sketches and some well-observed, though surely exaggerated, social background, the result is *comedy* rather than mere farce. The farcical elements then comprise merely part of the play, not the whole, and serve to make the dramatic action more vivid or exuberant or the comic idea sharper and more arresting. Shaw, for example, helps himself generously to farcical invention and detail in *Arms and the Man* (page 454) as did Molière in *The Pretentious Ladies* and in many other comedies. Even Chekhov, who was often somber in his plays and stories, employed farcical exaggeration for comic purposes, as in *The Harmful Effects of Smoking* (page 504), while, on other occasions, he blithely indulged in pure farce, as in *The Marriage Proposal* (page 496). Shakespeare, whose dramatic imagination was so comprehensive that it embraced nearly every mood and experience life has to offer, often resorted to farcical episodes and conversations. We can observe this in so weighty a history play as *Henry IV*, in which the security of a kingdom is at stake, as well as in so tender and lyrical a love-tragedy as *Romeo and Juliet*.

Comedy has often been predominantly imaginative, fanciful, and romantic, as in some of Shakespeare's best loved plays—*A Midsummer Night's Dream, As You Like It,* and *Twelfth Night*. At the same time that Shakespeare wrote his early comedies, however, his sturdy fellow-playwright Ben Jonson supplied the Elizabethan theatre with decidedly *unromantic* comedies of London life and character types whose idiosyncrasies or so-called humours earned his scorn. Shakespeare, at a later period in his career, also turned to a weightier and more realistic treatment of characters and themes, producing so-called *dark comedies*, such as his provocative *Measure for Measure*.

In the second half of the seventeenth century, the emphasis shifted to "comedy of manners," dealing with the foibles and intrigues of sophisticated society, chiefly the courtly world of Charles II in England (the "Restoration Period") and of Louis XIV in France. Comedy of manners, which contained much implied or even explicit social comment (although the comment was, as a rule, lighthearted), attained great brilliance in the work of Molière (page 383) in France and of William Congreve later on in England. Its vogue continued well on into the eighteenth century and was best represented in the English theatre by the comedies of Richard Brinsley Sheridan, notably *The Rivals* and *The School for Scandal* (see page 399), and in the French by Beaumarchais' two well-known plays *The Barber of Seville* and *The Marriage of Figaro*.

Comedy of manners began to be diluted and adulterated by sentimentality and moral platitudes in the same century, resulting in a type of so-called sentimental comedy which the French called "tearful comedy"—*comédie larmoyante*. In England its most representative playwright was the essayist Sir Richard Steele.

The art of comedy suffered a general decline during the nineteenth century, but a revival of the comic spirit occurred after 1860; and in England it was inaugurated and sustained by a number of gifted writers. The most talented were W. S. Gilbert, best known for the operettas for which Sir Arthur Sullivan wrote the music, Oscar Wilde (who wrote the wittiest farce in the English language, *The Importance of Being Earnest*), and Bernard Shaw who became England's most significant playwright after Shakespeare. In plays such as *Man and Superman* and *Pygmalion* (the source of the musical comedy *My Fair Lady*), Shaw developed a special kind of comedy of discussion, debate, and social analysis often designated as "comedy of ideas." But Shaw had a great forerunner in the Norwegian dramatist Ibsen, some of whose vigorous social dramas, most notably *An Enemy of the People*, were comedies or verged on comedy. Shaw, along with Sheridan, has had successors in the twentieth century theatre such as the English playwrights Somerset Maugham and Noel Coward and the Americans, Philip Barry and S. N. Behrman. Molière has had numerous successors in the theatres of continental Europe, especially Jean Giraudoux (see page 565), even though the latter's talent has been especially favorable to fantastic and philosophical comedy rather than to comedy of manners.

Everywhere in the twentieth century, moreover, there has been room for a more general type of drama that combines comedy of manners with comedy of character as well as with some social criticism. One of the most successful plays of this blend was Sidney Howard's *The Late Christopher Bean* (page 509), a comedy in which smug and egotistical characters are defeated and exposed to ridicule. Although the social background of the play is New England, it is nevertheless to be noted that it was based by the author on a French play set in France.

No country has had a monopoly on comic art and nothing appears to have exhausted its rich resources for delight and instruction.

MOLIÈRE (1622-1673)

Molière, generally considered the father of modern comedy, was born in Paris in 1622 and spent his early years in courtly circles. Well educated at the Jesuit College of Clermont and a student of law for a while, he turned to the stage first as an amateur, partly because he was enamored of an actress. But the theatre began to exert such an attraction that he made it his profession in 1643 and, changing his name from Jean Baptiste Poquelin to Molière, became the leader of a group of actors, the *Illustre Théâtre*, which struggled for twelve long years in the provinces as a touring company before it was able to establish itself in Paris. By then Molière had not only made himself the foremost comedian of the age but also his company's playwright. After composing numerous light-hearted farces particularly suited for performance by his fellow-actors in the provinces, he turned his attention to the vogue of exaggerated refinement that had been current for some time. The result was a one-act play, *Les Précieuses ridicules* (*The Pretentious Ladies*), which was a great success in Paris and won him the favor of King Louis XIV himself. Director as well as leading actor of his flourishing company, which, after his death, became a national institution (the subsidized *Comédie Française* is descended from it), Molière was often summoned to perform at court or to compose and stage some royal entertainment.

Although Molière was unhappily married, suffered from ill health, and experienced financial reverses, he managed to write twenty-eight plays between 1659 and the time of his death on February 17, 1673, when he collapsed on the stage while playing the title part of his last work, *The Imaginary Invalid*. Among these plays are a number of the best known masterpieces of comedy, such as *The School for Wives*, *The Misanthrope*, *Tartuffe*, and *The Would-Be Gentleman*. Always the enemy of pretense and quackery, a believer in naturalness in life and art, and a champion of reason and truth, Molière made himself the chief satirist of his age. His "thoughtful laughter" has continued to be heard on the French stage ever since.

INTRODUCTION TO *THE PRETENTIOUS LADIES*

The Pretentious Ladies was the first of Molière's masterpieces, and it is also the shortest of these chiefly for the reason that its scope is limited.

When it was first produced, however, the play was instantly effective because it struck at the social pretensions and extravagant refinement of the period sponsored by the literary salons of Paris and naively imitated in the French provinces. The sprightliness of this little work expresses the French spirit in the theatre—its spirit of comic detachment, its refined scepticism, and its mental agility.

The play is characteristically a work of Molière's mature artistry as a writer of comedies and illustrates the lively sense of the ridiculous with which he took the measure of the fashionable world and of mankind in general.

"The ridiculous is a facet of truth" in Molière's work here and in later comedies, and his laughter has been aptly described by one of his ablest critics (Ramon Fernandez) as an "evocation of the rational faculty." Molière began to make his comic art the proper instrument of truth and rationality when he resorted to satire in *The Pretentious Ladies*.

THE PRETENTIOUS LADIES

(Les Précieuses ridicules)

MOLIÈRE

Adaptation by JOHN GASSNER

CHARACTERS

LA GRANGE
DU CROISY
GORGIBUS, *a "citizen"*
THE MARQUIS DE MASCARILLE, *valet to La Grange*
THE VISCOUNT JODELET, *valet to Du Croisy*
ALMANZOR, *footman to the pretentious girls*
TWO CHAIRMEN
MUSICIANS (*fiddlers*)
MADELON, *daughter to Gorgibus*
CATHOS, *niece to Gorgibus*
MAROTTE, *maid to the pretentious girls*
LUCILE
CÉLIMÈNE

Scene: GORGIBUS' HOUSE IN PARIS

(LA GRANGE *and* DU CROISY, *two young gentlemen are standing in front of a house.*)

DU CROISY: Seigneur[1] La Grange.

LA GRANGE: What is it?

DU CROISY: What do you think of our visit? Are you pleased?

LA GRANGE: Does either of us have any reason to be pleased?

DU CROISY: None, to say the truth.

LA GRANGE: As for me, I must admit I am quite put out. Did ever anybody see country wenches giving themselves such ridiculous airs, and were ever two men treated with more contempt? I never saw such whispering, such yawning, such rubbing of the eyes, such asking what time of day it is.

DU CROISY: You seem to be annoyed.

LA GRANGE: So much so that I am resolved to be revenged. I know well enough why they depise us. Affectation has spread from Paris into the country. Our ridiculous damsels, fresh from the provinces, have sucked in their share of it, and combine coquetry and affection. Take my advice, and we shall play them such a trick as shall show them their folly, and teach them to deal with people more considerately.

DU CROISY: How will you do this?

LA GRANGE: I have a valet, Mascarille, who passes for a kind of wit; nowadays there's nothing easier. This extraordinary fellow has taken it into his head to ape persons of quality, prides himself on his elegance, writes poems, and despises the other servants; he goes so far as to call them "brutes."

DU CROISY: Well, what do you intend to accomplish through him?

LA GRANGE: What do I intend? I intend— ... but first, let us be gone.

(GORGIBUS *enters and greets* DU CROISY *and* LA GRANGE *effusively.*)

GORGIBUS: Well, gentlemen, you have now seen my niece and my daughter. How are matters getting on?

LA GRANGE: They can tell you better than we can. We thank you for the favor you have done us, and we remain your most humble servants.

DU CROISY: Your most humble servants.

(*The young men leave him unceremoniously.*)

GORGIBUS: (*left alone*) Hoity-toity! They seem put out. What can be the meaning of this? (*Yelling*) Hey, you, inside!

(MAROTTE *appears*)

MAROTTE: Did you call, sir?

GORGIBUS: Where are your mistresses?

MAROTTE: The young ladies are in their room.

GORGIBUS: What are they doing there?

MAROTTE: Making lip salve.

GORGIBUS: There is no end to their salves. Bid them come down. (*Alone.*) These hussies with their salves have a mind to ruin me. Everywhere in the house I see nothing but white of eggs or I don't know what! Since we have been here in Paris they have used up the lard of a dozen hogs at least. Four servants might live every day on the sheep's trotters they use up.

(MADELON *and* CATHOS *enter.*)

GORGIBUS: (*sarcastically*) I hope I am not disturbing you while you are wasting money to grease your faces! Please tell me, what you have done to those gentlemen I saw go away so unceremoniously? I ordered you to receive them well as persons I intended for you.

MADELON: Dear father, what consideration do you wish us to give to people who behave crudely?

CATHOS: How can a woman of ever so little understanding, uncle, reconcile herself to such unrefined persons.

GORGIBUS: What have they done wrong?

MADELON: Would you believe it? They began proposing marriage to us.

GORGIBUS: What would you have them begin doing?—propose to make you their chambermaids? Their proposal was a compliment to both of you, and to me as well. Can anything be more gallant? Do they not prove the honesty of their intentions?

MADELON: Oh, father! Nothing can be more vulgar; I am ashamed to hear you talk in such a manner; you should learn to know the *elegant* way of looking at things.

GORGIBUS: A lot I care for elegant ways! I tell you marriage is a holy state, and to start with marriage is to act like honest people.

MADELON: Good Heavens! If everybody thought like you a love-story would soon be over. What a fine thing it would have been if Cyrus had immediately espoused Mandane, and if Aronce had been married all at once to Clélie.[2]

GORGIBUS: (*to* CATHOS) Have you any idea what she is jabbering about?

MADELON: My cousin, father, will tell you as well as I that matrimony should come only after other adventures. A lover, to be agreeable, must know how to express fine sentiments and breathe soft, tender, and passionate vows. There are rules to be observed! In the first place, he should behold the fair one of whom he becomes enamored either at a place of worship or while out walking, or at some public ceremony; or he should be introduced to her by a relative or a friend as if by chance, and when he leaves her he should be in a pensive and melancholy mood. He should conceal his passion for a while from the object of his love, but pay her several visits, in every one of which he should introduce some subject to exercise the intellectual disposition of the company. When the time comes to propose to the lady—which generally should be contrived in some shady walk at some distance from the company—we are expected to react with anger, shown by our blushing, which should temporarily banish the lover from our presence. He should then find the proper means to placate us, and accustom us gradually to expressions of his passion until they draw from us the admission it embarrasses us to make. After that will come the adventures, the jealousies without foundation, the complaints, the despairs, the abductions and their consequences. That is how things are done in *good* society, and to disregard these rules is to be deficient in gallantry. But to come out point-blank with proposals of marriage—to make no love except with a marriage-contract in one's hand—is tantamount to beginning a novel at the wrong end. Nothing can be more tradesmanlike, nothing more common, father, so that the mere thought of it makes me sick at heart.

GORGIBUS: What nonsense is this? This is high-flown claptrap if there ever was any!

CATHOS: Uncle, my cousin has hit the nail on the head. How can we receive kindly those who are so deficient in gallantry? I could wager they have not even seen a map of the country of *Tenderness*, and that *Love-Letters*, *Trifling Attentions*, *Polite Epistles*, and *Pretty Verses* are regions to them unknown. A leg without any ornaments, a hat without feathers, a head with locks not artistically arranged, and a coat that hasn't a ribbon on it! Heavens! what lovers are these! and what barrenness of conversation! It is not to be borne; it simply should not be allowed. I also observed that their ruffs were altogether unfashionable and their breeches too narrow.

GORGIBUS: (*turning away in despair*) I think they are both mad. I don't understand a word of this gibberish. Cathos, and you Madelon. . . .

MADELON: Pray, father, do not use those strange names—

GORGIBUS: What do you mean by "strange names"? Are they not the names your godfathers and godmothers gave you?

MADELON: Good Heavens! how vulgar! I confess I sometimes wonder you could possibly be the father of a girl like me. Did anybody in literature ever talk of Cathos or of Madelon? These names would be sufficient to ruin the finest novel in the world.

CATHOS: It is quite true, uncle. A delicate ear suffers extremely at hearing these common names pronounced. You must admit that the name of Polixena, which my cousin has chosen, and that of Amintha, which I have adopted, possess a certain charm.

GORGIBUS: I have only one thing to say—just one word! I shall not allow you to take any other names than those that were given to you by your godfathers and godmothers. As for those gentlemen, I know their families and fortunes, and I am determined that they shall be your husbands. I am tired of having you on my hands. Looking after a couple of girls like you is simply too exhausting for a man of my years.

CATHOS: As for me, uncle, all I can say is that I think marriage a very shocking business.

MADELON: We arrived here, in Paris, only a short while ago, father. Let us breathe a little in the fashionable world. Allow us, please, to take our time in preparing the groundwork of our romance before we conclude it abruptly with a marriage.

GORGIBUS: (*aside*) There can be no doubt about it any longer, they are completely mad. (*Aloud.*) Once more, I tell you, I understand nothing at all of this gibberish. But I intend to be master in my household and shall put an end to this nonsense. You are either going to be married right away—*both* of you!— or march into a nunnery. (*He makes an angry exit, leaving the girls abruptly.*)

CATHOS: Good Heavens, my dear! What limited intelligence! What darkness of the soul!

MADELON: What can I do, my dear? I am utterly ashamed of him. I cannot bring myself to believe that I am his daughter. It wouldn't surprise me to discover one of these days that I am of noble descent.

CATHOS: It is very likely. As for myself, when I consider . . .

(*The maid* MAROTTE *enters briskly.*)

MAROTTE: There is a lackey[3] here who asks if you are at home. His master is coming to see you.

MADELON: Learn, you dunce, to express yourself a little less vulgarly. Say, "inquiring if it is commodious for you to become visible."

MAROTTE: I don't understand Latin, and I haven't learned philosophy out of *Cyrus*, as you have done.[4]

MADELON: Impertinent creature!

MAROTTE: He told me it was the Marquis de Mascarille.

MADELON: (*bubbling*) Ah, my dear! A marquis! a marquis! Go and tell him we are visible. This is certainly some fashionable man of wit who has heard of us.

CATHOS: Undoubtedly, my dear.

MADELON: We had better receive him here in this parlor at once! But let us at least arrange our hair a little first. Go, Marotte dear, and fetch us the Counsellor of the Graces.

MAROTTE: I do not know what sort of a beast that is; you must speak like a Christian if you want me to understand you.

CATHOS: Bring us the looking-glass, blockhead!, and take care not to contaminate its brightness with your image. (*They exit.*)

(MASCARILLE, *gorgeously dressed and wearing a hat with huge white plumes, enters, borne in a sedan chair by* TWO CHAIRMEN.)

MASCARILLE: Stop! Easy, easy! I think these boobies intend to shake me to pieces by bumping me against the walls.

FIRST CHAIRMAN: Ay, that's because the gate is narrow and you make us carry you in here.

MASCARILLE: Would you have me expose my plumes to the inclemency of the rainy season and let the mud besmirch my delicate shoes? (*He gets out of the chair.*) Begone; take away your chair.

SECOND CHAIRMAN: Then please to pay us, sir.

MASCARILLE: What?

SECOND CHAIRMAN: Sir, please to give us our money, I say.

MASCARILLE: (*giving him a box on the ear*) What, scoundrel, to ask money from a person of my rank!

SECOND CHAIRMAN: Is this the way poor people are to be paid? Will your rank get us dinner?

MASCARILLE: Ha, ha! I'll teach you to keep your place.

FIRST CHAIRMAN: (*picking up one of the poles of his chair*) Come, pay us quickly.

MASCARILLE: (*taken aback*) What?

FIRST CHAIRMAN: I mean to have my money at once.

MASCARILLE: (*retreating*) Now, now, there's a sensible fellow!

FIRST CHAIRMAN: Hurry up, then.

MASCARILLE: Ah, yes, you know how to speak properly—not like your mate.

(*Giving him some coins.*) There, are you satisfied?

FIRST CHAIRMAN: No, I am not satisfied; you boxed my friend's ears, and . . . (*holding up his pole*).

MASCARILLE: Gently! Gently! (*Giving him more money.*) Here is something for the box on the ear, too. People may get anything from me when they go about it the right way. Go now, but come back soon to carry me to the Louvre,[5] to attend the King's retirement.

(*The* CHAIRMEN *exit.*)

MAROTTE: (*entering*) Sir, my mistresses will come immediately.

MASCARILLE: Let them take their time. I am very comfortable here.

MAROTTE: Here they come.

(*Enter* MADELON, CATHOS *and* ALMANZOR.)

MASCARILLE: (*after bowing to them*) No doubt you will be surprised, ladies, at the boldness of my visit. But it is your reputation that has drawn this disagreeable visit upon you! Merit has such potent charms for me that I run after it.

MADELON: (*thrilled*) If you pursue merit you should not come to us.

CATHOS: If you find merit here amongst us, you must have brought it here yourself.

MASCARILLE: I object to these words. When fame mentioned your merits it spoke the truth.

MADELON: Your amiability goes a little too far in the liberality of its praises, and my cousin and I must take care not to give too much credit to your seductive adulation.

CATHOS: My dear, we should call for chairs.

MADELON: Almanzor!

ALMANZOR: Madam?

MADELON: Convey to us hither, instantly, the commodities of conversation. (ALMANZOR *stops to figure this out, grins with sudden realization, then brings chairs and arranges them.*[6])

MASCARILLE: But am I safe here?

(*Exit* ALMANZOR.)

CATHOS: What is it you fear?

MASCARILLE: Some larceny of my heart, some assault on my liberty. I behold here a pair of seductively sparkling eyes that cause enslavement and use a heart most barbarously. I shall scamper away unless assured that they will do me no mischief.

MADELON: My dear, what a charming facetiousness he has!

CATHOS: Fear nothing, our eyes have no wicked designs; your heart may rest in peace.

MADELON: But, pray, Sir, be not inexorable to the easy chair holding out its arms toward you. Pray yield to its desire of embracing you.

(*The girls make him sit down in the chair.*)

MASCARILLE: (*after having combed himself primly and adjusted the rolls of his stockings*) Well, ladies, and what do you think of Paris?

MADELON: Alas! What *can* we think? It would be the very antipodes of reason not to admit that Paris is the repository of marvels, the center of good taste, the capital of wit, and the emporium of gallantry.

MASCARILLE: As for me, I maintain that there is no salvation for the polite world outside Paris.

CATHOS: Most assuredly.

MASCARILLE: It is true that Paris is somewhat muddy; but that is what we have sedan chairs for.

MADELON: A sedan chair is indeed a wonderful defense against the offensiveness of bad weather.

MASCARILLE: I am sure you receive many visits. What eminent wit graces your company at present?

MADELON: We are not yet known, alas, but a lady of our acquaintance has promised us all the illustrious gentlemen who have contributed to that treasury of refinement the *Miscellanies of Select Poetry*.

CATHOS: And other gentlemen who are celebrated arbiters of all that is beautiful.

MASCARILLE: I can arrange visits for you better than anyone; I am so constantly visited that I never rise without having half-a-dozen wits at my levee.

MADELON: Good Heavens! you will place us under the greatest obligation if you will do us this kindness. Wits make or unmake a reputation at Paris; there are some wits whose visits alone suffice to start the report that you are a *connaisseuse*.[7] From these visits, we shall learn a hundred things which we ought to know, the latest scandal of the day, and the niceties in prose or verse. We should know *everything*, and at the right time; for instance, that So-and-so has adapted words to a tune, that a certain gentleman has written a madrigal on gaining some fair one's favor or an epigram yesterday evening to which she made reply this morning at eight o'clock; and so on. News of this sort procures you a reputation in good society.

CATHOS: That is true, indeed. I consider it the height of absurdity for any one who makes the least claim to cleverness not to know the slightest quatrain[8] that is made each day in Paris. I should be very much ashamed if anyone asked me if I have seen something new and I had not seen it. Without gossip your reputation isn't worth a nail.

MASCARILLE: It is really a shame not to be the first to know everything that is going on. But don't be distressed, ladies! I will establish an academy of wits at your house, and I can give you my word that not a single line of poetry shall be written in Paris that you won't be able to say by heart before anybody else. Indeed, I myself produce a great many verses—I amuse myself that way when I am in the humour. You may find handed about in fashionable assemblies two hundred songs, as many sonnets, four hundred epigrams, and more than a thousand madrigals that were made by me,—and I am not counting riddles and character sketches.

MADELON: I must acknowledge that I dote upon character sketches.

MASCARILLE: They are difficult to write, and call for a great deal of profundity; you shall see some of mine that will not displease you.

CATHOS: As for me, I am awfully fond of riddles.

MASCARILLE: They do exercise the intelligence; I have already written four of them this morning, which I will give you to guess.

MADELON: And madrigals are pretty when they are well turned.

MASCARILLE: Madrigals are my special talent; at present I am turning the whole of Roman history into madrigals!

MADELON: Goodness gracious! If you decide to publish it, please reserve a copy for me.

MASCARILLE: I promise you each a copy, in the handsomest of bindings. It does not, of course, become a man of my rank to write professionally. I do it only to help out the publishers.

MADELON: I fancy it is a delightful thing to see one's self in print.

MASCARILLE: That reminds me, I must repeat to you some extempore verses I made yesterday at the house of an acquaintance of mine, a duchess. I am rather good at extemporizing verses.

CATHOS: Extempore verses are certainly the touchstone of genius.

MASCARILLE: Listen then.

MADELON: We are all ears.

MASCARILLE: Oh! oh! how off my guard was I,
  When harmless you I chanced to spy.
    Slily your eyes
    Did my heart surprise.
  Stop thief! stop thief! stop thief! I cry!

CATHOS: Good Heavens! this is carried to the utmost height of elegance.

MASCARILLE: Everything I compose shows that it has been composed by a gentleman, not a pedant. Did you observe the beginning—the "oh! oh!"? There is something original in that "oh! oh!"—like a man who thinks of something all of a sudden, "oh! oh!" Taken by surprise as it were, oh! oh!

MADELON: Yes, indeed, the "oh! oh!" is admirable.

MASCARILLE: (*modestly*) Ah, it is a mere trifle, of course—a mere thing.

CATHOS: Good Heavens! How can you say so? It is simply invaluable.

MADELON: I would rather have written that "oh! oh!" than an epic poem.

MASCARILLE: You have good taste.

MADELON: (*modestly*) I hope not the worst.

MASCARILLE: But do you not also admire *quite off my guard was I?*—that is, I did not pay attention to anything; a natural way of saying "*of no harm thinking*"—that is, as I was going along, innocently, without malice, like a poor sheep when *you I chanced to spy*, that is to say, I amused myself with looking at you, with observing you, with contemplating you. *Slily your eyes.* . . . What do you think of that word "*slily*"—is it not well chosen?

CATHOS: Quite so.

MASCARILLE: Slily, stealthily; just like a cat watching a mouse—*slily*—then pouncing upon it suddenly.

MADELON: Superb.

MASCARILLE: *Did my heart surprise,* that is, carries it away from me, robs me of it. *Stop thief! stop thief! stop thief!* As if a man were shouting and running after a thief to catch him? *Stop thief! stop thief! stop thief!*

MADELON: This is certainly witty and sprightly.

MASCARILLE: Let me sing you the tune I made to it.

CATHOS: Oh! Have you studied music?

MASCARILLE: *I* study music? Not in the least.

CATHOS: How can you compose a tune then?

MASCARILLE: People of rank know everything without having learned anything.

MADELON: (*to* CATHOS) His lordship is quite right, my dear.

MASCARILLE: Tell me whether you like the tune: *hem, hem, la, la.* The inclemency of the season has greatly injured the delicacy of my voice; but no matter, this is purely informal. (*He sings:* "Oh! oh! how off my guard was I," *etc.*)

CATHOS: What passion breathes in this music. It is enough to make one expire.

MADELON: And there is something truly plaintive in it.

MASCARILLE: Do you not think that the tune expresses the sentiment perfectly —*Stop thief, stop thief!*? Then all at once like a person out of breath, *Stop thief.*

MADELON: (*gushing*) Altogether a wonderful performance; perfection itself, perfect perfection, the perfection of perfections. I am quite enchanted with the air and the words.

CATHOS: I am sure *I* never yet met with anything so excellent.

MASCARILLE: All that I do comes *naturally* to me; I do everything without ever having studied anything.

MADELON: You are Nature's favorite child; Nature has surely been a fond Mother to you.

MASCARILLE: (*abruptly shifting the subject*) How do you pass away the time, ladies?

CATHOS: Why, with nothing at all.

MADELON: Until now there has been a terrible famine of amusement[9] in our lives.

MASCARILLE: I am at your service to

accompany you to the theatre one of these days, if you wish. It so happens that there will be a new comedy soon to which I should be very glad to take you. But I beg of you to applaud it well, when we are there; for I have promised to give a helping hand. The author called upon me this very morning. It is the custom for authors to read their new plays to people of rank and solicit their approval in advance. The pit never dares to contradict us. As for me, I am very punctilious in these things, and when I have made a promise to a poet, I always cry out "Bravo," "How beautiful!," in the theatre the moment the candles are lit.[10]

MADELON: We couldn't possibly refuse your offer. Ah, Paris! A hundred things happen there everyday which people in the provinces, however clever they may be, have no idea of.

CATHOS: We shall consider it our duty ot applaud every word that is said on the stage.

MASCARILLE: (*looking at them with pretended concentration*) I wonder whether I could be mistaken, but you look to me like a person who has written a play herself.

MADELON: (*mysteriously*) Well—there may be something in what you say.

MASCARILLE: Ah! We must have a look at it before long! Between ourselves, I have written one which I intend to have brought out.

CATHOS: Wonderful! To what company do you mean to give your play?

MASCARILLE: Naturally, to the actors of the Hotel de Bourgogne.[11] Who else can do justice to a beautiful piece of writing? The other actors in Paris are ignoramuses who speak their lines as if they were people in everyday life. The other actors don't know how to declaim and point out the fine points of a play to the public by pausing significantly. How do they expect the public to know what is good or when to applaud!

CATHOS: (*very seriously*) Indeed! things are only prized when they are well set off.

MASCARILLE: (*showing off his costume like a model*) And while we're on that subject, pray tell me: What do you think of my top-knot, sword-knot, and rosettes? Do you think they harmonize with my coat?

CATHOS: Perfectly, perfectly!

MASCARILLE: Is the ribbon well chosen?

MADELON: Wonderfully well chosen.

MASCARILLE: What do you say to the ruffles over my knees?

MADELON: They look very fashionable.

MASCARILLE: I may at least boast that they are a good quarter of a yard wider than any that have been made.

MADELON: I never saw such elegance of dress before.

MASCARILLE: (*thrusting his gloves under the girls' noses*) Please apply your olfactory organ to these gloves.

MADELON: (*sniffing*) They smell tremendously fine!

CATHOS: (*also sniffing*) I have never inhaled a more delicious perfume.

MASCARILLE: And this? (*He gives them his powdered wig to smell.*)

MADELON: This has the true quality of odor; it is simply sublime!

MASCARILLE: You say nothing of my plumes. How do you like *them*?

CATHOS: Frightfully beautiful!

MASCARILLE: Every feather costs me a fortune. But I can't help it: I must have the best of everything.

MADELON: I sympathize with you. I myself am frightfully fastidious—right down to my stockings. My taste is so delicate that everything I wear must be bought at a fashionable shop.

MASCARILLE: (*crying out suddenly*) Oh! oh! oh! gently—easy there! Oh, ladies, you use me very ill; I have good reason to complain of your behavior, I have.

CATHOS: What is it? What is the matter?

MASCARILLE: What? How can you ask when both of you are assaulting my heart at the same time from right and left. This violates all the rules of warfare and is outrageously unfair. I am going to cry "Murder" if this assault doesn't stop.

CATHOS: (*thrilled to* MADELON) One must admit that he has a unique way of expressing himself. Such style!

MADELON: (*agreeing*) Such wit!

CATHOS: Sir, you have nothing to fear. Your heart cries out before it is wounded.

MASCARILLE: (*feigning dismay*) The Devil you say! My heart is already wounded from head to foot!

(MAROTTE *enters, full of excitement.*)

MAROTTE: Madame, a gentleman asks to see you.

MADELON: Who is it?

MAROTTE: The Viscount de Jodelet.

MASCARILLE: The Viscount de Jodelet?

MAROTTE: Yes, sir.

CATHOS: Do you know him?

MASCARILLE: Of course. He is my most intimate friend.

MADELON: Show him in immediately.

MASCARILLE: We have not seen each other for some time; I am delighted that this opportunity has arisen.

CATHOS: Here he comes.

(*Enter* JODELET, *got up as a nobleman, like* MASCARILLE, *but wearing his traditional white-face clown's make-up.*)

MASCARILLE: Ah, Viscount!

JODELET: Ah, Marquis!

MASCARILLE: How glad I am to meet you!

(*Embracing and kissing*[12] *each other.*)

JODELET: How happy I am to see you here.

MASCARILLE: Kiss me once more, I pray you, my friend.

MADELON: (*to* CATHOS) My dearest, we are beginning to be known in Paris when people of fashion find the way to our house.

MASCARILLE: Ladies, allow me to introduce this gentleman. He deserves the honor of your acquaintance.

JODELET: It is only right that we should come to pay our respects. Your charms, which possess seignorial rights, demand no less from all of Paris.

MADELON: (*twittering with delight*) Ah! You carry your civilities to the furthest bounds of flattery.

CATHOS: (*excitedly, to* MADELON) This happy day should be memorialized in our diaries.

MADELON: (*to* ALMANZOR) Must you always be told what to do? Don't you perceive that it is necessary to augment our furniture with a chair for his lordship?

MASCARILLE: (*referring to* JODELET'S *clown-like pallor*) You must not be astonished to see the Viscount thus; he has but lately recovered from an illness, which, as you perceive, has made him so pale.

JODELET: (*casually*) Oh nothing much—merely the consequence of staying up late at court and the fatigue of going to war.

MASCARILLE: In the Viscount, ladies, you behold one of the heroes of the age.

JODELET: Marquis, you are no less valiant. We all know what *you* can do.

MASCARILLE: (*winking at* JODELET, *and speaking with double meaning*) It is true we have seen one another at work.

JODELET: And in places where it was mighty hot.

MASCARILLE: (*looking at* CATHOS *and* MADELON) Ay, but not so hot as it is here. Ha, ha, ha!

JODELET: The first time we saw each

other he commanded a regiment of horse aboard the galleys of Malta.[13]

MASCARILLE: True, but for all that you were in the service before me. I was but a junior officer when you commanded two thousand horses.

JODELET: But, on my word, the court does not adequately reward men of merit like us.

MASCARILLE: That is why I intend to hang up my sword on the hook forever.

CATHOS: As for me, I have a tremendous liking for gentlemen of the army.

MADELON: I fancy them, too. But I like their valor to be seasoned with wit.

MASCARILLE: Do you remember, Viscount, our taking that half-moon from the enemy at the siege of Arras?

JODELET: What do you mean by a half-moon? It was a complete full moon.

MASCARILLE: I believe you are right.

JODELET: Upon my word, I have good reason to remember it. I was wounded in the leg by a hand-grenade, of which I still carry the marks. Pray, feel it a little here; you can tell what a wound it was.

CATHOS: (*putting her hand to the place*) The scar is really large.

MASCARILLE: Give me your hand for a moment, and feel this; right there, just at the back of my head. Do you feel it?

MADELON: Yes, I do feel something.

MASCARILLE: A musket shot, received during my last campaign.

JODELET: (*unbuttoning his breast*) And here is a wound which went quite through me at the attack of Gravelines.

MASCARILLE: (*putting his hand upon the button of his breeches*) I am going to show you a tremendous wound.

MADELON: (*withdrawing*) There is no need—we believe you.

MASCARILLE: (*turning to* CATHOS) Wounds like these show what a man is made of.

CATHOS: (*also drawing back*) We have not the least doubt of your valor.

MASCARILLE: (*changing his tactics*) Viscount, is your coach waiting?

JODELET: Why do you ask?

MASCARILLE: We might take these charming ladies for a drive outside the city gates and treat them to a country repast.

MADELON: We really cannot go out to-day.

MASCARILLE: Let us send for musicians then, and have a dance here.

JODELET: On my word, that is a happy thought.

MADELON: We have no objection, but we must have some additional company.

MASCARILLE: So ho! (*Pretending to call his servants, or "footmen."*) Champagne, Picard, Bourguignon, Cascaret, Basque, La Verdure, Lorrain, Provencal, La Violette. (*Getting no response*) I wish the deuce took all these footmen! I do not think there is a gentleman in France worse served than I am! These rascals are never around when you want them.

MADELON: Almanzor, go and fetch the musicians, and ask some of the gentlemen and ladies hereabouts to come here and populate the solitude of our ball.

(ALMANZOR *leaves*.)

MASCARILLE: Viscount, what do you think of those eyes?

JODELET: Why, Marquis, what do you think of them yourself?

MASCARILLE: I? I say that we shall find it difficult to preserve our liberty. My freedom is already in great jeopardy. And my heart hangs by a single thread.

MADELON: (*to* CATHOS, *thrilled*) He speaks so *naturally*! He gives everything such an agreeable turn.

CATHOS: Yes, and he is so witty!

MASCARILLE: To show you that I am in earnest, I shall make some impromptu verses upon my passion. (*He starts thinking hard.*)

CATHOS: (*eagerly*) Oh! by all means let us hear something made specially for us.

JODELET: (*embarrassed by his incompetence*) I shall be glad to do so too, but the quantity of blood I have lost lately has exhausted my poetic vein.

MASCARILLE: (*fumbling*) How annoying! I always make the first verse well, but I find the other verses more difficult. On my word, I mustn't be rushed like this. I will make you some impromptu verses at my leisure,[14] which you shall think the finest in the world.

JODELET: He is devilishly witty, you know!

MASCARILLE: Viscount, tell me, when did you see the Countess last?

JODELET: I have not paid her a visit these three weeks.

MASCARILLE: Do you know that the duke came to see me this morning, and that he was eager to take me into the country to hunt a stag with him?

MADELON: Here come our friends.
(*Enter two young ladies*, LUCILE *and* CÉLIMÈNE, MAROTTE, ALMANZOR, *and two or three* MUSICIANS.)

MADELON: (*to* LUCILE *and* CÉLIMÈNE) Oh, my dears, we beg your pardon. These gentlemen called for musicians to put life into our heels; so we sent for you to fill up the void in our numbers.

LUCILE: We are certainly much obliged to you for doing so.

MASCARILLE: This is a kind of impromptu ball, ladies. Have the musicians come?

ALMANZOR: Yes, sir, they are here.

CATHOS: Come then, my dears, take your places.

MASCARILLE: (*dancing by himself and singing*) La, la, la, la, la, la, la.

MADELON: What a very elegant shape he has.

CATHOS: He looks as if he were an exquisite dancer.

MASCARILLE: (*taking* MADELON *by the arm*) Play in time, musicians, *in time*. Oh, what ignorant wretches! There is no dancing with them. (*Stumbling.*) The devil take you all, can you not play in time? La, la, la, la, la, la, la, la? Steady, you fiddlers, you country-scrapers!

JODELET: (*dancing, but also stumbling*) Hold, do not play so fast. I have barely recovered from an illness.

(*Enter the valets' masters*, DU CROISY *and* LA GRANGE, *suddenly.*)

LA GRANGE: (*with a cane in his hand*) So here you are, you scoundrels. We have been looking for you these three hours. (*He beats* MASCARILLE.)

MASCARILLE: (*yelling*) Oh! oh! You didn't tell me that getting beaten was to be part of the game.

JODELET: (*who is also beaten*) Ouch! Ouch!

LA GRANGE: (*to* MASCARILLE) So you want to play the role of a gentleman, you rascal!

DU CROISY: (*to* JODELET) This will teach you to know your place.

(DU CROISY *and* LA GRANGE *go off as abruptly as they arrived.*)

MADELON: What is the meaning of this?

JODELET: It is a wager.

CATHOS: What, do gentlemen allow themselves to be beaten thus?

MASCARILLE: Good Heavens! I did not wish to appear to take any notice of it. I am by nature very violent and didn't want to be carried away by a passion; I might become dangerous.

MADELON: To be insulted like this, and in our presence, too!

MASCARILLE: A mere trifle, my lady. We have known one another for a long time; friends should not take offence so quickly.

(DU CROISY *and* LA GRANGE *return.*)

LA GRANGE: On my word, rascals, you shall not have the last laugh behind our backs, I promise you. Come in, you there.

(*Several men, hired by* DU CROISY *and* LA GRANGE, *enter.*)

MADELON: What means this impudence to come and disturb us in our own house?

DU CROISY: What, ladies? Shall we allow our lackeys to be received better than ourselves? Shall they be allowed to make love to you at our expense, and even give a ball in your honor?

MADELON: Your lackeys?

LA GRANGE: Yes, our lackeys; and permit us to say that it is very wrong of you to spoil our servants for us.

MADELON: (*flabbergasted*) O Heaven! such insolence!

LA GRANGE: (*going on with pretended anger*) But they shall not wear our clothes to dazzle your eyes. If you are determined to like them, it shall be for their handsome looks only. (*To the* MEN SERVANTS) Quick, let them be stripped immediately.

(*The* MEN SERVANTS *approach the two valets.*)

JODELET: (*ruefully*) Farewell, then, a long farewell to our fine clothes.

MASCARILLE: Alas, the marquisate and viscountship are at an end.[15]

DU CROISY: So, you knaves, you have had the impudence to become our rivals. You will have to go somewhere else to borrow the finery with which to make yourselves agreeable to your mistresses.

MASCARILLE: Oh, how fickle is Fortune! (*He submits to being undressed.*)

DU CROISY: (*to the* MEN SERVANTS, *pointing to* JODELET) Quick, pull everything off. (JODELET *is also promptly undressed.*)

LA GRANGE: And now, my highbrow ladies, you may continue your dalliance with them as long as you please. (*Pointing to* DU CROISY.) This gentleman and I give you our solemn promise that we shall not be jealous to the slightest degree.

(DU CROISY *and* LA GRANGE *go off, leaving behind the two valets, who have been stripped almost down to their underclothes, and the greatly puzzled* MUSICIANS.)

CATHOS: (*embarrassed*) What a predicament!

MADELON: (*raging*) I am simply bursting with vexation.

FIRST MUSICIAN: (*to* MASCARILLE) What is the meaning of all this? Who is going to pay us?

MASCARILLE: (*pointing to* JODELET) Ask my Lord the Viscount.

FIRST MUSICIAN: (*to* JODELET) Who is to give us our money.

JODELET: (*pointing to* MASCARILLE) Ask my Lord the Marquis!

(*Enter* GORGIBUS *in a temper, flourishing his cane.*)

GORGIBUS: (*to the* GIRLS) Ah! you hussies, you have surely put us in a nice pickle. I have heard about your fine goings on from the gentlemen who left.

MADELON: (*leaning against him and crying*) Oh, father, father! Those gentlemen have played a cruel trick on us.

GORGIBUS: I'll admit it is a cruel trick, but you can thank your impertinence for it. They have revenged themselves on you for the shameful way you treated them, and I, unhappy man, must put up with the affront we have received.

MADELON: We must be revenged, or I shall simply die of shame. (*To* MASCARILLE *and* JODELET.) And you, rascals, you dare remain here after all your insolence?

MASCARILLE: (*with mock indignation, brazening it out*) A nice way to treat a marquis! This is the way of the world: the least misfortune causes us to be slighted by those who made much of us. (*To* JODELET). Come away, dear comrade, let us seek our fortune somewhere else. I perceive that they love nothing here but outward show! Naked virtue is not appreciated!

(MASCARILLE *and* JODELET *depart huffily, their noses in the air—a comic exit since they are virtually in their underclothes. The* MUSICIANS *hesitate to follow them and turn to* GORGIBUS.)

FIRST MUSICIAN: Sir, since they have not paid us, we expect payment from you, for it was in your house we played.

GORGIBUS: *(beating them)* I shall satisfy you, of course. I am delighted to pay you and this *(beating him with his cane)* is the payment. *(The* MUSICIANS *make a hasty exit. Next* GORGIBUS *turns to the* GIRLS.) As for you, my fancy jades, I don't know what stops me from giving you the same treatment. The whole town is going to gossip about us and laugh at us, and you, my pretentious misses, have brought this on all of us with your idiotic behavior. *(Waving his cane.)* Out of my sight, go hide in shame. *(The girls run out, leaving him alone on the stage looking at the audience desperately, then addressing a small pile of books and papers in particular.)* And you that are the cause of all this nonsense, you trashy novels, songs, and sonnets, and sonatas or what else you're called, you can all go to the devil—the entire ridiculous lot of you.

CURTAIN

NOTES

1. Du Croisy is being facetious in addressing his friend by this title.
2. Characters in the popular 17th century romances *Grand Cyrus* and *Clélie* by Madeleine de Scudéry (1607-1701).
3. A footman or man servant who is formally dressed.
4. *Cyrus—The Great Cyrus,* a lengthy romantic novel by Madame de la Fayette that had a great vogue in 17th century France in upper class circles.
5. The Louvre in Paris (now a famous art museum) was a palace in the 17th century. The king's retiring to bed was a ceremonious occasion attended by the courtiers.
6. Chairs were not arranged in a room permanently in 17th century France.
7. A girl or woman who *knows* the fashion; literally, a knower, *connaisseuse* is derived from *connaître*—"to know."
8. A quatrain is a four-line stanza.
9. "A terrible famine of amusement"—"*un jeûne effroyable de divertissements*"—is a good example of the roundabout "precious," speech of the pretentious girls.
10. The stage was lit with candles in the 17th century.
11. Molière's rivals in Paris who declaimed and performed artificially while Molière favored relatively natural speech and behavior on the stage. He has his tongue in his cheek therefore when he praises the Hotel de Bourgogne acting company in the next line.
12. Kissing was fashionable at the time and was an accepted form of greeting friends in good society.
13. A regiment of cavalry on a galley is, of course, a patent absurdity.
14. "impromptu verses at my leisure" is an intentional contradiction.
15. Farewell, that is, to Mascarille's and Jodelet's pretense of being respectively a marquis and a viscount.

QUESTIONS

A. Understanding the Action:

1. What are Du Croisy and La Grange complaining about at the start of the play?
2. How does La Grange plan to seek revenge against his antagonists?
3. Mention some of the things Gorgibus complains about. Why is he angry with his daughter and his niece?
4. Madelon has some very definite ideas about love and matrimony. What are her ideas?
5. When Mascarille enters he gets into difficulty right away. Describe the situation, and explain why you think this scene is important to the play. What is the function of Mascarille to the play as a whole?

B. Understanding the Characters:

1. Who is the leading character in this play? Why?
2. The young ladies are obviously not members of courtly Parisian society. Whom do they represent? What is their real social station?

3. Are La Grange and Du Croisy too revengeful? Evidently Molière and his enthusiastic audiences did not think so. Can you think of some possible reasons to explain this?

4. Does Molière distinguish between the two pretentious girls? The two suitors? The two valets? Give your impressions.

C. Understanding the Approach:

1. What is "preciosity" and how is it represented in the play? How is it punished?

2. In expressing his scorn Molière employs exaggeration, the familiar device of burlesque. What other devices for comedy and satire does he use in the play? Explain how and where Molière employs these devices: contrast, contradiction, paradox, irony, reversals of situation, deflation of characters?

3. Why are the weaknesses and follies exposed in this play considered "universal" and "for all time" as some critics have claimed?

4. Why do you think Molière went to the trouble of writing *The Pretentious Ladies*, and why do you think it was so successfully received in 1659?

5. The essence of Molière's art was to burst a malignant social boil with the sharp scalpel of comedy. In your opinion do you see a need for this kind of comedy today? What are some of the areas that could benefit from Molière's dramatic technique? Explain your answer.

D. Comparisons:

1. List some of the similarities and differences between *The Pretentious Ladies*, and *The School for Scandal*. What is the real message or advice that each play offers? Discuss some of the differences of technique used by Molière and Sheridan to present their messages to an audience.

2. Which of the two plays is more effective for what is intended to be done? Discuss and explain your choice.

RICHARD BRINSLEY SHERIDAN (1751-1816)

The author of *School for Scandal*, Richard Brinsley Sheridan, was born of gifted parents in Dublin in 1751; the father was a distinguished actor and the mother wrote novels and plays. He was educated at Harrow, and then studied law. But he soon embarked on a literary career and won a reputation as a witty young man of the world, although far from an affluent one. Before long he became the talk of the town as a result of a romantic love affair which involved him in two duels with rivals and culminated in his eloping at the age of twenty-two with a beautiful concert singer, Elizabeth Linley, daughter of the singer and composer Dr. Linley. Two years later, he improved his financial position with the production of his successful comedy *The Rivals* in 1775. A year later, when he was twenty-five, he acquired part-ownership of the Drury Lane Theatre. He was twenty-six when he became England's outstanding playwright with *The School for Scandal*. He continued to write plays, but only one of these, a satire on the theatre, *The Critic* (1779), attained distinction.

Sheridan also won considerable reputation for a time when he became a member of Parliament in 1780 and made a rousing speech that resulted in the impeachment of Warren Hastings, the first governor-general of India, who was accused of corruption and oppression. Unfortunately his political career drained him of his energies; his management of Drury Lane, which involved him in costly conflicts with rival managers, was almost always in a state of bankruptcy; and his personal life was marred by misfortunes and misconduct. He lived on until 1816 with few gratifications and many aggravations. But he could look back upon some brilliant achievements in his youth when he earned the tribute of Lord Byron. "Whatever he tried," said Byron, "he did better than anyone else. He wrote the best comedy, *The School for Scandal*, the best opera, *The Duenna*, the best farce, *The Critic*, and the best address, the *Monologue on Garrick*. And to crown it all, he delivered the very best oration ever conceived or heard in this country, the famous Begum speech (the attack on Warren Hastings)."

INTRODUCTION TO *THE SCHOOL FOR SCANDAL*

The School for Scandal had its premiere in London on May 8, 1777, at the Drury Lane, the theatre that the great actor-manager David Garrick had sold to Sheridan the year before. The play was an instant success. A rival playwright, who was walking past the passage under the orchestra (the "pit-passage") on the opening night recorded his experience as follows: "I heard such a tremendous noise over my head that, fearing the theatre was proceeding to fall about it, I ran for my life; but found the next morning that the noise did not arise from the falling of the house, but from the falling of the screen in the fourth act, so violent and tumultuous were the applause and laughter."

The play has been called the greatest comedy in the English language, although this opinion is bound to be disputed by champions of Shakespeare, Ben Jonson, William Congreve, Oscar Wilde, and Bernard Shaw. It may be safer to say that *The School for Scandal* is the English masterpiece of a certain kind of comedy in prose called "comedy of manners." No English play came within hailing distance of it until 115 years later when Oscar Wilde's comedy *Lady Windermere's Fan* was presented in London in 1892.

THE SCHOOL FOR SCANDAL

RICHARD BRINSLEY SHERIDAN

CHARACTERS

SIR PETER TEAZLE
SIR OLIVER SURFACE
JOSEPH SURFACE
CHARLES SURFACE
CARELESS
SNAKE
SIR BENJAMIN BACKBITE
CRABTREE

ROWLEY
MOSES
TRIP
SIR TOBY BUMPER
LADY TEAZLE
MARIA
LADY SNEERWELL
MRS. CANDOUR

Gentlemen, Maid, *and* Servants

Scene: LONDON

ACT I SCENE I [LADY SNEERWELL'S *dressing-room*.]

(LADY SNEERWELL, *at her toilet*; SNAKE, *drinking chocolate*.)

LADY SNEERWELL: The paragraphs, you say, Mr. Snake, were all inserted?

SNAKE: They were, madam; and, as I copied them myself in a feigned hand, there can be no suspicion whence they came.

LADY SNEERWELL: Did you circulate the report of Lady Brittle's intrigue with Captain Boastall?

SNAKE: That's in as fine a train as your ladyship could wish. In the common course of things, I think it must reach Mrs. Clackitt's ears within four-and-twenty hours; and then, you know, the business is as good as done.

LADY SNEERWELL: Why, truly, Mrs. Clackitt has a very pretty talent, and a great deal of industry.

SNAKE: True, madam, and has been tolerably successful in her day. To my knowledge, she has been the cause of six matches being broken off, and three sons being disinherited; of four forced elopments, and as many close confinements; nine separate maintenances, and two divorces. Nay, I have more than once traced her causing a *tête-à-tête* in the *Town and Country Magazine*,[1] when the parties, perhaps, had never seen each other's face before in the course of their lives.

LADY SNEERWELL: She certainly has talents, but her manner is gross.

SNAKE: 'Tis very true. She generally designs well, has a free tongue and a bold invention; but her coloring is too dark, and her outlines often extravagant. She wants that delicacy of tint and mellowness of sneer which distinguish your ladyship's scandal.

LADY SNEERWELL: You are partial, Snake.

SNAKE: Not in the least; everybody allows that Lady Sneerwell can do more with a word or look than many can with the most labored detail, even when they happen to have a little truth on their side to support it.

LADY SNEERWELL: Yes, my dear Snake; and I am no hypocrite to deny the satisfaction I reap from the success of my efforts. Wounded myself in the early part of my life, by the envenomed tongue of slander, I confess I have since known no pleasure equal to the reducing others to the level of my own injured reputation.

SNAKE: Nothing can be more natural. But, Lady Sneerwell, there is one affair in which you have lately employed me, wherein, I confess, I am at a loss to guess your motives.

LADY SNEERWELL: I conceive you mean with respect to my neighbor, Sir Peter Teazle, and his family?

SNAKE: I do. Here are two young men, to whom Sir Peter has acted as a kind of guardian since their father's death; the eldest possessing the most amiable character, and universally well spoken of—the youngest, the most dissipated and extravagant young fellow in the kingdom, without friends or character: the former an avowed admirer of your ladyship, and apparently your favorite; the latter attached to Maria, Sir Peter's ward, and confessedly beloved by her. Now, on the face of these circumstances, it is utterly unaccountable to me why you, the widow of a city knight,[2] with a good jointure, should not close with the passion of a man of such character and expectations as Mr. Surface; and more so, why you should be so uncommonly earnest to destroy the mutual attachment subsisting between his brother Charles and Maria.

LADY SNEERWELL: Then, at once to unravel this mystery, I must inform you that love has no share whatever in the intercourse between Mr. Surface and me.

SNAKE: No!

LADY SNEERWELL: His real attachment is to Maria or her fortune; but, finding in his brother a favorite rival, he has been obliged to mask his pretensions and profit by my assistance.

SNAKE: Yet still I am more puzzled why you should interest yourself in his success.

LADY SNEERWELL: Heavens! how dull you are! Cannot you surmise the weakness which I hitherto, through shame, have concealed even from you? Must I confess that Charles—that libertine, that extravagant, that bankrupt in fortune and reputation—that he it is for whom I am thus anxious and malicious, and to gain whom I would sacrifice everything?

SNAKE: Now, indeed, your conduct appears consistent; but how came you and Mr. Surface so confidential?

LADY SNEERWELL: For our mutual interest. I have found him out a long time since. I know him to be artful, selfish, and malicious—in short, a sentimental knave; while with Sir Peter, and indeed with all his acquaintance, he passes for a youthful miracle of prudence, good sense, and benevolence.

SNAKE: Yes! yet Sir Peter vows he has not his equal in England; and, above all, he praises him as a man of sentiment.

LADY SNEERWELL: True; and with the assistance of his sentiment and hypocrisy he has brought Sir Peter entirely into his interest with regard to Maria; while poor Charles has no friend in the house—though, I fear, he has a powerful one in Maria's heart, against whom we must direct our schemes.

(*Enter* SERVANT.)

SERVANT: Mr. Surface.

LADY SNEERWELL: Show him up. (*Exit* SERVANT.) He generally calls about this time. I don't wonder at people giving him to me for a lover.

(*Enter* JOSEPH SURFACE.)

JOSEPH SURFACE: My dear Lady Sneerwell, how do you do today? Mr. Snake, your most obedient.

LADY SNEERWELL: Snake has just been rallying me on our mutual attachment; but I have informed him of our real views. You know how useful he has been to us; and, believe me, the confidence is not ill placed.

JOSEPH SURFACE: Madam, it is impossible for me to suspect a man of Mr. Snake's sensibility and discernment.

LADY SNEERWELL: Well, well, no compliments now; but tell me when you saw your mistress, Maria—or, what is more material to me, your brother.

JOSEPH SURFACE: I have not seen either since I left you; but I can inform you that they never meet. Some of your stories have taken a good effect on Maria.

LADY SNEERWELL: Ah, my dear Snake! the merit of this belongs to you. But do your brother's distresses increase?

JOSEPH SURFACE: Every hour. I am told he has had another execution in the house yesterday. In short, his dissipation and extravagance exceed anything I have ever heard of.

LADY SNEERWELL: Poor Charles!

JOSEPH SURFACE: True, madam; notwithstanding his vices, one can't help feeling for him. Poor Charles! I'm sure I wish it were in my power to be of any essential service to him; for the man who does not share in the distresses of a brother, even though merited by his own misconduct, deserves—

LADY SNEERWELL: O Lud! you are going to be moral and forget that you are among friends.

JOSEPH SURFACE: Egad, that's true! I'll keep that sentiment till I see Sir Peter. However, it is certainly a charity to rescue Maria from such a libertine, who, if he is to be reclaimed, can be so only by a person of your ladyship's superior accomplishments and understanding.

SNAKE: I believe, Lady Sneerwell, here's company coming. I'll go and copy the letter I mentioned to you. Mr. Surface, your most obedient.

JOSEPH SURFACE: Sir, your very devoted. (*Exit* SNAKE.) Lady Sneerwell, I am very sorry you have put any further confidence in that fellow.

LADY SNEERWELL: Why so?

JOSEPH SURFACE: I have lately detected him in frequent conference with old Rowley, who was formerly my father's steward and has never, you know, been a friend of mine.

LADY SNEERWELL: And do you think he would betray us?

JOSEPH SURFACE: Nothing more likely: take my word for't, Lady Sneerwell, that fellow hasn't virtue enough to be faithful even to his own villainy. Ah, Maria!

(*Enter* MARIA.)

LADY SNEERWELL: Maria, my dear, how do you do? What's the matter?

MARIA: Oh! there's that disagreeable lover of mine, Sir Benjamin Backbite, has just called at my guardian's with his odious uncle, Crabtree; so I slipped out and ran hither to avoid them.

LADY SNEERWELL: Is that all?

JOSEPH SURFACE: If my brother Charles had been of the party, madam, perhaps you would not have been so much alarmed.

LADY SNEERWELL: Nay, now you are severe; for I dare swear the truth of the matter is, Maria heard you were here. But, my dear, what has Sir Benjamin done that you should avoid him so?

MARIA: Oh, he has done nothing—but 'tis for what he has said. His conversation is a perpetual libel on all his acquaintance.

JOSEPH SURFACE: Ay, and the worst of it is, there is no advantage in not knowing him, for he'll abuse a stranger just as soon as his best friend; and his uncle's as bad.

LADY SNEERWELL: Nay, but we should make allowance; Sir Benjamin is a wit and a poet.

MARIA: For my part, I own, madam, wit loses its respect with me when I see it in company with malice. What do you think, Mr. Surface?

JOSEPH SURFACE: Certainly, madam. To smile at the jest which plants a thorn in another's breast is to become a principal in the mischief.

LADY SNEERWELL: Psha! there's no possibility of being witty without a little ill-nature. The malice of a good thing is the barb that makes it stick. What's your opinion, Mr. Surface?

JOSEPH SURFACE: To be sure, madam; that conversation, where the spirit of raillery is suppressed, will ever appear tedious and insipid.

MARIA: Well, I'll not debate how far scandal may be allowable; but in a man, I am sure, it is always contemptible. We have pride, envy, rivalship, and a thousand motives to depreciate each other; but the male slanderer must have the cowardice of a woman before he can traduce one.

(*Enter* SERVANT.)

SERVANT: Madam, Mrs. Candour is below, and, if your ladyship's at leisure, will leave her carriage.

LADY SNEERWELL: Beg her to walk in. (*Exit* SERVANT.) Now, Maria, here is a character to your taste; for, though Mrs. Candour is a little talkative, everybody knows her to be the best natured and best sort of woman.

MARIA: Yes, with a very gross affection of good nature and benevolence, she does more mischief than the direct malice of old Crabtree.

JOSEPH SURFACE: I'faith that's true, Lady Sneerwell: whenever I hear the current running against the characters of my friends, I never think them in such danger as when Candour undertakes their defence.

LADY SNEERWELL: Hush!—here she is!

(*Enter* MRS. CANDOUR.)

MRS. CANDOUR: My dear Lady Sneerwell, how have you been this century?— Mr. Surface, what news do you hear?— though indeed it is no matter, for I think one hears nothing else but scandal.

JOSEPH SURFACE: Just so, indeed, ma'am.

MRS. CANDOUR: Oh, Maria! child— what, is the whole affair off between you and Charles? His extravagance, I presume—the town talks of nothing else.

MARIA: I am very sorry, ma'am, the town has so little to do.

MRS. CANDOUR: True, true, child: but there's no stopping people's tongues. I own I was hurt to hear it, as I indeed was to learn, from the same quarter, that your guardians, Sir Peter, and Lady Teazle have not agreed lately as well as could be wished.

MARIA: 'Tis strangely impertinent for people to busy themselves so.

MRS. CANDOUR: Very true, child; but what's to be done? People will talk— there's no preventing it. Why, it was but yesterday I was told that Miss Gadabout had eloped with Sir Filagree Flirt. But, Lord! there's no minding what one hears; though, to be sure, I had this from very good authority.

MARIA: Such reports are highly scandalous.

MRS. CANDOUR: So they are, child— shameful, shameful! But the world is so censorious, no character escapes. Lord, now who would have suspected your friend, Miss Prim, of an indiscretion? Yet such is the ill-nature of people that they say her uncle stopped her last week just as she was stepping into the York diligence[3] with her dancing-master.

MARIA: I'll answer for't there are no grounds for that report.

MRS. CANDOUR: Ah, no foundation in the world, I dare swear: no more, probably, than for the story circulated last month, of Mrs. Festino's affair with Colonel Cassino—though, to be sure, that matter was never rightly cleared up.

JOSEPH SURFACE: The license of invention some people take is monstrous indeed.

MARIA: 'Tis so; but, in my opinion, those who report such things are equally culpable.

MRS. CANDOUR: To be sure they are; tale bearers are as bad as the tale makers—'tis an old observation and a very true one: but what's to be done, as I said before? how will you prevent people from talking? Today, Mrs. Clackitt assured me Mr. and Mrs. Honeymoon were at last become mere man and wife like the rest of their acquaintance. She likewise hinted that a certain widow in the next street had got rid of her dropsy and recovered her shape in a most surprising manner. And at the same time Miss Tattle, who was by, affirmed that Lord Buffalo had discovered his lady at a house of no extraordinary fame; and that Sir Harry Bouquet and Tom Saunter were to measure swords on a similar provocation. But, Lord, do you think I would report these things! No, no! tale bearers, as I said before, are just as bad as the tale makers.

JOSEPH SURFACE: Ah! Mrs. Candour, if everybody had your forbearance and good nature!

MRS. CANDOUR: I confess, Mr. Surface, I cannot bear to hear people attacked behind their backs; and when ugly circumstances come out against our acquaintance, I own I always love to think the best. By-the-bye, I hope 'tis not true that your brother is absolutely ruined?

JOSEPH SURFACE: I am afraid his circumstances are very bad indeed, ma'am.

MRS. CANDOUR: Ah!—I heard so—but you must tell him to keep up his spirits; everybody almost is in the same way: Lord Spindle, Sir Thomas Splint, Captain Quinze, and Mr. Nickit—all up, I hear, within this week; so, if Charles is undone, he'll find half his acquaintance ruined too; and that, you know, is a consolation.

JOSEPH SURFACE: Doubtless, ma'am—a very great one.

(*Enter* SERVANT.)

SERVANT: Mr. Crabtree and Sir Benjamin Backbite. (*Exit.*)

LADY SNEERWELL: So, Maria, you see your lover pursues you; positively you shan't escape.

(*Enter* CRABTREE *and* SIR BENJAMIN BACKBITE.)

CRABTREE: Lady Sneerwell, I kiss your hand. Mrs. Candour, I don't believe you are acquainted with my nephew, Sir Benjamin Backbite? Egad, ma'am, he has a pretty wit and is a pretty poet too. Isn't he, Lady Sneerwell?

SIR BENJAMIN: Oh, fie, uncle!

CRABTREE: Nay, egad it's true: I back him at a rebus or a charade against the best rhymer in the kingdom. Has your ladyship heard the epigram he wrote last week on Lady Frizzle's feather catching fire?—Do, Benjamin, repeat it, or the charade you made last night extempore at Mrs. Drowzie's *conversazione*.[3a] Come now; your first is the name of a fish, your second a great naval commander, and—

SIR BENJAMIN: Uncle, now—prithee—

CRABTREE: I'faith, ma'am, 'twould surprise you to hear how ready he is at all these sort of things.

LADY SNEERWELL: I wonder, Sir Benjamin, you never publish anything.

SIR BENJAMIN: To say truth, ma'am, 'tis very vulgar to print; and, as my little productions are mostly satires and lampoons on particular people, I find they circulate more by giving copies in confidence to the friends of the parties. However, I have some love elegies, which, when favored with this lady's smiles, I mean to give the public.

CRABTREE: (*to* MARIA) 'Fore heaven, ma'am, they'll immortalize you—you will be handed down to posterity like Petrarch's Laura,[4] or Waller's Sacharissa.[5]

SIR BENJAMIN: (*to* MARIA) Yes, madam, I think you will like them when you shall see them on a beautiful quarto page, where a neat rivulet of text shall meander through a meadow of margin. 'Fore gad, they will be the most elegant things of their kind!

CRABTREE: But, ladies, that's true—have you heard the news?

MRS. CANDOUR: What, sir, do you mean the report of—

CRABTREE: No, ma'am, that's not it. Miss Nicely is going to be married to her own footman.

MRS. CANDOUR: Impossible!

CRABTREE: Ask Sir Benjamin.

SIR BENJAMIN: 'Tis very true, ma'am: everything is fixed and the wedding liveries bespoke.

CRABTREE: Yes—and they do say there were pressing reasons for it.

LADY SNEERWELL: Why, I have heard something of this before.

MRS. CANDOUR: It can't be—and I wonder any one should believe such a story of so prudent a lady as Miss Nicely.

SIR BENJAMIN: O lud! ma'am, that's the very reason 'twas believed at once. She has always been so cautious and so reserved, that everybody was sure there was some reason for it at bottom.

MRS. CANDOUR: Why, to be sure, a tale of scandal is as fatal to the credit of a prudent lady of her stamp as a fever is generally to those of the strongest constitution. But there is a sort of puny, sickly reputation, that is always ailing, yet will outlive the robuster characters of a hundred prudes.

SIR BENJAMIN: True, madam, there are valetudinarians in reputation as well as constitution, who, being conscious of their weak part, avoid the least breath of air and supply their want of stamina by care and circumspection.

MRS. CANDOUR: Well, but this may be all a mistake. You know, Sir Benjamin, very trifling circumstances often give rise to the most injurious tales.

CRABTREE: That they do, I'll be sworn, ma'am. Did you ever hear how Miss Piper came to lose her lover and her character last summer at Tunbridge? Sir Benjamin, you remember it?

SIR BENJAMIN: Oh, to be sure!—the most whimsical circumstance.

LADY SNEERWELL: How was it, pray?

CRABTREE: Why, one evening at Mrs. Ponto's assembly, the conversation happened to turn on the breeding Nova Scotia sheep in this country. Says a young lady in company, "I have known instances of it; for Miss Letitia Piper, a first cousin of mine, had a Nova Scotia sheep that produced her twins." "What!" cries the Lady Dowager Dundizzy (who you know is as deaf as a post), "has Miss Piper had twins?" This mistake, as you may imagine, threw the whole company into a fit of laughter. However, 'twas the next morning everywhere reported, and in a few days believed by the whole town, that Miss Letitia Piper had actually been brought to bed of a fine boy and a girl: and in less than a week there were some people who could name the father, and the farm-house where the babies were put to nurse.

LADY SNEERWELL: Strange, indeed!

CRABTREE: Matter of fact, I assure you. O lud! Mr. Surface, pray is it true that your uncle, Sir Oliver, is coming home?

JOSEPH SURFACE: Not that I know of, indeed, sir.

CRABTREE: He has been in the East

Indies a long time. You can scarcely remember him, I believe? Sad comfort, whenever he returns, to hear how your brother has gone on!

JOSEPH SURFACE: Charles has been imprudent, sir, to be sure; but I hope no busy people have already prejudiced Sir Oliver against him. He may reform.

SIR BENJAMIN: To be sure he may. For my part I never believed him to be so utterly void of principle as people say; and though he has lost all his friends, I am told nobody is better spoken of by the Jews.

CRABTREE: That's true, egad, nephew. If the old Jewry was a ward, I believe Charles would be an alderman: no man more popular there, 'fore gad! I hear he pays as many annuities as the Irish tontine;[6] and that whenever he is sick they have prayers for the recovery of his health in all the synagogues.

SIR BENJAMIN: Yet no man lives in greater splendor. They tell me, when he entertains his friends he will sit down to dinner with a dozen of his own securities, have a score of tradesmen in the antechamber, and an officer behind every guest's chair.

JOSEPH SURFACE: This may be entertainment to you, gentlemen, but you pay very little regard to the feelings of a brother.

MARIA: (*aside*) Their malice is intolerable!—(*aloud*.) Lady Sneerwell, I must wish you a good morning: I'm not very well. (*Exit*.)

MRS. CANDOUR: O dear! she changes color very much.

LADY SNEERWELL: Do, Mrs. Candour, follow her; she may want assistance.

MRS. CANDOUR: That I will, with all my soul, ma'am. Poor dear girl, who knows what her situation may be! (*Exit*.)

LADY SNEERWELL: 'Twas nothing but that she could not bear to hear Charles reflected on, notwithstanding their difference.

SIR BENJAMIN: The young lady's *penchant* is obvious.

CRABTREE: But, Benjamin, you must not give up the pursuit for that: follow her and put her into good humor. Repeat her some of your own verses. Come, I'll assist you.

SIR BENJAMIN: Mr. Surface, I did not mean to hurt you; but depend on't your brother is utterly undone.

CRABTREE: O lud, ay! undone as ever man was—can't raise a guinea!

SIR BENJAMIN: And everything sold, I'm told, that was movable.

CRABTREE: I have seen one that was at his house. Not a thing left but some empty bottles that were overlooked and the family pictures which I believe are framed in the wainscots.

SIR BENJAMIN: And I'm very sorry also to hear some bad stories against him. (*Going*.)

CRABTREE: Oh, he has done many mean things, that's certain.

SIR BENJAMIN: But, however, as he's your brother— (*Going*.)

CRABTREE: We'll tell you all another opportunity.

(*Exeunt* CRABTREE *and* SIR BENJAMIN.)

LADY SNEERWELL: Ha, ha! 'tis very hard for them to leave a subject they have not quite run down.

JOSEPH SURFACE: And I believe the abuse was no more acceptable to your ladyship than to Maria.

LADY SNEERWELL: I doubt[7] her affections are further engaged than we imagine. But the family are to be here this evening, so you may as well dine where you are and we shall have an opportunity of observing further. In the meantime, I'll go and plot mischief and you shall study sentiment. (*Exeunt*.)

SCENE II [SIR PETER TEAZLE'S *house*.]

(*Enter* SIR PETER.)

SIR PETER: When an old bachelor marries a young wife, what is he to expect? 'Tis now six months since Lady Teazle made me the happiest of men—and I have been the most miserable dog ever since! We tift a little going to church and fairly quarrelled before the bells had done ringing. I was more than once nearly choked with gall during the honeymoon, and had lost all comfort in life before my friends had done wishing me joy. Yet I chose with caution—a girl bred wholly in the country, who never knew luxury beyond one silk gown, nor dissipation above the annual gala of a race ball. Yet she now plays her part in all the extravagant fopperies of fashion and the town, with as ready a grace as if she never had seen a bush or a grass-plot out of Grosvenor Square! I am sneered at by all my acquaintance and paragraphed in the newspapers. She dissipates my fortune, and contradicts all my humors; yet the worst of it is, I doubt I love her, or I should never bear all this. However, I'll never be weak enough to own it.

(*Enter* ROWLEY.)

ROWLEY: Oh! Sir Peter, your servant: how is it with you, sir?

SIR PETER: Very bad, Master Rowley, very bad. I meet with nothing but crosses and vexations.

ROWLEY: What can have happened to trouble you since yesterday?

SIR PETER: A good question to a married man!

ROWLEY: Nay, I'm sure, Sir Peter, your lady can't be the cause of your uneasiness.

SIR PETER: Why, has anybody told you she was dead?

ROWLEY: Come, come, Sir Peter, you love her, notwithstanding your tempers don't exactly agree.

SIR PETER: But the fault is entirely hers, Master Rowley. I am myself the sweetest tempered man alive, and hate a teasing temper; and so I tell her a hundred times a day.

ROWLEY: Indeed!

SIR PETER: Ay; and what is very extraordinary, in all our disputes she is always in the wrong! But Lady Sneerwell and the set she meets at her house encourage the perverseness of her disposition. Then, to complete my vexation, Maria, my ward, whom I ought to have the power of a father over, is determined to turn rebel too and absolutely refuses the man whom I have long resolved on for her husband; meaning, I suppose, to bestow herself on his profligate brother.

ROWLEY: You know, Sir Peter, I have always taken the liberty to differ with you on the subject of these two young gentlemen. I only wish you may not be deceived in your opinion of the elder. For Charles, my life on't! he will retrieve his errors yet. Their worthy father, once my honored master, was, at his years, nearly as wild a spark; yet, when he died, he did not leave a more benevolent heart to lament his loss.

SIR PETER: You are wrong, Master Rowley. On their father's death, you know, I acted as a kind of guardian to them both till their uncle Sir Oliver's liberality gave them an early independence. Of course no person could have more opportunities of judging of their hearts, and I was never mistaken in my life. Joseph is indeed a model for the young men of the age. He is a man of sentiment and acts up to the sentiments he professes; but, for the other, take my word for't, if he had any grain of virtue by descent, he has dissipated it with the rest of his inheritance. Ah! my old friend Sir Oliver will be deeply mortified when he finds how part of his bounty has been misapplied.

ROWLEY: I am sorry to find you so

violent against the young man, because this may be the most critical period of his fortune. I came hither with news that will surprise you.

SIR PETER: What! let me hear.

ROWLEY: Sir Oliver is arrived, and at this moment in town.

SIR PETER: How! you astonish me! I thought you did not expect him this month.

ROWLEY: I did not: but his passage has been remarkably quick.

SIR PETER: Egad, I shall rejoice to see my old friend. 'Tis sixteen years since we met. We have had many a day together: but does he still enjoin us not to inform his nephews of his arrival?

ROWLEY: Most strictly. He means, before it is known, to make some trial of their dispositions.

SIR PETER: Ah! There needs no art to discover their merits—however, he shall have his way; but, pray, does he know I am married?

ROWLEY: Yes, and will soon wish you joy.

SIR PETER: What, as we drink health to a friend in consumption! Ah, Oliver will laugh at me. We used to rail at matrimony together, but he has been steady to his text. Well, he must be soon at my house, though—I'll instantly give orders for his reception. But, Master Rowley, don't drop a word that Lady Teazle and I ever disagree.

ROWLEY: By no means.

SIR PETER: For I should never be able to stand Noll's jokes; so I'll have him think, Lord forgive me! that we are a very happy couple.

ROWLEY: I understand you: but then you must be very careful not to differ while he is in the house with you.

SIR PETER: Egad, and so we must—and that's impossible. Ah! Master Rowley, when an old bachelor marries a young wife, he deserves—no—the crime carries its punishment along with it. (*Exeunt.*)

ACT II SCENE I [SIR PETER TEAZLE'S *house.*]

(*Enter* SIR PETER *and* LADY TEAZLE.)

SIR PETER: Lady Teazle, Lady Teazle, I'll not bear it!

LADY TEAZLE: Sir Peter, Sir Peter, you may bear it or not as you please; but I ought to have my own way in everything, and what's more, I will too. What though I was educated in the country, I know very well that women of fashion in London are accountable to nobody after they are married.

SIR PETER: Very well, ma'am, very well; so a husband is to have no influence, no authority?

LADY TEAZLE: Authority! No, to be sure. If you wanted authority over me, you should have adopted me and not married me: I am sure you were old enough.

SIR PETER: Old enough!—ay, there it is! Well, well, Lady Teazle, though my life may be made unhappy by your temper, I'll not be ruined by your extravagance!

LADY TEAZLE: My extravagance! I'm sure I'm not more extravagant than a woman of fashion ought to be.

SIR PETER: No, no, madam, you shall throw away no more sums on such unmeaning luxury. 'Slife! to spend as much to furnish your dressing-room with flowers in winter as would suffice to turn the Pantheon[8] into a greenhouse, and give a *fête champêtre*[9] at Christmas.

LADY TEAZLE: And am I to blame, Sir Peter, because flowers are dear in cold weather? You should find fault with the climate, and not with me. For my part, I'm sure I wish it was spring all the year round and that roses grew under our feet!

SIR PETER: Oons! madam—if you had been born to this, I shouldn't wonder at your talking thus; but you forget what your situation was when I married you.

LADY TEAZLE: No, no, I don't; 'twas a very disagreeable one, or I should never have married you.

SIR PETER: Yes, yes, madam, you were then in somewhat a humbler style—the daughter of a plain country squire. Recollect, Lady Teazle, when I saw you first sitting at your tambour[10] in a pretty figured linen gown with a bunch of keys at your side, your hair combed smooth over a roll and your apartment hung round with fruits in worsted of your own working.

LADY TEAZLE: Oh, yes! I remember it very well, and a curious life I led. My daily occupation to inspect the dairy, superintend the poultry, make extracts from the family receipt-book, and comb my aunt Deborah's lapdog.

SIR PETER: Yes, yes, ma'am, 'twas so indeed.

LADY TEAZLE: And then, you know, my evening amusements! To draw patterns for ruffles, which I had not the materials to make up; to play Pope Joan[11] with the Curate; to read a sermon to my aunt; or to be stuck down to an old spinet to strum my father to sleep after a fox-chase.

SIR PETER: I am glad you have so good a memory. Yes, madam, these were the recreations I took you from; but now you must have your coach—*vis-à-vis*[12]—and three powdered footmen before your chair; and, in the summer, a pair of white cats[13] to draw you to Kensington Gardens. No recollection, I suppose, when you were content to ride double, behind the butler, on a docked coach-horse?

LADY TEAZLE: No—I swear I never did that; I deny the butler and the coach-horse.

SIR PETER: This, madam, was your situation; and what have I done for you? I have made you a woman of fashion, of fortune, of rank—in short, I have made you my wife.

LADY TEAZLE: Well, then, and there is but one thing more you can make me to add to the obligation, that is—

SIR PETER: My widow, I suppose?

LADY TEAZLE: Hem! hem!

SIR PETER: I thank you, madam—but don't flatter yourself; for, though your ill-conduct may disturb my peace it shall never break my heart, I promise you. However, I am equally obliged to you for the hint.

LADY TEAZLE: Then why will you endeavor to make yourself so disagreeable to me and thwart me in every little elegant expense?

SIR PETER: 'Slife, madam, I say; had you any of these little elegant expenses when you married me?

LADY TEAZLE: Lud, Sir Peter! would you have me be out of the fashion?

SIR PETER: The fashion, indeed! what had you to do with the fashion before you married me?

LADY TEAZLE: For my part, I should think you would like to have your wife thought a woman of taste.

SIR PETER: Ay—there again—taste! Zounds! madam, you had no taste when you married me!

LADY TEAZLE: That's very true, indeed, Sir Peter! and, after having married you, I should never pretend to taste again, I allow. But now, Sir Peter, since we have finished our daily jangle, I presume I may go to my engagement at Lady Sneerwell's?

SIR PETER: Ay, there's another precious circumstance—a charming set of acquaintance you have made there!

LADY TEAZLE: Nay, Sir Peter, they are all people of rank and fortune and remarkably tenacious of reputation.

SIR PETER: Yes, egad, they are tenacious of reputation with a vengeance; for they don't choose anybody should have a character but themselves! Such a crew! Ah! many a wretch has rid on a hurdle who has done less mischief than these utterers of forged tales, coiners of scandal, and clippers of reputation.

LADY TEAZLE: What, would you restrain the freedom of speech?

SIR PETER: Ah! they have made you just as bad as any one of the society.

LADY TEAZLE: Why, I believe I do bear a part with a tolerable grace. But I vow I bear no malice against the people I abuse: when I say an ill-natured thing, 'tis out of pure good humor; and I take it for granted they deal exactly in the same manner with me. But, Sir Peter, you know you promised to come to Lady Sneerwell's too.

SIR PETER: Well, well, I'll call in just to look after my own character.

LADY TEAZLE: Then, indeed, you must make haste after me or you'll be too late. So good-bye to ye. (*Exit.*)

SIR PETER: So—I have gained much by my intended expostulation! Yet with what a charming air she contradicts everything I say, and how pleasantly she shows her contempt for my authority! Well, though I can't make her love me, there is great satisfaction in quarrelling with her; and I think she never appears to such advantage as when she is doing everything in her power to plague me. (*Exit.*)

SCENE II   [LADY SNEERWELL'S *house*.]

(LADY SNEERWELL, MRS. CANDOUR, CRABTREE, SIR BENJAMIN BACKBITE, *and* JOSEPH SURFACE.)

LADY SNEERWELL: Nay, positively, we will hear it.

JOSEPH SURFACE: Yes, yes, the epigram, by all means.

SIR BENJAMIN: O plague on't, uncle! 'tis mere nonsense.

CRABTREE: No, no; 'fore gad, very clever for an extempore!

SIR BENJAMIN: But, ladies, you should be acquainted with the circumstance. You must know, that one day last week as Lady Betty Curricle was taking the dust in Hyde Park, in a sort of duodecimo phaeton, she desired me to write some verses on her ponies; upon which, I took out my pocketbook, and in one moment produced the following:—

> Sure never were seen two such beautiful ponies;
> Other horses are clowns, but these macaronies:[14]
> To give them this title I am sure can't be wrong.
> Their legs are so slim, and their tails are so long.

CRABTREE: There, ladies, done in the smack of a whip, and on horseback too.

JOSEPH SURFACE: A very Phœbus mounted—indeed, Sir Benjamin!

SIR BENJAMIN: Oh dear, sir!—trifles—trifles.

(*Enter* LADY TEAZLE *and* MARIA.)

MRS. CANDOUR: I must have a copy.

LADY SNEERWELL: Lady Teazle, I hope we shall see Sir Peter?

LADY TEAZLE: I believe he'll wait on your ladyship presently.

LADY SNEERWELL: Maria, my love, you look grave. Come, you shall sit down to piquet with Mr. Surface.

MARIA: I take very little pleasure in cards—however, I'll do as your ladyship pleases.

LADY TEAZLE: (*aside*) I am surprised Mr. Surface should sit down with her; I thought he would have embraced this opportunity of speaking to me before Sir Peter came.

MRS. CANDOUR: Now, I'll die; but you are so scandalous, I'll forswear your society.

LADY TEAZLE: What's the matter, Mrs. Candour?

MRS. CANDOUR: They'll not allow our friend Miss Vermillion to be handsome.

LADY SNEERWELL: Oh, surely she is a pretty woman.

CRABTREE: I am very glad you think so, ma'am.

MRS. CANDOUR: She has a charming fresh color.

LADY TEAZLE: Yes, when it is fresh put on.

MRS. CANDOUR: Oh, fie! I'll swear her color is natural: I have seen it come and go!

LADY TEAZLE: I dare swear you have, ma'am: it goes off at night and comes again in the morning.

SIR BENJAMIN: True, ma'am, it not only comes and goes; but, what's more, egad, her maid can fetch and carry it!

MRS. CANDOUR: Ha! ha! ha! how I hate to hear you talk so! But surely, now, her sister is, or was, very handsome.

CRABTREE: Who? Mrs. Evergreen? O Lord! she's six-and-fifty if she's an hour!

MRS. CANDOUR: Now positively you wrong her; fifty-two or fifty-three is the utmost—and I don't think she looks more.

SIR BENJAMIN: Ah! there's no judging by her looks, unless one could see her face.

LADY SNEERWELL: Well, well, if Mrs. Evergreen does take some pains to repair the ravages of time, you must allow she effects it with great ingenuity; and surely that's better than the careless manner in which the widow Ochre caulks her wrinkles.

SIR BENJAMIN: Nay, now, Lady Sneerwell, you are severe upon the widow. Come, come, 'tis not that she paints so ill —but, when she has finished her face, she joins it on so badly to her neck, that she looks like a mended statue, in which the connoisseur may see at once that the head's modern, though the trunk's antique!

CRABTREE: Ha! ha! ha! Well said, nephew!

MRS. CANDOUR: Ha! ha! ha! Well, you make me laugh; but I vow I hate you for it. What do you think of Miss Simper?

SIR BENJAMIN: Why, she has very pretty teeth.

LADY TEAZLE: Yes; and on that account, when she is neither speaking nor laughing (which very seldom happens), she never absolutely shuts her mouth, but leaves it always on ajar, as it were—thus. (*Shows her teeth.*)

MRS. CANDOUR: How can you be so ill-natured?

LADY TEAZLE: Nay, I allow even that's better than the pains Mrs. Prim takes to conceal her losses in front. She draws her mouth till it positively resembles the aperture of a poor's-box, and all her words appear to slide out edgewise, as it were—thus: *How do you do, madam? Yes, madam.*

LADY SNEERWELL: Very well, Lady Teazle; I see you can be a little severe.

LADY TEAZLE: In defense of a friend it is but justice. But here comes Sir Peter to spoil our pleasantry.

(*Enter* SIR PETER.)

SIR PETER: Ladies, your most obedient —(*aside.*) Mercy on me, here is the whole set! a character dead at every word, I suppose.

MRS. CANDOUR: I am rejoiced you are come, Sir Peter. They have been so censorious—and Lady Teazle as bad as any one.

SIR PETER: That must be very distressing to you, Mrs. Candour, I dare swear.

MRS. CANDOUR: Oh, they will allow good qualities to nobody; not even good nature to our friend Mrs. Pursy.

LADY TEAZLE: What, the fat dowager who was at Mrs. Quadrille's last night?

MRS. CANDOUR: Nay, her bulk is her misfortune; and, when she takes so much pains to get rid of it, you ought not to reflect on her.

LADY SNEERWELL: That's very true, indeed.

LADY TEAZLE: Yes, I know she almost

lives on acids and small whey; laces herself by pulleys; and often, in the hottest noon in summer, you may see her on a little squat pony, with her hair plaited up behind like a drummer's and puffing round the Ring[15] on a full trot.

MRS. CANDOUR: I thank you, Lady Teazle, for defending her.

SIR PETER: Yes, a good defence, truly.

MRS. CANDOUR: Truly, Lady Teazle is as censorious as Miss Sallow.

CRABTREE: Yes, and she is a curious being to pretend to be censorious—an awkward gawky without any one good point under heaven.

MRS. CANDOUR: Positively you shall not be so very severe. Miss Sallow is a near relation of mine by marriage, and, as for her person, great allowance is to be made; for, let me tell you, a woman labors under many disadvantages who tries to pass for a girl of six-and-thirty.

LADY SNEERWELL: Though, surely, she is handsome still—and for the weakness in her eyes, considering how much she reads by candlelight, it is not to be wondered at.

MRS. CANDOUR: True; and then as to her manner, upon my word, I think it is particularly graceful, considering she never had the least education; for you know her mother was a Welsh milliner, and her father a sugar-baker at Bristol.

SIR BENJAMIN: Ah! you are both of you too good-natured!

SIR PETER: (*aside*) Yes, damned good-natured! This their own relation! mercy on me!

MRS. CANDOUR: For my part, I own I cannot bear to hear a friend ill spoken of.

SIR PETER: No, to be sure.

SIR BENJAMIN: Oh! you are of a moral turn. Mrs. Candour and I can sit for an hour and hear Lady Stucco talk sentiment.

LADY TEAZLE: Nay, I vow Lady Stucco is very well with the dessert after dinner; for she's just like the French fruit[16] one cracks for mottoes—made up of paint and proverb.

MRS. CANDOUR: Well, I will never join in ridiculing a friend; and so I constantly tell my cousin Ogle, and you all know what pretensions she has to be critical on beauty.

CRABTREE: Oh, to be sure! she has herself the oddest countenance that ever was seen; 'tis a collection of features from all the different countries of the globe.

SIR BENJAMIN: So she has, indeed—an Irish front—

CRABTREE: Caledonian locks—

SIR BENJAMIN: Dutch nose—

CRABTREE: Austrian lips—

SIR BENJAMIN: Complexion of a Spaniard—

CRABTREE: And teeth *à la Chinoise*—

SIR BENJAMIN: In short, her face resembles a *table d'hôte* at Spa—where no two guests are of a nation—

CRABTREE: Or a congress at the close of a general war—wherein all the members, even to her eyes, appear to have a different interest, and her nose and chin are the only parties likely to join issue.

MRS. CANDOUR: Ha! ha! ha!

SIR PETER: (*aside*) Mercy on my life!—a person they dine with twice a week!

LADY SNEERWELL: Go—go—you are a couple of provoking toads.

MRS. CANDOUR: Nay, but I vow you shall not carry the laugh off so—for give me leave to say, that Mrs. Ogle—

SIR PETER: Madam, madam, I beg your pardon—there's no stopping these good gentlemen's tongues. But when I tell you, Mrs. Candour, that the lady they are abusing is a particular friend of mine, I hope you'll not take her part.

LADY SNEERWELL: Ha! ha! ha! well said, Sir Peter! but you are a cruel creature—too phlegmatic yourself for a jest, and too peevish to allow wit in others.

SIR PETER: Ah, madam, true wit is

more nearly allied to good nature than your ladyship is aware of.

LADY TEAZLE: True, Sir Peter: I believe they are so near akin that they can never be united.

SIR BENJAMIN: Or rather, madam, I suppose them man and wife because one seldom sees them together.

LADY TEAZLE: But Sir Peter is such an enemy to scandal, I believe he would have it put down by Parliament.

SIR PETER: 'Fore heaven, madam, if they were to consider the sporting with reputation of as much importance as poaching on manors, and pass an act for the preservation of fame, I believe many would thank them for the bill.

LADY SNEERWELL: O Lud! Sir Peter; would you deprive us of our privileges?

SIR PETER: Ay, madam; and then no person should be permitted to kill characters and run down reputations, but qualified old maids and disappointed widows.

LADY SNEERWELL: Go, you monster!

MRS. CANDOUR: But, surely, you would not be quite so severe on those who only report what they hear?

SIR PETER: Yes, madam, I would have law merchant[17] for them too; and in all cases of slander currency, whenever the drawer of the lie was not to be found, the injured parties should have a right to come on any of the indorsers.

CRABTREE: Well, for my part, I believe there never was a scandalous tale without some foundation.

LADY SNEERWELL: Come, ladies, shall we sit down to cards in the next room? (*Enter* SERVANT, *who whispers to* SIR PETER.)

SIR PETER: I'll be with them directly. —(*Exit* SERVANT.) (*Aside.*) I'll get away unperceived.

LADY SNEERWELL: Sir Peter, you are not going to leave us?

SIR PETER: Your ladyships must excuse me: I'm called away by particular business. But I leave my character behind me. (*Exit.*)

SIR BENJAMIN: Well—certainly, Lady Teazle, that lord of yours is a strange being. I could tell you some stories of him would make you laugh heartily if he were not your husband.

LADY TEAZLE: Oh, pray don't mind that; come, do let's hear them. (*Exeunt all but* JOSEPH SURFACE *and* MARIA.)

JOSEPH SURFACE: Maria, I see you have no satisfaction in this society.

MARIA: How is it possible I should? If to raise malicious smiles at the infirmities or misfortunes of those who have never injured us be the province of wit or humor, Heaven grant me a double portion of dullness!

JOSEPH SURFACE: Yet they appear more ill-natured than they are; they have no malice at heart.

MARIA: Then is their conduct still more contemptible; for, in my opinion, nothing could excuse the intemperance of their tongues but a natural and uncontrollable bitterness of mind.

JOSEPH SURFACE: Undoubtedly, madam; and it has always been a sentiment of mine that to propagate a malicious truth wantonly is more despicable than to falsify from revenge. But can you, Maria, feel thus for others, and be unkind to me alone? Is hope to be denied the tenderest passion?

MARIA: Why will you distress me by renewing this subject?

JOSEPH SURFACE: Ah, Maria! you would not treat me thus, and oppose your guardian, Sir Peter's will, but that I see that profligate Charles is still a favored rival.

MARIA: Ungenerously urged! But whatever my sentiments are for that unfortunate young man, be assured I shall not feel more bound to give him up, because his distresses have lost him the regard even of a brother.

JOSEPH SURFACE: Nay, but, Maria, do not leave me with a frown: by all that's honest, I swear— (*Kneels.*)

(*Enter* LADY TEAZLE.)

(*Aside.*) Gad's life, here's Lady Teazle. —(*Aloud to* MARIA.) You must not—no, you shall not—for, though I have the greatest regard for Lady Teazle—

MARIA: Lady Teazle!

JOSEPH SURFACE: Yet were Sir Peter to suspect—

LADY TEAZLE: (*coming forward*) What is this, pray? Do you take her for me?—Child, you are wanted in the next room.—(*Exit* MARIA.) What is all this, pray?

JOSEPH SURFACE: Oh, the most unlucky circumstance in nature! Maria has somehow suspected the tender concern I have for your happiness, and threatened to acquaint Sir Peter with her suspicions, and I was just endeavoring to reason with her when you came in.

LADY TEAZLE: Indeed! but you seemed to adopt a very tender mode of reasoning —do you usually argue on your knees?

JOSEPH SURFACE: Oh, she's a child and I thought a little bombast—but, Lady Teazle, when are you to give me your judgment on my library, as you promised?

LADY TEAZLE: No, no; I begin to think it would be imprudent, and you know I admit you as a lover no farther than fashion requires.

JOSEPH SURFACE: —True—a mere Platonic *cicisbeo*,[18] what every wife is entitled to.

LADY TEAZLE: Certainly, one must not be out of the fashion. However, I have so many of my country prejudices left that, though Sir Peter's ill humor may vex me ever so, it never shall provoke me to—

JOSEPH SURFACE: The only revenge in your power. Well, I applaud your moderation.

LADY TEAZLE: Go—you are an insinuating wretch! But we shall be missed —let us join the company.

JOSEPH SURFACE: But we had best not return together.

LADY TEAZLE: Well, don't stay; for Maria shan't come to hear any more of your reasoning, I promise you. (*Exit.*)

JOSEPH SURFACE: A curious dilemma, truly, my politics have run me into! I wanted, at first, only to ingratiate myself with Lady Teazle, that she might not be my enemy with Maria; and I have, I don't know how, become her serious lover. Sincerely I begin to wish I had never made such a point of gaining so very good a character; for it has led me into so many cursed rogueries that I doubt I shall be exposed at last. (*Exit.*)

SCENE III [SIR PETER TEAZLE'S *house.*]

(*Enter* SIR OLIVER SURFACE *and* ROWLEY.)

SIR OLIVER: Ha! ha! ha! so my old friend is married, hey?—a young wife out of the country. Ha! ha! ha! that he should have stood bluff[19] to old bachelor so long and sink into a husband at last!

ROWLEY: But you must not rally him on the subject, Sir Oliver; 'tis a tender point, I assure you, though he has been married only seven months.

SIR OLIVER: Then he has been just half a year on the stool of repentance!—Poor Peter! But you say he has entirely given up Charles—never sees him, hey?

ROWLEY: His prejudice against him is astonishing, and I am sure greatly increased by a jealousy of him with Lady Teazle, which he has industriously been led into by a scandalous society in the neighborhood, who have contributed not a little to Charles's ill name. Whereas the truth is, I believe, if the lady is partial to either of them, his brother is the favorite.

SIR OLIVER: Ay, I know there are a set of malicious, prating, prudent gossips, both male and female, who murder characters to kill time, and will rob a young fellow of his good name before he has years to know the value of it. But I am not to be prejudiced against my nephew by such, I promise you! No, no; if Charles has done nothing false or mean, I shall compound for his extravagance.

ROWLEY: Then, my life on't, you will reclaim him. Ah, sir, it gives me new life to find that your heart is not turned against him, and that the son of my good old master has one friend, however, left.

SIR OLIVER: What! shall I forget, Master Rowley, when I was at his years myself? Egad, my brother and I were neither of us very prudent youths; and yet, I believe, you have not seen many better men than your old master was?

ROWLEY: Sir, 'tis this reflection gives me assurance that Charles may yet be a credit to his family. But here comes Sir Peter.

SIR OLIVER: Egad, so he does! Mercy on me, he's greatly altered, and seems to have a settled married look! One may read *husband* in his face at this distance! (*Enter* SIR PETER.)

SIR PETER: Ha! Sir Oliver—my old friend! Welcome to England a thousand times!

SIR OLIVER: Thank you, thank you, Sir Peter! and i'faith I am glad to find you well, believe me!

SIR PETER: Oh! 'tis a long time since we met—fifteen years, I doubt, Sir Oliver, and many a cross accident in the time.

SIR OLIVER: Ay, I have had my share. But, what! I find you are married, hey, my old boy? Well, well, it can't be helped; and so—I wish you joy with all my heart!

SIR PETER: Thank you, thank you, Sir Oliver.—Yes, I have entered into—the happy state; but we'll not talk of that now.

SIR OLIVER: True, true, Sir Peter; old friends should not begin on grievances at first meeting. No, no, no.

ROWLEY: (*aside to* SIR OLIVER) Take care, pray, sir.

SIR OLIVER: Well, so one of my nephews is a wild rogue, hey?

SIR PETER: Wild! Ah! my old friend, I grieve for your disappointment there; he's a lost young man, indeed. However, his brother will make you amends; Joseph is, indeed, what a youth should be—everybody in the world speaks well of him.

SIR OLIVER: I am sorry to hear it; he has too good a character to be an honest fellow. Everybody speaks well of him! Psha! then he has bowed as low to knaves and fools as to the honest dignity of genius and virtue.

SIR PETER: What, Sir Oliver! do you blame him for not making enemies?

SIR OLIVER: Yes, if he has merit enough to deserve them.

SIR PETER: Well, well—you'll be convinced when you know him. 'Tis edification to hear him converse; he professes the noblest sentiments.

SIR OLIVER: Oh, plague of his sentiments! If he salutes me with a scrap of morality in his mouth, I shall be sick directly. But, however, don't mistake me, Sir Peter; I don't mean to defend Charles's errors: but, before I form my judgment of either of them, I intend to make a trial of their hearts; and my friend Rowley and I have planned something for the purpose.

ROWLEY: And Sir Peter shall own for once he has been mistaken.

SIR PETER: Oh, my life on Joseph's honor!

SIR OLIVER: Well—come, give us a bottle of good wine, and we'll drink the lads' health and tell you our scheme.

SIR PETER: *Allons*, then!

SIR OLIVER: And don't, Sir Peter, be

so severe against your old friends' son. Odds my life! I am not sorry that he has run out of the course a little. For my part, I hate to see prudence clinging to the green suckers of youth; 'tis like ivy round a sapling, and spoils the growth of the tree. (*Exeunt.*)

ACT III SCENE I [SIR PETER TEAZLE'S *house.*]

(*Enter* SIR PETER TEAZLE, SIR OLIVER SURFACE, *and* ROWLEY.)

SIR PETER: Well, then, we will see this fellow first and have our wine afterwards. But how is this, Master Rowley? I don't see the jet of your scheme.

ROWLEY: Why, sir, this Mr. Stanley, whom I was speaking of, is nearly related to them by their mother. He was once a merchant in Dublin, but has been ruined by a series of undeserved misfortunes. He has applied, by letter, since his confinement, both to Mr. Surface and Charles. From the former he has received nothing but evasive promises of future service, while Charles has done all that his extravagance has left him power to do; and he is, at this time, endeavoring to raise a sum of money, part of which, in the midst of his own distresses, I know he intends for the service of poor Stanley.

SIR OLIVER: Ah, he is my brother's son.

SIR PETER: Well, but how is Sir Oliver personally to—

ROWLEY: Why, sir, I will inform Charles and his brother that Stanley has obtained permission to apply personally to his friends; and, as they have neither of them ever seen him, let Sir Oliver assume his character, and he will have a fair opportunity of judging, at least, of the benevolence of their dispositions; and believe me, sir, you will find in the youngest brother one who, in the midst of folly and dissipation, has still, as our immortal bard expresses it,—

a tear for pity, and a hand
Open as day, for melting charity.[20]

SIR PETER: Psha! What signifies his having an open hand or purse either, when he has nothing left to give? Well, well, make the trial, if you please. But where is the fellow whom you brought for Sir Oliver to examine relative to Charles's affairs?

ROWLEY: Below, waiting his commands, and no one can give him better intelligence.—This, Sir Oliver, is a friendly Jew, who, to do him justice, has done everything in his power to bring your nephew to a proper sense of his extravagance.

SIR PETER: Pray let us have him in.

ROWLEY: (*calls to* SERVANT) Desire Mr. Moses to walk upstairs.

SIR PETER: But, pray, why should you suppose he will speak the truth?

ROWLEY: Oh, I have convinced him that he has no chance of recovering certain sums advanced to Charles but through the bounty of Sir Oliver, who he knows is arrived; so that you may depend on his fidelity to his own interests. I have also another evidence in my power, one Snake, whom I have detected in a matter little short of forgery and shall shortly produce to remove some of your prejudices, Sir Peter, relative to Charles and Lady Teazle.

SIR PETER: I have heard too much on that subject.

ROWLEY: Here comes the honest Israelite.

(*Enter* MOSES.)
—This is Sir Oliver.

SIR OLIVER: Sir, I understand you have lately had great dealings with my nephew Charles.

MOSES: Yes, Sir Oliver, I have done all I could for him; but he was ruined before he came to me for assistance.

SIR OLIVER: That was unlucky, truly; for you have had no opportunity of showing your talents.

MOSES: None at all; I hadn't the pleasure of knowing his distresses till he was some thousands worse than nothing.

SIR OLIVER: Unfortunate, indeed! But I suppose you have done all in your power for him, honest Moses?

MOSES: Yes, he knows that. This very evening I was to have brought him a gentleman from the city, who does not know him, and will, I believe, advance him some money.

SIR PETER: What, one Charles has never had money from before?

MOSES: Yes, Mr. Premium, of Crutched Friars, formerly a broker.

SIR PETER: Egad, Sir Oliver, a thought strikes me!—Charles, you say, does not know Mr. Premium?

MOSES: Not at all.

SIR PETER: Now then, Sir Oliver, you may have a better opportunity of satisfying yourself than by an old romancing tale of a poor relation. Go with my friend Moses and represent Premium, and then, I'll answer for it, you'll see your nephew in all his glory.

SIR OLIVER: Egad, I like this idea better than the other and I may visit Joseph afterwards as old Stanley.

SIR PETER: True—so you may.

ROWLEY: Well, this is taking Charles rather at a disadvantage, to be sure. However, Moses, you understand Sir Peter, and will be faithful.

MOSES: You may depend upon me.—This is near the time I was to have gone.

SIR OLIVER: I'll accompany you as soon as you please, Moses—But hold! I have forgot one thing—how the plague shall I be able to pass for a Jew?

MOSES: There's no need—the principal is Christian.

SIR OLIVER: Is he? I'm very sorry to hear it. But, then again, an't I rather too smartly dressed to look like a money-lender?

SIR PETER: Not at all; 'twould not be out of character, if you went in your carriage—would it, Moses?

MOSES: Not in the least.

SIR OLIVER: Well, but how must I talk? there's certainly some cant of usury and mode of treating that I ought to know.

SIR PETER: Oh, there's not much to learn. The great point, as I take it, is to be exorbitant enough in your demands. Hey, Moses?

MOSES: Yes, that's a very great point.

SIR OLIVER: I'll answer for't I'll not be wanting in that. I'll ask him eight or ten per cent. on the loan, at least.

MOSES: If you ask him no more than that, you'll be discovered immediately.

SIR OLIVER: Hey! what, the plague! how much then?

MOSES: That depends upon the circumstances. If he appears not very anxious for the supply, you should require only forty or fifty per cent.; but if you find him in great distress, and want the moneys very bad, you may ask double.

SIR PETER: A good honest trade you're learning, Sir Oliver!

SIR OLIVER: Truly I think so—and not unprofitable.

MOSES: Then, you know, you haven't the moneys yourself, but are forced to borrow them for him of a friend.

SIR OLIVER: Oh! I borrow it of a friend, do I?

MOSES: And your friend is an unconscionable dog: but you can't help that.

SIR OLIVER: My friend an unconscionable dog, is he?

MOSES: Yes, and he himself has not the moneys by him, but is forced to sell stocks at a great loss.

SIR OLIVER: He is forced to sell stocks at a great loss, is he? Well, that's very kind of him.

SIR PETER: I'faith, Sir Oliver—Mr. Premium, I mean—you'll soon be master of the trade. But, Moses! would not you have him run out a little against the Annuity Bill?[21] That would be in character, I should think.

MOSES: Very much.

ROWLEY: And lament that a young man now must be at years of discretion before he is suffered to ruin himself?

MOSES: Ay, great pity!

SIR PETER: And abuse the public for allowing merit to an act whose only object is to snatch misfortune and imprudence from the rapacious grip of usury, and give the minor a chance of inheriting his estate without being undone by coming into possession.

SIR OLIVER: So, so— Moses shall give me further instructions as we go together.

SIR PETER: You will not have much time, for your nephew lives hard by.

SIR OLIVER: Oh, never fear! my tutor appears so able that though Charles lived in the next street, it must be my own fault if I am not a complete rogue before I turn the corner. (*Exit with* MOSES.)

SIR PETER: So, now, I think Sir Oliver will be convinced; you are partial, Rowley, and would have prepared Charles for the other plot.

ROWLEY: No, upon my word, Sir Peter.

SIR PETER: Well, go bring me this Snake, and I'll hear what he has to say presently. I see Maria and want to speak with her.—(*Exit* ROWLEY.) I should be glad to be convinced my suspicions of Lady Teazle and Charles were unjust. I have never yet opened my mind on this subject to my friend Joseph—I am determined I will do it—he will give me his opinion sincerely.

(*Enter* MARIA.)

So, child, has Mr. Surface returned with you?

MARIA: No, sir; he was engaged.

SIR PETER: Well, Maria, do you not reflect, the more you converse with that amiable young man, what return his partiality for you deserves?

MARIA: Indeed, Sir Peter, your frequent importunity on this subject distresses me extremely—you compel me to declare that I know no man who has ever paid me a particular attention whom I would not prefer to Mr. Surface.

SIR PETER: So—here's perverseness! No, no, Maria, 'tis Charles only whom you would prefer. 'Tis evident his vices and follies have won your heart.

MARIA: This is unkind, sir. You know I have obeyed you in neither seeing nor corresponding with him: I have heard enough to convince me that he is unworthy my regard. Yet I cannot think it culpable, if, while my understanding severely condemns his vices, my heart suggests some pity for his distresses.

SIR PETER: Well, well, pity him as much as you please; but give your heart and hand to a worthier object.

MARIA: Never to his brother!

SIR PETER: Go, perverse and obstinate! But take care, madam; you have never yet known what the authority of a guardian is. Don't compel me to inform you of it.

MARIA: I can only say, you shall not have just reason. 'Tis true, by my father's will, I am for a short period bound to regard you as his substitute; but must cease to think you so, when you would compel me to be miserable. (*Exit.*)

SIR PETER: Was ever man so crossed as I am, everything conspiring to fret me! I had not been involved in matrimony a fortnight, before her father, a hale and hearty man, died, on purpose, I believe, for the pleasure of plaguing me with the care of his daughter.—(LADY TEAZLE *sings without.*) But here comes my helpmate! She appears in great good humor. How happy I should be if I could tease her into loving me, though but a little! (*Enter* LADY TEAZLE.)

LADY TEAZLE: Lud! Sir Peter, I hope you haven't been quarrelling with Maria? It is not using me well to be ill-humored when I am not by.

SIR PETER: Ah, Lady Teazle, you might have the power to make me good humored at all times.

LADY TEAZLE: I am sure I wish I had; for I want you to be in a charming sweet temper at this moment. Do be good humored now, and let me have two hundred pounds, will you?

SIR PETER: Two hundred pounds; what, an't I to be in a good humor without paying for it! But speak to me thus, and i'faith there's nothing I could refuse you. You shall have it; but seal me a bond for the repayment.

LADY TEAZLE: Oh, no—there—my note of hand will do as well. (*Offering her hand.*)

SIR PETER: And you shall no longer reproach me with not giving you an independent settlement. I mean shortly to surprise you; but shall we always live thus, hey?

LADY TEAZLE: If you please; I'm sure I don't care how soon we leave off quarrelling, provided you'll own you were tired first.

SIR PETER: Well—then let our future contest be, who shall be most obliging.

LADY TEAZLE: I assure you, Sir Peter, good nature becomes you. You look now as you did before we were married, when you used to walk with me under the elms, and tell me stories of what a gallant you were in your youth, and chuck me under the chin, you would; and ask me if I thought I could love an old fellow who would deny me nothing—didn't you?

SIR PETER: Yes, yes, and you were as kind and attentive—

LADY TEAZLE: Ay, so I was, and would always take your part, when my acquaintance used to abuse you and turn you into ridicule.

SIR PETER: Indeed!

LADY TEAZLE: Ay, and when my cousin Sophy has called you a stiff, peevish old bachelor, and laughed at me for thinking of marrying one who might be my father, I have always defended you, and said, I didn't think you so ugly by any means, and that I dared say you'd make a very good sort of a husband.

SIR PETER: And you prophesied right; and we shall now be the happiest couple—

LADY TEAZLE: And never differ again?

SIR PETER: No, never—though at the same time, indeed, my dear Lady Teazle, you must watch your temper very seriously; for in all our little quarrels, my dear, if you recollect, my love, you always began first.

LADY TEAZLE: I beg your pardon, my dear Sir Peter: indeed, you always gave the provocation.

SIR PETER: Now, see, my angel! take care—contradicting isn't the way to keep friends.

LADY TEAZLE: Then, don't you begin it, my love!

SIR PETER: There, now! you—you are going on. You don't perceive, my life, that you are just doing the very thing which you know always makes me angry.

LADY TEAZLE: Nay, you know if you will be angry without any reason, my dear—

SIR PETER: There! now you want to quarrel again.

LADY TEAZLE: No, I'm sure I don't; but, if you will be so peevish—

SIR PETER: There now! who begins first?

LADY TEAZLE: Why, you, to be sure. I said nothing—but there's no bearing your temper.

SIR PETER: No, no, madam: the fault's in your own temper.

LADY TEAZLE: Ay, you are just what my cousin Sophy said you would be.

SIR PETER: Your cousin Sophy is a forward, impertinent gipsy.

LADY TEAZLE: You are a great bear, I am sure, to abuse my relations.

SIR PETER: Now may all the plagues of marriage be doubled on me if ever I try to be friends with you any more!

LADY TEAZLE: So much the better.

SIR PETER: No, no, madam. 'Tis evident you never cared a pin for me, and I was a madman to marry you—a pert, rural coquette, that had refused half the honest 'squires in the neighborhood!

LADY TEAZLE: And I am sure I was a fool to marry you—an old dangling bachelor, who was single at fifty, only because he never could meet with any one who would have him.

SIR PETER: Ay, ay, madam; but you were pleased enough to listen to me: you never had such an offer before.

LADY TEAZLE: No! didn't I refuse Sir Tivy Terrier, who everybody said would have been a better match? for his estate is just as good as yours, and he has broke his neck since we have been married.

SIR PETER: I have done with you, madam! You are an unfeeling, ungrateful —but there's an end of everything. I believe you capable of everything that is bad. Yes, madam, I now believe the reports relative to you and Charles, madam. Yes, madam, you and Charles are, not without grounds—

LADY TEAZLE: Take care, Sir Peter! you had better not insinuate any such thing! I'll not be suspected without cause, I promise you.

SIR PETER: Very well, madam! very well! a separate maintenance as soon as you please. Yes, madam, or a divorce! I'll make an example of myself for the benefit of all old bachelors. Let us separate, madam.

LADY TEAZLE: Agreed! agreed! And now, my dear Sir Peter, we are of a mind once more, we may be the happiest couple, and never differ again, you know: ha! ha! ha! Well, you are going to be in a passion, I see, and I shall only interrupt you—so, bye! bye! (*Exit.*)

SIR PETER: Plagues and tortures! can't I make her angry either! Oh, I am the most miserable fellow! But I'll not bear her presuming to keep her temper: no! she may break my heart, but she shan't keep her temper. (*Exit.*)

SCENE II [CHARLES SURFACE'S *house*]

(*Enter* TRIP, MOSES, *and* SIR OLIVER SURFACE.)

TRIP: Here, Master Moses! if you'll stay a moment; I'll try whether—what's the gentleman's name?

SIR OLIVER: (*aside to* MOSES) Mr. Moses, what is my name?

MOSES: Mr. Premium.

TRIP: Premium—very well.

(*Exit, taking snuff.*)

SIR OLIVER: To judge by the servants, one wouldn't believe the master was ruined. But what!—sure, this was my brother's house?

MOSES: Yes, sir; Mr. Charles bought it of Mr. Joseph, with the furniture, pictures, etcetera, just as the old gentleman left it. Sir Peter thought it a piece of extravagance in him.

SIR OLIVER: In my mind, the other's economy in selling it to him was more reprehensible by half.

(*Re-enter* TRIP.)

TRIP: My master says you must wait, gentlemen: he has company, and can't speak with you yet.

SIR OLIVER: If he knew who it was wanted to see him, perhaps he would not send such a message?

TRIP: Yes, yes, sir; he knows you are here—I did not forget little Premium: no, no, no.

SIR OLIVER: Very well; and I pray, sir, what may be your name?

TRIP: Trip, sir; my name is Trip, at your service.

SIR OLIVER: Well, then, Mr. Trip, you have a pleasant sort of place here, I guess?

TRIP: Why, yes—here are three or four of us to pass our time agreeably enough; but then our wages are sometimes a little in arrear—and not very great either—but fifty pounds a year, and find our own bags and bouquets.[22]

SIR OLIVER: (*aside*) Bags and bouquets! halters and bastinadoes!

TRIP: And *à propos*, Moses, have you been able to get me that little bill discounted?

SIR OLIVER: (*aside*) Wants to raise money, too!—mercy on me! Has his distresses too, I warrant, like a lord, and affects creditors and duns.

MOSES: 'Twas not to be done, indeed, Mr. Trip.

TRIP: Good lack, you surprise me! My friend Brush has indorsed it, and I thought when he put his name at the back of a bill 'twas the same as cash.

MOSES: No, 'twouldn't do.

TRIP: A small sum—but twenty pounds. Hark'ee, Moses, do you think you couldn't get it me by way of annuity?

SIR OLIVER: (*aside*) An annuity! ha! ha! a footman raise money by way of annuity. Well done, luxury, egad!

MOSES: Well, but you must insure your place.

TRIP: Oh, with all my heart! I'll insure my place and my life too, if you please.

SIR OLIVER: (*aside*) It's more than I would your neck.

MOSES: But is there nothing you could deposit?

TRIP: Why, nothing capital of my master's wardrobe has dropped lately; but I could give you a mortgage on some of his winter clothes, with equity of redemption before November—or you shall have the reversion of the French velvet, or a post-obit[23] on the blue and silver. These, I should think, Moses, with a few pair of point ruffles, as a collateral security—hey, my little fellow?

MOSES: Well, well.
(*Bell rings.*)

TRIP: Egad. I heard the bell! I believe, gentlemen, I can now introduce you. Don't forget the annuity, little Moses! This way, gentlemen, I'll insure my place, you know.

SIR OLIVER: (*aside*) If the man be a shadow of the master, this is the temple of dissipation indeed!
(*Exeunt.*)

SCENE III [*Another room*]

(CHARLES SURFACE, CARELESS, &c., &c., *at a table with wine,* &c.)

CHARLES SURFACE: 'Fore heaven, 'tis true! there's the great degeneracy of the age. Many of our acquaintance have taste, spirit, and politeness; but plague on't they won't drink.

CARELESS: It is so, indeed, Charles! they give in to all the substantial luxuries of the table, and abstain from nothing but wine and wit. Oh, certainly society suffers by it intolerably! for now, instead of the social spirit of raillery that used to mantle over a glass of bright Burgundy, their conversation is become just like the Spa-water they drink, which has all the pertness and flatulency of champagne, without its spirit or flavor.

1 GENT: But what are they to do who love play better than wine?

CARELESS: True! there's Sir Harry

diets himself for gaming, and is now under a hazard regimen.

CHARLES SURFACE: Then he'll have the worst of it. What! you wouldn't train a horse for the course by keeping him from corn? For my part, egad, I'm never so successful as when I am a little merry. Let me throw on a bottle of champagne and I never lose—at least I never feel my losses, which is exactly the same thing.

2 GENT: Ay, that I believe.

CHARLES SURFACE: And then, what man can pretend to be a believer in love who is an abjurer of wine? 'Tis the test by which the lover knows his own heart. Fill a dozen bumpers to a dozen beauties, and she that floats at the top is the maid that has bewitched you.

CARELESS: Now then, Charles, be honest, and give us your real favorite.

CHARLES SURFACE: Why, I have withheld her only in compassion to you. If I toast her, you must give her a round of her peers, which is impossible—on earth.

CARELESS: Oh, then we'll find some canonized vestals or heathen goddesses that will do, I warrant!

CHARLES SURFACE: Here then, bumpers, you rogues! bumpers! Maria! Maria—

SIR TOBY: Maria who?

CHARLES SURFACE: Oh, damn the surname!—'tis too formal to be registered in Love's calendar—but now, Sir Toby, beware, we must have beauty superlative.

CARELESS: Nay, never study, Sir Toby: we'll stand to the toast, though your mistress should want an eye, and you know you have a song will excuse you.

SIR TOBY: Egad, so I have! and I'll give him the song instead of the lady. (*Sings.*)

   Here's to the maiden of bashful fifteen;
   Here's to the widow of fifty;
   Here's to the flaunting extravagant quean,[24]

   And here's to the housewife that's thrifty.

Chorus: Let the toast pass,
    Drink to the lass,
I'll warrant she'll prove an excuse for a glass!

   Here's to the charmer whose dimples we prize;
   Now to the maid who has none, sir;
   Here's to the girl with a pair of blue eyes,
   And here's to the nymph with but one, sir.

Chorus: Let the toast pass,
    Drink to the lass,
I'll warrant she'll prove an excuse for a glass.

   Here's to the maid with a bosom of snow;
   Now to her that's as brown as a berry;
   Here's to the wife with a face full of woe,
   And now to the damsel that's merry.

Chorus: Let the toast pass,
    Drink to the lass,
I'll warrant she'll prove an excuse for a glass.

   For let 'em be clumsy, or let 'em be slim,
   Young or ancient, I care not a feather;
   So fill a pint bumper quite up to the brim,
   And let us e'en toast them together.

Chorus: Let the toast pass,
    Drink to the lass,
I'll warrant she'll prove an excuse for a glass.

ALL: Bravo! Bravo!

(*Enter* TRIP, *and whispers to* CHARLES SURFACE.)

CHARLES SURFACE: Gentlemen, you must excuse me a little. Careless, take the chair, will you?

CARELESS: Nay, prithee, Charles, what now? This is one of your peerless beauties, I suppose, has dropped in by chance?

CHARLES SURFACE: No, faith! To tell you the truth, 'tis a Jew and a broker, who are come by appointment.

CARELESS: Oh, damn it! let's have the Jew in.

1 GENT: Ay, and the broker too, by all means.

2 GENT: Yes, yes, the Jew and the broker!

CHARLES SURFACE: Egad, with all my heart!—Trip, bid the gentlemen walk in. (*Exit* TRIP.) Though there's one of them a stranger I can tell you.

CARELESS: Charles, let us give them some generous Burgundy and perhaps they'll grow conscientious.

CHARLES SURFACE: Oh, hang 'em, no! wine does but draw forth a man's natural qualities; and to make them drink would only be to whet their knavery.

(*Enter* TRIP, *with* SIR OLIVER SURFACE *and* MOSES.)

CHARLES SURFACE: So, honest Moses; walk in, pray, Mr. Premium—that's the gentleman's name, isn't it, Moses?

MOSES: Yes, sir.

CHARLES SURFACE: Set chairs, Trip.—Sit down, Mr. Premium. Glasses, Trip.—Sit down, Moses.—Come, Mr. Premium, I'll give you a sentiment; here's *Success to usury!*—Moses, fill the gentleman a bumper.

MOSES: Success to usury!
(*Drinks.*)

CARELESS: Right, Moses—usury is prudence and industry, and deserves to succeed.

SIR OLIVER: Then here's—All the success it deserves!
(*Drinks.*)

CARELESS: No, no, that won't do! Mr. Premium, you have demurred at the toast, and must drink it in a pint bumper.

1 GENT: A pint bumper, at least!

MOSES: Oh, pray, sir, consider—Mr. Premium's a gentleman.

CARELESS: And therefore loves good wine.

2 GENT: Give Moses a quart glass—this is mutiny, and a high contempt for the chair.

CARELESS: Here, now for't! I'll see justice done, to the last drop of my bottle.

SIR OLIVER: Nay, pray, gentlemen—I did not expect this usage.

CHARLES SURFACE: No, hang it, you shan't; Mr. Premium's a stranger.

SIR OLIVER: (*aside*) Odd! I wish I was well out of their company.

CARELESS: Plague on 'em then! if they won't drink, we'll not sit down with them. Come, Toby, the dice are in the next room.—Charles, you'll join us when you have finished your business with the gentlemen?

CHARLES SURFACE: I will! I will!—(*Exeunt* GENTLEMEN.) Careless!

CARELESS: (*Returning*) Well?

CHARLES SURFACE: Perhaps I may want you.

CARELESS: Oh, you know I am always ready: word, note, or bond, 'tis all the same to me.
(*Exit.*)

MOSES: Sir, this is Mr. Premium, a gentleman of the strictest honor and secrecy; and always performs what he undertakes. Mr. Premium, this is—

CHARLES SURFACE: Psha! have done. Sir, my friend Moses is a very honest fellow, but a little slow at expression: he'll be an hour giving us our titles. Mr. Premium, the plain state of the matter is this: I am an extravagant young fellow who wants to borrow money; you I take to be a prudent old fellow, who has got money to lend. I am blockhead enough to give fifty per cent sooner than not have it! and you, I presume, are rogue enough to take a hundred if you can get it. Now, sir, you see we are acquainted at once, and may proceed to business without further ceremony.

SIR OLIVER: Exceeding frank, upon my word. I see, sir, you are not a man of many compliments.

CHARLES SURFACE: Oh, no, sir! plain dealing in business I always think best.

SIR OLIVER: Sir, I like you the better for it. However, you are mistaken in one thing. I have no money to lend, but I believe I could procure some of a friend; but then he's an unconscionable dog. Isn't he, Moses? And must sell stock to accommodate you. Mustn't he, Moses?

MOSES: Yes, indeed! You know I always speak the truth, and scorn to tell a lie!

CHARLES SURFACE: Right. People that speak truth generally do. But these are trifles, Mr. Premium. What! I know money isn't to be bought without paying for't!

SIR OLIVER: Well, but what security could you give? You have no land, I suppose?

CHARLES SURFACE: Not a mole-hill, nor a twig, but what's in the bough-pots[25] out of the window!

SIR OLIVER: Nor any stock, I presume?

CHARLES SURFACE: Nothing but live stock—and that's only a few pointers and ponies. But pray, Mr. Premium, are you acquainted at all with any of my connections?

SIR OLIVER: Why, to say the truth, I am.

CHARLES SURFACE: Then you must know that I have a devilish rich uncle in the East Indies, Sir Oliver Surface, from whom I have the greatest expectations?

SIR OLIVER: That you have a wealthy uncle, I have heard; but how your expectations will turn out is more, I believe, than you can tell.

CHARLES SURFACE: Oh, no!—there can be no doubt. They tell me I'm a prodigious favorite, and that he talks of leaving me everything.

SIR OLIVER: Indeed! this is the first I've heard of it.

CHARLES SURFACE: Yes, yes, 'tis just so. Moses knows 'tis true; don't you, Moses?

MOSES: Oh, yes! I'll swear to't.

SIR OLIVER: (*aside*) Egad, they'll persuade me presently I'm at Bengal.

CHARLES SURFACE: Now I propose, Mr. Premium, if it's agreeable to you, a post-obit on Sir Oliver's life: though at the same time the old fellow has been so liberal with me that I give you my word I should be very sorry to hear that anything had happened to him.

SIR OLIVER: Not more than I should, I assure you. But the bond you mention happens to be just the worst security you could offer me—for I might live to be a hundred and never see the principal.

CHARLES SURFACE: Oh, yes, you would! the moment Sir Oliver dies, you know, you would come on me for the money.

SIR OLIVER: Then I believe I should be the most unwelcome dun you ever had in your life.

CHARLES SURFACE: What! I suppose you're afraid that Sir Oliver is too good a life?

SIR OLIVER: No, indeed I am not; though I have heard he is as hale and healthy as any man of his years in Christendom.

CHARLES SURFACE: There again, now, you are misinformed. No, no, the climate has hurt him considerably, poor uncle Oliver. Yes, yes, he breaks apace, I'm told —and is so much altered lately that his nearest relations would not know him.

SIR OLIVER: No! Ha! ha! ha! so much altered lately that his nearest relation would not know him! Ha! ha! ha! egad —ha! ha! ha!

CHARLES SURFACE: Ha! ha!—you're glad to hear that, little Premium.

SIR OLIVER: No, no, I'm not.

CHARLES SURFACE: Yes, yes, you are—ha! ha! ha!—you know that mends your chance.

SIR OLIVER: But I'm told Sir Oliver is coming over; nay, some say he has actually arrived.

CHARLES SURFACE: Psha! sure I must know better than you whether he's come or not. No, no, rely on't he's at this moment at Calcutta. Isn't he, Moses?

MOSES: Oh, yes, certainly.

SIR OLIVER: Very true, as you say, you must know better than I, though I have it from a pretty good authority. Haven't I, Moses?

MOSES: Yes, most undoubted!

SIR OLIVER: But, sir, as I understand you want a few hundreds immediately, is there nothing you could dispose of?

CHARLES SURFACE: How do you mean?

SIR OLIVER: For instance, now, I have heard that your father left behind him a great quantity of massy old plate.

CHARLES SURFACE: O lud, that's gone long ago. Moses can tell you how better than I can.

SIR OLIVER: (*aside*) Good lack! all the family race-cups and corporation-bowls![26]—(*Aloud.*) Then it was also supposed that his library was one of the most valuable and compact.

CHARLES SURFACE: Yes, yes, so it was—vastly too much for a private gentleman. For my part, I was always of a communicative disposition, so I thought it a shame to keep so much knowledge to myself.

SIR OLIVER: (*aside*) Mercy upon me! learning that had run in the family like an heirloom!—(*Aloud.*) Pray, what has become of the books?

CHARLES SURFACE: You must inquire of the auctioneer, Master Premium, for I don't believe even Moses can direct you.

MOSES: I know nothing of books.

SIR OLIVER: So, so, nothing of the family property left, I suppose?

CHARLES SURFACE: Not much, indeed; unless you have a mind to the family pictures. I have got a room full of ancestors above; and if you have a taste for old paintings, egad, you shall have 'em a bargain!

SIR OLIVER: Hey! what the devil! sure, you wouldn't sell your forefathers, would you?

CHARLES SURFACE: Every man of them, to the best bidder.

SIR OLIVER: What! your great-uncles and aunts?

CHARLES SURFACE: Ay, and my great-grandfathers and grandmothers too.

SIR OLIVER: (*aside*) Now I give him up!—(*Aloud.*) What the plague, have you no bowels for your own kindred? Odd's life! do you take me for Shylock in the play, that you would raise money of me on your own flesh and blood?

CHARLES SURFACE: Nay, my little broker, don't be angry. What need you care, if you have your money's worth?

SIR OLIVER: Well, I'll be the purchaser. I think I can dispose of the family canvas.—(*Aside.*) Oh, I'll never forgive him this! never!

(*Enter* CARELESS.)

CARELESS: Come, Charles, what keeps you?

CHARLES SURFACE: I can't come yet. I'faith, we are going to have a sale above stairs; here's little Premium will buy all my ancestors!

CARELESS: Oh, burn your ancestors!

CHARLES SURFACE: No, he may do that afterwards, if he pleases. Stay, Careless, we want you: egad, you shall be auctioneer—so come along with us.

CARELESS: Oh, have with you, if that's the case. I can handle a hammer as well as a dice box!

SIR OLIVER: (*aside*) Oh, the profligates!

CHARLES SURFACE: Come, Moses, you shall be appraiser, if we want one. Gad's life, little Premium, you don't seem to like the business?

SIR OLIVER: Oh, yes, I do, vastly! Ha! ha! ha! yes, yes, I think it a rare joke to sell one's family by auction—ha! ha!— (*Aside.*) Oh, the prodigal!

CHARLES SURFACE: To be sure! when a man wants money, where the plague should he get assistance if he can't make free with his own relations?
(*Exeunt.*)

ACT IV   SCENE I   [*Picture Room at* CHARLES'S]

(*Enter* CHARLES SURFACE, SIR OLIVER SURFACE, MOSES, *and* CARELESS.)

CHARLES SURFACE: Walk in, gentlemen, pray walk in;—here they are, the family of the Surfaces up to the Conquest.

SIR OLIVER: And, in my opinion, a goodly collection.

CHARLES SURFACE: Ay, ay, these are done in the true spirit of portrait-painting; no *volontière grace* or expression. Not like the works of your modern Raphaels, who give you the strongest resemblance, yet contrive to make your portrait independent of you; so that you may sink the original and not hurt the picture. No, no; the merit of these is the inveterate likeness—all stiff and awkward as the originals, and like nothing in human nature besides.

SIR OLIVER: Ah! we shall never see such figures of men again.

CHARLES SURFACE: I hope not. Well, you see, Master Premium, what a domestic character I am; here I sit of an evening surrounded by my family. But come, get to your pulpit, Mr. Auctioneer; here's an old gouty chair of my grandfather's will answer the purpose.

CARELESS: Ay, ay, this will do. But, Charles, I haven't a hammer; and what's an auctioneer without his hammer?

CHARLES SURFACE: Egad, that's true. What parchment have we here? Oh, our genealogy in full. Here, Careless, you shall have no common bit of mahogany, here's the family tree for you, you rogue! This shall be your hammer, and now you may knock down my ancestors with their own pedigree.

SIR OLIVER: (*aside*) What an unnatural rogue!—an *ex post facto* parricide!

CARELESS: Yes, yes, here's a list of your generation indeed;—faith, Charles, this is the most convenient thing you could have found for the business, for 'twill not only serve as a hammer, but a catalogue into the bargain. Come, begin—A-going, a-going, a-going!

CHARLES SURFACE: Bravo, Careless! Well, here's my great uncle, Sir Richard Raveline, a marvellous good general in his day, I assure you. He served in all the Duke of Marlborough's wars, and got that cut over his eye at the battle of Malplaquet.[27] What say you, Mr. Premium? look at him—there's a hero! not cut out of his feathers, as your modern clipped captains are, but enveloped in wig and regimentals as a general should be. What do you bid?

MOSES: Mr. Premium would have you speak.

CHARLES SURFACE: Why, then, he shall have him for ten pounds, and I'm sure that's not dear for a staff-officer.

SIR OLIVER: (*aside*) Heaven deliver me! his famous uncle Richard for ten pounds!—(*Aloud.*) Very well, sir, I take him at that.

CHARLES SURFACE: Careless, knock down my uncle Richard.—Here, now, is a maiden sister of his, my great-aunt Deborah, done by Kneller,[28] in his best manner, and a very formidable likeness. There she is, you see, a shepherdess feeding her flock. You shall have her for five pounds ten—the sheep are worth the money.

SIR OLIVER: (*aside*) Ah! poor Deborah! a woman who set such a value on herself!—(*Aloud.*) Five pounds ten—she's mine.

CHARLES SURFACE: Knock down my aunt Deborah! Here, now, are two that were a sort of cousins of theirs.—You see, Moses, these pictures were done some time ago, when beaux wore wigs, and the ladies their own hair.

SIR OLIVER: Yes, truly, head-dresses appear to have been a little lower in those days.

CHARLES SURFACE: Well, take that couple for the same.

MOSES: 'Tis a good bargain.

CHARLES SURFACE: Careless!—This, now, is a grandfather of my mother's, a learned judge, well known on the western circuit.—What do you rate him at, Moses?

MOSES: Four guineas.

CHARLES SURFACE: Four guineas! Gad's life, you don't bid me the price of his wig.—Mr. Premium, you have more respect for the wool-sack,[29] do let us knock his Lordship down at fifteen.

SIR OLIVER: By all means.

CARELESS: Gone!

CHARLES SURFACE: And there are two brothers of his, William and Walter Blunt, Esquires, both members of Parliament, and noted speakers; and, what's very extraordinary, I believe, this is the first time they were ever bought or sold.

SIR OLIVER: That is very extraordinary, indeed! I'll take them at your own price, for the honor of Parliament.

CARELESS: Well said, little Premium! I'll knock them down at forty.

CHARLES SURFACE: Here's a jolly fellow—I don't know what relation, but he was mayor of Manchester: take him at eight pounds.

SIR OLIVER: No, no; six will do for the mayor.

CHARLES SURFACE: Come, make it guineas, and I'll throw you the two aldermen there into the bargain.

SIR OLIVER: They're mine.

CHARLES SURFACE: Careless, knock down the mayor and aldermen. But, plague on't! we shall be all day retailing in this manner; do let us deal wholesale: what say you, little Premium? Give me three hundred pounds for the rest of the family in the lump.

CARELESS: Ay ay, that will be the best way.

SIR OLIVER: Well, well, anything to accommodate you; they are mine. But there is one portrait which you have always passed over.

CARELESS: What, that ill-looking little fellow over the settee?

SIR OLIVER: Yes, sir, I mean that; though I don't think him so ill-looking a little fellow, by any means.

CHARLES SURFACE: What, that? Oh; that's my uncle Oliver! 'Twas done before he went to India.

CARELESS: Your uncle Oliver! Gad, then you'll never be friends, Charles. That, now, to me, is as stern a looking rogue as ever I saw; an unforgiving eye, and a damned disinheriting countenance! an inveterate knave, depend on't. Don't you think so, little Premium?

SIR OLIVER: Upon my soul, sir, I do not; I think it is as honest a looking face as any in the room, dead or alive. But I suppose uncle Oliver goes with the rest of the lumber?

CHARLES SURFACE: No, hang it! I'll not part with poor Noll. The old fellow has been very good to me, and, egad, I'll keep his picture while I've a room to put it in.

SIR OLIVER: (*aside*) The rogue's my nephew after all!—(*Aloud.*) But, sir, I have somehow taken a fancy to that picture.

CHARLES SURFACE: I'm sorry for't, for you certainly will not have it. Oons, haven't you got enough of them?

SIR OLIVER: (*aside*) I forgive him everything!—(*Aloud.*) But, sir, when I take a whim in my head, I don't value money. I'll give you as much for that as for all the rest.

CHARLES SURFACE: Don't tease me, master broker; I tell you I'll not part with it, and there's an end of it.

SIR OLIVER: (*aside*) How like his father the dog is!—(*Aloud.*) Well, well, I have done.—(*Aside.*) I did not perceive it before, but I think I never saw such a striking resemblance.—(*Aloud.*) Here is a draught for your sum.

CHARLES SURFACE: Why, 'tis for eight hundred pounds!

SIR OLIVER: You will not let Sir Oliver go?

CHARLES SURFACE: Zounds! no! I tell you, once more.

SIR OLIVER: Then never mind the difference, we'll balance that another time. But give me your hand on the bargain; you are an honest fellow, Charles—I beg pardon, sir, for being so free.—Come, Moses.

CHARLES SURFACE: Egad, this is a whimsical old fellow!—But hark'ee, Premium, you'll prepare lodgings for these gentlemen.

SIR OLIVER: Yes, yes, I'll send for them in a day or two.

CHARLES SURFACE: But hold; do now send a genteel conveyance for them, for, I assure you, they were most of them used to ride in their own carriages.

SIR OLIVER: I will, I will—for all but Oliver.

CHARLES SURFACE: Ay, all but the little nabob.

SIR OLIVER: You're fixed on that?

CHARLES SURFACE: Peremptorily.

SIR OLIVER: (*aside*) A dear extravagant rogue!—(*Aloud.*) Good day!—Come, Moses.—(*Aside.*) Let me hear now who dares call him profligate!

(*Exeunt* SIR OLIVER *and* MOSES.)

CARELESS: Why, this is the oddest genius of the sort I ever met with!

CHARLES SURFACE: Egad, he's the prince of brokers, I think. I wonder how the devil Moses got acquainted with so honest a fellow.—Ha! here's Rowley.—Do, Careless, say I'll join the company in a few moments.

CARELESS: I will—but don't let that old blockhead persuade you to squander any of that money on old musty debts, or any such nonsense; for tradesmen, Charles, are the most exorbitant fellows.

CHARLES SURFACE: Very true, and paying them is only encouraging them.

CARELESS: Nothing else.

CHARLES SURFACE: Ay, ay, never fear.—(*Exit* CARELESS.) So! this was an odd old fellow, indeed. Let me see, two-thirds of this is mine by right: five hundred and thirty-odd pounds. 'Fore heaven! I find one's ancestors are more valuable relations than I took them for!—Ladies and gentlemen, your most obedient and very grateful servant.

(*Bows to the pictures.*)
(*Enter* ROWLEY.)

Ha! old Rowley! egad, you are just come in time to take leave of your old acquaintance.

ROWLEY: Yes, I heard they were a-going. But I wonder you can have such spirits under so many distresses.

CHARLES SURFACE: Why, there's the point! my distresses are so many that I can't afford to part with my spirits; but I shall be rich and splenetic, all in good time. However, I suppose you are surprised that I am not more sorrowful at parting with so many near relations; to be sure, 'tis very affecting; but you see they never move a muscle, so why should I?

ROWLEY: There's no making you serious a moment.

CHARLES SURFACE: Yes, faith, I am so now. Here, my honest Rowley, here, get me this changed directly and take a hundred pounds of it immediately to old Stanley.

ROWLEY: A hundred pounds! Consider only—

CHARLES SURFACE: Gad's life, don't talk about it! poor Stanley's wants are pressing, and, if you don't make haste, we shall have some one call that has a better right to the money.

ROWLEY: Ah! there's the point! I never will cease dunning you with the old proverb—

CHARLES SURFACE: "Be just before you're generous."—Why, so I would if I could; but Justice is an old lame, hobbling beldame, and I can't get her to keep pace with Generosity, for the soul of me.

ROWLEY: Yet, Charles, believe me, one hour's reflection—

CHARLES SURFACE: Ay, ay, it's very true; but, hark'ee, Rowley, while I have, by Heaven I'll give; so, damn your economy! and now for hazard.
(*Exeunt.*)

SCENE II [*The parlor*]

(*Enter* SIR OLIVER SURFACE *and* MOSES.)

MOSES: Well, sir, I think, as Sir Peter said, you have seen Mr. Charles in high glory; 'tis great pity he's so extravagant.

SIR OLIVER: True, but he would not sell my picture.

MOSES: And loves wine and women so much.

SIR OLIVER: But he would not sell my picture.

MOSES: And games so deep.

SIR OLIVER: But he would not sell my picture. Oh, here's Rowley.

(*Enter* ROWLEY.)

ROWLEY: So, Sir Oliver, I find you have made a purchase—

SIR OLIVER: Yes, yes, our young rake has parted with his ancestors like old tapestry.

ROWLEY: And here has he commissioned me to re-deliver you part of the purchase-money—I mean, though, in your necessitous character of old Stanley.

MOSES: Ah! there is the pity of all: he is so damned charitable.

ROWLEY: And I left a hosier and two tailors in the hall, who, I'm sure, won't be paid, and this hundred would satisfy them.

SIR OLIVER: Well, well, I'll pay his debts, and his benevolence too. But now I am no more a broker, and you shall introduce me to the elder brother as old Stanley.

ROWLEY: Not yet awhile; Sir Peter, I know, means to call there about this time.

(*Enter* TRIP.)

TRIP: Oh, gentlemen, I beg pardon for not showing you out; this way—Moses, a word.

(*Exit with* MOSES.)

SIR OLIVER: There's a fellow for you! Would you believe it, that puppy intercepted the Jew on our coming, and wanted to raise money before he got to his master!

ROWLEY: Indeed.

SIR OLIVER: Yes, they are now planning an annuity business. Ah, Master Rowley, in my days servants were content with the follies of their masters when they were worn a little threadbare; but now they have their vices, like their birthday clothes,[30] with the gloss on.

(*Exeunt.*)

SCENE III [*A library in* JOSEPH SURFACE's *house*]

(*Enter* JOSEPH SURFACE *and* SERVANT.)

JOSEPH SURFACE: No letter from Lady Teazle?

SERVANT: No, sir.

JOSEPH SURFACE: (*Aside.*) I am surprised she has not sent, if she is prevented from coming. Sir Peter certainly does not suspect me. Yet I wish I may not lose the heiress through the scrape I have drawn myself into with the wife. However, Charles's imprudence and bad character are great points in my favour.

(*Knocking.*)

SERVANT: Sir, I believe that must be Lady Teazle.

JOSEPH SURFACE: Hold! See whether it is or not before you go to the door. I have a particular message for you if it should be my brother.

SERVANT: 'Tis her ladyship, sir; she always leaves the chair at the milliner's in the next street.

JOSEPH SURFACE: Stay, stay! Draw that screen before the window—that will do;—my opposite neighbour is a maiden lady of so curious a temper.—(SERVANT *draws the screen, and exit.*) I have a difficult hand to play in this affair. Lady Teazle has lately suspected my views on Maria; but she must by no means be let into that secret—at least, till I have her more in my power.

(*Enter* LADY TEAZLE.)

LADY TEAZLE: What, sentiment in soliloquy now? Have you been very impatient? O lud! don't pretend to look grave. I vow I couldn't come before.

JOSEPH SURFACE: O madam, punctuality is a species of constancy very unfashionable in a lady of quality.

LADY TEAZLE: Upon my word, you ought to pity me. Do you know Sir Peter is grown so ill-natured to me of late, and so jealous of Charles too—that's the best of the story, isn't it?

JOSEPH SURFACE: (*aside*) I am glad my scandalous friends keep that up.

LADY TEAZLE: I am sure I wish he would let Maria marry him, and then perhaps he would be convinced; don't you, Mr. Surface?

JOSEPH SURFACE: (*aside*) Indeed I do not.—(*Aloud.*) Oh, certainly I do! for then my dear Lady Teazle would also be convinced how wrong her suspicions were of my having any design on the silly girl.

LADY TEAZLE: Well, well, I'm inclined to believe you. But isn't it provoking to have the most ill-natured things said at one? And there's my friend Lady Sneerwell has circulated I don't know how many scandalous tales of me, and all without any foundation, too; that's what vexes me.

JOSEPH SURFACE: Ay, madam, to be sure, that is the provoking circumstance—without foundation; yes, yes, there's the mortification, indeed; for, when a scandalous story is believed against one, there certainly is no comfort like the consciousness of having deserved it.

LADY TEAZLE: No, to be sure, then I'd forgive their malice; but to attack me, who am really so innocent, and who never say an ill-natured thing of anybody—that is, of any friend; and then Sir Peter, too, to have him so peevish, and so suspicious, when I know the integrity of my own heart—indeed 'tis monstrous!

JOSEPH SURFACE: But, my dear Lady Teazle, 'tis your own fault if you suffer it. When a husband entertains a groundless suspicion of his wife, and withdraws his confidence from her, the original compact is broken, and she owes it to the honor of her sex to endeavor to outwit him.

LADY TEAZLE: Indeed! So that, if he suspects me without cause, it follows, that the best way of curing his jealousy is to give him reason for't?

JOSEPH SURFACE: Undoubtedly—for your husband should never be deceived in you: and in that case it becomes you to be frail in compliment to his discernment.

LADY TEAZLE: To be sure, what you say is very reasonable, and when the consciousness of my innocence—

JOSEPH SURFACE: Ah, my dear madam, there is the great mistake; 'tis this very conscious innocence that is of the greatest prejudice to you. What is it makes you negligent of forms, and careless of the world's opinion? why, the consciousness of your own innocence. What makes you thoughtless in your conduct and apt to run into a thousand little imprudences? why, the consciousness of your own innocence. What makes you impatient of Sir Peter's temper, and outrageous at his suspicions? why, the consciousness of your innocence.

LADY TEAZLE: 'Tis very true!

JOSEPH SURFACE: Now, my dear Lady Teazle, if you would but once make a trifling *faux pas*, you can't conceive how cautious you would grow, and how ready to humor and agree with your husband.

LADY TEAZLE: Do you think so?

JOSEPH SURFACE: Oh, I'm sure on't! and then you would find all scandal would cease at once, for—in short, your character at present is like a person in a plethora, absolutely dying from too much health.

LADY TEAZLE: So, so; then I perceive your prescription is that I must sin in my own defence, and part with my virtue to preserve my reputation?

JOSEPH SURFACE: Exactly so, upon my credit, ma'am.

LADY TEAZLE: Well, certainly this is the oddest doctrine, and the newest receipt for avoiding calumny!

JOSEPH SURFACE: An infallible one, believe me. Prudence, like experience, must be paid for.

LADY TEAZLE: Why, if my understanding were once convinced—

JOSEPH SURFACE: Oh, certainly, madam, your understanding should be convinced. Yes, yes—Heaven forbid I should persuade you to do anything you thought wrong. No, no, I have too much honor to desire it.

LADY TEAZLE: Don't you think we may as well leave honor out of the argument? (*Rises.*)

JOSEPH SURFACE: Ah, the ill effects of your country education, I see, still remain with you.

LADY TEAZLE: I doubt they do, indeed; and I will fairly own to you, that if I could be persuaded to do wrong, it would be by Sir Peter's ill usage sooner than your honorable logic, after all.

JOSEPH SURFACE: Then, by this hand, which he is unworthy of—
(*Taking her hand.*)
(*Enter* SERVANT.)
'Sdeath, you blockhead—what do you want?

SERVANT: I beg your pardon, sir, but I thought you would not choose Sir Peter to come up without announcing him.

JOSEPH SURFACE: Sir Peter!—Oons—the devil!

LADY TEAZLE: Sir Peter! O lud! I'm ruined! I'm ruined!

SERVANT: Sir, 'twasn't I let him in.

LADY TEAZLE: Oh! I'm quite undone! What will become of me now, Mr. Logic? —Oh! mercy, he's on the stairs—I'll get behind here—and if ever I'm so imprudent again—
(*Goes behind the screen.*)

JOSEPH SURFACE: Give me that book. (*Sits down.* SERVANT *pretends to adjust his chair.*)
(*Enter* SIR PETER TEAZLE.)

SIR PETER: Ay, ever improving himself. Mr. Surface, Mr. Surface—

JOSEPH SURFACE: Oh, my dear Sir

Peter, I beg your pardon. (*Gaping, throws away the book.*) I have been dozing over a stupid book. Well, I am much obliged to you for this call. You haven't been here, I believe, since I fitted up this room. Books, you know, are the only things I am a coxcomb in.

SIR PETER: 'Tis very neat indeed. Well, well, that's proper; and you can make even your screen a source of knowledge —hung, I perceive, with maps.

JOSEPH SURFACE: Oh, yes, I find great use in that screen.

SIR PETER: I dare say you must, certainly, when you want to find anything in a hurry.

JOSEPH SURFACE: (*aside*) Ay, or to hide anything in a hurry either.

SIR PETER: Well, I have a little private business—

JOSEPH SURFACE: (*to* SERVANT) You need not stay.

SERVANT: No, sir.
(*Exit.*)

JOSEPH SURFACE: Here's a chair, Sir Peter—I beg—

SIR PETER: Well, now we are alone, there is a subject, my dear friend, on which I wish to unburden my mind to you —a point of the greatest moment to my peace; in short, my good friend, Lady Teazle's conduct of late has made me very unhappy.

JOSEPH SURFACE: Indeed! I am very sorry to hear it.

SIR PETER: Yes, 'tis but too plain she has not the least regard for me; but, what's worse, I have pretty good authority to suppose she has formed an attachment to another.

JOSEPH SURFACE: Indeed! you astonish me!

SIR PETER: Yes! and, between ourselves, I think I've discovered the person.

JOSEPH SURFACE: How! you alarm me exceedingly.

SIR PETER: Ay, my dear friend, I knew you would sympathize with me!

JOSEPH SURFACE: Yes, believe me, Sir Peter, such a discovery would hurt me just as much as it would you.

SIR PETER: I am convinced of it. Ah! it is a happiness to have a friend whom we can trust even with one's family secrets. But have you no guess who I mean?

JOSEPH SURFACE: I haven't the most distant idea. It can't be Sir Benjamin Backbite!

SIR PETER: Oh, no! what say you to Charles?

JOSEPH SURFACE: My brother! impossible!

SIR PETER: Oh, my dear friend, the goodness of your own heart misleads you. You judge of others by yourself.

JOSEPH SURFACE: Certainly, Sir Peter, the heart that is conscious of its own integrity is ever slow to credit another's treachery.

SIR PETER: True; but your brother has no sentiment—you never hear him talk so.

JOSEPH SURFACE: Yet I can't but think Lady Teazle herself has too much principle.

SIR PETER: Ay; but what is principle against the flattery of a handsome, lively young fellow?

JOSEPH SURFACE: That's very true.

SIR PETER: And then, you know, the difference of our ages makes it very improbable that she should have any great affection for me; and if she were to be frail, and I were to make it public, why the town would only laugh at me, the foolish old bachelor who had married a girl.

JOSEPH SURFACE: That's true, to be sure—they would laugh.

SIR PETER: Laugh! ay, and make ballads, and paragraphs, and the devil knows what of me.

JOSEPH SURFACE: No, you must never make it public.

SIR PETER: But then again—that the nephew of my old friend, Sir Oliver, should be the person to attempt such a wrong, hurts me more nearly.

JOSEPH SURFACE: Ay, there's the point. When ingratitude barbs the dart of injury, the wound has double danger in it.

SIR PETER: Ay—I that was, in a manner, left his guardian, in whose house he had been so often entertained, who never in my life denied him—my advice!

JOSEPH SURFACE: Oh, 'tis not to be credited! There may be a man capable of such baseness, to be sure; but, for my part, till you can give me positive proofs, I cannot but doubt it. However, if it should be proved on him, he is no longer a brother of mine—I disclaim kindred with him: for the man who can break the laws of hospitality and tempt the wife of his friend, deserves to be branded as the pest of society.

SIR PETER: What a difference there is between you! What noble sentiments!

JOSEPH SURFACE: Yet I cannot suspect Lady Teazle's honor.

SIR PETER: I am sure I wish to think well of her, and to remove all ground of quarrel between us. She has lately reproached me more than once with having made no settlement on her; and, in our last quarrel, she almost hinted that she should not break her heart if I was dead. Now, as we seem to differ in our ideas of expense, I have resolved she shall have her own way and be her own mistress in that respect for the future; and, if I were to die, she will find I have not been inattentive to her interest while living. Here, my friend, are the drafts of two deeds, which I wish to have your opinion on. By one, she will enjoy eight hundred a year independent while I live; and, by the other, the bulk of my fortune at my death.

JOSEPH SURFACE: This conduct, Sir Peter, is indeed truly generous.—(*Aside*.) I wish it may not corrupt my pupil.

SIR PETER: Yes, I am determined she shall have no cause to complain, though I would not have her acquainted with the latter instance of my affection yet awhile.

JOSEPH SURFACE: (*aside*) Nor I, if I could help it.

SIR PETER: And now, my dear friend, if you please, we will talk over the situation of your hopes with Maria.

JOSEPH SURFACE: (*softly*) Oh, no, Sir Peter; another time, if you please.

SIR PETER: I am sensibly chagrined at the little progress you seem to make in her affections.

JOSEPH SURFACE: (*softly*) I beg you will not mention it. What are my disappointments when your happiness is in debate!—(*Aside*.) 'Sdeath, I shall be ruined every way!

SIR PETER: And though you are averse to my acquainting Lady Teazle with your passion, I'm sure she's not your enemy in the affair.

JOSEPH SURFACE: Pray, Sir Peter, now oblige me. I am really too much affected by the subject we have been speaking of to bestow a thought on my own concerns. The man who is entrusted with his friend's distresses can never—

(*Enter* SERVANT.)

Well, sir?

SERVANT: Your brother, sir, is speaking to a gentleman in the street, and says he knows you are within.

JOSEPH SURFACE: 'Sdeath, blockhead, I'm not within—I'm out for the day.

SIR PETER: Stay—hold—a thought has struck me: you shall be at home.

JOSEPH SURFACE: Well, well, let him up.—(*Exit* SERVANT.) (*Aside*.) He'll interrupt Sir Peter, however.

SIR PETER: Now, my good friend, oblige me, I entreat you. Before Charles comes, let me conceal myself somewhere, then do you tax him on the point we have been talking, and his answer may satisfy me at once.

JOSEPH SURFACE: Oh, fie, Sir Peter!

would you have me join in so mean a trick?—to trepan my bother too?

SIR PETER: Nay, you tell me you are sure he is innocent; if so, you do him the greatest service by giving him an opportunity to clear himself, and you will set my heart at rest. Come, you shall not refuse me: here, behind the screen will be—Hey! what the devil! there seems to be one listener here already—I'll swear I saw a petticoat!

JOSEPH SURFACE: Ha! ha! ha! Well, this is ridiculous enough. I'll tell you, Sir Peter, though I hold a man of intrigue to be a most despicable character, yet you know, it does not follow that one is to be an absolute Joseph either! Hark'ee, 'tis a little French milliner, a silly rogue that plagues me; and having some character to lose, on your coming, sir, she ran behind the screen.

SIR PETER: Ah, you rogue— But, egad, she has overheard all I have been saying of my wife.

JOSEPH SURFACE: Oh, 'twill never go any farther, you may depend upon it!

SIR PETER: No! then, faith, let her hear it out.—Here's a closet will do as well.

JOSEPH SURFACE: Well, go in there.

SIR PETER: Sly rogue! sly rogue!

(*Goes into the closet.*)

JOSEPH SURFACE: A narrow escape, indeed! and a curious situation I'm in, to part man and wife in this manner.

LADY TEAZLE: (*peeping*) Couldn't I steal off?

JOSEPH SURFACE: Keep close, my angel!

SIR PETER: (*peeping*) Joseph, tax him home!

JOSEPH SURFACE: Back, my dear friend!

LADY TEAZLE: (*peeping*) Couldn't you lock Sir Peter in?

JOSEPH SURFACE: Be still, my life!

SIR PETER: (*peeping*) You're sure the little milliner won't blab?

JOSEPH SURFACE: In, in, my dear Sir Peter!—'Fore gad, I wish I had a key to the door!

(*Enter* CHARLES SURFACE.)

CHARLES SURFACE: Holla! brother, what has been the matter? Your fellow would not let me up at first. What! have you had a Jew or a wench with you?

JOSEPH SURFACE: Neither, brother, I assure you.

CHARLES SURFACE: But what has made Sir Peter steal off? I thought he had been with you.

JOSEPH SURFACE: He was, brother; but, hearing you were coming, he did not choose to stay.

CHARLES SURFACE: What! was the old gentleman afraid I wanted to borrow money of him!

JOSEPH SURFACE: No, sir: but I am sorry to find, Charles, you have lately given that worthy man grounds for great uneasiness.

CHARLES SURFACE: Yes, they tell me I do that to a great many worthy men. But how so, pray?

JOSEPH SURFACE: To be plain with you, brother, he thinks you are endeavoring to gain Lady Teazle's affections from him.

CHARLES SURFACE: Who, I? O lud! not I, upon my word.—Ha! ha! ha! ha! so the old fellow has found out that he has got a young wife, has he?—or, what's worse, Lady Teazle has found out she has an old husband?

JOSEPH SURFACE: This is no subject to jest on, brother. He who can laugh—

CHARLES SURFACE: True, true, as you were going to say—then, seriously, I never had the least idea of what you charge me with, upon my honor.

JOSEPH SURFACE: (*in a loud voice*) Well, it will give Sir Peter great satisfaction to hear this.

CHARLES SURFACE: To be sure, I once thought the lady seemed to have taken a fancy to me; but, upon my soul, I never gave her the least encouragement. Besides, you know my attachment to Maria.

JOSEPH SURFACE: But sure, brother, even if Lady Teazle had betrayed the fondest partiality for you—

CHARLES SURFACE: Why, look'ee, Joseph, I hope I shall never deliberately do a dishonorable action; but if a pretty woman was purposely to throw herself in my way—and that pretty woman married to a man old enough to be her father—

JOSEPH SURFACE: Well!

CHARLES SURFACE: Why, I believe I should be obliged to borrow a little of your morality, that's all. But, brother, do you know now that you surprise me exceedingly by naming me with Lady Teazle; for i'faith, I always understood you were her favorite.

JOSEPH SURFACE: Oh, for shame, Charles! This retort is foolish.

CHARLES SURFACE: Nay, I swear I have seen you exchange such significant glances—

JOSEPH SURFACE: Nay, nay, sir, this is no jest.

CHARLES SURFACE: Egad, I'm serious! Don't you remember one day when I called here—

JOSEPH SURFACE: Nay, prithee, Charles—

CHARLES SURFACE: And found you together—

JOSEPH SURFACE: Zounds, sir, I insist—

CHARLES SURFACE: And another time, when your servant—

JOSEPH SURFACE: Brother, brother, a word with you! (*Aside.*) Gad, I must stop him.

CHARLES SURFACE: Informed, I say, that—

JOSEPH SURFACE: Hush! I beg your pardon, but Sir Peter has overheard all we have been saying. I knew you would clear yourself, or I should not have consented.

CHARLES SURFACE: How, Sir Peter! Where is he?

JOSEPH SURFACE: Softly, there! (*Points to the closet.*)

CHARLES SURFACE: Oh, 'fore Heaven, I'll have him out. Sir Peter, come forth!

JOSEPH SURFACE: No, no—

CHARLES SURFACE: I say, Sir Peter, come into court.—(*Pulls in* SIR PETER.) What! my old guardian!—What!—turn inquisitor and take evidence incog.?

SIR PETER: Give me your hand, Charles—I believe I have suspected you wrongfully; but you mustn't be angry with Joseph—'twas my plan!

CHARLES SURFACE: Indeed!

SIR PETER: But I acquit you. I promise you I don't think near so ill of you as I did. What I have heard has given me great satisfaction.

CHARLES SURFACE: Egad, then, 'twas lucky you didn't hear any more. Wasn't it, Joseph?

SIR PETER: Ah! you would have retorted on him.

CHARLES SURFACE: Ah, ay, that was a joke.

SIR PETER: Yes, yes, I know his honor too well.

CHARLES SURFACE: But you might as well have suspected him as me in this matter, for all that. Mightn't he, Joseph?

SIR PETER: Well, well, I believe you.

JOSEPH SURFACE: (*aside*) Would they were both out of the room!

SIR PETER: And in future, perhaps, we may not be such strangers.

(*Enter* SERVANT *and whispers to* JOSEPH SURFACE.)

JOSEPH SURFACE: Gentlemen, I beg pardon—I must wait on you downstairs; here's a person come on particular business.

CHARLES SURFACE: Well, you can see him in another room. Sir Peter and I have not met a long time, and I have something to say to him.

JOSEPH SURFACE: (*aside*) They must not be left together.—(*Aloud.*) I'll send Lady Sneerwell away, and return directly. —(*Aside to* SIR PETER.) Sir Peter, not a word of the French milliner.

SIR PETER: (*aside to* JOSEPH SURFACE) I! not for the world!—(*Exit* JOSEPH SURFACE.) Ah, Charles, if you associated more with your brother, one might indeed hope for your reformation. He is a man of sentiment. Well, there is nothing in the world so noble as a man of sentiment.

CHARLES SURFACE: Psha! he is too moral by half; and so apprehensive of his good name, as he calls it, that I suppose he would as soon let a priest into his house as a wench.

SIR PETER: No, no,—come, come,— you wrong him. No, no, Joseph is no rake, but he is no such saint either, in that respect.—(*Aside.*) I have a great mind to tell him—we should have such a laugh at Joseph.

CHARLES SURFACE: Oh, hang him! he's a very anchorite, a young hermit!

SIR PETER: Hark'ee—you must not abuse him: he may chance to hear of it again, I promise you.

CHARLES SURFACE: Why, you won't tell him?

SIR PETER: No—but—this way.— (*Aside.*) Egad, I'll tell him. (*Aloud.*) Hark'ee, have you a mind to have a good laugh at Joseph?

CHARLES SURFACE: I should like it of all things.

SIR PETER: Then, i'faith, we will! I'll be quit with him for discovering me. He had a girl with him when I called.

CHARLES SURFACE: What! Joseph? you jest.

SIR PETER: Hush!—a little French milliner—and the best of the jest is—she's in the room now.

CHARLES SURFACE: The devil she is!

SIR PETER: Hush! I tell you. (*Points to the screen.*)

CHARLES SURFACE: Behind the screen! S'life, let's unveil her!

SIR PETER: No, no, he's coming. You shan't, indeed!

CHARLES SURFACE: Oh, egad, we'll have a peep at the little milliner!

SIR PETER: Not for the world!— Joseph will never forgive me.

CHARLES SURFACE: I'll stand by you—

SIR PETER: Odds, here he is!

(JOSEPH SURFACE *enters just as* CHARLES *throws down the screen.*)

CHARLES SURFACE: Lady Teazle, by all that's wonderful!

SIR PETER: Lady Teazle, by all that's damnable!

CHARLES SURFACE: Sir Peter, this is one of the smartest French milliners I ever saw. Egad, you seem all to have been diverting yourselves here at hide and seek, and I don't see who is out of the secret. Shall I beg your ladyship to inform me? Not a word!—Brother, will you be pleased to explain this matter? What! is Morality dumb too?—Sir Peter, though I found you in the dark, perhaps you are not so now! All mute! Well—though I can make nothing of the affair, I suppose you perfectly understand one another; so I'll leave you to yourselves. (*Going.*) Brother, I'm sorry to find you have given that worthy man grounds for so much uneasiness.—Sir Peter! there's nothing in the world so noble as a man of sentiment! (*Exit.*)

(*They stand for some time looking at each other.*)

JOSEPH SURFACE: Sir Peter—notwithstanding—I confess—that appearances are against me—if you will afford me your patience—I make no doubt—but I shall explain everything to your satisfaction.

SIR PETER: If you please, sir.

JOSEPH SURFACE: The fact is, sir, that Lady Teazle, knowing my pretensions to your ward Maria—I say, sir, Lady Teazle, being apprehensive of the jealousy of your temper—and knowing my friendship to the family—she, sir, I say—called here —in order that—I might explain these pretensions—but on your coming—being apprehensive—as I said—of your jealousy —she withdrew—and this, you may depend on it, is the whole truth of the matter.

SIR PETER: A very clear account, upon my word; and I dare swear the lady will vouch for every article of it.

LADY TEAZLE: For not one word of it, Sir Peter!

SIR PETER: How! don't you think it worth while to agree in the lie?

LADY TEAZLE: There is not one syllable of truth in what that gentleman has told you.

SIR PETER: I believe you, upon my soul, ma'am!

JOSEPH SURFACE: (*aside to* LADY TEAZLE) 'Sdeath, madam, will you betray me?

LADY TEAZLE: Good Mr. Hypocrite, by your leave, I'll speak for myself.

SIR PETER: Ay, let her alone, sir; you'll find she'll make out a better story than you, without prompting.

LADY TEAZLE: Hear me, Sir Peter! I came here on no matter relating to your ward, and even ignorant of this gentleman's pretensions to her. But I came, seduced by his insidious arguments, at least to listen to his pretended passion, if not to sacrifice your honor to his baseness.

SIR PETER: Now, I believe, the truth is coming, indeed!

JOSEPH SURFACE: The woman's mad!

LADY TEAZLE: No, sir; she has recovered her senses, and your own arts have furnished her with the means. Sir Peter, I do not expect you to credit me— but the tenderness you expressed for me, when I am sure you could not think I was a witness to it, has penetrated so to my heart that had I left the place without the shame of this discovery, my future life should have spoken the sincerity of my gratitude. As for that smooth-tongued hypocrite, who would have seduced the wife of his too credulous friend, while he affected honorable addresses to his ward —I behold him now in a light so truly despicable that I shall never again respect myself for having listened to him.
(*Exit.*)

JOSEPH SURFACE: Notwithstanding all this, Sir Peter, Heaven knows—

SIR PETER: That you are a villain! and so I leave you to your conscience.

JOSEPH SURFACE: You are too rash, Sir Peter; you shall hear me. The man who shuts out conviction by refusing to—
(*Exeunt,* JOSEPH SURFACE *talking.*)

ACT V SCENE I [*The library in* JOSEPH SURFACE'S *house*]

(*Enter* JOSEPH SURFACE *and* SERVANT.)

JOSEPH SURFACE: Mr. Stanley! and why should you think I would see him? you must know he comes to ask something.

SERVANT: Sir, I should not have let him in, but that Mr. Rowley came to the door with him.

JOSEPH SURFACE: Psha! blockhead! to suppose that I should now be in a temper to receive visits from poor relations!—Well, why don't you show the fellow up?

SERVANT: I will, sir.—Why, sir, it was not my fault that Sir Peter discovered my lady—

JOSEPH SURFACE: Go, fool!—(*Exit* SERVANT.) Sure fortune never played a man of my policy such a trick before! My character with Sir Peter, my hopes with Maria, destroyed in a moment! I'm in a rare humor to listen to other people's distresses! I shan't be able to bestow even a benevolent sentiment on Stanley.—So! here he comes, and Rowley with him. I must try to recover myself, and put a little charity in my face, however.
(*Exit.*)
(*Enter* SIR OLIVER SURFACE *and* ROWLEY.)

SIR OLIVER: What! does he avoid us? That was he, was it not?

ROWLEY: It was, sir. But I doubt you are coming a little too abruptly. His nerves are so weak that the sight of a poor relation may be too much for him. I should have gone first to break it to him.

SIR OLIVER: Oh, plague of his nerves! Yet this is he whom Sir Peter extols as a man of the most benevolent way of thinking!

ROWLEY: As to his way of thinking, I cannot pretend to decide; for, to do him justice, he appears to have as much speculative benevolence as any private gentleman in the kingdom, though he is seldom so sensual as to indulge himself in the exercise of it.

SIR OLIVER: Yet he has a string of charitable sentiments at his fingers' ends.

ROWLEY: Or, rather, at his tongue's end, Sir Oliver; for I believe there is no sentiment he has such faith in as that "Charity begins at home."

SIR OLIVER: And his, I presume, is of that domestic sort which never stirs abroad at all.

ROWLEY: I doubt you'll find it so;—but he's coming. I mustn't seem to interrupt you; and you know, immediately as you leave him, I come in to announce your arrival in your real character.

SIR OLIVER: True; and afterwards you'll meet me at Sir Peter's.

ROWLEY: Without losing a moment. (*Exit.*)

SIR OLIVER: I don't like the complaisance of his features.
(*Enter* JOSEPH SURFACE.)

JOSEPH SURFACE: Sir, I beg you ten thousand pardons for keeping you a moment waiting.—Mr. Stanley, I presume.

SIR OLIVER: At your service.

JOSEPH SURFACE: Sir, I beg you will do me the honor to sit down—I entreat you, sir.

SIR OLIVER: Dear sir—there's no occasion.—(*Aside.*) Too civil by half!

JOSEPH SURFACE: I have not the pleasure of knowing you, Mr. Stanley; but I am extremely happy to see you look so well. You were nearly related to my mother, I think, Mr. Stanley?

SIR OLIVER: I was, sir; so nearly that my present poverty, I fear, may do discredit to her wealthy children, else I should not have presumed to trouble you.

JOSEPH SURFACE: Dear sir, there needs no apology: he that is in distress, though a stranger, has a right to claim kindred with the wealthy. I am sure I wish I was one of that class, and had it in my power to offer you even a small relief.

SIR OLIVER: If your uncle, Sir Oliver, were here, I should have a friend.

JOSEPH SURFACE: I wish he was, sir, with all my heart: you should not want an advocate with him, believe me, sir.

SIR OLIVER: I should not need one—my distresses would recommend me. But I imagined his bounty would enable you to become the agent of his charity.

JOSEPH SURFACE: My dear sir, you were strangely misinformed. Sir Oliver is a worthy man, a very worthy man, but avarice, Mr. Stanley, is the vice of age. I will tell you, my good sir, in confidence, what he has done for me has been a mere nothing; though people, I know, have thought otherwise; and, for my part, I never choose to contradict the report.

SIR OLIVER: What! has he never transmitted you bullion—rupees—pagodas?[31]

JOSEPH SURFACE: Oh, dear sir, nothing of the kind! No, no; a few presents now and then—china, shawls, congou tea,[32] avadavats,[33] and Indian crackers[34]—little more, believe me.

SIR OLIVER: (*aside*) Here's gratitude for twelve thousand pounds!—Avadavats and Indian crackers!

JOSEPH SURFACE: Then, my dear sir, you have heard, I doubt not, of the extravagance of my brother; there are very few would credit what I have done for that unfortunate young man.

SIR OLIVER: (*aside*) Not I, for one!

JOSEPH SURFACE: The sums I have lent him! Indeed I have been exceedingly to blame; it was an amiable weakness; however, I don't pretend to defend it—and now I feel it doubly culpable, since it has deprived me of the pleasure of serving you, Mr. Stanley, as my heart dictates.

SIR OLIVER: (*aside*) Dissembler!—(*Aloud.*) Then, sir, you can't assist me?

JOSEPH SURFACE: At present, it grieves me to say, I cannot; but, whenever I have the ability, you may depend upon hearing from me.

SIR OLIVER: I am extremely sorry—

JOSEPH SURFACE: Not more than I, believe me; to pity, without the power to relieve, is still more painful than to ask and be denied.

SIR OLIVER: Kind sir, your most obedient humble servant.

JOSEPH SURFACE: You leave me deeply affected, Mr. Stanley.—William, be ready to open the door.

SIR OLIVER: Oh, dear sir, no ceremony.

JOSEPH SURFACE: Your very obedient.

SIR OLIVER: Sir, your most obsequious.

JOSEPH SURFACE: You may depend upon hearing from me, whenever I can be of service.

SIR OLIVER: Sweet sir, you are too good.

JOSEPH SURFACE: In the meantime I wish you health and spirits.

SIR OLIVER: Your ever grateful and perpetual humble servant.

JOSEPH SURFACE: Sir, yours as sincerely.

SIR OLIVER: (*aside*) Charles!—you are my heir.
(*Exit.*)

JOSEPH SURFACE: This is one bad effect of a good character; it invites application from the unfortunate, and there needs no small degree of address to gain the reputation of benevolence without incurring the expense. The silver ore of pure charity is an expensive article in the catalogue of a man's good qualities; whereas the sentimental French plate I use instead of it makes just as good a show, and pays no tax.

(*Enter* ROWLEY.)

ROWLEY: Mr. Surface, your servant: I was apprehensive of interrupting you, though my business demands immediate attention, as this note will inform you.

JOSEPH SURFACE: Always happy to see Mr. Rowley.—(*Reads.*) Sir Oliver Surface!—My uncle arrived!

ROWLEY: He is, indeed: we have just parted—quite well, after a speedy voyage, and impatient to embrace his worthy nephew.

JOSEPH SURFACE: I am astonished!—William! stop Mr. Stanley, if he's not gone.

ROWLEY: Oh! he's out of reach, I believe.

JOSEPH SURFACE: Why did you not let me know this when you came in together?

ROWLEY: I thought you had particular business. But I must be gone to inform your brother and appoint him here to meet your uncle. He will be with you in a quarter of an hour.

JOSEPH SURFACE: So he says. Well, I am strangely overjoyed at his coming. —(*Aside*)—Never, to be sure, was anything so damned unlucky!

ROWLEY: You will be delighted to see how well he looks.

JOSEPH SURFACE: Oh! I'm overjoyed to hear it.—(*Aside*)—Just at this time!

ROWLEY: I'll tell him how impatiently you expect him.

JOSEPH SURFACE: Do, do; pray give my best duty and affection. Indeed, I cannot express the sensations I feel at the thought of seeing him.—(*Exit* ROWLEY.) Certainly his coming just at this time is the cruellest piece of ill fortune. (*Exit.*)

SCENE II [SIR PETER TEAZLE'S *house*]

(*Enter* MRS. CANDOUR *and* MAID.)

MAID: Indeed, ma'am, my lady will see nobody at present.

MRS. CANDOUR: Did you tell her it was her friend Mrs. Candour?

MAID: Yes, ma'am; but she begs you will excuse her.

MRS. CANDOUR: Do go again; I shall be glad to see her, if it be only for a moment, for I am sure she must be in great distress.—(*Exit* MAID.) Dear heart, how provoking! I'm not mistress of half the circumstances! We shall have the whole affair in the newspapers, with the names of the parties at length, before I have dropped the story at a dozen houses.

(*Enter* SIR BENJAMIN BACKBITE.)

Oh, dear Sir Benjamin! you have heard, I suppose—

SIR BENJAMIN: Of Lady Teazle and Mr. Surface—

MRS. CANDOUR: And Sir Peter's discovery—

SIR BENJAMIN: Oh, the strangest piece of business, to be sure!

MRS. CANDOUR: Well, I never was so surprised in my life. I am so sorry for all parties, indeed.

SIR BENJAMIN: Now, I don't pity Sir Peter at all: he was so extravagantly partial to Mr. Surface.

MRS. CANDOUR: Mr. Surface! Why, 'twas with Charles Lady Teazle was detected.

SIR BENJAMIN: No, no, I tell you: Mr. Surface is the gallant.

MRS. CANDOUR: No such thing! Charles is the man. 'Twas Mr. Surface brought Sir Peter on purpose to discover them.

SIR BENJAMIN: I tell you I had it from one—

MRS. CANDOUR: And I have it from one—

SIR BENJAMIN: Who had it from one, who had it—

MRS. CANDOUR: From one immediately —But here comes Lady Sneerwell; perhaps she knows the whole affair.

(*Enter* LADY SNEERWELL.)

LADY SNEERWELL: So, my dear Mrs. Candour, here's a sad affair of our friend Lady Teazle!

MRS. CANDOUR: Ay, my dear friend, who would have thought—

LADY SNEERWELL: Well, there is no trusting to appearances; though indeed, she was always too lively for me.

MRS. CANDOUR: To be sure, her manners were a little too free; but then she was so young!

LADY SNEERWELL: And had, indeed, some good qualities.

MRS. CANDOUR: So she had, indeed. But have you heard the particulars?

LADY SNEERWELL: No; but everybody says that Mr. Surface—

SIR BENJAMIN: Ay, there; I told you Mr. Surface was the man.

MRS. CANDOUR: No, no: indeed the assignation was with Charles.

LADY SNEERWELL: With Charles! You alarm me, Mrs. Candour.

MRS. CANDOUR: Yes, yes: he was the lover. Mr. Surface, to do him justice, was only the informer.

SIR BENJAMIN: Well, I'll not dispute with you, Mrs. Candour; but, be it which it may, I hope that Sir Peter's wound will not—

MRS. CANDOUR: Sir Peter's wound! Oh, mercy! I didn't hear a word of their fighting.

LADY SNEERWELL: Nor I, a syllable.

SIR BENJAMIN: No! what, no mention of the duel?

MRS. CANDOUR: Not a word.

SIR BENJAMIN: Oh, yes: they fought before they left the room.

LADY SNEERWELL: Pray let us hear.

MRS. CANDOUR: Ay, do oblige us with the duel.

SIR BENJAMIN: "Sir," says Sir Peter, immediately after the discovery, "you are a most ungrateful fellow."

MRS. CANDOUR: Ay, to Charles—

SIR BENJAMIN: No, no—to Mr. Surface—"a most ungrateful fellow; and old as I am, sir," says he, "I insist on immediate satisfaction."

MRS. CANDOUR: Ay, that must have been to Charles; for 'tis very unlikely Mr. Surface should fight in his own house.

SIR BENJAMIN: 'Gad's life, ma'am, not at all—"giving me immediate satisfaction."—On this, ma'am, Lady Teazle, seeing Sir Peter in such danger, ran out of the room in strong hysterics, and Charles after her, calling out for hartshorn and water; then, madam, they began to fight with swords—

(Enter CRABTREE.)

CRABTREE: With pistols, nephew—pistols! I have it from undoubted authority.

MRS. CANDOUR: Oh, Mr. Crabtree, then it is all true!

CRABTREE: Too true, indeed, madam, and Sir Peter is dangerously wounded—

SIR BENJAMIN: By a thrust in *seconde*[35] quite through his left side—

CRABTREE: By a bullet lodged in the thorax.

MRS. CANDOUR: Mercy on me! Poor Sir Peter!

CRABTREE: Yes, madam; though Charles would have avoided the matter, if he could.

MRS. CANDOUR: I knew Charles was the person.

SIR BENJAMIN: My uncle, I see, knows nothing of the matter.

CRABTREE: But Sir Peter taxed him with the basest ingratitude—

SIR BENJAMIN: That I told you, you know—

CRABTREE: Do, nephew, let me speak! —and insisted on immediate—

SIR BENJAMIN: Just as I said—

CRABTREE: Odds life, nephew, allow others to know something too! A pair of pistols lay on the bureau. (for Mr. Surface, it seems, had come home the night before late from Salthill where he had been to see the Montem[36] with a friend who has a son at Eton) so, unluckily, the pistols were left charged.

SIR BENJAMIN: I heard nothing of this.

CRABTREE: Sir Peter forced Charles to take one, and they fired, it seems, pretty nearly together. Charles's shot took effect, as I tell you, and Sir Peter's missed; but, what is very extraordinary, the ball struck against a little bronze Shakespeare that stood over the fireplace, grazed out of the window at a right angle, and wounded the postman who was just coming to the door with a double letter[37] from Northamptonshire.

SIR BENJAMIN: My uncle's account is more circumstantial, I confess; but I believe mine is the true one for all that.

LADY SNEERWELL: (*aside*) I am more interested in this affair than they imagine, and must have better information.
(*Exit.*)

SIR BENJAMIN: Ah! Lady Sneerwell's alarm is very easily accounted for.

CRABTREE: Yes, yes, they certainly do say—but that's neither here nor there.

MRS. CANDOUR: But, pray, where is Sir Peter at present?

CRABTREE: Oh! they brought him home, and he is now in the house, though the servants are ordered to deny him.

MRS. CANDOUR: I believe so, and Lady Teazle, I suppose, attending him.

CRABTREE: Yes, yes; and I saw one of the faculty[38] enter just before me.

SIR BENJAMIN: Hey! who comes here?

CRABTREE: Oh, this is he: the physician, depend on't.

MRS. CANDOUR: Oh, certainly! it must be the physician; and now we shall know.
(*Enter* SIR OLIVER SURFACE.)

CRABTREE: Well, doctor, what hopes?

MRS. CANDOUR: Ay, doctor, how's your patient?

SIR BENJAMIN: Now, doctor, isn't it a wound with a smallsword?

CRABTREE: A bullet lodged in the thorax, for a hundred!

SIR OLIVER: Doctor! a wound with a smallsword! and a bullet in the thorax?—Oons! are you mad, good people?

SIR BENJAMIN: Perhaps, sir, you are not a doctor?

SIR OLIVER: Truly, I am to thank you for my degree, if I am.

CRABTREE: Only a friend of Sir Peter's, then, I presume. But, sir, you must have heard of his accident?

SIR OLIVER: Not a word!

CRABTREE: Not of his being dangerously wounded?

SIR OLIVER: The devil he is!

SIR BENJAMIN: Run through the body—

CRABTREE: Shot in the breast—

SIR BENJAMIN: By one Mr. Surface—

CRABTREE: Ay, the younger.

SIR OLIVER: Hey! what the plague! you seem to differ strangely in your accounts: however, you agree that Sir Peter is dangerously wounded.

SIR BENJAMIN: Oh, yes, we agree there.

CRABTREE: Yes, yes, I believe there can be no doubt in that.

SIR OLIVER: Then, upon my word, for a person in that situation, he is the most imprudent man alive; for here he comes, walking as if nothing at all was the matter.
(*Enter* SIR PETER TEAZLE.)

Odds heart, Sir Peter! you are come in good time, I promise you; for we had just given you over!

SIR BENJAMIN: (*aside to* CRABTREE) Egad, uncle, this is the most sudden recovery!

SIR OLIVER: Why, man! what do you do out of bed with a smallsword through your body and a bullet lodged in your thorax?

SIR PETER: A smallsword and a bullet?

SIR OLIVER: Ay; these gentlemen would have killed you without law or physic, and wanted to dub me a doctor, to make me an accomplice.

SIR PETER: Why, what is all this?

SIR BENJAMIN: We rejoice, Sir Peter, that the story of the duel is not true and are sincerely sorry for your other misfortune.

SIR PETER: (*aside*) So, so; all over the town already.

CRABTREE: Though, Sir Peter, you were certainly vastly to blame to marry at your years.

SIR PETER: Sir, what business is that of yours?

MRS. CANDOUR: Though, indeed, as Sir Peter made so good a husband, he's very much to be pitied.

SIR PETER: Plague on your pity, ma'am! I desire none of it.

SIR BENJAMIN: However, Sir Peter, you must not mind the laughing and jests you will meet with on the occasion.

SIR PETER: Sir, sir! I desire to be master in my own house.

CRABTREE: 'Tis no uncommon case, that's one comfort.

SIR PETER: I insist on being left to myself. Without ceremony, I insist on your leaving my house directly!

MRS. CANDOUR: Well, well, we are going; and depend on't, we'll make the best report of it we can.

(*Exit.*)

SIR PETER: Leave my house!

CRABTREE: And tell how hardly you've been treated!

(*Exit.*)

SIR PETER: Leave my house!

SIR BENJAMIN: And how patiently you bear it.

(*Exit.*)

SIR PETER: Fiends! vipers! furies! Oh! that their own venom would choke them!

SIR OLIVER: They are very provoking indeed, Sir Peter.

(*Enter* ROWLEY.)

ROWLEY: I heard high words: what has ruffled you, sir?

SIR PETER: Psha! what signifies asking? Do I ever pass a day without my vexations?

ROWLEY: Well, I'm not inquisitive.

SIR OLIVER: Well, Sir Peter, I have seen both my nephews in the manner we proposed.

SIR PETER: A precious couple they are!

ROWLEY: Yes, and Sir Oliver is convinced that your judgment was right, Sir Peter.

SIR OLIVER: Yes, I find Joseph is indeed the man, after all.

ROWLEY: Ay, as Sir Peter says, he is a man of sentiment.

SIR OLIVER: And acts up to the sentiments he professes.

ROWLEY: It certainly is edification to hear him talk.

SIR OLIVER: Oh, he's a model for the young men of the age! But how's this, Sir Peter? you don't join us in your friend Joseph's praise, as I expected.

SIR PETER: Sir Oliver, we live in a damned wicked world, and the fewer we praise the better.

ROWLEY: What! do you say so, Sir Peter, who were never mistaken in your life?

SIR PETER: Psha! plague on you both! I see by your sneering you have heard the whole affair. I shall go mad among you!

ROWLEY: Then, to fret you no longer, Sir Peter, we are indeed acquainted with it all. I met Lady Teazle coming from Mr. Surface's so humbled, that she deigned to request me to be her advocate with you.

SIR PETER: And does Sir Oliver know all this?

SIR OLIVER: Every circumstance.

SIR PETER: What, of the closet and the screen, hey?

SIR OLIVER: Yes, yes, and the little French milliner. Oh, I have been vastly diverted with the story! ha! ha! ha!

SIR PETER: 'Twas very pleasant.

SIR OLIVER: I never laughed more in my life, I assure you: ha! ha! ha!

SIR PETER: Oh, vastly diverting! ha! ha! ha!

ROWLEY: To be sure, Joseph with his sentiments! ha! ha! ha!

SIR PETER: Yes, yes, his sentiments! ha! ha! ha! Hypocritical villain!

SIR OLIVER: Ay, and that rogue Charles to pull Sir Peter out of the closet: ha! ha! ha!

SIR PETER: Ha! ha! 'twas devilish entertaining, to be sure!

SIR OLIVER: Ha! ha! ha! Egad, Sir Peter, I should like to have seen your face when the screen was thrown down: ha! ha!

SIR PETER: Yes, yes, my face when the screen was thrown down: ha! ha! ha! Oh, I must never show my head again!

SIR OLIVER: But come, come, it isn't fair to laugh at you neither, my old friend; though, upon my soul, I can't help it.

SIR PETER: Oh, pray don't restrain your mirth on my account: it does not hurt me at all! I laugh at the whole affair myself. Yes, yes, I think being a standing jest for all one's acquaintance a very happy situation. Oh, yes, and then of a morning to read the paragraphs about Mr. S——, Lady T——, and Sir P——, will be so entertaining!

ROWLEY: Without affectation, Sir, Peter, you may despise the ridicule of fools. But I see Lady Teazle going towards the next room, I am sure you must desire a reconciliation as earnestly as she does.

SIR OLIVER: Perhaps my being here prevents her coming to you. Well, I'll leave honest Rowley to mediate between you; but he must bring you all presently to Mr. Surface's where I am now returning, if not to reclaim a libertine, at least to expose hypocrisy.

SIR PETER: Ah, I'll be present at your discovering yourself there with all my heart; though 'tis a vile unlucky place for discoveries.

ROWLEY: We'll follow.

(*Exit* SIR OLIVER.)

SIR PETER: She is not coming here, you see, Rowley.

ROWLEY: No, but she has left the door of that room open, you perceive. See, she is in tears.

SIR PETER: Certainly a little mortification appears very becoming in a wife. Don't you think it will do her good to let her pine a little?

ROWLEY: Oh, this is ungenerous in you!

SIR PETER: Well, I know not what to think. You remember the letter I found of hers evidently intended for Charles!

ROWLEY: A mere forgery, Sir Peter! laid in your way on purpose. This is one of the points which I intend Snake shall give you conviction of.

SIR PETER: I wish I were once satisfied of that. She looks this way. What a remarkably elegant turn of the head she has! Rowley, I'll go to her.

ROWLEY: Certainly.

SIR PETER: Though, when it is known that we are reconciled, people will laugh at me ten times more.

ROWLEY: Let them laugh, and retort their malice only by showing them you are happy in spite of it.

SIR PETER: I'faith, so I will! and, if I'm not mistaken, we may yet be the happiest couple in the country.

ROWLEY: Nay, Sir Peter, he who once lays aside suspicion——

SIR PETER: Hold, Master Rowley! if you have any regard for me, never let me hear you utter anything like a sentiment. I have had enough of them to serve me the rest of my life.

(*Exeunt.*)

SCENE III [*The library in* JOSEPH SURFACE's *house*]

(*Enter* JOSEPH SURFACE *and* LADY SNEERWELL.)

LADY SNEERWELL: Impossible! Will not Sir Peter immediately be reconciled to Charles, and of course no longer oppose his union with Maria? The thought is distraction to me.

JOSEPH SURFACE: Can passion furnish a remedy?

LADY SNEERWELL: No, nor cunning either. Oh, I was a fool, an idiot, to league with such a blunderer!

JOSEPH SURFACE: Sure, Lady Sneerwell, I am the greatest sufferer; yet you see I bear the accident with calmness.

LADY SNEERWELL: Because the disappointment doesn't reach your heart; your interest only attached you to Maria. Had you felt for her what I have for that ungrateful libertine, neither your temper nor hypocrisy could prevent your showing the sharpness of your vexation.

JOSEPH SURFACE: But why should your reproaches fall on me for this disappointment?

LADY SNEERWELL: Are you not the cause of it? Had you not a sufficient field for your roguery in imposing upon Sir Peter, and supplanting your brother, but you must endeavor to seduce his wife? I hate such an avarice of crimes; 'tis an unfair monopoly, and never prospers.

JOSEPH SURFACE: Well, I admit I have been to blame. I confess I deviated from the direct road of wrong, but I don't think we're so totally defeated either.

LADY SNEERWELL: No?

JOSEPH SURFACE: You tell me you have made a trial of Snake since we met, and that you still believe him faithful to us?

LADY SNEERWELL: I do believe so.

JOSEPH SURFACE: And that he has undertaken, should it be necessary, to swear and prove that Charles is at this time contracted by vows and honor to your ladyship, which some of his former letters to you will serve to support?

LADY SNEERWELL: This, indeed, might have assisted.

JOSEPH SURFACE: Come, come; it is not too late yet. (*Knocking at the door.*) But hark! this is probably my uncle, Sir Oliver: retire to that room; we'll consult further when he's gone.

LADY SNEERWELL: Well, but if he should find you out too.

JOSEPH SURFACE: Oh, I have no fear of that. Sir Peter will hold his tongue for his own credit's sake—and you may depend on it I shall soon discover Sir Oliver's weak side!

LADY SNEERWELL: I have no diffidence[39] of your abilities! only be constant to one roguery at a time.

(*Exit.*)

JOSEPH SURFACE: I will, I will! So! 'tis confounded hard, after such bad fortune, to be baited by one's confederate in evil. Well, at all events, my character is so much better than Charles's that I certainly—hey!—what—this is not Sir Oliver, but old Stanley again. Plague on't that he should return to tease me just now! I shall have Sir Oliver come and find him here—and—

(*Enter* SIR OLIVER SURFACE.)

Gad's life, Mr. Stanley, why have you come back to plague me at this time? You must not stay now, upon my word.

SIR OLIVER: Sir, I hear your uncle Oliver is expected here, and though he has been so penurious to you, I'll try what he'll do for me.

JOSEPH SURFACE: Sir, 'tis impossible for you to stay now, so I must beg—Come any other time, and I promise you, you shall be assisted.

SIR OLIVER: No: Sir Oliver and I must be acquainted.

JOSEPH SURFACE: Zounds, sir! then I insist on your quitting the room directly.

SIR OLIVER: Nay, sir—

JOSEPH SURFACE: Sir, I insist on't!—Here, William! show this gentleman out. Since you compel me, sir, not one moment—this is such insolence!

(*Going to push him out.*)

(*Enter* CHARLES SURFACE.)

CHARLES SURFACE: Heyday! what's the matter now? What the devil have you got hold of my little broker here? Zounds, brother, don't hurt little Premium. What's the matter, my little fellow?

JOSEPH SURFACE: So! he has been with you, too, has he?

CHARLES SURFACE: To be sure he has. Why, he's as honest a little—But sure, Joseph, you have not been borrowing money too, have you?

JOSEPH SURFACE: Borrowing! no! But, brother, you know we expect Sir Oliver here every—

CHARLES SURFACE: O gad, that's true! Noll mustn't find the little broker here, to be sure.

JOSEPH SURFACE: Yet, Mr. Stanley insists—

CHARLES SURFACE: Stanley! why his name's Premium.

JOSEPH SURFACE: No, sir, Stanley.

CHARLES SURFACE: No, no, Premium.

JOSEPH SURFACE: Well, no matter which—but—

CHARLES SURFACE: Ay, ay, Stanley or Premium, 'tis the same thing, as you say; for I suppose he goes by half a hundred names, besides A. B. at the coffee-house.[40]

(*Knocking.*)

JOSEPH SURFACE: 'Sdeath! here's Sir Oliver at the door. Now I beg, Mr. Stanley—

CHARLES SURFACE: Ay, ay, and I beg, Mr. Premium—

SIR OLIVER: Gentlemen—

JOSEPH SURFACE: Sir, by heaven you shall go!

CHARLES SURFACE: Ay, out with him, certainly!

SIR OLIVER: This violence—

JOSEPH SURFACE: Sir, 'tis your own fault.

CHARLES SURFACE: Out with him, to be sure!

(*Both forcing* SIR OLIVER *out.*)

(*Enter* SIR PETER *and* LADY TEAZLE, MARIA, *and* ROWLEY.)

SIR PETER: My old friend, Sir Oliver—hey! What in the name of wonder!—here are dutiful nephews—assault their uncle at first visit!

LADY TEAZLE: Indeed, Sir Oliver, 'twas well we came in to rescue you.

ROWLEY: Truly it was; for I perceive, Sir Oliver, the character of old Stanley was no protection to you.

SIR OLIVER: Nor of Premium either: the necessities of the former could not extort a shilling from that benevolent gentleman; and now, egad, I stood a chance of faring worse than my ancestors and being knocked down without being bid for.

JOSEPH SURFACE: Charles!

CHARLES SURFACE: Joseph!

JOSEPH SURFACE: 'Tis now complete!

CHARLES SURFACE: Very!

SIR OLIVER: Sir Peter, my friend, and Rowley too—look on that elder nephew of mine. You know what he has already received from my bounty; and you also know how gladly I would have regarded half my fortune as held in trust for him? judge, then, my disappointment in discovering him to be destitute of truth, charity, and gratitude!

SIR PETER: Sir Oliver, I should be more surprised at this declaration, if I had not myself found him to be mean, treacherous, and hypocritical.

LADY TEAZLE: And if the gentleman pleads not guilty to these, pray let him call me to his character.

SIR PETER: Then, I believe, we need add no more: if he knows himself, he will consider it as the most perfect punishment that he is known to the world.

CHARLES SURFACE: (*aside*) If they talk this way to Honesty, what will they say to me, by-and-by?

SIR OLIVER: As for that prodigal, his brother, there—

CHARLES SURFACE: (*aside*) Ay, now comes my turn: the damned family pictures will ruin me!

JOSEPH SURFACE: Sir Oliver—uncle, will you honor me with a hearing?

CHARLES SURFACE: (*aside*) Now, if Joseph would make one of his long speeches, I might recollect myself a little.

SIR OLIVER: (*to* JOSEPH) I suppose you would undertake to justify yourself entirely?

JOSEPH SURFACE: I trust I could.

SIR OLIVER: (*to* CHARLES) Well, sir! —and you could justify yourself too, I suppose?

CHARLES SURFACE: Not that I know of, Sir Oliver.

SIR OLIVER: What!—Little Premium has been let too much into the secret, I suppose?

CHARLES SURFACE: True, sir; but they were family secrets, and should not be mentioned again, you know.

ROWLEY: Come, Sir Oliver, I know you cannot speak of Charles's follies with anger.

SIR OLIVER: Odd's heart, no more I can; nor with gravity either. Sir Peter, do you know the rogue bargained with me for all his ancestors; sold me judges and generals by the foot, and maiden aunts as cheap as broken china.

CHARLES SURFACE: To be sure, Sir Oliver, I did make a little free with the family canvas, that's the truth on't. My ancestors may rise in judgment against me, there's no denying it; but believe me sincere when I tell you—and upon my soul I would not say so if I was not— that if I do not appear mortified at the exposure of my follies, it is because I feel at this moment the warmest satisfaction at seeing you, my liberal benefactor.

SIR OLIVER: Charles, I believe you. Give me your hand again: the ill-looking little fellow over the settee has made your peace.

CHARLES SURFACE: Then, sir, my gratitude to the original is still increased.

LADY TEAZLE: Yet, I believe, Sir Oliver, here is one whom Charles is still more anxious to be reconciled to.

(*Pointing to* MARIA.)

SIR OLIVER: Oh, I have heard of his attachment there; and, with the young lady's pardon, if I construe right—that blush—

SIR PETER: Well, child, speak your sentiments.

MARIA: Sir, I have little to say, but that I shall rejoice to hear that he is happy; for me, whatever claim I had to his attention, I willingly resign to one who has a better title.

CHARLES SURFACE: How, Maria!

SIR PETER: Heyday! what's the mystery now? While he appeared an incorrigible rake, you would give your hand to no one else; and now that he is likely to reform I'll warrant you won't have him.

MARIA: His own heart and Lady Sneerwell know the cause.

CHARLES SURFACE: Lady Sneerwell!

JOSEPH SURFACE: Brother, it is with great concern I am obliged to speak on this point, but my regard to justice compels me, and Lady Sneerwell's injuries can no longer be concealed.

(*Opens the door.*)

(*Enter* LADY SNEERWELL.)

SIR PETER: So! another French milliner! Egad, he has one in every room in the house, I suppose!

LADY SNEERWELL: Ungrateful Charles! Well may you be surprised, and feel for the indelicate situation your perfidy has forced me into.

CHARLES SURFACE: Pray, uncle, is this another plot of yours? For, as I have life, I don't understand it.

JOSEPH SURFACE: I believe, sir, there is but the evidence of one person more necessary to make it extremely clear.

SIR PETER: And that person, I imagine, is Mr. Snake. Rowley, you were perfectly right to bring him with us, and pray let him appear.

ROWLEY: Walk in, Mr. Snake.
(*Enter* SNAKE.)
I thought his testimony might be wanted; however, it happens unluckily, that he comes to confront Lady Sneerwell, not to support her.

LADY SNEERWELL: A villain! Treacherous to me at last! Speak, fellow, have you too conspired against me?

SNAKE: I beg your ladyship ten thousand pardons: you paid me extremely liberally for the lie in question; but I unfortunately have been offered double to speak the truth.

SIR PETER: Plot and counterplot, egad!

LADY SNEERWELL: The torments of shame and disappointment on you all!

LADY TEAZLE: Hold, Lady Sneerwell —before you go, let me thank you for the trouble you and that gentleman have taken in writing letters from me to Charles, and answering them yourself; and let me also request you to make my respects to the scandalous college, of which you are president, and inform them that Lady Teazle, licentiate, begs leave to return the diploma they granted her, as she leaves off practice and kills characters no longer.

LADY SNEERWELL: You too, madam! —provoking—insolent! May your husband live these fifty years!
(*Exit.*)

SIR PETER: Oons! what a fury!

LADY TEAZLE: A malicious creature, indeed!

SIR PETER: Hey! not for her last wish?

LADY TEAZLE: Oh, no!

SIR OLIVER: Well, sir, and what have you to say now?

JOSEPH SURFACE: Sir, I am so confounded, to find that Lady Sneerwell could be guilty of suborning Mr. Snake in this manner, to impose on us all, that I know not what to say: however, lest her revengeful spirit should prompt her to injure my brother, I had certainly better follow her directly.
(*Exit.*)

SIR PETER: Moral to the last drop!

SIR OLIVER: Ay, and marry her, Joseph, if you can. Oil and vinegar— egad, you'll do very well together.

ROWLEY: I believe we have no more occasion for Mr. Snake at present?

SNAKE: Before I go, I beg pardon once for all, for whatever uneasiness I have been the humble instrument of causing to the parties present.

SIR PETER: Well, well, you have made atonement by a good deed at last.

SNAKE: But I must request of the company, that it shall never be known.

SIR PETER: Hey! what the plague! are you ashamed of having done a right thing once in your life?

SNAKE: Ah, sir, consider—I live by the badness of my character; I have nothing but my infamy to depend on; and, if it were once known that I had been betrayed into an honest action, I should lose every friend I have in the world.

SIR OLIVER: Well, well—we'll not traduce you by saying anything in your praise, never fear.
(*Exit* SNAKE.)

SIR PETER: There's a precious rogue!

LADY TEAZLE: See, Sir Oliver, there needs no persuasion now to reconcile your nephew and Maria.

SIR OLIVER: Ay, ay, that's as it should be; and, egad, we'll have the wedding tomorrow morning.

CHARLES SURFACE: Thank you, dear uncle.

SIR PETER: What, you rogue! don't you ask the girl's consent first?

CHARLES SURFACE: Oh, I have done that a long time—a minute ago—and she has looked yes.

MARIA: For shame, Charles!—I protest, Sir Peter, there has not been a word—

SIR OLIVER: Well, then, the fewer the better: may your love for each other never know abatement.

SIR PETER: And may you live as happily together as Lady Teazle and I intend to do!

CHARLES SURFACE: Rowley, my old friend, I am sure you congratulate me; and I suspect that I owe you much.

SIR OLIVER: You do, indeed, Charles.

ROWLEY: If my efforts to serve you had not succeeded, you would have been in my debt for the attempt—but deserve to be happy—and you overpay me.

SIR PETER: Ay, honest Rowley always said you would reform.

CHARLES SURFACE: Why as to reforming, Sir Peter, I'll make no promises, and that I take to be a proof that I intend to set about it. But here shall be my monitor—my gentle guide.—Ah! can I leave the virtuous path those eyes illumine?

Though thou, dear maid, shouldst wave
  thy beauty's sway,
Thou still must rule, because I will obey:
An humble fugitive from Folly view,
No sanctuary near but Love—and you:
  (*To the audience.*)
You can, indeed, each anxious fear
  remove,
For even Scandal dies, if you approve.

CURTAIN

NOTES

1. sketches of people involved in society scandals.
2. a knighted merchant.
3. a public stagecoach.
3a. a social gathering usually for conversation about literature and art.
4. the lady of Petrarch's sonnet cycle.
5. The fanciful name of a lady celebrated by the seventeenth-century poet Edmund Waller (1606-1687) in a group of poems entitled *Sacharissa*.
6. Annuities sold by the Irish parliament.
7. doubt not, believe.
8. fashionable concert hall.
9. garden party.
10. embroidery frame.
11. an unfashionable game of cards.
12. a stylish carriage in which the occupants face each other.
13. ponies.
14. elegantly groomed ponies.
15. a drive in Hyde Park, London.
16. artificial fruits containing maxims: similar to the Chinese fortune cookies.
17. mercantile law under which endorsers are liable for debts not paid by debtor.
18. a married woman's lover.
19. firm, staunch.
20. *Henry IV*, Part II; Act IV, Scene iv.
21. intended to protect minors against unscrupulous sellers of annuities.
22. footmen's outfits.
23. to take effect after death.
24. harlot.
25. window boxes.
26. trophies and testimonial awards.
27. The Duke of Marlborough (1650-1722) led the English forces in the war with France (1702-1711) and won a great victory over the French at Blenheim (1704) and at the costly battle of Malplaquet in 1709.
28. a fashionable portrait painter.
29. the Lord Chancellor's seat—a symbol of the law.
30. elegant clothes worn at the king's birthday celebration.
31. coins of India.
32. a black Chinese tea.
33. small Indian songbirds.
34. firecrackers.
35. a position in parrying.
36. A carnival held at Salthill by the boys of Eton on Whit-Tuesday, every third year.
37. An overnight letter requiring extra postage.
38. the medical profession.
39. doubt.
40. appointments made under fictitious initials or assumed names.

QUESTIONS

A. *Understanding the Action:*

1. Sheridan is said to reveal an amiable and generous nature in *The School for Scandal.* Do you agree? Give reasons for your answer.

2. What standards of conduct are upheld by Sheridan in this play?

3. Why is the "screen scene" so essential to the play that it often is considered to be the climax of the play's action?

4. What is the serious conflict in *The School for Scandal?* Explain your answer.

5. What is the story line in this play? (See *The Oxford Companion to English Literature* for a brief summary.)

6. Describe several humorous scenes from the play. Why, in your opinion, are these scenes better than others? Explain your choices.

B. Understanding the Characters:

1. How does Sheridan present Lady Teazle, and what is her relationship with her husband?

2. What contrasts does Sheridan emphasize in the characterization of Charles and Joseph Surface?

3. Who is the dominant character . . . i.e., the protagonist in this play? Who is the antagonist? How do these characters come into conflict with each other?

4. What is the function of Sir Oliver Surface, the rich uncle from India?

5. Who are the leading members of the "scandalous college"?

C. Understanding the Approach:

1. On what grounds is this play considered a "comedy of manners"?

2. What is the dominant theme of the play, and how is it furthered a) by means of plot; b) by means of characterization; c) by means of contrasts; d) by means of irony?

D. Comparisons:

1. What elements of content does *The School for Scandal* have in common with George Bernard Shaw's *Arms and the Man?* What qualities of writing?

2. In what respects does *The School for Scandal* differ from the Chekhov play, *Then and Now,* presented on pages 496-507?

3. Which of the three plays mentioned above by Sheridan, Shaw, and Chekhov leans most towards pathos? Give your reasons.

GEORGE BERNARD SHAW (1856-1950)

George Bernard Shaw, like Sophocles, lived past his ninth decade. He was a prolific writer (he wrote more than forty plays, some of which are masterpieces) and made himself the leading dramatist of his age. But here the resemblance of the modern sage to the Attic dramatist ends. Sophocles in his philosophical outlook was a traditionalist; Shaw, an iconoclastic rebel. Down the centuries the deep-toned, tragic voice of Sophocles rings clear. Shaw with amazing virtuosity spoke with many voices. He was in turn novelist; art, music, and dramatic critic; Fabian socialist; polemicist for many causes; and playwright. Even as a dramatist he revealed great versatility, writing farces, comedies, melodramas, tragedies, historical and problem plays. Beginning his dramatic career as a disciple of Ibsen, Shaw liberated the English stage from its outworn romantic conventions just as his Norwegian predecessor had freed the European theatre.

Shaw's father, one of thirteen children, came of an old Protestant Irish family. A witty, unconventional suitor addicted to liquor, he proposed at the age of forty to Elizabeth Gurly, a singer half his age who gave up a large inheritance in order to marry him. On July 26, 1856, George Bernard Shaw was born in Dublin.

His childhood was not a very happy one. The family (Shaw had two older sisters) was shunned socially; the father's drunkenness and irresponsibility provoked frequent domestic quarrels, and the mother's musical ambitions frequently caused her to neglect the children. He disliked attendance at church and was bored by school. He did, however, develop early an intense love for music (especially Mozart's), art, and a passionate interest in books. He attended concerts, operas, the National Gallery, and the theatre. Thus like Shakespeare and Ibsen, Shaw, with his keen mind and enormous intellectual curiosity, educated himself. Later Shaw summed up his early life in a letter to Ellen Terry, the actress, "A devil of a childhood, rich only in dreams, frightful and loveless in realities."

Lack of money preventing his enrollment at the university, he obtained a job as a clerk in a land agent's office. By working efficiently at his boring task of collecting rents and keeping ledgers, he won a promotion but became increasingly unhappy. All around him he saw the twin evils of drink and poverty (which he railed against all his life). The religious and political squabbles and the drab provincialism of Dublin also depressed him. The family broke up when his mother and his two sisters moved to London to promote their musical careers. Fired by literary ambitions himself, Shaw at the age of twenty soon joined them. Thus like two other twentieth-century famous compatriots, James Joyce and Sean O'Casey, he became an expatriate for the rest of his life.

The next ten years were financially very difficult ones but not unexciting. He did some hack journalism and then doggedly wrote five unsuccessful novels. In 1881 he read the writings of the idealistic poet Shelley and became a vegetarian. The following year he heard a lecture on the single tax delivered by the American economist Henry George. Realizing his ignorance of economics, Shaw read George's *Progress and Poverty*, then Karl Marx's formidable *Capital*, and other writings that suggested cures for the ills of modern industrial society. In 1884 he joined the Fabian Society dedicated to the idea of gradually through education and political activity transforming society from a capitalist economy to a socialistic one. He became the secretary of the organization and wrote its constitution in the form of a militant manifesto. By speaking in Hyde Park and at many political meetings, Shaw overcame his shyness and developed formidable powers as a witty and accomplished public speaker. Some of the ideas expounded in his Fabian Society tracts later found expression in his plays. Much of the social legislation enacted by the Labor Party in England today is the direct result of the activity of the Fabian Society.

Shaw, however, did not lose his interest in the arts. In the next decade he wrote incisive, scintillating criticism on art for the *World*, on music for the *Star*, and on drama for *The Saturday Review*; unlike most ephemeral journalistic criticism, his critical writings can be read today with pleasure and profit. In two books, *The Perfect Wagnerite* and *The Quintessence of Ibsenism*, he effectively championed the nineteenth-century European rebels in music and drama.

At the age of thirty-six Shaw began his dramatic career with the production by the new Independent Theatre of the controversial *Widowers' Houses*, a problem play dealing with slum tenements and those who profited from them. The sensation this play created in England paralleled that of Ibsen's *Doll's House* in Norway thirteen years earlier. The following year, 1893, he wrote *Mrs. Warren's Profession*, a play exposing the economic roots of immorality. Because the official Censor would not grant permission to perform this play, the public did not see it until eight years later when the private Stage Society produced it for its subscription membership.

Shaw then showed his versatility by turning from problem plays to writing satirical comedies. In 1894 he wrote *Arms and the Man*, in 1895 the famous *Candida*, and in 1897 *The Devil's Disciple*, the latter, performed by Richard Mansfield in New York, bringing in £3,000 for Shaw. From this time on Shaw's fame and fortune were established.

In 1896 at the age of forty he fell in love with Miss Charlotte Payne-Townshend, an Irish millionairess turned Fabian. For a time she was his secretary, then his nurse. Two years later they were married. Their marriage, though childless, proved to be a very happy one, and their home became the social center for a host of celebrated friends. At her death she left a large part of her fortune to improve the artistic taste and the manners of the Irish.

His study of economics and of political systems naturally led him to a study of history. His interest in historical figures is evidenced by his *Caesar and Cleopatra* (1898) and *Saint Joan* (1924). In the former he created a down-to-earth Shavian Caesar, a lonely genius who combined high ethical principles with practical empire building, a witty diplomat and rational teacher who, however, only succeeded in developing young Cleopatra from a passionate kitten to a revengeful cat. In *Saint Joan* he portrayed in a series of dramatic scenes the clash of the individual soul with the powerful forces of institutionalized religion, emerging nationalism, and feudal war in medieval France.

In a quartet of philosophical plays Shaw used the theatre as forum to air his views on problems important to twentieth-century man. In *Man and Superman*, "A Comedy and a Philosophy," he showed how the Life Force working through woman the pursuer can with man's cooperation raise humanity to a higher level of existence if man will only learn to use his marvelous inventive power for constructive and not destructive ends. In *Major Barbara* (1905) he revealed the paradoxical relationships of poverty, religion, economics, and social reform in modern society. In *Heartbreak House*, which Shaw described as a "Fantasia in the Russian Manner on English Themes," written mostly in 1913, he portrayed a lethargic, spent society drifting toward war. Eight years later, Shaw dramatized his theory of creative evolution in *Back to Methuselah*.

Even during this period when he was writing serious plays, his comic gift did not desert him. In 1912 he wrote *Pygmalion*, which was later made into the most successful musical comedy, *My Fair Lady*. In his old age Shaw continued to write plays: *On the Rocks* (1933), *The Millionairess* (1937), *The Simpleton of the Unexpected Isles* (1935), *Geneva* (1938), and *In Good King Charles's Golden Days* (1939); but his last works do not bear comparison with his best earlier work.

Recognized internationally as the leading twentieth-century dramatist, he died in 1950.

At a first glance Shaw the man seems to be a mass of contradictions. Rationalist and mystic, individualist and collectivist, a jester who is serious, a pacifist perpetually at war, he was scornful of teachers, yet was himself a frustrated, disillusioned teacher. He once declared: "I have solved practically all the pressing questions of our time, but they keep on being propounded as insoluble as if I had never existed." Although fond of posing as an egoist, he was really a dedicated artist and thinker who combined moral passion with dramatic genius. Courageously for three generations he exposed and attacked the manifold evils of the complex modern world. In his hortatory prefaces and his paradoxical plays, he has used his caustic pen to reform society and save our shaky civilization. This modern-day prophet became our intellectual gadfly. Carrying on from where Ibsen left off and with more incisiveness and wit, Shaw rejuvenated the English theatre and made it once more an arena of ideas.

INTRODUCTION TO *ARMS AND THE MAN*

In writing *Widowers' Houses* and *Mrs. Warren's Profession*, Shaw gained a dubious reputation from the English public and an indignant blast from the Censor. He next turned to the writing of satiric comedy which could be produced in the commercial theatre. The result was *Arms and the Man* (1894), a play which bewildered both the actors and the audience. Since 1870 Europe had been embroiled in a series of wars, a picturesque one having recently occurred in the Balkans. By placing the scene in Bulgaria and introducing all the trappings of the typical romantic war play—beautiful women, thrilling pursuit and concealment, moonlight and love, handsome officers in uniform—, he cleverly placed his satirical time bombs that rocked the audience with laughter.

One of the most persistent follies of mankind he believed was the romantic concept of war, perhaps best expressed by Othello as

". . . the neighing steed, and the shrill trump,
The spirit-stirring drum, th' ear-piercing fife,
The royal banner, and all quality,
Pride, pomp, and circumstance of glorious war."

Causing almost as much havoc, was the sentimental concept of love romanticized by foolish poets and popular novelists. In a combination of farce, satire, and comedy, Shaw in *Arms and the Man* proceeded to destroy both of these illusions.

At the close of the nineteenth century, Shaw already saw how preposterous and obsolete colorful uniforms, shining swords, and romantic personal heroism were in modern war, which is mainly a matter of machines and logistics. When the romantic Sergius wants to fight a duel using his sword, the matter-of-fact Bluntschli suggests a machine gun. The sentimental love affair of Sergius and Raina, where both assume false heroic attitudes and spout bombastic endearments, is contrasted with the materialistic self-interest relationship of Louka and Nicola. In his portrayal of the Petkoffs Shaw also satirized the emergence of a *nouveauriche* aristocracy striving to enjoy the twin benefits of "culture" and cleanliness.

In this play Shaw revealed for the first time his skill in pouring new wine into old bottles. The Gilbert and Sullivan characters that he introduced into this play re-enact the old "boy meets girl" plot. Shaw's witty dialogue, sharp satire, and amusing paradoxes give the play its new sparkle.

ARMS AND THE MAN

GEORGE BERNARD SHAW

CHARACTERS

MAJOR PETKOFF
CATHERINE PETKOFF
RAINA PETKOFF
LOUKA

NICOLA
CAPTAIN BLUNTSCHLI
MAJOR SERGIUS SARANOFF
RUSSIAN OFFICER

ACT I*

Night. A lady's bedchamber in Bulgaria, in a small town near the Dragoman Pass, late in November in the year 1885. Through an open window with a little balcony a peak of the Balkans, wonderfully white and beautiful in the starlit snow, seems quite close at hand, though it is really miles away. The interior of the room is not like anything to be seen in the west of Europe. It is half rich Bulgarian, half cheap Viennese. Above the head of the bed, which stands against a little wall cutting off the left hand corner of the room, is a painted wooden shrine, blue and gold, with an ivory image of Christ, and a light hanging before it in a pierced metal ball suspended by three chains. The principal seat, placed towards the other side of the room and opposite the window, is a Turkish ottoman. The counterpane and hangings of the bed, the window curtains, the little carpet, and all the ornamental textile fabrics in the room are oriental and gorgeous; the paper on the walls is occidental and paltry. The washstand, against the wall on the side nearest the ottoman and window, consists of an enamelled iron basin with a pail beneath it in a painted metal frame, and a single towel on the rail at the side. The dressing table, between the bed and the window, is a common pine table, covered with a cloth of many colours, with an expensive toilet mirror on it. The door is on the side nearest the bed; and there is a chest of drawers between. This chest of drawers is also covered by a variegated native cloth; and on it there is a pile of paper backed novels, a box of chocolate creams, and a miniature easel with a large photograph of an extremely handsome officer, whose lofty bearing and magnetic glance can be felt even from the portrait.

---

* In reading this play, the student should bear in mind that Shaw's spelling here is somewhat unconventional, and reflects a phase of his artistic development. Thus, he dispenses with apostrophes where we normally employ them. He uses *"cant"* for can't, *"dont"* for don't, *"youll"* for you'll, *"Ive"* for I've, *"theyre"* for they're, *"theres"* for there's (there is), *"isnt"* for isn't, *"havent"* for haven't *"theyll"* for they'll (they will), *"theyd"* for they'd (they would), *"youve"* for you've (you have), *"thats"* for that's (that is), *"youd"* for you'd (you would), *"wed"* for we'd (we had), *"thats"* for that's (that is), *"lets"* for let's (let us), *"thatll"* for that'll (that will). Shaw also spells show or showing as *"shew"* or *"shewing,"* but the word is to be pronounced as it is ordinarily.

The room is lighted by a candle on the chest of drawers, and another on the dressing table with a box of matches beside it.

The window is hinged doorwise and stands wide open. Outside, a pair of wooden shutters, opening outwards, also stand open. On the balcony a young lady, intensely conscious of the romantic beauty of the night, and of the fact that her own youth and beauty are part of it, is gazing at the snowy Balkans. She is in her nightgown, well covered by a long mantle of furs, worth, on a moderate estimate, about three times the furniture of the room.

Her reverie is interrupted by her mother, CATHERINE PETKOFF, *a woman over forty, imperiously energetic, with magnificent black hair and eyes, who might be a very splendid specimen of the wife of a mountain farmer, but is determined to be a Viennese lady, and to that end wears a fashionable tea gown on all occasions.*

CATHERINE: (*entering hastily, full of good news*) Raina! (*She pronounces it Rah-eena, with the stress on the ee.*) Raina! (*She goes to the bed, expecting to find Raina there.*) Why, where—? (*Raina looks into the room.*) Heavens, child! are you out in the night air instead of in your bed? Youll catch your death. Louka told me you were asleep.

RAINA: (*dreamily*) I sent her away. I wanted to be alone. The stars are so beautiful! What is the matter?

CATHERINE: Such news! There has been a battle.

RAINA: (*her eyes dilating*) Ah! (*She comes eagerly to* CATHERINE.)

CATHERINE: A great battle at Slivnitza! A victory! And it was won by Sergius.

RAINA: (*with a cry of delight*) Ah! (*They embrace rapturously.*) Oh, mother! (*Then, with sudden anxiety.*) Is father safe?

CATHERINE: Of course! he sends me the news. Sergius is the hero of the hour, the idol of the regiment.

RAINA: Tell me, tell me. How was it? (*Ecstatically.*) Oh, mother! mother! mother! (*She pulls her mother down on the ottoman; and they kiss one another frantically.*)

CATHERINE: (*with surging enthusiasm*) You cant guess how splendid it is. A cavalry charge! think of that! He defied our Russian commanders—acted without orders—led a charge on his own responsibility—headed it himself—was the first man to sweep through their guns. Cant you see it, Raina: our gallant splendid Bulgarians with their swords and eyes flashing, thundering down like an avalanche and scattering the wretched Serbs and their dandified Austrian officers like chaff. And you! you kept Sergius waiting a year before you would be betrothed to him. Oh, if you have a drop of Bulgarian blood in your veins, you will worship him when he comes back.

RAINA: What will he care for my poor little worship after the acclamations of a whole army of heroes? But no matter: I am so happy! so proud! (*She rises and walks about excitedly.*) It proves that all our ideas were real after all.

CATHERINE: (*indignantly*) Our ideas real! What do you mean?

RAINA: Our ideas of what Sergius would do. Our patriotism. Our heroic ideals. I sometimes used to doubt whether they were anything but dreams. Oh, what faithless little creatures girls are! When I buckled on Sergius's sword he looked so noble: it was treason to think of disillusion or humiliation or failure. And yet—and yet—(*She sits down again suddenly.*) Promise me you'll never tell him.

CATHERINE: Don't ask me for promises until I know what I'm promising.

RAINA: Well, it came into my head just as he was holding me in his arms and looking into my eyes, that perhaps we only had our heroic ideas because we are so fond of reading Byron and Pushkin, and because we were so delighted with the opera that season at Bucharest. Real life is so seldom like that! indeed never, as far as I knew it then. (*Remorsefully.*) Only think, mother: I doubted him: I wondered whether all his heroic qualities and his soldiership might not prove mere imagination when he went into a real battle. I had an uneasy fear that he might cut a poor figure there beside all those clever officers from the Tsar's court.

CATHERINE: A poor figure! Shame on you! The Serbs have Austrian officers who are just as clever as the Russians; but we have beaten them in every battle for all that.

RAINA: (*laughing and snuggling against her mother*) Yes: I was only a prosaic little coward. Oh, to think that it was all true! that Sergius is just as splendid and noble as he looks! that the world is really a glorious world for women who can see its glory and men who can act its romance! What happiness! what unspeakable fulfilment!

(*They are interrupted by the entry of* LOUKA, *a handsome proud girl in a pretty Bulgarian peasant's dress with double apron, so defiant that her servility to* RAINA *is almost insolent. She is afraid of* CATHERINE, *but even with her goes as far as she dares.*)

LOUKA: If you please, madam, all the windows are to be closed and the shutters made fast. They say there may be shooting in the streets. (RAINA *and* CATHERINE *rise together, alarmed.*) The Serbs are being chased right back through the pass; and they say they may run into the town. Our cavalry will be after them; and our people will be ready for them, you may be sure, now theyre running away. (*She goes out on the balcony, and pulls the outside shutters to; then steps back into the room.*)

CATHERINE: (*businesslike, housekeeping instincts aroused*) I must see that everything is made safe downstairs.

RAINA: I wish our people were not so cruel. What glory is there in killing wretched fugitives?

CATHERINE: Cruel! Do you suppose they would hesitate to kill you—or worse?

RAINA: (*to* LOUKA) Leave the shutters so that I can just close them if I hear any noise.

CATHERINE: (*authoritatively, turning on her way to the door*) Oh no, dear: you must keep them fastened. You would be sure to drop off to sleep and leave them open. Make them fast, Louka.

LOUKA: Yes, madam. (*She fastens them.*)

RAINA: Dont be anxious about me. The moment I hear a shot, I shall blow out the candles and roll myself up in bed with my ears well covered.

CATHERINE: Quite the wisest thing you can do, my love. Goodnight.

RAINA: Goodnight. (*Her emotion comes back for a moment.*) Wish me joy. (*They kiss.*) This is the happiest night of my life—if only there are no fugitives.

CATHERINE: Go to bed, dear; and dont think of them. (*She goes out.*)

LOUKA: (*secretly to* RAINA) If you would like the shutters open, just give them a push like this (*She pushes them: they open: she pulls them to again.*) One of them ought to be bolted at the bottom; but the bolt's gone.

RAINA: (*with dignity, reproving her*) Thanks, Louka; but we must do what we are told. (LOUKA *makes a grimace.*) Goodnight.

LOUKA: (*carelessly*) Goodnight. (*She goes out, swaggering.*)

(RAINA, *left alone, takes off her fur cloak and throws it on the ottoman. Then she goes to the chest of drawers, and adores the portrait there with feelings that are beyond all expression. She does not kiss it or press it to her breast, or show it any mark of bodily affection; but she takes it in her hands and elevates it, like a priestess.*)

RAINA: *(looking up at the picture)* Oh, I shall never be unworthy of you any more, my soul's hero: never, never, never. *(She replaces it reverently. Then she selects a novel from the little pile of books. She turns over the leaves dreamily; finds her page; turns the book inside out at it; and, with a happy sigh, gets into bed and prepares to read herself to sleep. But before abandoning herself to fiction, she raises her eyes once more, thinking of the blessed reality, and murmurs.)* My hero! my hero!

(A distant shot breaks the quiet of the night. She starts, listening; and two more shots, much nearer, follow, startling her so that she scrambles out of bed, and hastily blows out the candle on the chest of drawers. Then, putting her fingers in her ears, she runs to the dressing table, blows out the light there, and hurries back to bed in the dark, nothing being visible but the glimmer of the light in the pierced ball before the image, and the starlight seen through the slits at the top of the shutters. The firing breaks out again: there is a startling fusillade quite close at hand. Whilst it is still echoing, the shutters disappear, pulled open from without; and for an instant the rectangle of snowy starlight flashes out with the figure of a man silhouetted in black upon it. The shutters close immediately; and the room is dark again. But the silence is now broken by the sound of panting. Then there is a scratch; and the flame of a match is seen in the middle of the room.)

RAINA: *(crouching on the bed)* Who's there? *(The match is out instantly)* Who's there? Who is that?

A MAN'S VOICE: *(in the darkness, subduedly, but threateningly)* Sh—sh! Dont call out; or youll be shot. Be good; and no harm will happen to you. *(She is heard leaving her bed, and making for the door.)* Take care: it's no use trying to run away.

RAINA: But who—

THE VOICE: *(warning)* Remember: if you raise your voice my revolver will go off. *(Commandingly.)* Strike a light and let me see you. Do you hear? *(Another moment of silence and darkness as she retreats to the chest of drawers. Then she lights a candle; and the mystery is at an end. He is a man of about 35, in a deplorable plight, bespattered with mud and blood and snow, his belt and the strap of his revolver case keeping together the torn ruins of the blue tunic of a Serbian artillery officer. All that the candlelight and his unwashed unkempt condition make it possible to discern is that he is of middling stature and undistinguished appearance, with strong neck and shoulders, roundish obstinate looking head covered with short crisp bronze curls, clear quick eyes and good brows and mouth, hopelessly prosaic nose like that of a strongminded baby, trim soldierlike carriage and energetic manner, and with all his wits about him in spite of his desperate predicament: even with a sense of the humor of it, without, however, the least intention of trifling with it or throwing away a chance. Reckoning up what he can guess about* RAINA: *her age, her social position, her character, and the extent to which she is frightened, he continues, more politely but still most determinedly.)* Excuse my disturbing you; but you recognize my uniform? Serb! If I'm caught I shall be killed. *(Menacingly.)* Do you understand that?

RAINA: Yes.

THE MAN: Well, I dont intend to get killed if I can help it. *(Still more formidably.)* Do you understand that? *(He locks the door quickly but quietly.)*

RAINA: *(disdainfully)* I suppose not. *(She draws herself up superbly, and looks him straight in the face, adding, with cutting emphasis.)* Some soldiers, I know, are afraid to die.

THE MAN: *(with grim good humor)* All of them, dear lady, all of them, believe me. It is our duty to live as long as we can. Now, if you raise an alarm—

RAINA: *(cutting him short)* You will

shoot me. How do you know that *I* am afraid to die?

THE MAN: (*cunningly*) Ah; but suppose I dont shoot you, what will happen then? A lot of your cavalry will burst into this pretty room of yours and slaughter me here like a pig; for I'll fight like a demon: they shant get me into the street to amuse themselves with: I know what they are. Are you prepared to receive that sort of company in your present undress? (RAINA, *suddenly conscious of her nightgown, instinctively shrinks and gathers it more closely about her neck. He watches her and adds pitilessly*) Hardly presentable, eh? (*She turns to the ottoman. He raises his pistol instantly, and cries*) Stop! (*She stops.*) Where are you going?

RAINA: (*with dignified patience*) Only to get my cloak.

THE MAN: (*passing swiftly to the ottoman and snatching the cloak*) A good idea! I'll keep the cloak; and you'll take care that nobody comes in and sees you without it. This is a better weapon than the revolver: eh? (*He throws the pistol down on the ottoman.*)

RAINA: (*revolted*) It is not the weapon of a gentleman!

THE MAN: It's good enough for a man with only you to stand between him and death. (*As they look at one another for a moment,* RAINA *hardly able to believe that even a Serbian officer can be so cynically and selfishly unchivalrous, they are startled by a sharp fusillade in the street. The chill of imminent death hushes the man's voice as he adds*) Do you hear? If you are going to bring those blackguards in on me you shall receive them as you are.

(*Clamor and disturbance. The pursuers in the street batter at the house door, shouting.* Open the door! Open the door! Wake up, will you! *A man servant's voice calls to them angrily from within.* This is Major Petkoff's house: you cant come in here; *but a renewal of the clamor, and a torrent of blows on the door, end with his letting a chain down with a clank, followed by a rush of heavy footsteps and a din of triumphant yells, dominated at last by the voice of* CATHERINE, *indignantly addressing an officer with* What does this mean, sir? Do you know where you are? *The noise subsides suddenly.*)

LOUKA: (*outside, knocking at the bedroom door*) My lady! my lady! get up quick and open the door. If you dont they will break it down.

(*The fugitive throws up his head with the gesture of a man who sees that it is all over with him, and drops the manner he has been assuming to intimidate* RAINA.)

THE MAN: (*sincerely and kindly*) No use, dear: I'm done for. (*Flinging the cloak to her.*) Quick! wrap yourself up: theyre coming.

RAINA: Oh, thank you. (*She wraps herself up with intense relief.*)

THE MAN: (*between his teeth*) Dont mention it.

RAINA: (*anxiously*) What will you do?

THE MAN: (*grimly*) The first man in will find out. Keep out of the way; and dont look. It wont last long; but it will not be nice. (*He draws his sabre and faces the door, waiting.*)

RAINA: (*impulsively*) I'll help you. I'll save you.

THE MAN: You cant.

RAINA: I can. I'll hide you. (*She drags him towards the window.*) Here! behind the curtains.

THE MAN: (*yielding to her*) Theres just half a chance, if you keep your head.

RAINA: (*drawing the curtain before him*) S-sh! (*She makes for the ottoman.*)

THE MAN: (*putting out his head*) Remember—

RAINA: (*running back to him*) Yes?

THE MAN: Nine soldiers out of ten are born fools.

RAINA: Oh! (*She draws the curtain angrily before him.*)

THE MAN: (*looking out at the other

side) If they find me, I promise you a fight: a devil of a fight.

(*She stamps at him. He disappears hastily. She takes off her cloak, and throws it across the foot of the bed. Then, with a sleepy, disturbed air, she opens the door.* LOUKA *enters excitedly.*)

LOUKA: One of those beasts of Serbs has been seen climbing up the waterpipe to your balcony. Our men want to search for him; and they are so wild and drunk and furious. (*She makes for the other side of the room to get as far from the door as possible.*) My lady says you are to dress at once and to— (*She sees the revolver lying on the ottoman, and stops, petrified.*)

RAINA: (*as if annoyed at being disturbed*) They shall not search here. Why have they been let in?

CATHERINE: (*coming in hastily*) Raina, darling, are you safe? Have you seen anyone or heard anything?

RAINA: I heard the shooting. Surely the soldiers will not dare come in here?

CATHERINE: I have found a Russian officer, thank Heaven: he knows Sergius. (*Speaking through the door to someone outside.*) Sir: will you come in now. My daughter will receive you.

(*A young Russian officer, in Bulgarian uniform, enters, sword in hand.*)

OFFICER: (*with soft feline politeness and stiff military carriage*) Good evening, gracious lady. I am sorry to intrude; but there is a Serb hiding on the balcony. Will you and the gracious lady your mother please to withdraw whilst we search?

RAINA: (*petulantly*) Nonsense, sir: you can see that there is no one on the balcony. (*She throws the shutters wide open and stands with her back to the curtain where the man is hidden, pointing to the moonlit balcony. A couple of shots are fired right under the window; and a bullet shatters the glass opposite* RAINA, *who winks and gasps, but stands her ground; whilst* CATHERINE *screams, and the officer, with a cry of* Take care! *rushes to the balcony.*)

THE OFFICER: (*on the balcony, shouting savagely down to the street*) Cease firing, you fools: do you hear? Cease firing, damn you! (*He glares down for a moment; then turns to* RAINA, *trying to resume his polite manner.*) Could anyone have got in without your knowledge? Were you asleep?

RAINA: No: I have not been to bed.

THE OFFICER: (*impatiently, coming back into the room*) Your neighbors have their heads so full of runaway Serbs that they see them everywhere. (*Politely.*) Gracious lady: a thousand pardons. Goodnight. (*Military bow, which* RAINA *returns coldly. Another to* CATHERINE, *who follows him out.*)

(RAINA *closes the shutters. She turns and sees* LOUKA, *who has been watching the scene curiously.*)

RAINA: Dont leave my mother, Louka, until the soldiers go away.

(LOUKA *glances at* RAINA, *at the ottoman, at the curtain; then purses her lips secretively, laughs insolently, and goes out.* RAINA, *highly offended by this demonstration, follows her to the door, and shuts it behind her with a slam, locking it violently. The man immediately steps out from behind the curtain, sheathing his sabre. Then, dismissing the danger from his mind in a businesslike way, he comes affably to* RAINA.)

THE MAN: A narrow shave; but a miss is as good as a mile. Dear young lady: your servant to the death. I wish for your sake I had joined the Bulgarian army instead of the other one. I am not a native Serb.

RAINA: (*haughtily*) No: you are one of the Austrians who set the Serbs on to rob us of our national liberty, and who officer their army for them. We hate them!

THE MAN: Austrian! not I. Dont hate me, dear young lady. I am a Swiss, fighting merely as a professional soldier. I joined the Serbs because they came first on the road from Switzerland. Be generous: you've beaten us hollow.

RAINA: Have I not been generous?

THE MAN: Noble! Heroic! But I'm not saved yet. This particular rush will soon pass through; but the pursuit will go on all night by fits and starts. I must take my chance to get off in a quiet interval. (*Pleasantly*) You dont mind my waiting just a minute or two, do you?

RAINA: (*putting on her most genteel society manner*) Oh, not at all. Wont you sit down?

THE MAN: Thanks. (*He sits on the foot of the bed.*)

(RAINA *walks with studied elegance to the ottoman and sits down. Unfortunately she sits on the pistol, and jumps up with a shriek. The man, all nerves, shies like a frightened horse to the other side of the room.*)

THE MAN: (*irritably*) Dont frighten me like that. What is it?

RAINA: Your revolver! It was staring that officer in the face all the time. What an escape!

THE MAN: (*vexed at being unnecessarily terrified*) Oh, is that all?

RAINA: (*staring at him rather superciliously as she conceives a poorer and poorer opinion of him, and feels proportionately more and more at her ease*) I am sorry I frightened you. (*She takes up the pistol and hands it to him.*) Pray take it to protect yourself against me.

THE MAN: (*grinning wearily at the sarcasm as he takes the pistol*) No use, dear young lady: there's nothing in it. It's not loaded. (*He makes a grimace at it, and drops it disparagingly into his revolver case.*)

RAINA: Load it by all means.

THE MAN: Ive no ammunition. What use are cartridges in battle? I always carry chocolate instead; and I finished the last cake of that hours ago.

RAINA: (*outraged in her most cherished ideals of manhood*) Chocolate! Do you stuff your pockets with sweets—like a schoolboy—even in the field?

THE MAN: (*grinning*) Yes: isnt it contemptible? (*Hungrily*) I wish I had some now.

RAINA: Allow me. (*She sails away scornfully to the chest of drawers, and returns with the box of confectionery in her hand.*) I am sorry I have eaten them all except these. (*She offers him the box.*)

THE MAN: (*ravenously*) Youre an angel! (*He gobbles the contents.*) Creams! Delicious! (*He looks anxiously to see whether there are any more. There are none: he can only scrape the box with his fingers and suck them. When that nourishment is exhausted he accepts the inevitable with pathetic good humor, and says, with grateful emotion*) Bless you, dear lady! You can always tell an old soldier by the inside of his holsters and cartridge boxes. The young ones carry pistols and cartridges: the old ones, grub. Thank you. (*He hands back the box. She snatches it contemptuously from him and throws it away. He shies again, as if she had meant to strike him.*) Ugh! Dont do things so suddenly, gracious lady. It's mean to revenge yourself because I frightened you just now.

RAINA: (*loftily*) Frighten me! Do you know, sir, that though I am only a woman, I think I am at heart as brave as you.

THE MAN: I should think so. You havent been under fire for three days as I have. I can stand two days without showing it much; but no man can stand three days: I'm as nervous as a mouse. (*He sits down on the ottoman, and takes his head in his hands.*) Would you like to see me cry?

RAINA: (*alarmed*) No.

THE MAN: If you would, all you have to do is to scold me just as if I were a little boy and you my nurse. If I were in camp now, theyd play all sorts of tricks on me.

RAINA: (*a little moved*) I'm sorry. I wont scold you. (*Touched by the sympathy in her tone, he raises his head and looks gratefully at her: she immediately draws back and says stiffly.*) You must excuse me: our soldiers are not like that. (*She moves away from the ottoman.*)

THE MAN: Oh yes they are. There are only two sorts of soldiers: old ones and young ones. Ive served fourteen years: half of your fellows never smelt powder before. Why, how is it that youve just beaten us? Sheer ignorance of the art of war, nothing else. (*Indignantly.*) I never saw anything so unprofessional.

RAINA: (*ironically*) Oh! was it unprofessional to beat you?

THE MAN: Well, come! is it professional to throw a regiment of cavalry on a battery of machine guns, with the dead certainty that if the guns go off not a horse or man will ever get within fifty yards of the fire? I couldnt believe my eyes when I saw it.

RAINA: (*eagerly turning to him, as all her enthusiasm and her dreams of glory rush back on her*) Did you see the great cavalry charge? Oh, tell me about it. Describe it to me.

THE MAN: You never saw a cavalry charge, did you?

RAINA: How could I?

THE MAN: Ah, perhaps not. No: of course not! Well, it's a funny sight. It's like slinging a handful of peas against a window pane: first one comes; then two or three close behind him; and then all the rest in a lump.

RAINA: (*her eyes dilating as she raises her clasped hands ecstatically*) Yes, first One! the bravest of the brave!

THE MAN: (*prosaically*) Hm! you should see the poor devil pulling at his horse.

RAINA: Why should he pull at his horse?

THE MAN: (*impatient of so stupid a question*) It's running away with him, of course; do you suppose the fellow wants to get there before the others and be killed? Then they all come. You can tell the young ones by their wildness and their slashing. The old ones come bunched up under the number one guard: they know that theyre mere projectiles, and that it's no use trying to fight. The wounds are mostly broken knees, from the horses cannoning together.

RAINA: Ugh! But I dont believe the first man is a coward. I know he is a hero!

THE MAN: (*goodhumoredly*) Thats what youd have said if youd seen the first man in the charge today.

RAINA: (*breathless, forgiving him everything*) Ah, I knew it! Tell me. Tell me about him.

THE MAN: He did it like an operatic tenor. A regular handsome fellow, with flashing eyes and lovely moustache, shouting his war-cry and charging like Don Quixote[1] at the windmills. We did laugh.

RAINA: You dared to laugh!

THE MAN: Yes; but when the sergeant ran up as white as a sheet, and told us theyd sent us the wrong ammunition, and that we couldnt fire a round for the next ten minutes, we laughed at the other side of our mouths. I never felt so sick in my life; though Ive been in one or two very tight places. And I hadnt even a revolver cartridge: only chocolate. Wed no bayonets: nothing. Of course, they just cut us to bits. And there was Don Quixote[1] flourishing like a drum major, thinking hed done the cleverest thing ever known, whereas he ought to be courtmartialled for it. Of all the fools ever let loose on a field of battle, that man must be the very maddest. He and his regiment simply committed suicide; only the pistol missed fire: that's all.

RAINA: (*deeply wounded, but steadfastly loyal to her ideals*) Indeed! Would you know him again if you saw him?

THE MAN: Shall I ever forget him!

(*She again goes to the chest of drawers.*

He watches her with a vague hope that she may have something more for him to eat. She takes the portrait from its stand and brings it to him.)

RAINA: That is a photograph of the gentleman—the patriot and hero—to whom I am betrothed.

THE MAN: (*recognizing it with a shock*) I'm really very sorry. (*Looking at her.*) Was it fair to lead me on? (*He looks at the portrait again.*) Yes: thats Don Quixote: not a doubt of it. (*He stifles a laugh.*)

RAINA: (*quickly*) Why do you laugh?

THE MAN: (*apologetic, but still greatly tickled*) I didnt laugh. I assure you. At least I didnt mean to. But when I think of him charging the windmills and imagining he was doing the finest thing— (*He chokes with suppressed laughter.*)

RAINA: (*sternly*) Give me back the portrait, sir.

THE MAN: (*with sincere remorse*) Of course. Certainly. I'm really very sorry. (*He hands her the picture. She deliberately kisses it and looks him straight in the face before returning to the chest of drawers to replace it. He follows her, apologizing.*) Perhaps I'm quite wrong, you know: no doubt I am. Most likely he had got wind of the cartridge business somehow, and knew it was a safe job.

RAINA: That is to say, he was a pretender and a coward! You did not dare say that before.

THE MAN: (*with a comic gesture of despair*) It's no use, dear lady: I cant make you see it from the professional point of view. (*As he turns away to get back to the ottoman, a couple of distant shots threaten renewed trouble.*)

RAINA: (*sternly, as she sees him listening to the shots*) So much the better for you!

THE MAN: (*turning*) How?

RAINA: You are my enemy; and you are at my mercy. What would I do if I were a professional soldier?

THE MAN: Ah, true, dear young lady: youre always right. I know how good youve been to me: to my last hour I shall remember those three chocolate creams. It was unsoldierly; but it was angelic.

RAINA: (*coldly*) Thank you. And now I will do a soldierly thing. You cannot stay here after what you have just said about my future husband; but I will go out on the balcony and see whether it is safe for you to climb down into the street. (*She turns to the window.*)

THE MAN: (*changing countenance*) Down that waterpipe! Stop! Wait! I cant! I darent! The very thought of it makes me giddy. I came up it fast enough with death behind me. But to face it now in cold blood—! (*He sinks on the ottoman.*) It's no use: I give up: I'm beaten. Give the alarm. (*He drops his head on his hands in the deepest dejection.*)

RAINA: (*disarmed by pity*) Come: dont be disheartened. (*She stoops over him almost maternally: he shakes his head.*) Oh, you are a very poor soldier: a chocolate cream soldier! Come, cheer up! it takes less courage to climb down than to face capture: remember that.

THE MAN: (*dreamily, lulled by her voice*) No: capture only means death; and death is sleep: oh, sleep, sleep, sleep, undisturbed sleep! Climbing down the pipe means doing something—exerting myself —thinking! Death ten times over first.

RAINA: (*softly and wonderingly, catching the rhythm of his weariness*) Are you as sleepy as that?

THE MAN: Ive not had two hours undisturbed sleep since I joined. I havent closed my eyes for forty-eight hours.

RAINA: (*at her wit's end*) But what am I to do with you?

THE MAN: (*staggering up, roused by her desperation*) Of course. I must do something. (*He shakes himself; pulls himself together; and speaks with rallied vigor and courage.*) You see, sleep or no sleep, hunger or no hunger, tired or not tired, you can always do a thing when you know it must be done. Well, that pipe must be got down: (*he hits himself on the chest*) do you hear that, you chocolate cream soldier? (*He turns to the window.*)

RAINA: (*anxiously*) But if you fall?

THE MAN: I shall sleep as if the stones were a feather bed. Goodbye. (*He makes boldly for the window; and his hand is on the shutter when there is a terrible burst of firing in the street beneath.*)

RAINA: (*rushing to him*) Stop! (*She seizes him recklessly, and pulls him quite round.*) Theyll kill you.

THE MAN: (*coolly, but attentively*) Never mind: this sort of thing is all in my day's work. I'm bound to take my chance. (*Decisively.*) Now do what I tell you. Put out the candle; so that they shant see the light when I open the shutters. And keep away from the window, whatever you do. If they see me theyre sure to have a shot at me.

RAINA: (*clinging to him*) Theyre sure to see you: it's bright moonlight. I'll save you. Oh, how can you be so indifferent! You want me to save you, dont you?

THE MAN: I really dont want to be troublesome. (*She shakes him in her impatience.*) I am not indifferent, dear young lady, I assure you. But how is it to be done?

RAINA: Come away from the window. (*She takes him firmly back to the middle of the room. The moment she releases him he turns mechanically towards the window again. She seizes him and turns him back, exclaiming*) Please! (*He becomes motionless, like a hypnotized rabbit, his fatigue gaining fast on him. She releases him, and addresses him patronizingly.*) Now listen. You must trust to our hospitality. You do not yet know in whose house you are. I am a Petkoff.

THE MAN: A pet what?

RAINA: (*rather indignantly*) I mean that I belong to the family of the Petkoffs, the richest and best known in our country.

THE MAN: Oh yes, of course. I beg your pardon. The Petkoffs, to be sure. How stupid of me!

RAINA: You know you never heard of them until this moment. How can you stoop to pretend!

THE MAN: Forgive me: I'm too tired to think; and the change of subject was too much for me. Dont scold me.

RAINA: I forgot. It might make you cry. (*He nods, quite seriously. She pouts and then resumes her patronizing tone.*) I must tell you that my father holds the highest command of any Bulgarian in our army. He is (*proudly*) a Major.

THE MAN: (*pretending to be deeply impressed*) A Major! Bless me! Think of that!

RAINA: You showed great ignorance in thinking that it was necessary to climb up to the balcony because ours is the only private house that has two rows of windows. There is a flight of stairs inside to get up and down by.

THE MAN: Stairs! How grand! You live in great luxury indeed, dear young lady.

RAINA: Do you know what a library is?

THE MAN: A library? A roomful of books?

RAINA: Yes. We have one, the only one in Bulgaria.

THE MAN: Actually a real library! I should like to see that.

RAINA: (*affectedly*) I tell you these things to show you that you are not in the house of ignorant country folk who would kill you the moment they saw your Serbian uniform, but among civilized people. We go to Bucharest every year for the opera season; and I have spent a whole month in Vienna.

THE MAN: I saw that, dear young lady. I saw at once that you knew the world.

RAINA: Have you ever seen the opera of *Ernani*?[2]

THE MAN: Is that the one with the devil in it in red velvet, and a soldiers' chorus?

RAINA: (*contemptuously*) No!

THE MAN: (*stifling a heavy sigh of weariness*) Then I dont know it.

RAINA: I thought you might have remembered the great scene where Ernani, flying from his foes just as you are tonight, takes refuge in the castle of his bitterest enemy, an old Castilian noble.[3] The noble refuses to give him up. His guest is sacred to him.

THE MAN: (*quickly, waking up a little*) Have your people got that notion?

RAINA: (*with dignity*) My mother and I can understand that notion, as you call it. And if instead of threatening me with your pistol as you did you had simply thrown yourself as a fugitive on our hospitality, you would have been as safe as in your father's house.

THE MAN: Quite sure?

RAINA: (*turning her back on him in disgust*) Oh, it is useless to try to make you understand.

THE MAN: Dont be angry: you see how awkward it would be for me if there was any mistake. My father is a very hospitable man: he keeps six hotels; but I couldnt trust him as far as that. What about your father?

RAINA: He is away at Slivnitza fighting for his country. I answer for your safety. There is my hand in pledge of it. Will that reassure you? (*She offers him her hand.*)

THE MAN: (*looking dubiously at his own hand*) Better not touch my hand, dear young lady. I must have a wash first.

RAINA: (*touched*) That is very nice of you. I see that you are a gentleman.

THE MAN: (*puzzled*) Eh?

RAINA: You must not think I am surprised. Bulgarians of really good standing—people in our position—wash their hands nearly every day. So you see I can appreciate your delicacy. You may take my hand. (*She offers it again.*)

THE MAN: (*kissing it with his hands behind his back*) Thanks, gracious young lady: I feel safe at last. And now would you mind breaking the news to your mother? I had better not stay here secretly longer than is necessary.

RAINA: If you will be so good as to keep perfectly still whilst I am away.

THE MAN: Certainly. (*He sits down on the ottoman.*)

(RAINA *goes to the bed and wraps herself in the fur cloak. His eyes close. She goes to the door. Turning for a last look at him, she sees that he is dropping off to sleep.*)

RAINA: (*at the door*) You are not going asleep, are you? (*He murmurs inarticulately: she runs to him and shakes him.*) Do you hear? Wake up: you are falling asleep.

THE MAN: Eh? Falling aslee—? Oh no: not the least in the world: I was only thinking. It's all right: I'm wide awake.

RAINA: (*severely*) Will you please stand up while I am away. (*He rises reluctantly.*) All the time, mind.

THE MAN: (*standing unsteadily*) Certainly. Certainly: you may depend on me. (RAINA *looks doubtfully at him. He smiles weakly. She goes reluctantly, turning again at the door, and almost catching him in the act of yawning. She goes out.*)

THE MAN: (*drowsily*) Sleep, sleep, sleep, sleep, slee— (*The words trail off into a murmur. He makes again with a shock on the point of falling.*) Where am I? Thats what I want to know: where am I? Must keep awake. Nothing keeps me awake except danger: remember that: (*intently*) danger, danger, danger, dan— (*trailing off again: another shock*) Wheres danger? Mus' find it. (*He starts off vaguely round the room in search of it.*) What am I looking for? Sleep—danger—dont know. (*He stumbles against the bed.*) Ah yes: now I know. All right now. I'm to go to bed, but not to sleep. Be sure not to sleep, because of danger. Not to lie down either, only sit down. (*He sits on the bed. A blissful expression comes into his face.*) Ah! (*With a happy sigh he sinks back at full length; lifts his boots into the bed with a final effort; and falls fast asleep instantly.*)

(CATHERINE *comes in, followed by* RAINA.)

RAINA: (*looking at the ottoman*) He's gone! I left him here.

CATHERINE: Here! Then he must have climbed down from the—

RAINA: (*seeing him*) Oh! (*She points.*)

CATHERINE: (*scandalized*) Well! (*She strides to the bed,* RAINA *following until she is opposite her on the other side.*) He's fast asleep. The brute!

RAINA: (*anxiously*) Sh!

CATHERINE: (*shaking him*) Sir! (*Shaking him again, harder.*) Sir!! (*Vehemently, shaking very hard.*) Sir!!!

RAINA: (*catching her arm*) Dont, mamma; the poor darling is worn out. Let him sleep.

CATHERINE: (*letting him go, and turning amazed to* RAINA) The poor darling! Raina!!! (*She looks sternly at her daughter.*)

(*The man sleeps profoundly.*)

ACT II

The sixth of March, 1886. In the garden of MAJOR PETKOFF's *house. It is a fine spring morning: the garden looks fresh and pretty. Beyond the paling the tops of a couple of minarets can be seen, shewing that there is a valley there, with the little town in it. A few miles further the Balkan mountains rise and shut in the landscape. Looking towards them from within the garden, the side of the house is seen on the left, with a garden door reached by a little flight of steps. On the right the stable yard, with its gateway, encroaches on the garden. There are fruit bushes along the paling and house, covered with washing spread out to dry. A path runs by the house, and rises by two steps at the corner, where it turns out of sight. In the middle, a small table, with two bent wood chairs at it, is laid for breakfast with Turkish coffee pot, cups, rolls, etc.; but the cups have been used and the bread broken. There is a wooden garden seat against the wall on the right.*

LOUKA, *smoking a cigaret, is standing between the table and the house, turning her back with angry disdain on a manservant who is lecturing her. He is a middle-aged man of cool temperament and low but clear and keen intelligence, with the complacency of the servant who values himself on his rank in servitude, and the imperturbability of the accurate calculator who has no illusions. He wears a white Bulgarian costume: jacket with embroidered border, sash, wide knickerbockers, and decorated gaiters. His head is shaved up to the crown, giving him a high Japanese forehead. His name is* NICOLA.

NICOLA: Be warned in time, Louka: mend your manners. I know the mistress. She is so grand that she never dreams that any servant could dare be disrespectful to her; but if she once suspects that you are defying her, out you go.

LOUKA: I do defy her. I will defy her. What do I care for her?

NICOLA: If you quarrel with the family, I never can marry you. It's the same as if you quarrelled with me!

LOUKA: You take her part against me, do you?

NICOLA: (*sedately*) I shall always be dependent on the good will of the family. When I leave their service and start a shop in Sofia, their custom will be half my capital: their bad word would ruin me.

LOUKA: You have no spirit. I should

like to catch them saying a word against me!

NICOLA: (*pityingly*) I should have expected more sense from you, Louka. But youre young: youre young!

LOUKA: Yes; and you like me the better for it, dont you? But I know some family secrets they wouldnt care to have told, young as I am. Let them quarrel with me if they dare!

NICOLA: (*with compassionate superiority*) Do you know what they would do if they heard you talk like that?

LOUKA: What could they do?

NICOLA: Discharge you for untruthfulness. Who would believe any stories you told after that? Who would give you another situation? Who in this house would dare be seen speaking to you ever again? How long would your father be left on his little farm? (*She impatiently throws away the end of her cigaret, and stamps on it.*) Child: you dont know the power such high people have over the like of you and me when we try to rise out of our poverty against them. (*He goes close to her and lowers his voice.*) Look at me, ten years in their service. Do you think I know no secrets? I know things about the mistress that she wouldnt have the master know for a thousand levas.[4] I know things about him that she wouldnt let him hear the last of for six months if I blabbed them to her. I know things about Raina that would break off her match with Sergius if—

LOUKA: (*turning on him quickly*) How do you know? I never told you!

NICOLA: (*opening his eyes cunningly*) So thats your little secret, is it? I thought it might be something like that. Well, you take my advice and be respectful; and make the mistress feel that no matter what you know or dont know, she can depend on you to hold your tongue and serve the family faithfully. Thats what they like; and thats how youll make most out of them.

LOUKA: (*with searching scorn*) You have the soul of a servant, Nicola.

NICOLA: (*complacently*) Yes: thats the secret of success in service.

(*A loud knocking with a whip handle on a wooden door is heard from the stable yard.*)

MALE VOICE OUTSIDE: Hollo! Hollo there! Nicola!

LOUKA: Master! back from the war!

NICOLA: (*quickly*) My word for it, Louka, the war's over. Off with you and get some fresh coffee. (*He runs out into the stable yard.*)

LOUKA: (*as she collects the coffee pot and cups on the tray, and carries it into the house*) Youll never put the soul of a servant into me.

(MAJOR PETKOFF *comes from the stable yard, followed by* NICOLA. *He is a cheerful, excitable, insignificant, unpolished man of about 50, naturally unambitious except as to his income and his importance in local society, but just now greatly pleased with the military rank which the war has thrust on him as a man of consequence in his town. The fever of plucky patriotism which the Serbian attack roused in all the Bulgarians has pulled him through the war; but he is obviously glad to be home again.*)

PETKOFF: (*pointing to the table with his whip*) Breakfast out here, eh?

NICOLA: Yes, sir. The mistress and Miss Raina have just gone in.

PETKOFF: (*sitting down and taking a roll*) Go in and say Ive come; and get me some fresh coffee.

NICOLA: It's coming, sir. (*He goes to the house door.* LOUKA, *with fresh coffee, a clean cup, and a brandy bottle on her tray, meets him.*) Have you told the mistress?

LOUKA: Yes: she's coming.

(NICOLA *goes into the house.* LOUKA *brings the coffee to the table.*)

PETKOFF: Well: the Serbs havnt run away with you, have they?

LOUKA: No, sir.

PETKOFF: Thats right. Have you brought me some cognac?

LOUKA: (*putting the bottle on the table*) Here, sir.

PETKOFF: Thats right. (*He pours some into his coffee.*)

(CATHERINE, *who, having at this early hour made only a very perfunctory toilet, wears a Bulgarian apron over a once brilliant but now half worn-out dressing gown, and a colored handkerchief tied over her thick black hair, comes from the house with Turkish slippers on her bare feet, looking astonishingly handsome and stately under all the circumstances.* LOUKA *goes into the house.*)

CATHERINE: My dear Paul: what a surprise for us! (*She stoops over the back of his chair to kiss him.*) Have they brought you fresh coffee?

PETKOFF: Yes: Louka's been looking after me. The war's over. The treaty was signed three days ago at Bucharest; and the decree for our army to demobilize was issued yesterday.

CATHERINE: (*springing erect, with flashing eyes*) Paul: have you let the Austrians force you to make peace?

PETKOFF: (*submissively*) My dear: they didnt consult me. What could *I* do? (*She sits down and turns away from him.*) But of course we saw to it that the treaty was an honorable one. It declares peace—

CATHERINE: (*outraged*) Peace!

PETKOFF: (*appeasing her*)—but not friendly relations: remember that. They wanted to put that in; but I insisted on its being struck out. What more could I do?

CATHERINE: You could have annexed Serbia and made Prince Alexander Emperor of the Balkans. Thats what I would have done.

PETKOFF: I dont doubt it in the least, my dear. But I should have had to subdue the whole Austrian Empire first; and that would have kept me too long away from you. I missed you greatly.

CATHERINE: (*relenting*) Ah! (*She stretches her hand affectionately across the table to squeeze his.*)

PETKOFF: And how have you been, my dear?

CATHERINE: Oh, my usual sore throats: thats all.

PETKOFF: (*with conviction*) That comes from washing your neck every day. Ive often told you so.

CATHERINE: Nonsense, Paul!

PETKOFF: (*over his coffee and cigaret*) I dont believe in going too far with these modern customs. All this washing cant be good for the health: it's not natural. There was an Englishman at Philippopolis who used to wet himself all over with cold water every morning when he got up. Disgusting! It all comes from the English: their climate makes them so dirty that they have to be perpetually washing themselves. Look at my father! he never had a bath in his life; and he lived to be ninety-eight, the healthiest man in Bulgaria. I dont mind a good wash once a week to keep up my position; but once a day is carrying the thing to a ridiculous extreme.

CATHERINE: You are a barbarian at heart still, Paul. I hope you behaved yourself before all those Russian officers.

PETKOFF: I did my best. I took care to let them know that we have a library.

CATHERINE: Ah; but you didnt tell them that we have an electric bell in it? I have had one put up.

PETKOFF: Whats an electric bell?

CATHERINE: You touch a button; something tinkles in the kitchen; and then Nicola comes up.

PETKOFF: Why not shout for him?

CATHERINE: Civilized people never shout for their servants. Ive learnt that while you were away.

PETKOFF: Well, I'll tell you something Ive learnt too. Civilized people dont hang out their washing to dry where visitors can see it; so youd better have all that (*indicating the clothes on the bushes*) put somewhere else.

CATHERINE: Oh, thats absurd, Paul: I dont believe really refined people notice such things.

SERGIUS: (*knocking at the stable gates*) Gate, Nicola!

PETKOFF: Theres Sergius. (*Shouting.*) Hollo, Nicola!

CATHERINE: Oh, dont shout, Paul: it really isnt nice.

PETKOFF: Bosh! (*He shouts louder than before.*) Nicola!

NICOLA: (*appearing at the house door*) Yes, sir.

PETKOFF: Are you deaf? Dont you hear Major Saranoff knocking? Bring him round this way. (*He pronounces the name with the stress on the second syllable:* SARAHNOFF.)

NICOLA: Yes, Major. (*He goes into the stable yard.*)

PETKOFF: You must talk to him, my dear, until Raina takes him off our hands. He bores my life out about our not promoting him. Over my head, if you please.

CATHERINE: He certainly ought to be promoted when he marries Raina. Besides, the country should insist on having at least one native general.

PETKOFF: Yes; so that he could throw away whole brigades instead of regiments. It's no use, my dear: he hasnt the slightest chance of promotion until we're quite sure that the peace will be a lasting one.

NICOLA: (*at the gate, announcing*) Major Sergius Saranoff! (*He goes into the house and returns presently with a third chair, which he places at the table. He then withdraws.*)

(MAJOR SERGIUS SARANOFF, *the original of the portrait in* RAINA'S *room, is a tall romantically handsome man, with the physical hardihood, the high spirit, and the susceptible imagination of an untamed mountaineer chieftain. But his remarkable personal distinction is of a characteristically civilized type. The ridges of his eyebrows, curving with an interrogative twist round the projections at the outer corners; his jealously observant eye; his nose, thin, keen, and apprehensive in spite of the pugnacious high bridge and large nostril; his assertive chin would not be out of place in a Parisian salon, showing that the clever imaginative barbarian has an acute critical faculty which has been thrown into intense activity by the arrival of western civilization in the Balkans. The result is precisely what the advent of nineteenth-century thought first produced in England: to wit, Byronism. By his brooding on the perpetual failure, not only of others, but of himself, to live up to his ideals; by his consequent cynical scorn for humanity; by his jejune credulity as to the absolute validity of his world in disregarding them; by his concepts and the unworthiness of the wincings and mockeries under the sting of the petty disillusions which every hour spent among men brings to his sensitive observation, he has acquired the half tragic, half ironic air, the mysterious moodiness, the suggestion of a strange and terrible history that has left nothing but undying remorse, by which Childe Harold fascinated the grandmothers of his English contemporaries. It is clear that here or nowhere is* RAINA'S *ideal hero.* CATHERINE *is hardly less enthusiastic about him than her daughter, and much less reserved in showing her enthusiasm. As he enters from the stable gate, she rises effusively to greet him.* PETKOFF *is distinctly less disposed to make a fuss about him.*)

PETKOFF: Here already, Sergius! Glad to see you.

CATHERINE: My dear Sergius! (*She holds out both her hands.*)

SERGIUS: (*kissing them with scrupulous gallantry*) My dear mother, if I may call you so.

PETKOFF: (*drily*) Mother-in-law,

Sergius: mother-in-law! Sit down; and have some coffee.

SERGIUS: Thank you: none for me. (*He gets away from the table with a certain distaste for* PETKOFF'S *enjoyment of it, and posts himself with conscious dignity against the rail of the steps leading to the house.*)

CATHERINE: You look superb. The campaign has improved you, Sergius. Everybody here is mad about you. We were all wild with enthusiasm about that magnificent cavalry charge.

SERGIUS: (*with grave irony*) Madam: it was the cradle and the grave of my military reputation.

CATHERINE: How so?

SERGIUS: I won the battle the wrong way when our worthy Russian generals were losing it the right way. In short, I upset their plans, and wounded their self-esteem. Two Cossack colonels had their regiments routed on the most correct principles of scientific warfare. Two major-generals got killed strictly according to military etiquette. The two colonels are now major-generals; and I am still a simple major.

CATHERINE: You shall not remain so, Sergius. The women are on your side; and they will see that justice is done you.

SERGIUS: It is too late. I have only waited for the peace to send in my resignation.

PETKOFF: (*dropping his cup in his amazement*) Your resignation!

CATHERINE: Oh, you must withdraw it!

SERGIUS: (*with resolute measured emphasis, folding his arms*) I never withdraw.

PETKOFF: (*vexed*) Now who could have supposed you were going to do such a thing?

SERGIUS: (*with fire*) Everyone that knew me. But enough of myself and my affairs. How is Raina; and where is Raina?

RAINA: (*suddenly coming round the corner of the house and standing at the top of the steps in the path*) Raina is here. (*She makes a charming picture as they turn to look at her. She wears an underdress of pale green silk, draped with an overdress of thin ecru canvas embroidered with gold. She is crowned with a dainty eastern cap of gold tinsel.* SERGIUS *goes impulsively to meet her. Posing regally, she presents her hand: he drops chivalrously on one knee and kisses it.*)

PETKOFF: (*aside to* CATHERINE, *beaming with parental pride*) Pretty, isnt it? She always appears at the right moment.

CATHERINE: (*impatiently*) Yes; she listens for it. It is an abominable habit. (SERGIUS *leads* RAINA *forward with splendid gallantry. When they arrive at the table, she turns to him with a bend of the head: he bows; and thus they separate, he coming to his place and she going behind her father's chair.*)

RAINA: (*stooping and kissing her father*) Dear father! Welcome home!

PETKOFF: (*patting her cheek*) My little pet girl. (*He kisses her. She goes to the chair left by* NICOLA *for* SERGIUS, *and sits down.*)

CATHERINE: And so youre no longer a soldier, Sergius.

SERGIUS: I am no longer a soldier. Soldiering, my dear madam, is the coward's art of attacking mercilessly when you are strong, and keeping out of harm's way when you are weak. That is the whole secret of successful fighting. Get your enemy at a disadvantage; and never, on any account, fight him on equal terms.

PETKOFF: They wouldnt let us make a fair stand-up fight of it. However, I suppose soldiering has to be a trade like any other trade.

SERGIUS: Precisely. But I have no ambition to shine as a tradesman; so I have taken the advice of that bagman of a captain that settled the exchange of prisoners with us at Pirot, and given it **up.**

PETKOFF: What! that Swiss fellow? Sergius: Ive often thought of that exchange since. He over-reached us about those horses.

SERGIUS: Of course he over-reached us. His father was a hotel and livery stable keeper; and he owed his first step to his knowledge of horse-dealing. (*With mock enthusiasm.*) Ah, he was a soldier: every inch a soldier! If only I had bought the horses for my regiment instead of foolishly leading it into danger, I should have been a field-marshal now!

CATHERINE: A Swiss? What was he doing in the Serbian army?

PETKOFF: A volunteer, of course: keen on picking up his profession. (*Chuckling.*) We shouldnt have been able to begin fighting if these foreigners hadnt shown us how to do it: we knew nothing about it; and neither did the Serbs. Egad, thered have been no war without them!

RAINA: Are there many Swiss officers in the Serbian Army?

PETKOFF: No. All Austrians, just as our officers were all Russians. This was the only Swiss I came across. I'll never trust a Swiss again. He humbugged us into giving him fifty ablebodied men for two hundred worn-out chargers. They werent even eatable!

SERGIUS: We were two children in the hands of that consummate soldier, Major: simply two innocent little children.

RAINA: What was he like?

CATHERINE: Oh, Raina, what a silly question!

SERGIUS: He was like a commercial traveller in uniform. Bourgeois to his boots!

PETKOFF: (*grinning*) Sergius: tell Catherine that queer story his friend told us about how he escaped after Slivnitza. You remember. About his being hid by two women.

SERGIUS: (*with bitter irony*) Oh yes: quite a romance! He was serving in the very battery I so unprofessionally charged. Being a thorough soldier, he ran away like the rest of them, with our cavalry at his heels. To escape their sabres he climbed a waterpipe and made his way into the bedroom of a young Bulgarian lady. The young lady was enchanted by his persuasive commercial traveller's manners. She very modestly entertained him for an hour or so, and then called in her mother lest her conduct should appear unmaidenly. The old lady was equally fascinated; and the fugitive was sent on his way in the morning, disguised in an old coat belonging to the master of the house, who was away at the war.

RAINA: (*rising with marked stateliness*) Your life in the camp has made you coarse, Sergius. I did not think you would have repeated such a story before me. (*She turns away coldly.*)

CATHERINE: (*also rising*) She is right, Sergius. If such women exist, we should be spared the knowledge of them.

PETKOFF: Pooh! nonsense! what does it matter?

SERGIUS: (*ashamed*) No, Petkoff: I was wrong. (*To* RAINA, *with earnest humility.*) I beg your pardon. I have behaved abominably. Forgive me, Raina. (*She bows reservedly.*) And you too, madam. (CATHERINE *bows graciously and sits down. He proceeds solemnly, again addressing* RAINA.) The glimpses I have had of the seamy side of life during the last few months have made me cynical; but I should not have brought my cynicism here: least of all into your presence, Raina. I—(*Here, turning to the others, he is evidently going to begin a long speech when the* MAJOR *interrupts him.*)

PETKOFF: Stuff and nonsense, Sergius! Thats quite enough fuss about nothing: a soldier's daughter should be able to stand up without flinching to a little strong conversation. (*He rises.*) Come: it's time for us to get to business. We have to make up our minds how those three regiments are to get back to Philippopolis: theres no forage for them on the Sofia route.

(*He goes towards the house.*) Come along. (SERGIUS *is about to follow him when* CATHERINE *rises and intervenes.*)

CATHERINE: Oh, Paul, cant you spare Sergius for a few moments? Raina has hardly seen him yet. Perhaps I can help you to settle about the regiments.

SERGIUS: (*protesting*) My dear madam, impossible: you—

CATHERINE: (*stopping him playfully*) You stay here, my dear Sergius: theres no hurry. I have a word or two to say to Paul. (SERGIUS *instantly bows and steps back.*) Now, dear (*taking* PETKOFF's *arm*): come and see the electric bell.

PETKOFF: Oh, very well, very well.

(*They go into the house together affectionately.* SERGIUS, *left alone with* RAINA, *looks anxiously at her, fearing that she is still offended. She smiles, and stretches out her arms to him.*)

SERGIUS: (*hastening to her*) Am I forgiven?

RAINA: (*placing her arms on his shoulders as she looks up at him with admiration and worship*) My hero! My king!

SERGIUS: My queen! (*He kisses her on the forehead.*)

RAINA: How I have envied you, Sergius! You have been out in the world, on the field of battle, able to prove yourself there worthy of any woman in the world; whilst I have had to sit at home inactive — dreaming — useless — doing nothing that could give me the right to call myself worthy of any man.

SERGIUS: Dearest: all my deeds have been yours. You inspired me. I have gone through the war like a knight in a tournament with his lady looking down at him!

RAINA: And you have never been absent from my thoughts for a moment. (*Very solemnly*) Sergius: I think we two have found the higher love. When I think of you, I feel that I could never do a base deed, or think an ignoble thought.

SERGIUS: My lady and my saint! (*He clasps her reverently.*)

RAINA: (*returning his embrace*) My lord and my—

SERGIUS: Sh—sh! Let me be the worshipper, dear. You little know how unworthy even the best man is of a girl's pure passion!

RAINA: I trust you. I love you. You will never disappoint me, Sergius. (LOUKA *is heard singing within the house. They quickly release each other.*) I cant pretend to talk indifferently before her: my heart is too full. (LOUKA *comes from the house with her tray. She goes to the table, and begins to clear it, with her back turned to them.*) I will get my hat; and then we can go out until lunch time. Wouldnt you like that?

SERGIUS: Be quick. If you are away five minutes, it will seem five hours. (RAINA *runs to the top of the steps, and turns there to exchange looks with him and wave him a kiss with both hands. He looks after her with emotion for a moment; then turns slowly away, his face radiant with the loftiest exaltation. The movement shifts his field of vision, into the corner of which there now comes the tail of* LOUKA's *double apron. His attention is arrested at once. He takes a stealthy look at her, and begins to twirl his moustache mischievously, with his left hand akimbo on his hip. Finally, striking the ground with his heels in something of a cavalry swagger, he strolls over to the other side of the table, opposite her, and says*) Louka: do you know what the higher love is?

LOUKA: (*astonished*) No, sir.

SERGIUS: Very fatiguing thing to keep up for any length of time, Louka. One feels the need of some relief after it.

LOUKA: (*innocently*) Perhaps you would like some coffee, sir? (*She stretches her hand across the table for the coffee pot.*)

SERGIUS: (*taking her hand*) Thank you, Louka.

LOUKA: (*pretending to pull*) Oh, sir, you know I didn't mean that. I'm surprised at you!

SERGIUS: (*coming clear of the table and drawing her with him*) I am surprised at myself, Louka. What would Sergius, the hero of Slivnitza, say if he saw me now? What would Sergius, the apostle of the higher love, say if he saw me now? What would the half dozen Sergiuses who keep popping in and out of this handsome figure of mine say if they caught us here? (*Letting go her hand and slipping his arm dexterously round her waist.*) Do you consider my figure handsome, Louka?

LOUKA: Let me go, sir. I shall be disgraced. (*She struggles: he holds her inexorably.*) Oh, will you let go?

SERGIUS: (*looking straight into her eyes*) No.

LOUKA: Then stand back where we cant be seen. Have you no common sense?

SERGIUS: Ah! thats reasonable. (*He takes her into the stable yard gateway, where they are hidden from the house.*)

LOUKA: (*plaintively*) I may be seen from the windows: Miss Raina is sure to be spying about after you.

SERGIUS: (*stung: letting her go*) Take care, Louka. I may be worthless enough to betray the higher love; but do not you insult it.

LOUKA: (*demurely*) Not for the world, sir, I'm sure. May I go on with my work, please, now?

SERGIUS: (*again putting his arm round her*) You are a provoking little witch, Louka. If you were in love with me, would you spy out of windows on me?

LOUKA: Well, you see, sir, since you say you are half a dozen different gentlemen all at once, I should have a great deal to look after.

SERGIUS: (*charmed*) Witty as well as pretty. (*He tries to kiss her.*)

LOUKA: (*avoiding him*) No: I dont want your kisses. Gentlefolk are all alike: you making love to me behind Miss Raina's back; and she doing the same behind yours.

SERGIUS: (*recoiling a step*) Louka!

LOUKA: It shows how little you really care.

SERGIUS: (*dropping his familiarity, and speaking with freezing politeness*) If our conversation is to continue, Louka, you will please remember that a gentleman does not discuss the conduct of the lady he is engaged to with her maid.

LOUKA: It's so hard to know what a gentleman considers right. I thought from your trying to kiss me that you had given up being so particular.

SERGIUS: (*turning away from her and striking his forehead as he comes back into the garden from the gateway*) Devil! devil!

LOUKA: Ha! ha! I expect one of the six of you is very like me, sir; though I am only Miss Raina's maid. (*She goes back to her work at the table, taking no further notice of him.*)

SERGIUS: (*speaking to himself*) Which of the six is the real man? thats the question that torments me. One of them is a hero, another a buffoon, another a humbug, another perhaps a bit of a blackguard. (*He pauses, and looks furtively at* LOUKA *as he adds, with deep bitterness*) And one, at least, is a coward: jealous, like all cowards. (*He goes to the table.*) Louka.

LOUKA: Yes?

SERGIUS: Who is my rival?

LOUKA: You shall never get that out of me, for love or money.

SERGIUS: Why?

LOUKA: Never mind why. Besides, you would tell that I told you; and I should lose my place.

SERGIUS: (*holding out his right hand in affirmation*) No! on the honor of a— (*He checks himself; and his hand drops, nerveless, as he concludes sardonically*)

—of a man capable of behaving as I have been behaving for the last five minutes. Who is he?

LOUKA: I don't know. I never saw him. I only heard his voice through the door of her room.

SERGIUS: Damnation! How dare you?

LOUKA: (*retreating*) Oh, I mean no harm: youve no right to take up my words like that. The mistress knows all about it. And I tell you that if that gentleman ever comes here again, Miss Raina will marry him, whether he likes it or not. I know the difference between the sort of manner you and she put on before one another and the real manner.

(SERGIUS *shivers as if she had stabbed him. Then, setting his face like iron, he strides grimly to her, and grips her above the elbows with both hands.*)

SERGIUS: Now you listen to me.

LOUKA: (*wincing*) Not so tight; youre hurting me.

SERGIUS: That doesnt matter. You have stained my honor by making me a party to your eavesdropping. And you have betrayed your mistress.

LOUKA: (*writhing*) Please—

SERGIUS: That shows that you are an abominable little clod of common clay, with the soul of a servant. (*He lets her go as if she were an unclean thing, and turns away, dusting his hands of her, to the bench by the wall, where he sits down with averted head, meditating gloomily.*)

LOUKA: (*whimpering angrily with her hands up her sleeves, feeling her bruised arms*) You know how to hurt with your tongue as well as with your hands. But I dont care, now Ive found out that whatever clay I'm made of, youre made of the same. As for her, she's a liar; and her fine airs are a cheat; and I'm worth six of her. (*She shakes the pain off hardily; tosses her head; and sets to work to put the things on the tray.*)

(*He looks doubtfully at her. She finishes packing the tray, and laps the cloth over the edges, so as to carry all out together. As she stoops to lift it, he rises.*)

SERGIUS: Louka! (*She stops and looks defiantly at him.*) A gentleman has no right to hurt a woman under any circumstances. (*With profound humility, uncovering his head.*) I beg your pardon.

LOUKA: That sort of apology may satisfy a lady. Of what use is it to a servant?

SERGIUS: (*rudely crossed in his chivalry, throws it off with a bitter laugh, and says slightingly*) Oh! you wish to be paid for the hurt! (*He puts on his shako, and takes some money from his pocket.*)

LOUKA: (*her eyes filling with tears in spite of herself*) No: I want my hurt made well.

SERGIUS: (*sobered by her tone*) How? (*She rolls up her left sleeve; clasps her arm with the thumb and fingers of her right hand; and looks down at the bruise. Then she raises her head and looks straight at him. Finally, with a superb gesture, she presents her arm to be kissed. Amazed, he looks at her; at the arm; at her again; hesitates; and then, with shuddering intensity, exclaims* Never! *and gets away as far as possible from her.*)

Her arm drops. Without a word, and with unaffected dignity, she takes her tray, and is approaching the house when RAINA *returns, wearing a hat and jacket in the height of the Vienna fashion of the previous year, 1885.* LOUKA *makes way proudly for her, and then goes into the house.*)

RAINA: I'm ready. Whats the matter? (*Gaily*) Have you been flirting with Louka?

SERGIUS: (*hastily*) No, no. How can you think such a thing?

RAINA: (*ashamed of herself*) Forgive me, dear: it was only a jest. I am so happy today.

(*He goes quickly to her, and kisses her hand remorsefully.* CATHERINE *comes out and calls to them from the top of the steps.*)

CATHERINE: (*coming down to them*) I am sorry to disturb you, children; but Paul is distracted over those three regiments. He doesnt know how to send them to Philippopolis; and he objects to every suggestion of mine. You must go and help him, Sergius. He is in the library.

RAINA: (*disappointed*) But we are just going out for a walk.

SERGIUS: I shall not be long. Wait for me just five minutes. (*He runs up the steps to the door.*)

RAINA: (*following him to the foot of the steps and looking up at him with timid coquetry*) I shall go round and wait in full view of the library windows. Be sure you draw father's attention to me. If you are a moment longer than five minutes, I shall go in and fetch you, regiments or no regiments.

SERGIUS: (*laughing*) Very well. (*He goes in.*)

(RAINA *watches him until he is out of her sight. Then, with a perceptible relaxation of manner, she begins to pace up and down the garden in a brown study.*)

CATHERINE: Imagine their meeting that Swiss and hearing the whole story! The very first thing your father asked for was the old coat we sent him off in. A nice mess you have got us into!

RAINA: (*gazing thoughtfully at the gravel as she walks*) The little beast!

CATHERINE: Little beast! What little beast?

RAINA: To go and tell! Oh, if I had him here, I'd cram him with chocolate creams til he couldnt ever speak again!

CATHERINE: Dont talk such stuff. Tell me the truth, Raina. How long was he in your room before you came to me?

RAINA: (*whisking round and recommencing her march in the opposite direction*) Oh, I forget.

CATHERINE: You cannot forget! Did he really climb up after the soldiers were gone; or was he there when that officer searched the room?

RAINA: No. Yes: I think he must have been there then.

CATHERINE: You think! Oh, Raina! Raina! Will anything ever make you straightforward? If Sergius finds out, it will be all over between you.

RAINA: (*with cool impertinence*) Oh, I know Sergius is your pet. I sometimes wish you could marry him instead of me. You would just suit him. You would pet him, and spoil him, and mother him to perfection.

CATHERINE: (*opening her eyes very widely indeed*) Well, upon my word!

RAINA: (*capriciously: half to herself*) I always feel a longing to do or say something dreadful to him—to shock his propriety—to scandalize the five senses out of him. (*To* CATHERINE, *perversely*) I dont care whether he finds out about the chocolate cream soldier or not. I half hope he may. (*She again turns and strolls flippantly away up the path to the corner of the house.*)

CATHERINE: And what should I be able to say to your father, pray?

RAINA: (*over her shoulder, from the top of the two steps*) Oh, poor father! As if he could help himself! (*She turns the corner and passes out of sight.*)

CATHERINE: (*looking after her, her fingers itching*) Oh, if you were only ten years younger! (LOUKA *comes from the house with a salver, which she carries hanging down by her side.*) Well?

LOUKA: Theres a gentleman just called, madam. A Serbian officer.

CATHERINE: (*flaming*) A Serb! And how dare he—(*checking herself bitterly*) Oh, I forgot. We are at peace now. I suppose we shall have them calling every day to pay their compliments. Well: if he is an officer why dont you tell your master? He is in the library with Major Saranoff. Why do you come to me?

LOUKA: But he asks for you, madam.

And I dont think he knows who you are: he said the lady of the house. He gave me this little ticket for you. (*She takes a card out of her bosom; puts it on the salver; and offers it to* CATHERINE.)

CATHERINE: (*reading*) "Captain Bluntschli"? That's a German name.

LOUKA: Swiss, madam, I think.

CATHERINE: (*with a bound that makes* LOUKA *jump back*) Swiss! What is he like?

LOUKA: (*timidly*) He has a big carpet bag, madam.

CATHERINE: Oh Heavens! he's come to return the coat. Send him away: say we're not at home: ask him to leave his address and I'll write to him. Oh stop: that will never do. Wait! (*She throws herself into a chair to think it out.* LOUKA *waits.*) The master and Major Saranoff are busy in the library, arnt they?

LOUKA: Yes, madam.

CATHERINE: (*decisively*) Bring the gentleman out here at once. (*Peremptorily*) And be very polite to him. Dont delay. Here (*impatiently snatching the salver from her*): leave that here; and go straight back to him.

LOUKA: Yes, madam (*going*).

CATHERINE: Louka!

LOUKA: (*stopping*) Yes, madam.

CATHERINE: Is the library door shut?

LOUKA: I think so, madam.

CATHERINE: If not, shut it as you pass through.

LOUKA: Yes, madam (*going*).

CATHERINE: Stop! (LOUKA *stops.*) He will have to go that way (*indicating the gate of the stable yard.*) Tell Nicola to bring his bag here after him. Don't forget.

LOUKA: (*surprised*) His bag?

CATHERINE: Yes: here: as soon as possible. (*Vehemently*) Be quick! (LOUKA *runs into the house.* CATHERINE *snatches her apron off and throws it behind a bush. She then takes up the salver and uses it as a mirror, with the result that the handkerchief tied round her head follows the apron. A touch to her hair and a shake to her dressing gown make her presentable.*) Oh, how? how? how can a man be such a fool! Such a moment to select! (LOUKA *appears at the door of the house, announcing* CAPTAIN BLUNTSCHLI. *She stands aside at the top of the steps to let him pass before she goes in again. He is the man of the midnight adventure in* RAINA'S *room, clean, well brushed, smartly uniformed, and out of trouble, but still unmistakably the same man. The moment* LOUKA'S *back is turned,* CATHERINE *swoops on him with impetuous, urgent, coaxing appeal.*) Captain Bluntschli: I am very glad to see you; but you must leave this house at once. (*He raises his eyebrows.*) My husband has just returned with my future son-in-law; and they know nothing. If they did, the consequences would be terrible. You are a foreigner: you do not feel our national animosities as we do. We still hate the Serbs: the effect of the peace on my husband has been to make him feel like a lion baulked of his prey. If he discovers our secret, he will never forgive me; and my daughter's life will hardly be safe. Will you, like the chivalrous gentleman and soldier you are, leave at once before he finds you here?

BLUNTSCHLI: (*disappointed, but philosophical*) At once, gracious lady. I only came to thank you and return the coat you lent me. If you will allow me to take it out of my bag and leave it with your servant as I pass out, I need detain you no further. (*He turns to go into the house.*)

CATHERINE: (*catching him by the sleeve*) Oh, you must not think of going back that way. (*Coaxing him across to the stable gate.*) This is the shortest way out. Many thanks. So glad to have been of service to you. Good-bye.

BLUNTSCHLI: But my bag?

CATHERINE: It shall be sent on. You will leave me your address.

BLUNTSCHLI: True. Allow me. (*He takes out his cardcase, and stops to write* his address, keeping CATHERINE *in an agony of impatience. As he hands her the card,* PETKOFF, *hatless, rushes from the house in a fluster of hospitality, followed by* SERGIUS.)

PETKOFF: (*as he hurries down the steps*) My dear Captain Bluntschli—

CATHERINE: Oh Heavens! (*She sinks on the seat against the wall.*)

PETKOFF: (*too preoccupied to notice her as he shakes* BLUNTSCHLI'S *hand heartily*) Those stupid people of mine thought I was out here, instead of in the —haw!—library (*he cannot mention the library without betraying how proud he is of it*). I saw you through the window. I was wondering why you didnt come in. Saranoff is with me: you remember him, dont you?

SERGIUS: (*saluting humorously, and then offering his hand with great charm of manner*) Welcome, our friend the enemy!

PETKOFF: No longer the enemy, happily. (*Rather anxiously*) I hope youve called as a friend, and not about horses or prisoners.

CATHERINE: Oh, quite as a friend, Paul. I was just asking Captain Bluntschli to stay to lunch; but he declares he must go at once.

SERGIUS: (*sardonically*) Impossible, Bluntschli. We want you here badly. We have to send on three cavalry regiments to Philippopolis; and we dont in the least know how to do it.

BLUNTSCHLI: (*suddenly attentive and businesslike*) Philippopolis? The forage is the trouble, I suppose.

PETKOFF: (*eagerly*) Yes: thats it. (*To* SERGIUS.) He sees the whole thing at once.

BLUNTSCHLI: I think I can show you how to manage that.

SERGIUS: Invaluable man! Come along! (*Towering over* BLUNTSCHLI, *he puts his hand on his shoulder and takes him to the steps,* PETKOFF *following.*)

(RAINA *comes from the house as* BLUNTSCHLI *puts his foot on the first step.*)

RAINA: Oh! The chocolate cream soldier!

(BLUNTSCHLI *stands rigid.* SERGIUS, *amazed, looks at* RAINA, *then at* PETKOFF, *who looks back at him and then at his wife.*)

CATHERINE: (*with commanding presence of mind*) My dear Raina, don't you see that we have a guest here? Captain Bluntschli: one of our new Serbian friends.

(RAINA *bows:* BLUNTSCHLI *bows.*)

RAINA: How silly of me! (*She comes down into the centre of the group, between* BLUNTSCHLI *and* PETKOFF.) I made a beautiful ornament this morning for the ice pudding; and that stupid Nicola has just put down a pile of plates on it and spoilt it. (*To* BLUNTSCHLI, *winningly*) I hope you didnt think that you were the chocolate cream soldier, Captain Bluntschli.

BLUNTSCHLI: (*laughing*) I assure you I did. (*Stealing a whimsical glance at her.*) Your explanation was a relief.

PETKOFF: (*suspiciously, to* RAINA) And since when, pray, have you taken to cooking?

CATHERINE: Oh, whilst you were away. It is her latest fancy.

PETKOFF: (*testily*) And has Nicola taken to drinking? He used to be careful enough. First he shows Captain Bluntschli out here when he knew quite well I was in the library; and then he goes downstairs and breaks Raina's chocolate soldier. He must—(NICOLA *appears at the top of the steps with the bag. He descends; places it respectfully before* BLUNTSCHLI; *and waits for further orders. General amazement.* NICOLA, *unconscious of the effect he is producing, looks perfectly satisfied with himself. When* PETKOFF *recovers his power of speech, he breaks out at him with*) Are you mad, Nicola?

NICOLA: (*taken aback*) Sir?

PETKOFF: What have you brought that for?

NICOLA: My lady's orders, major. Louka told me that—

CATHERINE: (*interrupting him*) My orders! Why should I order you to bring Captain Bluntschli's luggage out here? What are you thinking of, Nicola?

NICOLA: (*after a moment's bewilderment, picking up the bag as he addresses* BLUNTSCHLI *with the very perfection of servile discretion*) I beg your pardon, captain, I am sure. (*To* CATHERINE) My fault, madame: I hope youll overlook it. (*He bows, and is going to the steps with the bag, when* PETKOFF *addresses him angrily.*)

PETKOFF: Youd better go and slam that bag, too, down on Miss Raina's ice pudding! (*This is too much for* NICOLA. *The bag drops from his hand almost on his master's toes, eliciting a roar of*) Begone, you butter-fingered donkey.

NICOLA: (*snatching up the bag, and escaping into the house*) Yes, Major.

CATHERINE: Oh, never mind. Paul: dont be angry.

PETKOFF: (*blustering*) Scoundrel! He's got out of hand while I was away. I'll teach him. Infernal blackguard! The sack next Saturday! I'll clear out the whole establishment— (*He is stifled by the caresses of his wife and daughter, who hang round his neck, petting him.*)

CATHERINE }
RAINA   } (*together*) { Now, now, now, it
                          { Wow, wow, wow:

mustnt be angry. He meant no harm. Be good to please me, dear. Sh-sh-sh-sh! not on your first day at home. I'll make another ice pudding. Tch-ch-ch!

PETKOFF: (*yielding*) Oh well, never mind. Come, Bluntschli: lets have no more nonsense about going away. You know very well youre not going back to Switzerland yet. Until you do go back youll stay with us.

RAINA: Oh, do, Captain Bluntschli.

PETKOFF: (*to* CATHERINE) Now, Catherine: it's of you he's afraid. Press him: and he'll stay.

CATHERINE: Of course I shall be only too delighted if (*appealingly*) Captain Bluntschli really wishes to stay. He knows my wishes.

BLUNTSCHLI: (*in his driest military manner*) I am at madam's orders.

SERGIUS: (*cordially*) That settles it!

PETKOFF: (*heartily*) Of course!

RAINA: You see you must stay.

BLUNTSCHLI: (*smiling*) Well, if I must, I must.

(*Gesture of despair from* CATHERINE.)

ACT III

In the library after lunch. It is not much of a library. Its literary equipment consists of a single fixed shelf stocked with old paper-covered novels, broken-backed, coffee-stained, torn and thumbed; and a couple of little hanging shelves with a few gift books on them: the rest of the wall space being occupied by trophies of war and the chase. But it is a most comfortable sitting room. A row of three large windows shows a mountain panorama, just now seen in one of its friendliest aspects in the mellowing afternoon light. In the corner next the right hand window a square earthenware stove, a perfect tower of glistening pottery, rises nearly to the ceiling and guarantees plenty of warmth. The ottoman is like that in RAINA'S *room, and similarly placed; and the window seats are luxurious with decorated cushions. There is one object, however, hopelessly out of keeping with its surroundings. This is a small kitchen table, much the worse for wear, fitted as a writing* table with an old canister full of pens, an eggcup filled with ink, and a deplorable scrap of heavily used pink blotting paper.

At the side of this table, which stands to the left of anyone facing the window, BLUNTSCHLI *is hard at work with a couple of maps before him, writing orders. At the head of it sits* SERGIUS, *who is supposed to be also at work, but is actually gnawing the feather of a pen, and contemplating* BLUNTSCHLI'S *quick, sure, businesslike progress with a mixture of envious irritation at his own incapacity and awestruck wonder at an ability which seems to him almost miraculous, though its prosaic character forbids him to esteem it. The Major is comfortably established on the ottoman, with a newspaper in his hand and the tube of his hookah within easy reach.* CATHERINE *sits at the stove, with her back to them, embroidering.* RAINA, *reclining on the divan, is gazing in a daydream out at the Balkan landscape, with a neglected novel in her lap.*

The door is on the same side as the stove, farther from the window. The button of the electric bell is at the opposite side, behind BLUNTSCHLI.

PETKOFF: (*looking up from his paper to watch how they are getting on at the table*) Are you sure I cant help in any way, Bluntschli?

BLUNTSCHLI: (*without interrupting his writing or looking up*) Quite sure, thank you. Saranoff and I will manage it.

SERGIUS: (*grimly*) Yes: we'll manage it. He finds out what to do; draws up the orders; and I sign em. Division of labor! (BLUNTSCHLI *passes him a paper.*) Another one? Thank you. (*He plants the paper squarely before him; sets his chair carefully parallel to it; and signs with his cheek on his elbow and his protruded tongue following the movements of his pen.*) This hand is more accustomed to the sword than to the pen.

PETKOFF: It's very good of you, Bluntschli: it is indeed, to let yourself be put upon in this way. Now are you quite sure I can do nothing?

CATHERINE: (*in a low warning tone*) You can stop interrupting, Paul.

PETKOFF: (*starting and looking round at her*) Eh? Oh! Quite right. (*He takes his newspaper up again, but presently lets it drop.*) Ah, you havnt been campaigning, Catherine: you dont know how pleasant it is for us to sit here, after a good lunch, with nothing to do but enjoy ourselves. Theres only one thing I want to make me thoroughly comfortable.

CATHERINE: What is that?

PETKOFF: My old coat. I'm not at home in this one: I feel as if I were on parade.

CATHERINE: My dear Paul, how absurd you are about that old coat! It must be hanging in the blue closet where you left it.

PETKOFF: My dear Catherine, I tell you Ive looked there. Am I to believe my own eyes or not? (CATHERINE *rises and crosses the room to press the button of the electric bell.*) What are you showing off that bell for? (*She looks at him majestically, and silently resumes her chair and her needlework.*) My dear: if you think the obstinacy of your sex can make a coat out of two old dressing gowns of Raina's, your waterproof, and my mackintosh, youre mistaken. Thats exactly what the blue closet contains at present.

(NICOLA *presents himself.*)

CATHERINE: Nicola: go to the blue closet and bring your master's old coat here: the braided one he wears in the house.

NICOLA: Yes, madame. (*He goes out.*)

PETKOFF: Catherine.

CATHERINE: Yes, Paul.

PETKOFF: I bet you any piece of jewelry you like to order from Sofia against a week's housekeeping money that the coat isnt there.

CATHERINE: Done, Paul!

PETKOFF: (*excited by the prospect of a gamble*) Come: heres an opportunity for some sport. Wholl bet on it? Bluntschli: I'll give you six to one.

BLUNTSCHLI: (*imperturbably*) It would be robbing you, Major. Madame is sure to be right. (*Without looking up, he passes another batch of papers to* SERGIUS.)

SERGIUS: (*also excited*) Bravo, Switzerland! Major: I bet my best charger against an Arab mare for Raina that Nicola finds the coat in the blue closet.

PETKOFF: (*eagerly*) Your best char—

CATHERINE: (*hastily interrupting him*) Dont be foolish, Paul. An Arabian mare will cost you 50,000 levas.

RAINA: (*suddenly coming out of her picturesque revery*) Really, mother, if you are going to take the jewelery, I dont see why you should grudge me my Arab.

(NICOLA *comes back with the coat, and brings it to* PETKOFF, *who can hardly believe his eyes.*)

CATHERINE: Where was it, Nicola?

NICOLA: Hanging in the blue closet, madame.

PETKOFF: Well, I am d—

CATHERINE: (*stopping him*) Paul!

PETKOFF: I could have sworn it wasnt there. Age is beginning to tell on me. I'm getting hallucinations. (*To* NICOLA) Here: help me to change. Excuse me, Bluntschli. (*He begins changing coats,* NICOLA *acting as valet.*) Remember: I dont take that bet of yours, Sergius. Youd better give Raina that Arab steed yourself, since youve roused her expectations. Eh, Raina? (*He looks round at her; but she is again rapt in the landscape. With a little gush of parental affection and pride, he points her out to them, and says*) She's dreaming, as usual.

SERGIUS: Assuredly she shall not be the loser.

PETKOFF: So much the better for her. *I* shant come off so cheaply. I expect. (*The change is now complete.* NICOLA *goes out with the discarded coat.*) Ah, now I feel at home at last. (*He sits down and takes his newspaper with a grunt of relief.*)

BLUNTSCHLI: (*to* SERGIUS, *handing a paper*) Thats the last order.

PETKOFF: (*jumping up*) What! Finished?

BLUNTSCHLI: Finished.

PETKOFF: (*with childlike envy*) Havent you anything for me to sign?

BLUNTSCHLI: Not necessary. His signature will do.

PETKOFF: (*inflating his chest and thumping it*) Ah well, I think weve done a thundering good day's work. Can I do anything more?

BLUNTSCHLI: You had better both see the fellows that are to take these. (SERGIUS *rises.*) Pack them off at once; and show them that Ive marked on the orders the time they should hand them in by. Tell them that if they stop to drink or tell stories—if theyre five minutes late, theyll have the skin taken off their backs.

SERGIUS: (*stiffening indignantly*) I'll say so. (*He strides to the door.*) And if one of them is man enough to spit in my face for insulting him, I'll buy his discharge and give him a pension. (*He goes out.*)

BLUNTSCHLI: (*confidentially*) Just see that he talks to them properly, Major, will you?

PETKOFF: (*officiously*) Quite right, Bluntschli, quite right. I'll see to it. (*He goes to the door importantly, but hesitates on the threshold.*) By the bye, Catherine, you may as well come too. They'll be far more frightened of you than of me.

CATHERINE: (*putting down her embroidery*) I daresay I had better. You would only splutter at them. (*She goes out,* PETKOFF *holding the door for her and following her.*)

BLUNTSCHLI: What an army! They make cannons out of cherry trees; and the officers send for their wives to keep discipline! (*He begins to fold and docket the papers.*)

(RAINA, *who has risen from the divan, marches slowly down the room with her hands clasped behind her, and looks mischievously at him.*)

RAINA: You look ever so much nicer than when we last met. (*He looks up, surprised.*) What have you done to yourself?

BLUNTSCHLI: Washed; brushed; good night's sleep and breakfast. Thats all.

RAINA: Did you get back safely that morning?

BLUNTSCHLI: Quite, thanks.

RAINA: Were they angry with you for running away from Sergius's charge?

BLUNTSCHLI: (*grinning*) No: they were glad; because theyd all just run away themselves.

RAINA: (*going to the table, and leaning over it towards him*) It must have made a lovely story for them: all that about me and my room.

BLUNTSCHLI: Capital story. But I only told it to one of them: a particular friend.

RAINA: On whose discretion you could absolutely rely?

BLUNTSCHLI: Absolutely.

RAINA: Hm! He told it all to my father and Sergius the day you exchanged the prisoners. (*She turns away and strolls carelessly across to the other side of the room.*)

BLUNTSCHLI: (*deeply concerned, and half incredulous*) No! You dont mean that, do you?

RAINA: (*turning, with sudden earnestness*) I do indeed. But they dont know that it was in this house you took refuge. If Sergius knew, he would challenge you and kill you in a duel.

BLUNTSCHLI: Bless me! then dont tell him.

RAINA: Please be serious, Captain Bluntschli. Can you not realize what it is to me to deceive him? I want to be quite perfect with Sergius: no meanness, no smallness, no deceit. My relation to him is the one really beautiful and noble part of my life. I hope you can understand that.

BLUNTSCHLI: (*sceptically*) You mean that you wouldnt like him to find out that the story about the ice pudding was a—a—a—You know.

RAINA: (*wincing*) Ah, dont talk of it in that flippant way. I lied: I know it. But I did it to save your life. He would have killed you. That was the second time I ever uttered a falsehood. (BLUNTSCHLI *rises quickly and looks doubtfully and somewhat severely at her.*) Do you remember the first time?

BLUNTSCHLI: I! No. Was I present?

RAINA: Yes; and I told the officer who was searching for you that you were not present.

BLUNTSCHLI: True. I should have remembered it.

RAINA: (*greatly encouraged*) Ah, it is natural that you should forget it first. It cost you nothing: it cost me a lie! A lie! (*She sits down on the ottoman, looking straight before her with her hands clasped around her knee.* BLUNTSCHLI, *quite touched, goes to the ottoman with a particularly reassuring and considerate air, and sits down beside her.*)

BLUNTSCHLI: My dear young lady, dont let this worry you. Remember: I'm a soldier. Now what are the two things that happen to a soldier so often that he comes to think nothing of them? One is hearing people tell lies (RAINA *recoils*): the other is getting his life saved in all sorts of ways by all sorts of people.

RAINA: (*rising in indignant protest*) And so he becomes a creature incapable of faith and gratitude.

BLUNTSCHLI: (*making a wry face*) Do you like gratitude? I dont. If pity is akin to love, gratitude is akin to the other thing.

RAINA: Gratitude! (*Turning on him.*) If you are incapable of gratitude you are incapable of any noble sentiment. Even animals are grateful. Oh, I see now exactly what you think of me! You were not surprised to hear me lie. To you it was something I probably did every day! every hour! That is how men think of women. (*She paces the room tragically.*)

BLUNTSCHLI: (*dubiously*) Theres reason in everything. You said youd told only two lies in your whole life. Dear young lady: isnt that rather a short allowance? I'm quite a straightforward man myself; but it wouldnt last me a whole morning.

RAINA: (*staring haughtily at him*) Do you know, sir, that you are insulting me?

BLUNTSCHLI: I cant help it. When you strike that noble attitude and speak in that thrilling voice, I admire you; but I find it impossible to believe a single word you say.

RAINA: (*superbly*) Captain Bluntschli!

BLUNTSCHLI: (*unmoved*) Yes?

RAINA: (*standing over him, as if she could not believe her senses*) Do you mean what you said just now? Do you know what you said just now?

BLUNTSCHLI: I do.

RAINA: (*gasping*) I! I!!! (*She points to herself incredulously, meaning "I, Raina Petkoff tell lies!" He meets her gaze unflinchingly. She suddenly sits down beside him, and adds, with a complete change of manner from the heroic to a babyish familiarity*) How did you find me out?

BLUNTSCHLI: (*promptly*) Instinct, dear young lady. Instinct, and experience of the world.

RAINA: (*wonderingly*) Do you know, you are the first man I ever met who did not take me seriously?

BLUNTSCHLI: You mean, dont you, that I am the first man that has ever taken you quite seriously?

RAINA: Yes: I suppose I do mean that. (*Cosily, quite at her ease with him.*) How strange it is to be talked to in such a way! You know, Ive always gone on like that.

BLUNTSCHLI: You mean the—?

RAINA: I mean the noble attitude and the thrilling voice. (*They laugh together.*) I did it when I was a tiny child to my nurse. She believed in it. I do it before my parents. They believe in it. I do it before Sergius. He believes in it.

BLUNTSCHLI: Yes; he's a little in that line himself, isnt he?

RAINA: (*startled*) Oh! Do you think so?

BLUNTSCHLI: You know him better than I do.

RAINA: I wonder—I wonder is he? If I thought that—! (*Discouraged.*) Ah, well; what does it matter? I suppose, now youve found me out, you despise me.

BLUNTSCHLI: (*warmly, rising*) No, my dear young lady, no, no, no a thousand times. It's part of your youth: part of your charm. I'm like all the rest of them: the nurse, your parents, Sergius: I'm your infatuated admirer.

RAINA: (*pleased*) Really?

BLUNTSCHLI: (*slapping his breast smartly with his hand, German fashion*) Hand aufs Herz! Really and truly.

RAINA: (*very happy*) But what did you think of me for giving you my portrait?

BLUNTSCHLI: (*astonished*) Your portrait! you never gave me your portrait.

RAINA: (*quickly*) Do you mean to say you never got it?

BLUNTSCHLI: No. (*He sits down beside her, with renewed interest, and says, with some complacency*) When did you send it to me?

RAINA: (*indignantly*) I did not send it to you. (*She turns her head away, and adds, reluctantly*) It was in the pocket of that coat.

BLUNTSCHLI: (*pursing his lips and rounding his eyes*) Oh-o-oh! I never found it. It must be there still.

RAINA: (*springing up*) There still! for my father to find the first time he puts his hand in his pocket! Oh, how could you be so stupid?

BLUNTSCHLI: (*rising also*) It doesnt matter: I suppose it's only a photograph: how can he tell who it was intended for? Tell him he put it there himself.

RAINA: (*bitterly*) Yes: that is so clever! isnt it? (*Distractedly.*) Oh! what shall I do?

BLUNTSCHLI: Ah, I see. You wrote something on it. That was rash.

RAINA: (*vexed almost to tears*) Oh, to have done such a thing for you, who care no more—except to laugh at me—oh! Are you sure nobody has touched it?

BLUNTSCHLI: Well, I cant be quite sure. You see, I couldnt carry it about with me all the time: one cant take much luggage on active service.

RAINA: What did you do with it?

BLUNTSCHLI: When I got through to Pirot I had to put it in safe keeping somehow. I thought of the railway cloak room; but thats the surest place to get looted in modern warfare. So I pawned it.

RAINA: Pawned it!!!

BLUNTSCHLI: I know it doesnt sound nice: but it was much the safest plan. I redeemed it the day before yesterday. Heaven only knows whether the pawnbroker cleared out the pockets or not.

RAINA: (*furious: throwing the words right into his face*) You have a low shopkeeping mind. You think of things that would never come into a gentleman's head.

BLUNTSCHLI: (*phlegmatically*) Thats the Swiss national character, dear lady. (*He returns to the table.*)

RAINA: Oh, I wish I had never met you. (*She flounces away, and sits at the window fuming.*)

(LOUKA *comes in with a heap of letters and telegrams on her salver, and crosses, with her bold free gait, to the table. Her left sleeve is looped up to the shoulder with a brooch, shewing her naked arm, with a broad gilt bracelet covering the bruise.*)

LOUKA: (*to* BLUNTSCHLI) For you. (*She empties the salver with a fling on to the table.*) The messenger is waiting. (*She is determined not to be civil to an enemy, even if she must bring him his letters.*)

BLUNTSCHLI: (*to* RAINA) Will you excuse me: the last postal delivery that reached me was three weeks ago. These are the subsequent accumulations. Four telegrams: a week old. (*He opens one.*) Oho! Bad news!

RAINA: (*rising and advancing a little remorsefully*) Bad news?

BLUNTSCHLI: My father's dead. (*He looks at the telegram with his lips pursed, musing on the unexpected change in his arrangements.* LOUKA *crosses herself hastily.*)

RAINA: Oh, how very sad!

BLUNTSCHLI: Yes: I shall have to start for home in an hour. He has left a lot of big hotels behind him to be looked after. (*He takes up a fat letter in a long blue envelope.*) Here's a whacking letter from the family solicitor. (*He puts out the enclosures and glances over them.*) Great Heavens! Seventy! Two hundred! (*In a crescendo of dismay*) Four hundred! Four thousand!! Nine thousand six hundred!!! What on earth am I to do with them all?

RAINA: (*timidly*) Nine thousand hotels?

BLUNTSCHLI: Hotels! nonsense. If you only knew! Oh, it's too ridiculous! Excuse me: I must give my fellow orders about starting. (*He leaves the room hastily, with the documents in his hand.*)

LOUKA: (*knowing instinctively that she can annoy* RAINA *by disparaging* BLUNTSCHLI) He has not much heart, that Swiss. He has not a word of grief for his poor father.

RAINA: (*bitterly*) Grief! A man who has been doing nothing but killing people for years! What does he care? What does any soldier care? (*She goes to the door, restraining her tears with difficulty.*)

LOUKA: Major Saranoff has been fighting too; and he has plenty of heart left. (RAINA, *at the door, draws herself up haughtily and goes out.*) Aha! I thought you wouldnt get much feeling out of your soldier. (*She is following* RAINA *when* NICOLA *enters with an armful of logs for the stove.*)

NICOLA: (*grinning amorously at her*) Ive been trying all the afternoon to get a minute alone with you, my girl. (*His countenance changes as he notices her arm.*) Why, what fashion is that of wearing your sleeve, child?

LOUKA: (*proudly*) My own fashion.

NICOLA: Indeed! If the mistress catches you, she'll talk to you. (*He puts the logs down, and seats himself comfortably on the ottoman.*)

LOUKA: Is that any reason why you should take it on yourself to talk to me?

NICOLA: Come! dont be so contrary with me. Ive some good news for you. (*She sits down beside him. He takes out some paper money.* LOUKA, *with an eager gleam in her eyes, tries to snatch it; but he shifts it quickly to his left hand, out of her reach.*) See! a twenty leva[4] bill! Sergius gave me that, out of pure swagger. A fool and his money are soon parted. Theres ten levas more. The Swiss gave me that for backing up the mistress' and Raina's lies about him. He's no fool, he isnt. You should have heard old Catherine downstairs as polite as you please to me, telling me not to mind the Major being a little impatient; for they knew what a good servant I was—after making a fool and a liar of me before them all! The twenty will go to our savings; and you shall have the ten to spend if youll only talk to me so as to remind me I'm a human being. I get tired of being a servant occasionally.

LOUKA: Yes: sell your manhood for 30 levas and buy me for 10! (*Rising scornfully.*) Keep your money. You were born to be a servant. I was not. When you set up your shop you will only be everybody's servant instead of somebody's servant. (*She goes moodily to the table and seats herself regally in* SERGIUS's *chair.*)

NICOLA: (*picking up his logs, and going to the stove*) Ah, wait til you see. We shall have our evenings to ourselves; and I shall be master in my own house, I promise you. (*He throws the logs down and kneels at the stove.*)

LOUKA: You shall never be master in mine.

NICOLA: (*turning, still on his knees, and squatting down rather forlornly on his calves, daunted by her implacable disdain*) You have a great ambition in you, Louka. Remember: if any luck comes to you, it was I that made a woman of you.

LOUKA: You!

NICOLA: (*scrambling up and going to her*) Yes, me. Who was it made you give up wearing a couple of pounds of false black hair on your head and reddening your lips and cheeks like any other Bulgarian girl! I did. Who taught you to trim your nails, and keep your hands clean, and be dainty about yourself, like a fine Russian lady! Me: do you hear that? me! (*She tosses her head defiantly; and he turns away, adding more coolly*) Ive often thought that if Raina were out of the way, and you just a little less of a fool and Sergius just a little more of one, you might come to be one of my grandest customers, instead of only being my wife and costing me money.

LOUKA: I believe you would rather be my servant than my husband. You would make more out of me. Oh, I know that soul of yours.

NICOLA: (*going closer to her for greater emphasis*) Never you mind my soul; but just listen to my advice. If you want to be a lady, your present behavior to me wont do at all, unless when we're alone. It's too sharp and impudent; and impudence is a sort of familiarity: it shows affection for me. And dont you try being high and mighty with me, either. Youre like all country girls: you think it's genteel to treat a servant the way I treat a stableboy. Thats only your ignorance; and dont you forget it. And dont be so ready to defy everybody. Act as if you expected to have your own way, not as if you expected to be ordered about. The way to get on as a lady is the same as the way to get on as a servant: youve got to know your place: thats the secret of it. And you may depend on me to know my place if you get promoted. Think over it, my girl. I'll stand by you: one servant should always stand by another.

LOUKA: (*rising impatiently*) Oh, I must behave in my own way. You take all the courage out of me with your coldblooded wisdom. Go and put those logs in the fire: thats the sort of thing you understand.

(*Before* NICOLA *can retort,* SERGIUS *comes in. He checks himself a moment on seeing* LOUKA; *then goes to the stove.*)

SERGIUS: (*to* NICOLA) I am not in the way of your work, I hope.

NICOLA: (*in a smooth, elderly manner*) Oh no, sir: thank you kindly. I was only speaking to this foolish girl about her habit of running up here to the library whenever she gets a chance, to look at the books. Thats the worst of her education, sir: it gives her habits above her station. (*To* LOUKA.) Make that table tidy, Louka, for the Major. (*He goes out sedately.*)

(LOUKA, *without looking at* SERGIUS, *pretends to arrange the papers on the table. He crosses slowly to her, and studies the arrangement of her sleeve reflectively.*)

SERGIUS: Let me see: is there a mark there? (*He turns up the bracelet and sees the bruise made by his grasp. She stands motionless, not looking at him: fascinated, but on her guard.*) Ffff! Does it hurt?

LOUKA: Yes.

SERGIUS: Shall I cure it?

LOUKA: (*instantly withdrawing herself proudly, but still not looking at him*) No. You cannot cure it now.

SERGIUS: (*masterfully*) Quite sure? (*He makes a movement as if to take her in his arms.*)

LOUKA: Don't trifle with me, please. An officer should not trifle with a servant.

SERGIUS: (*indicating the bruise with a merciless stroke of his forefinger*) That was no trifle, Louka.

LOUKA: (*flinching; then looking at him for the first time*) Are you sorry?

SERGIUS: (*with measured emphasis, folding his arms*) I am never sorry.

LOUKA: (*wistfully*) I wish I could believe a man could be as unlike a woman as that. I wonder are you really a brave man?

SERGIUS: (*unaffectedly, relaxing his attitude*) Yes: I am a brave man. My heart jumped like a woman's at the first shot; but in the charge I found that I was brave. Yes: that at least is real about me.

LOUKA: Did you find in the charge that the men whose fathers are poor like mine were any less brave than the men who are rich like you?

SERGIUS: (*with bitter levity*) Not a bit. They all slashed and cursed and yelled like heroes. Psha! the courage to rage and kill is cheap. I have an English bull terrier who has as much of that sort of courage as the whole Bulgarian nation, and the whole Russian nation at its back. But he lets my groom thrash him, all the same. Thats your soldier all over! No, Louka: your poor men can cut throats; but they are afraid of their officers; they put up with insults and blows; they stand by and see one another punished like children: aye, and help to do it when they are ordered. And the officers!!! Well (*with a short harsh laugh*) *I* am an officer. Oh, (*fervently*) give me the man who will defy to the death any power on earth or in heaven that sets itself up against his own will and conscience: he alone is the brave man.

LOUKA: How easy it is to talk! Men never seem to me to grow up: they all have schoolboy's ideas. You don't know what true courage is.

SERGIUS: (*ironically*) Indeed! I am willing to be instructed. (*He sits on the ottoman, sprawling magnificently.*)

LOUKA: Look at me! How much am I allowed to have my own will? I have to get your room ready for you: to sweep and dust, to fetch and carry. How could that degrade me if it did not degrade you to have it done for you? But (*with subdued passion*) if I were Empress of Russia, above everyone in the world, then!! Ah then, though according to you I could show no courage at all, you should see, you should see.

SERGIUS: What would you do, most noble Empress?

LOUKA: I would marry the man I loved, which no other queen in Europe has the courage to do. If I loved you, though you would be as far beneath me as I am beneath you, I would dare to be the equal of my inferior. Would you dare as much if you loved me? No: if you felt the beginnings of love for me you would not let it grow. You would not dare: you would marry a rich man's daughter because you would be afraid of what other people would say of you.

SERGIUS: (*bounding up*) You lie: it is not so, by all the stars! If I loved you, and I were the Czar himself, I would set you on the throne by my side. You know that I love another woman, a woman as high above you as heaven is above earth. And you are jealous of her.

LOUKA: I have no reason to be. She will never marry you now. The man I told you of has come back. She will marry the Swiss.

SERGIUS: (*recoiling*) The Swiss!

LOUKA: A man worth ten of you. Then you can come to me; and I will refuse you. You are not good enough for me. (*She turns to the door.*)

SERGIUS: (*springing after her and catching her fiercely in his arms*) I will kill the Swiss; and afterwards I will do as I please with you.

LOUKA: (*in his arms, passive and steadfast*) The Swiss will kill you, perhaps. He has beaten you in love. He may beat you in war.

SERGIUS: (*tormentedly*) Do you think I believe that she—she! whose worst thoughts are higher than your best ones, is capable of trifling with another man behind my back?

LOUKA: Do you think she would believe the Swiss if he told her now that I am in your arms?

SERGIUS: (*releasing her in despair*) Damnation! Oh, damnation! Mockery! mockery everywhere! everything I think is mocked by everything I do. (*He strikes himself frantically on the breast.*) Coward! liar! fool! Shall I kill myself like a man, or live and pretend to laugh at myself? (*She again turns to go.*) Louka! (*She stops near the door.*) Remember: you belong to me.

LOUKA: (*turning*) What does that mean? An insult?

SERGIUS: (*commandingly*) It means that you love me, and that I have had you here in my arms, and will perhaps have you there again. Whether that is an insult I neither know nor care: take it as you please. But (*vehemently*) I will not be a coward and a trifler. If I choose to love you, I dare marry you, in spite of all Bulgaria. If these hands ever touch you again, they shall touch my affianced bride.

LOUKA: We shall see whether you dare keep your word. And take care. I will not wait long.

SERGIUS: (*again folding his arms and standing motionless in the middle of the room*) Yes: we shall see. And you shall wait my pleasure.

(BLUNTSCHLI, *much preoccupied, with his papers still in his hand, enters, leaving the door open for* LOUKA *to go out. He goes across to the table, glancing at her as he passes.* SERGIUS, *without altering his reso-*

lute attitude, watches him steadily. LOUKA *goes out, leaving the door open.*)

BLUNTSCHLI: (*absently, sitting at the table as before, and putting down his papers*) That's a remarkable looking young woman.

SERGIUS: (*gravely, without moving*) Captain Bluntschli.

BLUNTSCHLI: Eh?

SERGIUS: You have deceived me. You are my rival. I brook no rivals. At six o'clock I shall be in the drilling-ground on the Klissoura road, alone, on horseback, with my sabre. Do you understand?

BLUNTSCHLI: (*staring, but sitting quite at his ease*) Oh, thank you: thats a cavalry man's proposal. I'm in the artillery; and I have the choice of weapons. If I go, I shall take a machine gun. And there shall be no mistake about the cartridges this time.

SERGIUS: (*flushing, but with deadly coldness*) Take care, sir. It is not our custom in Bulgaria to allow invitations of that kind to be trifled with.

BLUNTSCHLI: (*warmly*) Pooh! dont talk to me about Bulgaria. You dont know what fighting is. But have it your own way. Bring your sabre along. I'll meet you.

SERGIUS: (*fiercely delighted to find his opponent a man of spirit*) Well said, Switzer. Shall I lend you my best horse?

BLUNTSCHLI: No; damn your horse! thank you all the same, my dear fellow. (RAINA *comes in, and hears the next sentence.*) I shall fight you on foot. Horseback's too dangerous; I dont want to kill you if I can help it.

RAINA: (*hurrying forward anxiously*) I have heard what Captain Bluntschli said, Sergius. You are going to fight. Why? (SERGIUS *turns away in silence, and goes to the stove, where he stands watching her as she continues, to* BLUNTSCHLI) What about?

BLUNTSCHLI: I dont know: he hasnt told me. Better not interfere, dear young lady. No harm will be done: Ive often acted as sword instructor. He wont be able to touch me; and I'll not hurt him. It will save explanations. In the morning I shall be off home; and youll never see me or hear of me again. You and he will then make it up and live happily ever after.

RAINA: (*turning away deeply hurt, almost with a sob in her voice*) I never said I wanted to see you again.

SERGIUS: (*striding forward*) Ha! That is a confession.

RAINA: (*haughtily*) What do you mean?

SERGIUS: You love that man!

RAINA: (*scandalized*) Sergius!

SERGIUS: You allow him to make love to you behind my back, just as you treat me as your affianced husband behind his. Bluntschli: you knew our relations; and you deceived me. It is for that that I call you to account, not for having received favors *I* never enjoyed.

BLUNTSCHLI: (*jumping up indignantly*) Stuff! Rubbish! I have received no favors. Why, the young lady doesnt even know whether I'm married or not.

RAINA: (*forgetting herself*) Oh! (*Collapsing on the ottoman.*) Are you?

SERGIUS: You see the young lady's concern, Captain Bluntschli. Denial is useless. You have enjoyed the privilege of being received in her own room, late at night—

BLUNTSCHLI: (*interrupting him pepperily*) Yes, you blockhead! she received me with a pistol at her head. Your cavalry were at my heels. I'd have blown out her brains if she'd uttered a cry.

SERGIUS: (*taken aback*) Bluntschli! Raina: is this true?

RAINA: (*rising in wrathful majesty*) Oh, how dare you, how dare you?

BLUNTSCHLI: Apologize, man: apologize. (*He resumes his seat at the table.*)

SERGIUS: (*with the old measured em-*

phasis, folding his arms) I never apologize!

RAINA: (*passionately*) This is the doing of that friend of yours, Captain Bluntschli. It is he who is spreading this horrible story about me. (*She walks about excitedly.*)

BLUNTSCHLI: No: he's dead. Burnt alive.

RAINA: (*stopping, shocked*) Burnt alive!

BLUNTSCHLI: Shot in the hip in a woodyard. Couldnt drag himself out. Your fellows' shells set the timber on fire and burnt him, with half a dozen other poor devils in the same predicament.

RAINA: How horrible!

SERGIUS: And how ridiculous! Oh, war! war! the dream of patriots and heroes! A fraud, Bluntschli. A hollow sham, like love.

RAINA: (*outraged*) Like love! You say that before me!

BLUNTSCHLI: Come, Saranoff: that matter is explained.

SERGIUS: A hollow sham, I say. Would you have come back here if nothing had passed between you except at the muzzle of your pistol? Raina is mistaken about your friend who was burnt. He was not my informant.

RAINA: Who then? (*Suddenly guessing the truth.*) Ah, Louka! my maid! my servant! You were with her this morning all that time after—after—Oh, what sort of god is this I have been worshipping! (*He meets her gaze with sardonic enjoyment of her disenchantment. Angered all the more, she goes closer to him, and says, in a lower, intenser tone*) Do you know that I looked out of the window as I went upstairs, to have another sight of my hero; and I saw something I did not understand then. I know now that you were making love to her.

SERGIUS: (*with grim humor*) You saw that?

RAINA: Only too well. (*She turns away, and throws herself on the divan under the centre window, quite overcome.*)

SERGIUS: (*cynically*) Raina: our romance is shattered. Life's a farce.

BLUNTSCHLI: (*to RAINA, whimsically*) You see: he's found himself out now.

SERGIUS: (*going to him*) Bluntschli: I have allowed you to call me a blockhead. You may now call me a coward as well. I refuse to fight you. Do you know why?

BLUNTSCHLI: No; but it doesnt matter. I didnt ask the reason when you cried *on*; and I dont ask the reason now that you cry *off*. I'm a professional soldier! I fight when I have to, and am very glad to get out of it when I havent to. Youre only an amateur: you think fighting's an amusement.

SERGIUS: (*sitting down at the table, nose to nose with him*) You shall hear the reason all the same, my professional. The reason is that it takes two men—real men —men of heart, blood and honor—to make a genuine combat. I could no more fight with you than I could make love to an ugly woman. Youve no magnetism: youre not a man: youre a machine.

BLUNTSCHLI: (*apologetically*) Quite true, quite true. I always was that sort of chap. I'm very sorry.

SERGIUS: Psha!

BLUNTSCHLI: But now that youve found that life isnt a farce, but something quite sensible and serious, what further obstacle is there to your happiness?

RAINA: (*rising*) You are very solicitous about my happiness and his. Do you forget his new love—Louka? It is not you that he must fight now, but his rival, Nicola.

SERGIUS: Rival!! (*bounding half across the room.*)

RAINA: Dont you know that theyre engaged?

SERGIUS: Nicola! Are fresh abysses opening? Nicola!

RAINA: (*sarcastically*) A shocking sacrifice, isnt it? Such beauty! such intellect! such modesty! wasted on a middle-aged servant man. Really, Sergius, you cannot stand by and allow such a thing. It would be unworthy of your chivalry.

SERGIUS: (*losing all self-control*) Viper! Viper! (*He rushes to and fro, raging.*)

BLUNTSCHLI: Look here, Saranoff: youre getting the worst of this.

RAINA: (*getting angrier*) Do you realize what he has done, Captain Bluntschli? He has set this girl as a spy on us; and her reward is that he makes love to her.

SERGIUS: False! Monstrous!

RAINA: Monstrous! (*Confronting him.*) Do you deny that she told you about Captain Bluntschli being in my room?

SERGIUS: No; but—

RAINA: (*interrupting*) Do you deny that you were making love to her when she told you?

SERGIUS: No; but I tell you—

RAINA: (*cutting him short contemptuously*) It is unnecessary to tell us anything more. That is quite enough for us. (*She turns away from him and sweeps majestically back to the window.*)

BLUNTSCHLI: (*quietly, as Sergius, in an agony of mortification, sinks on the ottoman, clutching his averted head between his fists*) I told you you were getting the worst of it, Saranoff.

SERGIUS: Tiger cat!

RAINA: (*running excitedly to* BLUNTSCHLI) You hear this man calling me names, Captain Bluntschli?

BLUNTSCHLI: What else can he do, dear lady? He must defend himself somehow. Come (*very persuasively*): dont quarrel. What good does it do?

(RAINA, *with a gasp, sits down on the ottoman, and after a vain effort to look vexedly at* BLUNTSCHLI, *falls a victim to her sense of humor, and actually leans back babyishly against the writhing shoulder of* SERGIUS.)

SERGIUS: Engaged to Nicola! Ha! ha! Ah well, Bluntschli, you are right to take this huge imposture of a world coolly.

RAINA: (*quaintly to* BLUNTSCHLI, *with an intuitive guess at his state of mind*) I daresay you think us a couple of grown-up babies, dont you?

SERGIUS: (*grinning savagely*) He does: he does. Swiss civilization nurse-tending Bulgarian barbarism, eh?

BLUNTSCHLI: (*blushing*) Not at all, I assure you. I'm only very glad to get you two quieted. There! there! let's be pleasant and talk it over in a friendly way. Where is this other young lady?

RAINA: Listening at the door, probably.

SERGIUS: (*shivering as if a bullet had struck him, and speaking with quiet but deep indignation*) I will prove that that, at least, is a calumny. (*He goes with dignity to the door and opens it. A yell of fury bursts from him as he looks out. He darts into the passage, and returns dragging in* LOUKA, *whom he flings violently against the table, exclaiming*) Judge her, Bluntschli. You, the cool impartial man: judge the eavesdropper.

(LOUKA *stands her ground, proud and silent.*)

BLUNTSCHLI: (*shaking his head*) I mustnt judge her. I once listened myself outside a tent when there was a mutiny brewing. It's all a question of the degree of provocation. My life was at stake.

LOUKA: My love was at stake. I am not ashamed.

RAINA: (*contemptuously*) Your love! Your curiosity, you mean.

LOUKA: (*facing her and returning her contempt with interest*) My love, stronger than anything you can feel, even for your chocolate cream soldier.

SERGIUS: (*with quick suspicion, to* LOUKA) What does that mean?

LOUKA: (*fiercely*) I mean—

SERGIUS: (*interrupting her slightingly*)

Oh, I remember: the ice pudding. A paltry taunt, girl!

(MAJOR PETKOFF *enters, in his shirtsleeves.*)

PETKOFF: Excuse my shirtsleeves, gentlemen. Raina: somebody has been wearing that coat of mine: I'll swear it. Somebody with a differently shaped back. It's all burst open at the sleeve. Your mother is mending it. I wish she'd make haste: I shall catch cold. (*He looks more attentively at them.*) Is anything the matter?

RAINA: No. (*She sits down at the stove, with a tranquil air.*)

SERGIUS: Oh no. (*He sits down at the end of the table, as at first.*)

BLUNTSCHLI: (*who is already seated*) Nothing. Nothing.

PETKOFF: (*sitting down on the ottoman in his old place*) Thats all right. (*He notices* LOUKA.) Anything the matter, Louka?

LOUKA: No, sir.

PETKOFF: (*genially*) Thats all right. (*He sneezes.*) Go and ask your mistress for my coat, like a good girl, will you?

(NICOLA *enters with the coat.* LOUKA *makes a pretense of having business in the room by taking the little table with the hookah away to the wall near the windows.*)

RAINA: (*rising quickly as she sees the coat on* NICOLA'S *arm*) Here it is, papa. Give it to me, Nicola; and do you put some more wood on the fire. (*She takes the coat, and brings it to the Major, who stands up to put it on.* NICOLA *attends to the fire.*)

PETKOFF: (*to* RAINA, *teasing her affectionately*) Aha! Going to be very good to poor old papa just for one day after his return from the wars, eh?

RAINA: (*with solemn reproach*) Ah, how can you say that to me, father?

PETKOFF: Well, well, only a joke, little one. Come: give me a kiss. (*She kisses him.*) Now give me the coat.

RAINA: No: I am going to put it on for you. Turn your back. (*He turns his back and feels behind him with his arms for the sleeves. She dexterously takes the photograph from the pocket and throws it on the table before* BLUNTSCHLI, *who covers it with a sheet of paper under the very nose of* SERGIUS, *who looks on amazed, with his suspicions roused in the highest degree. She then helps* PETKOFF *on with his coat.*) There, dear! Now are you comfortable?

PETKOFF: Quite, little love. Thanks. (*He sits down; and* RAINA *returns to her seat near the stove.*) Oh, by the bye, Ive found something funny. Whats the meaning of this? (*He puts his hand into the picked pocket.*) Eh? Hallo! (*He tries the other pocket.*) Well, I could have sworn—! (*Much puzzled, he tries the breast pocket.*) I wonder—(*trying the original pocket.*) Where can it—? (*He rises, exclaiming*) Your mother's taken it!

RAINA: (*very red*) Taken what?

PETKOFF: Your photograph, with the inscription: "Raina, to her Chocolate Cream Soldier: a Souvenir." Now you know theres something more in this than meets the eye; and I'm going to find it out. (*Shouting*) Nicola!

NICOLA: (*coming to him*) Sir!

PETKOFF: Did you spoil any pastry of Miss Raina's this morning?

NICOLA: You heard Miss Raina say that I did, sir.

PETKOFF: I know that, you idiot. Was it true?

NICOLA: I am sure Miss Raina is incapable of saying anything that is not true, sir.

PETKOFF: Are you? Then I'm not. (*Turning to the others.*) Come: do you think I dont see it all? (*He goes to* SERGIUS, *and slaps him on the shoulder.*) Sergius: youre the chocolate cream soldier, arnt you?

SERGIUS: (*starting up*) I! A chocolate cream soldier! Certainly not.

PETKOFF: Not! (*He looks at them. They are all very serious and very conscious.*) Do you mean to tell me that Raina sends things like that to other men?

SERGIUS: (*enigmatically*) The world is not such an innocent place as we used to think, Petkoff.

BLUNTSCHLI: (*rising*) It's all right, Major. I'm the chocolate cream soldier. (PETKOFF *and* SERGIUS *are equally astonished.*) The gracious young lady saved my life by giving me chocolate creams when I was starving: shall I ever forget their flavor! My late friend Stolz told you the story of Pirot. I was the fugitive.

PETKOFF: You! (*He gasps.*) Sergius: do you remember how those two women went on this morning when we mentioned it? (SERGIUS *smiles cynically.* PETKOFF *confronts* RAINA *severely.*) Youre a nice young woman, arnt you?

RAINA: (*bitterly*) Major Saranoff has changed his mind. And when I wrote that on the photograph, I did not know that Captain Bluntschli was married.

BLUNTSCHLI: (*startled into vehement protest*) I'm not married.

RAINA: (*with deep reproach*) You said you were.

BLUNTSCHLI: I did not. I positively did not. I never was married in my life.

PETKOFF: (*exasperated*) Raina: will you kindly inform me, if I am not asking too much, which of these gentlemen you are engaged to?

RAINA: To neither of them. This young lady (*introducing* LOUKA, *who faces them all proudly*) is the object of Major Saranoff's affections at present.

PETKOFF: Louka! Are you mad, Sergius? Why, this girl's engaged to Nicola.

NICOLA: I beg your pardon, sir. There is a mistake. Louka is not engaged to me.

PETKOFF: Not engaged to you, you scoundrel! Why, you had twenty-five levas from me on the day of your betrothal; and she had that gilt bracelet from Miss Raina.

NICOLA: (*with cool unction*) We gave it out so, sir. But it was only to give Louka protection. She had a soul above her station; and I have been no more than her confidential servant. I intend, as you know, sir, to set up a shop later on in Sofia; and I look forward to her custom and recommendation should she marry into the nobility. (*He goes out with impressive discretion, leaving them all staring after him.*)

PETKOFF: (*breaking the silence*) Well, I am—hm!

SERGIUS: This is either the finest heroism or the most crawling baseness. Which is it, Bluntschli?

BLUNTSCHLI: Never mind whether it's heroism or baseness. Nicola's the ablest man Ive met in Bulgaria. I'll make him manager of a hotel if he can speak French and German.

LOUKA: (*suddenly breaking out at* SERGIUS) I have been insulted by everyone here. You set them the example. You owe me an apology.

(SERGIUS, *like a repeating clock of which the spring has been touched, immediately begins to fold his arms.*)

BLUNTSCHLI: (*before he can speak*) It's no use. He never apologizes.

LOUKA: Not to you, his equal and his enemy. To me, his poor servant, he will not refuse to apologize.

SERGIUS: (*approvingly*) You are right. (*He bends his knee in his grandest manner.*) Forgive me.

LOUKA: I forgive you. (*She timidly gives him her hand, which he kisses.*) That touch makes me your affianced wife.

SERGIUS: (*springing up*) Ah! I forgot that.

LOUKA: (*coldly*) You can withdraw if you like.

SERGIUS: Withdraw! Never! You belong to me. (*He puts his arm about her.*) (CATHERINE *comes in and finds* LOUKA *in* SERGIUS' *arms, with all the rest gazing at them in bewildered astonishment.*)

CATHERINE: What does this mean? (SERGIUS *releases* LOUKA.)

PETKOFF: Well, my dear, it appears that Sergius is going to marry Louka instead of Raina. (*She is about to break out indignantly at him: he stops her by exclaiming testily*) Dont blame me: Ive nothing to do with it. (*He retreats to the stove.*)

CATHERINE: Marry Louka! Sergius: you are bound by your word to us!

SERGIUS: (*folding his arms*) Nothing binds me.

BLUNTSCHLI: (*much pleased by this piece of common sense*) Saranoff: your hand. My congratulations. These heroics of yours have their practical side after all. (*To* LOUKA) Gracious young lady: the best wishes of a good Republican! (*He kisses her hand, to* RAINA'S *great disgust, and returns to his seat.*)

CATHERINE: Louka: you have been telling stories.

LOUKA: I have done Raina no harm.

CATHERINE: (*haughtily*) Raina! (RAINA, *equally indignant, almost snorts at the liberty.*)

LOUKA: I have a right to call her Raina: she calls me Louka. I told Major Saranoff she would never marry him if the Swiss gentleman came back.

BLUNTSCHLI: (*rising, much surprised*) Hallo!

LOUKA: (*turning to* RAINA) I thought you were fonder of him than of Sergius. You know best whether I was right.

BLUNTSCHLI: What nonsense! I assure you, my dear Major, my dear Madame, the gracious young lady simply saved my life, nothing else. She never cared two straws for me. Why, bless my heart and soul, look at the young lady and look at me. She, rich, young, beautiful, with her imagination full of fairy princes and noble natures and cavalry charges and goodness knows what! And I, a commonplace Swiss soldier who hardly knows what a decent life is after fifteen years of barracks and battles: a vagabond, a man who has spoiled all his chances in life through an incurably romantic disposition, a man—

SERGIUS: (*starting as if a needle had pricked him and interrupting* BLUNTSCHLI *in incredulous amazement*) Excuse me, Bluntschli: what did you say had spoiled your chances in life?

BLUNTSCHLI: (*promptly*) An incurably romantic disposition. I ran away from home twice when I was a boy. I went into the army instead of into my father's business. I climbed the balcony of this house when a man of sense would have dived into the nearest cellar. I came sneaking back here to have another look at the young lady when any other man of my age would have sent the coat back—

PETKOFF: My coat!

BLUNTSCHLI:—yes: thats the coat I mean—would have sent it back and gone quietly home. Do you suppose I am the sort of fellow a young girl falls in love with? Why, look at our ages! I'm thirty-four: I dont suppose the young lady is much over seventeen. (*This estimate produces a marked sensation, all the rest turning and staring at one another. He proceeds innocently*) All that adventure which was life or death to me, was only a schoolgirl's game to her—chocolate creams and hide and seek. Heres the proof! (*He takes the photograph from the table.*) Now, I ask you, would a woman who took the affair seriously have sent me this and written on it "Raina, to her Chocolate Cream Soldier: a Souvenir"? (*He exhibits the photograph triumphantly, as if it settled the matter beyond all possibility of refutation.*)

PETKOFF: Thats what I was looking for. How the deuce did it get there? (*He comes from the stove to look at it, and sits down on the ottoman.*)

BLUNTSCHLI: (*to* RAINA, *complacently*) I have put everything right, I hope, gracious young lady.

RAINA: (*going to the table to face him*) I quite agree with your account of yourself. You are a romantic idiot. (BLUNTSCHLI *is unspeakably taken aback.*) Next time, I hope you will know the difference between a schoolgirl of seventeen and a woman of twenty-three.

BLUNTSCHLI: (*stupefied*) Twenty-three!

(RAINA *snaps the photograph contemptuously from his hand; tears it up; throws the pieces in his face; and sweeps back to her former place.*)

SERGIUS: (*with grim enjoyment of his rival's discomfiture*) Bluntschli: my one last belief is gone. Your sagacity is a fraud, like everything else. You have less sense than even I!

BLUNTSCHLI: (*overwhelmed*) Twenty-three! Twenty-three!! (*He considers.*) Hm. (*Swiftly making up his mind and coming to his host.*) In that case, Major Petkoff, I beg to propose formally to become a suitor for your daughter's hand, in place of Major Saranoff retired.

RAINA: You dare!

BLUNTSCHLI: If you were twenty-three when you said those things to me this afternoon, I shall take them seriously.

CATHERINE: (*loftily polite*) I doubt, sir, whether you quite realize either my daughter's position or that of Major Sergius Saranoff, whose place you propose to take. The Petkoffs and the Saranoffs are known as the richest and most important families in the country. Our position is almost historical: we can go back for twenty years.

PETKOFF: Oh, never mind that, Catherine. (*To* BLUNTSCHLI.) We should be most happy, Bluntschli, if it were only a question of your position; but hang it, you know, Raina is accustomed to a very comfortable establishment. Sergius keeps twenty horses.

BLUNTSCHLI: But who wants twenty horses? We're not going to keep a circus.

CATHERINE: (*severely*) My daughter, sir, is accustomed to a first-rate stable.

RAINA: Hush, mother: youre making me ridiculous.

BLUNTSCHLI: Oh well, if it comes to a question of an establishment, here goes! (*He darts impetuously to the table; seizes the papers in the blue envelope; and turns to* SERGIUS.) How many horses did you say?

SERGIUS: Twenty, noble Switzer.

BLUNTSCHLI: I have two hundred horses. (*They are amazed.*) How many carriages?

SERGIUS: Three.

BLUNTSCHLI: I have seventy. Twenty-four of them will hold twelve inside, besides two on the box, without counting the driver and conductor. How many table-cloths have you?

SERGIUS: How the deuce do I know?

BLUNTSCHLI: Have you four thousand?

SERGIUS: No.

BLUNTSCHLI: I have. I have nine thousand six hundred pairs of sheets and blankets, with two thousand four hundred eider-down quilts. I have ten thousand knives and forks, and the same quantity of dessert spoons. I have three hundred servants. I have six palatial establishments, besides two livery stables, a tea garden, and a private house. I have four medals for distinguished services; I have the rank of an officer and the standing of a gentleman; and I have three native languages. Show me any man in Bulgaria that can offer as much!

PETKOFF: (*with childish awe*) Are you Emperor of Switzerland?

BLUNTSCHLI: My rank is the highest known in Switzerland: I am a free citizen.

CATHERINE: Then, Captain Bluntschli, since you are my daughter's choice—

RAINA: (*mutinously*) He's not.

CATHERINE: (*ignoring her*)—I shall not stand in the way of her happiness.

(PETKOFF *is about to speak.*) That is Major Petkoff's feeling also.

PETKOFF: Oh, I shall be only too glad. Two hundred horses! Whew!

SERGIUS: What says the lady?

RAINA: (*pretending to sulk*) The lady says that he can keep his tablecloths and his omnibuses. I am not here to be sold to the highest bidder. (*She turns her back on him.*)

BLUNTSCHLI: I wont take that answer. I appealed to you as a fugitive, a beggar, and a starving man. You accepted me. You gave me your hand to kiss, your bed to sleep in, and your roof to shelter me.

RAINA: I did not give them to the Emperor of Switzerland.

BLUNTSCHLI: Thats just what I say.

(*He catches her by the shoulders and turns her face-to-face with him.*) Now tell us whom you did give them to.

RAINA: (*succumbing with a shy smile*) To my chocolate cream soldier.

BLUNTSCHLI: (*with a boyish laugh of delight*) Thatll do. Thank you. (*He looks at his watch and suddenly becomes businesslike.*) Time's up, Major. Youve managed those regiments so well that youre sure to be asked to get rid of some of the infantry of the Timok division. Send them home by way of Lom Palanka. Saranoff: dont get married until I come back: I shall be here punctually at five in the evening on Tuesday fortnight. Gracious ladies (*his heels click*) good evening. (*He makes them a military bow, and goes.*)

SERGIUS: What a man! Is he a man!

NOTES

1. The hero of Cervantes' reckless Spanish comic romance, or adventure-novel, published in two parts in 1605 and 1615. Don Quixote unrealistically tries to live up to the ideals of Knighthood or chivalry.
2. An opera, based on Victor Hugo's famous romantic drama *Hernani* (1830). The score was composed by Verdi, and the opera was produced in 1844.
3. A nobleman of the Kingdom of Castile, the central part of Spain.
4. A monetary unit of Bulgaria.

QUESTIONS

A. Understanding the Action:

1. What are the two main subjects that are given comic treatment in the play? What is the social and political background of the play? And why should Shaw have selected it?

2. What kind of society is caricatured in this play? What use does Shaw make of the overcoat in developing the plot?

B. Understanding the Characters:

1. Explain the statement that the play deals less with war than with "the pseudo-romance of war," and that it is an attack not on war but on foolish "romantic ideas." In what respect is *Arms and the Man* an anti-romantic and anti-heroic play? Nevertheless, would you agree that it is also a romantic play? Justify your answer.

2. What is Shaw's attitude toward: a) Sergius; and b) Raina.

3. In what sense can Louka be called "the New Woman" as of the time of the play (1894)? How would you explain that Nicola is an "economic man"?

4. Explain the statement that Shaw assumes that Man's behavior ought to be rational.

5. Taking the above view into consideration, explain why it can be maintained that the hero of *Arms and the Man* is Captain Bluntschli.

C. Understanding the Approach:

1. Are there any realistic elements or attitudes in *Arms and the Man*? Explain in detail. How would you describe Shaw's attitude toward *love* and *war* in the play? Is Shaw's attitude realistic?

2. How does Shaw employ a) comic reversals, b) paradoxes, c) exaggerations,

and d) comic contrasts in order to develop his subject or subjects?

3. What is meant by a statement (by the critic Louis Kronenberger) crediting Bernard Shaw with "sending accepted ideas before the firing squad" and "decapitating popular opinions and making grandiloquent emotion walk the gangplank"? How would you apply this statement to *Arms and the Man?*

4. In what sense of the term is *Arms and the Man* a *burlesque* or *travesty?* In what sense can *Arms and the Man* be considered a *farce* rather than a *comedy?* In what sense can it be called a comedy rather than a farce? What is the governing idea or theme of the play?

D. Comparisons:

1. What does *Arms and the Man* have in common with *The Pretentious Ladies* and *The Apollo of Bellac?*

E. Criticism:

1. Is *Arms and the Man* outmoded in any respect? if so, why should this be the case? What does critic Louis Kronenberger mean when he declares that, "Its satire, far from ever seeming startling today, is perhaps not even pertinent"? Do you agree or disagree with this critic? Explain and relate your answer to present social conditions.

2. *Arms and the Man* was transformed into one of the most successful operettas, *The Chocolate Soldier.* Can you advance reasons why this should have been possible?

3. What does Louis Kronenberger mean by the statement that, "In writing *Arms and the Man* Shaw was shrewd enough to realize that in order to take romantic folderol apart he had first to put it very neatly together. You cannot kill off what is not of itself alive"? Comment on this criticism.

ANTON CHEKHOV (1860-1904)

Anton Chekhov's grandfather was a serf, a peasant bound to the land and the nearest thing to being a slave in old Russia. Chekhov was born, in fact, just about the time when serfdom was abolished in the Russian empire. Although his father achieved prosperity for a time as a small businessman, the family's fortunes declined, and the future author's childhood was embittered by poverty and the personal tyranny of his father. "In my childhood," he once wrote, "I had no childhood." But Chekhov, who had a remarkably resilient character along with a truly sweet temperament that later won him the affection of many famous persons, did not allow himself to be suppressed by his depressing situation. Instead, he put himself through medical school and supported his family at the same time with a rapidly developing talent for short-story writing.

Since his early tales were light and humorous, they were easily sold to the periodicals and won great popularity for their author long before he could be considered a serious writer and an accomplished artist. At that time, moreover, Chekhov did not take himself very seriously as a writer of either stories or plays, which were mostly little entertainments called "vaudevilles." He took his medical degree in 1884 and he refrained from setting up a practice only because his writing for the periodicals became so lucrative. He won the coveted Pushkin Prize in Russia for his first published book, a collection of stories, two years later.

Although Chekhov's health was undermined by tuberculosis contracted while a student at the University of Moscow, he worked steadily at his writing. He wrote well over a thousand stories, and some of these, such as *The Duel* and the terrifying *Ward No. 6*, are actually short novels. Chekhov, indeed, came to be considered one of the great masters of the modern realistic short story. But he was also attracted to dramatic writing, and he became one of the greatest of modern playwrights with several full-length plays presented by the Moscow Art Theatre between 1899 and 1904 (*Uncle Vanya, The Sea Gull, The Three Sisters,* and *The Cherry Orchard*), as well as his earlier written one-act plays. Some of these (*The Boor* and *The Marriage Proposal*) are masterfully developed little farces. Others are either utterly serious pieces (*On the High Road*) or contain a blend of comedy and pathos.

INTRODUCTION TO *THEN AND NOW*

By connecting *The Marriage Proposal* with *The Harmful Effects of Smoking* (the latter is remarkable for its explosive power, and is both extremely funny and terribly sad), it is possible to show an example of Chekhov's humor and pathos.

The title "Then and Now" suggests that we encounter the characters later in their life when the husband has been quite thoroughly subdued by his spirited wife. Although this unifying idea is a liberty taken by the adapter, the theme itself, as well as the text, remains unaltered. It is the familiar subject of frustration that Chekhov dramatized in his longer plays and made famous with his art of making characters reveal their nature inadvertently, of allowing them to stray from their intentions, and of being foolish and touching at the same time.

THEN AND NOW

ANTON CHEKHOV

ADAPTED BY JOHN GASSNER *from* THE MARRIAGE PROPOSAL *and* THE HARMFUL EFFECTS OF SMOKING

PART ONE: *THEN* (The Marriage Proposal)

STEPAN STEPANOVITCH CHUBUKOV
IVAN VASSILEVITCH LOMOV
NATALYA STEPANOVA CHUBUKOV,
        Chubukov's daughter

PART TWO: *NOW* (The Harmful Effects of Smoking)

THE LECTURER (IVAN VASSILEVITCH LOMOV)

PART ONE

THEN: (The Marriage Proposal)
SCENE: THE DRAWING ROOM OF CHUBUKOV'S HOUSE IN THE COUNTRY

(*Enter* LOMOV, *a neighboring landowner, a robust man of about thirty-five. He is dressed formally and wears white gloves.* CHUBUKOV, *an ample man in his late fifties, wearing a smoking jacket and smoking a pipe, rises from his large rocking chair to greet him.*)

CHUBUKOV: My good fellow, how nice to see you! To what do I owe the honor, my dear Ivan? (*Pumping his hand vigorously.*) How are you?

LOMOV: (*nervously*) Thank you, thank you. And you—how are you getting along?

CHUBUKOV: We just get along, my friend, with the help of friends' prayers. (*Thrusting him into the rocker suddenly.*) Do sit down. (*Looking him over.*) But why so formal—evening clothes, white gloves, cravat, and so on? Going somewhere, Ivan Vassilevitch?

LOMOV: Only to you, dear Stepan Stepanovitch.

CHUBUKOV: To me? In evening clothes? It isn't Christmas!

LOMOV: (*rising and taking* CHUBUKOV'S *arm*) You see it's like this, honored Stepan Stepanovitch. I've come to trouble you with a special request. You have always helped me before. I've never knocked at your door in vain, you have always . . . Oh, I beg your pardon for running on like this, but this is a special occasion . . . May I have a drink of water? (*And he pours himself a drink from a decanter on the table as if his life depended on it.*)

CHUBUKOV: (*aside, while* LOMOV *is pouring glass after glass down his throat*) Wants to borrow money, of course. Won't

496

get any. (*Aloud.*) What is the matter, my young friend?

LOMOV: (*still flustered*) I beg your pardon, your ladyship—I mean, honored sir. Awfully excited—really—you see it's you alone who can help.—I don't deserve it ... haven't the right to ask it ... you know my condition ... but.

CHUBUKOV: Come now! ... just let it out. What is it you want?

LOMOV: ... I'll tell you in a minute ... The fact is—is—that I've come to ask for your daughter's honorable hand, for dear Natalya Stepanovna's hand. I hope I have made myself clear.

CHUBUKOV: (*joyfully*) As clear as can be. But say it again, Ivan Vassilevitch. I want to hear it again, just to enjoy it. (*Catching himself.*) I mean, I didn't quite hear it all.

LOMOV: (*formally*) I have the honor to request ...

CHUBUKOV: (*interrupting*) Good—that's all I wanted to hear. I know the rest of the formula—all that sort of flapdoodle. (*Embracing and kissing him.*) I've been hoping for it—I've been, in fact, expecting it—(*Wiping a tear running down his cheek.*) I've always loved you, dear boy, as if you were my own. May God bless you, make you fruitful—oh, what am I saying, why am I going on this way as if I were off my rocker (*he looks at the rocker and giving it a vigorous push sends it flying, whereupon he is puzzled and tries to collect his thoughts*)—rocker? What I mean is, I'll call the girl at once. (*He clears his throat, getting ready to call.*)

LOMOV: (*stopping him, somewhat fearfully*) Honored sir, are you sure I can count on her consent?

CHUBUKOV: (*cheerily*) Why not? Imagine her *not* consenting. She's in love—head-over-heels in love, if I'm any judge—and I *am*. (*Rushing out.*) Wait for me! (*He disappears at once.*)

LOMOV: (*left alone, in a state of extreme agitation*) Why are my teeth chattering? ... Why am I trembling all over as if I were up for an examination.... I have made up my mind, haven't I? *At once*—because if I give myself time to think it over, to analyze and consider, to look for an ideal—for *real love,* for example—then it's all over with me and I can forget about marrying altogether. (*His teeth chattering.*) Brrr—it's freezing in this room.—Besides, the girl is a fine housekeeper. She is efficient, hard-working, well educated, and not really bad looking. What more should a man want? And I simply must get married—I'm thirty-five, and it's essential to lead a peaceful, regular life—high time I did—I *am* excitable—get terribly upset over everything—there, I knew it, I've got a twitch again in my right eyebrow. And the worst of it is I don't sleep—something always tugs at my left side, the moment I climb into bed, and soon I begin to feel it in my shoulder and in the head. So I leap out of bed like a lunatic and start walking around a bit, but the moment I lie down again and start dozing the same damnable sensation starts all over. I can't postpone this any longer. There can be no doubt about it—I've *got* to get married. I don't want to, but ... (*He stops as* NATALYA, *a girl of about 25, wiping her hands on her apron, enters.*)

NATALYA: (*outwardly at least cool and composed, extending her hand which* LOMOV *kisses*) So it's you, after all. Papa said, "Go into the drawing room. There's a merchant there who has come for his goods." Papa is a terrible jokester! (*Politely.*) How are you, Ivan Vassilevitch?

LOMOV: How do you do, dear Natalya Stepanovna?

NATALYA: (*looking down at her dress*) You must excuse my dress—this awful apron!—you see, the maid and I, we've been shelling peas in the kitchen. Won't you sit down ... (*They both sit down.*) Will you have some lunch?

LOMOV: Oh, no—thank you very much—I have already lunched.

NATALYA: (*picking up a cigarette box from the side table and holding it for him*) In that case, a cigarette? (*He takes a cigarette but doesn't light it.*) The weather was so terrible yesterday the farm hands couldn't do a thing. It's nicer now, but— (*He can't speak and answers with an indefinable gesture.*) I meant to ask you—how much hay have you stacked on your farm? I am so upset—I was absolutely greedy the other day and had everything cut down, and now I am afraid that the hay is going to rot in the field if the wet weather returns. (*Observing him.*) But why are you in evening clothes? Going to a ball, are you?—you look a lot better that way, I'll admit. What's up?

LOMOV: You see, Natalya Stepanovna —I have resolved—I am determined to have you—that is, to have you hear me out . . . No doubt you will be surprised. I am afraid you will be angry, too, but— (*pausing*) you know it's really awfully cold here—

NATALYA: Now, what is the matter? (*A pause.*) Tell me!

LOMOV: I'll try to be brief. You know, of course, that I have had the honor of knowing your family for a long time. My deceased aunt and her husband, from whom I inherited my estate, were both attached to your father and to your late mother. So one might say—one could not say otherwise, to be sure—the Lomovs (*he points to himself*) and the Chubukovs —that is, your family, you understand —have had a great natural affection for each other. Also, you know, of course, that my lands adjoin yours—my Oxen Meadows, you know, touch your birchwoods!

NATALYA: (*visibly hardening*) *Your* Oxen Meadows, you say? *Your* meadows?

LOMOV: (*in a matter-of-fact manner*) Yes, of course.

NATALYA: Excuse me, but I don't understand what you are talking about. Surely the Oxen Meadows belong to us, not to you!

LOMOV: You are mistaken, honored Natalya Stepanovna, the Oxen Meadows are *mine*.

NATALYA: This is the first time I ever heard of it. What makes you imagine they are yours, I am really curious to know.

LOMOV: I am beginning to wonder whether you know what fields I am talking about? I am talking about the Oxen Meadows wedged in between the Marsh and your birchwoods.

NATALYA: Of course, and they're ours.

LOMOV: Oh, you're mistaken—they're definitely mine.

NATALYA: That is certainly odd. Since when have they been yours?

LOMOV: Since when? They've belonged to my family as long as I can remember.

NATALYA: Surely, you don't expect me to believe that.

LOMOV: You can tell at a glance from the documents. The possession of Oxen Meadows was disputed years ago, but now everybody knows that they belong to me. I'll explain it to you. (*Patiently.*) My aunt's grandmother gave the use of these meadows in perpetuity to your father's and grandfather's peasants.[1] In return, the peasants agreed to make bricks for her. Your father's grandfather's peasants, then, had the use of the meadows for forty years. So they formed the notion that the meadows actually belonged to themselves. That is how the whole misunderstanding started.

NATALYA: (*fiercely*) It isn't clear to me at all, not at all. All I know is that my grandfather and my great-grandfather always understood that their lands reached as far as the marsh—and this means that Oxen Meadows belonged to our family.

LOMOV: (*desperately*) I'll show you incontrovertible proof, documents!

NATALYA: Please don't bother. You are surely making fun of a simple girl like me, aren't you? We've occupied those lands for almost three centuries only to be suddenly told that it isn't ours. It's simply too fantastic, Ivan Vassilevitch ... Of course, those meadows don't mean anything to me—they're not extensive—a mere thirteen acres or so—and not really worth much. But when it's a question of justice! I simply can't endure unfairness—*(screaming)* I tell you I won't stand for it! *(She starts to walk out.)*

LOMOV: *(stopping her)* Please listen to me, I beg you. Your father's grandfather's serfs, as I had the honor of explaining a little while ago, used to bake bricks for my worthy aunt's grandmother. *(By now he is holding her.)*

NATALYA: Please let go of me—I don't understand a word of this business about your aunts and grandmothers and father's grandfathers when everything is perfectly simple. The meadows are ours, and there's an end to it.

LOMOV: *(wiping his perspiring forehead)* You are mistaken.

NATALYA: I am not! All your proofs will get you nowhere at all. I don't want to take anything from anybody, but, at the same time, I won't let anybody take anything from me.

LOMOV: *(trying to be patient)* Natalya Stepanova, please understand that I don't *want* the meadows. I am just acting on principle. I would be delighted to *give* them to you—as a present.

NATALYA: *(huffily)* If I should like, *I* can give them to *you* as a present, because they're mine—*mine*. I can only marvel at your attitude. Up to this hour I always thought of you as a good neighbor and friend. Last year I even lent you our threshing machine although it became necessary to put off our own threshing as a result; and now you are treating us as if we were gypsies. To offer to give me my own land is not in the least neighborly—. One might even call it, so to speak, an impertinence.

LOMOV: *(flaring)* And you want to make out that I am a robber and land-grabber, which is certainly an impertinence. I want you to know, Madam, that I have never in my life grabbed anyone's land. But the fact remains *(he helps himself to more water)* that Oxen Meadows belongs to me, and to me alone.

NATALYA: And to prove that they are *mine* I am going to send my people out to mow the meadows this very day *(and she makes a move toward the door with a determined stride).*

LOMOV: *(standing in her way)* I'd advise you not to.

NATALYA: My mowers will be there, nevertheless.

LOMOV: They'll get their necks broken, I promise you.

NATALYA: *(glaring)* You wouldn't dare!

LOMOV: *(clutching at his heart)* There—you've done it—my palpitations have returned; I owe them to you and no one else. Nevertheless, *(shouting)* Oxen Meadows are mine—*mine!*

NATALYA: Please do your shouting in your own house, not in mine. (CHUBUKOV *enters in a fright.)*

CHUBUKOV: What's all the shouting about?

NATALYA: *(hurling herself at him)* Oh, papa, papa—please tell this gentleman who the owners of the Oxen Meadows are.

CHUBUKOV: *(puzzled)* They are ours, of course. Why do you ask, darling?

LOMOV: *(flabbergasted)* But, Stepan Stepanovitch, how can that be? Please reflect that my aunt's grandmother gave your great-grandfather's peasants free use of the land only *temporarily*. The peasants who got used to working the land for some forty years just stupidly assumed that they belonged to your family ...

CHUBUKOV: *(calmly)* It is true enough that this land was once in dispute. But the matter was settled in our favor ages ago, and now everybody knows that the meadows belong to us. (NATALYA *nods vigorously in agreement.*)

LOMOV: (*frantic*) This is impossible. They're mine!

CHUBUKOV: My good fellow, yelling won't prove anything. Not that I care—I'd rather give the land to the peasants than argue about it.

LOMOV: (*indignantly*) Give Oxen Meadows to the peasants? One doesn't give away somebody else's property, one just doesn't do such things! (*Stamping his foot.*) I simply won't allow it.

CHUBUKOV: (*on his dignity*) Now, look here, I am not used to being spoken to like that, young man. I am twice your age—

LOMOV: (*plaintively, clutching at his heart*) But how can I talk calmly when you call my land yours—my property, my *inheritance*. This just isn't neighborly—for a neighbor to be a common land-grabber.

CHUBUKOV: (*dangerously*) What's that you say?

NATALYA: Papa, please send the mowers out to Oxen Meadows at once!

CHUBUKOV: (*paying no attention to her in his rage, and moving threateningly toward* LOMOV) What's that you say?

NATALYA: (*doing likewise*) We won't give up the meadows, we won't, we won't, we won't!

LOMOV: (*retreating*) Well, then, why don't we let the courts decide.

CHUBUKOV: The courts? You'd like that, wouldn't you. Your entire family was like that—always going to court.

LOMOV: Never mind *my* family, Stepan Stepanovitch. No one in my family was ever tried for embezzlement—like your grandfather.

CHUBUKOV: There's been lunacy in your family. It is well known that all the Lomovs are crazy.

NATALYA: (*supporting her father, screaming*) Yes, all of you, *all, all!*

CHUBUKOV: And what about your grandfather, the notorious drunkard—and your aunt, the younger one, who ran away with a worthless fellow—(*contemptuously*) an *architect!*

NATALYA: That she did! If ever there was a scandal—

LOMOV: What difference does it make, Stepan Stepanovitch? Please consider, my dear sir, that your mother was a hunchback! (*Clutching at his heart.*) Oh that tug again at my heart ... Help! (*He goes to the table to pour himself some water only to find that he has used up the last drop.*) Some water—quick.

CHUBUKOV: (*paying no attention*) And the whole world knows your father was a gambler and drunkard.

NATALYA: That's right. And that other aunt of yours!—there's nobody to equal her backbiting from here to Tokyo.

LOMOV: (*jumping*) See what you have done to me!—Pins and needles, my foot's fallen asleep ... (*to* CHUBUKOV) And it's an open secret you stuffed the ballot box at the last local election ... Ah, my head! I am beginning to see stars. (*As he looks frantically around*) Where's my hat? Don't you understand me?—Please, my hat. (*He finds his hat where he left it, on the side table.*) Which way? Where's that blasted door? Think of it, having a parlor without a single door!

CHUBUKOV: (*striding toward the door and pointing*) Here is one if you would be good enough to look where you should. And don't you dare set foot in here again.

LOMOV: (*staggering out*) Oh, my heart —oh, my head.

NATALYA: (*calling after him*) And don't forget to take it to court so that everyone can see what a monster you are, *fathead!* (*To her father*) And that scarecrow had the nerve to abuse our family just because grandmother was a hunchback! It was such a little hump! Only a low-down scoundrel talks that way to his neighbors.

CHUBUKOV: And just imagine, that blind rooster had the impertinence to come here to propose.

NATALYA: (*on the alert*) Propose, you say? Propose what? (*An edge in her voice.*) To whom, father?

CHUBUKOV: To you, of course.

NATALYA: (*her hands going to her face and adjusting the hair on her forehead, which makes her look plainer*) Propose to me? (*Wailing*) Father, what have you done?

CHUBUKOV: What have *I* done?— Done? What wouldn't I like to *do* to that stuffed sausage in evening clothes! Tfoo!

NATALYA: (*dropping into the rocker, imperiously*) Back, father! (*He doesn't understand.*) Bring him back!

CHUBUKOV: (*reacting to her determined look*) Oh—all right, I suppose. I am going at once. (*He goes out.*)

NATALYA: (*rising up and glaring after him*) What has that old fool of a father gone and done? Nothing at all except *kill* me! (*Walking up and down furiously.*) I'll hang myself . . . I'll shoot all of us . . . I'll—

CHUBUKOV: (*running in*) He's coming back. You can talk to him yourself. I won't have anything to do with it.

NATALYA: Bring him in, father. Quick.

CHUBUKOV: I don't carry him in my pocket, do I? What a bother to have a grown-up daughter, especially one that fights with people all the time.—After all, it's you who railed at him and drove him out!

NATALYA: (*frantically*) No, it was you —you!

CHUBUKOV: What do you want of me? I'll cut my throat, I will.—Here he comes.

NATALYA: (*with deadly calm*) Leave us alone, father.

CHUBUKOV: (*intimidated*) I tell you it wasn't my fault. (*Edging out of the room.*) All right, I am going!

LOMOV: (*colliding with* CHUBUKOV) I am back, you see . . . I have such palpitations—and my eyebrow is twitching!

NATALYA: Sit down, Ivan Vassilevitch. (*She pushes him into the rocker and he drops into it heavily, caught by surprise, so that he rocks helplessly.*)

LOMOV: (*puzzled*) Confounded rocker! Why does everybody push me into it?

NATALYA: (*impatiently*) Forgive us, Vassilevitch! Oxen Meadows is really yours. I just remembered.

LOMOV: What did you say? Oh, my heart! Now *both* my eyebrows are twitching!

NATALYA: We got overexcited—that's all. Oxen Meadows is really yours. Do you understand me? I say it is yours. *Yours!*

LOMOV: (*puzzled*) Mine? Oh, (*Recollecting*) that's all right—I don't care any more.—It was the principle of the thing.—

NATALYA: Yes, I understand, the principle—just so.

LOMOV: The land isn't really worth anything to me, you know.

NATALYA: Nor to me! And now let us talk about something else.

LOMOV: Just principle, you know!

NATALYA: Right! But let us talk about *something else*.

LOMOV: Something else? What "else"? —Oh, I have proof. My aunt's grandmother gave those meadows to your father's grandmother's peasants—

NATALYA: (*interrupting*) Yes, we know all about that now. But as to the *something else*—if you can't come out with it, begin by telling me when you're starting the hunting season (*when he doesn't respond*) —when are you going hunting, I mean— "ahunting we shall go . . . ahunting we shall go"—you understand?

LOMOV: ("*getting it*" *and beaming*) Oh—I am thinking of having a go at it right after the harvest. (*After a pause.*) But you must have heard of my misfortune. My best hunting dog's gone lame. I am distressed about Geyser—I mean, Guesser; especially since I paid a small fortune for him—125 rubles.

NATALYA: (*sharply*) Far too much, Ivan Vassilevitch.

LOMOV: Oh, no. Dirt cheap, I think. He's a first-rate dog.

NATALYA: Why, papa paid only 80 rubles for Squeezer, who is a better dog.

LOMOV: Squeezer a *better* dog? You can't mean that. (*Laughing.*) What an idea!

NATALYA: (*earnestly*) I don't know why you are laughing! Squeezer is younger and he can develop a bit yet, while on pedigree and on points he is way ahead of Guesser.

LOMOV: But you forget that Squeezer is, so to speak, overshot, Natalya Stepanova, and that means the dog is a bad hunter.

NATALYA: Overshot? It's the first I've heard of it.

LOMOV: Well, you hear it now. Just look at his lower jaw—it is shorter than the upper. He's all right at tracking down or following. But if you expect him to get hold of something with his mouth, you are sure to be disappointed. Squeezer's lower jaw is much too small.

NATALYA: But look at his pedigree, while your dog doesn't even have a pedigree. And, to top it off, he is old and worn out.

LOMOV: Old, yes. Worn out, definitely no. I wouldn't exchange him for five of your Squeezers. Guesser is a real dog while Squeezer—a dog like him can be found under any bush.

NATALYA: (*glaring at* LOMOV) I see you are determined to contradict me no matter what I say; there's a demon of contradiction in you this afternoon. First you pretend that Oxen Meadows belong to you, and now you claim that your Guesser is better than our Squeezer. You know perfectly well that it isn't so when you consider his pedigree. (*Screaming.*) It just can't be!

LOMOV: (*huffily*) Why are you shouting at me?

NATALYA: Tell me, please, why you talk such rot? (*Violently.*) Oh, I wish that Guesser of yours was dead. It's high time the old beast was put out of his misery with a bullet!

LOMOV: (*terribly upset again, pressing his side*) Excuse me. I simply cannot continue this discussion. I am out of breath and my heart is pounding away as though it were going to pieces.

NATALYA: Why, then, did you wear yourself out unnecessarily? All you had to do is to admit that our Squeezer is a hundred times better than your filthy Guesser, who's half-dead already.

LOMOV: (*pleading*) Please!—Let us say no more about him.

NATALYA: (*flaring*) You shall not shut me up. (*Screaming.*) I'll not allow it. (CHUBUKOV *enters hastily, alarmed.*)

CHUBUKOV: What's the matter now?

NATALYA: (*appealing*) Papa, be a dear and tell us truly which is the better dog, Squeezer or Guesser?

CHUBUKOV: (*stumped for a moment*) I don't understand.

LOMOV: (*also appealing to him*) Stepan Stepanovitch, I implore you—is Squeezer overshot or not? Yes, or No?

CHUBUKOV: (*innocently*) Of course not. Whoever said such a thing? Besides, what difference does it make? Isn't he the best dog in the province even so?

LOMOV: (*flabbergasted*) Really now! I never heard such a thing.

CHUBUKOV: But there is no need to excite yourself. Who says your Guesser isn't also a fine dog?—Sturdy legs, well-sprung ribs, no doubt about it. But he *is* old—that is a fact!—and he does have *one* defect.

LOMOV: A *defect?*

CHUBUKOV: You must admit he's

short in the muzzle, unfortunately.

LOMOV: But consider last month's hunt. My Guesser was way out front, neck and neck with Count Marunsky's dog while Squeezer was nearly a mile behind.

CHUBUKOV: Naturally, he limped because the Count's crazy whipper-in struck him with the whip.

LOMOV: Squeezer got what he deserved. (*Excited, as if hunting were his passion, and gesticulating wildly.*) The dogs are chasing the fox when Squeezer takes it into his stupid head to start running after a sheep. That's one thing Guesser, you may be sure, would never do.

CHUBUKOV: That's a lie—I mean . . . I beg your pardon. Please let's change the subject before I lose my temper. You aren't a hunter anyway.

NATALYA: That's right. What sort of hunter could you be with one foot always falling asleep, your eternal stitches in the side, and your everlasting palpitations!

LOMOV: So I'm not a hunter! What do I care? (*To* CHUBUKOV.) And are *you* a hunter? Everyone knows you go hunting only to stay on the good side of the Count, with whom you have been carrying on some sort of intrigue against other landowners of the province these many years.

NATALYA: (*flaring*) You have the nerve to call papa an intriguer!

CHUBUKOV: (*to her*) Bah! Pay no attention to the puppy.

NATALYA: And *you* can't even sit on a horse!

LOMOV: Oh, my heart again! (*He drops into the rocking chair, which flies backward. It would topple over if* NATALYA *didn't catch it from behind and give it such a push forward that it strikes* CHUBUKOV *on the shin.*)

CHUBUKOV: (*crying out*) Now you've done it—you've just killed me, you fool! Give me air! (*He leans against a chair.*)

NATALYA: Now see what you have done, murderer!

LOMOV: (*rises from the rocker in a daze*) How? What have I done? (*He takes one step toward* CHUBUKOV *and faints away.*)

NATALYA: Papa, look what he's gone and done. (*Shaking* LOMOV.) Ivan Vassilevitch, wake up, *wake up!* (*She becomes hysterical.*) Quick, get a doctor, papa!

CHUBUKOV: (*coming out of a daze*) Hey! What's going on?

NATALYA: Father, he is dead. Ivan Vassilevitch is dead!

CHUBUKOV: (*looking down on* LOMOV *in surprise*) Why, so he is! How did he do it? (*He tries to pour water down his throat.*) Drink!—He doesn't drink—he's surely dead, then. Did I do any violence to him in my rage? If I did, I'll put a bullet into my brain.—What am I waiting for? Give me a pistol!

LOMOV: (*moving*) Where am I? I see . . . nebulae . . . star dust.

CHUBUKOV: (*resolutely*) Look here, Lomov, let's put a stop to all this nonsense right now. My daughter accepts your proposal of marriage and there's an end to it. And please do me a favor: Get married at once and start quarreling afterward! I am not as strong as I used to be, I can't take any more bickering.

LOMOV: (*rising*) Married? *Whom* shall I marry?

CHUBUKOV: (*smiling benignly while pushing him toward* NATALYA) Nincompoop, go ahead, kiss her.

LOMOV: *Whom* shall I kiss?

NATALYA: (*cornering* LOMOV *imperiously*) *I am waiting*, Ivan Vassilevitch!

LOMOV: (*kissing her*) This is very nice. May I do it again?

NATALYA: (*smiling*) You may. You shall!

LOMOV: (*kissing her again*) This makes me very happy. Natalya Stepanovna, let me kiss your hand, too.

NATALYA: (*giving him her hand*) Go ahead. But still you'll admit—that Guesser is no match for Squeezer.

LOMOV: Not at all.

NATALYA: You might as well admit it.

CHUBUKOV: (*shouting*) Bring the champagne somebody.

LOMOV: Guesser is good.

NATALYA: (*loudly*) Squeezer is—(*she subsides a trifle*)—better.

CHUBUKOV: (*beaming as a blouse-wearing* SERVANT *brings the champagne*) Just keep on arguing, my children. Start your happiness the right way—and take my blessings both of you *as soon as you leave my house!* Drink up!

(LOMOV *and* NATALYA *glare at each other, then lift their champagne glasses as the Curtain falls quickly.*)

PART TWO

NOW: (The Harmful Effects of Smoking)

A provincial Lecture Hall.
Later. A LECTURER, *whom we may identify as the once-fiery* LOMOV,* *now middle-aged, hen-pecked, and perhaps balding, dressed formally in a frock coat, comes determinedly on the stage, which is to be considered the lecturer's platform. The audience of the theatre, which he faces and addresses, is to be considered the audience of a provincial lecture hall. On the platform (the stage) sit several worthy gentlemen, as if they were the presiding officers of the function or possibly the honored guests of the assembly; and one of these gentlemen, an old man, is*

---

* In Chekhov's original play, the LECTURER is not identified, nor is any member of the audience.—J.G.

CHUBUKOV, *greatly aged and given to dozing; in fact, he dozes throughout most of the* LECTURER'S *speech, awaking only now and then and applauding guiltily—usually at the wrong time.*

THE LECTURER: Ladies and gentlemen, as it were! Somebody—(*glaring at the audience reproachfully*) I don't know who, but I wish I did!—told my wife that I should give a public lecture to support our provincial United Charities drive. So lecture I must whether I like it or not, and it's all the same to me whether I lecture or don't.

(*He seems a trifle unsteady, as if he had taken one drink too many, and steadies himself against the lectern.*)

Yet I must confess I have been pondering on scientific problems for a long time now and working on them even to the detriment of my health. I have done this even though I am not a professor, as you know, and no university has given me a degree. I am a *thinking* man—a man who thinks, you know—and I even compose scientific articles. Well, perhaps not exactly scientific—that is, not in the scientific sense of scientific, I mean—but they are almost scientific. For instance, I wrote a long article the other day called The Harmfulness of Certain Insects. My daughters, bless their little hearts, liked my article immensely—especially the part that dealt with the life-cycle of insects. But I tore it up anyhow. No matter how well you write about insects you still need an insecticide. After all, *we've* got bugs almost everywhere—even in the piano.

(CHUBUKOV,[2] *who awoke and remained awake long enough to hear the last statement, clucks and nods his head disapprovingly. He is about to rise to remonstrate with the* LECTURER. *But it is too much of an effort and he leans back instead and dozes off again.*)

I trust you know, of course, that I have taken for the subject of my present lecture the evils—I mean the harmful effects—of smoking. I myself do a lot of smoking these days (*he fumbles for a cigarette and*

lights up), but my wife wanted me to talk about smoking—so here I am talking about smoking. There isn't a thing I can do about it. That is no reason, however, why you should refuse me your attention; something unexpected—I don't know what —might happen any moment. At the same time, I wouldn't stop you if you were afraid of being bored and wanted to leave. *(Noticing that his father-in-law has come out of his comatose condition, the* LECTURER *coughs and adjusts his tie nervously.)*
I especially plead for the attention of members of the medical profession whom I could provide with a vast amount of useful information on the subject, since despite the harmful effects of the tars and the nicotine, tobacco has medicinal properties, if you know what I mean—*(under his breath)* which is more than I do. For example, if you place a living fly in a tobacco pouch or a snuff-box, it is certain to die of a derangement of its nervous system. To begin with—tobacco is, in essence by its nature, a *plant* ...
(Someone in the audience, evidently a female, titters.)
I am absolutely serious about this and didn't intend to seem frivolous and wink at anyone. You mustn't take any notice if I should wink at you, for I usually wink with my right eye when I address an audience—it's an old habit of mine. I am, generally speaking, an extremely nervous person. As a matter of fact, I know exactly when I started winking. It started back in 1889—if you want to be exact about it, on the thirteenth of September of that year, when my wife presented me with our *fourth* daughter, Barbara. I really don't know how to explain how all my daughters managed to get born on the 13th.— It's no reflection on them, of course, though what all of them have been doing to me, you understand, passes comprehension.
(He bows to CHUBUKOV, *who stirs restlessly and calls out "Hurrah.")*
But in view of the little time left for my lecture I must stop digressing. I shall only digress long enough to add that my daughters are the reason my wife decided to start a boarding school for girls in the city. Daughters, as you well know, are extravagantly expensive and my wife— this is strictly between ourselves *(he notices with satisfaction that his father-in-law* CHUBUKOV *is sound asleep),*—my wife, who has about 50,000 rubles of her own money hidden away somewhere, likes to fancy herself in dire straits. To tell the truth, she *is* a trifle miserly, but it doesn't do me any good to complain. She has me looking after the school like a hired housekeeper. I buy the provisions for the school, I keep the ledger, and I even stitch together the exercise-books, aside from exterminating the bugs for her, catching the mice, and walking the poodle. And, at that, she expects me to save money by eating the left-overs from the pupils' bill-of-fare. Yesterday, for instance, three of the girl boarders had swollen glands and we had some pancakes to spare. So my wife had the cook give them to me instead of dinner. They were cold and pasty, but I had to gulp them down all the same. My swallowing made her cry out, "It's simply no use feeding you, scarecrow that you are." She has a beastly temper when she is crossed—I mean *(looking fearfully at the recumbent figure of his father-in-law)* my wife is a woman of spirit.
However, I do think I have strayed a little from my subject and—*tempus fugit*, you know—time is fleeting, as it were. *(He looks at his watch, and frowning, puts it to his ear; apparently making it go, since he smiles fondly at the watch and puts it back in his pocket.)*
I forgot to say, however, that at the boarding school I save my wife a pretty penny by filling in as a teacher of mathematics *(he starts counting on his fingers)*, chemistry, physics, geography, physics (I mean, history!), choral singing, and the classics, although I don't really *read* Latin —I merely *quote* from it. My wife, by the

way, charges extra for teaching the pupils Latin!—Also, for drawing, singing, and dancing, and I teach those subjects, too. But I am not at all bad at it, and should you want to observe the pupils please feel free to visit the school any morning—in fact, I happen to have a few prospectuses in my breast pocket—my wife saw to that —*she would!* (*He starts pulling papers out of his pocket, but drops them on the floor.*) I forgot to give you the address, however. It's number thirteen Dobermann Lane. And I don't mind admitting that it's a real dog's life I lead there. Everything involving me has the unlucky number thirteen attached to it; wouldn't you just know it! The school—and it's our home, too, I forgot to say—is number 13, three of my daughters were born on the thirteenth day of the month, and, believe it or not, our loathsome house has *thirteen* windows.

There is no doubt about it, I am a failure in every conceivable respect, and I would be the first to be surprised if I weren't. And I was once a sprightly fellow, if I say so myself; what a temper I had—I could shake the rafters with it. The day I came to her house to propose . . . what a battle we had . . . *what fun!* But I have grown old—and tired—maybe even stupid. Don't I look the jolly fellow standing here in front of you, although I have a great desire to lie down and bay at the moon or just break down and cry. (*Pulling himself together.*) But please forgive me—I am just one of those unfortunates who gets drunk on a single glass of ordinary wine. It gets hold of me in a mysterious way and then I remember my happy youth as a bachelor and I become sentimental. (*He wipes his eyes.*) And then I want to run away and leave everything behind.

Don't ask me where I want to go, because I don't know. And it doesn't matter where, provided I am far away from the vile life I am leading, the life that has turned me into an imbecile who is losing his hair along with his hopes. (*By now his voice is quite loud.*) All I know (*and he looks defiantly at the old man who, having awakened, has started applauding idiotically*)—all I know is that I would give anything to run away from that spiteful miser of a wife who has been my misfortune these many years. . . . I even studied at the university for a while; I had dreams and expectations; I was a man then. . . . How I long to run away and come to a stop somewhere far away in a green field, where I could stand stock-still under the sky and become rooted like a tree. A garden-variety of scarecrow would suit me too, with the moon bathing me in its pale light all night long, making me forget my tiresome past. (*Violently.*) And how I long to tear off this shabby old coat (*he starts tearing off his frock coat*), which I wear at all these ridiculous lectures I am expected to give for charity in order to make my wife's shabby boarding school better known in the county. (*His coat is now off his back; he flings it to the ground and stamps on it, while his father-in-law stands up in amazement, blinking stupidly.*) Yes, idiotic old uniform, take that! (*He steps on it again. But suddenly he freezes as he peers at the back of the house.*) But—oh no!—(*He hastily gets back into his frock coat.*) There she comes in full regalia—just in time to drag me home as usual. (*Softly and pathetically.*) Please tell her, if she asks, that the lecture has come off well. (*Raising his voice, and smiling to the back rows, where his wife is now presumably seated.*) In conclusion, therefore, there can be no doubt whatsoever that tobacco contains a dreadful poison. Smoking should be absolutely prohibited by law as a punishable offense. In view of what I have told you at such great length, ladies and gentlemen, I can only trust that my lecture on the harmful effects of tobacco will put you on your guard against this insidious weed and be of some benefit to you. I have finished! (*Winking mischievously to someone in the front rows of the auditorium*) Dixi et animam levavi.[3]—That is all! (*He bows and exits slowly.*)

NOTES

1. By "peasants" he means *serfs*—that is, peasants *owned* by a landowner, bought and sold by him like slaves, until the emancipation of the serfs in Russia in 1861.
2. Chubukov does not appear in the original play.
3. I have had my say and got a "load off my mind."

QUESTIONS

A. Understanding the Action:

1. The element of "plot" rarely plays an important part in Chekhov's work. In what way does this generalization receive any support from the text of *Then and Now?*

2. To what degree, if any, does the action of *Then and Now* and of each of the two individual plays of *Then and Now* stem from "situation," from "character," or from "environment"?

3. Are any follies, excesses, or pretensions exposed to ridicule in the two short plays of *Then and Now?* Describe them, and explain how Chekhov deals with them.

B. Understanding the Characters:

1. Is there any affection in the work on the part of the characters or on the part of the author? For whom? How is it demonstrated?

2. How do the characters change in the two plays? Is the change consistent with what the characters are, i.e., do they seem to "grow" in a logical or in a contrived manner? Explain your observation.

3. Why do the characters seem comic? What is it about any of them that is pathetic?

C. Understanding the Approach:

1. What is meant by Chekhov's "centrifugal" style of writing? Where is it present in *Then and Now,* and for what purpose or purposes is it employed?

2. Which of the two small plays in *Then and Now* is farcical, and which is pathetic?

3. What are the ingredients of farce in the one and of pathos in the other?

4. Why is the *combined* effect of the two individual plays comic rather than farcical?

D. Comparisons:

1. Is there any resemblance between *Then and Now* and *The School for Scandal?* Also, with *Arms and the Man?* Are there any differences between the two plays?

2. Describe the essential differences between *Then and Now* and *The Apollo of Bellac.*

SIDNEY HOWARD (1891-1939)

Most responsible for the success of the play, *The Late Christopher Bean*, was the man who adapted the original for the Broadway stage, Sidney Howard. Born in Oakland, California, he graduated from the University of California. After spending a year in Switzerland, he enrolled in Professor George Pierce Baker's class in playwriting at Harvard in 1916, but soon resigned from the course to become an ambulance driver in World War I. Later during the war he joined the American air force stationed in France and was entrusted with the command of a squadron. Subsequently, he became a journalist and came to know life in America at first hand; he covered such subjects as narcotic rings and a coal miners' strike and published a social study, *The Labor Spy*.

After writing a romantic play, *Swords*, in 1921, he began to turn out successful realistic plays about life in different parts of the United States: The first of these, *They Knew What They Wanted*, in 1924, was a comedy rich in sympathetic characterization and local color, the action being set in the Napal Valley in California. Sidney Howard won the Pulitzer Prize with this play.

Another play, *Ned McCobb's Daughter* (1926), had an authentic and extremely appealing New England background. In 1926 he also wrote a good family study, *The Silver Cord*, in which he exposed the selfishness of a possessive mother who tries to deprive her sons of friendship, love, and marriage.

Sidney Howard became one of the most effective adapters of novels and other books for the stage. Among the best of these were *Dodsworth* (based on the novel of the same name by Sinclair Lewis) and *Yellowjack*, based on a chapter on the fight against yellow fever in Paul de Kruif's *Microbe Hunters*.

INTRODUCTION TO *THE LATE CHRISTOPHER BEAN*

Howard also made English adaptations of foreign plays, and the best known of these was *The Late Christopher Bean*. He changed the French provincial background to New England, and he based his comedy on the sturdy character of a sympathetic country woman and the comic greed of the persons who try to deceive and cheat her. The result was one of the most acute American comedies of character and environment. The play represents a particularly happy marriage of sympathy and satire, and blends character-drama and humor.

The Late Christopher Bean originated as a light comedy, under the title of *Prenez garde à la peinture*, by the popular Parisian playwright René Fauchois, who was born in 1882.

Fauchois was first known as a writer of verse plays, and his biographical drama *Beethoven* was staged in Paris in 1909 and in New York in 1910. After the failure of a second biographical play in 1911, he turned to the writing of inconsequential light comedies. He would probably have had little success in the American theatre if *The Late Christopher Bean* had not appeared on Broadway in the fall of 1932 in an excellent adaptation and with an attractive cast that included Walter Connolly and Pauline Lord.

THE LATE CHRISTOPHER BEAN

SIDNEY HOWARD

BASED ON RENÉ FAUCHOIS' PRENEZ GARDE À LA PEINTURE

CHARACTERS

DR. HAGGETT
SUSAN HAGGETT
ABBY
MRS. HAGGETT
ADA HAGGETT

WARREN CREAMER
TALLANT
ROSEN
DAVENPORT

ACT ONE: *Morning.*
ACT TWO: *Noon.*
ACT THREE: *Afternoon.*

ACT I

SCENE: *The dining room of an old house, not far from Boston.*

Double doors in the rear wall, to the Left of Center, give on the entry, from which the stair ascends to the bedroom floor. The newel post of the stair and the front door are seen. When the front door is opened, a small porch with lattice-work and ivy vine is seen. To the Right of the double doors is a large fireplace and mantel in natural old pine. Fire logs and a pair of andirons are seen in the fireplace. The Right wall, downstage, contains the door to the "L," where the kitchen is located. To the Left of the Left Center double doors, the rear wall jogs down, then carries off Left. In this section of the rear wall is located a window, through which is seen an elm-shaded yard with trees, grass, bushes and flowers, and a picket fence. A large bay window is located in the Left wall and gives on the same view. The rear wall, from the Right joint to the joint where it jogs down, is in natural old

CAUTION: Professionals and amateurs are hereby warned that "The Late Christopher Bean," being fully protected under the copyright laws of the United States of America, the British Empire, including the Dominion of Canada, and all other countries of the Copyright Union, is subject to a royalty. All rights, including professional, amateur, motion pictures, recitation, public reading, radio and television broadcasting, and the rights of translation into foreign languages are strictly reserved. Amateurs may produce this play upon payment of a royalty of twenty-five dollars for each performance payable one week before the play is to be given to Samuel French, Inc., at 25 West 45th Street, New York, N.Y. 10036, or 7623 Sunset Boulevard, Hollywood, California, or, if in Canada, to Samuel French (Canada) Ltd., 27 Grenville Street, Toronto, Ontario.

pine. *Above and on both sides of the fireplace, the wall is panelled. The remaining walls are covered with wall-paper.*

The room is worthy of more tasteful furnishing than the Haggett family has given it. Mingled with the few old pieces is much of less merit and more recent date. Added to this again, and producing an atmosphere of some confusion both in the entry and in the room itself, are the desk and other furnishings of the doctor's office from which they have been moved in honor of painting and papering, evidences of which (in the form of a ladder, buckets, brushes and a sign on the front door which reads "Paint!") clutter the entry. Below the door down Right and against the wall is a highback chair. Above the door, against the wall, is a sideboard. To the Right of the fireplace is a wicker basket with firewood. To the Left of the fireplace is a small footstool. Just Right of the double doors, against the rear wall, is a wooden medical cabinet. Exactly Right Center is the dining table with four chairs placed about it. To the Left of the double doors is a small bench or stool. There is a large corner cabinet set in the corner where the wall jogs down. On the shelves of the cabinet are many ornaments. Below this cabinet is an armchair facing down Right. The dining table is balanced on the Left side of the room by the doctor's desk with the knee hole facing Right. A swivel chair is placed at the desk. Below the desk is a side chair facing Right. Above the bay window, set in the corner, is a low-back side chair. On the wall over the mantel is a framed oil painting of a bowl of buttercup flowers.

On the wall over the door down Right is a large framed etching. On the wall over the double doors is a framed oil painting study of a dog's head. A small framed photograph is hung on the wall above the bay windows. There are simple white pullback curtains on all the windows and a pair of tapestry drapes on the bay window. The floor is entirely covered by a well-worn carpet of old-fashioned design, with rag rugs placed just beyond the threshold of the three doors.

The light out of doors is of early morning in October. The stage is empty. The door Right leading to kitchen is only partly open. The double doors Left Center to the entry are both open. After a moment of silence, the front door opens to admit DR. HAGGETT, *a stout, undistinguished rural medical man of fifty. He closes the door, then removes his hat and overcoat and places them on a table in the entry. Then—*

DR. HAGGETT: Hannah!

MRS. HAGGETT: (*from upstairs*) That you, Milton?

DR. HAGGETT: Yes, it is.

MRS. HAGGETT: (*as before*) Back already, are you?

DR. HAGGETT: Yes, I am. (*Enters the room.*)

MRS. HAGGETT: (*as before*) Had your breakfast?

DR. HAGGETT: No, I haven't. (*Goes to desk to set his doctor's satchel on it*)

MRS. HAGGETT: (*as before, calling loudly*) Abby! (*Something on* DR. HAGGETT'S *hands annoys him. Smelling them, he gets a strip of gauze from a glass jar on desk and goes to medicine cabinet*) Abby!! (HAGGETT *opens drawer in cabinet; gets out a bottle; proceeds to clean his hands with contents, drying them with gauze*) Abby!!! Get Doctor Haggett his breakfast! He ain't had none! (SUSAN HAGGETT, *a pretty girl of nineteen, comes down the stair*) Better help Abby get your Pa's breakfast for him, Susie!

SUSAN: (*enters room and crosses to above table*) I will.

DR. HAGGETT: (*throws piece of gauze into firelog carrier next to fireplace*) What ails Abby that she wants help to get my breakfast?

SUSAN: Oh, Abby's terrible upset!

DR. HAGGETT: What about? (*Sits Left of table*)

SUSAN: Why, Pa! About leaving us!

DR. HAGGETT: That's right! Today *is* Thursday! I clean forgot! There's been enough talk about it, too! (SUSAN *moves a few steps Right*) So Abby's leaving us after all these years! (*He is looking toward Right door as* ABBY *enters, carrying a tin tray with coffee pot, cup and saucer, cream and sugar, napkins.*)

ABBY: (*wears a smile that decreases in plausibility as it increases in determination. She is the help of the* HAGGETT *family, a Yankee villager, aged vaguely between youth and maturity, of a wistful prettiness, simple and serious. Speaking as she crosses to above table and Right of him*). I got strong coffee hot and ready for you, Doctor Haggett. Think of you going all this time on an empty stomach. Did everything come out all right?

DR. HAGGETT: Yes. Boy, eight pounds, three ounces, come out.

ABBY: (*setting coffee things out on table*) Well, that's just lovely! I expect the Jordans must be real pleased it's a boy! I expect most parents'd sooner have boys than girls, and I don't know as I blame 'em. You just sit there, Doctor Haggett, and Susie, you fix your Pa his coffee while I get the rest of his breakfast. (*Starts to move toward Right door.* SUSAN *goes to above the table and Right of* HAGGETT. ABBY *points to the newspaper and telegram lying on table*) There's his Boston paper handy for him, And there's a telegram with it that just come. (*She has vanished again, carrying the empty tray, on the last word.* SUSAN *pours a cup of coffee*)

DR. HAGGETT: She appears to be making quite an effort for the last day. (*He reaches for the telegram and opens it.*)

SUSAN: Well, Abby would! It's going to seem like losing one of the family, ain't it? (*Moves a step Right. The contents of the telegram bring forth a low exclamation from* HAGGETT. SUSAN *stops and turns to him*) Pa, what is it?

DR. HAGGETT: It's from New York.

SUSAN: No!

DR. HAGGETT: Yes, it is. (*He reads*) "An admirer of the late Christopher Bean will do himself the honor of calling on you at noon on Thursday." Signed, Maxwell Davenport.

SUSAN: (*thoughtful*) Chris Bean. (*Goes to Right of table and sits*)

DR. HAGGETT: I haven't thought of Chris Bean for years.

SUSAN: Chris Bean who painted all them pictures—

DR. HAGGETT: Guess *he* thought they was pictures when he wasn't too drunk to think! But who's Maxwell Davenport? Guess I ain't supposed to know him, but— (*Puts telegram in his left coat pocket. He accepts coffee which* SUSAN *has poured for him*)

MRS. HAGGETT: (*comes down the stairs. Like her husband, she is Yankee, and they are about of an age. Unlike him, however, she has assumed certain citified airs in dress and bearing which, so she feels, lift her above the standards of her native village. Distastefully viewing the debris in the entrance as she descends*) Why ain't that painter-paperhanger come round like he said he would to fetch his stuff away? (*While speaking she picks up the two paint cans containing brushes which are placed against Left Center door, and puts them down by step-ladder. Next, she picks up end of canvas trailing on the floor at foot of the ladder and tucks it under the ladder*) He was all finished up when he went home last night, and he gave me his word he'd be here first thing this morning. (*Enters room and crosses to above table*) Deliver me from any more painters in the house! Your sister Ada's lying up in her bed this minute with the sick headache this paint smell's given her. (*Sits above table*) When I think of the work's got to be done in this house today, moving your Pa's things back into his office and all!

ABBY: (*returns from kitchen, bringing a tray containing balance of* HAG-

GETT's *breakfast. She sets the tray on the lower end of the sideboard; gets the dish of cereal*) Here you are, Doctor Haggett.

MRS. HAGGETT: (*still plaintive*) And Abby leaving us this afternoon—

ABBY: I'd as soon you didn't speak about me leaving, if you got no objection, Mrs. Haggett. (ABBY *crosses Right of* MRS. HAGGETT. *She leans over table and places dish before* HAGGETT. *He eats his breakfast during the ensuing scene*)

MRS. HAGGETT: Well, you are leaving, ain't you?

ABBY: Yes, I am. But you know I don't want to, and I wouldn't neither only it's the will of God. (*Returns to sideboard and gets covered dish of wheatcakes*) And the only way I can get through with it is if nobody speaks to me about it. But if you keep reminding me, I—I— (*Returns to table; places dish in front of* HAGGETT. *Goes Left of* MRS. HAGGETT, *who looks up.* SUSAN *lays a warning hand on her mother's arm.* ABBY *just manages to control herself. She smiles bravely, then goes to sideboard for plate of butter*) What I want is to hear about Mrs. Jordan's baby. She didn't get married none too soon, did she? (*Returns to table; places dish, then returns to sideboard*) I should think when a baby comes that quick after a wedding you'd pretty near have to brush the rice off it. (*Returns to table with syrup jug, which she places before* HAGGETT; *crosses in between* MRS. HAGGETT *and* SUSAN) Was she in labor long?

DR. HAGGETT: Not so long.

ABBY: (*continuing*) Did she have just a terrible time? You look kind of washed out yourself, Doctor Haggett. Well, it couldn't have been more than four o'clock when they called you out. Seems like babies is always getting you up or keeping you up, don't it?

(ADA HAGGETT, *a girl of twenty-six, who fancies her baby prettiness and babylike manner, comes down the stairs slowly.*)

SUSAN: (*puts her arm about* ABBY's *waist*) If you feel so bad about leaving us, Abby, why don't you stay?

ABBY: You're all so good to me! I don't want to go. It's the will of God.

DR. HAGGETT: The first time I ever heard of the will of God sending a woman off to live in Chicago. (ADA *enters room and goes to Left of medicine cabinet*)

ABBY: It couldn't have been nothing less to make my poor brother's wife take sick and die and leave him with four little children and no woman in the house. You know it wouldn't be my way to will a thing like that.

DR. HAGGETT: Well, don't let's be going over it again. You're leaving us. We're sorry to have you go. We'll save our tears till the time comes for you to take your train. What time is it?

ABBY: The five-o'clock to Boston.

SUSAN: We're going to miss you, Abby.

ABBY: And me? What about me leaving this place where I been so long? Fifteen years I been here!

DR. HAGGETT: (*exasperated*) Don't keep on going over it!

ABBY: (*turns and crosses toward Right door*) No, I don't want to go over it, either. I just can't stand—

(*Exits Right.*)

SUSAN: Poor Abby! (*Rises*) We'll never get another like her.

(*Exits Right, closing door.*)

DR. HAGGETT: Well, that wouldn't be such a bad idea.

MRS. HAGGETT: Want us to do without no help, I suppose!

DR. HAGGETT: Don't see why not. Three women in the house. I'll undertake to make *my* bed mornings.

ADA: (*moves down a step*) But, Pa! Have you thought what folks'd say?

DR. HAGGETT: What *would* they say?

MRS. HAGGETT: That Doctor Haggett's

practice has fallen off so bad he can't afford to keep help.

DR. HAGGETT: You keep house, Hannah, and I'll keep my practice.

MRS. HAGGETT: You'd set back and let everything go to the dogs if it wasn't for me. How long was I after you to have that office and entry painted and papered?

DR. HAGGETT: (*peace at any price*) Yes. I know, Hannah.

MRS. HAGGETT: (*continuing, her voice rising*) Who was it, you or me, found we could sell that *old* wall-paper for more than enough to give you a nice clean office sick folks could enjoy?

DR. HAGGETT: Oh, I know! I know!

MRS. HAGGETT: Now you want to spoil the *whole* impression by making your wife and daughters do their own work.

DR. HAGGETT: I know, Hannah, I know. And if you could find some way to make my patients pay the *bills* they owe me—

MRS. HAGGETT: If folks won't pay you, don't take care of them. (*Begins to read the newspaper*)

DR. HAGGETT: And what would happen to my practice then?

MRS. HAGGETT: God Almighty! There just ain't no reasoning with him.

DR. HAGGETT: Doctors have to care for the sick even if they can't pay. It's the ones who can and don't, these days—

MRS. HAGGETT: (*quietly*) Ada, you better go upstairs. I see I got to talk private with your Pa. (ADA *goes into entry and starts upstairs; pauses on stair, listening.* HAGGETT *rises and crosses toward desk. As he does he takes his tobacco pouch and his pipe from his coat pocket and begins to fill the pipe*)

DR. HAGGETT: If you could find new help for the same as we pay Abby—

MRS. HAGGETT: The new one I found won't cost us much more.

DR. HAGGETT: (*stops and turns to her*) You haven't gone and got a new one already!

MRS. HAGGETT: Oh, yes, I have. Last week when I went to Boston.

DR. HAGGETT: Have you got help in Boston?

MRS. HAGGETT: (*puts newspaper down on table*) Can't you understand, Milton, that it's in bad times like these you got to keep up appearances most of all? (*He sits uncomfortably in his chair at desk. She rises and crosses down to just Right of him*) I ain't sorry to see Abby leaving. (*He lights his pipe*) She's been here long enough. Mebbe fine for her to feel she's one of the family and call the girls by their first names and all. But you know she hasn't got a mite of style or dash about her. The new one ain't like that. She's a real city maid that can answer the doorbell proper!

DR. HAGGETT: (*looks up at her*) How much more does she cost?

MRS. HAGGETT: If you'll stop to think of all the girls and me are saving, making every stitch of our clothes for Florida!

DR. HAGGETT: (*sits back, his glance sharpening to a very fine point*) Oh, you're still talking *Florida* this winter?

MRS. HAGGETT: (*flustered*) Why—wouldn't I—be?

DR. HAGGETT: Well, the girls and you *ain't going to Florida,* nor any other place, till times get better.

ADA: (*bursts in from upstairs. As she enters*) Did I hear Pa say we can't go to Florida? (*Slowly moves to Left of table*)

DR. HAGGETT: Yes, you did, Ada. And it ain't the first time neither. Maybe I do sit by and let your Ma paint and paper up my office, and *maybe* your Ma is going to have a maid from Boston—maybe. But as long as I can't collect the bills my patients owe me, there ain't no use of no more *Florida* talk. I take my stand on that.

MRS. HAGGETT: Well, I take my stand

too, Milton Haggett, and I wouldn't be no mother if I give it up.

DR. HAGGETT: What's Florida got to do with being a mother?

MRS HAGGETT: You may not care if your daughters get married or not, but I do.

ADA: *And so do they!*

DR. HAGGETT: You don't have to go to Florida to get married.

ADA: Maybe not, but the opportunities down there are exceptional.

DR. HAGGETT: (*irritably*) Stuff and nonsense.

MRS. HAGGETT: No, it ain't, Milton. Them Miami beaches is just alive with boys who don't give a thought to nothing but romance and getting married.

DR. HAGGETT: Most boys get them ideas most any place.

MRS. HAGGETT: Not in New England in the winter time. (*Goes to armchair and sits*)

DR. HAGGETT: The girls can wait for spring, then.

ADA: (*to mother*) Pa wants for me to grow up an old maid.

DR. HAGGETT: (*getting a little testy*) I don't want no such thing.

ADA: (*to him*) I'm pretty near an old maid already.

DR. HAGGETT: You're not more than a baby.

ADA: I'm twenty-four.

DR. HAGGETT: No, you're not. You're twenty-six.

ADA: (*sits Left of table*) That makes it all the worse!

DR. HAGGETT: Well, if you're in such a hurry to get married, go down to the Post Office and put up a notice.

ADA: (*turns to him*) Pa!

MRS. HAGGETT: After all the advantages we gave our girls, would you want to see 'em married to village boys?

DR. HAGGETT: What's wrong with village boys? You married one.

MRS. HAGGETT: Well, I hadn't been to Miami then. (*A short pause*)

DR. HAGGETT: I thank you, Hannah. I thank you. But if Ada can do half as well as you've done—

ADA: There ain't no boys to speak of in this place. And what there is don't like me.

DR. HAGGETT: What is it makes Florida boys like you better? Is it because they seen you in your swimming suit? All right, give the boys here a chance. Invite 'em in, put on your swimming suit, and set by the fire. (SUSAN *enters Right; goes to chair Right of table*)

MRS. HAGGETT: (*rises; crosses to chair above table*) Well, your Pa's got the best of us again. There ain't no hope of Florida this winter. I'll have to make 'em take back my flowered foulard.

SUSAN: (*cheerfully*) Well, that's too bad. But I don't see as it matters. (*Sits*)

ADA: It does matter! It does! (MRS. HAGGETT *sits*) Pa says I'm only a baby. But what he really wants is for me to grow up an old maid.

DR. HAGGETT: (*rises; crosses Center*) I don't want no— (*Paces to and fro, muttering to himself*)

ADA: (*her voice rising*) If we stay here, Susie'll get married before me, because the boys here like her better than they like me, and if she gets married before me I'll just die. I'll die. I know I'll die.

(*Sobbing, she lowers her head on table.* HAGGETT *stops his mutterings and pacings*)

MRS. HAGGETT: (*rises, comes to above* ADA *and pats her on the shoulder*) It's this forever having just enough and not one mite over for—

DR. HAGGETT: (*sorrowfully*) Greed, Hannah! Greed! (*Crosses up to Left Center doorway, then returns to Left of table*)

MRS. HAGGETT: (*savagely*) Maybe I am greedy! But it's only *fools* and *wastrels* who don't try to get all they can out of life.

(ABBY *enters Right, her eye cocked malevolently. She goes to sideboard and gets empty tray*)

DR. HAGGETT: No man has never called me greedy for money, Hannah. And I hope no man ever does. I'll go upstairs now and shave. (*Goes out Left Center and upstairs*)

ABBY: (*moves to above table and with her tray goes about gathering up* HAGGETT'S *breakfast dishes*) I declare, if folks ain't peculiar, though! There I was crying and carrying on over going away and you're doing the very same as me because you got to stay.

MRS. HAGGETT: I'll thank you, Abby, not to make observations and remarks.

ABBY: Mrs. Haggett, don't mind me! I'm only help, without a mite of style about me, and I call the girls by their first names like one of the family. And now you got a real city maid coming from Boston. And she knows how to answer the doorbell proper. (*She carries filled tray to lower end of sideboard*)

MRS. HAGGETT: (*above and Left of table. Furious*) You're a common, impudent girl, and I discharge you for listening at keyholes.

ABBY: You can't discharge me because I discharged myself already. I won't go till I'm good and ready.

MRS. HAGGETT: I'll take no more back talk from you, young lady. You'll go now.

ABBY: I'll go this afternoon.

(WARREN CREAMER, *the village painter and paperhanger, has come into the entry from behind Right. He is a personable, self-satisfied youth in his early twenties*)

WARREN: (*in doorway*) Morning, Mrs. Haggett.

MRS. HAGGETT: Oh! It's the paperhanger!

WARREN: (*continuing*) Morning, Ada. Morning, Susie.

MRS. HAGGETT: (*as the girls return his greetings*) I was just saying it was about time you showed up.

ABBY: Warren ain't so late you need fret about it. (MRS. HAGGETT *swings on her again*)

WARREN: (*placid*) Weather's getting sharp. Guess winter must be coming. Had trouble starting the old truck this morning.

MRS. HAGGETT: (*turns back from* ABBY *with great dignity, then crosses up to Right of* WARREN *and indicates his materials in entry*) Well, get your stuff on out of here. I'm sick of the smell of paint.

ABBY: (*picks up the tray and starts for Right door*) There's plenty of things in this house smells worse than paint does. (*Exits; closes door*)

WARREN: (*still calmly*) *I come* to get my stuff out, Mrs. Haggett. And I brought you each a little present too.

ADA: Did you, Warren? What?

WARREN: Well, I brought each of you girls one of my pictures. (*He produces two small framed oil paintings of still life from under his arm, as he crosses to Left of table*)

SUSAN: (*delighted*) Oh!

ADA: A picture of you, Warren?

WARREN: No, not of me. They're pictures I painted. (*Hands a picture to each of the girls*)

MRS. HAGGETT: (*crosses round to Left of table, behind Ada and examines her picture*) It's a *dead fish!*

SUSAN: (*leans over to see it*) Looks like salmon you caught last Sunday, Warren.

WARREN: That's what it is.

MRS. HAGGETT: (*to* SUSAN) What's yours? (SUSAN *tilts picture for her to see*) *A dead duck!* Better swap round with your sister, Susie. Fish always makes Ada break out terrible.

ADA: Oh, not in pictures, Ma! (*Turns to* WARREN *with a too-ingratiating smile*) And they're your *own* work, Warren?

WARREN: Yeah.

ADA: The *frames* too? (MRS. HAGGETT *goes up a few steps*)

WARREN: (*nodding*) They're first-rate painting. I thought maybe you'd like to hang 'em up over the sideboard. I thought they'd look kind of suitable.

MRS. HAGGETT: I wouldn't have no appetite if I had to look up at a dead fish and a dead duck.

ADA: No! Warren's right, Ma. They'd look just lovely! (*Turns her fatal flattery on* WARREN) To think I never knowed you was a picture painter!

WARREN: (*blandly*) Seems like all kinds of painting comes natural to me.

ADA: (*same tactics*) I can see that. My! I hadn't no idea you was so clever. I didn't know the boys here were like *you*, Warren.

WARREN: They ain't! (MRS. HAGGETT *goes to desk; begins to arrange the papers, etc.*)

ADA: Why, you could paint real well, if you was to study. I'm only a baby, but I used to take painting lessons myself. Did you know that, Warren?

WARREN: No.

ADA: That flower-piece there on the wall is my work. (*Points to it.* ABBY *returns from kitchen, goes to sideboard, gets vase of flowers, crosses to table and sets it there*) It took a prize, it looked so natural. I guess I could give you some pointers, if you'd like.

ABBY: What are you giving him pointers about, Ada? Is it about pictures? (*Sees the two paintings on the table*) Did you paint these, Warren? Let's see, Susie.

WARREN: (*above table, Left of* ABBY) They're what's called still life.

ABBY: Still life. That's a painting term, still life.

MRS. HAGGETT: (*turns from desk*) What do you know about painting terms?

ABBY: Oh, I know. See this, Susie? (*She points*) Know how he did that? He didn't use his brush. No, he stuck his thumb in the paint and went like this— (*She indicates*) —and like this.

WARREN: That's right.

ABBY: (*to* WARREN) Oh, I know. I know.

ADA: (*her mother's dignity*) Don't notice her, Ma. Let her go out in the kitchen and wash Pa's dishes and let Susie go out and help her. And you go up to Pa and leave Warren and me to hang the pictures together. (*Picks up pictures and starts to rise.* WARREN *turns his back on her.* ABBY *takes newspaper to mantel, then empties ashtray on medicine cabinet into fireplace.* MRS. HAGGETT *starts for the stairs.* HAGGETT *comes downstairs in his shirt-sleeves*)

DR. HAGGETT: I was trying to shave, but there's no hot water. Morning, Warren.

MRS. HAGGETT: Susie, you get the kettle for your Pa. (SUSAN *rises; starts to move toward kitchen*)

ABBY: Don't you trouble, Susie. I don't mind fetching for your Pa and you.

MRS. HAGGETT: (*crosses above table toward* ABBY. *Quickly*) No, but if it was me I suppose you'd tell me to shave in cold water. (ABBY *sweeps into the kitchen, closing door.* MRS. HAGGETT *goes to sideboard and puts napkins and table-runner in drawer*)

SUSAN: (*quickly*) 'Tain't nothing, Pa. (*Picks up her painting, crosses below table, picks up* ADA'S *painting, goes to* HAGGETT *and hands them to him*) Just Ma and ABBY having one of their regular spats. Look at what Warren's painted for the dining room.

DR. HAGGETT: (*examines the pictures without much pleasure. Between* SUSAN *and* WARREN) Hmmm— Hmmm—

WARREN: (*right of him*) If you don't

like this pair, I got plenty more I painted down at the shop. I guess I must have close on a hundred. (SUSAN *takes paintings and places them by corner cabinet, then stands below armchair*)

DR. HAGGETT: A hundred? You must have taken a good bit of time off regular painting to get that many pictures painted.

WARREN: I don't mind how much time I take for painting pictures. I'm too good to stay with paper-hanging.

MRS. HAGGETT: (*a step to above chair Right of table*) You ain't fixing to be an artist, I hope?

WARREN: You bet I am, and I'll be a good one, too!

MRS. HAGGETT: (*with wise decision.* ADA *offers chair*) No, Ada. No, I guess I'll set right here. (*Does in chair Right of table*) I'd rather have a real painter in the family than a picture-painter.

WARREN: (*a step Right*) I was thinking of painting the dooryard fence for you, Mrs. Haggett, but—

MRS. HAGGETT: (*breaking in sharply*) Free?

WARREN: Yeah. But I got a better idea now. I'll paint you a portrait of the girls instead.

SUSAN: (*left*) Oh, Warren, will you?

ADA: (*seated chair Left of table. Turns and nods at* SUSAN) Does Susie have to be in it?

WARREN: Yeah. The both of you.

DR. HAGGETT: Warren, what's made you get so generous all of a sudden?

WARREN: (*turns to* HAGGETT) I got to thinking over what good care you took of my Ma the time she died and how you ain't never been paid for that, and so—

MRS. HAGGETT: If you're that grateful, mebbe you'd let us have the job you just done in the office free.

WARREN: Well, I ain't that grateful.

MRS. HAGGETT: Could you paint the girls *and* the dooryard fence?

WARREN: If you'd buy the paint for the fence, I could.

MRS. HAGGETT: Couldn't you use the portrait paint on the fence?

WARREN: 'Tain't the same kind.

MRS. HAGGETT: Then I guess we'll let the fence wait for spring.

ADA: How about the portrait?

MRS. HAGGETT: I got no use for it, but I got nothing against it.

SUSAN: How will you paint us, Warren? (*He turns to them and sees that with* ADA *seated in an old chair and* SUSAN *behind her, the pair of them, both in color and composition, would make a picture*)

DR. HAGGETT: (*moves a few steps up*) Now that's a question.

WARREN: Well, I don't know—I'd have to think. Ada, you go over and sit in that chair by Susie. (ADA *goes to armchair and sits*)

DR. HAGGETT: If Ada was listening to a sea-shell and Susie looking on—

WARREN: No—

MRS. HAGGETT: Or both of them looking off into the future like.

DR. HAGGETT: (*a step to* WARREN) You ought to paint Mrs. Haggett with them. She don't take up much room.

WARREN: (*decision*) I'll paint them just like they are.

ADA: Not in this dress! I got a lovely new one.

WARREN: I like that dress. I like the color. (*Has become thoroughly professional*) Yours and Susie's and that old chair together. I like that fine. Just give me a scrap of paper. Any old scrap and a pencil— (*Looks about him, goes to desk and finds a large pad there. He takes an artist's drawing pencil from his coat pocket as he returns to chair above table, watching the girls meanwhile*)

ADA: (*rises. To* SUSAN *as she pulls her down into the chair*) You sit down and I'll stand behind. (*The girls exchange places,* ADA *arranging herself over the back of the chair*) I'm such a baby, Warren wouldn't want you towering over me, would you, Warren?

WARREN: Either way. (*Crosses to* ADA *and poses her*) There, that's all right. (*Returns to chair above table and sits*) Now, Mrs. Haggett, just to give you an idea of what I can do. (*To girls as he begins to sketch excitedly*) Don't move, now! (*Pause*)

MRS. HAGGETT: Won't you even let Ada hold a bunch of flowers?

ADA: It's Warren's picture, Ma. If he likes me the way I am—

DR. HAGGETT: (*leans over* WARREN'S *shoulder*) Look, Hannah! You got to admit the boy's quick with his pencil. You can see which girl is which already.

MRS. HAGGETT: (*rises and joins him*) Which *is* which?

ADA: Does it look like me, Ma?

DR. HAGGETT: Give the boy time. You don't get likenesses as quick as that.

MRS. HAGGETT: What do you know about it?

DR. HAGGETT: Guess I know that much. Look at that, Hannah! (*Pulls* MRS. HAGGETT *nearer*) You're quite an artist, Warren. You'll be painting patriotic pictures before you're through. Ever seen the pictures in the Boston State House? (MRS. HAGGETT *reseats herself Right of table*) They got fine patriotic pictures there. (WARREN *stops sketching for a moment and squints over his pencil at girls in a typical artist's manner*) Figures life size! Frames thirty feet long! Pictures that make you proud to be an American! "Bunker Hill" and "The Spirit of '76"! I could give you ideas for pictures if you wanted, Warren. "The First Thanksgiving!" (WARREN *repeats the same business*) Now, that would be a good picture for a dining room. Look at that, will you, Hannah? Where ever did you learn such tricks, Warren?

WARREN: (*still working*) You remember that painter here named Chris Bean?

DR. HAGGETT: Chris Bean! Patient of mine! I had a telegram about him this morning. (*Fumbles for his coat pocket and finds that he is coatless*)

MRS. HAGGETT: About Chris Bean?

DR. HAGGETT: Yes. A man who calls himself an admirer of his.

MRS. HAGGETT: Wonder what he finds to admire him for? (ABBY *enters with the kettle. Stops still by the sideboard as* WARREN *speaks*)

WARREN: Chris started me off on a painting when I was a kid. He'd let me follow him wherever he went and sit beside him and draw the same things he did. He gave me lessons, all I ever had. I try to remember what he taught me and— (ABBY *has fairly yearned toward* WARREN)

MRS. HAGGETT: Hope he didn't teach you to drink like he did!

ABBY: (*stiffens*) Well, if he— (MRS. HAGGETT *looks sharply at* ABBY) Here's your hot-water bottle, Doctor Haggett. (*Crosses to above table and gives it to him*)

DR. HAGGETT: What do I want with—? That's so! I *was* shaving. Well, I better get back to it and get round to making my calls. (*Takes kettle and crosses toward Left Center door*) Thank you, Abby. (*Goes up the stair.* ABBY *and* MRS. HAGGETT *exchange a venomous glance as* ABBY *turns back toward Right door.*)

ABBY: Oh, Mrs. Haggett, I forgot to tell you. The real city maid from Boston's out in the kitchen. I found her in back when I went to fetch the kettle. I don't hardly think she'll stay after what I told her about the place. (*She exits Right*)

MRS. HAGGETT: (*rises; crosses to Right door*) If Abby's gone and poisoned that new maid's mind! (*Exits Right*)

ADA: (*crosses above table*) You'll have to excuse me, Warren. This is important. Oh, Ma! Do you think— (*She follows mother out, closing door*)

SUSAN: (*rises and moves a step to him*) Will you let me see?

WARREN: (*rises; crosses to her*) Sure, if you want to. (*She looks*) It's just rough.

SUSAN: Looks to me like it isn't quite fair to Ada.

WARREN: Well, as long as it's fair to you—

SUSAN: (*a step Left*) Oh, no, Warren! Be fair to Ada or you'll get Ma down on you.

WARREN: I paint pictures to suit myself, not your Ma. I don't care shucks for your Ma nor Ada neither. I guess you know why I'm painting this picture.

SUSAN: (*drawing back*) You said you wanted to give Ma a present.

WARREN: All I want's an excuse to see you every day.

SUSAN: You've known me a long time to talk that way, Warren.

WARREN: Guess you know me long enough to know what I think about you.

SUSAN: Guess you'd better not say any more.

WARREN: *You* say you'll marry me and I won't.

SUSAN: Warren!

WARREN: What?

SUSAN: I wouldn't be any wife for you. Not if you're going to be an artist, I wouldn't.

WARREN: Why not? I'm a hard worker and I'm going to be a *good* artist.

SUSAN: But I don't even know if I like art much.

WARREN: I'll teach you to like it.

SUSAN: You haven't even said you loved me.

WARREN: Do I have to say that?

SUSAN: Well, I think you ought to.

WARREN: Can't you take my word for it?

SUSAN: All right, Warren. Only there's one thing. We'd have to wait till Ada gets married first. (*He turns and crosses to table; puts drawing there*) We wouldn't have any peace if we didn't do that.

WARREN: (*turns to her*) Guess I'd better kiss you.

SUSAN: Why?

WARREN: Well, I'm marrying you, not Ada, and I'm awful busy and I got no time to waste. And I guess being kissed'll make you stop your nonsense.

SUSAN: Well, mebbe it will.

WARREN: You ain't afraid?

SUSAN: (*smiles*) No.

WARREN: All right, I'll do it, then. (*Goes to her, Left Center; takes her in his arms rather stiffly; kisses her with little passion. The Right door opens and* ADA *appears*)

ADA: Well, Warren, here I am back— (*A gasp. Then a step on*) Pa! (*Turns to kitchen*) Ma! Come here this minute! (SUSAN *breaks away to down Left*)

DR. HAGGETT: (*off stage on stairs*) What is it?

WARREN: (*quickly*) It's Ada messing in other people's business.

ADA: Don't you dast speak to me.

MRS. HAGGETT: (*appears in Right door, closing it*) Ada, don't you know I'm busy?

ADA: (*beside herself*) I don't care if you are! There's things going on in here I want 'tending to!

DR. HAGGETT: (*still in shirt-sleeves, and minus his collar, comes downstairs and enters room*) What's come over this house of mine this morning?

ADA: There I was in the kitchen, Pa, with the new maid and Ma, and I come back and I caught him and Susie—

WARREN: Don't tell 'em what I was doing, Ada. (*Stepping forward undismayed to* SUSAN'S *side*) I'd sooner show 'em. (*Takes the terrified* SUSAN *in his arms again and again kisses her, this time with real passion. A gasp from* MRS. HAGGETT)

DR. HAGGETT: (*above chair Left of table*) God bless my soul!

MRS. HAGGETT: (*crosses below table to Center. Furiously*) You pack your stuff up and clear out of here.

WARREN: (*turns to her*) All right. I don't mind. (*To* SUSAN) Coming with me, Susie? Susie and me are going to get married.

ADA: (*a step Left. A scream*) Ma, if you let Susie get married ahead of me—!

MRS. HAGGETT: Susie ain't going to marry no Warren Creamer. My daughter's too good to waste on any starving dead beat of an artist.

WARREN: You ain't talking about me, Mrs. Haggett? I'm the best bet for marriage in this whole country. I'm going far and Susie's coming with me. I guess she's old enough to know her own mind.

SUSAN: Go along now, Warren. This won't help things any.

WARREN: I won't go unless you come with me.

MRS. HAGGETT: (*snorts as she crosses to Left of* HAGGETT) Milton, if he ain't out of this house before I count ten, I—

SUSAN: There won't be no need for throwing Warren out, Pa. Please go, Warren. I'll see you later.

WARREN: (*as steadily as ever*) When?

SUSAN: I'll get word to you.

DR. HAGGETT: (*crosses to* WARREN) Better go, Warren, and let things simmer down.

WARREN: (*crosses to table*) All right. Give me my drawing, and—

MRS. HAGGETT: (*snatches the drawing off table just as* WARREN *reaches for it, and crumples it. A general gasp*) There'll be no more painting portraits in this house.

WARREN: (*picks up his hat from table and puts it on; crosses into entry. Sullen*) I'll go to keep the peace for Susie's sake. (*Opens the front door, then begins picking up his materials*) But she'd ought to come with me. Because we *are* going to get married. (*Takes a step into room*) And as for you, you're what they call a Philistine, Mrs. Haggett. Yes, a Philistine! I'll go now. But I'll show you yet. (*Turns and goes out through front door, slamming it.* SUSAN *bursts into tears*)

MRS. HAGGETT: (*above table. Throws drawing toward fireplace*) Well, I may be a Philistine, but I guess I nipped that romance in the bud. (SUSAN *sits in desk chair.* HAGGETT *goes to Right of her*)

DR. HAGGETT: Clear out, you two, and leave Susie and me alone. (*Ada looks at* SUSAN)

MRS. HAGGETT: (*crosses above table to Right door*) I said this was going to be a terrible upsetting morning, but I hadn't no idea how terrible— (ADA *follows* MRS. HAGGETT *into the kitchen; closes door.* SUSAN *continues sobbing.* HAGGETT *looks down on her*)

DR. HAGGETT: (*patting her on shoulder*) Don't take on, Susie.

SUSAN: He loves me, Pa, and I love him.

DR. HAGGETT: That's too bad. If he wasn't so hell-bent to be an artist—

SUSAN: What's wrong with artists?

DR. HAGGETT: Not a thing but the cost of food and lodging.

SUSAN: Not if he's a good one! And he *will* be a good one.

(TALLANT *is seen passing by outside windows Left.*)

DR. HAGGETT: He's got conceit enough. But the best of 'em is poor providers, from all I hear, *and these days*—

SUSAN: (*rises. Passionately, with her head on his shoulder*) "These days!" That's all you ever say! "These days!" If it wasn't for these days you and Ma wouldn't have nothing against Warren, and Ma and Ada could go to Florida—

DR. HAGGETT: And I could get a little peace. (*The doorbell rings*) Here we are talking, and I ought to be making my calls. (*Both move toward the stair*) Come upstairs and wash your face, and I'll get my coat on. I'll have a talk with Warren and see what's what. (*Over his shoulder as* ABBY *comes from Right through room into entry. Very concerned and solicitous*) If that's a patient, Abby, show him in here in the dining room and keep the others out. I'll be right down. (*Disappears with* SUSAN *upstairs*)

(ABBY *opens the front door to admit* TALLANT, *a smooth, youngish and shabbily-dressed New Yorker.*)

ABBY: Will you step in here? (TALLANT *comes into the entry*) The Doctor'll be right down. (*She closes front door*)

TALLANT: Thank you. I'll wait, then. (*Enters to Left of medicine cabinet and casually glances about the room*)

ABBY: (*crosses to behind armchair*) You can have a chair. The waiting-room magazines got lost in the moving on account of the office being painted, but he won't keep you long. (*Is going below table toward kitchen. He smiles*)

TALLANT: You must be Abby. (*Very casually*)

ABBY: (*surprised*) I've never seen you before that I remember.

TALLANT: (*places hat on top of medicine cabinet*) No, this is the first time we've ever met.

ABBY: (*stops at Center*) How do you walk right in and call me by my name?

TALLANT: (*crosses Left Center*) Ever hear of mind readers?

ABBY: (*continues on her way to kitchen*) You're not one of them, are you?

TALLANT: Only in a small way.

ABBY: Whatever you are, you're fresh as paint. (*Exits Right, closing door*)

DR. HAGGETT: (*comes downstairs, now fully dressed, and enters to Left of* TALLANT) Good morning, sir.

TALLANT: Is this Doctor Haggett?

DR. HAGGETT: Yes, it is. (*They shake hands*)

TALLANT: (*over-elaborate*) I'm very glad to meet you, Doctor Haggett.

DR. HAGGETT: Sit down, won't you? (*Gestures toward patients' chair below desk as he crosses to desk chair*) I'm sorry my office is out of commission.

TALLANT: Don't apologize, Doctor. I've come to see you because I feel— (*Moves a step to him*)

DR. HAGGETT: A little bilious? You look it. (*Gestures again to chair below desk*) Can't fool me on a sluggish liver. (*Takes his place professionally at his desk*)

TALLANT: I daresay you're right, Doctor, but—

DR. HAGGETT: (*turns to him. Indicates patients' chair*) Sit down and put out your tongue. Headache? Nausea? Bowels all right?

TALLANT: You don't understand, Doctor. I'm not sick.

DR. HAGGETT: (*sits up in surprise*) Well, if you're not sick, what do you want with me?

TALLANT: (*sits in armchair, Left Center*) I was just coming to that, Doctor.

DR. HAGGETT: (*rises. Impatiently*) Might as well tell you I don't want no insurance.

TALLANT: (*reassuring*) I'm not here to sell *insurance*. I'm not here to sell *anything*. I'm here solely for the pleasure of making your acquaintance.

DR. HAGGETT: (*surly*) You don't tell me!

TALLANT: Oh, yes, I do! I happened to be motoring through your lovely State, enjoying the glory of its autumn foliage. (HAGGETT *shows signs of impatience*) And as I came to this village I realized that I'd stumbled upon an opportunity to perform a duty I've postponed *too long*.

DR. HAGGETT: What's that?

TALLANT: The *payment* of a sacred *debt* I owe you, Doctor.

DR. HAGGETT: (*re-seats himself. Astonished*) What *debt* do you owe me?

TALLANT: A matter of ten years ago

you had as a patient a man whom I called and still call my dearest friend.

DR. HAGGETT: Did I now!

TALLANT: A man known by a good Yankee name. An excellent Yankee name! Christopher Bean!

DR. HAGGETT: (*enlightened*) Oh, it's *you*, is it?

TALLANT: (*startled*) I beg your pardon!

DR. HAGGETT: (*laughs*) Funny, me taking you for a patient. But I wasn't expecting you for some hours yet.

TALLANT: (*very much on his guard*) You *were* expecting me?

DR. HAGGETT: Well, I got your telegram, Mr— (*Fumbling in his Right pocket for the wire*) Let's see, what was the name? (*He takes out telegram and unfolds it*)

TALLANT: (*rises, a step to him. Quickly*) Is that the telegram? May I see it? They so often mix them up—

DR. HAGGETT: (*looks up in surprise. Reads it carefully*) That there seems clear enough. (*He hands it to* TALLANT)

TALLANT: (*as he reads it quickly*) Oh, yes. Quite! I forgot that I'd said "noon"! (*Returns telegram to* HAGGETT) It took me less time to get here than I thought. (*Sits again*) I hurried. (*He smiles, his affability restored*) I was afraid that you might go out on your rounds of visiting the sick and that I might miss you. And I was so eager, you see, so very eager—

DR. HAGGETT: (*looking at the telegram*) You say here you're an admirer of Chris Bean's.

TALLANT: That's putting it pretty mildly, Doctor Haggett.

DR. HAGGETT: I was just wondering if your Chris Bean's the same one I know.

TALLANT: Oh, I'm certain.

DR. HAGGETT: Well, I don't know now. As my wife said when this telegram came: "Can't see what he finds to *admire* about Chris Bean!" *Not* that Chris wasn't a likeable lad. I was fond of him.

TALLANT: Of course you were.

DR. HAGGETT: I just wanted to make sure, though. (*Quickly*) Did the fellow you're thinking of think he was a painter?

TALLANT: (*surprised*) You might put it that way.

DR. HAGGETT: It's the same, then. (*Places telegram on desk*)

TALLANT: Poor chap.

DR. HAGGETT: (*confidentially*) Oh, I always humored him about his pictures. You got to humor folks when they're sick as he was.

TALLANT: I know you did everything you could for him.

DR. HAGGETT: Well, I hope I done my duty for him. Of course, a case like his— This ain't no climate for tuberculosis. If he'd had the money to get himself out West he might have had some chance, if he'd quit drinking. But as it was, there wasn't much I could do.

TALLANT: We're all mortal, Doctor.

DR. HAGGETT: There's no denying that.

TALLANT: It delights me that you remember him with affection.

DR. HAGGETT: Oh, we ain't none of us forgot him. Why, we was speaking of him just a few minutes past. My wife, she took a real fancy to him. He kind of appealed to her, I guess, seeing as we ain't got no sons of our own only two daughters. And him coming to live here, sick like he was and an orphan without no family. She took him right to her heart, and gave him the old barn for his studio. He painted most everything round the place. They was terrible bad, though, them pictures of his. (*Laughs reminiscently*) Mebbe if he'd had some training—

TALLANT: (*quickly*) Oh, very like. (*Then, more seriously*) Recently, though, Doctor, only the other day in fact, as I was going through an old desk of mine, I came across some letters Chris wrote to me while he was living here. And in the last of them—it's disgraceful I should have neglected it all these years—he spoke of your kindness to him and his gratitude and asked if I couldn't help him pay what he owed you.

DR. HAGGETT: (*very pleased*) Well, that's like Chris. Never a penny to his name and forever borrowing! He didn't even own a hat.

TALLANT: Let me see—the sum came to—

DR. HAGGETT: (*quite sincerely*) I don't remember.

TALLANT: (*firmly*) Exactly a hundred dollars.

DR. HAGGETT: Mebbe so. Likely he asked me how much he owed me, and likely I told him if ever he had a hundred he could spare— (*Rises*)

TALLANT: Allow me, Doctor. (*He rises and hands two fifty-dollar bills to* HAGGETT.) A little late, but paid in full.

DR. HAGGETT: (*amazed*) Well, God Almighty!

TALLANT: And all my apologies for keeping you waiting.

DR. HAGGETT: (*rises*) My dear sir—

TALLANT: Well, the debt's paid at last. I shall go home to New York a happier man.

DR. HAGGETT: (*completely flabbergasted as he turns to desk*) I'll give you a receipt.

TALLANT: (*protesting*) Oh, Doctor, please!

DR. HAGGETT: (*turns to* TALLANT) Would you allow me to shake you by the hand?

TALLANT: I should be honored, Doctor. (*They shake hands*)

DR. HAGGETT: Just a minute— (*Crosses to below table and calls*) Hannah! Ada! Come back in here a minute! (*Turns back to* TALLANT) I want you to meet my family, Mr.—Mr.—Davenport!

TALLANT: I'm sorry I left my cards at the hotel.

DR. HAGGETT: I don't need no visiting card of yours. (*Touching his heart*) Your name's engraved here, Mr. Davenport. (MRS. HAGGETT *and* ADA *come in Right*) My wife. (MRS. HAGGETT *crosses below table to Right of* TALLANT *and shakes hands with him*) My daughter, Ada. My younger daughter Susan—she's not so well this morning. (ADA *crosses to below chair below table. To the two women as* TALLANT *bows*) I called you in, though, to show you an honest man.

TALLANT: (*Left of* MRS. HAGGETT) Don't be alarmed, please, ladies!

DR. HAGGETT: Mr. Davenport here, who sent me that telegram from New York, is a friend of your old friend, Chris Bean. And now, ten years after poor Chris's death, this loyal friend, this more than honest man, has paid me the little debt poor Chris owed me. A hundred dollars. Here! You see! (*Turns to* ADA *and hands her the money*) You take it, Ada. You take it down and put it in the bank. Such things don't happen every day.

MRS. HAGGETT: (*profoundly impressed*) Well, I should say they don't!

DR. HAGGETT: Let this be an example and inspiration to both of you.

ADA: Yes, Pa.

MRS. HAGGETT: Oh, it will be. Indeed, it will be, Milton. Won't you rest yourself? (TALLANT *to armchair.* MRS. HAGGETT *sits Left of table.* ADA *sits below table*)

DR. HAGGETT: (*crosses to desk chair*) And don't neither of you never forget the name of—the name of—

TALLANT: (*sits armchair*) Davenport.

DR. HAGGETT: That's right. Davenport. (*He sits*)

TALLANT: You cover me with confusion, Doctor. I see nothing extraordinary in what I've done.

DR. HAGGETT: You ain't tried collecting doctors' bills these days. (*Picks up his cash book, makes entry in it and mutters gleefully*) A hundred dollars!

TALLANT: But I told you how much my friend meant to me. (*Long pause as all look solemn. The merest afterthought*) I'm just wondering if he didn't leave some of his pictures to remember him by. Of course you've told me what you thought of them. (MRS. HAGGETT *looks down*) And Chris wrote how even the village boys laughed at him when they watched him painting—

DR. HAGGETT: It seems mean to say so now, but I'm afraid *they* did.

MRS. HAGGETT: We never let him see *us* laugh.

TALLANT: (*to her*) They'd have a special sentimental value for me. You can understand.

DR. HAGGETT: There ain't nothing to be ashamed of in that.

TALLANT: (*to him*) Then if you *have* any, do you think I might take them away with me? (*More specific*) His letters mention six or seven he left here.

DR. HAGGETT: Oh, there was all of six or seven.

MRS. HAGGETT: Milton, I believe there's one out in the chicken house, *still*.

TALLANT: (*to her. Barely suppressed horror*) In the chicken house!

DR. HAGGETT: Hannah, you're right. There is. (*Apologetically to* TALLANT) But I hate to think what condition it must be in.

TALLANT: (*the least pause. Then, quickly*) I'd like to have it, Doctor. No matter what shape it's in, I'd like to have it. It *is* a souvenir, you know.

MRS. HAGGETT: (*rises*) You come with me, Ada. We'll see if we can't get it for Mr. Davenport. (ADA *rises and follows her mother out off Right in the entry*)

DR. HAGGETT: I remember now. There was a leak in the chicken house tar-paper roof. I was looking round for something watertight, and I found that picture. Fine, solid, thick oil paint, you know, and there wasn't no reason to set much store by it.

TALLANT: No.

DR. HAGGETT: (*rises*) Wait! (*Calling*) Abby! (*He turns back to* TALLANT) I just thought of something else. (ABBY *enters and crosses above table to up Center*) Run up in the attic and look in that corner behind the north dormer. Seems to me like a few years ago we put one of them pictures of Chris Bean's in there to stop up that leak, too.

ABBY: (*starts guiltily and gulps*) What do you want with it, Doctor Haggett?

DR. HAGGETT: Mr. Davenport here wants it to take along home with him.

ABBY: Mr. Davenport does?

DR. HAGGETT: Mr. Davenport was Chris Bean's closest friend.

ABBY: Mr. Davenport was?

DR. HAGGETT: See if you can get that picture off without tearing it. Then bring it down here.

ABBY: For Mr. Davenport?

DR. HAGGETT: That's what I said.

ABBY: Yes, Doctor Haggett. (ABBY *goes upstairs.* HAGGETT *reseats himself*)

TALLANT: I'm sorry to cause your household so much trouble.

DR. HAGGETT: A man like you ain't no trouble to us. I only hope we can find what you're after. (MRS. HAGGETT *and* ADA *return, through entry.* TALLANT *rises*)

ADA: Well, we got it.

MRS. HAGGETT: (*extending a filthy square of canvas as she enters to Right of* TALLANT) It's kind of dirty. But you know chicken houses! (ADA *crosses to above table*)

DR. HAGGETT: (*rises*) Just let Abby get at it with some *soap* and a *scrubbing brush*—

TALLANT: (*hastily*) No! No! No! No! That won't be necessary!

MRS. HAGGETT: 'Twon't be no trouble.

TALLANT: Oh, no, please! I'd be afraid— (*Takes canvas from* MRS. HAGGETT) I mean I'd rather clean it up myself.

DR. HAGGETT: But you can't carry it off all nasty like that!

TALLANT: Don't you see, Doctor, what it will mean to me to bring the picture back to life? It will seem almost as though Chris himself— (*There is a pause in honor of his emotion*)

MRS. HAGGETT: Oh, yes. (*She points toward wall, Left Center*) Did you think of Ada's picture there?

DR. HAGGETT: But Mr. Davenport don't want Ada's pictures.

ADA: (*below fireplace*) Of course he don't want pictures painted by little me. (TALLANT *looks at her*) But Ma means I turned one of Chris Bean's pictures over to paint my flower piece on the back. (*Points to picture over fireplace.* TALLANT *looks at it*)

DR. HAGGETT: I didn't know that. Now ain't that a pity, Mr. Davenport? (*Crosses up to below fireplace. He turns to* TALLANT) There's another we might have given you if Ada hadn't gone splotching. (HAGGETT *takes the picture from the wall and considers it*)

TALLANT: (*puts old canvas on chair Left of table, then crosses up to Left of* HAGGETT) Did you paint this, Miss Haggett?

ADA: (*right of* HAGGETT. *Archly*) If you can *call* it painting, I did.

TALLANT: (*takes painting from* HAGGETT) This lovely, living thing!

ADA: Oh, Mr. Davenport! I did take a few lessons once, but—

TALLANT: You did this little masterpiece on a few lessons?

ADA: (*happily*) It isn't no masterpiece, Mr. Davenport! At least *I* wouldn't think it was.

TALLANT: My dear Miss Haggett, don't underrate your gifts. The exquisite texture of those buttercups is not to be underrated.

ADA: (*excited*) Ma, do you hear what Mr. Davenport's saying?

TALLANT: Of course I didn't mean that you won't do better things in the future or that you won't go farther. But here, already, I, the connoisseur, sense the spark of *genius*.

DR. HAGGETT: Of genius!

TALLANT: I do indeed!

MRS. HAGGETT: (*left Center*) Now don't you go making our Ada into an artist. (TALLANT *crosses down to Right of her, still holding painting.* HAGGETT *comes down to above chair Left of table*)

TALLANT: (*to her*) Of course I know you won't want to part with it, but if you'd let me buy it—

MRS. HAGGETT: (*quickly*) What's it worth?

TALLANT: (*looking at it*) That's hard to say. Her name's not known, of course, but I should think the better dealers of New York would sell a thing like this for—let me see—fifty dollars. (*Quickly*) Not that it isn't worth much more!

ADA: (*right*) *Fifty dollars!*

TALLANT: (*quickly*) Well, say, forty!

ADA: But I could do one like it every day.

TALLANT: (*a step Right to table*) Don't hesitate, then, Miss Haggett. Your fortune's made.

DR. HAGGETT: (*crosses to Left of* MRS. HAGGETT. *Oddly dubious*) It strikes me kind of funny, you coming in here and paying Chris Bean's bill and then offering my daughter *forty dollars—*

MRS. HAGGETT: Fifty dollars.

DR. HAGGETT: (*to her*) He said forty.

MRS. HAGGETT: He said fifty first, and fifty's Ada's price.

TALLANT: (*places picture on table*) I will of course pay fifty dollars if you'll sell it. (*To* ADA) And you may be sure that orders for more will follow. (*Has again produced a roll of bills from his pocket and extracts several bills.* ADA *crosses below table, nearer him*)

DR. HAGGETT: I don't know as she ought to take it, Hannah.

ADA: But Pa! A young girl like me can spend fifty dollars even if we don't go South. (*Takes the money from* TALLANT) Thank you.

TALLANT: Thank *you* for the very great pleasure of discovering a new artist, Miss Haggett.

DR. HAGGETT: (*somewhat ashamed*) She gets it all from me. I always did have a kind of weakness for *art*, even though I am a doctor.

ADA: And you got Chris Bean's picture on the other side of mine.

TALLANT: (*false laugh. Picks up picture*) By Jove, so I have! Do you know— (*Turns the picture over*)—in my enthusiasm for your work I'd quite forgotten—(*We see that he is struck by its beauty*)

DR. HAGGETT: (*a step down to below and Left of* TALLANT) What do you think he was getting at that time?

ADA: (*a step nearer*) Isn't that meant to be the old covered bridge up the back river?

MRS. HAGGETT: (*pulls* HAGGETT *by arm so that he is in proper position to see picture*) Why don't you try looking at it right side up, Milton?

DR. HAGGETT: Looks the same to me either way. (*Then remembering. To* TALLANT) I beg your pardon, Mr. Davenport. I shouldn't have said that about a dead man. (*They all look solemn*) Not with you feeling for him the way you do. (MRS. HAGGETT *crosses to armchair and sits*)

ABBY: (*comes downstairs and enters, still eyeing* TALLANT *with suspicion. Above armchair*) I couldn't find a thing in the attic. There's no pictures up there of any kind.

DR. HAGGETT: (*turns to her*) But I know darn well I— (TALLANT *drops the picture to his side*)

MRS. HAGGETT: Mebbe the mice have et it.

DR. HAGGETT: (*a step to her*) It was on the left of the north dormer—

ABBY: (*very steady*) There's nothing there now but some tin cracker boxes Mrs. Haggett's saving.

DR. HAGGETT: But I tell you I'm positive.

ABBY: (*not to be shaken*) I've been over every inch of that attic, Doctor. I didn't find a thing but the old trundle bed used to be in the front room before you got the brass bed, and the trunk with your Ma's pewter in it and the other trunk—

DR. HAGGETT: I could have sworn! Well, it's too bad. That's all, Abby. (*Turns to* TALLANT. ABBY *crosses to above desk*) I'm sorry, sir. I'd have liked to show you how much I appreciate what you've done, but there you are. No man can do better than his best. (ABBY *draws back, her gaze fixed on* TALLANT)

TALLANT: I'm more than satisfied with what I've *got*, Doctor Haggett. (*Turns and picks up roll of canvas from chair Left of table*) And I repeat I'm only sorry to have caused so much trouble— (*The ladies brush his apologies aside with low exclamations. He bows*) Mrs. Haggett. Miss Haggett.

DR. HAGGETT: (*crosses up to Left of* TALLANT *and escorts him to the Left Center door*) Mr. Davenport, your call this morning is going to stand out as one of the happiest memories of my medical career!

TALLANT: (*gets his hat from top of medical cabinet and puts it on*) Doctor, you and I are going to be much better acquainted. And it occurs to me that we might go into business together. (MRS. HAGGETT *looks around at them*) Business which might be highly profitable to both.

DR. HAGGETT: I ain't got no capital.

TALLANT: It will require nothing more of you than—(*Laughs*) —friendly co-operation.

DR. HAGGETT: (*smiles*) I got a plenty of that!

TALLANT: (*they move up to front door*) Then we're rich men, Doctor Haggett, we're rich men! (*They shake hands, then* TALLANT *exits by front door*)

MRS. HAGGETT: (*rises*) Well! (*Crosses to above the table*) At this rate we'll mebbe get to Florida after all. (HAGGETT *returns to room and crosses to desk.* TALLANT *is seen passing outside windows Left*)

DR. HAGGETT: Well, after this morning, I'm not so sure you won't. Wish I knew what the business is he's got in mind—

ADA: (*below and Right of table*) I don't care what it is if it makes us rich. (ADA *goes to window and watches* TALLANT)

DR. HAGGETT: (*sententiously*) Ada, that's no kind of talk for my daughter. If there's one thing I can't abide it's greed for money.

ADA: Let's get on to our marketing, Ma, before Pa gets started. (*He looks at her; turns away*)

MRS. HAGGETT: Yes, Ada, come upstairs and get your hat on. (*Starts upstairs with* ADA) If anything ever did happen to make us rich I wouldn't worry much what it was. (ADA *laughs. They disappear*)

DR. HAGGETT: (*listens, standing beside his desk. He picks up his case and moves away Right a few steps, where he pauses and smiles dreamily. Suddenly he rouses himself and turns to* ABBY) You seen my call book, Abby?

ABBY: (*turns away from bay window, goes to desk, takes it out of drawer and gives it to him*) Here it is, Doctor Haggett.

DR. HAGGETT: (*glancing at the open page*) I'll go out to the Jordans' farm again first. After that the rest of 'em's all in town. (*Puts it in his coat pocket*)

ABBY: (*pointing to another pad on desk*) I got 'em all written down, Doctor Haggett.

DR. HAGGETT: (*moves away Right a step*) Then you know where to reach me if I'm wanted. (*Slips away again into his daydream. Again he recalls himself, laughing apologetically*) There I go daydreaming again. (*Crosses up Left Center*) That man Davenport's got me all off doctoring.

ABBY: (*crosses to him*) If I was you, Doctor Haggett, I'd watch him careful.

DR. HAGGETT: What makes you say that?

ABBY: Strikes me it's always a good idea to watch folks careful when they know as much as he does.

DR. HAGGETT: (*testily*) I declare, Abby, I think Mrs. Haggett's pretty near right about the way you meddle. Didn't I get a telegram from him this morning? (ABBY *says nothing. He goes out into the entry, picks up hat and coat and leaves. He passes outside windows Left.* ABBY *stands still; glances toward window and then at telegram lying on the desk; starts toward it and picks it up. Before she can read it, however,* MRS. HAGGETT *and* ADA *come chattering downstairs, dressed for going out.* ABBY *drops the telegram and quickly goes to armchair and moves it a trifle upstage*)

MRS. HAGGETT: I don't believe I'll take back that flowered foulard just yet, Ada.

ADA: Oh, I wouldn't, Ma. You heard Pa say we might get to Florida after all. We might even get as far as California now! It's always been my dream. (*They go out front door, closing it.* ABBY *then crosses to upstage end of desk and begins to arrange papers, books, etc., on desk, meanwhile watching* MRS. HAGGETT *and* ADA *as they pass outside window Left. As they pass from sight, she again picks up* the telegram. *This time she reads it through, pronouncing each word inaudibly to herself. A clock strikes ten.* SUSAN *comes sobbing downstairs.* ABBY *quickly drops telegram on desk.* SUSAN, *however, is too miserable to notice* ABBY, *and runs sobbing and snivelling to the fireplace*)

ABBY: Susie! (*She crosses to below armchair*)

SUSAN: (*picks up piece of paper by fireplace*) Oh, Abby, I never knowed I *could* be so miserable.

ABBY: (*crosses to above* SUSAN) Oh, folks can be awful miserable sometimes.

SUSAN: (*sits Right chair and lovingly smooths out the drawing*) But look at poor Warren's drawing, all mussed up!

ABBY: He'll make another. (SUSAN *looks at her*) Artists always do.

SUSAN: Abby, *you* ain't got nothing against *artists*, have you?

ABBY: Me? No! (*Crosses toward kitchen*) No! *Not me*— (*Smiles to herself. The Curtain falls*)

ACT II

It is only a little later. The furniture is arranged exactly as in the preceding Act. There are dishes, cups and saucers, glasses and a plate of crackers on the sideboard. On the dining table is a bowl of flowers. Bright sunshine pours into the room through the windows. The Right door is closed but the Left Center entry doors are open.

As the Curtain rises, ABBY *crosses above the table, into the entry, and opens the front door to admit* TALLANT. *She stands with her hand on the knob of the open door, eyeing him suspiciously.*

ABBY: Doctor's still out making calls and Mrs. Haggett and Ada's out to market.

TALLANT: (*comes into entry to Right of her*) It was *you* I came back to see, Abby.

ABBY: (*surprised*) Me? (*She eyes him more narrowly than ever, as she closes the door*)

TALLANT: (*enters the room and places his hat on the medicine cabinet*) I'd like to talk to you if you can spare a moment.

ABBY: (*follows to Left of him. Challengingly*) Whatever have you got to say to me? (*A pause, then he takes a step to her and puts his left hand on her right shoulder*)

TALLANT: "Thank you."

ABBY: What are you thanking me for?

TALLANT: For being kind once to a friend of mine. For giving him things that other women denied him. You gave him all the good things that have no name. All the warm, tender things he so sorely needed. (*She draws back a step. He drops his hand*)

ABBY: (*really frightened*) What do you know about me?

TALLANT: (*simply*) Only what he told me. Except for you, I was the best friend he ever had.

ABBY: (*with swift, low intensity*) I never heard him name no Davenport. He used to talk lots about his friend Bert Davis. But I never heard of you.

TALLANT: I'm Davis.

ABBY: (*gasps*) If you're Bert Davis, what are you calling yourself Davenport for?

TALLANT: (*floridly*) Davenport's my professional name. I needed a name people would remember, and Maxwell Davenport's—

ABBY: (*scornfully*) If you *was* Bert Davis that wouldn't be why you changed.

TALLANT: If you know a better reason I'd like to hear it.

ABBY: Well, I do know Bert Davis got in trouble. Chris told me that he owed a lot more money than he could pay. So he skipped out of the place he was living in. Anyways, that's how Chris said it was.

TALLANT: You remember all that, do you?

ABBY: I haven't forgotten nothing Chris ever told me. (*She turns and goes to above desk*) You don't look like I expected Bert Davis to look, neither.

TALLANT: (*flattering*) You look exactly as I expected you to, Abby, only younger and prettier. And I knew your name too. Don't forget that.

ABBY: Yes, that's so. (*She returns to Left of him*)

TALLANT: I don't deny I used to skip my rent. I've done it often and got in *plenty* of trouble. Wouldn't you expect that of a friend of Chris's? (*Both laugh*) I wouldn't have put it beyond Chris himself!

ABBY: (*smiling*) Guess mebbe I was wrong to be so wary of you. (*She forgets her suspicions in her pleasure*) Did Chris really mention my name to you? I wouldn't have expected him to mention my name. That was nice of Chris.

TALLANT: Chris was fond of you.

ABBY: Did he say that, too?

TALLANT: Over and over. Weren't you fond of him?

ABBY: He was the only man that ever took me serious and talked to me. He didn't talk so much. But what he said was awful pithy. And to think of you being Bert Davis! It certainly is a pleasure to make your acquaintance. I never expected to meet up with you. Don't you think we better shake hands on it? (*They do*) Set down, Mr. Davis, and I'll set down with you. (*She sits in armchair. He sits Left of table*) Mrs. Haggett don't favor the help setting in the setting room, but she's citified that way. And she ain't home anyhow and what she don't know won't hurt her. (*Her eyes shine as they take him in*) Bert Davis! My, don't that name bring things back, though?

TALLANT: What kind of things?

ABBY: (*laughs*) Oh, this and that!

TALLANT: Chris wrote me that you were the *only one* who ever liked his painting, or got what he was after.

ABBY: (*nodding with delight*) Oh, yes, I liked it! Oh, I had to learn to like it. But he taught me. Oh, he taught me lots. And there wasn't nothing about him I didn't like.

TALLANT: (*lightly. Leaning forward*) If you liked his *pictures* so much, why didn't you take better care of them? Why did you let so many of them get lost?

ABBY: (*draws back. Casually*) Now, I'd rather not go into that if you got no objection.

TALLANT: (*pause. Covering himself*) He *taught* you things, you said?

ABBY: Oh, yes, he taught me. Not that he set up to be a teacher. But you couldn't be with him and not pick up a mite here and a mite there.

TALLANT: What did he teach you? I'd be interested to hear, if you remember.

ABBY: (*only too eager to tell*) Oh, I remember! It was mostly things to see, I guess. Like the rust color the marshes get this time of year when the sky gets the color of that old blue platter. (*She points to the platter on the cabinet shelf, adding proudly*) That's cobalt blue! That's a painting term, cobalt blue! (*She continues*) And he showed me the old red barn and the covered bridge that he was forever painting and I was used to all my life and never noticed. And he taught me that old chairs may be more than just old chairs to be thrown away. That some of 'em may be beautiful. He used to say them very words about the old doors in the brick houses up along the Common. That was when they began taking the old doors out and putting in new ones ordered from Sears-Roebuck. And did you know that old brick houses ain't red but mostly green and brown and that moonlight and snow ain't white at all but all kinds of colors and that elm trees is most—decorative when their leaves come off? He taught me. (*Her reminiscence becomes more personal*) He taught me that a man can get drunk and not be no different only just more so and that everybody's got more good qualities than bad. Oh, he taught me lots. And I ain't never forgotten none of it. I lived over and over that time he spent here. Over and over it ever since he died.

TALLANT: (*a pause. Then, cautiously leading up to the point again*) Did he leave you much to remember him by?

ABBY: I just now told you.

TALLANT: But I was thinking of more *substantial* things.

ABBY: (*not understanding*) Substantial—in what way?

TALLANT: (*as though accepting a correction*) You're right there, Abby. Our memories *are* the most substantial things we have. They're the only things no one can take from us. *Still*, there are other kinds—souvenirs—

ABBY: (*almost to herself*) I wonder if you're right about memories, though. I know nobody can't take 'em away from us. But what happens to 'em when we take 'em away from the place they belong in? Don't they kind of get left behind? (*Pulls her chair nearer him*) I been kind of worried about that question lately.

TALLANT: Why have you?

ABBY: Because I'm going away from here, Mr. Davis. I'm going to Chicago, this afternoon. My brother's wife died and left him with four small children, and I got to go. It's the will of God. But I don't want to go one bit. (*She laughs*) The Haggetts, they think that's on their account.

TALLANT: I shouldn't worry. You'll carry your memories with you wherever you go.

ABBY: (*looks away*) But I won't see the red barn no more, nor the brick houses, nor the covered bridge, nor the hill pasture, nor any of 'em!

TALLANT: The places he liked to paint.

ABBY: Yes. (*Leans forward*) I used to take him hot coffee while he was painting.

TALLANT: And you knitted a sweater for him.

ABBY: Did he write you about that sweater?

TALLANT: You *must* know he'd have written me everything.

ABBY: Everything about me?

TALLANT: I was his closest friend.

ABBY: (*a pause, then*) I was pretty once.

TALLANT: (*playfully*) You don't need to explain.

ABBY: I'm not ashamed. Only I'd sooner you wouldn't tell Doctor or Mrs. Haggett or the girls. You know how folks thought about him here—him being only an artist and all. And they never understood him. And they wouldn't have understood him no better for liking me. And I wanted to keep their good opinion and my place here with Doctor Haggett. But I'm not ashamed.

TALLANT: I wouldn't tell, Abby. I'd respect your memories. But you must have things of his, too. Little sketches, for instance.

ABBY: (*proudly*) I could show you something a lot better than sketches.

TALLANT: Oh? What would that be?

ABBY: He painted a picture of me life size. (*She holds her right hand up to indicate size of portrait*) It's hung over my bed all these years.

TALLANT: I should certainly like to see *that*, Abby. Abby, show me the portrait. Show it to me now.

ABBY: (*rises*) I'll show it to you. It's that makes me feel worst about leaving here. (*She starts toward the kitchen*) You've got to come out to my room to see it. Out this way. (*He rises and follows* her. *She stops abruptly as she nears the door and turns to him*) I forgot!

TALLANT: Is somebody out there?

ABBY: That city maid who's come to take my place! I wouldn't have her see me take a man into my room where I lived fourteen years.

TALLANT: (*smiles*) What harm would it do?

ABBY: She'd tell Mrs. Haggett.

TALLANT: (*moves away Left a few steps*) Oh! Well, *I'd* rather the Haggetts didn't know about our talk. When can I see you again?

ABBY: (*a step after him*) Where are you living?

TALLANT: At the hotel. Can you come there to see me?

ABBY: I'll get around after dinner.

TALLANT: And bring the portrait with you.

ABBY: What? That great big portrait?

TALLANT: (*quickly*) Abby, if ever you need money—I'm no rich man. You know that— But I've been doing a little better these last few years, and as I say, if ever you *are* in need, I'd buy *anything* of Chris's you had to sell.

ABBY: (*quickly*) Oh, I wouldn't sell nothing, Mr. Davis!

TALLANT: Not to a stranger, Abby. I know you wouldn't. But to his friend. In memory of him and the old days—

ABBY: Why, I couldn't take money for the things he left.

TALLANT: Think it over, Abby. (*He takes a step up and looks away*) I'm trying to get all his works together in one place, where they'll keep each other company.

ABBY: Is that what you're doing? (*He turns to her as she follows up a step*) Oh, I think that's just lovely of you. I couldn't sell you nothing, but I might give you—

TALLANT: (*too quickly. Breathlessly*) What? The portrait?

ABBY: (*startled*) Oh, I didn't mean that. I'd have to think a lot to part with that.

TALLANT: (*pressing her*) Of course you would. But to his best friend!

ABBY: If it was anyone on earth but you— (*She turns at the sound of a door closing off Right*) Here comes one of 'em through the kitchen now. (TALLANT *goes up to medicine cabinet and gets his hat there as* ABBY *crosses to Right door*)

TALLANT: (*turns to her*) Abby, I'm counting on you.

ABBY: Yeah— Better get along if you don't want 'em to see you. (*As he goes into entry* ABBY *quickly crosses above table to him*) Mr. Davis! And don't tell nobody what you know about Chris and me. (*He pats her on her arm and exits front door.* ABBY *re-enters room and goes to above desk*)

SUSAN: (*comes quickly downstairs*) That wasn't Ma, was it?

ABBY: (*startled*) No. It wasn't nobody worth mentioning. (WARREN CREAMER *enters Right*) Now, I haven't got no time for—

SUSAN: (*sees* WARREN) Watch the front, Abby! (*She goes quickly below table to* WARREN, *who takes a few steps toward her. They embrace and kiss*)

ABBY: You're taking awful chances. You can't mix me up in this, my last day. What's he doing here? (*She moves to behind armchair*)

SUSAN: I seen him standing out by the red barn.

WARREN: I seen you wave. What was it you wanted?

ABBY: What do *you* want hanging 'round our barn? There'll be just a terrible row.

WARREN: I had something to tell her.

SUSAN: What? What was it, Warren?

WARREN: I just come to an important decision in my life.

ABBY: (*advancing, interested, down to*

below and Left of them) You come to an important decision, Warren?

SUSAN: (*turns to* ABBY) Watch the door, Abby.

ABBY: How can I watch the door when Warren gets me so interested?

WARREN: 'Tain't no affair of yours.

ABBY: I wouldn't *be* so interested if it was. (*She goes huffily up to window above desk*) If you don't want me to hear, though, I'll—

SUSAN: We ain't got no secrets from you, Abby. What is it, Warren?

WARREN: Harold Sherman's been after me to sell my stock and business so as he can have all the contracting 'round here. He only wants to pay me five hundred dollars—

SUSAN: Oh!

WARREN: —It ain't enough, but I made up my mind to take it! (ABBY *turns and looks at them*)

SUSAN: Now, what do you want to go and do that for, Warren?

WARREN: So as I can get to New York and study art.

SUSAN: Oh, Warren! That's an awful rash step to take. (*Drops her head*) And that means you'll be going away from here.

WARREN: I wouldn't do it only on one condition.

SUSAN: What *is* the condition?

WARREN: *You've* got to come with me.

SUSAN: Warren, you know Ma'll never let me go. Didn't you hear the way she took on this morning?

WARREN: I wasn't figuring to let your Ma know nothing about it.

ABBY: (*moves to above armchair*) Warren Creamer! You ain't proposing to elope!

WARREN: If Susie likes me much as she says she does, she won't take no chances on letting me go off without her. (SUSAN *takes his hand*)

ABBY: As if there hadn't been enough happening in this house this morning you bringing in this eloping talk and getting Susie all upset again!

WARREN: This ain't no talk. Her Ma got me good and mad this morning and I'm a-going to show her. And there ain't no use of me wasting no time about it.

SUSAN: Oh, Warren, I think you're wonderful! (*He smiles. She turns to* ABBY) Don't you think so, Abby?

ABBY: He wants taking down, but I do kind of admire him for it. (ABBY *moves to bay window, then back to above desk*)

WARREN: *You* give your clothes to Abby to take with her when she goes on the train to Boston tonight. Then I'll bring the truck here to fetch Abby's trunk. And you come along with me like you was seeing her off. Then I drive you out to the junction and put you on the train there. And then I meet the both of you in Boston and we get married. Guess there ain't much wrong with that scheme.

ABBY: Susie! If you listen to one more word of this, I'll tell your Ma.

SUSAN: (*frightened*) You wouldn't do that, Abby!

ABBY: (*moves down to below armchair*) Why wouldn't I? It's my bounden duty.

SUSAN: (*pleading*) You said you hadn't nothing against artists.

ABBY: Mebbe I haven't, but all the folks here have.

SUSAN: Haven't you never cared for any man, Abby?

ABBY: Do you think I'd be watching this front door now if I hadn't? (*Crosses to above table*)

WARREN: Say you'll help her, Abby.

ABBY: If I do it wouldn't be on your account, young man. When a girl gets in the state you got Susie in, she needs someone to look after her and see to it that she does get married and not just fly off the handle regardless. I've been in love! I know— (*The doorbell rings. They freeze —all three*) Better get along now, Warren Creamer, before you get caught. (*Goes to the window above desk and looks out*)

WARREN: (*a step Right*) I'll have the truck at the door at four-thirty.

SUSAN: (*moves to him*) That early, Warren?

WARREN: That ain't too soon if Abby's taking the five-o'clock to Boston. (*The young people kiss again.* ABBY *turns from window and sees them*)

ABBY: Susie! Stop doing that. (*To* SUSAN) You get upstairs and fix yourself. (SUSAN *runs into the entry and disappears upstairs*) If you let your Ma and Pa see you in this state—

WARREN: Four-thirty. (*He exits Right, closing door*)

ABBY: (*goes to front door*) I'd like to know what's come over this house this morning. (*She opens the door to admit* ROSEN, *an oily and too affable gentleman of middle age*)

ROSEN: (*outside*) This is where Doctor Haggett lives, I believe.

ABBY: It's where he's *been* living for thirty years.

ROSEN: (*a step inside*) I wonder if I can see him for a minute?

ABBY: You could if he was here, but he ain't here.

ROSEN: Will he be long?

ABBY: I wouldn't think so very. The Haggett family's awful prompt to meals.

ROSEN: I'll come in and wait, then, if you'll allow me. (*Hands her his hat and enters room*)

ABBY: Watch out for the paint? (*Closes front door and puts hat on hall table*)

ROSEN: I'm used to paint. (*Looks about the room.* ABBY *enters and crosses to behind armchair and watches him. He turns and meets her gaze*) You must be Abby.

ABBY: (*surprised*) You don't know me!

ROSEN: No, but I've heard an awful lot about you.

ABBY: (*a step to him*) What did you hear and where did you hear it?

ROSEN: Well, I heard you've got a kind *nature* and appreciate *modern painting*—

ABBY: That I appreciate— (*Goes to desk and sits*) I'll see if I can't get the doctor on the telephone. He ought never to have left this house today! (*She picks up* HAGGETT's *call book*)

ROSEN: Don't hurry him, Abby. Let me enjoy myself. Well, I've seen the *"old brick fronts"* on the Common— (*She looks at him*) —and *"the red barn"* behind this house and now I've seen you. (*Casually*) Only I expected you to be wearing a gingham dress.

ABBY: (*questioning*) A gingham dress?

ROSEN: You know, red and white checked gingham, the *same* as you *used* to wear.

ABBY: What do you know what I used to wear— (HAGGETT, MRS. HAGGETT *and* ADA *enter front door. The two women continue on their way upstairs.* HAGGETT *places hat and satchel on table in entry.* ABBY *rises and crosses into entry to Left of him*) Well, I'm not sorry to see you come home, Doctor. There's too much going on around here that I can't grasp. I guess I'll get back to my kitchen and stay there! (*She disappears into entry, passing off Right.* HAGGETT *looks after her, puzzled, then comes into the room, Left of* ROSEN)

ROSEN: (*a step up*) So *this* is Doctor Haggett?

DR. HAGGETT: (*nods his head*) What can I do for you?

ROSEN: My card. (*Presents it.* HAGGETT *looks at it, then turns and crosses toward desk, gesturing meanwhile to chair below desk*)

DR. HAGGETT: Won't you sit down, Mr. Rosen? (ROSEN *follows after him a few steps.* HAGGETT *stops and turns to him*) A patient?

ROSEN: (*shakes his head*) No, no, no. (HAGGETT *then points to armchair and seats himself at his desk*) Thank you. (*He sits*) Doctor Haggett, in the course of your professional career, you once *had* a patient, a young friend of mine. A painter— (HAGGETT *pricks up his ears*) A painter with whom I confess I had personal difficulties. Ten years ago *his death* left me with that regret we all feel in such cases. Recently I have come across some letters— (HAGGETT *shifts his chair forward, staring at* ROSEN *in amazement*) Letters which he wrote to me while he lived under your care. They showed me how in a small way I might ease my conscience regarding him. Doctor Haggett, my friend Christopher Bean died owing you one hundred dollars. I have computed the interest on the unpaid bill at six per cent, and the total for ten years comes to exactly one hundred and sixty dollars. Allow me to offer you my check for the sum. (*He presents the check*)

DR. HAGGETT: (*takes check—reads it, then almost breathless*) I thank you, sir.

ROSEN: Don't mention it. In paying this I fulfill a sacred duty to a poor devil whom I might have helped before he passed beyond all human aid. Of course I know that we're all mortal, but I shall go back to New York feeling—

DR. HAGGETT: A happier man?

ROSEN: You take the words out of my mouth, Doctor Haggett.

DR. HAGGETT: Mr. Rosen. I'm delighted to make your acquaintance and I see that artists make better paying patients than what I thought. (*As he pockets the check*) But there's a question occurs to me that I'd like to ask you.

ROSEN: Don't hesitate, Doctor Haggett! *Anything!*

DR. HAGGETT: (*timorous*) Are you, by any chance, on the point of inquiring if I haven't got *something* in the way of pic-

tures poor Chris Bean left behind him that you can take away as souvenirs?

ROSEN: (*protests*) No, no, no! I don't do things that way. I don't come begging.

DR. HAGGETT: (*with humility*) I never said you did. I only asked you—

ROSEN: (*gives him a look. Then lifting his hand so graciously*) Well, if you'll allow me to be businesslike, I *was* on the point of asking you about any such pictures you may still have in your possession. (HAGGETT *sits up.* ROSEN *assumes a businesslike manner*) I assume, of course, that they are your property. The boy had no family and any pictures he left here, even those which he did not give you personally, may be considered security for that unpaid bill and so forfeit to you. Doctor Haggett, I'll give you a *thousand dollars* for the lot!

DR. HAGGETT: (*stunned*) A thousand dollars!

ROSEN: For the lot, understand.

DR. HAGGETT: *A thousand dollars!* For Chris Bean's pictures?

ROSEN: I can't go any higher. I hope you don't *exaggerate* their value.

DR. HAGGETT: (*quite voiceless*) A thou—

ROSEN: That is my offer. Take it or leave it. I consider it very generous.

DR. HAGGETT: (*quickly*) I'm not saying a word *against* your offer, Mr. Rosen. The only trouble is you ain't the first. There was a man here not two hours ago—

ROSEN: (*leaning forward*) With the same proposition?

DR. HAGGETT: No, not quite the same.

ROSEN: You didn't sell *him* your Christopher Bean pictures!

DR. HAGGETT: No. I gave 'em to him.

ROSEN: *What?!!*

DR. HAGGETT: There was one Chris painted of the old covered bridge—and there was another—

ROSEN: (*rises. Breaks in. Clutching his*

brow, or the equivalent) You gave away "The Covered Bridge"! Doctor Haggett, you've been *swindled*!

DR. HAGGETT: You don't have to tell me that.

ROSEN: But how in God's name did you—

DR. HAGGETT: He sent me a telegram he was coming from New York.

ROSEN: What was his name?

DR. HAGGETT: I ain't much good at remembering names— (*Fumbles through his pockets*) I ought to have his telegram some place, though. (*Sees telegram on desk and picks it up*) Here it is now. (*He reads*) "Maxwell Davenport." That was his name. Maxwell Davenport.

ROSEN: (*staggered*) Maxwell Davenport?

DR. HAGGETT: That's right. Yes.

ROSEN: (*incredulous*) You mean to say Maxwell Davenport let you *give* him—

DR. HAGGETT: I thought they wasn't no good. He *said* they wasn't.

ROSEN: (*unable to believe his hearing*) Davenport said that?

DR. HAGGETT: Yes! Davenport! Here— (*Rises and hands telegram to* ROSEN) If you don't believe me! Do you know him?

ROSEN: (*as he reads it*) Do I know Davenport? Yes! Of course I know him. (*Moves away Right a step*) But I never would have believed such a thing of him. (*He sniffs the smell of powder*) Have you got witnesses?

DR. HAGGETT: I got my wife and daughter.

ROSEN: (*grinning and confidential*) Then I tell you, Doctor, this may not be so serious. (*Returns telegram to* HAGGETT. *They reseat themselves*) I think I see how we can fix Davenport. He's the art critic on the *New York Tribune*, the best we've got down in the big city and everybody's looking up to him. Now, he would hardly care to have it known what a dirty trick he played on you to get those pictures free when they're worth—a thousand dollars. So this is what *we* do. (*Rises and extracts papers from his pocket and explains.* HAGGETT *listening attentively*) I have here with me a bill of sale for what he took, all made out in advance by my lawyer. (*The doorbell rings*) You sign it and I give you my check for a thousand dollars. *Then* we get you and your wife and daughter and go down to the Court House and swear out an affidavit about every word that great art critic said. *Especially* that the pictures were no good. You leave the rest to me. (ABBY *passes through the entry from Right and goes to the front door.* ROSEN *laughs*) I think we can fix Mr. Davenport!

(ABBY *admits* MAXWELL DAVENPORT, *an elderly and distinguished gentleman, carrying a coat on his arm.*)

DAVENPORT: Is Doctor Haggett in? He's expecting me. (*Steps into the entry.* ABBY *shuts door.* DAVENPORT *comes into room to Left of table.* HAGGETT *looks up, but* ROSEN *silences him with a gesture and goes up Left.* ABBY *enters to Right of* DAVENPORT)

ABBY: He's got a gentleman with him. (*Indicates chair Left of table*) Won't you have a chair and rest yourself? (*Moves away to above table.* ROSEN *recognizes* DAVENPORT, *smiles and moves up to corner cabinet and stands with his back partly to* DAVENPORT)

DAVENPORT: (*at table*) Oh, thank you. That's very kind of you. Tell me, are you by any chance the famous *Abby*?

ABBY: (*pause. Above table at the Right. Practically annihilated*) Does everybody from New York know me?

DAVENPORT: Then you *are*! What luck that you're still here! "The Covered Bridge," "The Brick Houses" on the Common, "The Red Barn," and now, Abby, herself!

ABBY: (*crosses to behind chair Right of table*) Doctor Haggett, I can't stand no more folks who never saw me before in my life streaming in here and calling me by name. (*Crosses toward Right door*)

DAVENPORT: Don't be alarmed, please, Abby. (*She bursts out of the room in a panic; closes door.* DAVENPORT *places his coat over the back of chair Left of table, turns and moves a few steps toward* HAGGETT) Is this Doctor Haggett?

DR. HAGGETT: (*rises*) Yes, it is.

DAVENPORT: I'm Davenport.

DR. HAGGETT: (*sharply*) *Who?!!*

DAVENPORT: Maxwell Davenport. I sent you a night letter yesterday from New York. Don't let me disturb you, though. (*Moves up a step as he indicates* ROSEN) I'll wait outside.

DR. HAGGETT: (*a step toward him*) No! No! No! Don't you go! (*Turns and crosses up to* ROSEN. *Lowly*) Is *this* Davenport?

ROSEN: (*nodding*) Yes. It's Davenport.

DR. HAGGETT: *But it ain't the same!!!*

ROSEN: *What?!!!*

DR. HAGGETT: It ain't the same, I tell you! And if this is Davenport, *who* was the other?

ROSEN: (*quickly to* HAGGETT *as he calms him*) Don't say any more, Doctor Haggett! (*Confidentially*) Don't say another word! Wait till we find out where we stand. (*Pockets his papers hastily and turns, smirking*)

DAVENPORT: Rosen!! (ROSEN *turns to face* DAVENPORT. *Disgust*) May I ask what the devil you're doing here?

ROSEN: (*crosses to* DAVENPORT) Do you think you ought to swear at me, Mr. Davenport? You've got no cause to swear at me in public. *Print* what you like about me, but don't insult me to my face!

DAVENPORT: I might have known the scavengers would be gathering. (*Turns to* HAGGETT, *who makes a strong gesture*) I beg your pardon, Doctor, but this man, who exploits artists and treats their work like so much merchandise—

ROSEN: It's not the *artists* I exploit. It's the *customers*. And it's men like me who justify the existence of you art critics. Where would you be, writing about your *tactile* values, *limpid* shadows, your something or other highlights, if you didn't have *us* to create interest in art by building up prices?

DAVENPORT: You befoul the whole business of dealing in art with your tricks and forgeries, and— (ROSEN *snorts; turns away a step.* HAGGETT *brushes him aside as he crosses up to Left of* DAVENPORT)

DR. HAGGETT: (*floundering*) Just a minute, please! This is my house and I got a right to know what's going on. (ROSEN *returns to behind armchair*) You say you're Mr. Davenport. And Mr. Rosen says you are. All right, you must be. But will you please tell me what this is all about?

DAVENPORT: It's about one of the world's greatest injustices, Doctor Haggett, which I am doing my small part to set right. You once had for your patient a poor boy, a painter—

DR. HAGGETT: Yes, I know. Chris Bean.

DAVENPORT: (*surprised*) Oh, I'm glad, Doctor, that you remember him. Now, this boy that I mention—

DR. HAGGETT: (*breaks in. Points his finger on* DAVENPORT'S *chest*) Died owing me a hundred dollars, and you come to pay it.

DAVENPORT: No, Doctor! No! *Don't* say that Bean owed any man anything. It is *we*—(DAVENPORT *taps* HAGGETT *on shoulder with his left hand*)—all of us, who stand in everlasting debt to him. As the world always stands in debt to its men of *genius*.

DR. HAGGETT: Genius? Chris Bean a— (*Turns, moves toward desk, stops, turns and motions* DAVENPORT *to be seated in armchair.* DAVENPORT *sits.* HAGGETT *sits at desk*)

DAVENPORT: (*then, more quietly*) I've come to gather any details that I may find concerning his life here for a critical biography of him that I am writing.

DR. HAGGETT: You're writing a book about Chris Bean!

DAVENPORT: That is my occupation at the moment, yes.

DR. HAGGETT: Whatever gave you that idea?

DAVENPORT: Haven't you read of the sensation his pictures have been making in New York? (ROSEN *gives* DAVENPORT *a look of annoyance.* HAGGETT *shakes his head dizzily*) Haven't you seen the last *Atlantic Monthly*?

ROSEN: (*a step down, below armchair*) That only came out yesterday, Mr. Davenport.

DAVENPORT: Quite! (ROSEN *moves to above desk and takes out cigarette case*) Well, Doctor Haggett, art is long, and the world is often slow to recognize it. Only *now*, ten years after his death, has Christopher Bean had his first exhibition in New York. Only now do we realize that he was not merely the greatest *American* painter, but one of the great masters of all times.

DR. HAGGETT: Our Chris Bean was?

DAVENPORT: Your Chris Bean, who painted and drank and—coughed his short life away here in this village. From which he wrote to his friend, Davis, alas, also dead, the exquisite group of letters published yesterday in the *Atlantic Monthly*. (ROSEN *takes out lighter and lights a cigarette*)

DR. HAGGETT: Our Chris Bean! (*A pause. Then turns to* ROSEN) So them's the letters you folks has been finding going through your desks! (MRS. HAGGETT *comes downstairs*)

ROSEN: You guessed it, Doctor. (HAGGETT *gives him an indignant look, turns and sees* MRS. HAGGETT)

DR. HAGGETT: Oh! Hannah, come in here! (MRS. HAGGETT *comes down to Right of* DAVENPORT, *who rises*) This is my wife, Mr. Davenport.

MRS. HAGGETT: (*stares at the name*) Mr. Davenport?

DR. HAGGETT: (*quickly*) No, don't say a word, Hannah. I'll explain later. And Mr. Rosen. (*Turns to the company with fine, simple dignity*) Mr. Davenport, we live a long way from New York. (ADA *comes downstairs*) I'm nothing but just a simple country doctor. I'll have to admit that much as I liked Chris Bean, I never would have expected him to get nowheres. (ADA *slowly enters; crosses above table to Right of it*)

DAVENPORT: I'm not exaggerating, Doctor, when I say that no painter of our times has got so far as he.

MRS. HAGGETT: (*is dumbfounded*) Does this mean folks is paying money for Chris Bean's pictures?

DAVENPORT: (*to her*) If only the dealers could find *more* to sell! There are so few they bring large prices even in these days.

ADA: As much as fifty dollars?

DAVENPORT: Not less than five, as much as ten thousand.

ADA: *Dollars?!*

MRS. HAGGETT: *Each!* (ADA *sits above table*)

DR. HAGGETT: (*to* ROSEN) And you offered me a measly *thousand for the lot!*

ROSEN: Remember, Doctor, I wasn't the first and say no more. (HAGGETT *turns away, dazed*)

DAVENPORT: A very generous offer, for Mr. Rosen. I hope I arrived in time to stop his game.

MRS. HAGGETT: (*a sudden scream of anguish*) God Almighty, I just remembered—

DR. HAGGETT: What?

MRS. HAGGETT: No, I won't say no more, neither. I don't feel well. (*Sits Left of table, staring in horror before her.* ABBY *passes along entry from Right and enters the room*)

ABBY: (*crosses down to above* HAG-

GETT) Here's another telegram, just come for you, Doctor Haggett.

DR. HAGGETT: (*weakly*) Another telegram? (*Opens telegram.* ABBY *goes into entry and disappears to Right*)

DAVENPORT: Now, really, Rosen, I think you might have gone higher than a thousand.

ROSEN: (*pleasantly*) I'm not a rich man, Mr. Davenport. And my business is a small one.

DAVENPORT: Stick to your forgeries. They're more respectable than swindling *honest men* who aren't equipped to defend themselves. (*Turns to* HAGGETT. *Crisply*) Now, Doctor! I don't usually mix in buying and selling, but to protect you I will gladly put proper values on any *Christopher Beans* you may have.

DR. HAGGETT: (*breaks in. Haggard as he looks from the telegram in his hand*) Would you mind explaining this telegram to me?

DAVENPORT: May I see it? (*Takes it. Then as he reads telegram*) Why, it's clear enough. The Metropolitan Museum—(*Looks at* HAGGETT)—that's in New York—offers you seven thousand five hundred dollars for the choice of your Christopher Bean canvases. (*Returns telegram to* HAGGETT)

DR. HAGGETT: (*pause. Quietly*) Mr. Davenport, you see in me a desperate man.

DAVENPORT: Desperate, Doctor? The owner of pictures worth a fortune!

DR. HAGGETT: How do you know I got any such pictures?

DAVENPORT: From the *Atlantic Monthly.* Bean in his letters, enumerates—(HAGGETT *looks up and winces*) —seven of the pictures he painted and left behind him here. "*The Hill Pasture,*" "*The Covered Bridge,*" "*The Red Barn,*" "*The Brick—*"

DR. HAGGETT: (*breaks in*) I guess I didn't take 'em as serious as I should have—

DAVENPORT: Don't reproach yourself, Doctor. You weren't the only one. (HAGGETT *draws in his breath and gives him an agonized look.* DAVENPORT, *suddenly alarmed*) Doctor, for God's sake! You haven't let anything happen to them! (MRS. HAGGETT *feels even worse*)

DR. HAGGETT: (*rises. On the rack*) I must have 'em *somewheres.* There's two I can't account for just at the moment. But if he left *seven* I must have the rest. Did you ever hear of folks throwing away oil paintings? Valuable oil paintings? (*Sets his teeth grimly, rallying*) I'll have a look for 'em! I'll find 'em! And when I do, I'll pay 'em the honor they deserve. I'll hang 'em all up here in the dining room! And I don't know as I'm interested in selling 'em. Not now that I know what they're worth, I don't! At least— (*with a glare toward* ROSEN) At least, not for no small sums like I've been offered! (*Falls exhaustedly into his chair*) But now I'd like for you all to go away. And leave me to eat my dinner in peace, and talk matters over with my family. This is all kind of sudden. I got to think.

DAVENPORT: (*still anxious*) But you'll let me come in again this afternoon?

DR. HAGGETT: What for?

DAVENPORT: Why, to get your recollections of Bean's life here. (*Turns and goes to chair where* MRS. HAGGETT *is seated*)

DR. HAGGETT: (*suffering*) After I've had my dinner.

DAVENPORT: (*tries to pick up his coat, but* MRS. HAGGETT *is seated on part of it*) Oh, excuse me. (*She barely rises and does not look at him*) Thank you. (*As he moves toward* HAGGETT *he takes a copy of "The Atlantic Monthly" out of a pocket in his coat*) Let me leave this number of the *Atlantic* with you. You'll find Bean's letters in it. I brought it along for the list of pictures he mentions—(*Extends it to* HAGGETT, *then returns to Center*) —but you'll enjoy reading what he says about *you.*

DR. HAGGETT: Thanks. (*Lays the magazine on the desk*)

DAVENPORT: (*looks about, embarrassed*) Well—good-by. (*Exits front door*)

ROSEN: (*the moment the front door closes,* ROSEN *goes up to entry, then returns to above* HAGGETT) Now about that man who was here before me. If you don't know his real name, what did he look like?

DR. HAGGETT: *You* get out too!

ROSEN: (*conciliatory*) All right, Doctor. All right. (*Goes into entry and gets his hat*) But I'll be back. (*Looks into room*) And don't do anything final till you see me. (*Goes; passes by outside window Left*)

DR. HAGGETT: (*a pause*) The one chance I ever had to make any money, and it's slipped through my fingers!

ADA: (*rises and goes up a step*) I can't look at that spot on the wall where my picture was without just boiling.

MRS. HAGGETT: I'm going upstairs to my room to lay down. (*Rises and starts for stairs wearily.* ABBY *enters Right, closes door and crosses to Right of table. Takes flower vase to sideboard, returns to table and begins removing table-cover*)

ABBY: Now that all them city folks is gone, I guess I better set the table for dinner.

MRS. HAGGETT: (*back to audience. Weakly*) I don't want no dinner. (ABBY *folds the table-cover*)

DR. HAGGETT: (*indignant*) You don't! You don't! Who's to blame for this? (ABBY *looks up, astonished*)

MRS. HAGGETT: (*turns to him*) You can't blame me.

DR. HAGGETT: Which one of us was it took him in and gave him the old barn to paint in?

MRS. HAGGETT: You didn't have no more use for his pictures than I did.

ABBY: (*crosses to sideboard and opens drawer*) I can't have you quarreling this way on my last day! (*Puts cover in drawer*)

DR. HAGGETT: Mrs. Haggett and I'll quarrel, if we want to, without any help from you, young lady.

ABBY: (*slams sideboard drawer shut*) Doctor Haggett, you ain't never spoke to me like that before.

DR. HAGGETT: (*practically screaming*) Get back in your kitchen. I can't stand no more talk. (ABBY *runs for her life, slamming Right door*)

ADA: (*by chair above table*) Now, the important thing is for us not to lose our heads. There's only two things that matter. The first man wasn't Mr. Davenport. And since he wasn't, who was he?

MRS. HAGGETT: (*up Center*) What's that matter? Your Pa *gave* the pictures to him.

ADA: It matters a lot. He got 'em out of Pa under false pretenses.

DR. HAGGETT: (*rises*) That's right. He did.

MRS. HAGGETT: Then we can get 'em back.

DR. HAGGETT: If it wasn't for that fifty dollars he gave Ada.

ADA: That fifty dollars wasn't for the *back* side.

MRS. HAGGETT: (*crosses down to Right of him*) You got to find him, Milton.

DR. HAGGETT: How? I don't even know what his real name is. All I know is he's gone back to New York a happier man. (*Through his teeth*) I'll find him somehow, though. And when I find him I'll give him a *thrashing* he'll remember.

MRS. HAGGETT: He's younger than you are. He'll give you the thrashing.

DR. HAGGETT: (*strides to and fro as he forms his plan*) All right, then. I'll get a lawyer. (*Crosses to desk and lifts phone*) I'll get a lawyer after him and bring suit against him. (*He pauses*) Lawsuits cost money if you ain't sure of winning. (*Drops phone*) 'Tain't as though we minded parting with what he took.

MRS. HAGGETT: But he didn't know what it was worth.

DR. HAGGETT: And I called the both of you in to have a good look at an honest man. (*Croaks hoarsely*)

ADA: The wicked, sneaking, thieving, *greedy* scoundrel. It just makes me sick —that's what it does.

DR. HAGGETT: (*breaks in. Snatching at the straw of comfort*) That's it, Ada. Our baby's said it, Hannah. It's the *greed* of it that turns my stomach. The *greed!* If Davenport ain't lying—I let that greedy crook snatch between ten and twenty thousand dollars out of my hands.

MRS. HAGGETT: (*crosses to him*) Milton, he said he was going into business with you. Couldn't you tell him you won't have no more dealings with him unless he brings back the pictures?

ADA: (*scornfully*) Wasn't all that business talk jest to pull the *wool* over Pa's eyes?

MRS. HAGGETT: (*breaks in. Returns to Left of table*) Oh, the wicked, scheming, greedy—

ADA: (*to* HAGGETT) How many pictures did Chris Bean leave here? (MRS. HAGGETT's *strange alarm revives*)

DR. HAGGETT: Davenport said seven.

ADA: And *you* said folks don't *throw away* oil paintings. Well, what's become of the other five?

DR. HAGGETT: That's right, Ada. (*To his wife*) Our baby's got more head than either of us. (*He calls*) Abby! Abby! Come in here! (ABBY *enters Right*) Are you sure you made a thorough search of that attic?

ABBY: (*in doorway. Frightened*) Of the attic, Doctor Haggett?

DR. HAGGETT: Yes. When that first fellow came here this morning?

ABBY: Yes, Doctor Haggett.

DR. HAGGETT: And you didn't see *no* sign of no pictures up there?

ABBY: I didn't see no sign, Doctor Haggett.

DR. HAGGETT: Get out! (ABBY *goes out Right as before; closes door*) Ada, you go look. (ADA *runs up the stairs.* HAGGETT *crosses up a step and calls again*) Susie!! Come down here, Susie!

MRS. HAGGETT: Now, what do you want with Susie? (*Sits Left of table*)

DR. HAGGETT: (*moves down to his desk*) We ain't asked Susie yet. She may know something.

SUSAN: (*comes downstairs and enters to Upper Right. Frightened*) What is it, Pa? What do you want?

DR. HAGGETT: (*below armchair*) Have you seen any old pictures of Chris Bean's laying around?

SUSAN: (*relieved*) Oh, is that all? (*Moves away toward above table*)

DR. HAGGETT: (*crosses to Left of her*) "Is that all? Is that *all?*" Don't talk like a fool!

SUSAN: (*turns to him*) Pa, what's come over you, hollering this way?

DR. HAGGETT: Answer my question.

SUSAN: Yes, of course I have.

MRS. HAGGETT: *What?!* } (*Simultane-*
DR. HAGGETT: *Where!?* } *ously*)

SUSAN: Last time I seen 'em they was in the barn. (MRS. HAGGETT *seems on the point of fainting*)

DR. HAGGETT: In the *barn!*

SUSAN: Yes, Pa.

DR. HAGGETT: How many?

SUSAN: I don't know rightly. Eight or ten, I guess.

DR. HAGGETT: *Eight* or *ten!*

SUSAN: Yes, they was in the old box stall.

DR. HAGGETT: I'm in and out of that barn all day long. (*Moves away a few steps*) Taking the Ford out and putting it up again. *I* ain't seen no pictures! (*Re-*

turns to SUSAN) When did you see 'em last?

SUSAN: It couldn't have been so long ago. (*Then guiltily*) I remember showing 'em to Warren Creamer.

DR. HAGGETT: (*wildly excited*) Aha! Then that's what's become of 'em. Warren Creamer's stole 'em.

SUSAN: (*indignant*) He ain't! He wouldn't!

DR. HAGGETT: They was in the barn. You showed 'em to Warren. They ain't there now and I'd have seen 'em. Warren *must* have stole 'em.

SUSAN: No!

DR. HAGGETT: You get your Warren over here this minute. No! Here! I'll get him. (*Crosses quickly to desk and sits*)

SUSAN: (*follows quickly to Right of him*) Pa! Please!— (*He snatches up the phone*)

MRS. HAGGETT: (*suffocating*) It ain't no use, Milton.

DR. HAGGETT: Why ain't it? (*Turns to her*)

MRS. HAGGETT: Warren didn't steal 'em.

DR. HAGGETT: How do you know he didn't?

MRS. HAGGETT: (*pause*) I burnt 'em.

DR. HAGGETT: (*pause, as he looks at her, speechless with horror. Rises*) You what?

MRS. HAGGETT: I put 'em on the bonfire and burnt 'em.

DR. HAGGETT: All eight or ten?

MRS. HAGGETT: I'd have thought there was more.

DR. HAGGETT: (*no longer able to control himself*) You'd have thought there was more. At ten thousand and over for every one. You'd have thought there was more.

MRS. HAGGETT: You thought they were *terrible pictures too,* Milton.

DR. HAGGETT: (*screaming*) Don't keep on saying that! (*Drops into his chair*) You ought to get down on your knees, Hannah, and beg forgiveness of both your children. (*After a moment his eye falls upon the "Atlantic Monthly" lying on his desk. He picks it up and begins to glance through it*)

ADA: (*comes down the stairs and enters to Left of* MRS. HAGGETT) Abby was right. There isn't a single picture in the attic.

MRS. HAGGETT: Your Pa knows that. There ain't none anywheres. (*Apologetic*) They took up so much room I burnt the lot.

ADA: (*a pause*) You never! Then we'll have to get to work and get back that pair we gave away this morning! (HAGGETT *holds up his hand for attention.* ADA *turns to him*) Pa!— (*Breaks off as she sees his outstretched hand.* SUSAN *moves nearer to* HAGGETT)

DR. HAGGETT: (*reading aloud*) "Doctor H. takes conscientious care of me. He knows nothing of medicine but looks like a gargoyle and that amuses me."

SUSAN: (*frightened*) What's he saying, Ma?

DR. HAGGETT: Doctor H. is me! That's what Chris Bean wrote about me in his letters. (*He continues reading*) "I beg him to let me do a portrait of him, but all my pleading avails me nothing. His notions of art belong to the lower animals."

MRS. HAGGETT: Mebbe if you'd let him paint your portrait you'd be better off now. You wouldn't have used no portrait of *yourself* to patch the chicken-house roof.

DR. HAGGETT: (*loftily extending the magazine to* SUSAN) You can read the rest, Susie. Mebbe he says something kind about your Ma. (SUSAN *takes magazine and sits in armchair.* ADA *crosses to above chair and leans over* SUSAN's *shoulder*)

SUSAN: (*reading*) "This angel of devotion is both sister and nurse to me, and more than both. I know that her care is adding months to my life, all the more because she, and only she, sees merit in what I paint. She is the single comfort I have found in my life here and in her own way she is beautiful."

MRS. HAGGETT: (*Her smile broadens*) Well, I liked the boy and I encouraged him.

ADA: (*reading over her sister's shoulder*) But, Ma! That ain't *you*. It's Abby! (MRS. HAGGETT's *smile fades*. ADA *reads on*) "When I go into the fields these chill autumn mornings, she brings me out hot coffee to drink."

MRS. HAGGETT: *Our* coffee.

DR. HAGGETT: (*slowly*) It don't matter now.

MRS. HAGGETT: It matters to me that a man I took kindly to carried on behind my back with the help.

SUSAN: But Ma, it don't say that.

MRS. HAGGETT: It says she was beautiful. She never was.

DR. HAGGETT: (*springing to his feet again*) Good God Almighty!

ADA: Pa!
SUSAN: What is it?
MRS. HAGGETT: You hadn't ought to screech that way, Milton!
(*Simultaneously*)

DR. HAGGETT: Chris Bean did paint one portrait while he was here. I remember he did.

ADA: Who did he paint it *of?*

DR. HAGGETT: Of Abby! (*Sensation*)

MRS. HAGGETT: That's so, he did!

ADA: It's a great *big* portrait.

DR. HAGGETT: What's become of it?

MRS. HAGGETT: She's had it hanging in her room ever since he died.

DR. HAGGETT: Ada, go in and see if it's still there. (ADA *crosses above table on her way to kitchen*)

SUSAN: (*quickly*) But, *Pa*, if it is, it must belong to Abby. Ada, wait— (ADA *stops above table and turns to them.* HAGGETT *goes to* SUSAN *and bends over her*)

DR. HAGGETT: (*savagely*) Here we are, at the worst crisis of the Depression, with a fortune in the house and you try to tell me it belongs to Abby! Is Abby capable of knowing what that picture's worth?

MRS. HAGGETT: (*angrily*) Susie! I'm surprised at you, after your Pa's just been swindled himself this morning!

ADA: I think it's about time Pa stood up for his rights. (HAGGETT *paces up and down behind armchair*)

SUSAN: But that picture's Abby's rights.

DR. HAGGETT: (*to* SUSAN, *loud and querulous*) I ain't going to do nothing that ain't fair and square—(*Then quietly as he bends over her again*)—and don't talk so loud. Do you want Abby to hear?

SUSAN: (*rises*) Well, I *won't* stand by and see you take advantage of Abby. (*She flashes out into entry and upstairs.* HAGGETT *takes several steps after her as if to stop her*)

MRS. HAGGETT: (*rises and crosses to him*) Never mind her, Milton! We got one thing, and one thing only, to do now. And that is find out if Abby's planning to take that portrait to Chicago with her.

DR. HAGGETT: Call her in and ask her.

ADA: She'd get on to you.

DR. HAGGETT: That's right. Not that we got anything shameful to conceal, but she would get on to us.

MRS. HAGGETT: If it was me I wouldn't hesitate. I'd walk right into Abby's room and take that picture like it wasn't no account.

DR. HAGGETT: (*crosses to swivel chair*) There's a point of conscience here. I got to think. (*Sits*)

MRS. HAGGETT: (*follows to Right of him*) Shut your eyes, Milton. You know you always think best with your eyes shut. (*He has obeyed*) That's right. (*Slight pause*) Now—what?

DR. HAGGETT: Well, one way of looking at it the portrait is *our* property, too. Abby's no artist's model. She's our help. We was paying her thirty dollars a month and keep—

MRS. HAGGETT: We only paid her fifteen in those days—

DR. HAGGETT: The principle's the same. And the question is, did she have any *right* to let him paint it on the time we paid for?

MRS. HAGGETT: Your conscience is clear, Milton. There ain't no doubt but that portrait belongs to us. (*Crosses to Left of* ADA) Ada, go into Abby's room and get it.

ADA: But what will Abby say?

MRS. HAGGETT: (*giving her imagination free rein*) Wreck the room! Tear down the window curtains! Turn the bed over! Then your Pa can tell her a *burglar* must have got it.

DR. HAGGETT: (*breaks in. Uncomfortably*) I'm only a simple country doctor. I don't care for money. It's only for my loved ones I got to have it.

MRS. HAGGETT: (*to him*) We've got to get a move on! (*She pushes* ADA *ahead of her as they both go to Right door*) Go along, Ada. Take it out the back way and upstairs. (ADA *goes out Right*. MRS. HAGGETT *closes door and crosses below table to Left of it*) Once we get it we'll hide it under your bed.

DR. HAGGETT: (*to himself*) If Abby feels bad I can give her a little something.

ADA: (*returns; closes door*) Abby's out there.

MRS. HAGGETT: How about the picture?

ADA: That's there too.

DR. HAGGETT: (*rises*) What's it like?

ADA: You know. Terrible!

DR. HAGGETT: Well, it's some comfort to know it's still all right.

MRS. HAGGETT: What's Abby doing?

ADA: Packing her trunk.

MRS. HAGGETT: Tell her she ought to be getting dinner ready.

ADA: But if she stays out there in the kitchen—

MRS. HAGGETT: Tell her to come in and set the table.

ADA: You call her. (ADA *moves to below sideboard*. HAGGETT *reseats himself.* MRS. HAGGETT *looks at him for approval. He gestures for her to "go ahead"*)

MRS. HAGGETT: (*in her sweetest tones as she crosses below table to Right door*) Abby! (*Opens door*) Abby! (*Closes door and turns to her husband*) You got to talk to her. (*Moves to Right of table. All three watch Center door.* ABBY *enters, still in a state of terror*)

DR. HAGGETT: (*sits swivel chair. An heroic effort at play-acting*) I'm sorry I spoke so rough to you just now, Abby.

ABBY: (*crosses to below chair Right of table. Eyeing him askance*) Oh, that's all right.

MRS. HAGGETT: (*also play-acting*) No, Abby. Doctor Haggett couldn't rest till he'd apologized. (*Gets the tablecloth from a drawer in the sideboard*)

ABBY: (*eyeing her*) It's all right.

MRS. HAGGETT: (*drops folded cloth on table*) And you can go ahead now and set the table for dinner.

ABBY: Yeah. (*Proceeds to spread the cloth.* MRS. HAGGETT *nods to* ADA, *who slips into the kitchen, then* MRS. HAGGETT *moves over to Right door, closes it and blocks it*)

DR. HAGGETT: (*as before*) It's nice of you to wait on us your last day, Abby.

ABBY: Oh, it's nothing.

MRS. HAGGETT: (*as before*) Yes, it is, Abby. And we appreciate it. Doctor Haggett and me, with the new maid here and all.

ABBY: It's nothing. (*Crosses to sideboard drawer and takes out napkins*)

DR. HAGGETT: It wouldn't have seemed

natural to have the new maid waiting on the table with you still in the house, Abby.

ABBY: No, I guess not. (*Returns to table; places napkins on it*)

ADA: (*returns. A whisper*) Ma! The new maid's there!!

MRS. HAGGETT: Tell her to go out and take a walk around the village. (ADA *turns to door*) And Ada— (ADA *turns to her Mother*) Never mind the burglar. (ADA *exits Right; closes the door*)

ABBY: (*left of table*) What about a burglar—

MRS. HAGGETT: (*laughs*) No, Abby, it's just a little joke between—you'll hear about it later. (HAGGETT *laughs.* ABBY *crosses below table toward kitchen*) Where're you going, Abby?

ABBY: Just out to the kitchen to get the mustard pickles.

MRS. HAGGETT: (*blocking door. Pleasantly*) Oh, I don't think we need mustard pickles for dinner. Do you think we do, Milton?

DR. HAGGETT: I'll be frank with you Abby, them mustard pickles don't seem to set good with me. (ABBY *starts again for the kitchen. He rises and moves to Center*) Abby! (*She stops and turns back again*) Didn't you hear us, Abby? We said we didn't care for mustard pickles.

ABBY: I was going to get some watermelon preserves. You always liked my watermelon preserves.

MRS. HAGGETT: (*stumped*) That's so, Milton! You always have liked *them* particular.

DR. HAGGETT: (*breaks in, likewise stumped*) I know I have. And I can't think of a thing against 'em now.

MRS. HAGGETT: (*helpful*) I thought you wanted to talk to Abby, Milton?

DR. HAGGETT: That's right, Hannah, I did.

ABBY: (*a step to him*) What was it you wanted to talk to me about?

DR. HAGGETT: (*at a total loss*) Well, about several things. Let me see, now. To begin with, I—

ADA: (*returns. A whisper*) Ma!

MRS. HAGGETT: What is it?

ADA: She says she *don't want* to take a walk.

MRS. HAGGETT: Tell her either she takes a walk or goes back to Boston. (ADA *exits Right; closes door*)

ABBY: (*turns to* MRS. HAGGETT) Back to Boston?

DR. HAGGETT: (*quickly*) I know what it was I wanted to talk about, Abby. It was about that new maid. What do you think of her?

ABBY: Oh, she's a nice girl.

DR. HAGGETT: Of course she's a nice girl. A very nice girl. Mrs. Haggett wouldn't have chosen anything else. (*He becomes confidential*) But, Abby—think now—think carefully. Will she give the same satisfaction *you've* given us.

ABBY: Now, that's real kind of you to say that, Doctor Haggett. Of course, in fairness you got to remember I had fifteen years to study your manners and ways. And I'm not saying she'll be on to the way you like your chowder nor things like that without being told. But she's a nice girl, and if she finds she likes the place enough—

MRS. HAGGETT: Don't you think she will, Abby?

ABBY: Well, mebbe she will and mebbe she won't, Mrs. Haggett. I'll get dinner on the table first and talk afterwards. (*Again she starts for Right door. He takes a step after her, helplessly*)

MRS. HAGGETT: But, Abby, you ain't even got the table set!

ABBY: (*brushing* MRS. HAGGETT *aside*) I know, but I can't stand here talking with my biscuits burning up. (*Goes into kitchen; closes door*)

MRS. HAGGETT: Why didn't you stop her?

DR. HAGGETT: How could I? Why didn't you stop her?

MRS. HAGGETT: You seen me try, didn't you? Now you'll just have to face it. It was a cowardly way to get round her, at that.

DR. HAGGETT: It was your idea. I never would have done it. (SUSAN *comes downstairs enters room to up Center and regards them distastefully*)

MRS. HAGGETT: Keep quiet! Listen! (*Listens at Right door*)

DR. HAGGETT: Can you hear anything?

MRS. HAGGETT: Not a sound!

DR. HAGGETT: Ada must be in the room now. She'll come out with the picture in her hands and Abby— Hannah, go out there and do something—

MRS. HAGGETT: I can't! You go yourself! (*Phone rings.* HAGGETT *turns and moves Left a step*)

DR. HAGGETT: I got to answer.

MRS. HAGGETT: No, you don't. Susie, you answer that. (*He stops.* SUSAN *crosses toward desk. Just as she nears it phone rings again*)

DR. HAGGETT: (*to his wife*) Call her back in here. I'll talk to her some more.

MRS. HAGGETT: What have you got to talk to her about?

SUSAN: (*into the phone*) Hello.

DR. HAGGETT: Let me think. (*Sits below table*) Don't hurry me. I'll think of something.

SUSAN: (*into the phone*) Yes?

MRS. HAGGETT: (*a step to him*) You can't take all day.

SUSAN: What?

MRS. HAGGETT: (*continuing*) —Once she catches Ada—

DR. HAGGETT: I'll ask her not to leave.

SUSAN: This is Doctor Haggett's.

DR. HAGGETT: (*continuing*) —That's what I'll do! I'll plead with her—!

MRS. HAGGETT: No! Then she might not leave. And if she doesn't *leave* it will be twice as hard.

DR. HAGGETT: (*breaks in*) Call her. I'll think of something. (ADA *returns, tottering; leaves door open*)

MRS. HAGGETT: (*starts to call*) Ab—! (*Her voice catches as she sees* ADA. ADA *crosses to Right of* HAGGETT. MRS. HAGGETT *rushes to door and closes it*)

SUSAN: (*into phone*) Just a minute. I'll call him.

MRS. HAGGETT: (*turns to* ADA) Did you get it?

ADA: (*gasping, her hand on her heart*) No!

DR. HAGGETT: She didn't catch you?

SUSAN: Pa!

ADA: No. But if the biscuits hadn't been burning she would have caught me. I was just lifting it off the hook when I looked over my shoulder and there she stood with her head in the oven.

SUSAN: *Pa!* (HAGGETT *gestures for* SUSAN *to be quiet*)

MRS. HAGGETT: We'll just have to try again. (SUSAN *puts receiver down, and moves away Right a step*) We'll eat dinner quiet as if nothing happened. I'll send her out on an errand. Come on, Ada. We'll finish setting the table. (*She turns to upstage end of sideboard and begins taking silverware out of a drawer.* ADA *goes to lower end and gets a stack of soup plates*)

SUSAN: *When you're done* plotting and whispering over there, New York's calling Pa.

MRS. HAGGETT: (*at sideboard. Turns*) New York—*again!*

SUSAN: I can't get the name. It sounds to me like Knoedler & Company.

DR. HAGGETT: (*very agitated*) I won't speak to him! I won't speak to no more from New York! Tell him I'm out! Tell him I've gone away! Tell him— (MRS. HAGGETT *crosses and places silverware on table*)

SUSAN: You can tell your *own* lies, Pa! (*Moves to above armchair.* ADA *brings plates and glasses to table*)

DR. HAGGETT: All right, I will. (*Rises and crosses to desk; takes phone and sits*) A lot of help I get from you, young lady. (MRS. HAGGETT *and* ADA *continue setting the table mechanically, straining to hear every word*) Hello— Yes. This is Doctor Haggett— Who?—Go ahead— Can't hear you— What—? *"The Covered Bridge"*? (*A pause*) How much? (MRS. HAGGETT *and* ADA *pause and listen intently*) How much? (*Another pause. Then, dully*) I'll think it over. Call me tomorrow. (*Rings off, dazed*)

MRS. HAGGETT: (*by chair Left of table. Stammering*) What—what is it, Milton?

DR. HAGGETT: (*weakly*) He wants to pay me twelve thousand dollars for Chris Bean's picture of *"The Covered Bridge"* if it's in good condition— (*A desperate echo*) In *good* condition! (*Then hysterically*) Can you beat that? In *good* condition.

MRS. HAGGETT: (*leans on the table. Also hysterical*) Twelve thousand! Twelve thou—!

ADA: (*above table, also hysterical*) That's the one I painted my picture on the back of and sold for *fifty dollars!*

DR. HAGGETT: (*screaming*) I know it is! (ABBY *enters Right, carrying a soup tureen*)

ABBY: Well, I got dinner ready, folks. You can set down! (*She places the tureen at* MRS. HAGGETT'S *place on the Right side of the table. She then moves to the Right a few steps. The* HAGGETTS *fail to stir*) You can all set down. Dinner's ready— (*She eyes them with surprise.*)

(*Finally the* HAGGETTS *move mechanically, as though under a spell, toward their respective places at the table.* MRS. HAGGETT *goes below the table to her chair on the Right.* ADA *goes to her place below the table.* SUSAN *sits above table and* HAGGETT *sits Left of table.* SUSAN *is the only one who unrolls her napkin. Then she and* ADA *both lean forward on the table, staring down dejectedly.* MRS. HAGGETT *removes the lid of the tureen and hands it to* ABBY, *who has taken a position at the table between* MRS. HAGGETT *and* SUSAN. ABBY *takes the lid to the sideboard and places it there. She then returns to the same position at the table.* MRS. HAGGETT *slowly serves the first bowl of soup and hands it to* ABBY, *who solicitously places her other arm about* SUSAN'S *shoulder and bends over to serve her.* SUSAN, *however, pushes the plate away. Then* ABBY *hands it to* HAGGETT, *who has been following her every move with great concentration. Startled, he takes it very quickly.* MRS. HAGGETT *hands the next bowl to* ABBY, *who goes to* ADA, *who seems unaware of* ABBY'S *presence at her side.* ABBY, *vexed at the strange behaviour of the* HAGGETTS, *slaps* ADA *roughly on the shoulder.* ADA *then sits back and* ABBY *places the bowl before her. However, neither* HAGGETT *nor* ADA *touch the soup.* MRS. HAGGETT *does not serve herself but drops her head in her hands in despair.* ABBY *looks at them queerly, then goes to the sideboard and gets a plate of crackers and returns to the table. More mystified than ever, she bends over and peers into* MRS. HAGGETT'S *face; looks at* HAGGETT, *who invokes the blessing*)

CURTAIN

ACT III

AT RISE: *The afternoon of the same day is well advanced. Furniture retains same arrangement as in the preceding Act. Sunshine of less brightness still pours into the room.*

DAVENPORT *is discovered standing at the fireplace with his back to the audience, waiting for* HAGGETT'S *return.* SUSAN *comes downstairs and enters the room to up Center.*

SUSAN: How do you do?

DAVENPORT: (*turns*) Oh, how do you do?

SUSAN: We haven't met, Mr. Davenport. I'm the other daughter, Susan. Ma said for me to apologize for keeping you waiting so long. Pa went out after dinner. We don't know where he is nor what's become of him.

DAVENPORT: (*crosses to just Right of her*) I don't mind waiting and if your father's errand is what I hope it is, I pray it may prove successful.

SUSAN: (*a step to him*) Yes. Well, seeing as you aren't doing much at the moment I've got a kind of a funny *favor* to ask you.

DAVENPORT: Please!

SUSAN: (*quickly*) You wouldn't tell Ma or Pa I asked it, would you?

DAVENPORT: (*smiles*) I can keep a secret.

SUSAN: I was thinking of eloping this afternoon.

DAVENPORT: My dear child!

SUSAN: Yeah. And it's just providential *you* turning up today because all I need's an *art critic*.

DAVENPORT: If you're counting on me to break the news to your parents—

SUSAN: (*quickly*) Oh, nothing like that!

DAVENPORT: Suppose you explain more fully, then. There's always some reason for an elopement. Either that the man's married or that the girl's father and mother don't approve of him.

SUSAN: That's *my* reason.

DAVENPORT: Why don't they?

SUSAN: Because he's an artist and they got no use for artists.

DAVENPORT: Is he a *good* artist?

SUSAN: (*seriously*) He thinks he is, but I'm not fit to judge. So I thought you'd mebbe run around and look at his pictures and tell me what you think.

DAVENPORT: (*sadly*) You're a Yankee, too!

SUSAN: What do you mean by that?

DAVENPORT: Well, I naturally conclude that if his pictures don't measure up, you'll think twice before you marry him.

SUSAN: (*with determination*) Oh, I'd have him anyways! I'd have him if he was the most terrible painter in the world! I just want to know the *worst* for my own information!

DAVENPORT: I see you belong to the *higher* type of Yankee.

SUSAN: I don't understand.

DAVENPORT: Fearless of both risk and reality.

SUSAN: No, I only want to know whether he ought to paint pictures or houses.

DAVENPORT: (*laughs*) Let it pass. I warn you that if I don't like the pictures—

SUSAN: Don't tell him.

DAVENPORT: Are you wise to want to know the truth yourself?

SUSAN: I'll show you I'm not afraid. (*Goes to above desk and picks up the two paintings brought in by* WARREN *in Act I*) I've got two of Warren's pictures here. (*Moves a step down and Left*) They're only little ones, so they don't do him justice. (*Returns to Left of him*) But you can tell me what you think right to my face. (*Extends them for his inspection*) This one's my dead duck and this one's my sister's salmon.

DAVENPORT: (*takes them*) Let's see. (*He examines first one, then the other*) Curious! Very curious! (*He turns to* SUSAN) I'd certainly say a pupil of Christopher Bean's.

SUSAN: Yes, he was. When he was a little boy, thirteen years old. But he's been painting on his own ever since.

DAVENPORT: Oh, they've got their own individuality, too.

SUSAN: Does that mean they're bad?

DAVENPORT: No, no, it means they make me want to see *more* of his work. And to meet him. (*Hands pictures back to her*)

SUSAN: That's easy! (*Replaces pictures above desk*) I'll show you where! I'll take you! Will you come now? (*Returns to him*) You see, there isn't much time!

DAVENPORT: At what time *is* the elopement?

SUSAN: At four-thirty. So I can catch the Boston train with Abby.

DAVENPORT: Is Abby leaving too? (HAGGETT *enters through the front door*)

SUSAN: Yeah. Abby's going to Chicago, and— (*Puts out her hand to warn him*) Shhh! Here's Pa! (HAGGETT *enters room, haggard; gives them a look of agony; crosses to chair Left of table and sinks wearily into it*) Why, Pa! What's the matter? Where have you been?

DR. HAGGETT: I've been around. (*A pause*)

SUSAN: You look awful.

DR. HAGGETT: I feel awful.

DAVENPORT: Oh—yes—

SUSAN: I'm just taking Mr. Davenport out to see the village, Pa.

DR. HAGGETT: Yes, take him out.

SUSAN: (*to* DAVENPORT) You don't object? (*They turn and start for the front door*)

DAVENPORT: No, your young man should certainly have things to tell me. I must talk with Abby, too, before she leaves. (*They both get their coats and hats from table in entry*)

SUSAN: (*gaily*) You'll have plenty of time to see Abby. It's just across the street.

DAVENPORT: Which way, left or right?

SUSAN: This way, Mr. Davenport.

(*They exit front door and to Right.* MRS. HAGGETT *comes in from the kitchen and crosses to below chair Right of table*)

MRS. HAGGETT: Well, Milton?

DR. HAGGETT: I been all over. Up to the hill pasture. Down to the covered bridge. Up to the *graveyard*.

MRS. HAGGETT: What'd you go *there* for?

DR. HAGGETT: Looking for that scoundrel who robbed me this morning.

MRS. HAGGETT: You didn't think he'd died and *buried* himself, did you?

DR. HAGGETT: He's still there. Painting somewhere.

MRS. HAGGETT: Painting?

DR. HAGGETT: I found out that much at the hotel. He checked in there this morning and he ain't checked out!

MRS. HAGGETT: Well, if the pictures are in his room, why didn't you get them?

DR. HAGGETT: He took 'em to the bank. They're in the vault. The bank wouldn't let me have 'em. Now he's gone out again. He's got his lunch and painting things with him. His name's Tallant.

MRS. HAGGETT: Tallant. With two "L's" or one?

DR. HAGGETT: (*looks up to her*) Two. (*He calls*) Abby! (*To his wife*) I've been running and running all afternoon. (ABBY *enters Right.* MRS. HAGGETT *crosses to above table.*) Bring me a cracker and a glass of milk.

ABBY: Wouldn't you like something hot, Doctor Haggett?

DR. HAGGETT: I got no time for anything hot. (ABBY *returns to the kitchen; closes the door*)

MRS. HAGGETT: There was three more telephone calls from New York while you was out. (*Crosses toward desk*) And there's seven more telegrams that come—

DR. HAGGETT: (*testily, as he turns to her*) I got no time for telegrams neither. (MRS. HAGGETT *stops by lower end of desk.*) Look! (*She turns to him. Pathet-*

ically he holds up his trembling hand) This kind of thing is not good for no man of my age. This morning I was a peaceful country doctor filled with gentle thoughts of a medical description and I coveted nothing, not even my collections. Look at me now. (*The shaking hand again*) Hannah, if a patient came in with an appendix now I'd miss it so far I'd put his eye out! (*Concludes desperately*) Once you get *started on* a thing like this, though— Once you let it get a *hold* on you—

MRS. HAGGETT: (*crosses to back of him. Exasperated*) Oh, stick to business.

DR. HAGGETT: That's what I'm doing. I remembered Abby leaves at five o'clock, and we can't let her take that portrait with her. It's the *only* one we can be *sure* to get our hands on.

MRS. HAGGETT: *You'll* have to work on her, then. I ain't up to no more today.

DR. HAGGETT: That's just what I come back home to do. Leave it to me. You started it, but I got to finish it. I got everything all thought out. (ABBY *enters Right with glass of milk and a cracker; closes door*) I thank you, Abby. (*She crosses to above table; places glass before him*) That's just what I need.

ABBY: But I got a nice pork chop I could heat up for you.

DR. HAGGETT: (*shudders*) Look! (*He shows* ABBY *his hand.* MRS. HAGGETT *goes up to window above desk and looks out*)

ABBY: I never seen you in such a state, Doctor Haggett. It's all them New York folks coming here.

DR. HAGGETT: (*deep self-pity*) And they're all coming back any minute, too.

ABBY: Why do you bother with 'em, Doctor Haggett?

DR. HAGGETT: Can't avoid responsibilities in this life, Abby. (*With unaccountable intention*) Wouldn't mind so much if this room looked right. It's that *patch* over the fireplace where Ada's picture was. (MRS. HAGGETT *crosses to below armchair*)

ABBY: (*a step up to fireplace*) I'll wash off where it's smoked.

DR. HAGGETT: No. There isn't time.

MRS. HAGGETT: You could hang one of Warren Creamer's pictures— (*Points to pictures at upstage end of desk*)

DR. HAGGETT: No, Hannah! Warren's pictures ain't big enough for that. What we need is something to cover up the *whole* place. A *big* picture.

ABBY: Well, then, I— (*Starts for kitchen. He stops her. She turns*)

DR. HAGGETT: (*as though a thought struck him suddenly*) Abby, ain't you got a picture Chris Bean painted of you before he died? (MRS. HAGGETT *starts*)

ABBY: I got my portrait.

DR. HAGGETT: Well, if that isn't just the thing! We'll hang *that* there.

ABBY: Oh, Doctor Haggett!

DR. HAGGETT: Just till you go.

ABBY: I'd like very much to oblige. I certainly would like to oblige. But, Doctor— (*Is covered with embarrassment*) Why, I couldn't have my picture hanging in there. It wouldn't look right.

DR. HAGGETT: Why wouldn't it?

ABBY: What'll people say if they come into your dining room and seen a picture of me hanging there scraping carrots?

DR. HAGGETT: What do I care what people'd say? Ain't this a democracy? I'd rather have you there scraping carrots than half these society women who can't do nothing.

ABBY: But my portrait hasn't even got no frame, Doctor Haggett.

DR. HAGGETT: That don't matter, either. Anything to cover up that patch!

MRS. HAGGETT: (*crosses to chair above table. Joining in persuasively*) Don't refuse him, Abby!

DR. HAGGETT: (*piteously*) Look, Abby! (*Holds up his trembling hand again*)

ABBY: I never could say "no" to Doctor Haggett. (*Goes out Right; closes door. They catch each other's eyes*)

DR. HAGGETT: A much better way than stealing it would have been. This has got to be done. But it's got to be done *legitimate*.

MRS. HAGGETT: She ain't give it up to you yet.

DR. HAGGETT: She will— Only you can't take more than one step at a time. I got it all thought out.

ABBY: (*returns, carrying portrait; closes door; crosses to chair Right of table and props portrait against it. Back of portrait facing audience*) Well, here it is!

DR. HAGGETT: (*rises*) That's very nice of you, Abby. I appreciate that.

ABBY: It'd look better if it had a frame.

DR. HAGGETT: There's no time for frames either.

MRS. HAGGETT: (*to* HAGGETT) That picture of your Ma in the upstairs hall's about the size of this, and it's got a beautiful frame.

ABBY: Why don't you hang that up?

MRS. HAGGETT: No, she's been dead so long, she's just as happy in the upstairs hall. (HAGGETT *turns and goes up a few steps as though he were going for the frame*) You go and get it, Abby.

ABBY: But I wouldn't want for Doctor Haggett to take the frame off his Ma's picture.

DR. HAGGETT: (*moves down again*) It gives me real pleasure, Abby, to show you this little mark of my esteem.

ABBY: (*covered with confusion*) But my picture'll look too dressed up in that frame.

DR. HAGGETT: (*with great dignity*) Abby, if I put my mother's frame around your picture, it's not for you to say that it isn't fitting.

ABBY: (*apologetically*) I didn't mean no offense, Doctor Haggett. I guess you know best. (*She crosses above table and goes upstairs.* MRS. HAGGETT *looks at the portrait*)

DR. HAGGETT: (*to himself*) I said I'd pay her something, and I will. I'll give her twenty-five dollars.

MRS. HAGGETT: (*shakes her head in negation*) You'll *never* get your money back.

DR. HAGGETT: (*moves to above table*) It ain't for you, who burnt up a fortune, to fret me for risking twenty-five dollars. (*Looks at portrait*) I'll be frank with you, though. If it hadn't been for them telegrams and telephone calls, I wouldn't be risking twenty-five cents on it.

MRS. HAGGETT: (*bends over*) Look at that dab of red on the nose, will you. And the hands is blue.

DR. HAGGETT: Mebbe she just done the wash. (*Bends over to examine it closely*) What's that she's holding?

MRS. HAGGETT: A knife. She is scraping carrots.

ABBY: (*comes downstairs, carrying a large, old-fashioned frame*) Well, here it is. I feel so embarrassed, Mrs. Haggett. (*Enters and moves toward Left side of table.* HAGGETT *turns and crosses to her*)

DR. HAGGETT: Oh, that's too heavy for you, Abby. (*Takes part of the frame and helps her place it face down on the table*)

MRS. HAGGETT: (*inaudibly*) I'll just clear these away— (*She quickly takes the bowl of flowers and glass of milk to sideboard. Then she returns to Right side of table*)

DR. HAGGETT: Now! We'll see if it fits. (*Lifts the painting and places it face down into the frame. He then uses his fist to hammer stretcher into place. Both* ABBY *and* MRS. HAGGETT *crowd about him, aiding him*)

ABBY: Take care not to scratch yourself on them rusty nails.

DR. HAGGETT: Oh, that wouldn't matter now, Abby.

MRS. HAGGETT: Oh, it's too small.

DR. HAGGETT: (*quiets her*) No, Hannah, it's a little tight up there, maybe. That's funny! It was always *loose* on Ma. (*They finally get the painting set firmly in the frame*) Look! Now, wouldn't you say that frame had just been made for it? (*Picks up frame as he moves above table to Left of it and leans the frame against table, with back of picture to audience. He backs away a few steps*) Now we'll just have a look. (*The effect is admired, too warmly, by the* HAGGETTS, *ecstatically by* ABBY)

ABBY: (*left of him*) Who'd ever have thought my portrait could look like that?

MRS. HAGGETT: (*moves to Right of him*) Wouldn't Chris Bean be proud to see it like that?

ABBY: I wish he could see it.

DR. HAGGETT: It's like you, Abby. There's no denying that.

ABBY: (*proudly*) All the time he was painting it he kept saying: "Abby, this is my masterpiece I'm painting now!"

MRS. HAGGETT: (*sharp*) Do you hear that, Milton?

DR. HAGGETT: (*sharper*) Are you sure he said that?

ABBY: Oh, yes—! And when it was all done he thanked me. He thanked me just like I'd done something for him! (*Voice choking*) Boys like him— 'Tain't right for boys like him to die so young!

MRS. HAGGETT: Don't cry, Abby. You'll have me crying too. (*Goes to chair Right of table and sits*)

DR. HAGGETT: You'll have us all crying. (*Crosses up to entry and calls*) Ada! Come down here and see Abby's portrait! (*Crosses down to Left and below* ABBY)

ABBY: (*so gratefully*) You're all so good to me! (ADA *appears on the stairs and enters to Right of* ABBY)

DR. HAGGETT: We're fond of you, Abby. We're fond of you, Abby. Look Ada! Don't you think that makes a handsome effect?

ADA: I should say so—

DR. HAGGETT: We got *two* Abbies in here now. One of 'em standing here in flesh and blood and the other there in an oil painting. (*They all laugh*) Seems a pity to let the both of 'em leave us, don't it?

ABBY: Oh, Doctor Haggett! I don't know how to thank you. And I won't never forget—

DR. HAGGETT: If seeing the both don't give me an idea!

MRS. HAGGETT: (*swallowing*) I'll bet it's a good one, Milton.

ABBY: Doctor Haggett couldn't have nothing but good ideas.

DR. HAGGETT: Well, I'll let you have it just as it come to me. Since you're going away after all these years it'd be awful nice for you to leave your portrait behind you here with us.

ABBY: (*unable to grasp*) Leave it here for good! Go away without it!

DR. HAGGETT: (*explaining quickly*) Oh, I wouldn't ask you to make such a sacrifice without giving you something in return.

ABBY: (*incredulous*) How could you give me anything in return?

DR. HAGGETT: (*on the spot again*) Oh, I don't say I could give you anything equal to what the portrait would mean to *us*. But I guess twenty-five dollars would come in kind of handy in Chicago. (ABBY *shakes her head*)

ADA: Make it *fifty*, Pa. (MRS. HAGGETT *reaches out and grasps* ADA'S *arm*)

DR. HAGGETT: All right, I *will* make it fifty. Yes, I will, Abby. It comes pretty hard to be handing out presents that size these days. I'll make it fifty. I guess you ain't got much to say against that!

ABBY: (*embarrassed*) No, Doctor Haggett, I ain't got nothing to say against it. It's real generous of you—

DR. HAGGETT: (*turning to* MRS. HAGGETT) There, you see! It's settled.

MRS. HAGGETT: Milton, you're wonderful!

DR. HAGGETT: (*no relief like a guilty conscience put to rest*) Everything open and above-board!

ABBY: Oh, but I couldn't never see my way to giving up my portrait. (ADA *reacts to this*)

DR. HAGGETT: Abby, you *amaze* me.

ABBY: Well, I'm funny that way about things I had so long.

DR. HAGGETT: (*gravely paternal*) You'd better think twice, Abby, before you refuse what I must say is a generous offer.

ADA: (*quickly*) How'd it be, Abby, if we had a nice *photograph* made of it, and gave *that* to you to keep with you in Chicago?

MRS. HAGGETT: (*delighted*) Now, ain't that a clever idea of Ada's, Milton? I declare I never would have thought of that myself.

ABBY: (*distracted*) You got me too upset to know what to do. I *hadn't* no idea you was so fond of me.

MRS. HAGGETT: *Abby!*

ABBY: No, I hadn't, Mrs. Haggett. I knew Susie was, but I hadn't no idea about you and Ada and the Doctor. And it's awful hard for me to deny you, only—

DR. HAGGETT: (*so warmly*) Then don't deny us, Abby. Say yes and shake hands on it.

ABBY: (*a slight pause*) Oh! I know what we'll do. *I'll* get the photograph for *you*. I'll get it *made* in Chicago and send it back.

DR. HAGGETT: (*controlling his impatience*) But don't you see, Abby, it's the—

ADA: The color and all makes it so much—

MRS. HAGGETT: No photograph'd ever give us the comforting feeling that we still had *you* with us.

(*Simultaneously*)

ABBY: Would it really mean so much to all of you to have me hanging there in an oil painting?

MRS. HAGGETT: Would we want *anyone* we didn't love in our dining room?

ABBY: But I got so used to looking at that portrait!

DR. HAGGETT: Why, Abby! That's no better than if you was to sit all day in front of a looking-glass.

ABBY: But it ain't me I see. It's—it's—it's the time when I was young. It's all how things used to be in the old days. It's—it's—I couldn't say it. I couldn't say it. (*The doorbell rings*)

MRS. HAGGETT: (*inaudibly*) There's someone at the door.

ADA: (*a step left*) Don't disappoint us, Abby.

DR. HAGGETT: She won't. You know you won't, Abby. You'll say "yes." Think! Fifty dollars!

ABBY: Well, if you're all so set— (*The doorbell rings again*) If you're so set on having it—

MRS. HAGGETT: (*smiles, to her Husband*) Now our own dear Abby's speaking.

ABBY: (*to* MRS. HAGGETT) No. I still got to think.

DR. HAGGETT: (*silences his two women with a gesture*) Of course you have, Abby. And I want you to think, and I know you won't reach no wrong decision. (*The front door opens and* TALLANT *appears, a painting dangling carefully from his right hand*) You go set alone in your room for ten minutes. (*A general gasp from the three* HAGGETTS)

TALLANT: (*as he enters*) No one answered the bell, but I took the liberty of— (*Puts picture, back to audience, against medicine cabinet. Places hat on top of cabinet*)

ABBY: (*crosses to him*) If you come for my portrait, I can't let you have it. (TALLANT *comes down Center; looks at portrait*) I made up my mind I couldn't anyway, and now it looks like I got to make other arrangements. So if you'll excuse me, Mr. Davis— (*Crosses above table and disappears quickly into kitchen; closes door*)

ADA: Was *you* after Abby's portrait, as well as what you got?

MRS. HAGGETT: (*breaks in quickly*) You said you was Davenport. She called you Davis. Who in *blazes* are you?

DR. HAGGETT: (*breaks in*) I didn't expect you to come here of your own free will, Mr. Tallant.

TALLANT: (*a step down to* HAGGETT) Would you ask the ladies to leave us alone together?

MRS. HAGGETT: (*quickly*) Have you got secrets?

TALLANT: (*to her*) Of the most delicate nature. (*Returns to his scrutiny of the portrait*)

DR. HAGGETT: (*to his wife and daughter*) You can leave *me* to attend to him. (*Points to* TALLANT, *then turns and crosses to desk*)

ADA: (*crosses above table toward Left Center door*) Watch out, Pa! If he tries to get that, too, *shoot* him. (MRS. HAGGETT *rises; crosses above table, behind* ADA)

MRS. HAGGETT: Just call out, Milton. *We'll* be listening.

TALLANT: (*moves up to her*) I'm certain you will. But your husband and I are going to be friends now. (*Bows them into the entry.* ADA *and* MRS. HAGGETT *go upstairs.* TALLANT *closes the Left Center doors*)

DR. HAGGETT: (*crosses up to* TALLANT) Don't take much stock in that last remark, Mr. Tallant. You as good as stole a pile of money from me this morning.

TALLANT: (*looking at picture*) I must ask you to be more careful with your language, Doctor Haggett.

DR. HAGGETT: What's your opinion of the trick you played on me?

TALLANT: (*still looking at picture*) It was a simple business operation, carried through in the classic tradition of art collecting. Not a day passes but some collector finds some *rare* and *unappreciated* work of art—

DR. HAGGETT: Did you even *know* Chris Bean?

TALLANT: (*turns and smiles at* HAGGETT) I never heard of him till a month ago.

DR. HAGGETT: Well, you certainly have got your nerve with you.

TALLANT: (*a step down to* HAGGETT) Quite! But to come down to business— How much have you told Davenport about the pictures Bean left here?

DR. HAGGETT: Didn't tell him nothing. I was still hoping I might find the rest.

TALLANT: You haven't succeeded?

DR. HAGGETT: (*a groan*) They've been *burnt!* All but the two you got and that one there! (*Indicates the portrait*)

TALLANT: (*goes up and looks at it. Admiring*) A masterpiece!

DR. HAGGETT: I'm glad you like it.

TALLANT: Oh, you and I can hardly hope to reach that height.

DR. HAGGETT: You and I? What are you driving at?

TALLANT: (*returns to Left of* HAGGETT) Corot. (HAGGETT *does not see light*) The name means nothing to you?

DR. HAGGETT: Not a thing.

TALLANT: Corot was a French painter of landscapes. *He died in eighteen seventy-five.* The bulk of his painting has been done *since* then. (HAGGETT *is startled*) The same is true of the late Cézanne. He died in nineteen hundred and six. I know a dozen *excellent* Cézannes, all painted in the last year. (*Goes for the picture he brought in with him*) I spoke this morning of a business partnership between us. Allow me— (*He exhibits it*) "The Hill Pasture" by the late Christopher Bean. (HAGGETT *starts to take it from him*) Careful! Don't touch it! It's not dry yet! (HAGGETT *draws back*)

DR. HAGGETT: Where did you find it?

TALLANT: I *painted it*.

DR. HAGGETT: *What* are you?

TALLANT: A *forger*. (*Drops picture to his side. Light dawns on* HAGGETT) I see that you begin to understand. Those letters in the *Atlantic* tell us about the pictures Bean left here. The originals are lost. Thanks to *my* peculiar gifts, their loss needn't disturb us. (HAGGETT *gasps*) I assure you, Doctor Haggett, I am offering you a *gold* mine. We have an *absolute* corner on Christopher Bean. (HAGGETT *looks at him*) Because you cannot only vouch for *my* forgeries, but can also discredit my competitors. (*He turns and places the painting against the medicine cabinet, showing to audience. Then he returns to* HAGGETT) Have I made myself clear?

DR. HAGGETT: (*A pause, then* HAGGETT *wrings his hands*) It's too *risky!* (*Turns and goes toward desk chair*)

TALLANT: Not at all. (*Follows down to Right of* HAGGETT)

DR. HAGGETT: (*turns*) It's *criminal!*

TALLANT: Perhaps. But no picture-collecting sucker ever admits that he's been "stung," so—

DR. HAGGETT: (*sits*) I don't like the *sound* of it. I was all right this morning before you come in. I was respected by the world and at peace with myself, and I wasn't tempted by nothing nor no man.

TALLANT: As I remarked this morning, we are all mortals, Doctor. You have a wife and two lovely daughters—

DR. HAGGETT: (*brightening*) That's so. I have. And being tempted for your loved ones ain't as bad as if it was just on your own account. (*An uneasy glance toward the portrait*) How much would I get from this scheme of yours?

TALLANT: I thought twenty percent.

DR. HAGGETT: 'Tain't worth it.

TALLANT: I'll be liberal. Twenty-five.

DR. HAGGETT: Not a cent under *fifty!*

TALLANT: (*drawing himself up*) If you persist in letting *your greed* come between you and—

DR. HAGGETT: (*rises*) My greed! Mine! (*A pause, then he adds craftily*) You can't work this scheme of yours without my help. Because *I'm* in a position to discredit *you!*

TALLANT: (*holding out his hand*) Doctor Haggett, it's done! (HAGGETT *starts to take hand; stops, then takes it*)

(*Voices are audible in the entry.* ROSEN *opens Left Center doors and enters living room to Left of table.*)

MRS. HAGGETT: (*in entry*) There's someone else in there but I guess you can go in—

DR. HAGGETT: (*shaking* TALLANT's *hand*) I better warn Hannah and Ada not to talk—

ROSEN: (*down Center to* TALLANT) *You* up here too?

TALLANT: (*smiling*) I got here first, Rosen.

ROSEN: So it was you beat me to it! I might have known it!

DR. HAGGETT: You two acquainted with each other?

TALLANT: Mr. Rosen will be the selling end of our firm.

DR. HAGGETT: (*to his Wife and* ADA, *who are visible in the entry*) Hannah! Shut that door and keep out! (MRS. HAGGETT *closes the Left Center doors*)

TALLANT: We've just organized, Rosen. Coming in on the ground floor?

ROSEN: I'm not talking your kind of business today. I've come up here after the *real* thing, and I'm going to *get* it!

TALLANT: (*indicating* ABBY's *portrait*) There it is—if you can pay the price for it. (ROSEN *crosses up to portrait*)

ROSEN: Aha! (*Bends over to examine it*) It isn't signed.

TALLANT: That's easily fixed.

ROSEN: Oh, one of *yours*, is it?

TALLANT: (*winks at* HAGGETT) Thanks.

DR. HAGGETT: I should say not! It's—

TALLANT: (*turns to* HAGGETT) Leave him be, Doctor! He's not one of the "suckers." I forge most of the pictures he sells.

ROSEN: I know you're *good*, Tallant, but I never knew you were *this* good!

TALLANT: (*crosses to below table. Delighted*) You do recognize my brushwork then?

ROSEN: (*laughs*) You can't fool me! (*To* HAGGETT) If it was *real* I'd buy it, but— (*He moves down to Center*)

DR. HAGGETT: It is real!

ROSEN: (*pointing to* TALLANT) With him on the premises!

TALLANT: Word of honor!

ROSEN: Yours?

DR. HAGGETT: Mine!

TALLANT: There you are. (ROSEN *looks at the portrait*) We'll take twenty thousand for it. (HAGGETT *gasps.* ROSEN *moves down a step*)

ROSEN: (*amused*) Now, isn't that good of you? Would you throw in the frame?

TALLANT: You'll get twice twenty thousand in a year.

ROSEN: If it was genuine I might.

DR. HAGGETT: But I assure you, Mr. Rosen, it is genuine. Only trouble is I ain't in a position—

ROSEN: Excuse me for doubting your word, Doctor Haggett, but— (*Indicating* TALLANT. TALLANT *takes a step toward* ROSEN)

TALLANT: (*quickly*) Come on, now, Rosen. Admit you don't know. (ROSEN *crosses up to portrait and looks at it.* TALLANT *laughs at him*)

ROSEN: (*explodes*) Well! *Which* is it? *Genuine* or *not*?

(*The Left Center door is opened and* DAVENPORT *appears. He is speaking to* SUSAN, *who has come back with him and is on her way upstairs*)

TALLANT: (*laughs; indicates* DAVENPORT) Here's Davenport back again. Ask *him*. (TALLANT *moves away Right a few steps*)

DAVENPORT: (*comes into room, to up Center*) Well, Doctor Haggett, have you found the missing treasures? (HAGGETT *gestures to the portrait.* DAVENPORT *turns and sees it*) Ah! (*To* ROSEN, *who is in front of portrait*) Allow me? (ROSEN *takes a step Right*) And the man who painted this died miserably. Here is all womanhood. It's nobility! (*Drops down to one knee*) It's tenderness and it's strength. This is beautiful as only—only— (*Rises*) Damn comparisons! The thing's beautiful. (*Backs up stage a step*)

ROSEN: That's *all* I need to hear. Doctor Haggett, I'll give you *seventy-five hundred* for it. (MRS. HAGGETT *opens Right double Left Center door and enters to above armchair.* HAGGETT *drops down into armchair*)

DAVENPORT: (*turns to* ROSEN, *who is on his Right*) You're not buying it, Rosen?

ROSEN: Yes, I am, Mr. Davenport, and I'm glad to have you here to see me do it.

DAVENPORT: What do *you* want with it? (ADA *appears in the entry; enters to just Left of medicine cabinet*)

ROSEN: (*exultant*) To show it in my gallery. A one-man show! A one-picture show! For a whole month before *I try* to sell it. I'm going to bring all Duveen's customers over to Lexington Avenue.

DAVENPORT: (*laughs*) Are you going to force me to respect you at last?

ROSEN: Yes, I am, Davenport. If it ruins me! (*Crosses above table to chair Right of table and sits*) Come on, now, Doctor! Be reasonable and I'll talk business. (DAVENPORT *moves a step toward portrait and looks at it.* SUSAN *comes downstairs and enters to Left of* ADA)

DR. HAGGETT: (*utterly distracted*) I—I—I'd like to sell it to you, but— You see I ain't in a position—

SUSAN: (*a few steps down*) Don't you

do nothing you'd be ashamed of, Pa. (MRS. HAGGETT *moves up a step and grasps* SUSAN'S *arm*)

DR. HAGGETT: You get out of here. I won't have no child of mine criticizing me.

DAVENPORT: Doctor Haggett, please!

DR. HAGGETT: I can't talk business with womenfolks around.

ROSEN: Ten thousand, Doctor Haggett!

DR. HAGGETT: I tell you I ain't in a position to sell it yet.

MRS. HAGGETT: (*crosses down a step and bends over him*) You ain't got much time. Her train goes at five.

DR. HAGGETT: I know it does. Where *is* Abby?

MRS. HAGGETT: (*points*) She's out there in the kitchen.

DR. HAGGETT: (*he changes his mind and rises*) No, never mind her. (*To* TALLANT *as he crosses to chair Left of table*) Might as well be hanged for a sheep as a lamb.

TALLANT: Leave this to *me*, partner. I'll handle it.

DR. HAGGETT: You shut up too. You got no part in this deal. (*Glances nervously toward Right door, then turns to* ROSEN *and goes off the deep end; sits chair Left of table.* TALLANT *goes up to below fireplace*) Ten thousand ain't enough.

ROSEN: Don't be foolish.

DR. HAGGETT: It ain't enough.

ROSEN: You've got to think of my expenses.

DR. HAGGETT: Don't care about 'em. Ten thousand ain't—

ROSEN: How do I know I'll ever be able to sell it?

DR. HAGGETT: I ain't so anxious to sell—

ADA: (*in Left Center doorway*) *Pa!*

MRS. HAGGETT: (*crosses to Left of him*) Remember you risked *fifty dollars* on it.

DR. HAGGETT: I ain't risked it yet. (MRS. HAGGETT *a step down to look at kitchen door*)

ROSEN: Twelve thousand, then, but *that's* the top.

DR. HAGGETT: *No!*

ROSEN: How much *do* you want?

DR. HAGGETT: (*another anxious glance toward Right door*) I ain't quite ready to sell this yet, but if I'm going to sell it you got to make it worth my while. (*Gulps*) I'd take forty thousand! (*A gasp from the* HAGGETT *ladies*)

ROSEN: (*laughs*) You're crazy!

DR. HAGGETT: *Thirty-five.*

ROSEN: Even *that*, Mr. Davenport—

DAVENPORT: (*above table*) A little high.

DR. HAGGETT: All right. *Thirty!*

MRS. HAGGETT: (*behind* HAGGETT) Don't be easy, Milton.

DR. HAGGETT: (*to her*) I won't go no lower— (*A nervous glance toward Right door. To* ROSEN) And you got to be quick about it!!

ROSEN: *Fifteen!*

MRS. HAGGETT *and* ADA: (*together*) *No!*

ROSEN: Seventeen and a half!

ALL THREE HAGGETTS: No!

DAVENPORT: (*to* ROSEN) You're dealing with a *united* family.

SUSAN: (*a step to* DAVENPORT) Not with *me*, Mr. Davenport! And I want to say that I got *no use* for any one trying to—

DR. HAGGETT: (*beside himself*) Go up to your room. You'll get what's coming to you for mixing in matters you can't grasp!!

SUSAN: I don't care. I just can't *stand* to see Abby— (*Goes upstairs indignantly*)

ADA: (*looks at* SUSAN *and then turns to* DAVENPORT. *Covering quickly*) My sister ain't right on account of falling on her head when she was a baby.

MRS. HAGGETT: (*crosses up to Left of*

ADA) She's a sentimental fool, that's all she is. (*Pushes* ADA *ahead of her, front of table, toward kitchen*) She just can't bear to part with this after having it 'round so long.

DR. HAGGETT: *I* can part with it, though. (*Looks at his watch*) Good God Almighty!

MRS. HAGGETT: (*low to* ADA) Keep Abby out of here. (ADA *goes into kitchen, closing door.* MRS. HAGGETT *turns and watches* HAGGETT)

DR. HAGGETT: Thirty thousand, Mr. Rosen! Take it or leave it.

ROSEN: Well, I certainly won't take it.

DAVENPORT: (*to* ROSEN) You've met your match this time.

ROSEN: *Twenty!*

DR. HAGGETT: *Thirty!*

ROSEN: *Cash in three days!*

DR. HAGGETT: (*quickly*) Twenty-nine!

MRS. HAGGETT: (*quickly as she totters a step Left*) Milton, don't slip!

ROSEN: *Twenty-three!* Half of it down and the balance tomorrow!

DR. HAGGETT: *Twenty-five* on the same terms.

ROSEN: (*a slight pause. Pounds the table with his fist*) Done!

DAVENPORT: (*above table*) Good work, Rosen!

DR. HAGGETT: (*on the verge of collapse but still painfully conscious of that kitchen door*) Let's see the money.

ROSEN: (*truculently*) Good God, give me time. (*Takes his checkbook, a fountain pen and the bills-of-sale out of his coat pocket.* ADA *returns Right; closes door*)

ADA: Ma!

MRS. HAGGETT: What is it?

ADA: The new maid from Boston—

MRS. HAGGETT: What about her?

ADA: She's going *back* to Boston.

MRS. HAGGETT: Let her go! We're going to get a *butler* now! (*The doorbell rings*) See who that is. If it's a patient,

tell him your Pa has retired from doctoring. (ADA *goes above table and out Left Center to answer*)

ROSEN: (*breaks in*) Now, I had that bill-of-sale all ready made out for— (*He looks at his checkbook*) Oh, I see—a thousand dollars. Well, I'll just have to alter it to fit. (*Writes.* HAGGETT *watches him, fascinated.* ADA *admits* WARREN CREAMER *by front door*)

ADA: What are you doing here, Warren? (WARREN *enters to Left side Left Center door.* ADA *closes front door and enters to Right side Left Center door*)

WARREN: I've come for Abby's trunk.

DAVENPORT: (*moves a few steps Left*) Ah, the boy marvel!

MRS. HAGGETT: Who? Warren?

WARREN: Hello, Mr. Davenport.

DAVENPORT: (*moves to Center*) I've been looking at his pictures, Mrs. Haggett. You produce *talented* painters in this village.

MRS. HAGGETT: (*incredulous*) Are his pictures good too? (*Her eyes shine. She quickly moves up toward the entry, brushing* DAVENPORT *aside as she passes him. She calls out in her sweetest tones*) Susie! Warren's here! (*Returns to below door, Right of* WARREN) Come in, Warren. Don't be afraid. We kind of *changed* our minds about artists since this morning! (ADA *glares at* WARREN)

WARREN: (*still truculent*) Guess I'll just get that trunk. (*He goes through the entry to Right.* SUSAN *hurries downstairs and follows him out*)

ROSEN: (*to* HAGGETT) Now, you sign here. (*He hands pen and bill-of-sale paper to* HAGGETT, *who glances toward the kitchen door and signs*) And here's the check. (*He delivers*)

MRS. HAGGETT: (*crosses down to Left of him*) Let's see it, Milton.

DR. HAGGETT: How do I know I get the balance tomorrow? (MRS. HAGGETT *crosses to Right door, then returns to below table*)

ROSEN: My God, it's in writing, isn't it?

DR. HAGGETT: Well, so long as you get that picture on out of here before— (*Another uneasy glance toward Right door*)

ROSEN: (*rises; crosses above table to portrait*) That's what I'm going to do. (*Begins removing the portrait from the frame*)

DR. HAGGETT: (*rises*) Hannah, watch that door— (ABBY *enters, Right, dressed for her departure, and carrying a small suitcase.* MRS. HAGGETT *gasps with dismay; crosses to Left Center.* HAGGETT *goes to Left of* ABBY)

ABBY: Please excuse me for interrupting, Doctor Haggett, but it's time for me to go— (*Puts bag down, below sideboard*) And I had to tell you that much as I hate denying you what you asked, I made up my mind—

DR. HAGGETT: (*breaks in*) I knew it was all right, Abby. I knew it was. (*He fumbles bills out of his pocket*) And here's the fifty dollars I promised you! (*Forces the money into her hand*) God bless you, Abby! (*Is hurrying her toward Right door*)

ABBY: (*wrenching free from* HAGGETT) What's that man doing there with my portrait?

ROSEN: (*blandly*) Taking it to New York, Abby! To exhibit it! (*She slowly crosses below table to Left of it*) Where everybody will come to look at it! Could you let me have some string and wrapping paper?

ABBY: What right have you got to take it away?

ROSEN: Well, I never paid *more* for a right in my life.

ABBY: (*flatly*) It belongs to me. (*Sensation. Pause. Then:*)

ROSEN: How's that? (TALLANT *smirks*)

ABBY: It *belongs* to me.

DR. HAGGETT: (*right of her*) What's come over you, Abby? Did anyone ask you to come in like this? What are you after in here anyway?

ABBY: I come in to say goodbye and get my portrait, and I seen him fixing to go off with it—

DR. HAGGETT: (*right of her*) But you just sold it to *me*.

ABBY: I never! I never!

MRS. HAGGETT: (*left Center*) You got the money there in your hand, Abby.

DAVENPORT: (*above table*) Oh, Doctor Haggett! It can't be that you—

ABBY: (*violently*) Here! Take this money back! Go on, take it! (*He takes it*) You said you wanted my portrait to remember me by. *I* said I'd think about giving it to you. And I have thought. And I ain't never going to part with it. And now you're trying to sell it behind my back. I'd be ashamed. (HAGGETT *lowers his head*)

MRS. HAGGETT: Abby!

ABBY: I'd be ashamed. Of all the sharp, *underhanded* tricks!

DR. HAGGETT: (*breaks in, explosively*) This house is mine and everything in it's mine, and you're my paid help. (ROSEN *replaces portrait to against table*)

DAVENPORT: (*indignantly*) Good God!

ABBY: (*fortissimo*) My portrait ain't yours.

DR. HAGGETT: (*desperately*) If you'd all step into the entry, Mr. Davenport, and leave me to explain things quickly to Abby! There won't be no more difficulty. Just five minutes, Hannah! (GENERAL *murmurs as* MRS. HAGGETT *and* HAGGETT *urge the company out into entry*)

ROSEN: (*protesting*) Damn it, Doctor, I just gave you a check for—

DR. HAGGETT: Now don't you get upset, Mr. Rosen. There's just a little misunderstanding here. (*Closes the Left Center door upon them, mops his brow and turns to* ABBY. ABBY *moves to above portrait*) You ain't showing much gratitude for all we done for you, Abby, all these years. (*Crosses down to Left of her*)

ABBY: (*at bay, low*) I can't help that. I won't part with my portrait.

DR. HAGGETT: And I was just working up such a nice surprise for you.

ABBY: Well, I caught you at it. And I'd be *ashamed*.

DR. HAGGETT: You think I was trying to do something sneaky.

ABBY: *Sneaky and greedy!* I knew your wife and Ada was both greedy. But I never knew you was.

DR. HAGGETT: (*hurt*) Oh, Abby, how could you say that of me? When I was only trying to make some money for you! I don't mean that fifty. That was just for fun. I was really going to give you a thousand dollars. *A thousand dollars.* Abby!

ABBY: And you were going to get it by selling my portrait?

DR. HAGGETT: People in your circumstance ain't got no right to own things that are worth so much money.

ABBY: *That may be!* But my portrait's all I got in the world. The boy who painted it—Well, I ain't ashamed to say it now, it's so long ago. I loved him and I still love him. And he died just after he finished painting it, so it was the last thing he ever painted. That's why it means so much to me. It means all the happiness I ever had. And you know that I ain't had so much, Doctor Haggett. Now I guess I better go and catch my train. (*Moves down to below the table*)

DR. HAGGETT: (*follows and grasps her arm. She stops*) Abby, you're thinking only of yourself. How about your poor brother and his children? He's a poor man, Abby.

ABBY: I know he is.

DR. HAGGETT: And he ain't got work now.

ABBY: I know that.

DR. HAGGETT: You'll all be poor out there in Chicago.

ABBY: I can't help it, Doctor.

DR. HAGGETT: And his children. Wouldn't you like to give 'em advantages?

ABBY: (*breaks in*) But I promised Chris Bean I'd never part with it. The last time I ever seen him I promised him that. He painted it for *me*.

DR. HAGGETT: Who's being *greedy* now? Who would your brother's children say was greedy?

ABBY: Don't keep after me. Let me go and catch—

DR. HAGGETT: (*a gulp, then his tone changes*) Abby, there's something else you ain't thought of! That portrait don't even belong to you. (ABBY *grasps. He drives on*) It was time I paid for, you wasted sitting for Chris Bean to paint it when you'd ought to have been working.

ABBY: (*indignantly*) It ain't so! I worked every minute he was painting. Every minute! I remember how we used to set out in that barn, me working and him painting.

DR. HAGGETT: You used to take him out *our* coffee to drink.

ABBY: I *never*. You know how Mrs. Haggett always watched the coffee. That was *my own* breakfast coffee that I saved for him and took out to him. It was all I ever had to give him, my coffee was! There now! What more meanness can you think up?

DR. HAGGETT: I'll be honest with you. Honesty's the best policy, after all. They want to pay me twenty-five thousand for your portrait.

ABBY: (*stunned*) Twenty-five thou—

DR. HAGGETT: Divide with me, Abby. (*Poignant*) Take half and give me half. If it wasn't for me you wouldn't have none of it.

ABBY: (*decisively*) *No!*

DR. HAGGETT: (*desperately*) Take *more* than half! Take *fifteen* thousand! Think what you could do for your brother's children with *fifteen* thousand.

ABBY: (*backing away from him*) No! No, I tell you.

DR. HAGGETT: (*grasps her arm*) Take twenty thousand!

ABBY: Let go of my dress.

DR. HAGGETT: Greed, Abby, greed!

ABBY: (*fortissimo*) It ain't greed! I wouldn't take a million. You ought to be ashamed!!!

DR. HAGGETT: (*a despairing gesture*) I am. (*Turns, crosses to armchair and sits*)

ABBY: (*long pause. Follows to Right of him*) Well, now will you let me go?

DR. HAGGETT: Yes, God help me, I'll have to let you go.

ABBY: (*looks lovingly at the portrait*) He was so poor, Chris was. He never had no good coat nor nothing warm, only that one sweater I knitted for him. He never had no warm room to sleep in nights, nor nothing he needed, he was so poor. If he could have afforded to go away from here down South he needn't have died. I used to pray that we'd get an early thaw just for Chris's sake. How is it a man dies so poor when he painted pictures that's worth so much?

DR. HAGGETT: Because nobody had any use for his pictures while he was living.

ABBY: I always liked 'em. That's why I kept so many. (DR. HAGGETT *has turned slowly*) No, only just because— (*She crosses below table towards her suitcase*)

DR. HAGGETT: (*rises, a step after her*) You kept so many?

ABBY: (*stops below table; turns to him*) Yes, I kept them.

DR. HAGGETT: (*crosses to her, wetting his dry lips feverishly*) How did you get them?

ABBY: Mrs. Haggett she put 'em on the bonfire but *I* took them off.

DR. HAGGETT: Where are they now?

ABBY: In my trunk. I rolled 'em up. But they're all right. (*Starts again for her bag*)

DR. HAGGETT: (*all but voiceless*) How many are there?

ABBY: (*stops again*) There's seventeen.

DR. HAGGETT: (*gasps*) Seventeen, Abby? Did you say seventeen? (*Turns and crosses up toward Left Center door, shouting*) Hannah! Ada! Mr. Rosen! Come back in here! (*The Left Center door is opened from without and the others pour back into the room*)

MRS. HAGGETT: (*enters and crosses to* HAGGETT) What is it, Milton?

ADA: (*enters to up Center*) Pa!

ROSEN: (*enters to Left of table*) Good God, what now?

DR. HAGGETT: Never mind the *portrait!* The *other* pictures have been *found.* (DAVENPORT *enters to above* ROSEN)

TALLANT: (*enters to above* HAGGETT) No! (ABBY *listens in confusion and alarm*)

DR. HAGGETT: The ones you burned, Hannah! (*Hugs her*)

MRS. HAGGETT: Milton!

DR. HAGGETT: Only you *never* burned 'em. Abby's got 'em in her trunk. *There's seventeen of 'em.*

DAVENPORT: *Seventeen new* Christopher Beans! (ABBY *moves up to below the fireplace.* WARREN *comes into the entry from the Right carrying* ABBY's *old leather trunk, tied up with rope.* SUSAN *following to steer it clear of the paint*)

MRS. HAGGETT: It's a *fortune*, Milton.

ADA: And it's *ours!*

DR. HAGGETT: (*breaking loose from his wife*) Put that trunk down and open it! (*Charges the entry*)

WARREN: (*stops*) I just roped it up!

DR. HAGGETT: Unrope it! Got a knife, ain't you! (WARREN *puts the trunk down, takes out a pocket knife and bends over the trunk. The others all move up closer to the trunk*)

ABBY: (*crosses above table to* HAG-

GETT) You'll make me miss my train, Doctor Haggett.

ADA: Talking about *trains* at a time like this!

WARREN: (*cutting the rope*) There!

DR. HAGGETT: (*throws up the lid of the trunk*) Now, Abby, where are they?

ABBY: (*goes up to trunk*) Better let me, Doctor Haggett. I don't like for folks to go messing in my trunk. (*Silence. She bends over the trunk and takes out a flattish roll of canvases from beneath several articles of wearing apparel*)

DR. HAGGETT: Ha! (*Snatches them from her and comes down to* ROSEN, *who is by chair Left of table.*) Now I'll talk business with you, Mr. Rosen.

ROSEN: Excuse me, Doctor Haggett, but I am the picture dealer. (*Takes pictures from* HAGGETT, *turns and crosses to desk. Sits in swivel chair; places paintings on desk and unrolls them.* HAGGETT *crosses to above desk.* MRS. HAGGETT *follows to below desk.* ADA *goes above the desk to Left of it.* TALLANT *moves to rear of armchair*)

ROSEN: Well, Doctor Haggett, I wasn't prepared for any such deal as this!

DAVENPORT: *Carefully* now! (*Crosses to Right of* HAGGETT *and peers over his shoulder*) Don't harm them. (*As the roll opens out flat*) Ah!

DR. HAGGETT: What would you say it's worth, Mr. Davenport?

DAVENPORT: Well, now, I don't know—

ABBY: (*to* WARREN) Will you rope up my trunk for me again, please, Warren? (WARREN *ropes up the trunk,* SUSAN *assisting.* ABBY *looks from the trunk to the group at the desk indeterminately*)

DR. HAGGETT: You promised you'd tell me. Is it worth ten thousand?

DAVENPORT: *Easily,* I should say.

DR. HAGGETT: (*wildly excited*) Do you hear that, Hannah! Easily ten thousand for the first one on the pile! And *seventeen* of 'em!

ADA: (*comes down a step and puts an arm about her mother*) We're *rich*, Ma! We're *rich!* (ROSEN *turns over a new picture*)

DAVENPORT: *Oh!*

MRS. HAGGETT: (*sits below desk*) Seems like we must be, but it kind of gets my stomach. (*During the following scene,* ABBY *makes repeated attempts to interrupt the proceedings at desk but her every effort to attract their attention is drowned in another outburst from them. Their attitude is one of complete indifference to her presence and they pay no heed to her pitiful attempts to edge in*)

ABBY: (*crosses down to Right of desk Right of Group*) Were you aiming to sell those too, Doctor Haggett?

DR. HAGGETT: What's that?

DAVENPORT: (*bends over the second canvas*) "The Hill Pasture." It *must* be "*The Hill Pasture*"!

DR. HAGGETT: Certainly it's "*The Hill Pasture*"! (TALLANT *looks over* DAVENPORT'S *shoulder at the painting, shrugs his shoulder, and crosses to the medicine cabinet*)

ABBY: I saved them— (*Stops as she sees* TALLANT *pick up his forgery of "The Hill Pasture," put on hat, and go into entry*)

DAVENPORT: (*as he sees another painting*) Oh, *look!*

ABBY: —I saved those from burning and I thought they are mine to keep!

ROSEN: (*to* HAGGETT) Say, now, before we start talking business, I got to know if you really are the rightful owner this time. (TALLANT *goes out front door.* SUSAN *and* WARREN *watch* TALLANT *exit*)

MRS. HAGGETT: Who would be if he ain't?

DR. HAGGETT: I got your word for it they're mine. And wasn't they left here against an unpaid bill?

DAVENPORT: Yes, Rosen, I expect they *do* belong to him.

ABBY: Oh!

DR. HAGGETT: *There*, you see!

ABBY: Well—

DAVENPORT: Let's look through the rest. (*No one pays the slightest attention to* ABBY)

ROSEN: Well—as I say, I never tackled anything this big before. A corner in *Christopher Bean*.

ABBY: Goodbye, Doctor Haggett. I'll be going now.

DR. HAGGETT: That's what it is, Mr. Rosen! (*He laughs*) A *corner*!

ABBY: My train will be going, Doctor Haggett. That's why I—

DAVENPORT: I wouldn't be in any hurry to sell, Doctor. Not the lot, anyway.

ROSEN: I wasn't figuring on that, Mr. Davenport.

ABBY: Goodbye, Ada— Goodbye, Mrs. Haggett—

ROSEN: Why, he may have a couple of hundred thousand in this pile.

ADA: Ma.

ROSEN: (*pounds top of desk with his fist*) I don't know, though. I might get the deal financed. Would you give me time?

DR. HAGGETT: Don't know about giving time.

ABBY: Goodbye. I got to be going now— Well— (*Turns back to* WARREN *with a pathetic little laugh*) I guess I'll just go. I guess there ain't nothing else to do.

ROSEN: (*to himself*) Schmidt might come in on this—and there's Goldstein, I might put him down for a— (*The group at the desk turn over another and another with low exclamations of delighted amazement*)

ABBY: Will you take my trunk out, Warren? (WARREN *nods to* SUSAN, *who exits front door.* WARREN *picks up the trunk and goes out front door; leaves door open.* ABBY *goes for her suitcase, picks it up and stands for a moment looking about her down Left*)

ROSEN: I tell you what, Doctor Haggett. Suppose you keep that check for a thirty-day option?

DR. HAGGETT: Well, if you set a price on the lot now. But a *good* price, mind.

ROSEN: Let me figure up. (DAVENPORT *turns away from the group at the desk and sees* ABBY *picking up the bag*)

DR. HAGGETT: (*laughs*) You go right ahead, Mr. Rosen, we're not going to stop your figuring. (ROSEN *proceeds to do so, all the others watching over his shoulder.* ABBY *returns to above the portrait*)

DAVENPORT: Oh, Abby! (*Goes to Left of her*) You're not going, are you? (*Stoops and puts bag down in front of portrait*)

ABBY: Yes, I'm going. I tried to say goodbye, but they're so busy.

DAVENPORT: Will you let me say just one word to you about your portrait? (*She turns away from him*) Oh, I'm not trying to take it from you. But, Abby, a work of art like that is a responsibility. It's *yours*, but only yours in trust for the future. Take it with you to Chicago by all means. But when you get there, don't keep it where it won't be safe. Lend it to the Chicago Art Institute. You could go and see it *every* day, you know. Would you do that, Abby?

ABBY: I'd think about it.

ROSEN: (*looking up from his figures*) A hundred and eighty thousand.

DR. HAGGETT: You said two hundred!

ROSEN: (*turns to* DAVENPORT) I appeal to Mr. Davenport! (HAGGETT *also turns to face* DAVENPORT)

DAVENPORT: (*holding up his hand for silence.* MRS. HAGGETT *looks up and rises*) Please, Abby! I know it's more than a work of art to you. I *know* the *bond* there must have existed between you and Chris Bean when he painted it.

MRS. HAGGETT: (*a supercilious sniff*) *Bond*, huh! *Carryings on!* If you call that a bond!

ABBY: (*looks at her, but turns back with her own dignity to answer* DAVENPORT) Mr. Davenport, he was the only man ever asked me to marry him. (*Though her words are spoken shyly, they fall like lead upon the room's sudden attention*)

DR. HAGGETT: (*pause. All but speechless*) You— (*He moves toward her*) You didn't marry him, though, Abby? (MRS. HAGGETT *moves a step Right.* ADA *moves to below desk*)

ABBY: He was so sick. I couldn't refuse him nothing. (*The idea strikes all simultaneously*)

DAVENPORT: (*pleased surprise*) Then you're his *widow*? (ROSEN *rolls up the paintings*)

ABBY: I know I am. (WARREN *enters front door, gets the portrait and the suitcase, then exits. All of the following speeches are spoken simultaneously*)

DR. HAGGETT: (*shaking his head*) She's got to prove it! She's got to prove it! She's got to prove it!

DAVENPORT: (*to* DOCTOR) I believe she can! I certainly believe she can! (*To* ABBY) And you never told! But, Abby! Why didn't you?—This is magnificent! And it's certainly turning out just like Chris Bean would have—

ROSEN: (*to* MRS. HAGGETT) In that case these pictures belong to *her!* My God; I can't do business this way! If they don't know the— (MRS. HAGGETT *tears the roll of paintings out of his hands*) Well, I give it up.

MRS. HAGGETT: (*clasping the paintings tightly in her arms*) Well, she doesn't get 'em away from me! Not over my dead body—

ADA: Ma! Does that mean Pa can't— Ma, answer me! Aren't these pictures ours to sell? Oh, it isn't fair! It just isn't fair! I don't think it's—

ABBY: (*to* HAGGETT) Certainly I can. I got my marriage lines out in my— (*Points towards the front door through which* WARREN *has taken her trunk*) Do you want to see— And my wedding ring on a— (*Pulls out her wedding ring on a ribbon from her bosom*) Look! (HAGGETT *throws up his hands in defeat, turns and goes toward* MRS. HAGGETT. ABBY *follows down after him a few steps*) I wanted to hold folks' good opinion and my— But I don't care who knows it now, that I'm Mrs. Christopher Bean— That's who I am, just as much as Mrs. Haggett's Mrs.— (HAGGETT *tears the roll of paintings away from his wife, turns and goes to* ABBY) And I never carried on with— (*He hands the paintings to her. The Curtain starts to fall*)

DR. HAGGETT: *There!!!*

ABBY: Oh, are you giving me back my— (*She takes the roll of paintings, smiles her appreciation; turns and moves toward the front door.* DAVENPORT *bows her out.* ADA *bursts into tears*)

CURTAIN

QUESTIONS

A. Understanding the Action:

1. Is the action of the play strongly localized? If so, why should the environment receive special attention in this particular play? What details are given in the play?

2. What did you learn about Christopher Bean? What did you learn about the treatment he received when he was alive?

3. What is the place of art in this community? Does the play contain an actual or implied comment on social values in general? What are they?

4. Who is the main character (the "protagonist") of the play, and why?

5. Who is the "antagonist" in the play, and why? Are there several antagonists? Does the play contain any downright villains or scoundrels? Explain in detail.

6. Summarize and explain the humorous and satirical elements of this play. Which of

these two elements is more pertinent? Explain.

B. *Understanding the Characters:*

1. Describe the character of Dr. Haggett and Mrs. Haggett.

2. Why can Davenport and Tallant be called comic characters?

3. Ada "bursts into tears" as the curtain falls on the last act. How would you justify her action? Is she also a comic?

4. Abby is considered to be an extremely appealing character. Why? Why did she conceal the fact that she was "Mrs. Christopher Bean"? Is she also a comic character? If so, is she comic in the same sense that her employers are?

C. *Understanding the Approach:*

1. One master of comedy, Shakespeare's fellow-playwright Ben Jonson, declared that the moving of laughter is not always the ultimate aim [purpose] of comedy, nor is the moving of laughter always the end [goal] of the comedy. How would you apply this statement to *The Late Christopher Bean*?

2. What is the meaning of the title of the play? What did one reviewer mean when he wrote that the play had "pungency under the surface and surprise around the edges"?

3. What is the comic technique of the play? Does the comedy depend upon exaggeration or on characterization? Does the action follow expected lines of development or contain reversals and surprises?

D. *Comparisons:*

1. How is *The Late Christopher Bean* the same or different as a comedy from the following plays: *The Pretentious Ladies; The School for Scandal; Arms and the Man;* and *The Apollo of Bellac?*

JEAN GIRAUDOUX (1882-1944)

One of the most interesting dramatists that France has produced in the twentieth century was Jean Giraudoux, the diplomat and novelist. Born in the Limousin district in the little town of Bellac, which he has immortalized, he retained an abiding love for the provincial aspects of life even though he lived in many countries and enjoyed the intellectual delights of the great cities of the world. In his youth the family moved to another small town near Vichy, where his father was the tax collector and his brother, the town physician. Genius can see the great in the little; Blake could see the world in a grain of sand. In the provincial town the poetic and imaginative Giraudoux observed on a small scale all the woes and joys, all the problems and complexities of the human condition. In the fields surrounding the town, under an open sky, he felt the beauty and mystery of nature.

He received an excellent education at the École Normale Supérieure, specializing in German literature and winning the highest academic honors. After graduation he was awarded a scholarship to study in Munich. Germany both attracted and repelled him. In his work he tried to achieve the union of discordant elements, a rapprochement of Gallic clarity and logic with German restlessness and romanticism. After his stay in Germany he lectured for a year at Harvard, where ten years later he returned during World War I as a military instructor.

He began his literary career at the age of twenty-five by publishing three stories entitled characteristically *Provinciales*. Two years later, intelligent, good-humored, sophisticated, and reserved, he entered the French foreign service. Giraudoux worked the rest of his life for the government in various capacities. He was Chief of the Press in the Foreign Ministry under Poincaré and a cabinet member (Minister of Propaganda) under Daladier, a post he held from 1939 until the German occupation.

In spare time from his diplomatic duties Giraudoux pursued a separate literary career, publishing stories, essays, and novels, some thirty titles in all before he turned to writing plays in 1928. He was fortunate in his association with Louis Jouvet, the famous French actor and director, who staged virtually all of Giraudoux's plays in Paris. Giraudoux's first theatrical success was *Siegfried*, a dramatization of one of his novels. The play is a study of dual personality, of a victim of amnesia searching for his true identity and trying to discover after his participation in the war (World War I) whether he is German or French.

Following the tradition of his famous seventeenth-century predecessors, Corneille and Racine, of reinterpreting classic Greek subject-matter, Giraudoux wrote three plays that reveal his verbal virtuosity and his dramatic versatility. *Amphitryon 38* (so-called because the author claimed it was the thirty-eighth treatment of this famed love triangle involving Zeus, the mortal woman Alcmene and her mortal husband) was a farcical, sophisticated comedy successfully performed first in Paris in 1928 and in New York in 1937 by the Lunts. In 1935 Giraudoux wrote a powerful satire *The Trojan War Will Not Take Place* (renamed in the English productions as *Tiger at the Gates*). Considered cynical at the time of its writing, the play proved to be tragically prophetic when World War II broke out four years later. Giraudoux then turned to writing tragedy. His *Electra*, like his *Siegfried*, showed the futility of revenge and a deep abhorrence of violence in settling human problems. When Electra, obsessed by her mother Clytemnestra's guilt and her own passion for revenge, drives her brother to slay Clytemnestra and the latter's lover Aegisthus in the name of justice, she brings about the destruction of her country.

Realism and fantasy, which play so important a part in Giraudoux's plays, found their best expression in *The Madwoman of Chaillot*, written a year before his death. In this poetic fable and satire the urbane dramatist attacked the materialism of twentieth-century society which was destroying the joy of simple loving. Paradoxically in a supposedly mad world, perhaps only the insane in this play show some rationality. Other plays of Giraudoux which have been produced in America are *The Enchanted* (1933) and *Ondine* (1939), with Audrey Hepburn in the leading role of a water-sprite who falls in love with a mortal.

INTRODUCTION TO *THE APOLLO OF BELLAC*

Giraudoux wrote *The Apollo of Bellac* in 1942, two years before his death. Although this one-act play is not one of his major contributions to the theatre, it serves as a good introduction to his work, for in its smaller configuration it reveals typical aspects of his mind and technique.

In it we find the usual Giraudoux ingredients of satire, poetic fantasy, realism, and humor combined artistically in a framework of theatrical effectiveness. His style ranges from conciseness of expression to rhetorical floweriness or preciosity. Under the urbanity of its surface, the play deals with philosophical problems universally faced by humanity in the course of its troubled existence: the ephemeral nature of beauty, the search for happiness, the eternal conflict of reality and dream, the clash of the material and the transcendental worlds. Giraudoux has characterized himself as the "journalist of the theatre," but perhaps an apter appellation would be the "philosopher in the theatre," except that his work possesses the stylistic polish of a Santayana rather than the ponderousness of a Hegel. Practicing a kind of inverse pantheism, he has defended his preciosity "which causes him to treat objects as if they were human, humans as if they were gods, and gods as if they were cats or weasels."

In *The Apollo of Bellac* we find the archetypal figure of the young girl who is, in the adapter Maurice Valency's opinion, "Giraudoux's supreme achievement as a dramatist." We first see Agnes as a frightened, naïve girl in the first bloom of youth, but after her strange meeting with an immortal Apollo she quickly achieves self-knowledge and a mature understanding of the world. Forever she carries with her the dazzling vision of the ideal, but with mature common sense adjusts quickly to the commonplace of the real. For a moment she transfigures the dull lives of people before they sink back to the monotony of everyday living. In this charming comedy Giraudoux has successfully summed up the duality of human existence.

THE APOLLO OF BELLAC

A Play in One Act

ADAPTED BY MAURICE VALENCY
FROM THE FRENCH OF JEAN GIRAUDOUX

CHARACTERS

AGNES
THERESE
THE CLERK
THE MAN*
THE VICE PRESIDENT
MR. CRACHETON

MR. LEPEDURA
MR. RASEMUTTE
MR. SCHULTZ
THE PRESIDENT
CHEVREDENT
THE CHAIRMAN OF THE BOARD

Scene: THE RECEPTION ROOM OF THE INTERNATIONAL
BUREAU OF INVENTIONS, S.A.

This is a large, well-appointed room on the second floor of a magnificent office building in Paris. The French windows are open and afford us a view of treetops. There is an elaborate crystal chandelier hanging from the ceiling. The morning sun plays upon it. On a pedestal large enough to conceal a man a bust of Archimedes is set. Four doors open off the room. Three of them are marked Private. These lead into the office of the President, Right, and the First Vice President rear Right, and the Directors' Conference Room rear Left. The effect is French and very elegant, perhaps a trifle oppressive in its opulence.

Behind a period desk sits the RECEPTION CLERK. *The desk has an ivory telephone and a row of signal lights. It has also a period blotter on which the clerk is writing something in an appointment book. The* CLERK *is well on in years and his face makes one think of a caricature by Daumier.*

TIME: *Autumn in Paris. The present or shortly before.*

AT RISE: THE CLERK *is writing with a meticulous air. The outer door opens.* AGNES *comes in timidly from outer door, and stands in front of the desk.* THE CLERK *does not look up.*

AGNES: Er—

CLERK: Yes?

---

* Note: The reader should bear in mind that Apollo, the Greek God of Music, Poetry, Prophecy, and Medicine (later also considered the God of the Sun) was believed to be the prototype of Manly Beauty, and could therefore be regarded as the God of Beauty as well.

567

AGNES: Is this the International Bureau of Inventions, Incorporated?

CLERK: Yes.

AGNES: Could I please see the Chairman of the Board?

CLERK: (*looks up*) The Chairman of the Board? No one sees the Chairman of the Board.

AGNES: Oh.

(*The outer door opens again.* THERESE *sweeps into the room. She is blonde, shapely, thirty-five, dressed in expensive mink.* CLERK *rises respectfully.*)

CLERK: Good morning, Madame.

THERESE: Is the President in?

CLERK: Yes, Madame. Of course.

(THERESE *walks haughtily to* PRESIDENT'S *door.* CLERK *opens it for her and closes it behind her. He goes back to his desk where* AGNES *is waiting.*)

AGNES: Could I see the President?

CLERK: No one sees the President.

AGNES: But I have—

CLERK: What type of invention? Major? Intermediate? Minor?

AGNES: I beg pardon?

CLERK: Assistant Secretary to the Third Vice President. Come back Tuesday. Name?

AGNES: My name?

CLERK: You have a name, I presume?

(THE MAN FROM BELLAC *appears suddenly from outer door. He is nondescript, mercurial, shabby.*)

MAN: Yes. The young lady has a name. But what permits you to conclude that the young lady's invention is as minor as all that?

CLERK: Who are you?

MAN: What chiefly distinguishes the inventor is modesty. You should know that by now. Pride is the invention of non-inventors.

(A STREET SINGER, *accompanied by violin and accordion, begins* "La Seine" *outside the windows.* CLERK *crosses to close them.*)

AGNES: (*to the* MAN) Thanks very much, but—

MAN: To the characteristic modesty of the inventor, the young lady adds the charming modesty of her sex— (*He smiles at* AGNES) But—

(CLERK *closes one of the windows.*)

how can you be sure, you, that she has not brought us at last the invention which is destined to transform the modern world?

CLERK: (*closes the other window*) For world-transformations it's the Second Vice President. Mondays ten to twelve.

MAN: Today is Tuesday.

CLERK: Now how can I help that?

MAN: So! While all humanity awaits with anguish the discovery which will at last utilize the moon's gravitation for the removal of corns, and when we have every reason to believe that in all likelihood Mademoiselle—Mademoiselle?

AGNES: Agnes.

MAN: Mademoiselle Agnes has this discovery in her handbag— You tell her to come back Monday.

CLERK: (*nervously*) There is going to be a Directors' meeting in just a few minutes. The Chairman of the Board is coming. I must beg you to be quiet.

MAN: I will not be quiet. I am quiet Mondays.

CLERK: Now, please. I don't want any trouble.

MAN: And the Universal Vegetable? Five continents are languishing in the hope of the Universal Vegetable which will once and for all put an end to the ridiculous specialization of the turnip, the leek and the stringbean, which will be at one and the same time bread, meat, wine and coffee, and yield with equal facility cotton, potassium, ivory and wool. The Universal Vegetable which Paracelsus could not, and Burbank dared not, imagine! Yes, my friend. And while in this handbag, which with understandable concern she clutches to her charming bosom, the seeds of the Universal Vegetable await only the signal of your President to burst upon an expectant world, you say—come back Monday.

AGNES: Really, sir—

CLERK: If you wish an appointment for Monday, Mademoiselle—

MAN: She does not wish an appointment for Monday.

CLERK: (*shrugs*) Then she can go jump in the lake.

MAN: What did you say?

CLERK: I said: She can go jump in the lake. Is that clear?

MAN: That's clear. Perfectly clear. As clear as it was to Columbus when— (*The* BUZZER *sounds on the* CLERK'S *desk. A* LIGHT *flashes on.*)

CLERK: Excuse me. (*He crosses to the* VICE PRESIDENT'S *door, knocks and enters.*)

(MAN *smiles.* AGNES *smiles back wanly.*)

AGNES: But I'm not the inventor of the Universal Vegetable.

MAN: I know. I am.

AGNES: I'm just looking for a job.

MAN: Typist?

AGNES: Not really.

MAN: Stenographer?

AGNES: Not at all.

MAN: Copy-reader, translator, bookkeeper, editor, file-clerk—stop me when I come to it.

AGNES: You could go on like that for years before I could stop you.

MAN: Well then—your specialty? Charm? Coquetry, devotion, seduction, flirtation, passion, romance?

AGNES: That's getting warmer.

MAN: Splendid. The best career for a female is to be a woman.

AGNES: Yes, but—men frighten me.

MAN: Men frighten you?

AGNES: They make me feel weak all over.

MAN: That clerk frightens you?

AGNES: Clerks, presidents, janitors, soldiers. All a man has to do is to look at me, and I feel like a shoplifter caught in the act.

MAN: Caught in what act?

AGNES: I don't know.

MAN: Perhaps it's their clothes that frighten you. Their vests? Their trousers?

AGNES: (*shakes her head*) I feel the same panic on the beach when they don't wear their trousers.

MAN: Perhaps you don't like men.

AGNES: Oh, no, I like them. I like their dog-like eyes, their hairiness, their big feet. And they have special organs which inspire tenderness in a woman—. Their Adam's apple, for instance, when they eat dinner or make speeches. But the moment they speak to me, I begin to tremble—

MAN: (*he looks appraisingly at her a moment*) You would like to stop trembling?

AGNES: Oh yes. But— (*She shrugs hopelessly.*)

MAN: Would you like me to teach you the secret?

AGNES: Secret?

MAN: Of not trembling before men. Of getting whatever you want out of them. Of making the directors jump, the presidents kneel and offer you diamonds?

AGNES: Are there such secrets?

MAN: One only. It is infallible.

AGNES: Will you really tell it to me?

MAN: Without this secret a girl has a bad time of it on this earth. With it, she becomes Empress of the World.

AGNES: Oh tell it to me quickly.

MAN: (*peering about the room*) No one is listening?

AGNES: (*whispers*) No one.

MAN: Tell them they're handsome.

AGNES: You mean, flatter them? Tell them they're handsome, intelligent, kind?

MAN: No. As for the intelligence and the kindness, they can shift for themselves. Tell them they're handsome.

AGNES: All?

MAN: All. The foolish, the wise, the modest, the vain, the young, the old. Say it to the professor of philosophy and he will give you a diploma. Say it to the butcher and he will give you a steak. Say it to the president here, and he will give you a job.

AGNES: But to say a thing like that, one has to know a person well—

MAN: Not at all. Say it right off. Say it before he has a chance even to open his mouth.

AGNES: But one doesn't say a thing like that before people.

MAN: Before people. Before all the world. The more witnesses, the better.

AGNES: But if they're not handsome—and for the most part they're not, you know—how can I tell them that they are?

MAN: Surely you're not narrow-minded, Agnes?

(*She shrugs, not quite sure.*)
The ugly, the pimply, the crippled, the fat. Do you wish to get on in this world? Tell them they're handsome.

AGNES: Will they believe it?

MAN: They will believe it because they've always known it. Every man, even the ugliest, feels in his heart a secret alliance with beauty. When you tell him he's handsome, he will simply hear outwardly the voice he has been listening to inwardly all his life. And those who believe it the least will be the most grateful. No matter how ugly they may have thought themselves, the moment they find a woman who thinks them handsome, they grapple her to their hearts with hooks of steel. For them, she is the magic glass of truth, the princess of an enchanted world. When you see a woman who can go nowhere without a staff of admirers, it is not so much because they think she is beautiful, it is because she has told them they are handsome.

AGNES: There are women then who already know this secret?

MAN: Yes. But they know it without really knowing it. And usually they evade the issue, they go beside the point. They tell the hunchback he is generous, the wall-eyed that he's strong. There's no profit in that. I've seen a woman throw away a cool million in diamonds and emeralds because she told a clubfooted lover that he walked swiftly, when all he wanted to hear was—you know what. And now—to work. The President is in every day to those who come to tell him he's handsome.

AGNES: I'd better come back another day. I have to have training. I have a cousin who's not at all bad-looking— I'll practice on him tomorrow, and then the next day I'll—

MAN: You can practice right now. On the receptionist.

AGNES: That monster?

MAN: The monster is perfect for your purpose. After that, the Vice President. I know him. He's even better. Then the President.

(*The* VICE PRESIDENT'S *door opens. The* CLERK *comes in.*)

CLERK: (*into the doorway*) Very good, sir.

VOICE: And another thing—

CLERK: (*turns*) Yes sir?

VOICE: When the Chairman of the Board—

(CLERK *goes back in and closes the door.*)

AGNES: No, I can't!

MAN: (*indicating the bust of Archimedes at rear*) Begin with this bust then.

AGNES: Whose is it?

MAN: What does it matter? It's the bust of a man. It's all ears. Speak!

AGNES: (*shuddering*) It has a beard.

MAN: Begin with what you like. With this chair. With this clock.

AGNES: They're not listening.

MAN: This fly, then. See? He's on your glove. He's listening.

AGNES: Is he a male?

MAN: Yes. Speak. Tell him.

AGNES: (*with an effort*) How handsome he is!

MAN: No, no, no. Say it to him.

AGNES: How handsome you are!

MAN: You see? He's twirling his moustache. Go on. More. More. What is a fly especially vain of?

AGNES: His wings? His eyes?

MAN: That's it. Tell him.

AGNES: How beautiful your wings are, beautiful fly! They sparkle in the sun like jewels. And your eyes—so large, so sad, so sensitive!

MAN: Splendid. Shoo him away now. Here comes the clerk.

AGNES: He won't go. He's clinging to me.

MAN: Naturally.

AGNES: (*to the fly*) You're bowlegged. (*she smiles*) He's gone.

MAN: You see? And now—
(*The* VICE PRESIDENT'S *door opens slowly.*) Here he comes.

AGNES: (*in panic*) What must I say?

MAN: "How handsome you are."
(CLERK *comes in and walks to his desk.* MAN *disappears behind the bust of Archimedes.*)

AGNES: (*after an agony of indecision*) How handsome you are!

CLERK: (*stops dead*) What?

AGNES: I said, how handsome you are!

CLERK: Do you get this way often?

AGNES: It's the first time in my life that I've ever—

CLERK: (*finishing the sentence for her*) Called a chimpanzee handsome? Thanks for the compliment. But—why?

AGNES: You're right. Handsome is not the word. I should have said beautiful. Because, mind you, I never judge a face by the shape of the nose or the arch of the brow. To me, what counts is the ensemble.

CLERK: So what you're telling me is: your features are ugly, but they go beautifully together. Is that it?

AGNES: It serves me right. Very well— It's the first time I've ever told a man he was handsome. And it's going to be the last.

CLERK: Now don't get excited, please. I know girls. At your age a girl doesn't calculate; she says whatever comes into her head. I know you meant it. Only— why did you say it so badly?
(MAN *sticks his head out and makes a face at* AGNES *behind the* CLERK'S *back.*)

AGNES: (*to the* MAN) Did I say it badly? (*to the* CLERK, *who thinks it is said to him*) I thought you were handsome. I may have been wrong.

CLERK: Women are blind as bats. Even if there were something good about me, they'd never see it. What's so good about me? My face? God, no. My figure? Not at all. Only my shadow. But of course you didn't notice that.

AGNES: Is that what you think? And when you leaned over to close the window, I suppose your shadow didn't lean over with you? And when you walked into the Vice President's office, did you put your shadow away in a drawer? (*She strokes his shadow with her hand*) How could I help noticing a shadow like that?

CLERK: You notice it now because I direct your attention to it.

AGNES: Have it your way. I thought I was looking at you, but what I saw was your shadow.

CLERK: Then you shouldn't say, what a handsome man. You should say, what a handsome shadow.
(*He opens the window, the room is filled with music. It is still "La Seine."*)

AGNES: From now on, I shall say no more about it.

CLERK: (*returning to desk*) Don't be angry, my dear. It's only because I'm a man of years and I have a right to warn you. I have a daughter of your age. I know what girls are. One day they see a fine shadow, and at once their heads are turned, the silly geese, and they think the man himself is handsome. Oh, I don't deny it, it's a rare thing, a fine shadow. And believe me it lasts—you don't keep your hair, you don't keep your skin, but your shadow lasts all your life. Even longer, they say. But that's not the point. These little fools invariably insist on confusing the shadow with the man, and if the idiot lets himself be talked into it, in a moment it's all over and they've ruined their lives for nothing, the nitwits. No, my dear. Heed an old man's warning. You can't live your life among shadows. (MAN *sticks out his head and lifts an admonishing finger.*)

AGNES: How handsome you are!

CLERK: You know why? It's because when I'm angry I show my teeth. And the fact is, they are rather good. My dentist says they're perfect. It's no credit to me— It's because I eat hard foods. And when you—

(*The buzzer sounds again.*)

Ah—the Vice President needs me again. Wait just a minute, my dear. I'll make sure that he sees you at once. I'll say it's my niece.

AGNES: (*as he bends over to close a drawer*) How beautiful it is, your shadow, when it leans over. One would say it belonged to Rodin's Thinker!

CLERK: (*delighted*) Come, now, that will do. If you were my daughter, I'd give you a good slap on the—. Sit down a minute. I'll get him for you. (*Crosses to the* VICE PRESIDENT'S *door and goes out.*) (MAN *comes out from behind the bust. The music stops.*)

MAN: Well, it's a start.

AGNES: I think I'm better with flies.

MAN: Because in your mind the idea of beauty is inseparable from the idea of the caress. Women have no sense of the abstract—a woman admiring the sky is a woman caressing the sky. In a woman's mind beauty is something she needs to touch. And you didn't want to touch the clerk, not even his shadow.

AGNES: No.

MAN: With my method, it's not your hands that must speak, nor your cheek, nor your lips—. It's your brain.

AGNES: I had a narrow squeak. I almost lost him.

MAN: Yes, he had you there with his shadow. You're not ready to tackle a Vice President. No. Not yet.

AGNES: But there's no time. What shall I do?

MAN: Practice. Practice on me.

AGNES: You expect me to tell you you're handsome?

MAN: Is it so difficult?

AGNES: Not at all. Only—

MAN: Think. Think before you speak.

AGNES: Oh, you're not bad at all, you know, when you tease one like this.

MAN: Very feeble. Why when I tease one like this? The rest of the time, I'm not handsome?

AGNES: Oh yes. Always. Always.

MAN: Better. Now it's no longer your hands that are speaking.

AGNES: With you, all the same, they murmur a little something.

MAN: Good.

AGNES: The mass of your body is beautiful. The outline is beautiful. The face matters little.

MAN: What nonsense is this? My face matters little?

AGNES: (*recovering quickly*) No more than the face of Rodin's Thinker.

MAN: In his case, doubtless the feet have more importance. Look here, Agnes, these little allusions to famous statues are ingenious. But is Rodin's Thinker the only one you know?

AGNES: Except for the Venus of Milo. But she wouldn't be much use to me with men.

MAN: That remains to be seen. In any case, we'd better extend your repertory. Forget The Thinker. Michelangelo's David is very good. Or his Moses. But best of all—the Apollo of Bellac—

AGNES: The Apollo of Bellac?

MAN: It doesn't exist. It will do perfectly.

AGNES: What does it look like?

MAN: A little like me, I think. I too come from Bellac. It's a little town in Limousin. I was born there.

AGNES: But they say the men of Limousin are so ugly. How does it happen that you are so handsome?

MAN: My father was a very handsome man, and he— Oh-oh. Good for you. (*He applauds.*)

AGNES: (*pursuing her advantage*) Oh never! Not with you! You taught me the secret. With you I could be no other than honest.

MAN: At last. You understand.

(*The* VICE PRESIDENT'S *door opens.*)

Here we are. (*Goes behind the bust.*)

CLERK: (*comes in, smiling tenderly*) The Vice President will be out in a moment, my dear. No need to put yourself out. A shadow like his, you may see every day—in the zoo. (*He takes some papers from his desk and goes into where the Directors will meet.*)

AGNES: (*whispers*) Help! Help!

(MAN *thrusts his head out.*)

I feel faint!

MAN: Practice. Practice.

AGNES: (*desperately*) On whom? On what?

MAN: On anything. The telephone.

AGNES: (*she speaks to the telephone*) How handsome you are, my little telephone! (*She strokes it gently.*)

MAN: No! Not with the hands.

AGNES: But it's so much easier that way.

MAN: I know. Try the chandelier. That's one thing you can't touch.

AGNES: How handsome you are, my little, my great chandelier!

(*The music begins again. Another tune.*) Only when you're all lit up? Oh, don't say that. Other chandeliers, yes. Street lamps, store-fixtures, yes. Not you. See— you are full of sunshine. You are the chandelier of the sun. A desk lamp needs to be lit. A planet needs to be lit. But you have radiance of your own. You are as beautiful as a galaxy of stars, even more beautiful, for a galaxy is only an imitation chandelier, a cluster of uncertain lights swinging precariously in the eternal darkness. But you are a creature of crystal with limbs of ivory and gold, a living miracle!

(*The chandelier lights up by itself.*)

MAN: Bravo!

VICE PRESIDENT: (*The door opens. The* VICE PRESIDENT *comes in. His manner is important. His face is that of a gargoyle*) My dear young lady, I have exactly two minutes to give you. (*He crosses to close the window.*)

AGNES: (*whispering in awe*) Oh!

VICE PRESIDENT: (*Stops and turns*) Why do you stare at me like that? You've seen me before?

AGNES: (*In a tone of wonder*) No! On the contrary.

VICE PRESIDENT: And what does that mean, no, on the contrary?

AGNES: I was expecting to see the usual Vice President, stoop-shouldered, paunchy, bald— And all at once, I see you!

(VICE PRESIDENT *freezes in his tracks.* MAN *thrusts out his head. He raises a warning finger.*)

(*Hastily*) How handsome you are!

VICE PRESIDENT: What? (*He turns.*)

AGNES: Nothing. I beg your pardon.

VICE PRESIDENT: I heard you distinctly. You said I was handsome. Don't deny it. (*He steps closer to her.*)

(*Music swells up.*)

You know, it gave me rather a shock to hear you say it. However, it can't be true. If I were really—what you said—wouldn't some woman have told me before this?

AGNES: Oh, the fools! The fools!

VICE PRESIDENT: Whom are you calling fools, Mademoiselle? My sister, my mother, my niece?

AGNES: (*Giving up all at once. In a formal tone*) Mr. Vice President, the truth is I am looking for a position. And I happened to hear through a friend of one of your directors, Mr. Lepedura—

(MAN *thrusts out his head.*)

VICE PRESIDENT: Never mind Monsieur Lepedura. We are discussing me. As you probably know, I am one of the world's authorities in the fields of dreams. It is I who work with those who are able to invent only while they sleep, and I have been able to extract from their dreams such extraordinary devices as the book that reads itself and the adjustable Martini, wonders of modern science which without my help would have remained mere figments of the imagination. If you appeared to me in a dream and told me I was handsome, I should have understood at once. But we are in a waking state, or are we? One moment. (*He pinches himself*) Ow! I am awake. Permit me. (*Pinches her.*)

AGNES: Ow!

VICE PRESIDENT: We're not dreaming, Mademoiselle. And now, my dear— (*He takes her hand*) Why did you say I was handsome? To flatter me?—I can see you are incapable of such baseness. To make fun of me? No—your eye is gentle, your lips attract— Why did you say it, Mademoiselle?

AGNES: I say you are handsome because you are handsome. If your mother finds you ugly that's not my concern.

VICE PRESIDENT: I cannot permit you to form so low an opinion of my mother's taste. Even when I was a boy, my mother used to say I had the hands of an artist.

AGNES: If your niece prefers Charles Boyer—

VICE PRESIDENT: My niece? Only yesterday at dinner she was saying that my eyebrows could have been drawn by El Greco.

AGNES: If your sister—

VICE PRESIDENT: My sister has never quite admitted that I am handsome, no, but she has always said that there was something distinctive about my face. A friend of hers, a history teacher, told her it's because in certain lights, I resemble Lodovico Sforza. (*He makes a deprecating gesture.*)

AGNES: Lodovico Sforza? Never. The Apollo of Bellac, yes.

VICE PRESIDENT: The Apollo of Bellac?

AGNES: Wouldn't you say? Quite objectively?

VICE PRESIDENT: Well—if you really think so—perhaps just a little. Although Lodovico Sforza, you know—I've seen engravings—

AGNES: When I say the Apollo of Bellac, I mean, naturally, the Apollo of Bellac in a beautifully tailored suit. You see, I am frank. I say what I think. Yes, Mr. Vice President. You have the fault of all really handsome men—you dress carelessly.

VICE PRESIDENT: (*smiling*) What insolence! And this from a girl who tells every man she meets that he's handsome!

AGNES: I have said that to two men only in all my life. You are the second. (CLERK *comes in.*)

VICE PRESIDENT: What is it? Don't you see I'm busy?

CLERK: The Directors are on the way up, sir. It's time for the meeting.

VICE PRESIDENT: I'll be right in.
(CLERK *goes into the Directors' room.*)
I'm sorry, Mademoiselle. I must go to this meeting. But we must certainly continue this wonderful conversation. Won't you come back and lunch with me? You know, my secretary is impossible. I'm having her transferred to the sales department. Now you're a first-rate typist, I'm told—

AGNES: I don't type. I play the piano.

VICE PRESIDENT: Ah, that's wonderful. And you take dictation?

AGNES: In longhand, yes.

VICE PRESIDENT: That's much the best way. That gives one time to think. Would you like to be my secretary?

AGNES: On one condition.

VICE PRESIDENT: A condition?

AGNES: On condition that you never wear this awful jacket again. When I think of these wonderful shoulders in that ill-fitting suit—!

VICE PRESIDENT: I have a beautiful blue silk suit. But it's for summer— It's a little light for the season.

AGNES: As you please.

VICE PRESIDENT: I'll wear it tomorrow.

AGNES: Goodbye.

VICE PRESIDENT: Don't forget. Lunch. (*He goes out, smiling, by way of the door to the Directors' room. The street music stops.*)
(MAN *peers out from behind the bust.*)

AGNES: I kept my hands behind my back the whole time. I pretended I had no hands. Now I can hardly move my fingers.

MAN: Here come the rest of the apes. Go to work.

AGNES: On the first?

MAN: On all. One after the other.

AGNES: But—

(CLERK *throws open the doors of the Directors' room. The street music starts again. We have a glimpse of the Directors' table with chairs pulled back ready to receive the Directors. The* VICE PRESIDENT *is seen inside. He is posturing in front of a bookcase in the glass door of which he sees himself reflected, and he is trying vainly to give a smartly tailored appearance to his coat.* CLERK *glances at him in astonishment, then he stands by the outer door to announce the Directors as they appear. They come in through the outer door and cross the length of the reception room, one by one in time to the music, which is a waltz.*)

CLERK: Mr. Cracheton.

(MR. CRACHETON *comes in, a lugubrious type, stiff and melancholy.*)

AGNES: How handsome he is!

CRACHETON: (*He snaps his head about as if shot. His expression changes. He smiles. In a low voice*) Charming girl! (*He goes into the Directors' room, looking all the while over his shoulder.*)

CLERK: Mr. Lepedura.

LEPEDURA: (*Appears. He has a face full of suspicion and worry. As he passes* AGNES, *he tips his derby perfunctorily, recognizing her*) Good morning.

AGNES: How handsome you are!

LEPEDURA: (*stops dead*) Who says so?

AGNES: Your wife's friend, the Baroness Chagrobis. She thinks you're wonderful.

LEPEDURA: (*a changed man, gallant and charming*) She thinks I'm wonderful? Well, well, give her my love when you see her. And tell her I mean to call her up shortly myself. She has a pretty thin time of it with the Baron, you know. We have to be nice to her. Is she still at the same address?

AGNES: Oh yes. I'll tell her you're as handsome as ever.

LEPEDURA: Now don't exaggerate, my dear. We don't want to disappoint her. (*He gives her a radiant smile, and goes in, fully six inches taller and many pounds lighter. To the* CLERK) Delightful girl!

CLERK: Mr. Rasemutte and Mr. Schultz.
(*They enter together, Mutt and Jeff.*)
AGNES: How handsome he is!
(*Both stop as if at a signal.*)
RASEMUTTE: To which of us, Mademoiselle—
SCHULTZ: —Do you refer?
AGNES: Look at each other. You will see.
(*They look at each other anxiously, and both smile radiantly.*)
RASEMUTTE: Charming creature!
SCHULTZ: Lovely girl!
(SCHULTZ *offers* RASEMUTTE *his arm. They walk into the Directors' room arm in arm like characters in "Alt Wien."* CLERK *blows* AGNES *a kiss, follows them in and closes the doors behind them.* MAN *pokes his head out from behind Archimedes. He shakes his head ruefully.*)
AGNES: I'm not doing it well? You're sad?
MAN: You're doing it much too well. I'm frightened.
AGNES: You?
MAN: Like Frankenstein.
(*The door of the Directors' room is flung open.*)
CLERK: The President!
(*As the* PRESIDENT *enters the room, we catch a glimpse of the* DIRECTORS. *Each has a mirror in his hand. While one combs his hair into waves, another settles his tie. Another preens his whiskers. The* VICE PRESIDENT *has taken off his jacket.*)
PRESIDENT: So you're the cause of it all, Miss— Miss—?
AGNES: Agnes.
PRESIDENT: Miss Agnes, for fifteen years this organization has been steeped in melancholy, jealousy and suspicion. And now suddenly this morning, everything is changed. My reception clerk, ordinarily a species of hyena—
(*The* CLERK *smiles affably.*)
has become so affable he even bows to his own shadow on the wall—
(CLERK *contemplates his silhouette in the sunshine with a nod of approval. It nods back.*)
The First Vice President, whose reputation for stuffiness and formality has never been seriously challenged, insists on sitting at the Directors' meeting in his shirtsleeves, God knows why. In the Directors' room, around the table, mirrors flash like sunbeams in a forest, and my Directors gaze into them with rapture. Mr. Lepedura contemplates with joy the Adam's apple of Mr. Lepedura. Mr. Rasemutte stares with pride at the nose of Mr. Rasemutte. They are all in love with themselves and with each other. How in the world did you bring about this miracle, Miss Agnes? What was it you said to them?
AGNES: How handsome you are!
PRESIDENT: I beg your pardon?
AGNES: I said to them, to each of them, "How handsome you are!"
PRESIDENT: Ah! You conveyed it to them subtly by means of a smile, a wink, a promise—
AGNES: I said it in a loud clear voice. Like this: How handsome you are!
(*In the Directors' room, all heads turn suddenly.* CLERK *closes the doors.*)
PRESIDENT: I see. Like a child winding up a mechanical doll. Well, well! No wonder my mannikins are quivering with the joy of life.
(*There is a round of applause from the Directors' room.*)
Listen to that. It's Mr. Cracheton proposing the purchase of a new three-way mirror for the men's room. Miss Agnes, I thank you. You have made a wonderful discovery.
AGNES: (*modestly*) Oh, it was nothing.
PRESIDENT: And the President? How does it happen that you don't tell the President?

AGNES: How handsome he is?

PRESIDENT: He's not worth the trouble, is that it? (*She looks at him with a smile full of meaning.*) You've had enough of masculine vanity for one morning?

AGNES: Oh, Mr. President—you know the reason as well as I.

PRESIDENT: No. I assure you.

AGNES: But—I don't need to tell *you*. You *are* handsome.

PRESIDENT: (*Seriously*) Would you mind repeating that?

AGNES: You are handsome.

PRESIDENT: Think carefully, Miss Agnes. This is a serious matter. Are you quite sure that to you I seem handsome?

AGNES: You don't seem handsome. You are handsome.

PRESIDENT: You would be ready to repeat that before witnesses? Think. Much depends upon your answer. I have grave decisions to make today, and the outcome depends entirely upon you. Have you thought? Are you still of the same opinion?

AGNES: Completely.

PRESIDENT: Thank heaven. (*He goes to his private door, opens it and calls*) Chevredent!

(CHEVREDENT *comes in. She is a thin, sour woman with an insolent air. Her nose is pinched. Her chin is high. Her hair is drawn up tightly. When she opens her mouth she appears to be about to bite.*)

CHEVREDENT: Yes? (*She looks at* AGNES *and sniffs audibly.*)

PRESIDENT: Chevredent, how long have you been my private secretary?

CHEVREDENT: Three years and two months. Why?

PRESIDENT: In all that time there has never been a morning when the prospect of finding you in my office has not made me shudder.

CHEVREDENT: Thanks very much. Same to you.

PRESIDENT: I wouldn't have put up with you for ten minutes if it had ever occurred to me that I was handsome.

CHEVREDENT: Ha-ha.

PRESIDENT: But because I thought I was ugly, I took your meanness for generosity. Because I thought I was ugly, I assumed that your evil temper concealed a good heart. I thought it was kind of you even to look at me. For I am ugly, am I not?

(CHEVREDENT *sneers maliciously.*)

Thank you. And now listen to me. This young lady seems to be far better equipped to see than you. Her eyelids are not red like yours, her pupils are clear, her glance is limpid. Miss Agnes, look at me. Am I ugly?

AGNES: You are beautiful.

(CHEVREDENT *shrugs.*)

PRESIDENT: This young lady's disinterested appraisal of my manly charms has no effect on your opinion?

CHEVREDENT: I never heard such rubbish in my life!

PRESIDENT: Quite so. Well, here is the problem that confronts us. I have the choice of spending my working time with an ugly old shrew who thinks I'm hideous or a delightful young girl who thinks I'm handsome. What do you advise?

CHEVREDENT: You intend to replace me with this little fool?

PRESIDENT: At once.

CHEVREDENT: We'll soon see about that, Mr. President. You may have forgotten, but your wife is inside in your office reading your mail. She should know about this.

PRESIDENT: She should. Tell her.

CHEVREDENT: With pleasure. (*She rushes into the President's office, slamming the door after her.*)

AGNES: I'm terribly sorry, Mr. President.

PRESIDENT: My dear, you come like an angel from heaven at the critical moment of my life. Today is my fifteenth wedding anniversary. My wife, with whose fury Chevredent threatens us, is going to celebrate the occasion by lunching with my Directors. I am going to present her with a gift. A diamond. (*He takes out a case and opens it*) Like it?

AGNES: How handsome it is!

PRESIDENT: Extraordinary! You praised the diamond in exactly the same tone you used for me. Is it yellow, by any chance? Is it flawed?

AGNES: It is beautiful. Like you.

PRESIDENT: (*His door opens*) We are about to become less so, both of us. (*He puts the case in his pocket*) Here is my wife.

THERESE: (THERESE, *the blonde lady, comes in with icy majesty. She looks* AGNES *up and down*) So.

PRESIDENT: Therese, my dear, permit me to present—

THERESE: Quite unnecessary. That will be all, Mademoiselle. You may go.

PRESIDENT: Agnes is staying, my dear. She is replacing Chevredent.

THERESE: Agnes! So she is already Agnes!

PRESIDENT: Why not?

THERESE: And why is Agnes replacing Chevredent?

PRESIDENT: Because she thinks I'm handsome.

THERESE: Are you mad?

PRESIDENT: No. Handsome.

THERESE: (*To* AGNES) You think he's handsome?

AGNES: Oh, yes.

THERESE: He makes you think of Galahad? Of Lancelot?

AGNES: Oh, no. His type is classic. The Apollo of Bellac.

THERESE: The Apollo of Bellac?

PRESIDENT: Have you ever stopped to wonder, Therese, why the good Lord made women? Obviously they were not torn from our ribs in order to make life a torment for us. Women exist in order to tell men they are handsome. And those who say it the most are those who are most beautiful. Agnes tells me I'm handsome. It's because she's beautiful. You tell me I'm ugly. Why?

MAN: (*Appears. He applauds*) Bravo! Bravo!

THERESE: Who is this maniac?

MAN: When one hears a voice which goes to the very heart of humanity, it is impossible to keep silent.

PRESIDENT: My friend—

MAN: From the time of Adam and Eve, of Samson and Delilah, of Antony and Cleopatra, the problem of man and woman has made an impenetrable barrier between man and woman. If, as it seems, we are able to solve this problem once and for all, it will be a work of immeasurable benefit to the human race.

THERESE: And you think we're getting somewhere with it today, is that it?

MAN: Oh, yes.

THERESE: You don't think the final solution could be deferred until tomorrow?

MAN: Till tomorrow? When the President has just posed the problem so beautifully?

AGNES: So beautifully!

THERESE: The beautiful man poses a beautiful problem, eh, Mademoiselle?

AGNES: I didn't say it. But I can say it. I say what I think.

THERESE: Little cheat!

PRESIDENT: I forbid you to insult Agnes!

THERESE: It's she who insults me!

PRESIDENT: When I'm called handsome, it's an insult to you—is that it?

THERESE: I'm no liar.

PRESIDENT: No. You show us the bottom of your heart.

MAN: Agnes is telling the President the truth, Madame. Just as Cleopatra told the truth, just as Isolt told the truth. The truth about men is, they are beautiful, every last one of them; and your husband is right, Madame, the woman who tells it to them never lies.

THERESE: So I am the liar!

MAN: (*Gently*) It's only because you don't see clearly. All you have to do to see the beauty of men is to watch as they breathe and move their limbs. Each has his special grace. His beauty of body. The heavy ones—how powerfully they hold the ground! The light ones—how well they hang from the sky! His beauty of position. A hunchback on the ridge of Notre Dame makes a masterpiece of Gothic sculpture. All you have to do is to get him up there. And, finally, his beauty of function. The steamfitter has the beauty of a steamfitter. The president has the beauty of a president. There is ugliness only when these beauties become confused—when the steamfitter has the beauty of a president, the president the beauty of a steamfitter.

AGNES: But there is no such confusion here.

THERESE: No. He has the beauty of a garbageman.

PRESIDENT: Thanks very much.

THERESE: My dear, I have known you too long to deceive you. You have many good qualities. But you're ugly.

PRESIDENT: Quiet!

THERESE: Yes. Yes. Ugly! This girl, whatever her motives, is just able to force her lips to whisper her lies. But with every part of me—my heart, my lungs, my arms, my eyes—I scream the truth at you. My legs! You're ugly! Do you hear?

PRESIDENT: I've heard nothing else for years.

THERESE: Because it's true.

MAN: There. And at last she's confessed.

THERESE: Confessed what? What have I confessed?

MAN: Your crime, Madame. You have injured this man. How could you expect him to be handsome in an environment that screamed at him constantly that he was ugly?

PRESIDENT: Ah! Now I understand!

THERESE: What do you understand? What's the matter with you all? What have I done?

PRESIDENT: Now I understand why I am always embarrassed not only in your presence, but in the presence of everything that belongs to you.

THERESE: Do you know what he is talking about?

PRESIDENT: The sight of your skirt on the back of a chair shortens my spine by three inches. Can you expect me to stand up like a man when you come in? Your stockings on the bureau tell me that I'm knock-kneed and thick-ankled. Is it any wonder if I stumble? Your nail file on my desk hisses at me that my fingers are thick and my gestures clumsy. What do you expect of me after that? And your onyx clock with the Dying Gaul on the mantelpiece—no wonder I always shiver when I go near the fire. Imagine—for fifteen years that Dying Gaul has been sneering at me in my own house, and I never realized why I was uncomfortable. Well, at last I understand. And this very evening—

THERESE: Don't you dare!

PRESIDENT: This very evening your Dying Gaul shall die. You will find him in the garbage with the rest of the conspiracy. Your Dresden china shepherd, your Arab sheik, your directoire chairs with their scratchy bottoms—

THERESE: Those chairs belonged to my grandmother!

PRESIDENT: From now on they belong to the garbage. What are your chairs covered with, Agnes?

AGNES: Yellow satin.

PRESIDENT: I knew it. And the statues on your table?

AGNES: There is only a bowl of fresh flowers on my table. Today it is white carnations.

PRESIDENT: Of course. And over your fireplace?

AGNES: A mirror.

PRESIDENT: Naturally.

THERESE: I warn you, if you so much as touch my chairs, I'll leave you forever.

PRESIDENT: As you please, my dear.

THERESE: I see. So this is my anniversary gift after fifteen years of devotion. Very well. Only tell me, what have you to complain of? In all these years has it ever happened that your roast was too rare? Did I ever give you your coffee too cold, too hot, too light, too sweet? Thanks to me, you are known as a man whose handkerchief is always fresh, whose socks are always new. Have you ever known what it was to have a hole in your toe? Has anyone ever seen a spot on your vest? And yet how you splash in your gravy, my friend! How you go through your socks!

PRESIDENT: Tell me one thing. Do you say I am ugly because you think I am ugly or merely to spite me?

THERESE: Because you are ugly.

PRESIDENT: Thank you, Therese. Go on.

THERESE: Then this woman appears. And at the first glance we can guess the fate of the unhappy creature who marries her. We see it all—the slippers with the inner sole curled up in a scroll. The nightly battle over the newspaper. The pajamas without buttons and always too small. The headaches without aspirin, the soup without salt, the shower without towels—

PRESIDENT: Agnes, one question. Do you tell me I'm handsome because you think I'm handsome or only to make fun of me?

AGNES: Because you're handsome.

PRESIDENT: Thank you, Agnes.

THERESE: You mean because he's rich.

AGNES: If he were the richest man in the world, I'd still say he was handsome.

THERESE: Very well. Marry her if she thinks you're so handsome. Well? What are you waiting for?

PRESIDENT: Nothing.

THERESE: Take him, you, with my compliments. After fifteen years I've had enough. If you like to hear snoring at night—

AGNES: You snore? How wonderful!

THERESE: If you like bony knees—

AGNES: I like legs that have character.

THERESE: Look at that face! Now tell me he has the brow of a Roman Senator.

AGNES: No, Madame.

THERESE: No?

AGNES: The brow of a king.

THERESE: I give up. Goodbye.

PRESIDENT: Goodbye, my love.

(THERESE *rushes out through outer door.*) And now, Agnes, in token of a happy future, accept this diamond. For me, one life has ended, and another begins.

(CLERK *comes in and signs to him.*) Forgive me just one moment, Agnes. I must address the Directors. The Chairman of the Board is evidently not coming. I'll be right back. (*He crosses to the door. To the* CLERK) Send down to the florist. I want all the white carnations he has. Agnes, you have made me the happiest of men.

AGNES: The handsomest.

(*The* PRESIDENT *goes out by his door, the* CLERK *by outer door.*)

MAN: Well, there you are, my dear.

You have everything—a job, a husband and a diamond. I can leave?

AGNES: Oh no!

(*The street music starts afresh.*)

MAN: But what more do you want?

AGNES: Look at me. I have changed—haven't I?

MAN: Perhaps just a little. That can't be helped.

AGNES: It's your fault. I have told so many lies! I must tell the truth at last or I shall burst!

MAN: What truth do you want to tell?

AGNES: I want to tell someone who is really beautiful that he is beautiful. I want to tell the most beautiful man in the world that he is the most beautiful man in the world.

MAN: And to caress him, perhaps, just a little?

AGNES: Just a little.

MAN: There is the Apollo of Bellac.

AGNES: He doesn't exist.

MAN: What does it matter whether or not he exists? His beauty is the supreme beauty. Tell him.

AGNES: I can't. Unless I touch a thing I don't see it. You know that. I have no imagination.

MAN: Close your eyes.

AGNES: (*Closes them*) Yes?

MAN: Suppose, Agnes, it were the God of Beauty himself who visited you this morning. Don't be astonished. Perhaps it's true. Where else could this terrible power have come from? Or this extraordinary emotion you feel? Or this sense of oppression? And suppose that now the god reveals himself?

AGNES: It is you?

MAN: Don't open your eyes. Suppose I stand before you now in all my truth and all my splendor.

AGNES: I see you.

MAN: Call me thou.

AGNES: I see thee.

MAN: How do I seem?

AGNES: You seem—

MAN: I am taller than mortal men. My head is small and fringed with golden ringlets. From the line of my shoulders, the geometricians derived the idea of the square. From my eyebrows the bowmen drew the concept of the arc. I am nude and this nudity inspired in the musicians the idea of harmony.

AGNES: Your heels are winged, are they not?

MAN: They are not. You are thinking of the Hermes of St. Yrieix.

AGNES: I don't see your eyes.

MAN: As for the eyes, it's as well you don't see them. The eyes of beauty are implacable. My eyeballs are silver. My pupils are graphite. From the eyes of beauty poets derived the idea of death. But the feet of beauty are enchanting. They are not feet that touch the ground. They are never soiled and never captive. The toes are slender, and from them artists derived the idea of symmetry. Do you see me now?

AGNES: You dazzle my eyes.

MAN: But your heart sees me.

AGNES: I'm not so sure. Do not count on me too much, God of Beauty. My life is small. My days are long, and when I come back to my room each evening, there are five flights to climb in the greasy twilight amid smells of cooking. These five flights mark the beginning and the end of every event of my life, and oh, if you knew, Apollo, how lonely I am! Sometimes I find a cat waiting in a doorway. I kneel and stroke it for a moment, we purr together and it fills the rest of my day with joy. Sometimes I see a milk bottle that has fallen on its side. I set it right and the gesture comforts me. If I smell gas in the hallway I run and speak to the janitor. It is so good to speak to someone about something. Between the second story and the third, the steps sag. At this turning one abandons hope. At this turning one loses one's balance, and catches at the bannister, gasping with the anguish of those more fortunate ones who clutch at the rail on the heaving deck of a ship. That is my life, Apollo, a thing of shadows and tortured flesh. That is my conscience, Apollo, a staircase full of stale odors. If I hesitate to see you as you are, O beautiful god, it is because I need so much and I have so little and I must defend myself.

MAN: But I have rescued you, Agnes. You possess the secret.

AGNES: I know. From now on, my staircase will be new and full of light, the treads carpeted in velvet and adorned with initials. But to climb it with you would be unthinkable. Go away, God of Beauty. Leave me for always.

MAN: You wish that?

AGNES: If you were merely a handsome man, Apollo, thick and human in your flesh, with what joy I would take you in my arms! How I would love you! But you are too brilliant and too great for my staircase. I would do better to look at my diamond. Go, Apollo. Go away. Before I open my eyes, I implore you, vanish.

MAN: When I vanish, you will see before you an ordinary creature like yourself, covered with skin, covered with clothes.

AGNES: That is my destiny, and I prefer it. Let me kiss your lips, Apollo. And then—

MAN: (*he kisses her*) Open your eyes, my dear. Apollo is gone. And I am going.

AGNES: How handsome you are!

MAN: Dear Agnes!

AGNES: Don't go. I will make you rich. I will order the President to buy your invention.

MAN: Which one?

AGNES: The Universal Vegetable. There must be a fortune in it.

MAN: I haven't quite got the hang of it yet. The roots don't hold the earth. I'll be back the moment I've perfected it.

AGNES: You promise?

MAN: We shall plant it together. And now—

AGNES: You are really leaving me? You think I shall marry the President?

MAN: No.

AGNES: Why not?

MAN: He's already married. And his wife has learned a lesson. You will see.

AGNES: Then whom shall I marry, if not the President?

CLERK: (*Enters. He crosses to the Directors' room and throws open the door. Announces*) The Chairman of the Board! (*The* CHAIRMAN *enters from outer door.*)

MAN: (*whispers*) He is a bachelor.

AGNES: How handsome he is!

MAN: Yes. (*He vanishes.*)

CHAIRMAN: Mademoiselle—

PRESIDENT: (*The* PRESIDENT *comes in quickly in great excitement*) Agnes! Agnes! A miracle! My wife has just telephoned. I don't know what has come over her. She has thrown out the Dying Gaul and the china shepherd.

AGNES: Give her this diamond.

PRESIDENT: Thank you, Agnes. Thank you.

CHAIRMAN: (*taking her hand*) And who is this charming girl who gives away diamonds?

AGNES: Her name is Agnes.

CHAIRMAN: Dear Agnes!

PRESIDENT: But what's happened to our friend? He isn't here?

AGNES: He is gone.

PRESIDENT: Call him back. He must have lunch with us. Do you know his name?

AGNES: His first name only. Apollo.

PRESIDENT: (*runs to the outer door*) Apollo! Apollo!
(*The* DIRECTORS *come in, all adorned with white carnations.*)
Gentlemen, gentlemen, let's call him! We can't let him go like that. Apollo!
(*They each go to a door or a window save* AGNES *and the* CHAIRMAN *who remain standing hand in hand.*)

PRESIDENT *and* DIRECTORS: Apollo! Apollo!

CHAIRMAN: But whom are they shouting at? Is Apollo here?

AGNES: No. He just passed by.

CURTAIN

QUESTIONS

A. Understanding the Action:

1. What is Giraudoux's point in naming the play after something that does not exist?
2. Why is a bust of Archimedes set up in the reception room?
3. On what individuals, insect, and objects does Agnes practice her skill?
4. Is the theme of this play (a) a satire on male vanity?, (b) love for beauty exists in every soul? ("Every man, even the ugliest, feels in his heart a secret alliance with beauty"), or (c) the impossibility of living with ideal beauty in a material world? Justify your opinion.

B. Understanding the Characters:

1. Why does Agnes dismiss the vision she has of Apollo, the God of Beauty?
2. Contrast the attitude of Chevredent and Therese toward men with that of Agnes.
3. Why does the Man from Bellac applaud the President's speech to Therese?
4. Bergson, the French philosopher, believed that one of the sources of laughter was human automatism (i.e., when men act like puppets or wound-up, mechanical dolls, they are funny). Do the directors illustrate this theory of comedy, or do they function as a chorus does in Greek plays?

C. Understanding the Approach:

1. Giraudoux has been praised for his poetic fancy and condemned for his preciosity. Find examples of each.
2. Explain: "There is ugliness only . . . when the steamfitter has the beauty of a president, the president the beauty of a steamfitter."
3. Explain: "The eyes of beauty are implacable . . . From the eyes of beauty poets derived the idea of death."
4. Is this play simply an intellectual version of the old Cinderella story? Is the ending a happy one or not?

D. Comparisons:

1. What is Giraudoux satirizing in The International Bureau of Inventions? Compare with Swift's *Gulliver's Travels* (Voyage to Laputa, etc.) or Huxley's *Brave New World*.